80.00

FOR REFERENCE

Do Not Take
From This Room

Encyclopedia of World Cultures

Volume IV

EUROPE

ENCYCLOPEDIA OF WORLD CULTURES

David Levinson
Editor in Chief

North America
Oceania
South Asia
Europe (Central, Western, and Southeastern Europe)
East and Southeast Asia
Russia and Eurasia / China
South America
Middle America and the Caribbean
Africa and the Middle East
Bibliography

The Encyclopedia of World Cultures was prepared under the auspices and with the support of the Human Relations Area Files at Yale University. HRAF, the foremost international research organization in the field of cultural anthropology, is a not-for-profit consortium of twenty-three sponsoring members and 300 participating member institutions in twenty-five countries. The HRAF archive, established in 1949, contains nearly one million pages of information on the cultures of the world.

Encyclopedia of World Cultures

Volume IV

EUROPE
(Central, Western, and Southeastern Europe)

Linda A. Bennett
Volume Editor

G.K. Hall & Co.
Boston, Massachusetts

MEASUREMENT CONVERSIONS

When You Know	Multiply By	To Find
LENGTH		
inches	2.54	centimeters
feet	30	centimeters
yards	0.9	meters
miles	1.6	kilometers
millimeters	0.04	inches
centimeters	0.4	inches
meters	3.3	feet
meters	1.1	yards
kilometers	0.6	miles
AREA		
square feet	0.09	square meters
square yards	0.8	square meters
square miles	2.6	square kilometers
acres	0.4	hectares
hectares	2.5	acres
square meters	1.2	square yards
square kilometers	0.4	square miles

TEMPERATURE

$°C = (°F - 32) \times .555$

$°F = (°C \times 1.8) + 32$

© 1992 by the Human Relations Area Files, Inc.

First published 1992
by G.K. Hall & Co., an imprint of Macmillan Inc.
866 Third Avenue
New York, NY 10022

10 9 8 7 6 5 4
Macmillan, Inc., is part of the Maxwell Communication Group of Companies.

Library of Congress Cataloging-in-Publication Data
(Revised for vol. 4)

Encyclopedia of world cultures.

Includes bibliographical references, filmographies, and indexes.
Contents: v. 1. North America / Timothy J. O'Leary, David Levinson, volume editors—   —v. 3. South Asia / Paul Hockings, volume editor—v. 4. Europe (central, western, and southeastern Europe) / Linda A. Bennett, volume editor.
1. Ethnology—Encyclopedias. I. Levinson, David, 1947–
GN307.E53   1991   306'.097   90–49123
ISBN 0-8168-8840-X (set : alk. paper)
ISBN 0-8161-1808-6 (v. 1 : alk. paper)
ISBN 0-8161-1812-4 (v. 3 : alk. paper)

The paper used in this publication meets the minimum requirements of American National Standard for Information Sciences—Permanence of Paper for Printed Library Materials. ANSI Z39.48-1984.

MANUFACTURED IN THE UNITED STATES OF AMERICA

Contents

Contributors

Peter S. Allen
Department of Anthropology and Geography
Rhode Island College
Providence, Rhode Island
United States

Peloponnesians

Robert W. Allison
Bates College
Lewiston, Maine
United States

Mount Athos

Myrdene Anderson
Department of Sociology and Anthropology
Purdue University
West Lafayette, Indiana
United States

Saami

Robert Anderson
Department of Anthropology
Mills College
Oakland, California
United States

Danes

Stanley Anderson
Department of Political Science
University of California, Santa Barbara
Santa Barbara, California
United States

Danes

Hugh Beach
Department of Cultural Anthropology
Uppsala University
Uppsala
Sweden

Saami

Sam Beck
Field and International Study Program
New York State College of Human Ecology
Cornell University
Ithaca, New York
United States

Cape Verdeans

Jeremy Boissevain   **Maltese**
Anthropological-Sociological Centre
University of Amsterdam
Amsterdam
The Netherlands

Jonathan Boyarin   **Ashkenazic Jews**
Graduate Faculty of Political and Social Science
New School for Social Research
New York, New York
United States

Caroline B. Brettell   **Portuguese**
Department of Anthropology
Southern Methodist University
Dallas, Texas
United States

Carles Carreras   **Catalans (Països Catalans)**
Catedrátic de Geografia Humana
Universitat de Barcelona
Barcelona
Spain

Janeen Arnold Costa   **Ionians**
Department of Marketing
Graduate School of Business and College of Business
University of Utah
Salt Lake City, Utah
United States

Gerald W. Creed   **Bulgarians**
Anthropology Program
City University of New York Graduate School
New York, New York
United States

Carole L. Crumley   **Burgundians**
Department of Anthropology
University of North Carolina at Chapel Hill
Chapel Hill, North Carolina
United States

Heidi Dahles   **Dutch**
Institute for Social Research
Catholic University of Brabant
Tilburg
The Netherlands

William A. Douglass   **Basques**
Basque Studies Program
University of Nevada—Reno
Reno, Nevada
United States

Jill Dubisch   **Cyclades**
Department of Sociology, Anthropology, and Social Work
University of North Carolina at Charlotte
Charlotte, North Carolina
United States

E. Paul Durrenberger
Department of Anthropology
University of Iowa
Iowa City, Iowa
United States

Icelanders

L. M. Edelsward
Mediterranean Anthropological Research Equipe
Department of Anthropology
McGill University
Montreal, Quebec
Canada

Corsicans; Sardinians

John R. Eidson
Department of Anthropology
University of Maryland at College Park
College Park, Maryland
United States

Germans

Fernando Estévez
Unidad Departamental de Antropologia Cultural
Universidad de la Laguna
La Laguna, Tenerife
Canary Islands

Canarians

Merielle K. Flood
Office of the President
University of California
Oakland, California
United States

Flemish

Bernard Formoso
Maître de Conférences
Université de Paris
Paris
France

Piemontese Sinti

Robin Fox
Department of Anthropology
Rutgers University
New Brunswick, New Jersey
United States

Tory Islanders

Susan Tax Freeman
Department of Anthropology
University of Illinois at Chicago
Chicago, Illinois
United States

Pasiegos

Annette B. Fromm
Folklore Institute
Indiana University
Bloomington, Indiana
United States

Greek-Speaking Jews of Greece

Vesna Garber
Department of Anthropology
University of Illinois at Chicago
Chicago, Illinois
United States

Slav Macedonians

Ervan G. Garrison   **German Swiss**
Department of Civil Engineering
Texas A&M University
College Station, Texas
United States

Lena Gerholm   **Swedes**
Institute of Ethnology
Stockholm
Sweden

Patricia R. Gibson   **Bavarians**
Department of Anthropology
The University of the South
Sewanee, Tennessee
United States

Sharon Gmelch   **Irish Travellers**
Department of Sociology and Anthropology
Union College
Schenectady, New York
United States

Joan Gross   **Walloons**
Department of Anthropology
Oregon State University
Corvallis, Oregon
United States

Arthur W. Helwig   **English**
Department of Anthropology
Western Michigan University
Kalamazoo, Michigan
United States

Michael Herzfeld   **Cretans**
Department of Anthropology
Indiana University
Bloomington, Indiana
United States

Paul Hockings   **Gaels (Irish)**
Department of Anthropology
University of Illinois at Chicago
Chicago, Illinois
United States

Milena Hübschmannová   **Rom of Czechoslovakia**
Prague
Czechoslovakia

Éva Huseby-Darvas   **Hungarians**
Department of Behavioral Sciences
The University of Michigan—Dearborn
Dearborn, Michigan
United States

Robert Jarvenpa   **Finns**
Department of Anthropology
State University of New York at Albany
Albany, New York
United States

Miriam Lee Kaprow   **Gitanos**
Department of Anthropology
John Jay College of Criminal Justice
The City University of New York
New York, New York
United States

David Kideckel   **Romanians**
Department of Anthropology
Central Connecticut State University
New Britain, Connecticut
United States

Ed Knipe   **Highland Scots**
Department of Anthropology
Virginia Commonwealth University
Richmond, Virginia
United States

Karen Larson   **Norwegians**
Gustavus Adolphus College
Saint Peter, Minnesota
United States

David Levinson   **Sephardic Jews**
Human Relations Area Files
New Haven, Connecticut
United States

Leo Lucassen   **Gypsies and Caravan Dwellers in the Netherlands**
University of Leiden
Leiden
The Netherlands

Jean Ludtke   **Azoreans; Madeirans**
Hyannis Port, Massachusetts
United States

Gary W. McDonogh   **Catalans (Països Catalans)**
Department of Anthropology
New College, University of South Florida
Sarasota, Florida
United States

F. David Mulcahy   **Spanish Rom**
Polytechnic University
Brooklyn, New York
United States

David G. Nixon   **Manx**
Department of Anthropology
University of Massachusetts at Amherst
Amherst, Massachusetts
United States

Maria B. Olujić   **Dalmatians**
San Mateo, California
United States

Leonardo Piasere *Peripatetics; Slovensko Roma; Xoraxané Romá*
Instituto di Psicologia
Universita Delgi Studi di Verona
Verona
Italy

Janet Pollak **Slovaks**
Department of Sociology/Anthropology and Geography
William Patterson College
Wayne, New Jersey
United States

Irene Portis-Winner **Slovenes**
Massachusetts College of Art
Boston, Massachusetts
United States

Pamela Quaggiotto **Sicilians**
Department of Sociology and Anthropology
Randolph-Macon Woman's College
Lynchburg, Virginia
United States

Deborah Reed-Danahay **Auvergnats**
Department of Anthropology
Emory University
Atlanta, Georgia
United States

Susan Carol Rogers **Aveyronnais**
Institute of French Studies
New York University
New York, New York
United States

Robert Rotenberg **Austrians**
Department of Sociology
DePaul University
Chicago, Illinois
United States

Philip Carl Salzman **Sardinians**
Mediterranean Anthropological Research Equipe
Department of Anthropology
McGill University
Montreal, Quebec
Canada

Zdenek Salzmann **Czechs**
Department of Anthropology
University of Massachusetts at Amherst
Amherst, Massachusetts
United States

Stephanie Schwander **Albanians**
Institut für Ethnologie
Freie Universität Berlin
Berlin
Germany

Andris Skreija   **Poles**
Department of Sociology and Anthropology
University of Nebraska at Omaha
Omaha, Nebraska
United States

Carol Silverman   **Bulgarian Gypsies; Pomaks**
Department of Anthropology
University of Oregon
Eugene, Oregon
United States

Michael Stewart   **Vlach Gypsies of Hungary**
Department of Social Anthropology
University of Cambridge
Cambridge
England

Anita Sujoldžić   **Vlachs**
Institute for Anthropological Research
University of Zagreb
Zagreb
Croatia

Olga Supek   **Croats**
Department of Ethnology
University of Zagreb
Zagreb
Croatia

Susan Buck Sutton   **Greeks**
Department of Anthropology
Indiana University/Purdue University
Indianapolis, Indiana
United States

Lawrence J. Taylor   **Irish**
Department of Anthropology and Sociology
Lafayette College
Easton, Pennsylvania
United States

Robert J. Theodoratus   **Orcadians; Shetlanders; Welsh**
Department of Anthropology
Colorado State University
Fort Collins, Colorado
United States

Lenora A. Timm   **Bretons**
Department of Linguistics
University of California, Davis
Davis, California
United States

Robert C. Ulin   **Aquitaine**
Department of Sociology and Anthropology
Allegheny College
Meadville, Pennsylvania
United States

Eugene Valentine
Department of Communication
Arizona State University
Tempe, Arizona
United States

Galicians

Kristin B. Valentine
Department of Communication
Arizona State University
Tempe, Arizona
United States

Galicians

Katherine Verdery
Department of Anthropology
Johns Hopkins University
Baltimore, Maryland
United States

Transylvanian Ethnic Groups

Joan Vincent
Department of Anthropology
Barnard College
New York, New York
United States

Northern Irish

Richard Wagner
Smith College
Northhampton, Massachusetts
United States

Montenegrins; Serbs

Barbara Waldis
Seminaire D'Ethnologie
Université de Fribourg
Fribourg
Switzerland

Swiss, Italian

Wim Willems
University of Leiden
Leiden
The Netherlands

Gypsies and Caravan Dwellers in the Netherlands

Jonathan Wylie
Anthropology/Archaeology Program
Massachusetts Institute of Technology
Cambridge, Massachusetts
United States

Faroe Islanders

Preface

This project began in 1987 with the goal of assembling a basic reference source that provides accurate, clear, and concise descriptions of the cultures of the world. We wanted to be as comprehensive and authoritative as possible: comprehensive, by providing descriptions of all the cultures of each region of the world or by describing a representative sample of cultures for regions where full coverage is impossible, and authoritative by providing accurate descriptions of the cultures for both the past and the present.

The publication of the *Encyclopedia of World Cultures* in the last decade of the twentieth century is especially timely. The political, economic, and social changes of the past fifty years have produced a world more complex and fluid than at any time in human history. Three sweeping transformations of the worldwide cultural landscape are especially significant.

First is what some social scientists are calling the "New Diaspora"—the dispersal of cultural groups to new locations across the world. This dispersal affects all nations and takes a wide variety of forms: in East African nations, the formation of new towns inhabited by people from dozens of different ethnic groups; in Micronesia and Polynesia, the movement of islanders to cities in New Zealand and the United States; in North America, the replacement by Asians and Latin Americans of Europeans as the most numerous immigrants; in Europe, the increased reliance on workers from the Middle East and North Africa; and so on.

Second, and related to this dispersal, is the internal division of what were once single, unified cultural groups into two or more relatively distinct groups. This pattern of internal division is most dramatic among indigenous or third or fourth world cultures whose traditional ways of life have been altered by contact with the outside world. Underlying this division are both the population dispersion mentioned above and sustained contact with the economically developed world. The result is that groups who at one time saw themselves and were seen by others as single cultural groups have been transformed into two or more distinct groups. Thus, in many cultural groups, we find deep and probably permanent divisions between those who live in the country and those who live in cities, those who follow the traditional religion and those who have converted to Christianity, those who live inland and those who live on the seacoast, and those who live by means of a subsistence economy and those now enmeshed in a cash economy.

The third important transformation of the worldwide cultural landscape is the revival of ethnic nationalism, with many peoples claiming and fighting for political freedom and territorial integrity on the basis of ethnic solidarity and ethnic-based claims to their traditional homeland. Although most attention has focused recently on ethnic nationalism in Eastern Europe and the Soviet Union, the trend is nonetheless a worldwide phenomenon involving, for example, American Indian cultures in North and South America, the Basques in Spain and France, the Tamil and Sinhalese in Sri Lanka, and the Tutsi and Hutu in Burundi, among others.

To be informed citizens of our rapidly changing multicultural world we must understand the ways of life of people from cultures different from our own. "We" is used here in the broadest sense, to include not just scholars who study the cultures of the world and businesspeople and government officials who work in the world community but also the average citizen who reads or hears about multicultural events in the news every day and young people who are growing up in this complex cultural world. For all of these people—which means all of us—there is a pressing need for information on the cultures of the world. This encyclopedia provides this information in two ways. First, its descriptions of the traditional ways of life of the world's cultures can serve as a baseline against which cultural change can be measured and understood. Second, it acquaints the reader with the contemporary ways of life throughout the world.

We are able to provide this information largely through the efforts of the volume editors and the nearly one thousand contributors who wrote the cultural summaries that are the heart of the book. The contributors are social scientists (anthropologists, sociologists, historians, and geographers) as well as educators, government officials, and missionaries who usually have firsthand research-based knowledge of the cultures they write about. In many cases they are the major expert or one of the leading experts on the culture, and some are themselves members of the cultures. As experts, they are able to provide accurate, up-to-date information. This is crucial for many parts of the world where indigenous cultures may be overlooked by official information seekers such as government census takers. These experts have often lived among the people they write about, conducting participant-observations with them and speaking their language. Thus they are able to provide integrated, holistic descriptions of the cultures, not just a list of facts. Their portraits of the cultures leave the reader with a real sense of what it means to be a "Taos" or a "Rom" or a "Sicilian."

Those summaries not written by an expert on the culture have usually been written by a researcher at the Human Relations Area Files, Inc., working from primary source materials. The Human Relations Area Files, an international educational and research institute, is recognized by professionals in the social and behavioral sciences, humanities, and medical sciences as a major source of information on the cultures of the world.

Uses of the Encyclopedia

This encyclopedia is meant to be used by a variety of people for a variety of purposes. It can be used both to gain a general understanding of a culture and to find a specific piece of information by looking it up under the relevant subheading in a summary. It can also be used to learn about a particular region or subregion of the world and the social, economic, and political forces that have shaped the cultures in that region. The encyclopedia is also a resource guide that leads readers who want a deeper understanding of particular cultures to additional sources of information. Resource guides in the encyclopedia include ethnonyms listed in each summary, which can be used as entry points into the social science literature where the culture may sometimes be identified by a different name; a bibliography at the end of each summary, which lists books and articles about the culture; and a filmography at the end of each volume, which lists films and videos on many of the cultures.

Beyond being a basic reference resource, the encyclopedia also serves readers with more focused needs. For researchers interested in comparing cultures, the encyclopedia serves as the most complete and up-to-date sampling frame from which to select cultures for further study. For those interested in international studies, the encyclopedia leads one quickly into the relevant social science literature as well as providing a state-of-the-art assessment of our knowledge of the cultures of a particular region. For curriculum developers and teachers seeking to internationalize their curriculum, the encyclopedia is itself a basic reference and educational resource as well as a directory to other materials. For government officials, it is a repository of information not likely to be available in any other single publication or, in some cases, not available at all. For students, from high school through graduate school, it provides background and bibliographic information for term papers and class projects. And for travelers, it provides an introduction into the ways of life of the indigenous peoples in the area of the world they will be visiting.

Format of the Encyclopedia

The encyclopedia comprises ten volumes, ordered by geographical regions of the world. The order of publication is not meant to represent any sort of priority. Volumes 1 through 9 contain a total of about fifteen hundred summaries along with maps, glossaries, and indexes of alternate names for the cultural groups. The tenth and final volume contains cumulative lists of the cultures of the world, their alternate names, and a bibliography of selected publications pertaining to those groups.

North America covers the cultures of Canada, Greenland, and the United States of America.
Oceania covers the cultures of Australia, New Zealand, Melanesia, Micronesia, and Polynesia.
South Asia covers the cultures of Bangladesh, India, Pakistan, Sri Lanka and other South Asian islands and the Himalayan states.
Europe covers the cultures of Europe.

East and Southeast Asia covers the cultures of Japan, Korea, mainland and insular Southeast Asia, and Taiwan.
Russia and Eurasia/China covers the cultures of Mongolia, the People's Republic of China, and the former Union of Soviet Socialist Republics.
South America covers the cultures of South America.
Middle America and the Caribbean covers the cultures of Central America, Mexico, and the Caribbean islands.
Africa and the Middle East covers the cultures of Madagascar and sub-Saharan Africa, North Africa, the Middle East, and south-central Asia.

Format of the Volumes

Each volume contains this preface, an introductory essay by the volume editor, the cultural summaries ranging from a few lines to several pages each, maps pinpointing the location of the cultures, a filmography, an ethnonym index of alternate names for the cultures, and a glossary of scientific and technical terms. All entries are listed in alphabetical order and are extensively cross-referenced.

Cultures Covered

A central issue in selecting cultures for coverage in the encyclopedia has been how to define what we mean by a cultural group. The questions of what a culture is and what criteria can be used to classify a particular social group (such as a religious group, ethnic group, nationality, or territorial group) as a cultural group have long perplexed social scientists and have yet to be answered to everyone's satisfaction. Two realities account for why the questions cannot be answered definitively. First, a wide variety of different types of cultures exist around the world. Among common types are national cultures, regional cultures, ethnic groups, indigenous societies, religious groups, and unassimilated immigrant groups. No single criterion or marker of cultural uniqueness can consistently distinguish among the hundreds of cultures that fit into these general types. Second, as noted above, single cultures or what were at one time identified as single cultures can and do vary internally over time and place. Thus a marker that may identify a specific group as a culture in one location or at one time may not work for that culture in another place or at another time. For example, use of the Yiddish language would have been a marker of Jewish cultural identity in Eastern Europe in the nineteenth century, but it would not serve as a marker for Jews in the twentieth-century United States, where most speak English. Similarly, residence on one of the Cook Islands in Polynesia would have been a marker of Cook Islander identity in the eighteenth century, but not in the twentieth century when two-thirds of Cook Islanders live in New Zealand and elsewhere.

Given these considerations, no attempt has been made to develop and use a single definition of a cultural unit or to develop and use a fixed list of criteria for identifying cultural units. Instead, the task of selecting cultures was left to the volume editors, and the criteria and procedures they used are discussed in their introductory essays. In general, however, six criteria were used, sometimes alone and sometimes in combination to classify social groups as cultural groups: (1) geographical localization, (2) identification in the social science literature as a distinct group, (3) distinct language, (4) shared traditions, religion, folklore, or values, (5) maintenance of group identity in the face of strong assimilative pressures, and (6) previous listing in an inventory of the world's cultures such as _Ethnographic Atlas_ (Murdock 1967) or the _Outline of World Cultures_ (Murdock 1983).

In general, we have been "lumpers" rather than "splitters" in writing the summaries. That is, if there is some question about whether a particular group is really one culture or two related cultures, we have more often than not treated it as a single culture, with internal differences noted in the summary. Similarly, we have sometimes chosen to describe a number of very similar cultures in a single summary rather than in a series of summaries that would be mostly redundant. There is, however, some variation from one region to another in this approach, and the rationale for each region is discussed in the volume editor's essay.

Two categories of cultures are usually not covered in the encyclopedia. First, extinct cultures, especially those that have not existed as distinct cultural units for some time, are usually not described. Cultural extinction is often, though certainly not always, indicated by the disappearance of the culture's language. So, for example, the Aztec are not covered, although living descendants of the Aztec, the Nahuat-speakers of central Mexico, are described.

Second, the ways of life of immigrant groups are usually not described in much detail, unless there is a long history of resistance to assimilation and the group has maintained its distinct identity, as have the Amish in North America. These cultures are, however, described in the location where they traditionally lived and, for the most part, continue to live, and migration patterns are noted. For example, the Hmong in Laos are described in the Southeast Asia volume, but the refugee communities in the United States and Canada are covered only in the general summaries on Southeast Asians in those two countries in the North America volume. Although it would be ideal to provide descriptions of all the immigrant cultures or communities of the world, that is an undertaking well beyond the scope of this encyclopedia, for there are probably more than five thousand such communities in the world.

Finally, it should be noted that not all nationalities are covered, only those that are also distinct cultures as well as political entities. For example, the Vietnamese and Burmese are included but Indians (citizens of the Republic of India) are not, because the latter is a political entity made up of a great mix of cultural groups. In the case of nations whose populations include a number of different, relatively unassimilated groups or cultural regions, each of the groups is described separately. For example, there is no summary for Italians as such in the Europe volume, but there are summaries for the regional cultures of Italy, such as the Tuscans, Sicilians, and Tirolians, and other cultures such as the Sinti Piemontese.

Cultural Summaries

The heart of this encyclopedia is the descriptive summaries of the cultures, which range from a few lines to five or six pages in length. They provide a mix of demographic, historical, social, economic, political, and religious information on the cultures. Their emphasis or flavor is cultural; that is, they focus on the ways of life of the people—both past and present—and the factors that have caused the culture to change over time and place.

A key issue has been how to decide which cultures should be described by longer summaries and which by shorter ones. This decision was made by the volume editors, who had to balance a number of intellectual and practical considerations. Again, the rationale for these decisions is discussed in their essays. But among the factors that were considered by all the editors were the total number of cultures in their region, the availability of experts to write summaries, the availability of information on the cultures, the degree of similarity between cultures, and the importance of a culture in a scientific or political sense.

The summary authors followed a standardized outline so that each summary provides information on a core list of topics. The authors, however, had some leeway in deciding how much attention was to be given each topic and whether additional information should be included. Summaries usually provide information on the following topics:

CULTURE NAME: The name used most often in the social science literature to refer to the culture or the name the group uses for itself.

ETHNONYMS: Alternate names for the culture including names used by outsiders, the self-name, and alternate spellings, within reasonable limits.

ORIENTATION
Identification. Location of the culture and the derivation of its name and ethnonyms.
Location. Where the culture is located and a description of the physical environment.
Demography. Population history and the most recent reliable population figures or estimates.
Linguistic Affiliation. The name of the language spoken and/or written by the culture, its place in an international language classification system, and internal variation in language use.

HISTORY AND CULTURAL RELATIONS: A tracing of the origins and history of the culture and the past and current nature of relationships with other groups.

SETTLEMENTS: The location of settlements, types of settlements, types of structures, housing design and materials.

ECONOMY
Subsistence and Commercial Activities. The primary methods of obtaining, consuming, and distributing money, food, and other necessities.
Industrial Arts. Implements and objects produced by the culture either for its own use or for sale or trade.
Trade. Products traded and patterns of trade with other groups.
Division of Labor. How basic economic tasks are assigned by age, sex, ability, occupational specialization, or status.
Land Tenure. Rules and practices concerning the allocation of land and land-use rights to members of the culture and to outsiders.

KINSHIP
Kin Groups and Descent. Rules and practices concerning kin-based features of social organization such as lineages and clans and alliances between these groups.
Kinship Terminology. Classification of the kinship terminological system on the basis of either cousin terms or genera-

tion, and information about any unique aspects of kinship terminology.

MARRIAGE AND FAMILY

Marriage. Rules and practices concerning reasons for marriage, types of marriage, economic aspects of marriage, postmarital residence, divorce, and remarriage.

Domestic Unit. Description of the basic household unit including type, size, and composition.

Inheritance. Rules and practices concerning the inheritance of property.

Socialization. Rules and practices concerning child rearing including caretakers, values inculcated, child-rearing methods, initiation rites, and education.

SOCIOPOLITICAL ORGANIZATION

Social Organization. Rules and practices concerning the internal organization of the culture, including social status, primary and secondary groups, and social stratification.

Political Organization. Rules and practices concerning leadership, politics, governmental organizations, and decision making.

Social Control. The sources of conflict within the culture and informal and formal social control mechanisms.

Conflict. The sources of conflict with other groups and informal and formal means of resolving conflicts.

RELIGION AND EXPRESSIVE CULTURE

Religious Beliefs. The nature of religious beliefs including beliefs in supernatural entities, traditional beliefs, and the effects of major religions.

Religious Practitioners. The types, sources of power, and activities of religious specialists such as shamans and priests.

Ceremonies. The nature, type, and frequency of religious and other ceremonies and rites.

Arts. The nature, types, and characteristics of artistic activities including literature, music, dance, carving, and so on.

Medicine. The nature of traditional medical beliefs and practices and the influence of scientific medicine.

Death and Afterlife. The nature of beliefs and practices concerning death, the deceased, funerals, and the afterlife.

BIBLIOGRAPHY: A selected list of publications about the culture. The list usually includes publications that describe both the traditional and the contemporary culture.

AUTHOR'S NAME: The name of the summary author.

Maps

Each regional volume contains maps pinpointing the current location of the cultures described in that volume. The first map in each volume is usually an overview, showing the countries in that region. The other maps provide more detail by marking the locations of the cultures in four or five subregions.

Filmography

Each volume contains a list of films and videos about cultures covered in that volume. This list is provided as a service and in no way indicates an endorsement by the editor, volume editor, or the summary authors. Addresses of distributors are provided so that information about availability and prices can be readily obtained.

Ethnonym Index

Each volume contains an ethnonym index for the cultures covered in that volume. As mentioned above, ethnonyms are alternative names for the culture—that is, names different from those used here as the summary headings. Ethnonyms may be alternative spellings of the culture name, a totally different name used by outsiders, a name used in the past but no longer used, or the name in another language. It is not unusual that some ethnonyms are considered degrading and insulting by the people to whom they refer. These names may nevertheless be included here because they do identify the group and may help some users locate the summary or additional information on the culture in other sources. Ethnonyms are cross-referenced to the culture name in the index.

Glossary

Each volume contains a glossary of technical and scientific terms found in the summaries. Both general social science terms and region-specific terms are included.

Special Considerations

In a project of this magnitude, decisions had to be made about the handling of some information that cannot easily be standardized for all areas of the world. The two most troublesome matters concerned population figures and units of measure.

Population Figures

We have tried to be as up-to-date and as accurate as possible in reporting population figures. This is no easy task, as some groups are not counted in official government censuses, some groups are very likely undercounted, and in some cases the definition of a cultural group used by the census takers differs from the definition we have used. In general, we have relied on population figures supplied by the summary authors. When other population data sources have been used in a volume, they are so noted by the volume editor. If the reported figure is from an earlier date—say, the 1970s—it is usually because it is the most accurate figure that could be found.

Units of Measure

In an international encyclopedia, editors encounter the problem of how to report distances, units of space, and temperature. In much of the world, the metric system is used, but scientists prefer the International System of Units (similar to the metric system), and in Great Britain and North America the English system is usually used. We decided to use English measures in the North America volume and metric measures in the other volumes. Each volume contains a conversion table.

Acknowledgments

In a project of this size, there are many people to acknowledge and thank for their contributions. In its planning stages, members of the research staff of the Human Relations Area Files provided many useful ideas. These included Timothy J. O'Leary, Marlene Martin, John Beierle, Gerald Reid, Delores Walters, Richard Wagner, and Christopher Latham. The advisory editors, of course, also played a major role in planning the project, and not just for their own volumes but also for the project as a whole. Timothy O'Leary, Terence Hays, and Paul Hockings deserve special thanks for their comments on this preface and the glossary, as does Melvin Ember, president of the Human Relations Area Files. Members of the office and technical staff also must be thanked for so quickly and carefully attending to the many tasks a project of this size inevitably generates. They are Erlinda Maramba, Abraham Maramba, Victoria Crocco, Nancy Gratton, and Douglas Black. At Macmillan and G. K. Hall, the encyclopedia has benefited from the wise and careful editorial management of Elly Dickason, Elizabeth Kubik, and Elizabeth Holthaus, and the editorial and production management of Ara Salibian.

Finally, I would like to thank Melvin Ember and the board of directors of the Human Relations Area Files for their administrative and intellectual support for this project.

DAVID LEVINSON

References

Murdock, George Peter (1967). _Ethnographic Atlas._ Pittsburgh, Penn., University of Pittsburgh Press.

Murdock, George Peter (1983). _Outline of World Cultures._ 6th rev. ed. New Haven, Conn., Human Relations Area Files.

Introduction

Europe is in tremendous flux. Political boundaries and designations are changing with dizzying speed. Population mobility is altering the human landscape in astonishing and unpredictable ways. To publish this volume on European cultures at this particular historical juncture provides both a wonderful opportunity to offer a much-needed resource to help interpret these phenomenal changes as well as an awesome challenge to include information that is as up-to-date as possible.

The volume covers 116 cultures of western, northern, central, Mediterranean, and southeastern Europe. Also included here are island cultures in the Mediterranean Sea and the Atlantic Ocean that traditionally have been affiliated sociopolitically with mainland European cultures. The locations of many of these cultures are shown on maps 2–4. Not included in this volume are cultures in North Africa, mainland Turkey, or within the former Soviet Union. The cultures in the European section of the former Soviet Union, such as Estonia, Georgia, and Ukraine, are covered in volume 6.

Our decision about which cultures to cover in this volume were based on several considerations. First, cultures that might be considered "European" but that fall within the geographical scope of another volume are not covered here (for example, the former Soviet Union as noted earlier). Second, we understand that readers will hold varying points of view as to what constitutes a distinct culture within the European context. With the acceleration of nationalistic sentiments and movements across Europe over the past decade, the ambiguity about where to draw boundaries between one cultural group and another and whether one group should encompass another has become more obvious and more difficult to clarify. As this volume goes to press, growing divisions—both peaceful and violent, ethnic and nationalistic—serve as a counterpoint to the evolution of the European Community as a coalescing political-economic force within Europe.

Given this situation, our tendency in selecting cultures for coverage here has been in the direction of "splitting" rather than "lumping" and in being inclusive rather than exclusive. In general, we have opted to cover a particular culture whenever (1) European anthropologists have treated it as a distinct culture; (2) anthropological research has been conducted on the culture; (3) an anthropologist or other scholar was available to contribute an article on that cultural group; and (4) sufficient published information was available on the group to enable a staff researcher to write an article on the group in the absence of a scholar to do the same.

Boundaries between cultures are often fuzzy, depending on specific criteria used for defining a particular group (e.g., territory, social ascription, behavior, language, historical tradition, or self-definition). For example, some readers might view France as constituting a single culture (the "French"); however, for this volume we have chosen to provide several separate articles on particular cultural regions of France—Alsace, Aquitaine, Auvergne, Aveyron, Brittany, Burgundy, and Occitan. We have followed a similar strategy for other nations such as Greece, Spain, and Italy. In other situations where there is a regional culture that is a part of a wider cultural group (such as Dalmatians and Croatians or Bavarians and Germans) we have often included both, especially when scholars could be found to write the entries. Thus, we have decided to err on the side of inclusion rather than exclusion in order to provide the richest possible information about the breadth of cultures in contemporary Europe.

This strategy has led us to include a number of different "types" of cultures: (1) national cultures such as Austrians, Germans, Greeks, and Poles; (2) regional cultures such as Andalusians, Burgundians, Frisians, and Tuscans; (3) linguistic minorities such as Basques, Ladins, and Bretons; (4) language isolates such as Pontics; and (5) geographically isolated cultures such as Azoreans, Mount Athos, and Tory Islanders. We have also covered Jews and Gypsy and Traveller (Peripatetic) peoples. We should also note that unlike other regions of the world whose cultures have been the subject of anthropological inquiry since the early twentieth century, cultures in Europe have been the subject of intensive anthropological study only in the last few decades. Thus, the current state of our anthropological knowledge of the cultures of Europe may differ widely in breadth, time depth, and topical focus from one culture to another.

The Physical Environment

Europe is the second-smallest continent; only Australia is smaller. With the European part of the former USSR included, Europe covers 10,360,000 square miles; excluding the former USSR, it has a landmass of 3,800,000 square miles. It is physically contiguous with Asia; together, they are often considered to form the single continent of Eurasia. Given the way we have defined "Europe" in this volume and the cultures we have covered, Europe is demarcated by the following boundaries and approximate distances from the meridian line in England (see map 1). On the north, Europe is bounded by the Arctic Ocean, with North Cape, Norway, being the farthest northern point at 71°10′20″ N. To the east, Europe is delimited by the eastern border of Finland (31°30′ E) with Russia in the north, and by the eastern border of Romania (30° E) with Moldova in the south. The Black Sea lies to the east of Romania. While the main southern boundary for continental Europe is the Mediterranean Sea (with many island cultures such as Crete located in the sea), Europe, as defined here, also encompasses the Cape Verde Islands (17°12′ N and 14°48′ N) off the coast of Africa. To the west, Europe is bounded by the Atlantic Ocean and includes Iceland in the north (13°–25° W) and the Azore Islands in the south (36°–39° N, 24°–31° W). The farthest western point of continental Europe is Cape Roca, Portugal (9°30′ W) in the south and mainland Scotland (6° W) and Dunmore Head, Ireland (10°30′ W) in the northern areas. The most southerly point of the mainland is Point Tarifa, Spain, at 36°01′ N.

The bodies of water surrounding Europe include the Black Sea, the Sea of Marmara, and the Aegean Sea in the east, the Mediterranean Sea to the south, the North Atlantic Ocean to the west, and the North Sea, the Norwegian Sea, and the Barents Sea to the north. The English Channel and Strait of Dover separate the British Isles from continental Europe. The Strait of Gibraltar lies between North Africa and southern Spain. Turkey is divided from Europe by the narrow straits of the Dardanelles, the Bosporus, and the Sea of Marmara.

The areas occupied by the European countries covered here and those of the former USSR (covered in volume 6) are mainly continuous in physiographic features and types of environment. For example, no distinct physical features distinguish Finland from the neighboring Karelia region of Russia; instead, both are composed of woodlands (mainly coniferous forests), similar rock formations (metamorphic and intrusive igneous rocks), and numerous lakes. Similarly, Poland has much the same environment as Belarus, Ukraine, and Lithuania—one of open plains, lowlands, croplands, woodlands of a mixed-forest (deciduous and coniferous) variety, and similar sedimentary rock deposits. Thus, geographic continuity rather than differentiation characterizes much of western-central Europe and the European regions of the former USSR. This conformity has had a profound effect on the shifting of political borders in the past and the movement of large populations, as many groups have moved across these open spaces, often displacing existing populations or settling among them.

Geographically, Europe can be divided into six different regions: Scandinavia (including Iceland, Norway, Sweden, Denmark, and Finland); the British Isles (the United Kingdom and Ireland); western Europe (France, the Netherlands, Belgium, Luxembourg, and Monaco); central Europe (Switzerland, Germany, Poland, Liechtenstein, Austria, Hungary, and the Czech and Slovak Federative Republic); southern Europe (Portugal, Spain, Italy, Malta, Andorra, San Marino, and Vatican City); and southeastern Europe (Slovenia, Croatia, Bosnia and Herzegovina, Yugoslavia, Albania, Macedonia, Greece, Bulgaria, and Romania). With respect to the European sections of Eurasia, the European part of Turkey can be placed within southeastern Europe, and the European parts of the former Soviet Union can be placed within central or eastern and southeastern Europe.

Europe contains numerous mountain ranges: the Cantabrian Mountains (Spain); the Pyrenees (Spain and France); the Grampians (Scotland); the Alps (Switzerland, France, Italy, and Austria); the Apennines (Italy); the Dinaric Alps (Albania, Bosnia and Herzegovina, Croatia, Slovenia, and Yugoslavia); the Pindus Mountains (Greece); the Rhodope and Balkan mountains (Bulgaria); the Transylvanian Mountains (Romania); and the Carpathian Mountains (the Czech and Slovak Federative Republic, Poland, and Romania). Mont Blanc is the highest point (4,807 meters) in this part of Europe; in the wider definition of Europe, Mount Elbrus (5,633 meters) in the Caucasus Mountains in Russia is the highest peak. These ranges have played a major role in the cultural history of Europe—isolating some groups, separating others, and directing migration routes of still others. Many of the more traditional cultural groups of contemporary Europe are found in mountain areas, including the Pasiegos in Spain, the Sarakatsani in Greece, and the Ladins in Italy.

Between the mountainous Scandinavian Peninsula in the north and the Alpine mountain chain in the south, the Great European Plain runs from the Atlantic Ocean on the west to the Ural Mountains in the east. This rich agricultural plain includes steppe lands in the north and east, which consist of forests, lakes, and tundra. Three mountainous peninsulas lie south of the Alpine region: Iberia, Italy, and the Balkans. The continent of Europe includes two other major plains, both of which contain rich agricultural lands. The Po Plain lies between the Alps and the Apennines in Italy and the Danubian Plain runs from the Alps to the Carpathians.

The primary rivers of Europe are the Tagus and Douro in Portugal and Spain; the Guadalquivir and Ebro in Spain; the Garonne, Loire, Rhone, and Seine in France; the Po and Tiber in Italy; the Rhine and Elbe in Germany; the Oder of Germany, Poland, and the Czech and Slovak Federative Republic; the Thames in England; the Tisza in Hungary, Romania, and Yugoslavia; the Vistula in Poland; the Drina in Bosnia and Herzegovina and Yugoslavia; the Severn in England and Wales; and the Danube, which after the Volga in Russia is the second-longest river in Europe. The Danube flows eastward from Germany through Austria, Hungary, Yugoslavia, Romania, Bulgaria, and into the Black Sea. It forms the boundary between parts of Romania and Bulgaria. Numerous lakes are found in Finland, Sweden, and Switzerland.

European climatic regions range from arctic in the far north to subtropical in the south. Subarctic and tundra climates are found in the northeast region. Continental weather characterizes central and eastern Europe, with high humidity and cool summers. Northwestern Europe has a humid moderate marine-forest climate, with mild winters and cool summers. The Mediterranean region has warm, dry weather, with rain falling mainly in the winter. Because of the warming westerly winds blowing in from the Atlantic Ocean, Europe has a more moderate climate than that found in similar latitudes in other parts of the world.

Excluding the former USSR, Europe's landmass of 3,800,000 square miles covers 6.6 percent of the Earth's surface. In comparison, North America covers more than 16.2 percent of the Earth's surface and includes 5.1 percent of the Earth's population. As more thoroughly described in the following section on population, Europe is a particularly densely populated continent (second only to Asia).

Population

According to 1990 estimates, the total population of Europe (excluding the former Soviet Union) is between 450 and 500 million people, or 8.4 percent of the world's total population. (Population figures reported here are mostly taken from the 1992 *World Almanac* and the 1992 *Universal Almanac*.) By 1995, the total population of Europe is expected to reach 506,500,000. As of 1989, Europe had an overall population density of 180 people per square mile (*Goode's World Atlas* 1990). The most densely populated countries are: Monaco (28,072 people/square mile); Malta (2,900 people/square mile); San Marino (958 people/square mile); the Netherlands (931 people/square mile); Belgium (840 people/square mile); United Kingdom (610 people/square mile); Italy (493 people/square mile); Liechtenstein (483 people/square mile); Switzerland (406 people/square mile); Poland (317 people/square mile).

The least densely populated countries include: Iceland (6 people/square mile); Norway (33 people/square mile); Finland (38 people/square mile); Sweden (48 people/square mile).

In 1990, the most populous countries with more than 30,000,000 inhabitants were: Germany (79,070,000); Italy (57,657,000); United Kingdom (57,121,000); France (56,184,000); Spain (39,623,000); and Poland (38,363,000).

Europe is a highly urbanized continent. The most populous metropolitan areas of Europe having at least 1 million inhabitants living in the greater metropolitan area are: London, United Kingdom (9,170,000); Paris, France (8,709,000); Essen-Dortmund, Germany (7,474,000); Milan, Italy (4,738,000); Barcelona, Spain (4,163,000); Manchester, England (4,050,000); Athens, Greece (3,469,000); Madrid, Spain (3,451,000); Greater Berlin, Germany (3,022,000); Rome, Italy (3,021,000); Naples, Italy (2,960,000); Lisbon, Portugal (2,396,000); Vienna, Austria (2,313,000); Budapest, Hungary (2,301,000); Birmingham, England (2,170,000); Bucharest, Romania (2,150,000); Warsaw, Poland (1,600,000); Hamburg, Germany (1,600,000); Porto, Portugal (1,500,000); Belgrade, Yugoslavia (1,300,000); Munich, Germany (1,300,000); Prague, Czech and Slovak Federative Republic (1,200,000); Sofia, Bulgaria (1,200,000); and Turin, Italy (1,000,000).

In addition, there are 25 cities with populations between 500,000 and 1 million.

Among those six countries having the greatest total population (Germany, the United Kingdom, Italy, France, Spain, and Poland), the United Kingdom and Italy are particularly densely populated (601 and 493 per square mile, respectively). The metropolitan areas of these six countries also have major population concentrations. For example, the United Kingdom includes three metropolitan areas with over 2 million people (London, Manchester, and Birmingham); Italy, three such metropolitan areas (Milan, Rome, and Naples); Germany, two (Essen and Greater Berlin); Spain, two (Madrid and Barcelona); and France, one (Paris). Poland, while not having a city with over 2 million inhabitants, does have five cities with between half a million and 2 million people (Warsaw, Lódź, Kraków, Wrocław, and Poznań).

The clustering of substantial populations into metropolitan regions is a distinctive demographic feature of Europe. In 1990, 73 percent of Europe's population lived in urban areas. In comparison, the entire population of the planet is only 43 percent urban; more developed regions have 72 percent and less developed regions have 33 percent of their populations living in urban areas. In this regard, Europe is most like North America (74 percent urban), Latin America (72 percent urban), Oceania (70 percent), and the former USSR (67 percent). It is least like Africa (34 percent urban) and Asia (29 percent urban).

Within Europe, the northern regions (including Denmark, Finland, Ireland, Norway, Sweden, and the United Kingdom) and western regions (Austria, Belgium, France, the former West Germany, the Netherlands, and Switzerland) are the most urbanized (87 percent and 80 percent, respectively). In contrast, the southern regions (Albania, Greece, Italy, Portugal, Spain, and the former Yugoslavia) and eastern regions (Bulgaria, the Czech and Slovak Federative Republic, the former East Germany, Hungary, Poland, and Romania) are the least urbanized overall (64 percent and 63 percent, respectively). These regional statistics, however, do not reflect accurately the situation in all the constituent countries. For example, although the countries with the highest percentage of their populations living in urban areas are located in northern and western regions of Europe (Belgium, 96 percent; the United Kingdom, 92 percent; the Netherlands, 88 percent; the former West Germany, 86 percent; Denmark, 86 percent; and Sweden, 83 percent), not all those countries having 60 percent or less of their population living in urban areas are found in southern and eastern regions of Europe. Those nations with 60 percent or less are, in fact, scattered throughout the four regions: Portugal (33 percent), Albania (35 percent), the former Yugoslavia (50 percent), Romania (50 percent), Austria (57 percent), Switzerland (59 percent), Ireland (59 percent), and Hungary (60 percent).

While urbanization has been a notable characteristic of European society for centuries, the trend toward industrialization and urbanization has accelerated phenomenally since World War II. London and Paris, for example, have been major urban centers for centuries, but many other European cities have experienced rapid expansion of their populations only since the late 1940s. Thus, in countries such as Poland, Italy, and Spain—which were largely agricultural and rural before World War II—we find that many of their cities have now become home to large numbers of people. For example, among those 99 cities having the largest estimated populations in 1990, those listed for Italy and Spain, in particular, experienced substantial increases between 1960 and 1990, in comparison with more moderate increases for most cities in the former West Germany, France, and the United Kingdom. In Spain (with 78 percent of the 1990 population living in urban areas), Madrid's population increased from 2,220,000 in 1960 to 4,950,000 in 1990, and Barcelona's grew from 1,940,000 to 3,240,000. In Italy (68 percent urban), Milan increased from 4,510,000 to 7,530,000, Naples from 3,200,000 to 4,150,000, Rome from 2,330,000 to 3,750,000, and Turin from 1,250,000 to 2,400,000 over these three decades. Movement from rural to urban areas in the postwar era was extremely common throughout most parts of Europe. Albania is a notable exception, with only 35 percent of its people living in urban areas. Portugal, with only two major metropolitan areas (Lisbon and Porto), remains predominantly rural.

Migration

Migration—including legal and illegal immigration, migration under contracts between countries for guest workers, and political and economic refugee movements—from within Europe and from other countries has swelled the urban population of many European countries. This is particularly true in cities in Austria, Belgium, France, Germany, Hungary, Italy, the Netherlands, Sweden, Switzerland, and the United Kingdom. In Germany, for example, the former West Berlin as of 1987 had approximately 224,000 foreign-national residents, 11.1 percent of its entire population. Other German cities with an even greater proportion of their residents being foreign nationals included Cologne, Dusseldorf, Frankfurt, Munich, and Stuttgart. In the former West Berlin, Turks constituted the largest foreign-national group of residents, numbering 112,000 in 1987. At that time, 29,000 people from what was then Yugoslavia also lived there, as well as smaller numbers of people from Poland, Italy, and Greece (*Outlook Berlin* 1989, 8).

In western Germany, *Gastarbeiter* or guest workers have been a major segment of the labor force since the early 1960s. Because of labor shortages in a rapidly expanding economy, the government contracted with the governments of several other countries that had a surplus of labor and struggling economies to send workers—sometimes with their families and sometimes without—as temporary residents to work for set periods of time. Even though many guest workers and their families remain in Germany, they do not hold German citizenship and have limited political rights. As of 1990, the former West Germany and East Germany together had substantial numbers of guest workers from Turkey (1,612,623 workers and family members); the former Yugoslavia (610,499); Italy (519,548); various Asian countries, including Vietnam (442,056); Greece (293,649); Poland (226,943); various African countries including Mozambique (179,005); and approximately 1,000,000 from other countries, including Cuba. This amounted to close to 5 million people, or 6.5 percent of their joint population of about 77 million (Graff 1990).

Vast political transformations that have taken place in central, eastern, and southern Europe and the former USSR—including the ongoing war in the former Yugoslavia—already have had major implications for the fate of these guest workers. Their future is now highly uncertain. With the huge influx of Germans from the former East Germany into the former West Germany, for example, the need to retain so many non-German workers is being questioned seriously. Although this problem is seen most notably in Germany, several other countries also are questioning the need for retaining their guest workers.

Several European countries have absorbed a substantial number of refugees—defined as "people who are in need of protection and/or assistance" and not including those people who have resettled thus far within the new country—from various countries. With the fall of the Berlin Wall in 1989 and the political, economic, and social upheaval in central, eastern, and southern Europe that followed, the refugee situation also has reached crisis proportion. As a consequence,

population movements from one part of Europe to another since 1989 present a major problem for European countries individually and collectively, especially for the European Community (Ghosh 1991; Miller 1991).

In 1989 alone, 1.3 million people moved from eastern and southern Europe to countries in western Europe. This trend has persisted over the past two years because of economic and political upheavals and shows no signs of abating. Austria, France, Germany, and Italy have experienced a tremendous increase in the number of people requesting political asylum between 1988 and 1991. From 1987 to 1990 the number of people seeking asylum in western Europe increased from about 180,000 to 400,000 (Ghosh 1991, 80). In Italy alone, the number increased from 1,366 in 1988 to 27,000 during the first six months of 1991 (Miller 1991, 81). Germany's requests jumped from an already high figure of over 100,000 in 1988 to 193,000 in 1990 and to 203,321 in the first ten months of 1991 (Miller 1991, 81; *Newsweek*, 9 December 1991, p. 36).

Most recently, the war in the former Yugoslavia has produced an overwhelming number of refugees: an estimated 600,000 from Croatia and 700,000 from Bosnia and Herzegovina as of late spring 1992. Many of these refugees are displaced within the territories of former Yugoslavia. Many others, however, have left for other countries. The sheer magnitude of these numbers has taxed the resources and overflowed the refugee camps of border countries especially. The extraordinary number of refugees from the former Yugoslavia has created great difficulties and challenges for Hungary, for example, as it has attempted to host people displaced from the war zones across its border.

Recent news accounts (late 1991 and early 1992) regarding migrational movements in Europe emphasize the critical effects of this trend. The European Community is contending with its consequences in terms of considering new frontier policies. Throughout Europe, on the one hand, certain forces encourage continuing immigration. With the general aging of the population of Europe (described later), many countries such as France have labor shortages and will continue to need to import additional workers. However, a substantial native backlash against having so many foreign-national residents is now evident in many countries. Italy, for example, is one of the least restrictive countries in Europe regarding the free movement of people. However, it is reconsidering its relatively liberal policy in light of the large number of illegal immigrants living in Italy and because of the thousands of Albanians who arrived by boat in 1991. After accepting one boatload of 20,000 Albanian people in March, Italy turned back a second boat (carrying 10,000 people) that arrived later in the year. Furthermore, an estimated 400,000 illegal immigrants are already living in Italy. With its extensive coastal area, it is almost impossible for Italy to control illegal entry (Miller 1991, 81). Many European countries are faced with thorny practical and ethical questions in their attempt to gain some semblance of balance over migrational forces.

Amid the euphoria surrounding the fall of the Berlin Wall and the demise of Communist governments in Europe and the former USSR, certain segments of the European population have reacted very strongly and negatively toward the influx of "foreigners" into their countries. Some of these counterreactions have received considerable attention in the media. Often referred to as "Europe's New Right" (*News-*

week, 27 April 1992), these movements are gaining substantial voter support in several countries, including, but not limited to, Austria, Belgium, Denmark, France, Germany, and Italy. Thus, the early 1990s is a time of great uncertainty with respect to the continuing acceptance of "outsiders" by the more developed countries of Europe. Europeans typically contrast their own countries with the "immigrant" nature of the United States and value the relative homogeneity of their constituent populations. They are now faced with the possibility of becoming multiethnic and multiracial, and it is vividly clear that many Europeans do not welcome such a change (Ghosh 1991; Miller 1991; *Newsweek,* 9 December 1991; *Newsweek,* 27 April 1992).

Demographic Trends

With regard to 1990 vital statistics, Europe has the lowest birthrate (12 live births/1,000 people) in the world; North America's rate is 113/1,000. In contrast, the birthrate of Africa is 43; Latin America, 26; Asia, 26; and Oceania, 19. The fertility rate for Europe is similarly the lowest in the world (1.7/1,000 women of child-bearing age). In contrast, Europe's mortality rate (10/1,000 people) is midway between that of Latin America (7), North America (8), and Asia (8) at one end of the scale and Africa (13) at the other end. Life expectancy for the current population of Europe is 75 years, in contrast to 53 for Africa, 63 for Asia, 67 for Latin America, and 76 for both North America and Oceania. The European mid-range death rate reflects a balance between a high standard of health care and the aging structure. Generally speaking, Europe's population is aging. In the decade between 1980 and 1990, for example, the percentage of people under the age of 15 living in the twelve countries of the European Community dropped from approximately 22.5 percent to 18.5 percent of the total population; in contrast, the percentage of people over 65 increased from approximately 13 percent to 14.5 percent. This trend is expected to continue into the twenty-first century (Monod, Gyllenhammar, and Dekker 1991, 16). The aging of Europe's population is a result of the low birthrates and death rates as well as the high life expectancy.

Although Europe has an overall low birthrate, this is not a consistent pattern throughout the continent. Four countries that have birthrates higher than 13 and fertility rates higher than 2.0 are: Albania (21, 2.7); Ireland (17, 2.4); Romania (15, 2.0); and Poland (14.1). The position of religion in these societies and government policy regarding birth control and abortion influence their birthrates.

Albania clearly stands out as not fitting a typical European "demographic" profile with respect to vital statistics. Compared with the other European countries, it has the highest birthrates and fertility rates, the lowest death rate (5/1,000 people, compared with 10 overall for Europe), and among the lowest life expectancies (72).

Contemporary Languages of Europe

At least fifty different languages are spoken today in those parts of Europe covered in this volume. We have been comprehensive, rather than restrictive, in the following outline of European languages. Hence, whenever there is no consensus about whether a particular linguistic entity constitutes one language or two, we have usually identified both. For example, we have identified both Macedonian and Bulgarian as different South Slavic languages; many people would argue that they should not be separated. Following the same line of thinking, we have listed both Croatian and Serbian. There are many such cases throughout the outline.

Similarly, whenever a language is in revival as a spoken language or is still spoken now by only a very small number of people—as reported in the articles of this volume—we have included that language in the outline. In most cases, we have tried to follow general linguistic divisions in our organization of the identification of different languages. With nationalistic sentiments being increasingly expressed throughout Europe, language identification carries particularly strong meaning, prompting us to be as inclusive as possible. However, we have not included in the outline those languages that are spoken mainly for religious purposes in Europe, including Hebrew, Latin, and Old Church Slavonic.

The following outline is based mainly on the language divisions as reported by Comrie (1987), Stephens (1976), Ruhlen (1991), and Zaborski's "European Languages" in *Goode's World Atlas* (1990).

I. Indo-European Language Family
   A. Teutonic Language Group
      (1) English Group
         English
         Frisian
      (2) Scandinavian Language Group
         Swedish
         Norwegian
         Danish
         Faroese
         Icelandic
      (3) German-Dutch Language Group
         Dutch
         Flemish
         Low German
         Middle German
         High German
         Yiddish
   B. Romanic Language Group
      (1) Spanish Language Group
         Castilian
         Catalan
         Ladino
      (2) Portuguese Language Group
         Portuguese
         Galician
      (3) French Language Group
         French Walloon
         Northern French
         Southern French
         Occitan
      (4) Italian Language Group
         Italian
         Sardinian
         Corsican
         Sicilian
      (5) Romansch Language Group
         Rhaeto-Romance
         Ladin
         Friulian
      (6) Romanian Language Group

Romanian
Vlach
Istro-Romanian (Dalmatian)
   C. Celtic Language Group
      (1) Gaelic Language Group
          Irish
          Scots Gaelic
          Manx
      (2) Brittanic Language Group
          Welsh
          Breton
          Cornish (extinct)
   D. Slavic Language Group
      (1) Western Slavic Language Group
          Polish
          Slovak
          Czech
          Sorbian (Lusatian) (Upper and Lower)
      (2) Eastern Slavic Language Group (mostly not covered in this volume—See volume 6)
          Russian
          Ukrainian
          Byelo-Ruthenian (or Belorussian, White Russian)
      (3) Southern Slavic Language Group
          Slovenian
          Croatian
          Serbian
          Macedonian
          Bulgarian
          Pomak
   E. Illyrian Language Group
      Albanian
   F. Hellenic (Greek) Language Group
      Demotiki
      Katharevousa
   G. Baltic Language Group (covered in volume 6)
      Lithuanian
      Latvian
   H. Indo-Iranian Language Group
      Romany
II. Uralic Language Family
   A. Finnic Language Group
      (1) Northwest Language Group (covered mainly in volume 6)
          Finnish
          Karelian
          Estonian
          Livian
          Vepsian
          Izhorian (Ingrian)
          Vodian
      (2) Northeast Language Group (covered in volume 6)
      (3) Southeast or Volga Language Group (covered in volume 6)
   B. Ugrian Language Group
      Hungarian
   C. Lapp Language Group
      Lapponian
III. Altaic Language Family
   A. Southwest (Oguz) Language Group

Osman Turks (covered in volumes 6 and 9)
Gagauz (covered in volume 6)
Azerbayjanian (covered in volume 6)
Turkmenian (covered in volume 6)
IV. Semitic Language Family
      Maltese
V. Basque Language Family
      Basque
VI. Language Isolate
      Pontic

European Prehistory and History

At the time of the early discoveries of hominid fossils in the nineteenth century, many scientists considered Europe the likely place of origin of the ancestors of *Homo sapiens*. In the twentieth century, the discoveries of hominid fossils in Africa and Asia that clearly predated any of those found in Europe, as well as the debunking in the 1950s of Piltdown as a possible European transitional man-ape, led scientists to agree that the earliest humans definitely did not originate in Europe. While Miocene-period ape fossils dating back approximately 22 million years have been found in several parts of southern and central Europe, paleontologists have never found any evidence of the earliest hominid australopithecines or *Homo habilis* being in any part of Europe. Evidence clearly points to Africa for hominid origins.

Paleontologists disagree as to whether the range of human forms called *Homo erectus* extended into Europe. Those few fossils found in Europe that had been considered by some to belong to *H. erectus* exhibit traits that suggest that they are related to *H. sapiens*. Although they clearly are not anatomically modern, these particular fossils display "a mosaic of primitive and late traits that mark them as archaic *H. sapiens*" (Nelson and Jurmain 1991, 490). Most recently, paleontologists have tended to include these fossils among *H. sapiens* and not *H. erectus*. Dispute persists as to how to classify them. In short, there are no unequivocal *H. erectus* fossils in Europe.

Archaic *H. sapiens* began to appear in Europe about 500,000 or so years ago during the Middle Pleistocene geological epoch. Some of these fossil finds resemble later Neanderthals, leading to the possible interpretation that they were ancestral to Neanderthals. The Mauer mandible from Germany, the Petralona skull from Greece (with an estimated cranial capacity of 1,320 cubic centimeters), and the Arago partial skull (with an estimated cranial capacity of 1,050–1,150 cubic centimeters) are among the earliest human fossils found so far in Europe.

Earlier Middle Pleistocene human fossils are more robust than later ones and possess more features characteristic of *H. erectus* than of *H. sapiens*. Since we cannot be certain of the dates associated with finds from the Middle Pleistocene, the evolutionary sequence remains muddled. Even though more archaeological excavation for fossils has been carried out in Europe than any other part of the world, the fossil record remains ambiguous for these early time periods. Since evidence of tool assemblages predates any hominid fossil finds, figures provided for earliest known human activities in Europe cannot be generalized to any particular hominid form.

Based upon a combination of fossil finds and stone tool deposits, it is clear that human groups had dispersed throughout central and western Europe by 350,000 years or so ago. Acheulean-type technology predominated through the Middle Pleistocene, becoming somewhat more sophisticated by the end of the epoch. The basic tools consisted of choppers and flake tools constructed in a variety of forms. During the latter periods of the Middle Pleistocene, archaic *H. sapiens* in Europe and Africa developed the Levalloisian, or prepared-core, technique. Using this method, hominids could anticipate the size and shape of the flake before striking the core, indicating improved cognitive capacity. Archaic *H. sapiens* inhabited open-air sites and caves; it is not clear whether they controlled fire. Three major Middle Pleistocene Acheulean sites include Terra Amata in southern France and Torralba and Ambrona in Spain.

NEANDERTHALS AND THE UPPER PLEISTOCENE

Approximately 125,000 years ago during the Middle Paleolithic, Neanderthals began to appear in Europe during the Riss-Wurm interglacial. Over the course of the Wurm glaciation, they remained widespread throughout most parts of Europe until they disappeared about 35,000 years ago. Since the discovery of hominid fossils in the Neander Valley in Germany in 1856, considerable confusion and controversy has surrounded Neanderthals. Their place in human history—especially their relationship to modern humans—remains far from clear. While Neanderthals evidenced considerable physical commonality with modern hominids, they also had quite distinctive traits. Neanderthal average cranial capacity actually exceeded that of modern humans. They had an upright stature and a fully bipedal gait. There is considerable variability among Neanderthal fossils. Generally, however, their cranial and postcranial bones tended to be quite robust with a series of specific features: e.g. large, protruding face; prominent torus above the eye orbits; occipital bun and torus at the lower back of the skull, and the lack of a chin.

The Neanderthals developed a new stone-tool tradition called Mousterian, drawing upon the disc-core technique. They lived during a particularly cold period (Wurm, the last glacial period). Archaeological data indicates that they lived in caves and open-air sites, built fires, made and wore clothing, and were skillful hunters. Ranging far into the northern reaches of Europe, they relied mainly upon hunting of large game animals such as mammoths, reindeer, and woolly rhinoceroses. They buried at least some of their deceased members, leading some anthropologists to conclude that Neanderthals believed in some sort of spiritual world or afterlife.

The most recent Neanderthal fossils date back about 35,000 years and were found at Saint Cesaire in southwestern France, in association with an Upper Paleolithic tool tradition. Since anatomically modern hominids inhabited parts of western Europe by this time, we are faced with the perplexing question of the exact relationship between Neanderthals and modern hominids. It appears that both forms coexisted in time and space for several thousand years. The nature of the contact—both cultural and biological—between the two groups remains a matter of intense scientific dispute.

ANATOMICALLY MODERN HUMANS IN EUROPE

A large assemblage of *Homo sapiens sapiens* has been found in both central and western Europe. In central Europe, especially, fossils from several sites evidence both modern and Neanderthal features; certain paleontologists interpret that as evidence of a local transition from Neanderthal to modern hominids. Many of the early modern hominids in central Europe have robust features and archaic traits. The fossil finds called Mladec from the Czech and Slovak Federative Republic, dated at about 33,000 years ago, represent an earlier modern hominid. In part because of sexual dimorphism, the three male and two female skulls from this site evidence considerable variation. More recent modern hominids show a combination of both archaic and more gracile traits. In contrast to the local continuity explanation for this evidence, other paleontologists argue that these more gracile traits were a result of migrations of hominids from Africa. Cro-Magnon is not the earliest modern human for this part of Europe.

Several problems plague scientific efforts to relate Neanderthal accurately to modern hominids: limitations of dating techniques, insufficient fossils that clearly connect the two, incompleteness of the fossils available, and poor excavation techniques at the time of early discoveries.

Approximately 12,000 years ago the Wurm glacier retreated, the "affluent hunter-gatherer" Mesolithic commenced, and the way of life for the anatomically modern hominids began to shift substantially. While the Neolithic culture emerged in southern parts of Europe soon thereafter, the Mesolithic culture persisted in northwestern Europe until approximately 5,500 years ago. In the meantime, domestication of animals and agriculture had spread from Anatolia to the Balkan Peninsula by about 8,000–9,000 years ago. Thus, at that time the Neolithic revolution was under way in Europe, at least in some parts of Europe.

CHRONOLOGICAL SUMMARY OF CRITICAL CULTURAL DEVELOPMENTS AND HISTORICAL EVENTS

The cultural summaries in the volume provide information about the prehistory and history of the major cultural groups of Europe. The following time line, beginning with 32,000 B.P., provides a summary of major events (mainly political and economic) that have shaped Europe. The time line draws heavily from Wetterau (1990) as well as Grun (1975, 1979, 1991), Vidal-Naquet (1987), and the *World Almanac*.

Prehistoric Period from the Upper Paleolithic

32,000 B.P.   Rapid transition from Middle to Upper Paleolithic with great diversity in cultural traditions. Artistic traditions thrive for 20,000 years, demonstrated in remains by a complex symbolic relationship between human beings, their physical environment, and other animals; these traditions last until about 13,000 years ago.

30,000 B.P.   First appearance of Upper Paleolithic cave art in northern Spain and southwestern France.

16,000–5000 B.P.   Magdalenian cultural tradition flourishes with complex artistic achievements. Extraordinary technological advances occur, including the barbed harpoon. Highest population density to date in Europe.

10,300 B.P.   Mesolithic period begins with the retreat of glaciers; low-lying areas are flooded and become natural environments for new flora and fauna. An increase in use of microlithic tools.

c. 8500 B.P.   Neolithic begins in Europe with evidence of agriculture in the southeastern areas. Cultivation of cereals and domestication of sheep and goats appears to have diffused from Anatolia. By 8300 B.P., villages appear in the central and western parts of the Mediterranean. By approximately 8000 B.P. Anatolian peoples have moved across the Aegean Sea into Thessaly and onto Crete. Two routes of colonization are followed: along the Mediterranean littoral (7,000–8,000 years ago) and north-westwardly through the Vardar-Danube-Rhine river corridors to the plains of northern Europe (6,000–7,000 years ago). The sea levels rise about this time, and Britain is separated from the European continent.

7200 B.P.   Agriculture is being practiced as far north as the Netherlands. Two economic belts develop: a northern belt, in which cereals (particularly wheat) and sheep and cattle dominate, and a southern belt stressing maritime trade, fishing, and wine and olive production.

6500 B.P.   People in the Balkans are making gold and copper objects. In eastern and central Europe, individual burial sites hold rich materials, including the large Varna Cemetery in Bulgaria that holds copper and gold artifacts. In the lower Danube, people are using cattle as plow animals. In western Europe, appearance of first megalithic tombs. Dolmens appear in the regions of Brittany and Portugal.

6000–5000 B.P.   Rapid population movement into western Europe and expansion of agriculture, as far as Spain, the British Isles, the Netherlands, northern Poland, northern Germany, France, and southern Scandinavia.

5500 B.P.   With the development and spread of new farming patterns and technology, the ard (simple plow) is found throughout western and northern Europe and animals are being used for food, transport, and their wool and hides.

c. 5200 B.P.   Appearance of the wheel in Europe, with evidence in the form of pottery models in places such as Hungary and Transylvania. In northwest France and the British Isles, megalithic stone circular structures appear.

5000 B.P.   Walled citadels are built in Mediterranean Europe.

4300 B.P.   Bronze Age begins in Europe.

4000 B.P.   Stonehenge is created in England.

c. 4000 B.P.   Migration of Indo-European populations—including the Celts, Illyrians, Thracians, Germans, Balts, Italic speakers, Slavs, and Veneti—is under way from central Asia and eventually reaches Europe.

4000 B.P.   State formation on Crete (Minoan culture). By 3900 B.P. evidence of hieroglyphic writing in Minoan culture.

3500 B.P.   Mycenaean period commences in Greece.

c. 3000 B.P.   Bronze-using agriculturalists are located throughout Europe. Two areas become particularly developed in terms of metal industries and artistic traditions: southern Scandinavia and the east-central region.

2850 B.P.   First evidence of a settlement at the later site of Rome.

c. 2800 B.P.   Celtic-speaking people begin to spread throughout north-central Europe and later well into many parts of western Europe. Celtic Iron Age established, as seen at Hallstatt site in Austria.

2800 B.P.   In central Italy, Etruscan city-states begin to develop.

2750 B.P.   First evidence of Greek alphabet; Greek colonization begins to spread throughout the Mediterranean. Ironworking develops in Britain.

2700 B.P.   Greek Archaic period.

c. 2600 B.P.   Greeks found a trading colony at contemporary site of Marseilles.

2600 B.P.   Celts are located north and west of the Alps trading with western Mediterranean Greek colonies. Rome is established as an urban center; first evidence of Latin alphabet. In northern Europe, central lowlands are settled.

c. 2500 B.P.   Celts invade the Iberian Peninsula.

2450 B.P.   Athens city-state at height of its cultural influence. Parthenon is built 1432 B.P.

2400 B.P.   Celts in northern Italy; in 2432 B.P. they pillage Rome. In turn, Rome greatly improves its defenses by construction of Servian Wall.

2250 B.P.   Rome controls the Italian Peninsula.

c. 2250 B.P.   Carthage establishes commercial concerns in Iberian Peninsula.

2218–2201 B.P.   During the Second Punic War, the Romans conquer the Iberian Peninsula, later occupying it.

2146 B.P.   Destruction of Greek city-states by Rome. Greek culture continues to flourish.

2058–2051 B.P.   Under Julius Caesar, the Romans conquer Gaul (modern France).

c. 2084–2043 B.P.   Romans subjugate the British Isles, establishing Londinium (modern London) as a successful trading center.

First through Seventh Centuries A.D.

50   Rome's population reaches one million, making it the most populous city in the world.

100   Roman legions at their height, consisting of 300,000 soldiers. By 117 the Roman Empire has expanded to its maximum geographic influence.

125   Hadrian's Wall constructed in northern Britain.

285   Roman Empire divided into eastern and western sectors.

c. 300   Iron production well advanced in northern Europe.

c. 400   Germanic tribes invade Iberian Peninsula.

419–711   Visigoths overthrow Germanic tribes and found their own kingdom in the Iberian Peninsula.

476   Roman Empire in the west collapses following the Battle of Pavia.

500s   Germanic peoples establish Anglo-Saxon kingdoms on the British Isles (in location of contemporary England).

Eighth Century

711   North African Muslims invade the Iberian Peninsula.

751–754   Carolingian kingdom founded under the rulership of Pepin the Short, unifying the Frankish territories.

756   Pepin gives conquered lands around Rome to the pope. This land becomes the nucleus of the Papal States.

768–814   Holy Roman Emperor Charlemagne extends Carolingian empire to the northwest, encompassing lands of contemporary northern Italy, France, Germany, Belgium, Luxembourg, and the Netherlands.

Ninth Century

787–c. 1000 Danish Norsemen attack England. By 800 they control much of the modern British Isles.
800s Moravian Empire unifies contemporary lands of Czechoslovakia. Norsemen invade Russia and found Rurik dynasty.
843 Charlemagne's empire divided at the Treaty of Verdun.
c. 845 Norsemen invade modern France and settle Normandy.
c. 863 Development of Cyrillic alphabet.
871–99 London captured from the Danes by Alfred the Great, English king.

Tenth Century

930 Vikings establish Althing in Iceland. This is the first representative governmental body in Europe.
962 Otto I crowned emperor of the Holy Roman Empire (H.R.E.) by Pope John XII, strengthening the relationship between the church and European monarchies. H.R.E. later becomes Germany.
983 Eastward expansion of the German Empire under way.
987–996 As first of the Capetian kings of the Western Franks, Hugh Capet establishes Paris as his capital.

Eleventh Century

c. 1000 Venice, Genoa, and Naples develop into strong maritime powers and successfully battle the Muslims on the seas. They become economically prosperous through trade.
1016 Danes conquer England.
1042 Anglo-Saxon rule is reestablished.
1066 William I the Conqueror leads the Norman Conquest, invades England, and claims the English throne.
1075 Pope Gregory VII establishes reforms—including denying the right of Holy Roman Emperor Henry IV to appoint church bishops—that provoke power struggles between emperors and popes that last until 1122.
c. 1080 Central authority breaks down in Italy, resulting in establishment of separate city-republics such as Pisa.

Twelfth Century

1096–1291 The Crusades, during which time the English and French kings unsuccessfully attempt to recapture the Holy Land.
c. 1100 Population expansion in Europe.
1122 The Diet of Worms determines that the Catholic church has authority over the Holy Roman Empire.
1169 Normans invade Ireland and establish English control.

Thirteenth Century

1198–1216 Papal power at its zenith. Holy Roman Emperor Otto IV is excommunicated in 1210.

1200 Mongols invade and begin centuries-long domination of Russian kingdoms.
1200s Austrian dynasty is established by Hapsburg King Rudolf I. The dynasty will rule for 700 years.
1209 Crusaders massacre 20,000 people at Bezier, France.
1212 Aragon and Christian kingdoms of Leon and Castile gain control of Spain, leaving the Muslims in control of Granada.
1215 English king John signs the Magna Carta. The Magna Carta has major impact on the development of English law and guarantees many basic liberties.
1236–1241 Mongol invasion of Europe (Polish, Hungarian, Serbian, and Bulgarian territories).
1254–1273 During the unrest of the Great Interregnum, nobles gain considerable power in the Holy Roman Empire.
1261 Restoration of Greek Empire in Constantinople.
1284 Wales is formally annexed to England.

Fourteenth Century

1300 Climate deteriorates, causing problems in agriculture in parts of Europe.
c. 1300 Business institutions and the mercantile class operations emerge in Italy.
1314 Robert the Bruce, Scottish revolutionary, defeats the English at the Battle of Bannockburn, establishing Scottish independence and him as king of the Scots.
1337–1453 Following the Hundred Years' War, France obtains control over all the English continental kingdoms. French visionary Joan of Arc is a rallying force for the French armies.
1348 The plague (the Black Death) starts to spread throughout Europe, eventually killing a quarter of Europe's population.
c. 1350 The Renaissance begins to develop in Italy and spreads eventually throughout Europe.
1356 The Holy Roman Empire is reorganized under the Golden Bull of 1356; the emperor maintains control of only his personal territory.
1380 Russians are victorious over the Mongols.
1381 The Peasants' Revolt takes place in England, reflecting popular discord over the poll tax and legal control of wages.
1397 Sweden, Norway, and Denmark are united into the Kalmar Union by Queen Margaret of Denmark.

Fifteenth Century

1431 The English capture Joan of Arc and burn her at the stake for heresy.
1438–1439 Albert II is crowned the first Hapsburg emperor.
1453 Fall of the Byzantine Empire as the Ottoman Turks take control of Constantinople and conquer Greece; the beginning of 350 years of Ottoman rule.
1455–1485 War of the Roses in England.
1461–1483 During the reign of Louis XI in France, later absolute French monarchy set in motion.
1462–1505 Reign of Ivan III (the Great) in Russia.
1478 Spanish Inquisition commences. Ottoman Turks conquer Albania; rule continues until 1912.
1492 Spain expels Arabs and Jews. Genoese explorer

Christopher Columbus reaches the New World on behalf of Spain.

1494–1559 Italian Wars.

1495 French soldiers spread syphilis epidemic from Florence throughout Europe. Two years later, Florence experiences severe famine.

Sixteenth Century

1500s The emergence of Copenhagen as a cultural and commercial center.

1509 Constantinople destroyed by earthquake. Trade in slaves from Africa begins.

1516 King Charles I is crowned the first king of a united Spain. When later he becomes Charles V, he reigns over both Spain and the Holy Roman Empire.

1517 Martin Luther, German theologian, protests against corruption in the Roman Catholic church and sets in motion the Protestant Reformation. Coffee arrives in Europe.

1520 Anabaptist movement develops in Germany and Switzerland, leading to their persecution by Lutherans and Catholics.

1525 Potato introduced from South America.

1526 Hapsburgs take control of Bohemia.

1526–1529 Ottoman Turks push westward and invade Holy Roman Empire, defeating the Hungarians and reaching as far as the walls of Vienna, where they are finally stopped and turned back.

1528 Plague breaks out in England.

1533–1584 The reign of the first Russian czar, Ivan IV (the Terrible).

1534 King Henry VIII breaks from the Roman Catholic church and establishes the Church of England over a conflict with the pope regarding an annulment of the king's marriage.

1545–1563 With the Council of Trent, beginning of Catholic Counter-Reformation.

1558–1603 Protestantism is restored in England under reign of Elizabeth I. Development of Puritan movement.

1588 In effort to eradicate Protestantism, Spanish Armada attacks English navy and, in turn, is destroyed.

1598 Edict of Nantes marks the demise of the European religious wars and religious freedom for Protestants.

Seventeenth Century

1600s–1700s Paris is Europe's cultural center and the center from which the Enlightenment emerges.

1602 Dutch East India Company formed.

1613 Beginning of Romanov line in Russia, which lasts until 1917.

1618–1648 Thirty Years' War; Holy Roman Empire is destroyed. France becomes the leading military and political power in Europe. Ends with Peace of Westphalia, which divides Germany into Protestant and Roman Catholic sectors and gives Belgium and the Netherlands their independence.

1640 Portuguese freedom from Spain.

1643–1715 Rule of Louis XVI in France.

1649 Following the end of English King Charles I's rule, Oliver Cromwell takes the leadership of the newly established republican government (the Commonwealth).

c. 1650 The Dutch create a world empire in Asia, Africa, and the New World.

1660 English Parliament restores the monarchy, and the reign of Charles II begins.

1664 The Great Plague of London begins and eventually kills over 100,000 people.

1666 The Great Fire of London.

1676–1878 Russo-Turkish Wars. At the end of this long period of warfare, the Ottoman Empire had weakened considerably and the Russian borders had expanded substantially.

1680s Ottomans driven out of Hungary by the Hapsburgs, who establish their own rule in the Hungarian territory.

Eighteenth Century

1700s Age of Enlightenment, with an emphasis on rationalism initiated by the French.

1703 Buckingham Palace built.

1707 England and Scotland unified.

1712 Czar Peter founds the city of Saint Petersburg and moves the Russian capital there. Saint Petersburg is the capital city of Russia until 1918. Moscow retains its status as center of Russian commerce and culture.

1752 18,000 buildings burn in a great fire in Moscow.

1789 Storming of the Bastille in Paris and publication of *The Declaration of the Rights of Man and Citizen*, which specifies freedom of the press, religion, and speech and the right of representation.

1792 French Revolution begins.

1793 Execution of Louis XVI in France for treason.

1793–1794 Reign of Terror; at least 40,000 royalists and other people executed by French revolutionaries.

Nineteenth Century

1803–1815 Napoleonic Wars. Substantial part of continental Europe controlled by Napoleon while campaign to conquer Russia fails.

1804 Napoleon proclaims himself emperor of the newly founded French Empire. Napoleonic Code established and becomes basis of French civil law.

1815 Napoleon exiled after his defeat at Waterloo. New Treaty of Paris results in loss of territory for France. Congress of Vienna reestablishes Spanish and Austrian control of Italy. Restoration of Papal States. Kingdom of Netherlands established. Norway gains independence from Sweden. Following Napoleonic Wars, Austria becomes the dominant power of the German states.

1821–1827 Greek rebellion against the Ottomans leads to Greek independence.

1833 End of slavery throughout the British Empire.

1840s Irish potato famine, leading to starvation of over a million people (1846–1851) and emigration of 1.5 million people.

1848 Karl Marx, German philosopher, and Friedrich Engels, German businessman, predict end of capitalism in the *Communist Manifesto*.

1853–1856 In the Crimean War, France and Great Britain (with other countries) keep Russia from invading Ottoman Empire.

1861 Through the Edict of Emancipation, Russian serfs are freed. Unification of Italy.

1867 Austro-Hungarian monarchy established.

1870–1871 Franco-Prussian War.
1871 Rome named the capital city of Italy.
1894 Dreyfus Affair. Alfred Dreyfus, French army officer, wrongly charged with treason; conviction overturned in 1906.

Twentieth Century

1903 Assassination of King Alexander I and Queen Draga of Serbia.
1910 Nicholas I becomes king of newly proclaimed kingdom of Montenegro.
1912–1913 Balkan Wars, with Serbia, Greece, and Bulgaria at war with the Ottoman Turks.
1913 Treaty of Bucharest confirms the withdrawal of Turkey from Balkan territories after almost 500 years of rule.
1914 Heir to the throne of Austria Archduke Francis Ferdinand and his wife are assassinated in Sarajevo by a Serbian nationalist, leading to the outbreak of World War I. Following the assassination, over the course of 1914, Austria-Hungary declares war on Serbia; Germany declares war on Russia and France, and then invades Belgium; Britain declares war on Germany and later Austria; Austria, on Russia; Serbia and Montenegro, on Germany; France, on Austria; Russia, on Turkey; and France and Britain, on Turkey.
1914–1918 World War I.
1916 Irish Easter Rebellion leading to guerrilla warfare in opposition to British rule. Within the Commonwealth of Britain, Ireland becomes an independent dominion.
1917 United States declares war against Germany.
1917–1922 October Revolution in Russia and outbreak of Russian Civil War. Czar Nicholas abdicates and Bolsheviks take control. Continuing hostilities between Communists and the counterrevolutionaries.
1917–1924 Lenin becomes head of the Soviet Communist party, moves the capital to Moscow, and commences collectivization and nationalization policies.
1918 Women's suffrage legislation passed in Great Britain for women over 30. Iceland established as a sovereign state. Treaty of Versailles establishes the new nation-state of Czechoslovakia. Proclamation of the union between Serbs, Croats, and Slovenes as the Kingdom of the Serbs, Croats and Slovenes (later Yugoslavia). Allies and Austria-Hungary sign armistice. Bolsheviks execute ex-Czar Nicholas II and his family in Russia. With half of its population dead at the close of the war, Hungary gives up three-quarters of its prewar lands in war reparations to Czechoslovakia, Romania, and Yugoslavia.
1919 Comintern created by Lenin.
1920 Home rule granted to Ireland (Irish Free State). Northern Ireland created.
1921 In Germany, Hitler organizes Nazi party; in Italy Mussolini founds the Fascist party.
1924 After Lenin's death, Stalin becomes leader of USSR.
1926 Trotsky ousted, strengthening Stalin's power.
1930s Great Depression, especially severe in Germany, France, and Great Britain.
1933 Beginning of Nazi concentration camps.
1935 Rhineland invaded by Germans.
1936–1939 Spanish Civil War.
1938 Following Munich Pact, Germany permitted gradu-

ally to occupy Sudetenland; with the invasion of Czechoslovakia and Poland in 1939, pact is nullified.
1939 Alliance between Italy and Germany strengthened through Pact of Steel. Albania invaded by Italy.
1939–1945 World War II. Germany begins the war with its invasion of Poland in 1939. Initially an ally of Germany, the USSR is invaded by the Germans and then joins the Allies. After France falls in 1940, Italy becomes an ally of Germany. Italy's campaigns in North Africa fail, and Italy is invaded by the Allies in 1943.
1939–1975 Dictatorship of Franco in Spain, which ends upon his death.
1944–1949 Greek Civil War, during which Britain and the United States help the resistance against Communists.
1945 World War II ends in Europe with Allied occupation of Germany. Hitler commits suicide, and the Partisans kill Mussolini. As the head of the Partisan movement during the war, Tito takes political leadership of the newly formed Federal People's Republic of Yugoslavia.
1946 New constitution enacted in France and Fourth Republic formed.
1947 During the Meeting of the Big Four (the USSR, Britain, France, and the United States), disagreements arise between the USSR and the other three powers over plans for Germany.
1948 After expelling Soviet military advisers, Tito is expelled from the Comintern, breaking formal ties between the USSR and Yugoslavia. Creation of Soviet satellites in central and eastern Europe.
1948–1949 USSR blockades Berlin; U.S. airlift to West Berlin.
1949 West Germany (Federal Republic of Germany) established from the British, French, and U.S. occupation zones. East Germany (German Democratic Republic) created by the USSR from its occupation zone.
1955 Warsaw Pact signed between East German satellite countries and the USSR.
1956 Soviet invasion of Hungary.
1957 *Sputnik I* launched by USSR. European Economic Community established through the Treaty of Rome.
1960s–1990s Persistent and intense guerrilla warfare in Northern Ireland.
1961 Berlin wall constructed by the USSR.
1968 Invasion of Czechoslovakia by the USSR.
1970 Great Britain becomes member of Common Market. East and West German leaders meet.
1972 During Munich Olympics, eleven Israeli athletes killed by Arab terrorists.
1972–1974 Britain establishes direct rule in Northern Ireland after intense unrest.
1973 Diplomatic relations established between East and West Germany.
1977 First free Spanish elections since the civil war, leading to constitutional monarchy in 1978.
1980 Death of Tito in Yugoslavia, followed later by economic and political instability.
1981 Martial law established by USSR in Poland.
1985 Gorbachev becomes leader of USSR and establishes policies of *glasnost* and *perestroika*.
1987 Intermediate Nuclear Forces (INF) Treaty signed. With Gorbachev's agreement to reduce the military forces of

the USSR in Europe, serious arms reduction talks between the United States and the USSR become possible.

1989   Multiparty system established in Hungary. In Poland, the Solidarity party is victorious in elections, and first non-Communist government is established. In Czechoslovakia, a predominantly non-Communist government takes power, with Vaclav Havel as president and Alexander Dubcek as chair of the parliament. Thousands of East Germans escape through Hungary to West Germany. Resignation of East German Communist government and East German President Erich Honecker. Fall of the Berlin Wall. Romanian Communist government is overthrown and Ceausescu and his wife are tried and executed. In Kosovo Province of Serbian Republic of Yugoslavia clashes between ethnic Albanians and police lead to direct Serbian control of the province's police and courts. Violent demonstrations ensue.

1990   Albania's borders are opened. Free elections are held in Romania. First free elections in Czechoslovakia. Reunification of Germany. Poles overwhelmingly elect Lech Walesa (leader of Solidarity) president. General strike in Bulgaria leads to resignation of Socialist (previously Communist) premier; political independent elected premier by parliament. Charter of Paris for a New Europe signed by U.S. President Bush and Gorbachev. Treaty on Conventional Armed Forces in Europe signed by Bush and Gorbachev and NATO and Warsaw Pact leaders.

1991   Crackdown by Soviet troops in the Baltics leads to demonstrations and violence. Lithuanians, Latvians, and Estonians vote to secede from USSR; their independence is recognized later in the year by the United Nations. Resignation of Communist government of Albania. Slovenia and Croatia declare independence; war ensues between the Yugoslav military in Slovenia and later in Croatia; civil war in Croatia continues through the year. Soviet troops vacate Hungary and Czechoslovakia. Warsaw Pact abolished. Thousands of Albanians try to find refuge in Italy; some are turned back.

Reference Resources
GENERAL RESOURCES

As far as we know, there is no English-language, book-length survey of either the cultural anthropology or ethnography of Europe. Relevant review articles include Cole (1977) on community studies, Gilmore (1982) on the Mediterranean region, Gullestad (1989) on Scandinavia, and Halpern and Kideckel (1983) on eastern Europe. There are also a number of good bibliographies, although none are up-to-date: Dickenson and Pempe (1981), Sweet and O'Leary (1969), Theodoratus (1969), and Kuter (1978). Other, more general resources that go beyond the scope of anthropology are Horak (1985), Horecky (1969a, 1969b), and Jelavich (1969).

PHYSICAL ENVIRONMENT

While no single source provides complete information about the physical environment of Europe, each of the following references provides certain types of specific information. Among the following references, the best general description of Europe is found in *The New Columbia Encyclopedia. Chambers World Gazetteer: An A–Z of Geographical Informa-*

tion is a comprehensive and relatively detailed directory of physical locations throughout the world. Country entries include maps with political subdivisions indicated and identified. It is very useful for a brief but moderately in-depth overview of each country.

The *Euro-Atlas* is an up-to-date, detailed, clearly drawn, readable, and well-indexed road atlas of all sections of Europe, including the United Kingdom and the European part of the former USSR, but excluding Iceland. It also includes city maps. *Goode's World Atlas* is a moderately sized and well-indexed atlas that is very convenient to use. The maps are easy to decipher owing to clarity of drawing and printing. It has several notable features, including excellent thematic maps (including a well-drawn and keyed language map for Europe) and a glossary of foreign geographic terms.

The New York Times Atlas of the World is a large, very detailed atlas, with an excellent index that permits the reader to identify locations easily on any particular map. It is especially helpful when used in conjunction with *Goode's*.

Webster's New Geographical Dictionary is a very handy, comprehensive, quick-reference type of dictionary. The 47,000 entries are short, but they provide a good beginning point for more intensive investigation in other sources, such as the *Chambers Gazetteer* and the *World Atlas*. The *1992 World Almanac and Book of Facts* and the *World Atlas* provide less detail for each entry regarding physical locations than does the *Chambers Gazetteer*, but the latter has an extensive section of maps (thematic, environmental, and historical).

CONTEMPORARY LANGUAGES OF EUROPE

Three basic sources for Europe are Chadwick (1973), Comrie (1987), and Stephens (1976). Although the Stephens volume does not encompass all languages spoken in Europe, it does provide the contextual background and status of minority languages in sixteen countries. For example, the chapter on Austria covers the Slovenes living in Carinthia and the Croats and Magyars in Burgenland, and the chapter on Spain includes Galicians, Basques, and Catalans. Britain, Italy, and France are covered especially well. Furthermore, the book includes a good bibliography organized by country and by culture. For scholars interested in the cultural context of languages, this is a particularly good overview for Europe.

Ruhlen's *A Guide to the World's Languages*, volume 1, *Classification* (1991) is an invaluable one-of-a-kind resource for classifying the languages of the world. The chapter on Europe includes historical and linguistic background and then separately discusses the Indo-Hittite (Indo-European), Uralic-Yukaghir, and Caucasian language families, with extensive bibliographies on languages in each group. The final chapter presents a detailed classification of the world's languages (encompassing over 50 pages). Three indices cover personal names, language groups, and languages. Classifications of languages vary from one source to another, but this book is so comprehensive that it provides a solid basis for comparison with other phyla. Upcoming volumes are to be published on language data and on language universals.

Zaborski's "Europe Languages" in *Goode's World Atlas* (1990) provides an extremely useful language map of Europe, including the western former USSR, parts of North Africa, Turkey, Syria, and parts of Iran and Iraq. The combination of a thematic color differentiation for language groups, a number designation for particular languages, and a clearly indexed key make this an indispensable map for scholars interested in languages in Europe. As noted above with respect to the Ruhlen classification, the reader will find certain variations from other language sources in the organization and terminology used on this map. However, this is one of the most concise and easily discernible visual outlines of European languages available.

PREHISTORY

General references to prehistory and human evolution that can be drawn on for details about early hominids and their associated culture in Europe include Barraclough (1988), Fagan (1989), Klein (1989), Nelson and Jurmain (1991), Sherratt (1980), and Vidal-Naquet (1987). Other works focusing mainly on the human biology of later Europeans include Ammerman and Cavalli-Sforza (1984).

General references to the cultural prehistory of Europe, which especially cover archaeological materials, include Barraclough (1988), Champion et al. (1984), Fagan (1989), Kinder and Hilgemann (1974), Scarre (1988), and Sherratt (1980). Specific regions and times of European prehistory are covered in Ammerman and Cavalli-Sforza (1984), Barraclough (1988), Borde (1968), Champion et al. (1984), Childe (1957), Clark (1952, 1979), Coles and Harding (1979), Collis (1984), Crosby (1986), Cunliffe (1974), Dennell (1983), Gamble (1986), Gimbutas (1971), Grasiosi (1960), Phillips (1980), Piggott (1965), Pirenne (1952), Renfrew (1973), Scarre (1988), Sherratt (1980), Stringer (1988), Trump (1980), Ucko and Rosenfeld (1967), and Whittle (1985).

GENERAL EUROPEAN HISTORY

Stearns (1967) is an excellent and readable overview of the social history of Europe during its transition from a preindustrial to an industrial society, covering the industrialization of Europe as a whole up to the early 1960s. It pays close attention to change among the peasantry, aristocracy, middle class, artisans, workers, and other significant social groups over the past two centuries. The bibliography is organized by topical category such as "labor movements," "population change and urbanization," "agriculture and the peasantry," and "interwar period."

Gilbert (1984) is a good companion to the Stearns book. Gilbert focuses on the past century's political, economic, and social history. Considerable attention is drawn to developments among the most powerful countries, including what are called the parliamentary governments of Great Britain, France, Spain, and Italy and the authoritarian governments of Germany, the Hapsburg monarchy, and Russia in the pre-1914 period. The second part deals with the "Peace That Failed" or the interwar period and the forces leading to and continuing through World War II. In the third part, the book covers the period from the first years after World War II through the early 1980s. It includes a useful annotated bibliography of recommended further readings. Grun's *The Timetables of History: A Horizontal Linkage of People and Events* (new 3rd rev. ed.) is a rich and handy-to-use resource based on Werner Stein's *Kulturfahrplan* originally published in 1946 in Germany. Beginning with 5000 B.C. and continuing

into 1990, the volume is divided into seven categories: history and politics; literature and theater; religion, philosophy, and learning; visual arts; music; science, technology, and growth; and daily life. The themes run vertically and the years horizontally throughout the book. Because of this organization, the book is easy to use and is able to accommodate a phenomenal amount of information. It also includes a detailed index. Wetterau (1990) is a unique resource, several parts of which pertain to European history and prehistory. In particular, however, the section on nations and empires of Europe is especially pertinent. In addition to a 25-page chronology of main developments, this section includes a list of all the Holy Roman emperors, British monarchs and prime ministers, and rulers and heads of state for Spain, Germany, Italy, and Russia and the former USSR. The historical chronology is more condensed than that of Grun. Other resources of use on general European history include Hood (1973), MacQueen (1987), McEvedy (1967), Meyer (1989), Renfrew (1972), Taylour (1969), Vidal-Naquet (1987), and Warren (1975). Rothschild (1974) and Seton-Watson (1962) cover European history for the period between the world wars.

SPECIAL TOPICS IN HISTORY

There is a large literature on focused topics in European history. Family history and demographic change has been a major topic of study. Some representative general works are Aries (1962), Boswell (1988), Fox (1967), Goody (1983), Hallett (1984), Herligy (1985), Kertzer and Saller (1991), Lasslett (1972), Levin (1989), Lynch (1986), Macfarlane (1978), Pollock (1987), Rawson (1986), and Wall and Laslett (1983). A second topical area of relevance to this volume is nationalism. Useful works include Chadwick (1973), Esman (1977), Hayes (1949), Janowsky (1945), Kohn (1960, 1961), Ramet (1984), Seton-Watson (1964), Snyder (1990), and Sugar and Lederer (1969).

Acknowledgments

Since we had no prior model for Europe to draw upon in planning this volume, we were particularly fortunate to have the enthusiastic cooperation of many scholars. I am especially grateful to the scores of contributors from North America and Europe who wrote articles for this volume. Because of the fast-breaking developments in Europe at the end of the 1980s and the beginning of the 1990s, many articles had to be revised shortly before publication to be reasonably current. Contributors were extremely cooperative in making these last-minute changes, and we greatly appreciate their responsiveness. Working with members of the research staff at the Human Relations Area Files (HRAF) has been a real pleasure. Some articles were written by HRAF researchers, in particular Nancy Gratton. I very much enjoyed having David Levinson as a colleague on this project; he remained persistently patient throughout. Ross Sackett is thanked for his assistance on the early hominid and prehistory sections. Paul Hockings, Timothy J. O'Leary, Matt Salo, Sharon Gmelch, and Walter Zenner provided useful advice on various matters. Dozens of members of the two anthropological organizations that focus on European cultures—the Society for the Anthropology of Europe and the American Anthropological Association and the East European Anthropology Group—

provided substantial assistance in selecting cultures for coverage and in identifying scholars to write about the cultures. I very much appreciate their participation in this project.

References

Ammerman, Albert J., and L. L. Cavalli-Sforza (1984). *The Neolithic Transition and the Genetics of Populations in Europe.* Princeton: Princeton University Press.

Aries, Philippe (1962). *Centuries of Childhood.* Translated by Robert Baldick. New York: Knopf.

Barraclough, Geoffrey, ed. (1988). *The Times Concise Atlas of World Prehistory.* Maplewood, N.J.: Hammond.

Bordes, François (1968). *The Old Stone Age.* New York: McGraw-Hill.

Boswell, John (1988). *The Kindness of Strangers: The Abandonment of Children in Western Europe from Late Antiquity to the Renaissance.* New York: Pantheon.

Chadwick, H. Munro (1973). *The Nationalities of Europe and the Growth of National Ideologies.* New York: Cooper Square Publishers.

Chambers World Gazetteer: An A–Z of Geographical Information (1988). Cambridge: W. & R. Chambers; Cambridge University Press.

Champion, T. G., et al. (1984). *Prehistoric Europe.* New York: Academic Press.

Childe, V. Gordon (1957). *The Dawn of European Civilization.* New York: Knopf.

Clark, J. G. D. (1952). *Prehistoric Europe: The Economic Basis.* Palo Alto, Calif.: Stanford University Press.

Clark, J. G. D. (1975). *The Earlier Stone Age Settlement of Scandinavia.* Cambridge: Cambridge University Press.

Clark, J. G. D. (1979). *Mesolithic Prelude.* Edinburgh: Edinburgh University Press.

Cole, John (1977). "Anthropology Comes Part Way Home: Community Studies in Europe." *Annual Review of Anthropology* 6:349–378.

Coles, J. M., and A. F. Harding (1979). *The Bronze Age in Europe.* London: Methuen.

Collis, John (1984). *The European Iron Age.* London: Batsford.

Comrie, Bernard (1987). *The World's Major Languages.* New York: Oxford University Press.

Crosby, Alfred W. (1986). *Ecological Imperialism: The Biological Expansion of Europe, 900–1900.* Cambridge: Cambridge University Press.

Cunliffe, Barry (1974). *Iron Age Communities in Britain.* London: Routledge & Kegan Paul.

Dennell, Robin C. (1983). *European Economic Prehistory: A New Approach.* New York: Academic Press.

Dickenson, Dennis, and Ruta Pempe (1981). "Europe Bibliographies." In *Europe Bibliographies: A Selected Guide,* 144–170. South Salem, N.Y.: Redgrave.

Esman, Milton J., ed. (1977). *Ethnic Conflict in the Western World.* Ithaca, N.Y.: Cornell University Press.

Euro-Atlas (n.d.). Bern: Kummerly & Frey.

"Europe's New Right" (1992). *Newsweek,* 27 April.

Fagan, Brian M. (1989). *People of the Earth: An Introduction to World Prehistory.* Glenview, Ill.: Scott, Foresman & Co.

"A Fortress Mentality" (1991). *Newsweek,* 9 December.

Fox, Robin (1967). *Kinship and Marriage: An Anthropological Perspective.* Harmondsworth, England: Penguin.

Gamble, Clive (1986). *The Paleolithic Settlement of Europe.* Cambridge: Cambridge University Press.

Ghosh, Bimal (1991). "The Immigrant Tide." *European Affairs* 5(6): 78–82.

Gilbert, Felix (1984). *The End of the European Era, 1980 to the Present.* New York: W. W. Norton & Co.

Gilmore, David D. (1982). "Anthropology and the Mediterranean Area." *Annual Review of Anthropology* 11:175–205.

Gimbutas, Marija (1971). *The Slavs.* London: Thames & Hudson.

Goode's World Atlas (1990). 18th ed. Edited by Edward B. Espenshade, Jr. New York, Chicago, and San Francisco: Rand McNally.

Goody, Jack (1983). *The Development of the Family and Marriage in Europe.* Cambridge: Cambridge University Press.

Graff, James L. (1990). "Strangers in a Strange New Land." *Time,* 25 June. [International edition; no page numbers.]

Grasiosi, Paolo (1960). *Palaeolithic Art.* New York: Abrams.

Grun, Bernard (1975, 1979, 1991 English editions). *The Timetables of History: A Horizontal Linkage of People and Events.* New 3rd rev. ed. New York: Simon & Schuster.

Gullestad, Marianne (1989). "Small Facts and Large Issues: The Anthropology of Contemporary Scandinavian Society." *Annual Review of Anthropology* 18:71–93.

Hallett, Judith P. (1984). *Fathers and Daughters in Roman So-*

ciety: Women and the Elite Family. Princeton: Princeton University Press.

Halpern, Joel M., and David A. Kideckel (1983). "Anthropology of Eastern Europe." *Annual Reviews of Anthropology* 12:377–402.

Hayes, J. H. (1949). *The Historical Evolution of Modern Nationalism*. 2nd ed. New York: Macmillan.

Herligy, David (1985). *Medieval Households*. Cambridge, Mass.: Harvard University Press.

Hood, Sinclair (1973). *The Minoans*. London: Thames & Hudson.

Horak, Stephan M. (1985). *Eastern European National Minorities, 1919/1980: A Handbook*. Littleton, Colo.: Libraries Unlimited.

Horecky, Paul L., ed. (1969a). *East Central Europe: A Guide to Basic Publications*. Chicago: University of Chicago Press.

Horecky, Paul L., ed. (1969b). *Southeastern Europe: A Guide to Basic Publications*. Chicago: University of Chicago Press.

Janowsky, Oscar J. (1945). *Nationalities and National Minorities*. New York: Macmillan.

Jelavich, Charles, ed. (1969). *Language and Area Studies, East Central and Southeastern Europe*. Chicago: University of Chicago Press.

Kertzer, David I., and Richard P. Saller (1991). *The Family in Italy from Antiquity to the Present*. New Haven, Conn.: Yale University Press.

Kinder, Hermann, and Hilgemann, Werner (1974). *The Anchor Atlas of World History*. Vol. 1, *From the Stone Age to the Eve of the French Revolution*. New York: Doubleday, Anchor Books.

Klein, Richard G. (1989). *The Human Career: Human Biological and Cultural Origins*. Chicago: University of Chicago Press.

Kohn, Hans (1960). *Pan-Slavism: Its History and Ideology*. 2nd ed. New York: Vintage Books.

Kohn, Hans (1961). *The Idea of Nationalism*. 2nd ed. New York: Macmillan.

Kuter, Lois (1978). *The Anthropology of Western Europe: A Selected Bibliography*. Bloomington: Indiana University, Western European Studies.

Laslett, Peter, ed., with assistance of Richard Wall (1972). *Household and Family in Past Time: Comparative Studies in the Size and Structure of the Domestic Group over the Last Three Centuries in England, France, Serbia, Japan, and Colonial North America, with Further Materials from Western Europe*. Cambridge: Cambridge University Press.

Leroi-Gourhan, A. *The Dawn of European Art: An Introduction to Palaeolithic Cave Painting*. Cambridge: Cambridge University Press.

Levin, Eve (1989). *Sex and Society in the World of the Orthodox Slavs, 900–1700*. Ithaca, N.Y.: Cornell University Press.

Lynch, J. M. (1986). *Godparents and Kinship in Early Medieval Europe*. Princeton: Princeton University Press.

MacQueen, J. G. (1987). *The Hittites*. London: Thames & Hudson.

McEvedy, Colin (1967). *The Penguin Atlas of Ancient History*. London: Penguin Books.

Meyer, Marc Anthony (1989). *A Documentary History of Western Civilization from Ancient Times to the Present*. Lanham, Md.: University Press of America.

Miller, Judith (1991). "Strangers at the Gate: Europe's Immigration Crisis." *New York Times Magazine*, 15 September, pp. 32–86.

Monod, Jerome, Pehr Gyllenhammar, and Wisse Dekker (1991). "Reshaping Europe." *European Affairs* 5(6): 12–16.

Nelson, Harry, and Jurmain, Robert (1991). *Introduction to Physical Anthropology*. St. Paul, Minn.: West Publishing Co.

The New Columbia Encyclopedia (1975). New York: Columbia University Press.

The New York Times Atlas of the World (1989). London: John Bartholomew & Son.

1992 World Almanac and Book of Facts (1991). New York: Pharos Books.

Phillips, Patricia (1980). *The Prehistory of Europe*. Bloomington: Indiana University Press.

Piggott, Stuart (1965). *Ancient Europe: From the Beginnings of Agriculture to Classical Antiquity*. Chicago: Aldine Publishing Co.

Pirenne, Henri (1952). *Medieval Cities: Their Origins and the Revival of Trade*. Translated by Frank D. Halsey. Princeton: Princeton University Press. [Originally published in French in 1925.]

Pollock, Linda A. (1987). *A Lasting Relationship: Parents and Children over Three Centuries*. London: Fourth Estate.

Ramet, Pedro, ed. (1984). *Religion and Nationalism in Soviet and East European Politics*. Durham, N.C.: Duke University Press.

Rawson, Beryl, ed. (1986). *The Family in Ancient Rome: New Perspectives*. Ithaca, N.Y.: Cornell University Press.

Renfrew, Colin (1972). *The Emergence of Civilization.* London: Methuen.

Renfrew, Colin (1973). *Before Civilization.* New York: Knopf.

Rothschild, Joseph (1974). *A History of East Central Europe.* Vol. 9, *East Central Europe between the Two World Wars.* Seattle: University of Washington Press.

Ruhlen, Merritt (1991). *A Guide to the World's Languages.* Vol. 1, *Classification.* Stanford, Calif.: Stanford University Press.

Scarre, Chris, ed. (1988). *Past Worlds: The Times Atlas of Archaeology.* Maplewood, N.J.: Hammond.

Seton-Watson, Hugh (1962). *Eastern Europe between the Wars, 1918-1941.* 3rd ed. Hamden, Conn.: Archon Books.

Seton-Watson, Hugh (1964). *Nationalism and Communism: Essays, 1946-63.* London: Methuen & Co.

Sherratt, Andrew, ed. (1980). *The Cambridge Encyclopedia of Archaeology.* New York: Crown Publishers; Cambridge University Press.

Snyder, Louis L. (1990). *Encyclopedia of Nationalism.* New York: Paragon House.

Stearns, Peter N. (1967). *European Society in Upheaval: Social History since 1800.* New York: Macmillan.

Stephens, Meic (1976). *Linguistic Minorities in Western Europe.* Llandysul Dufed, Wales: Gomer Press.

Stringer, Chris (1988). *The Neanderthals.* London: Thames & Hudson.

Sugar, Peter F., and Ivo J. Lederer, eds. (1969). *Nationalism in Eastern Europe.* Seattle: University of Washington Press.

Sweet, Louise E., and Timothy J. O'Leary (1969). *Circum-Mediterranean Peasantry: Introductory Bibliographies.* New Haven: HRAF Press.

Taylour, Lord William (1969). *The Mycenaeans.* London: Thames & Hudson.

Theodoratus, Robert J. (1969). *Europe: A Selected Ethnographic Bibliography.* New Haven: HRAF Press.

Trump, David (1980). *The Prehistory of the Mediterranean.* New Haven: Yale University Press.

Ucko, Peter J., and Andree Rosenfeld (1967). *Palaeolithic Cave Art.* New York: McGraw-Hill.

Vidal-Naquet, Pierre, ed. (1987). *The Harper Atlas of World History.* New York: Harper & Row.

Wall, Richard, Jean Robin, and Peter Laslett, eds. (1983). *Family Forms in Historic Europe.* Cambridge: Cambridge University Press.

Warren, Peter (1975). *The Aegean Civilizations.* Oxford: Elsevier Phaidon.

Webster's New Geographical Dictionary (1988). Springfield, Mass.: Merriam-Webster.

Wetterau, Bruce, first ed. (1990). *The New York Public Library Book of Chronologies.* New York: Prentice Hall.

Wetzlaugk, Udo, ed. (1989). *Outlook Berlin.* Translated by Joan Glenn. 3rd ed. Berlin: Berlin Information Center.

Whittle, Alastair (1985). *Neolithic Europe: A Survey.* Cambridge: Cambridge University Press.

World Atlas (1987). New York: Rand McNally.

Wright, John W., gen. ed. (1991). *1992 Universal Almanac.* Kansas City, Mo.: Andrews & McMeel.

LINDA A. BENNETT

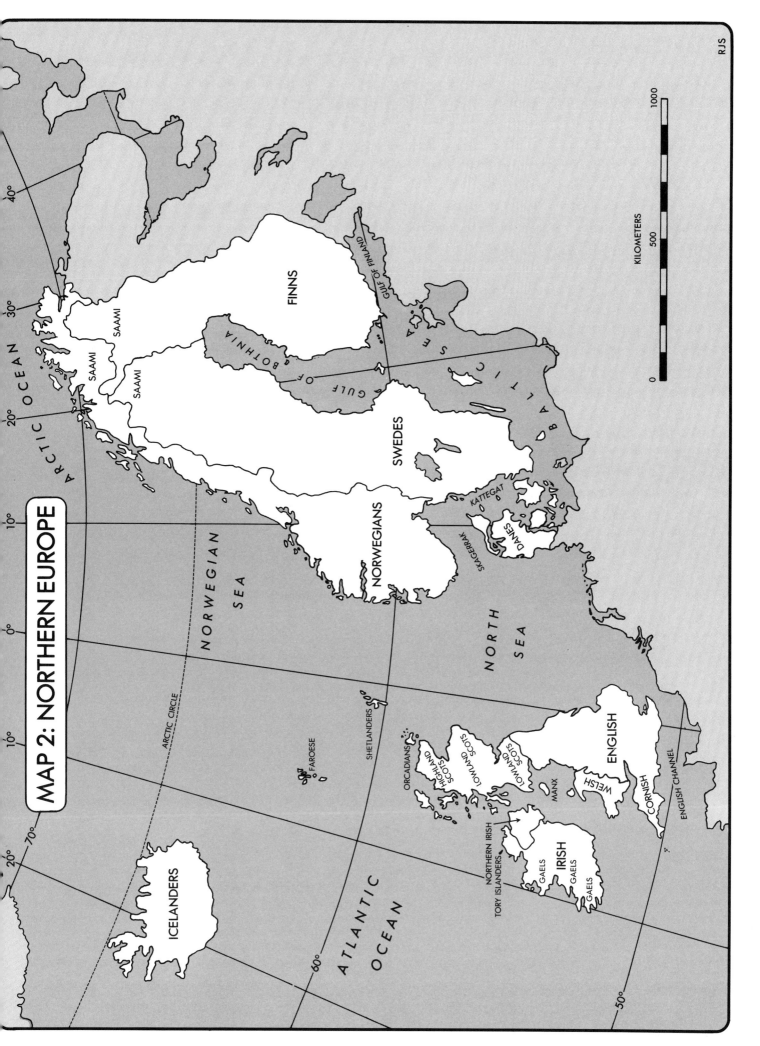

MAP 2: NORTHERN EUROPE

ARCTIC OCEAN

SAAMI

SAAMI

SAAMI

SAAMI

FINNS

GULF OF FINLAND

GULF OF BOTHNIA

BALTIC SEA

SWEDES

NORWEGIANS

NORWEGIAN SEA

ARCTIC CIRCLE

KATTEGAT

SKAGERRAK

DANES

NORTH SEA

FAROESE

SHETLANDERS

ORCADIANS

HIGHLAND SCOTS

LOWLAND SCOTS

LOWLAND SCOTS

NORTHERN IRISH

TORY ISLANDERS

GAELS

IRISH

GAELS

GAELS

MANX

WELSH

ENGLISH

CORNISH

ENGLISH CHANNEL

ATLANTIC OCEAN

ICELANDERS

ATLANTIC OCEAN

40°

30°

20°

10°

0°

10°

20°

70°

60°

50°

KILOMETERS

0   500   1000

RJS

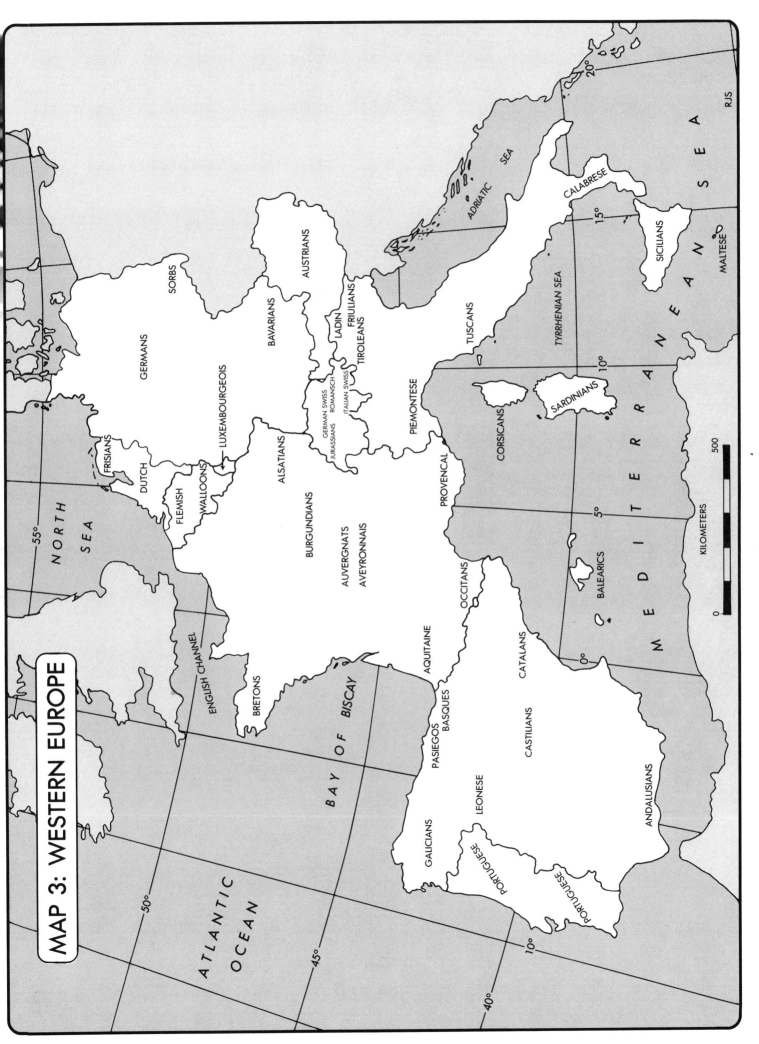

MAP 3: WESTERN EUROPE

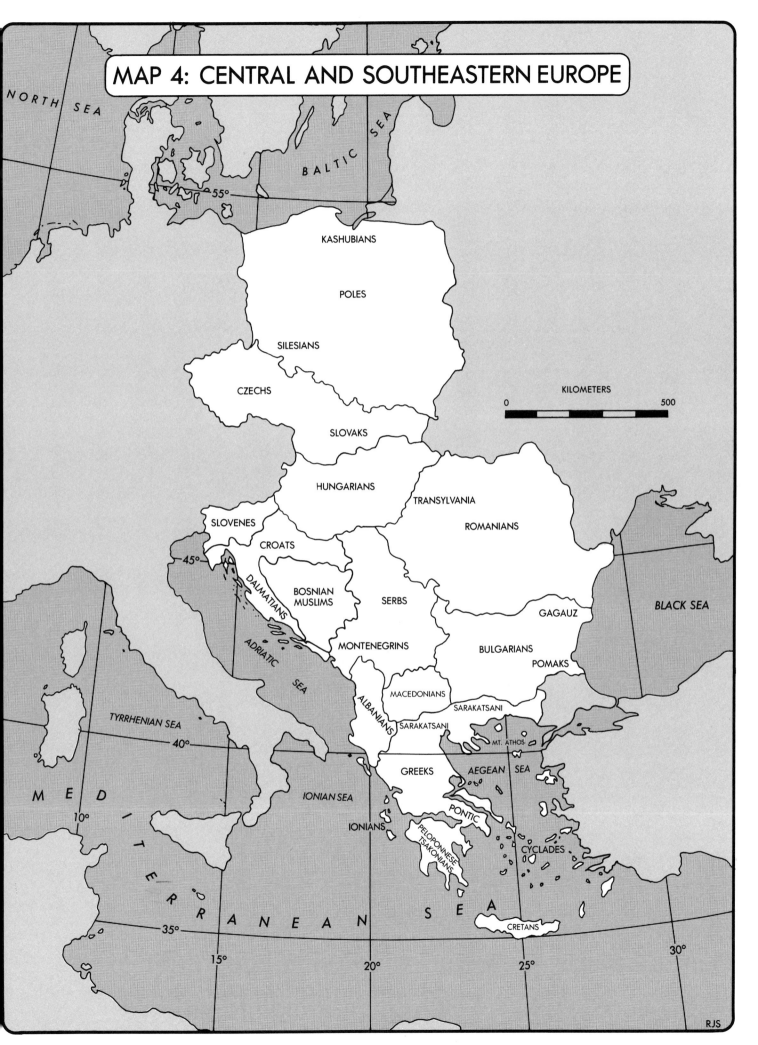

MAP 4: CENTRAL AND SOUTHEASTERN EUROPE

NORTH SEA

BALTIC SEA

55°

KASHUBIANS

POLES

SILESIANS

CZECHS

SLOVAKS

HUNGARIANS

TRANSYLVANIA

ROMANIANS

SLOVENES

CROATS

45°

DALMATIANS

BOSNIAN MUSLIMS

SERBS

GAGAUZ

BLACK SEA

ADRIATIC

SEA

MONTENEGRINS

BULGARIANS

POMAKS

ALBANIANS

MACEDONIANS

SARAKATSANI

TYRRHENIAN SEA

40°

SARAKATSANI

MT. ATHOS

GREEKS

AEGEAN SEA

IONIAN SEA

M E D

10°

PONTIC

IONIANS

PELOPONNESE TSAKONIANS

CYCLADES

I T E R R A N E A N   S E A

35°

CRETANS

KILOMETERS

0   500

15°

20°

25°

30°

RJS

Encyclopedia of World Cultures

Volume IV

EUROPE

Albanians

ETHNONYMS: Albanois, Arbëresh, Arnauts, Arvanits, Illyrians, Shiptare

Orientation

Identification.   The name "Albanian" derives from the ancient town of Albanopolis, mentioned by Ptolemy in the second century B.C. and located within present-day Albania. Etymologically this derives from the Latin *albus*, "white," a possible reference to the whiteness of the nearby mountains. "Arbëresh" comes from Albanian *arbër*, a term for Albanians in Italy. "Arbanit," "Arvanit"—designating Greek Albanians—changed to "Arbërit" and "Arbëreshët," which were initially names for Catholic Albanians only. "Arnaut" derives from the Ottoman designation and—like "Albanoi," the original French name—is to be found in older sources. "Illyrian" is the name for the autochthonous population that lived partly on modern Albanian territory, from the time of the Iron Age, and it is sometimes used in Albanian nationalist literature as a designation for "ancestral Albanians." "Shiptare," "sons of the eagle," originally the self-designation of the people of the northern highlands only, is in modern Albanian the correct ethnonym for all Albanian people.

Location.   Present-day Albania covers an area of 28,748 square kilometers located between 39°38' and 42°39' N and 19°16' and 21°4' E and is bordered by the Adriatic and Ionian seas to the west, Montenegro, Serbia, and Macedonia to the north and east, and Greece to the south. Seventy-six percent of Albania is hill and mountain, 23.4 percent plains. The climate is Mediterranean in the coastal plains and foothills. In the mountain area of inner Albania, the climate becomes more continental, with less dry summers and cooler, often snowy winters.

Demography.   In 1990 there were about 3.25 million Albanians in Albania, 35 percent of them urban. The population growth rate is up to 2 percent per year with an extremely high birthrate of 24 per 1,000 inhabitants (1985–1990 average). The population has the youngest average age in Europe, with 33.9 percent under 14, 51.8 percent between 15 and 49, and only 14.3 percent above 50 in 1985. Life expectancy is 69 for men and 74 for women. More than a third of all Albanians live outside Albania's political borders, which were fixed in 1913 after the Balkan Wars. More than 2 million Albanians live in Kosovo in the Republic of Serbia, Yugoslavia, with others Montenegro and Macedonia. There is also a large Albanian community in Greece, mainly in the Tshamaria (Greek Epirus), in the Peloponnesos, in Thrace, in Greek Macedonia, and on the islands of Angistri, Euboea, Hydra, Poros, Spetsai, etc. There are another 100,000 in south Italy and Sicily, descendants of religious refugees from the Ottoman advance in the fifteenth and sixteenth centuries. Thousands of Albanians have come very recently (1990–1991) as political refugees to Greece, Italy, and other western European states. There are also Albanian enclaves in Turkey, Egypt, Russia, and the United States.

Linguistic Affiliation.   Albanian is the sole member of one branch of Indo-European languages. There are two main dialects whose names are also the names of the two main regional groups in Albania, which are also differentiated by their traditional social organization: Tosk, influenced by Turkish, roughly to the south of the Shkumbin River; and Gheg, with many Romance, Greek, and Slavonic influences, to the north. The modern official Albanian language dates from the period 1908 to 1912, when, as a result of the nation-building process, the language was standardized on the Tosk variant and the Latin alphabet was introduced.

History and Cultural Relations

Archaeological and prehistoric evidence for Illyrian settlements on Albanian territory date from the second millennium B.C. At first influenced by ancient Greek civilization, Illyria belonged to the Roman Empire after 168 B.C. From the fourth to the sixth centuries the Illyrians suffered Hun and Gothic invasions, and from the sixth century Slavs began to settle on Illyrian territory. In Kosovo the plains settlers withdrew into the mountains, thus laying the historical foundations for modern territorial disputes between Serbs and Albanians in Yugoslavia. From 750 the area was under Byzantine rule, and from 851 to 1014 it belonged to the Bulgarian Empire. Later came the Normans (1081–1185) and Neapolitans (the "Regnum Albaniae" of Charles of Anjou in coastal Albania, 1271), and the country became part of the Great Serbian Empire from 1334 to 1347 under Stefan Dušan. The Venetians then claimed the area until 1393, when the Ottoman Empire absorbed it; the area finally declared its independence in 1912.

Today Albania is relatively homogeneous ethnically. The 1976 Albanian constitution recognizes national minorities and guarantees minority rights concerning language, folklore, and tradition, but not religion. The Greeks (5.2 percent) live mainly in the Albanian Epirus. Thousands of Albanian Greeks have gone to Greece since the end of 1990 over a border that had been virtually closed for decades. The Balkan

Romanians (0.5 percent), also known as Aromuns or Vlachs, are regarded as an assimilated minority. Their earlier nomadic pastoralism came to an end through restrictions on their mobility after World War II, when political borders were closed, and through the socialist government's collectivization of agriculture. In the thirteenth century, Vlach pastoralists, artisans, and traders founded their capital, Voskopoja, in southern Albania, which in the seventeenth and eighteenth centuries became a center for international trade and cultural relations (with Venice, Vienna, and Budapest) with an educated class. More than 100,000 Vlachs were still recorded in Albania around the turn of the century. There are also groups of Macedonians (0.4 percent) and Montenegrins (0.2 percent). The Gypsies (less than 0.2 percent), both Sinti and Roma (Albanian *evgjitë*, a reference to a formerly assumed Egyptian origin, or *kurbetë*), were compelled by state programs to settle down permanently. In the cities they live in apartment blocks or single dispersed apartments, though separate residential quarters for Gypsies can still be found. Traditionally basket makers, smiths, and tinkers, today they are employed as street cleaners or in road construction, being socially marginalized. A very few Blacks (Albanian *arigi*), the descendants of Ottoman slaves, also live in Albania. Many Jews were taken from Albania to Israel in January 1991 by Operation Flying Carpet.

Settlements

Today 35.5 percent of the Albanian population is urban, 64.5 percent rural. The relatively low urbanization rate is probably a result of state restrictions on mobility. Virilocal marriage leads many Albanian women to live in urban areas. About 80 percent of the population today lives in apartment blocks built in the Socialist period. Besides the capital, Tirana, the main regional centers are Durrës (the main port), Shkodër, Elbasan, Vlorë, and Korcë. In presocialist days villages were composed of groups of houses surrounded by farmland and pastures. Stone and wood were the main materials used in house building. The Ottoman influence can clearly be seen in the widespread enclosure of houses by stone walls for religious reasons and the use of stone, originally for defensive purposes, in the first floor, timber in the second. Also typical of Albania is the *kula*, a fortified dwelling of stone with slits for windows in the lower floor and closable windows above, adapted to the threat of brigandage, foreign (especially Ottoman) invasions, and, above all, feuds. The one-room house of stone and timber with a central fireplace is the basic unit, sometimes extended with additional buildings into larger farms. Because of the sloping terrain, many houses are built perpendicularly on several levels against the slope, thus utilizing all possible space. In areas with a more Mediterranean climate, a veranda added to the basic unit serves in summer as a place for cooking, sleeping, and living. In the south one also finds the manor houses of the former feudal rulers (patrons) in both rural and urban areas, some of which were built for defense. In the plains both these and ordinary houses often show the influence of Italian architecture.

Economy

Subsistence and Commercial Activities. The extended household was basically self-sufficient, with property and labor held in common. Surplus produce was sold in some-times distant markets to provide weapons, household utensils, bride-wealth, etc. During the Socialist period farming and stock raising were carried out by cooperatives and collective farms, and many villagers commuted to jobs in industry and state services. Privatization started in the early 1980s, after expropriations had led to the slaughter of stock by protesting farmers and consequent meat shortages. As a result, the government introduced a *brigade* economy (a brigade being a cooperative workers' unit representing approximately the population of a former village), and workers sold the surplus products at state shops at prices guaranteed by the state. No research has been carried out on the secondary economy in Albania, but people evidently provided themselves with *raki* (a spirit), vegetables, herbs, and fruits on the black market. Since 1990, a transformation toward a free-market economy has been going on. Industrial production declined by about 50 percent in 1991. Strikes, especially in the mines, the worthlessness of the Albanian currency, and a 60 percent unemployment rate currently are the main features of a very unstable economic situation.

Industrial Arts. In the past there were urban centers and certain streets in the cities where male artisans and specialists sold various products of pottery, metal, and wood: for example, agricultural and household tools, instruments, religious icons in Eastern Orthodox areas, ironwork, silver and gold filigree, embroidery, and other needlework. Ottoman style influenced carvings in wood for interior decoration all over Albania. Shepherds carved their crooks. Farmers produced and carved wooden spoons, pipes, distaffs, spindles, and musical instruments such as flutes, the *cifteli* (a two-stringed mandolin), and the *lahuta* (a one-stringed instrument); some regions were famous for their ornamented carved wooden chairs, cradles, and bridal chests. Women worked for family needs and in many urban and rural regions for the market, specializing in textiles.

Trade. Until the fall of Constantinople in 1453, an important trade route between Rome and Byzantium, the Via Egnatia, passed through Durrës. In the nineteenth century, Orthodox Greek and Vlach citizens in the southern parts of Albania traded with the Ottoman Empire, economic centers in the north being Shkodër and Prizren (the latter now in Kosovo). Economic relations with Yugoslavia ended two years after the proclamation of the Albanian Socialist People's Republic in 1946. From 1949 Albania was a member of the Soviet–East European Council of Mutual Economic Assistance, and the Soviet Union was the most important trading partner until 1961, when relations were broken off. Economic assistance was provided by China from 1961 until 1978, when it ended and Chinese experts withdrew. In 1968 Albania left the Warsaw Pact. Until May 1990 the constitution did not permit the raising of foreign loans, and this restricted foreign investment. In recent years Albania has exported different types of ore and metals (primarily iron ore and chromite), electricity, gas, agricultural products, some finished goods (textiles, handicrafts, etc.), building materials, chemical products, plastics, and cigarettes and tobacco. Grain, luxury goods, machinery, vehicles, chemical and electromechanical products were imported. The principle of "no import without export," broadly realized until 1987, was intended to guarantee economic autarchy. The increasing deterioration of Eastern European economies—Albania's major trading partners—together with the problems of drought and an inflexible system of central planning, have led to severe shortages. Since September 1991 the Albanian population has been supported largely through European Community programs designed to avoid further movements of refugees.

Division of Labor. In general, the men of the clan society were concerned with agriculture and stock raising. Transhumant pastoralism, lumbering, and hunting were men's seasonal tasks. In addition to housekeeping, women were responsible for small-scale production such as weaving and sewing for the household or for one's dowry, plus dairy farming and child care. Often, when a family was involved in a feud, the men went into hiding and the women took over their work too. The household head was allowed a horse in order to represent the family to the outside world, and he also decided the organization of labor among the agnates. He appointed his female counterpart, the "mistress of the house" (_zonjë_, not necessarily his wife), who was similarly responsible for the female labor of the household. In modern times, the socialist constitution declared women equal to men. In reality this principle often creates an added burden for women, because in public life they are employed equally with men in agricultural and industrial production and in civilian and military service, whereas their emancipation in private life, though official policy, is often more theory than fact.

Land Tenure. In the clan society land was owned jointly by the clan and owned locally by the agnates of an extended household. In the plains latifundia (_çiftlics_) developed when the formerly independent villages were integrated into the patronage system in Ottoman times. With the weakening of the Ottoman Empire, regional feudal rulers (beys), Albanian converts to Islam with lucrative positions in the Ottoman administration, extended their power and kept the mostly Eastern Orthodox peasants under their control as tenants. Endogamous family aristocracies arose, the best-known from 1778 being the Bushatli family, with large properties around Shkodër in northern Albania, and the family of Ali Pasha of Tepelena (1785–1822), with extensive landholdings in present-day Greek and Albanian Epirus. In the area around the city of Tirana up to the neighboring mountainous district of Mati, the two systems met and a mixed system of land tenure developed. Family heads were already known as beys, and some estates belonged to wealthier families, but in general land still was communally held by the different clans. The Albanian beys were expropriated after the war, when socialist land reforms in 1946 divided the land among farmers formerly dependent on feudal landlords. Later, the land was nationalized and collectivized in state farms, though this action was delayed somewhat in mountain areas because of a combination of underdeveloped infrastructure and popular resistance. People were organized in cooperatives, first on the level of single villages and later in groups of villages. Since the collapse of socialism, a process of privatization of land has been set in motion, accompanied and hampered by numerous conflicts.

Kinship

Kin Groups and Descent. Gheg clan society lasted until the 1950s in northern Albania. Those who claimed descent from a common, sometimes mythical or fictitious male ances-

tor were organized in an ideally exogamous patriclan or _fis_ found in many villages with lineages at the village or _mehala_ level. Understood as a "brotherhood" or _vellezeri_, these included a variable number of communal extended households, called _shpi_ or _shtëpi_ (literally, "house"), each consisting of the nuclear families of a number of brothers, with up to ninety individuals in some cases. Genealogies, understood as a tree, were carefully remembered and handed down through the generations through epic songs and tales as origin myths.

Kinship Terminology. Kin ties were defined by blood given to the children only through the patriline. A wife's or mother's kin were her parental family; her father and brothers were responsible for her until she married. Accordingly, mother's brother and mother's son had special terms, but apparently there was no specific kin terminology for their children. All matrilateral cousins, cross as well as parallel, were potential marriage partners but not any patrilateral cousins, relations with whom constituted incest. In the traditional extended household, patrilateral cousins of any degree were called brothers and sisters, patrilateral uncles of any degree fathers or uncles. When the actual father and mother became very old, the eldest brother and sister were given the terms for father and mother. Thus the terminology was at least partly classificatory, with bifurcate-merging features.

Marriage and Family

Marriage. Residence in Albanian clan society was strictly virilocal. Marriage arrangements were always exogamous and made by the head of the household. Children were betrothed sometimes even before birth, often in respect of an existing alliance or in order to establish friendship or peace with another clan. Religious differences between the families were no obstacle. A part of the bride-price was paid after the girl was born, the balance when she was old enough to be handed over to the bridegroom's relatives, who picked her up in a marriage procession. Girls were married between the ages of 13 and 16, boys between 15 and 18. Regionally, dowry also was given to the girl by her family, and if she was widowed and sent home, she could take with her whatever remained. Levirate was also practiced. Sometimes young widows were resold, the profit being shared between her former husband's family and her own. A wife was regarded as her husband's property, as were her children; unmarried women belonged to their fathers. If a wife failed to give birth to a son, her husband was allowed to divorce her by cutting off a piece of her dress and sending her home to her family. Such a woman was considered worthless and she had almost no chance of being married again. Church influence ended the practice of taking a woman without marrying her until she proved her fertility. A woman's only possibility of escaping an unwanted marriage without causing bloodshed between the families involved was to promise perpetual virginity as a _verdzin_, which entailed the difficult task of finding a number (which varied according to region) of co-jurors from her own clan who would agree to feud if she failed to maintain her oath. A verdzin was allowed to take over male responsibilities and duties, and in some areas she dressed like a man. In the mountains there was often a shortage of women, causing a regional explosion in the amount of bride-price, which in turn led to marriage by capture in some cases. Socialism prohibited traditional customs concerning marriage and promised the free choice of partner to both sexes.

Domestic Unit.   In the anthropological literature the extended household organized by fraternal principle is known by the original Serb word *zadruga* (see "Kin Groups and Descent").

Inheritance.   Leadership positions traditionally were not inherited but achieved. One exception was the public post of a *bayraktar* or standard-bearer (see "Political Organization"), though even here, merit was the basis of a holder's choice of his successor from among his sons. Another exception was the position of captain (*kapedan*), or head of the clan, which was transmitted hereditarily through the Gjomarkaj family of the large clan of Mirditë, who were the keepers of all knowledge about the "Kanun" or traditional law (see "Social Control"). The Kanun also regulated inheritance for the household and specified that land and other property never be divided up but always remain communal within the agnatic group, with the household head having control over its use. Land could not be bequeathed to the church by anyone without permission of the clan assembly. In the event of the deaths of their husbands or fathers, women were left to the charge of their respective agnates. In the case of the minority of a sole male heir or of the total lack of male heirs, an elder sister could choose to become a *verdzin* as a classificatory male household head to care for the property and keep it together for subsequent generations.

Socialization.   On the third day after birth (*poganik*) three fairies would predict a child's fortune, according to traditional belief. Although baptized after three to four weeks, the child was actually initiated into the community of the house through the ritual of the first haircut when the child was about one year old. A lack of sons or of children altogether was regarded as a misfortune. Ritual techniques and amulets protected children from the evil eye. Fathers often exchanged their young sons to raise them even more strictly, and children were only allowed to speak when spoken to. A man had to carry weapons (a rifle or pistol) to be taken seriously. Girls were introduced to domestic work very early. The main concerns of child care and education were developing toughness and respect for elders, especially men. Initially the socialist government faced high rates of illiteracy, which has now almost vanished. Today children normally attend a crèche from about 6 months old, before going to kindergarten and then, from the age of about 6, to school. Socialist state education stressed the symbolic "triangle of education, productive work, and physical and military training."

Sociopolitical Organization

Social Organization.   The agnatic descent system has already been discussed under "Kin Groups and Descent." The institutions of godparenthood, arising out of the rites of a child's first haircut and baptism, and blood brotherhood extended social ties further for the whole family.

Political Organization.   The lord of the house or *zot i shpis* represented his extended family in the assembly of village elders, no member of which had any wealth or other privileges. One or more of its most respected members (*plak* or *dryeplak*) also represented the village in the assembly of clan elders (*kuvënd*). Each clan also had one or more "standard-bearers" or bayraktars, military leaders with administrative and juridical functions in times of peace. The area in which the zot i shpis recruited his followers was known as a *bayrak*, which might or might not coincide with a clan (fis) territory. Some clans therefore had more than one standard-bearer, while in other cases one bayraktar would be responsible for more than one clan. He had the right to convene the clan assembly and preside over it for military purposes. The assembly had executive and juridical functions concerning the community (questions of territory, religion, politics, and law), whereas cases concerning single persons or lineages were decided at village assembly level. In the plains these traditional forms of political organization were replaced by the Ottoman administration, which introduced a feudal structure. Under socialism, the state and the Communist party organized politics on the local level. As part of the collapse of socialism in Eastern Europe in the early 1990s, Albania is moving rapidly toward a democratic system. In 1991 Albania became a member of the Conference on Security and Cooperation in Europe, and in March 1992 the Democratic party, which had been founded only in 1990, won the second free election in Albania with a majority of more than 70 percent.

Social Control.   Gheg customary law was transmitted orally. The clan and village assemblies administrated and modified justice for 500 years by always referring to a territorial ruler, to Lek Dukagjin, or in certain areas to Skanderbeg, both of whom were said to have codified existing customary law. In 1913 the Franciscan scholar Shtjefen Gjecov collected the laws referring to Dukagjin in the Mirdita clan's area, where it was said to have been preserved best. In 1933, many years after Gjecov's mysterious death, this collection was published as *Kanuni i Lek Dukagjinit*, a code based on the concepts of honor and blood. A person had to guard the honor of his family and clan, which was conceptualized through the patriline as consisting of the same blood, and the honor of wives. There was also a collective liability lasting generations regarding the actions of any clan member, maintained through an internal hierarchy reflecting the closeness of kin. The doctrine of "blood for blood" found in the Kanun led to institutionalized feud, which clearly defined the responsibilities of the "debtor of the blood" and the "master of the blood" and their respective successors in vengeance.

Conflict.   Moral death was more threatening than any intervention by the church, as this Albanian saying makes clear: "You fast for the soul and you kill for honor." The idea of feud as ultimately producing family cohesion and at the same time preventing crime and disputes must be seen in the context of a system that took no action in relation to disputes or murders within a household. Since the latter concerned blood within a family, no feud would result. Quarrels arose through disputes about marriage arrangements, territory, theft, murder, and slander, whose respective values were also defined by the Kanun. For example, a guest's security had to be extremely well maintained according to strict regulations, which ensured mobility for all in an insecure environment. Misfortune for or the mistreatment of a guest could provoke blood vengeance or bring forth sanctions (such as burning the host's house) following a decision of the village community. Blood payments or an oath of allegiance, *besa*, were among the institutionalized ways of ending a feud, with regional variations regarding the degree to which this was consistent with one's honor.

Religion and Expressive Culture

Religious Beliefs. In 1967 Albania was proclaimed the first atheist state in the world, and it remained so until December 1990, when the process of democratization under the head of state and party leader, Ramiz Alia, allowed people to admit their faith freely. About 70 percent were registered in a presocialist census as being of Muslim origin, 20 percent Eastern Orthodox, especially in the south, and the rest Catholic. Today there seems to be a tendency to define oneself as Catholic, motivated by a desire to move closer to the West. The old Albanian sayings, "Where the sword is, is the faith," and "The belief of an Albanian is to be an Albanian"—the latter being current right up to and including the socialist period, when it was used for political purposes—throw some light on conversions such as those from the seventeenth to the nineteenth centuries under Ottoman rule, when observance of the Islamic religion became the key to the possession of civic rights. Under Ottoman rule, "Crypto-Christianity" and religious syncretism became very common. After the schism of 1054 north Albania became Roman Catholic, the south Greek Orthodox. Under the Ottomans Catholicism survived only in remoter areas. Four autocephalous Orthodox dioceses were maintained in Tirana, Berat, Gjirokastër, and Korcë until 1967, when atheism was proclaimed. From the fifteenth century on, the Bektashis, a Shiite pantheistic order of dervishes who did not distinguish between Muslim and non-Muslim members, attained great popularity, their monasteries or _tekkë_ being spread all over Albania, with their center at the holy tomb of Saint Sari Saltik in Krujë. Typical of the pre-Christian traditional beliefs is the dichotomy of light and dark, equivalents to male and female, sun and moon, good and evil, as can be seen in symbols and figures used in legends, myths, fairy tales (e.g., _kulshedra_, "monster," versus _dragoni_), oaths, curses, tattoos, amulets, handicrafts, on gravestones, etc. There were also beliefs concerning vampires and witchcraft, the interpretation of omens, the observation of natural phenomena for predictions, etc. Taboos of an apotropaic character were also found; for example, the wolf's name was never pronounced out loud.

Religious Practitioners. Neither Catholic priests nor bishops, nor Muslim clergymen (_hoxha_ and _sheikh_ among the Sunnis), nor abbots (_baba_, sing.; _baballar_, pl.) among the Bektashis, could supply every village. Some were wanderers, all were respected as God's men, and there is evidence that the nearest available were consulted by people of any faith when necessary. Clerics were not allowed to keep house dogs because their houses had to be open all night to parishioners or passing strangers, though Eastern Orthodox and Muslim priests' houses were not considered sacred, and theft from them therefore was not considered sacrilegious. Besides their more or less important role in life-cycle rites and as consultants, priests had an educational role, since the Ottoman administration allowed religious bodies (Franciscans, Jesuits) to run schools. Jesuits sometimes succeeded in ending feuds, because of the belief that they were sent by the pope and had the power to take away God's blessing for one's family for generations to come. In the years after World War II many religious leaders were sent to prison or executed.

Ceremonies. Life-cycle rites traditionally occurred at birth, the first haircut, sometimes the first nail cutting, marriage, and death. Further rites included the swearing of an oath on a rock, a gravestone, an altar, the doorstep of a church, a meteor, a glowing coal, and on natural phenomena such as the sun, moon, fire, plains, mountains, etc., as well as the besa or renunciation of feud. Rites of the yearly cycle consisted of pre-Christian customs as well as church festivals and processions, which were often shared by people of every faith. Some days involved taboos on certain activities or certain food. Other occasions involved the lustration and blessing of water, farmland, the harvest, agricultural instruments, livestock, houses, children, plants, etc. Under socialist rule religious ceremonies were prohibited and replaced by military and nationalist public celebrations such as First May Day processions, the birthday of the former party leader Enver Hoxha, the anniversary of his death, etc. New Year's Day became the most important festivity of the year.

Arts. Albanian epic songs were the original vehicle for tradition and local history in a culture without writing. Typical heroic epics (e.g., the epic cycle "The Brothers Muji and Halili," songs of Skanderbeg) were monophonic and sung by professional wandering artists on social occasions, or by private musicians in the family or with friends, who accompanied themselves with the one-stringed lahuta. The telling of fairy tales for adults as well as for children was popular and assured the survival of both cosmological conceptions and old legends. Norms and values were also transmitted through anecdotes, sayings, and riddles. These traditional features are still cultivated and are performed every five years at a major festival of folklore in Gjirokastër, an old city in the south. Also still performed are, for example, the women's "vessel song," polyphonic and monophonic songs with specific regional features, and likewise a variety of men's and women's dances. The best-known modern Albanian writer is Ismail Kadare, born in 1939, who in his novels brings to life traditional conditions in Albania and the individual's experiences under the Ottomans.

Medicine. Medicine was traditionally practiced either by local specialized folk doctors (_hekim_), by dervishes, or by "wise old women" with herbal knowledge and knowledge of necessary ritual incantations said to have been inherited from their ancestors. Doctors were highly regarded and were often also considered soothsayers. Christian and Muslim saints were appealed to for help through pilgrimages to holy places such as monasteries, saintly tombs, holy waters and springs, etc. Diseases were attributed to evil forces and malevolent ghosts (_vila_). The latter had a deadly touch, could cast the evil eye, and often symbolized the illness itself. Under socialism the replacement of these traditions through the continuous development of a network of hospitals, medical research institutions, care centers, and maternity stations was regarded as one of the government's most challenging tasks. Modern medicine emphasizes information and prevention. The state bears the expenses for medical treatment and medicine. There were about 714 inhabitants per doctor in 1983, a figure that approximates the European standard.

Death and Afterlife. Wailing, scratching one's face, cutting or tearing out one's hair, wearing clothes inside out, etc. are all recognized modes of mourning. Usually this is done by female dependents and neighbors, rarely also by men, and sometimes female mourners are hired. In the south some mourning takes the form of a repeated antiphonal two-verse song sung by a leading mourner followed by a female chorus. Burial follows on the same day or, if a person dies in the afternoon, on the next morning, after a procession to church. Females bid farewell with a last kiss in front of the door, men inside the church. In some areas the bodies of important males are dressed in their most typical costume, with their rifle and other things associated with them (like a cigarette in the corner of the mouth), and then seated in their own yard on a chair to say their last goodbye to those who gather there. Mourning is continued for forty days in the house of the deceased and repeated at certain intervals at the graveside. In Eastern Orthodox areas traditionally the remains were exhumed after three years and the bones placed in a bone house. The good are believed to have an easy death, the bad a hard one. Life is thought to leave a person through the mouth. As well as having a decorated wooden cross, the grave is surrounded by stones either as a protection from the corpse becoming a vampire (the stones hold the corpse down) or as stepping-stones leading the dead on their way to the other world. To make their voyage easier the dead also have coins placed in their mouths (in some areas also apples or other travel supplies). In the mountains, the sites associated with particular murders, especially those resulting from feuds, are indicated with mounds of stones, called *murana*.

Bibliography

Çabej, Eqrem (1966). "Albanische Volkskunde." In *Südost-Forschungen*, edited by M. Bernath, 333–387. Vol. 25. Munich: R. Oldenbourg.

Durham, Edith (1909). *High Albania*. Boston: Beacon Press.

Hahn, J. G. von (1854). *Albanesische Studien*. Vol. 3. Jena.

Hasluck, Margaret (1954). *The Unwritten Law in Albania*. London: Cambridge University Press.

Lienau, Cay, and Günter Prinzing, eds. (1986). *Albanien: Beiträge zur Geographie und Geschichte*. Berichte aus dem Arbeitsgebiet Entwicklungsforschung am Institut für Geographie Münster, vol. 12. Münster: Verlag Dr. Cay Lienau.

Shytock, Andrew J. (1988). "Autonomy, Entanglement, and the Feud: Prestige Structures and Gender Value in Highland Albania." *Anthropological Quarterly* 61: 113–118.

Whitaker, Ian (1968). "Tribal Structure and National Politics in Albania, 1910–1950." In *History and Social Anthropology*, edited by I. M. Lewis. London and New York: Tavistock.

STEPHANIE SCHWANDNER

Alsatians

ETHNONYMS: none

Alsatians are the German-speaking people of the French region of Alsace, located between the Vosges Mountains and the German border in the departments of Bas-Rhin and Haut-Rhin. There are perhaps 1.5 million speakers of German dialects in this region. There is no single Alsatian dialectal variant, although High German is used as the written standard. Today, most Alsatians are bilingual, French as the official language having grown rapidly in the region since the 1940s.

The region was historically and culturally long part of the Rhineland—throughout the Roman era and that of the Holy Roman Empire. In the ninth and tenth centuries it was part of Lotharingia, and later of the duchy of Swabia. In the mid-1600s it was ceded to France at the end of the Thirty Years' War. In 1791 the whole region became part of France, only to be ceded once again to Germany eighty years later at the end of the Franco-German War. Although it changed political hands often between France and Germany, its cultural affiliation never wavered from a Germanic focus, there being little effort on the part of the French government to disrupt traditional and linguistic practice in the region (except in religious matters) until the late 1700s. This situation changed dramatically with the French Revolution, during which a decree was issued that all citizens unable to speak French were to be shot or deported to the interior. Still, supporters of the retention of an Alsatian identity, including a linguistic identity, remained—among them the Catholic church. It was not until the 1850s that French became the official language of primary instruction, and German never ceased being the language of the people at home, for worship, and in day-to-day affairs. Severe upheavals began in the mid- to late 1800s, as Alsace became the focus of territorial dispute between France and Germany, and the region changed political hands four times more. However much Alsatians resisted cultural and linguistic assimilation into France, they equally resisted Germanization during their periods under Teutonic control. The "Alsatian predicament" was a difficult one by this period. While political and territorial disputes raged over their heads, the people maintained that their traditional loyalty belonged to the region, rather than the region's rulers. In this century, the tensions between the two elements of Alsatian culture heightened, and Alsatian society was torn—as a war memorial in Strasbourg, depicting a woman grieving for her two fallen brothers, profoundly expresses. The male figures of the statue are represented as having fought, and died, on opposing sides. After World War I, when control of the region reverted to the French, a period of repression of Germanic culture ensued, giving rise to strong regionalist movements that coalesced in the formation of political parties seeking regional autonomy, even separation and self-rule. Through the late 1920s and early 1930s, these movements reached their height, but with the rise of Hitler's Nazi party, attention again turned to the region's vulnerability to invasion and conquest. Alsace was one of Germany's earliest French conquests during World War II, and it has been said that the imposition of Nazi rule did more to further French loyalty than any French administrative or political action could ever have done. Although some local leaders collaborated with the occupiers, the region's general population participated heavily in the Resistance. In 1945, in reaction to the brutality of the German occupation, the people of Alsace turned away from autonomist movements for a time. Even the teaching of German in the schools was legally suspended for nearly a decade, so that while the language remained current in spoken form, literacy in German fell to about 20 percent. In the 1970s, a new movement toward reviving the Germanic aspects of Alsatian tradition arose, as did a nascent autonomist movement—the latter inspired largely as reaction against the centralism of the French state.

Although its lands are fertile, and the region's iron and coal mines have long constituted a source of wealth, Alsace's long history of political insecurity and the devastation wrought by the two world wars have impoverished the region. Its heavy industry, which is based on iron and textiles, consists primarily of small enterprises that are not fully competitive with their more highly developed counterparts in Switzerland, Germany, and the Netherlands. The new autonomist movements seek to turn this situation around by gaining greater control over economic and social development policy.

Paralleling this desire to increase the regional voice in economic decision making has been a resurgence of interest in promoting the region's linguistic heritage and establishing a recognized body charged with the preservation and development of Alsatian culture. Although the issues of separatism that arose in the prewar years do not form a part of the new movement, the French government has been less than supportive to date, holding that the "unitary state" of France depends upon assimilation.

Bibliography

Boehler, Jean-Michel, Dominique Lerch, and Jean Vogt (1983). _Histoire de l'Alsace rurale._ Strasbourg: ISTRA.

Bonnet, Jocelyn (1988). _La terre des femmes et ses magies._ Paris: R. Laffont.

Stevens, Meic (1976). _Linguistic Minorities in Western Europe._ Llandysul, Dyfed, Wales: Gomer Press.

Wolf, Lothar, and Paul Fischer (1983). _Le français régional d'Alsace: Étude critique des alsacianismes._ Bibliothèque Française et Romane, Série A, Manuels d'Études Linguistiques, 45. Paris.

Zind, Pierre (1977). _Brève histoire de l'Alsace._ Paris: Éditions Albatros.

NANCY E. GRATTON

Andalusians

ETHNONYM: Andalucians

Orientation

Identification. Andalusians are the people of the eight southernmost provinces of Spain: Huelva, Seville, Cadiz, Cordoba, Malaga, Jaen, Granada, and Almeria.

Location. Andalusia borders the Portuguese Algarve on the west; the Spanish provinces of the Estremadura, Castile-La-Mancha, and Murcia on the northwest, north, and northeast; the Gulf of Cadiz to the southwest; and the Mediterranean on the southeast. Most of the region (Huelva, Cadiz, Seville, Cordoba, and Jaen) lies on the flat tablelands of the _meseta_ and consists of rolling expanses of fields largely given over to cereal crops and olive groves. Malaga and Granada are hilly, even mountainous in places, and Almeria, at the southeastern extremity of the region, is arid and largely barren. The climate on the meseta is one of extended hot, dry summers and rains, heavy at times, in autumn and early winter.

Linguistic Affiliation. Andalusian is a Spanish dialect, strongly flavored with Arabic-derived words, reflecting the long Moorish occupation of the region.

History and Cultural Relations

There is evidence that as long ago as 1000 B.C. there were thriving trade relations between the peoples of this region and Phoenicia. This early civilization is the "Tarshish" of the Old Testament (called Tartessos by the Greeks), and it may well date back to the time of the Minoans, or even earlier. Its earliest peoples were of Celtiberian stock and may have come from the east. As long ago as the fourth or fifth millennium, Aegean ships began to arrive at Almeria, seeking to trade for Andalusia's rich copper resources. While it is unclear whether the trade in copper and other Andalusian minerals stimulated the development of Tartessan civilization or whether sociopolitical organization predated the trade, by the middle of the third millennium or the start of the second, a loose confederation of tribes existed. After the Aegeans came the Phoenicians, who established a trading post at what is now Cadiz by 1100 B.C. The Phoenicians and their colonists (especially the Carthaginians) held sway in the region until the coming of the Romans in 206 B.C. Along with their trade and language, they brought many other eastern Mediterranean peoples to the region. Of singular importance to the region's developing economy and culture were the Jewish wine and olive growers and traders who established colonies of their own. These Sephardic Jews flourished in Andalusia throughout the times of Phoenician, Roman, and Muslim rule.

By the time of the Roman conquest, Andalusia was the home of great ethnic diversity, being comprised of Africans, Jews, Phoenicians, and Greeks, as well as descendants of the indigenous Celtiberian peoples. Roman rule did not diminish this diversity but simply provided an integrative political and economic framework within which it could function. The Muslims conquered these Roman territories of southern Spain in the early eighth century A.D. Much of the population converted to Islam under the Moors, but there was tolerance on the part of the new rulers, so conversion was not forced. Thus the Sephardic enclaves remained vital participants in the region's economy and formed the essential core of its trade, crafts, and merchant classes. Moorish occupation in Andalusia, which lasted until nearly the end of the fifteenth century, had the positive effect of sparing Andalusia from the "Dark Ages" of the rest of Europe, for Andalusia participated in the Islamic high culture of the time and became a center for advances in philosophy, theology, the sciences, medicine, and the arts. It was not until the expansion of Castilian-based Christianity into the region, which began in the 1100s but was not fully successful until the late 1500s, that the rich and vibrant culture of Andalusia was cut off from its eastern sources. The persecutions, forced conversions, and suppression of all things Moorish that ensued in the course of this Castilian-based crusade resulted in the destruction of much of this culture. In addition, with the expulsion of the Jews, Moors, and *moriscos* (Jewish converts to Islam) and the confiscation of much of their property and wealth, an economic decline of the region began that has persisted to this day. At some time in the late 1400s, Gypsies arrived in the region. Although found throughout Europe, the Gypsies became more settled and assimilated in Andalusia than they did elsewhere in the world, a fact that enabled them to influence the development of Andalusian cultural forms, particularly music.

Whereas northern Spain looked to Europe for its cultural influences, Andalusia retained its strongly Mediterranean flavor. This development was perhaps partly the result of the concentration of the new Spanish nobility in Castile and their general unwillingness to settle in a region like Andalusia, so far from the attractions of the royal court. Andalusia itself was thus left free to develop its own cultural style, elaborating upon the diverse traditions of its long history and preserving, with modifications, elements of all of them. The fact that Spain as a whole remained outside the early industrialization and drive toward "progress" that gripped Europe during the Industrial Revolution, using the wealth it derived from its overseas colonies for consumption rather than for investment and modernization, has been cited as the cause of the nation's "stagnation." Indeed, Andalusia has become impoverished because of its reliance until well into the twentieth century upon ancient agricultural techniques and a weak industrial base. Yet this "stagnation" also provided an environment in which Andalusian culture was able to elaborate upon its unique cultural traditions, so that today it retains a distinctive flavor. The region's "backwardness" was encouraged, even enforced, by the Franco regime—as well as by the entire country's isolation from the United States and the rest of Western Europe during the postwar years, owing to the Allies' disdain for Franco's fascism. With Franco's death and the end of the fascist regime in the 1970s, and especially with Spain's entry into the European Economic Community, economic development has begun to make inroads in the region with the introduction of modern agricultural technology and a move—however halting and small-scale—to establish industry in the region. The 1980s brought to all of Spain a new constitution, which, among other things, sought to accomplish the decentralization of power from Castile to a series of autonomous communities. Andalusia achieved autonomous status by the middle of the decade. Retaining ties to the larger Spanish polity, Andalusia is now able to make social and economic development decisions for itself.

Settlements

The principal settlement form in Andalusia is the *pueblo*, a relatively small municipal and residential center with a strongly agrarian economic focus. In most of Andalusia these population centers are geographically isolated from each other, being situated in the approximate center of the extensive lands associated with latifundia (large estate farms). What one finds is a central municipality harboring the local church, administrative buildings, shops and taverns, and dwellings, but little or no industrial focus. The majority of the residents in these population centers consists of landless agricultural laborers and their families. Scattered in the surrounding countryside are the large estate farms with their extensive fields of cereal crops or corn. Associated with each estate, usually built on an elevated site at the approximate center of the property, are the farm buildings: the owner's manor (generally occupied by a manager, for absentee landlordism has long been the rule in the region); outbuildings for crop storage and livestock; olive and/or grape arbors; and buildings for the processing of agricultural and animal products. In addition, one or more small clusters of dwellings may be found on the property, owned by the landlord but housing permanent staff or long-term contract employees and their families, as well as one or more market gardens, watered by wells.

Economy

Subsistence and Commercial Activities.   Most of Andalusia traditionally has been devoted to estate-based, extensive cultivation of cereals, with olives and sunflowers constituting additional important crops. Cereal cropping is carried out in conjunction with sheepherding, although the flocks have declined dramatically over the last several decades and are now found only on the largest of the region's estates. Chickens and pigs are raised on a small scale. The vast majority of economic activity in Andalusia is agriculturally related, and this situation has become more and more exacerbated in recent years as local artisans faced competition from goods brought in from beyond the local community. On the great farms, most of the agricultural produce is destined for market, and the available work consists largely of unskilled, repetitive tasks such as sowing and harvesting. Local economies never have been capable of providing full employment, and many young men (fewer women) leave to seek work in the cities or elsewhere.

Industrial Arts.   Large-scale industry is uncommon in the region, but local milling and processing of olive oil, wine making, and other such enterprises are still common. Buildings are, for the most part, constructed of local materials—including wood-frame and, more commonly, mud-walled (stucco) structures—although the older estates are often made of stone.

Trade.   Nearly all of Andalusia's agricultural product is destined for market, either sold directly to processors in raw state or processed locally and sold to urban markets in final form (e.g., olive oil and wine). Little is left of the great mineral trade upon which the earliest economy of the region was based. Locally there are still weekly markets for agricultural produce and livestock, as well as for some locally produced crafts.

Division of Labor. The _casa_, or coresident kinship group, is the basic economic production unit, and each member is expected to contribute labor toward securing the livelihood of the whole. There is a strong sexual division of labor organizing the economic roles of household members, but the nature of such gender-specific roles varies according to the class to which a household belongs. Among landed families, where the combination of current income and inherited wealth reduces the need for supplemental income, management of the household economy falls entirely to the male head of household, while his wife concerns herself with the administration of the household and does not usually work outside of the home. In the households of agricultural laborers, the administration of the family budget falls to the wife, who may also work in the fields alongside her sons and husband. Still, regardless of the economic class to which the family belongs, there is a strong sense that home-management tasks (housekeeping, child rearing, and the like) are the exclusive province of women, an assumption that it is best for women to remain, as far as possible, in the domestic sphere, and a strong cultural proscription for men to participate in any domestic tasks whatsoever.

Land Tenure. Land tenure takes one of three forms. Direct ownership is the preferred and the most common form. Leaseholds, traditionally for six years although variations in terms of the lease are not infrequent, are secured for payments in cash or kind (although today it is rare for agreements to be based upon the latter). Rents have soared in recent decades, and the lessor must often pay a substantial annual rent without certainty of the future profits at the harvest. Together, these factors have contributed to the decline in popularity of this form of land tenure. Sharecropping—in which an individual shares in the profits of the farm in return for the contribution of his labor in producing the crop—was once far more common than it is today, partly because of the mechanization of many farming tasks, which has reduced the need for outside labor. When sharecropping does occur, the proceeds of the sale of farm products are generally split, 50-50, between the landowner and the sharecropper.

Kinship

Kin Groups and Descent. Kinship is reckoned bilaterally and extends across five generations—an individual reckons as part of his/her kindred all lineal consanguines in the categories of grandchildren, children, siblings and some collaterals, parents and parents' siblings and collaterals, and grandparents. Collateral kin relations are not counted as particularly significant beyond first cousins.

Kinship Terminology. There is no distinction made between maternal and paternal kin, referentially, but the difference between first cousins (part of the kindred) and second cousins (recognized as relatives but not considered to be particularly close) is marked terminologically: first cousins are called _primos hermanos_ (brother cousins) while all cousins further removed are collectively referred to merely as _primos_ (cousins). People recognized as members of one's kindred are referred to as _parientes_, alternatively as _familiares_. Spiritual kinship is important in Andalusia. For instance, godparents are chosen at two stages of an individual's life: as sponsors for baptism, and as sponsors at marriage. However, in Andalusia these individuals are usually also the grandparents of the sponsored person, so that godparenthood does not usually draw into the kinship network anyone not already a part of it.

Marriage and Family

Marriage. The decision to marry is made by the potential spouses, but not without the active involvement of the parents of both in the selection process. Courtship is carried out by the men, but it is held that the woman usually initiates it by expressing her interest in a potential suitor through discreet flirting. Although traditional laws stipulating that only church weddings were legitimate have been changed to recognize civil unions, the church wedding is still the rule. Despite the fact that informal liaisons are not officially or religiously recognized, common-law marriage among landless laborers is not unusual, and couples living together in this fashion are often tacitly accepted without serious damage to their reputations as long as they comport themselves as a properly married pair (i.e., maintain a monogamous union). They are expected to make every effort to regularize such a union when a child is imminent. Because of the strong social pressures to conform to the twin precepts of _honore_ and _verguenza_ (honor and shame), adultery and/or premarital sex are traditionally negatively sanctioned—a situation that both church and state have long reinforced. Divorce was legally prohibited until very recently and remains repugnant to the church, but it does happen on occasion. It is much less likely for a wife to try to divorce her husband than for the reverse to occur. Postmarital residence is neolocal but tends to be in the same community—quite frequently the same neighborhood—as that of the wife's family.

Domestic Unit. The domestic unit is, minimally, the nuclear family—a man, his wife, their children. Although this form of household is the most common, extended families do occur and usually consist of a nuclear family and a member or members of the grandparental generation. Even when not coresident, the households of a woman and her married daughter tend to maintain strong ties, based on their close emotional relationship and proximity, which lead to the cooperation of the two in their day-to-day work and personal lives.

Inheritance. In Andalusia, heritable property is divided equally among all heirs, with no distinction made on the basis of order of birth or gender.

Socialization. Child rearing is the responsibility of the mother because the cultural proscription against male participation in the domestic sphere is strong. A father's relationship with his children is generally remote, to the point of formality. This distant relationship remains in place even after a son achieves maturity. In early childhood, the mother-child tie is very strong, but it gradually weakens between mother and son as the boy approaches his teenage years. At this time, young men are expected to begin to establish an increasingly "public" identity, spending greater and greater amounts of time away from the house in the company of their male contemporaries. Still, however much independence a young man achieves, as a "good son" he is expected to revere his mother throughout his life. A daughter rarely undergoes such a separation from her mother. Rather, upon reaching puberty a daughter is expected to retire further and further into the life of the casa, lest she risk incurring gossip. Thus, the mother-daughter bond is strengthened, rather than weakened, as the daughter achieves adulthood.

Sociopolitical Organization

Social Organization. Traditional Andalusian society has been said to operate primarily according to principles of patron-clientage, according to which those with greater access to wealth, power, or other resources are recruited by those with lesser access, to provide assistance. The terms used to justify such relationships may be fictive kin (by making the patron godparent to one's child) or loyalty and friendship (as between employer/employee). In modern Andalusia, more explicitly class-based factors appear to comprise the primary organizing principle. The institution of the *cofradia* (brotherhood, fraternal order) has importance in organizing cooperative efforts in preparing for ritual occasions and as a kind of mutual-aid society for its members; it is a village-based organization of men, united for specific purposes or tasks. Each man is born into the cofradia of his father.

Political Organization. Andalusia today, as an autonomous community within the larger national polity, has its own representative who brings to the attention of the state the interests of the region and who heads a regional board that makes decisions regarding Andalusian social and economic issues. Local communities are under the jurisdiction of the municipality or township, the minimal administrative level. The municipal-level political organization centers on the town hall, and the leading official is the mayor.

Social Control and Conflict. As is true for many rural, face-to-face communities, one of the strongest mechanisms for social control is local gossip and other informal expressions of public censure. There is also recourse to municipal authorities.

Religion and Expressive Culture

Religious Beliefs. In Spain as a whole, the Catholic church was long the only religion; freedom of worship became permissible by law only in recent decades. Andalusia is known for having its own emotionally charged and personalized brand of Catholicism, best exemplified in the extravagant Holy Week (Santa Semana) celebrations. There is a strong Madonna focus organizing Andalusian religious beliefs, and some scholars of the region trace the preeminence of the Virgin Mary to pre-Christian religious beliefs and practices in which a nurturant mother-goddess (variously personified as Aphrodite [Greek], Astarte [Phoenician], and Tanit [Carthaginian]) is paired with a son/father/consort figure (Apollo, Melkart, Hercules), citing these pairs as prefiguring the later emphasis upon Madonna and Christ figures. Traditional Holy Week *saetas* (lyric verses with a religious theme) make strong use of invocations of the Madonna's powers to intervene and protect the people, as well as commemorating her status as the grieving mother of the crucified Christ. The belief that saintly figures, and particularly the Madonna, are capable of being recruited to assist the faithful in daily life is strong throughout the Iberian peninsula, but it finds its most extreme expression in Andalusian religious practice. There are strong undercurrents of acceptance of the miraculous and belief in the power of penitence, which together form an essential element of Andalusian religion.

Religious Practitioners. Religious practitioners are the duly ordained priests of the Catholic church, but they are assisted by members of lay brotherhoods and sisterhoods.

Ceremonies. Life-cycle events such as baptism, marriage, and death are attended by church ritual. In the past, such ceremonies might have involved the entire village population, although today baptisms and marriages tend to be much more a family affair. Although church attendance is not strictly observed on a day-to-day basis, particularly among men, the High Holy Days of the Catholic liturgical calendar still tend to bring out the majority of parishioners, and the Lenten period is in practice the single most important ceremonial occasion. The Santa Semana masses are attended by nearly everyone, but the more secular processions and fiestas held during that week evoke the greatest degree of enthusiasm and participation among the people. Massive floats bearing the likenesses of the Madonna and the Christ figure are borne along the streets, each sponsored, prepared, and carried by a particular cofradia, and there is a strong competitive flavor to the comparisons (often couched in the verses of saetas) among the Madonnas of the different cofradias.

Arts. The "quintessentially Spanish" art forms of bullfighting and, especially, flamenco are in fact "quintessentially Andalusian" in origin. It is in Andalusia that the fighting black bulls were first bred, and long before the development of bullfighting as we currently know it, bull rituals and bull cults were established in the region—predating the Mithraic cult of the Roman empire and perhaps deriving from prehistoric practices. At least, there are prehistoric Andalusian cave paintings and stone carvings of bulls that have an extremely early provenance. Flamenco, too, has an ancient tradition. "The dancers of Gades [Cadiz]" were known as far back as the second century B.C., and the "puellae Gaditanae" ("girls of Cadiz") are referred to by Strabo, Martial, and Juvenal. This Andalusian tradition of the dance formed the basis upon which the Gypsies, who arrived in the region in the 1400s, elaborated and stylized to yield the form we know today as flamenco. But the region's artistic production is not limited to modern variations on ancient artistic practice. Andalusia was, after all, the birthplace of Picasso, and it has been claimed that the region provided the greatest inspiration for the development of his art. Outside of the sphere of formal performance, Andalusia also has a long tradition of folk composition, particularly represented in lyric verse (secular *coplas* and the more religiously oriented saetas), both of which are strongly emotional in content.

Death and Afterlife. Andalusian attitudes toward death are strongly colored by Catholic beliefs, and funerary ritual is oriented around the Catholic sacraments of confession and extreme unction. Masses must be said for the deceased, and there has long been a tradition of charitable donations as commemoration for the dead. The expenses for both of these practices are borne by the cofradia to which the deceased belonged during his or her lifetime.

See also Gitanos; Sephardic Jews

Bibliography

Brandes, Stanley (1980). *Metaphors of Masculinity: Sex and Status in Andalusian Folklore*. Philadelphia: University of Pennsylvania Press.

Gilmore, David (1980). *The People of the Plain: Class and Community in Lower Andalusia*. New York: Columbia University Press.

Gilmore, David (1987). *Aggression and Community: Paradoxes of Andalusian Culture*. New Haven: Yale University Press.

Josephs, Allen (1983). *White Wall of Spain: The Mysteries of Andalusian Culture*. Ames: Iowa State University Press.

Mitchell, Timothy (1990). *Passional Culture: Emotion, Religion, and Society in Southern Spain*. Philadelphia: University of Pennsylvania Press.

Pitt-Rivers, Julian A. (1971). *The People of the Sierra*. 2nd ed. Chicago: University of Chicago Press.

NANCY E. GRATTON

Aquitaine

ETHNONYMS: none

Orientation

Identification. The southwest of France, or Aquitaine, is geographically and culturally diverse. It consists of the departments (political divisions) of the Gironde, Perigord, Lot et Garonne, Landes, and Pyrénées-Atlantiques. The southwest, however, should not be understood simply as a natural entity having eternal geographical boundaries: its specific identity has been socially and historically constructed, subject to continuous renegotiation. As a cultural area, the southwest reflects not only long-standing regional relations and inequalities but also a struggle for autonomy between a local region and a strong centralized state that since the sixteenth and seventeenth centuries has sought to construct and impose a French national identity. While the struggle for regional identity is often experienced in political and economic terms, its quotidian dimension is also apparent in terms of dialect and pronunciation—often a subject of ridicule in Paris. A further complicating factor in the cultural identity of the southwest is the presence of immigrants from neighboring European countries and from former French colonies who have made the southwest their home since the Second World War. These groups have struggled to maintain their identities in the midst of changing regional, national, cultural, and political dynamics.

Location. The southwest of France is bordered on the south by the Basque country, the Pyrenees Mountains, and Spain, on the west by the Atlantic Ocean, on the north by the regions of Poitou-Charentes and the Limousin, and on the east again by the Midi-Pyrenees. The capital of the Aquitaine, Bordeaux, is approximately on the same latitude as New York City. Geographically, the southwest is spread over 41,308 square kilometers incorporating mountains, rolling hills, and two important rivers in the Garonne and the Dordogne. It is also renowned for its caves, which were the homes of prehistoric peoples. The Aquitaine exhibits a strong cool and wet oceanic influence in the cold season and a Mediterranean climate in summer. Winters are mild and moist, summers hot and dry. Average annual rainfall is 58.2 centimeters with average temperatures ranging from 5° C in January to 20° C in July.

Demography. The population of the Aquitaine is approximately 2,718,200. The largest upward trend in population has been since the Second World War. Immigrants account for roughly 8 percent of the population.

Linguistic Affiliation. The principal language spoken in the southwest is French. However, prior to the second half of the nineteenth century, numerous dialects were spoken. These included Provençal or Occitan, which is divided into North Occitan, Middle Occitan, and Gascon. These dialects only approximate ancient political boundaries. The French language itself spread first among the nobility and bourgeoisie of the eighteenth century and only appeared in the countryside as an administrative language. The centralization of power, culture, and the economy in the French state served to suppress but not to eradicate regional dialects.

History and Cultural Relations

The history of the southwest of France, like that of France in general, is marked by a series of invasions and conquests. Apart from prehistoric peoples—largely in the Perigord—the earliest inhabitants of the southwest were Gauls, a Celtic people. The Gauls maintained control of the southwest until conquered by the Romans in 52 B.C. Rome controlled the Aquitaine until its capital and power shifted east to Constantinople, at which time the borders of Gaul were overrun by Germanic invaders who divided the land into small chiefdoms. While the territory of Gaul was reunified under the Frankish king Clovis, who ascended the throne in A.D. 481, a succession of French kings—including the emperor Charlemagne, who was a force in the revival of Latin culture—struggled with variable success until the period of Absolutism in the seventeenth century to bring France under unified rule. The southwest was characterized by fiercely independent landlords or seigneurs who used their feudal domains and local power over the peasantry with some success to hold at bay the French crown. They were gradually less able to resist assimilation as a national market took shape during the sixteenth and seventeenth centuries. The twelfth to fifteenth centuries witnessed the occupation of the southwest by the English. This period was important for the growth of the southwest French wine trade as winegrowers found an eager clientele for claret among the English aristocracy. The importance of the wine trade can be recognized in the fact that English warships of this period were measured by the quantity of wine they could carry. The Aquitaine also served as a stronghold for the Protestant Huguenots during the sixteenth and seventeenth centuries, who suffered persecution at the hands of the Catholic church. The Huguenots called upon the English crown for assistance against the Catholic Cardinal Richelieu. The profound cultural and economic ties of the southwest of France to England, beginning with the occupation and reinforced during the religious wars, persist today, as evidenced by the numerous English people who have settled in this region. From the period of French Absolutism onward through the French Revolution, which was well supported in the southwest, the Napoleonic empires, and now the Fifth Republic, the Aquitaine's history—but not its complete cultural identity—converges with that of the French nation-state. The southwest is ethnically diverse, especially in urban areas. Periods of recent economic hardship, however, have led to racial and ethnic tensions in the Aquitaine.

Settlements

Until the later part of the nineteenth century, many people in the southwest lived in small villages. However, the twentieth century has initiated a progressive urbanization, with approximately 75 percent of the population now living in cities. This change has come from the industrialization of towns and mining areas, the destruction of many rural crafts, and the widespread modernization of agriculture, all leading to the destruction of communal lands and a general exodus to the cities. Villages today tend to consist of densely packed houses surrounded by farmland that is often dispersed. Tourism, ranging from specialized communities to independent homes, has also affected the settlement patterns.

Economy

Subsistence and Commercial Activities. Owing to the importance of the wine trade, capitalist agriculture coexisted with subsistence production throughout most of the nineteenth century. Today, virtually all segments of French agriculture have been thoroughly integrated into capitalist markets and social relations. The most important commercial activity continues to be wine making, which divides the southwest into areas of quality and ordinary production. Most areas of the southwest are regions of polyculture where the cultivation of cereals, fruits, vegetables, truffles, and tobacco and the raising of livestock are among the most important activities. There is also some light industry. Many rural households earn a living through a combination of agricultural production and nonagricultural pursuits such as work in a local factory or domestic labor. The smallest farms are made viable through the numerous agricultural cooperatives that are prevalent in the southwest.

Industrial Arts. The southwest is home to many artists and to those who orient their production to the tourist trade.

Trade. The southwest has since the early Middle Ages been tied into international markets. Today, it is France's membership in the European Community (EC) that is most important for the Aquitaine. Membership in the EC has both highlighted aspects of development in the southwest and created problems with neighboring states, for example the importation of inexpensive Spanish and Italian wines. Membership in the EC has also revitalized regional consciousness and made it more difficult for the French government to inter-

vene, as prices and guidelines for the circulation of agricultural goods and workers are often set at the international level.

Division of Labor. While a division of labor based on gender has long existed in the countryside, the modernization of agriculture has established an almost exclusively domestic role for women. Although urban areas avowedly offer more opportunities for women, numerous inequalities in pay and opportunities for advancement reflect the sexual division of labor. The division of labor in manufacture and service industries is specialized and hierarchical.

Land Tenure. Although France is known for its preservation of the small family tenure, the average is actually larger than many other countries in the EC. The southwest has witnessed a consolidation of tenures as a result both of government planning and of the failure of small family farms. Nevertheless, it is still quite common to find small- and medium-sized farms whose tenures are divided into small units spread over a wide area. Private property is jealously guarded even by those farmers who are members of cooperatives.

Kinship, Marriage, and Family

Kin Groups and Descent. The nuclear family predominates in both rural and urban areas. Extended family units can be found in the countryside and among low-income groups in cities. Descent is recognized equally through both male and female lines.

Kinship Terminology. Kin terms follow the Eskimo system.

Marriage. Men and women in the countryside typically marry in their early twenties; marriage in urban areas is often delayed until later because of the demands of education and career. Postmarital residence is almost exclusively neolocal. Marriage laws date from the Napoleonic era and tend to favor the rights of men. Divorce and remarriage have become common.

Domestic Unit. The nuclear household is the most common domestic unit, although extended households can be found in rural and urban areas. Although many scholars argue that households in the past were large because of the need for agricultural labor, this is a topic of great debate.

Inheritance. In the past, it was common for men to inherit the family farm while daughters were given a dowry. Today, men and women have equal claims to the family estate.

Socialization. The primary means of socialization are the family, school, and peer groups. Elders no longer command the esteem and authority that they once did.

Sociopolitical Organization

Social Organization. The southwest, like France in general, is class-stratified. While post–World War II economic development has produced new wealth, approximately 1.56 percent of households in France possess 25 percent of the nation's wealth. It is reported that 10 percent of households share 50 percent of the nation's wealth, while the poorest 25 percent share only 6 percent of the wealth. Consolidation of peasant tenures as well as marked differences in agricultural production within the Aquitaine make the southwest a mirror of class stratification in France.

Political Organization. France is a republic, or constitutional democracy, with a National Assembly consisting of 577 deputies elected by direct suffrage and a Senate consisting of 319 members elected by indirect suffrage. The president of the republic is elected every seven years and, besides appointing the prime minister, is responsible for protecting the constitution, the national independence, and the territorial sovereignty of France.

France is divided into communes, cantons, arrondissements, and departments, of which the first and the last are the most significant. All of these political divisions are represented in the southwest. The communes are local in focus and traditionally represented groupings of villages or agricultural settlements, whereas the departments serve principally as administrative arms of the state. Departments and communes have come under criticism for their inadequacy as spatial units of administration and for their arbitrary boundaries, respectively. Consequently, to facilitate administration and state planning, regions were introduced as a unit in three stages, in 1964, 1972, and 1982. Apart from being identifiable as a cultural area, the Aquitaine now serves as a region. Regions were partially decentralized by the socialist government in 1982 as a means of enhancing their autonomy.

Social Control. The French legal system at the local and national level serves as a primary instrument of social control. This is reinforced, especially in villages, by the power of gossip and public opinion.

Conflict. Regional identity periodically surfaces as a source of tension with the nation-state, in addition to differences that emerge within the region as a result of political and economic inequalities. More recently, the many immigrants who have settled in the southwest have served as a source of tension and debate among political parties and the general citizenry.

Religion and Expressive Culture

Religious Beliefs. France recognizes the separation of church and state, so there is no state religion. Catholicism and Protestantism are the two largest religions within France, although virtually all world religions are represented. The saints play an important role in certain parts of the southwest as guardians of the crops. Agricultural modernization has done much to eliminate traditional ceremonies associated with planting and the harvest. Periodically, these ceremonies reappear as orchestrated by local bureaus of tourism. Important holidays are Christmas, New Year's Day, Easter, May Day, Ascension Day, and Independence Day.

Religious Practitioners. Apart from the clergy of the established religions in France, there are numerous practitioners representative of pagan religions. Witchcraft, for example, is practiced in certain rural sectors of the Aquitaine.

Arts. There is tremendous diversity within the southwest with respect to local arts. Today, the arts are dominated by artisans from all over France who have made the southwest their home. Some of the traditional arts are kept alive by local bureaus of tourism.

Medicine. France has a fully Westernized system of medicine with excellent social services subsidized by the government. In the countryside, many traditional healers carry on their trades with explanations of illness in moral rather than exclusively medical terms.

Death and Afterlife. The Catholic and Protestant churches have done much to shape attitudes toward death and an afterlife. However, the rituals surrounding death and disposal of bodies have been thoroughly modernized and medicalized and are now largely carried out by undertakers.

Bibliography

Guiraud, Pierre (1968). _Patois et dialectes français_. Paris: Presses Universitaires de France.

Herzfeld, Michael (1987). _Anthropology through the Looking Glass: Critical Ethnography in the Margins of Europe_. Cambridge: Cambridge University Press.

Pinchemel, Philippe (1987). _France: A Geographical, Social, and Economic Survey_. Translated by Dorothy Elkins. Cambridge: Cambridge University Press.

Segalen, Martine (1986). _Historical Anthropology of the Family_. Cambridge: Cambridge University Press.

Ulin, Robert C. (1987). "Writing and Power: The Recovery of Winegrowing Histories in the Southwest of France." _Anthropological Quarterly_ 60: 77–82.

Ulin, Robert C. (1988). "Cooperation or Cooptation: A Southwest French Wine Cooperative." _Dialectical Anthropology_ 13: 253–267.

ROBERT C. ULIN

Ashkenazic Jews

ETHNONYMS: none

Orientation

The term "Ashkenaz" is derived from a geographic designation in the Hebrew Bible. It is an ethnonym that at one time was applied rather precisely to the German-speaking areas, especially the Rhineland. Ashkenazic Jews have lived across most of northern, central, and eastern Europe, and they have been culturally distinctive roughly since the time of the Holy Roman Empire. However, no group of Jewish communities fits neatly into the standard concept of a "cultural region." With the exception of contemporary Israel, it has been many centuries since Jews constituted a cultural majority within a given territorial region. In fact, it would be more appropriate to speak of Ashkenazim using Mikhail Bakhtin's notion of the chronotope—a field of human interaction defined synthetically along the dimensions of time and space—which would allow us to see these Jews in their interaction with cultural and historical developments among the surrounding populations.

This becomes clear when we try to define the boundaries of Ashkenazic Jewry, which are coterminous with the boundaries of the Yiddish language area. In the seventeenth and eighteenth centuries, Amsterdam and Venice were major Yiddish publishing centers. Dialects of Yiddish were spoken as far north as northern Germany. After the first partition of Poland at the end of the eighteenth century, masses of Jews were incorporated into the westernmost portions of the Russian Empire. The "center of gravity" of Ashkenazic Jewry shifted steadily eastward during the latter parts of the eighteenth and nineteenth centuries for two reasons. First, the western European Ashkenazic communities lost cultural vigor and distinctiveness with the rise of the western European Enlightenment and the possibility of legal emancipation. Second, the Jews of the Russian and Austro-Hungarian empires experienced a massive growth in population. We might employ geological imagery, therefore, and think of Ashkenazic Jewry as a continent that became largely submerged in the modern period, leaving islands in western Europe—particularly Alsace, where Yiddish was spoken until World War II—and that experienced a gradual buildup and then sudden eruption of a mountain range on its eastern borders.

Owing to assimilation, emigration, and genocide, memoir literature generally constitutes the best source of ethnographic information on Ashkenazic Jews. The only extant communities that should properly be called "Ashkenazic" are those in which Yiddish is still spoken. These fall into two categories. The first consists of groups of elderly, usually secularist eastern European Jewish émigrés, centered in Israel, France, the United States, Canada, and a few other countries. The second includes a number of flourishing Hasidic communities, especially in Israel and New York City. The Hasidic communities utilize Yiddish in newspapers and in schools and adult religious study, and many Hasidic families continue to speak Yiddish at home.

Like Middle Eastern Jews, Ashkenazim display four of the major criteria of a distinctive cultural entity: religion, region, language, and political-economic position.

Religion

The cultural-religious system of Ashkenazic Jewry represents a fundamental continuity of the Rabbinic Judaism encapsulated in the Mishnah and the Babylonian Talmud. These compendiums concentrate to a large degree on the problem of adapting Biblical law, intended for a free Israelite polity centered on the temple rituals, to a situation in which Jewish communities were dispersed in other lands and lacked a ritual center. Therefore, they serve Diaspora Jews as a model for cultural adaptation and reconstitution in changing circumstances, and they help explain the persistence of Jewish collective identity through the centuries. The Talmud in particular also contains a great deal of narrative, biographical, and legendary material. The great focus in traditional Ashkenazic culture on Talmud and Bible study fostered an imaginative identification with the past generations whose lives were described therein. Furthermore, the Talmudic model of

textual interrogation and dialogue contributed to a close link between textual and oral culture. While in principle Talmudic learning was open to all Jewish males, social stratification and economic pressures generally kept it the province of an elite. In certain periods and places, women were encouraged especially to study the Prophets and Chronicles.

The Ashkenazic sense of time and space was conditioned to a large extent by reiterations of the belief that the Messiah might come at any time to gather all the dispersed Jews in the land of Israel. The ritual cycle remained fixed to the lunar calendar, maintaining powerful associations with the agricultural cycle of Palestine. This system ensured both a rough correspondence between the celebration of festivals and the seasons of the year and also a certain disjuncture between the Jewish calendar on the one hand and the secular and Christian solar calendars on the other. Jewish interaction with the coterritorial populations was also shaped by the significant place of Jews in the folklore and religion of Christianity.

During periods of relative peace and prosperity, it was possible for marriage patterns to conform somewhat to ideals that stressed both the means of engaging in commerce and the leisure and competence to engage in Talmudic scholarship. The ideal marriage, therefore, was one between a young scholar who had studied full-time into his teens and the daughter of a successful merchant capitalist. The bride's family was expected to provide a dowry, often including support of the couple for a few years so the husband could continue his study, after which he would either go into business or find a rabbinic position. This pattern, to the degree it ever held as a norm, failed in largely the modern period under the combined pressures of increased pauperization, communal dislocation, and the ideology of personal choice.

Between the late eighteenth and the early twentieth century, religious Ashkenazic Jews were profoundly divided between Hasidim—enthusiastic, often mystical, and in a sense "populist" followers of the eighteenth-century charismatic leader known as Baal Shem Tov (Master of the Good Name)—and Misnagdim (literally, "opponents"), who fiercely defended traditional standards of social hierarchy, learning, worship, and observance.

Beginning in the nineteenth century, various movements arose as problematic syntheses of Ashkenazic culture—especially the Yiddish language—and the Enlightened or sometimes Social Democratic ideologies of modern Europe. A particularly powerful modern Yiddish culture briefly flourished, grounded in generations of Jews who experienced traditional religious childhood and education and then sought to frame new ideals within the older idioms of Ashkenazic Judaism. Zionism, the only such movement that proved to be an effective historical experiment, synthesized the traditional motif of the messianic return to the land of Israel with modern European ideologies of nationalism and colonialism.

Religious roles in Ashkenazic society were highly segregated according to gender. Separate seating was maintained at synagogue services. To varying degrees, rules governing women's modesty (shaving the head after marriage, not singing in public) were strictly maintained. Since domestic life was governed by religious law, women nevertheless had major "religious" responsibilities, and they often possessed informal authority in various matters.

Region

Ashkenazic Jews generally inhabited all of Europe, except for Iberia and the Mediterranean lands. Yiddish folklore displays a high consciousness of the regional variations among Ashkenazic Jews. Some of the most prominent markers of variation are dialect and culinary style. In recent times, these regional variations have become hypostatized into a contrast between "Litvaks"—Jews from the northeastern portion of the Russian Pale of Settlement (those eastern portions of the Russian Empire to which Jewish residents were legally confined), comprising historic Lithuania—and "Galicianers"—Jews in the Austro-Hungarian province of Galicia. Other ethnically significant regional designations include White Russia, the Ukraine, Bukovina, Hungary, and central ("Congress") Poland.

Ashkenazic Jewry since the late nineteenth century has been overwhelmingly associated with eastern Europe. In the decades before World War II, Poland, with 3.3 million Jews, had a larger Jewish population than any other country in the world. Other nations with large pre–World War II Jewish populations were Hungary (825,000), Romania (609,000), Germany (566,000), and France (350,000). In 1986, Poland had only 6,000 Jews, Hungary 80,000, Romania 45,000, and Germany 38,000. The largest population remaining in pregenocide "Ashkenazic" lands is located in the nations that were previously republics of the Soviet Union, especially Russia, Belarus, and Ukraine; though the Jews there are currently emigrating in large numbers. Major populations of descendants of Ashkenazic immigrants are located in Israel, the United States, France, Canada, South Africa, Australia, and Latin America. Except in Israel and to a much lesser degree France, the ethnic designation "Ashkenazic" (insofar as it ever had significant currency) has lost ground to the more general designation "Jewish."

Language

The Yiddish language, which is the single most distinctive marker of Ashkenazim, was the most widely used of numerous Diaspora Jewish languages, each of which synthesized Hebrew and Aramaic elements with lexical and syntactic bases of the coterritorial languages or dialects. It should not be supposed that the Hebrew and Aramaic elements were mere remnants of a time when those languages were Jewish vernaculars. Rather, the fact that Bible and Talmud study were at the heart of Ashkenazic culture meant that words, phrases, and loan translations from the religious texts were constantly interacting with the vernacular and shaping the evolution of the Jewish language.

Nor is Yiddish a variant of any single Germanic dialect belonging to a single time or place. Yiddish served to unify Jews within particular communities, and it also provided a means of communication between Jews living across a huge territory, among populations speaking a wide range of different languages. The distinctiveness of Yiddish became more obvious when Jews from Germanic-speaking lands moved into Slavic territories. Yet the language was as porous as the people were separatist, and it thus contains within itself traces of the entire cultural history of the Ashkenazim. The distinctiveness of the Hebrew alphabet also helped identify distinctive Jewish language use, even (or especially) in "secular" texts whose lexical corpus is almost indistinguishable from non-Jewish German usages.

Women and "uneducated" men were the earliest intended audience of Yiddish texts. Religious books in Yiddish, such as formalized supplications to God and an interpretive translation of the Bible, were popular long before the nineteenth century, as were Yiddish versions of the postmedieval adventure-story collections. These texts served as the basis for the growth of a secularist Yiddish literature in the nineteenth and early twentieth century.

Political-Economic Situation

In the "classic" period of Ashkenazic Jewry—before the massive shocks of industrialization, Enlightenment, nationalism, and world wars—Ashkenazim fulfilled the role of a middleman minority. In western Europe, they were variously bankers, peddlers, artisans, and the like. In eastern Europe, they fulfilled all these roles as well, but they were also utilized by the nobility as agents in the development and extraction of capital from new agricultural territories. Thus, Jews had a large percentage of state liquor monopolies in the nineteenth-century Russian Empire, and they often managed the estates of absentee nobility. Jews also served as cultural intermediaries, bringing news of the world especially to isolated peasants.

During the "classic" period, the Jewish communities were marked by a high degree of self-definition and communal autonomy. Their right to settle in a given location and to engage in business was granted by various local authorities, whether bishop, noble, or king. They were sometimes protected by these authorities and sometimes harassed or expelled at the instigation of coterritorial commercial classes or religiously inspired mobs. The rights of particular Jewish families to settle or go into business in a certain spot were frequently controlled by the community itself, which was able to deploy sanctions of Jewish law such as the *khazoke* (proprietary rights to a given "concession") and the *herem hayishuv* (ban on free settlement).

The loss of the middleman-minority sociocultural "slot," the increased threats to Jewish well-being over the course of perhaps three centuries, and the erosion of Ashkenazic Jewish cultural distinctiveness are closely and causally linked. The authority of the traditional texts and the rabbinic elite were undermined by the progressivist philosophy of the Enlightenment. The corporatist status of the premodern Jewish communities was rendered obsolete by the evolution of the inclusive Western nation-state. The masses of Jews in eastern Europe lost the artisanal and petty-commercial bases of their livelihoods, and they found little alternative opportunity in the new industrialism. Today, those descendants of the Ashkenazim who value their distinctive cultural heritage are struggling to find new ways to integrate past and present.

Bibliography

Gutman, Israel, ed. (1990). *The Encyclopedia of the Holocaust.* 4 vols. New York: Macmillan.

Katz, Jacob (1971). *Tradition and Crisis.* New York: Shocken.

Kugelmass, Jack, and Jonathan Boyarin (1983). *From a Ru-*

ined Garden: The Memorial Books of Polish Jewry. New York: Schocken.

Memoirs of Glueckel of Hameln (1932). Translated, with introduction and notes, by Marvin Lowenthal. New York: Harper Brothers.

Tillem, Ivan L., ed. (1987). *The 1987–88 Jewish Almanac.* New York: Pacific Press.

Weinreich, Max (1980). *The History of the Yiddish Language.* Chicago: University of Chicago Press.

Zborowski, Mark, and Elizabeth Herzog (1952). *Life Is with People: The Culture of the Shtetl.* New York: Shocken.

JONATHAN BOYARIN

Austrians

ETHNONYMS: Burgenländer, Kärntner, Niederösterreicher, Oberösterreicher, Österreicher, Salzburger, Steierer, Tiroler, Vorarlberger, Wiener

Orientation

Identification. Austria is a national culture of early twentieth-century origin (1919). It was created out of the six German-speaking provinces of the Austro-Hungarian Empire and the city of Vienna. An eighth province, containing many Hungarian and Croatian speakers, Burgenland, was added in 1945. The national culture is created by a communication system that tries to generate implicit agreement on a small set of values, especially those emphasizing historic, linguistic, and cultural similarities. This system includes the centralized curriculum of the schools, the programming of the national media monopoly, the discourse surrounding national and provincial elections and similar issues reported in the popular press, and customs of various types, including those regarding clothing, food and drink, recreational tastes, and use of dialect. In spite of these linguistic and cultural similarities, the provinces retain social, political, and ideological identities that have resisted complete integration. Also, the national culture is rejected by a growing minority that seeks unification with Germany. The forging of a national identity has fallen disproportionately on the urban centers, notably Vienna.

Location. Austria is bounded on the north by the Czech and Slovak Federative Republic and Germany; on the east by Hungary; on the south by Slovenia, Croatia, and Italy; and on the west by Switzerland and Liechtenstein. Its location is approximately 46° to 49° N and 9° to 17° E. The spine of the Alps runs west to east through the center of Austria. Only the extreme east and northeast edges of the area are hilly lowland plains. The mountains drain primarily north into the Danube

River system. Most of the country has alpine climate with a restricted growing season. In the lowlands, the climate is continental with warm, dry summers, humid autumns, and cold, wet winters. Average high temperature in January is −1° C, while in June it is 18° C. Elevation is a stronger determinant of local climate than latitude.

Demography. The total population in the 1981 census was 7,574,085. Vienna had the largest concentration of population at 1,524,510, followed by Lower Austria (1,431,400), Upper Austria (1,276,807), Steiermark (1,188,878), Tirol (591,069), Carinthia (537,137), Salzburg (446,981), Vorarlberg (307,220), and Burgenland (270,083). Through migration and changing birthrates, the western provinces and highland areas have lost population to the eastern provinces and urban areas. Twenty-three percent of the population lives in villages of 2,500 or less, 32 percent in market towns of 2,500 to 10,000, 15 percent in cities of 10,000 to 100,000, and 30 percent in cities of 100,000 or more. The population structure has been altered by the mortality of two highly destructive wars in this century and the differential male mortality of advanced industrial societies.

Linguistic Affiliation. Most Austrians speak the Southern (Bavarian) dialect of German, a branch of the Indo-European Language Family. Vorarlbergers speak the Alemannic dialect of German more commonly found in northern Switzerland and Swabia. In border provinces, one can find concentrations of speakers of Italian, Slovene, Croatian, Hungarian, and Czech. In Vienna one can find established enclaves of these languages, as well as speakers of Turkish, Serbian, Greek, Russian, Polish, French, Spanish, Arabic dialects, Persian, and English.

History and Cultural Relations

Although each province has a documentary history stretching back to the Roman occupation, the events relevant to the formation of the national culture begin after the First World War. After losing the war, the Austro-Hungarian Empire disintegrated into a number of nation-states—Hungary, Czechoslovakia, and Yugoslavia—based primarily on language affiliation. The German-speaking provinces, some with sizable non-German populations, became the (First) Republic of Austria. Other provinces, some with large German populations, especially in the regional centers, were ceded to Italy (South Tirol), Poland (Galicia), and Romania (Transylvania). National integration was hampered by postwar famine, disease, the loss of provincial markets and areas of supply, and the inflationary cycle and depression of 1926–1938. Pan-German nationalist political ideologies that linked the small, vulnerable Austria to the more powerful German state to the north were popular alternatives to Austrian nationalism, and in 1938 a majority of the country welcomed "Anschluss," the annexation of Austria by the Third Reich. The struggle between German and Austrian nationalism led to cultural warfare that severely damaged—or even, in some cases, destroyed—the country's Jewish, Gypsy, Croatian, and Slovene communities during World War II. After the war, the four Allied powers each occupied a separate sector of the country and of Vienna. In 1955, sovereignty was returned to Austria under the condition of perpetual political neutrality. The war experience, the failure of Pan-Germanism, the permanent neutrality, and the legacy of the destruction of the minority communities became the basis for a new national identity in the Second Republic of Austria.

Germany remains the most significant cultural focus outside Austria. The Austrian schilling is tied to the German mark in international money markets. German corporations are heavily invested in the Austrian economy. The German press is read and German trends in government, society, and consumption are closely monitored. Austria also has important relationships with Hungary and the Czech and Slovak Federative Republic. Although relations were strained after the dissolution of the Austro-Hungarian Empire and the erection of political barriers in the 1950s and 1960s, the three countries now maintain a cordial association. Currently, their citizens may freely cross their frontiers without visas. Ethnic conflicts have created difficult relations with three other neighbors. In northern Italy (South Tirol), German-speaking Tirolese separatists still wage guerrilla actions against Italian institutions from Austria. Although the Austrian government deplores these actions and has successfully prosecuted offenders, relations with Italy have been strained for many years. German nationalist sentiment has also antagonized Yugoslavia. Croatian minorities in Burgenland and Slovene communities in Carinthia have been subject to discrimination by local and provincial officials. Of all its neighbors, Romania has the most strained relations with Austria. A large number of Protestant Upper Austrians migrated to Transylvania after the Counter-Reformation, but they maintained links to their original communities. These new communities were under the direct threat of "Romanianization" and the destruction of their ethnic identities. After the 1989 rebellion in Romania, however, the threat was mitigated and relations between the countries improved.

Settlements

Austrian ethnographers speak of six identifiable rural settlement forms: (1) single, isolated farms with field blocks; (2) hamlets with tenant holdings; (3) nucleated villages with strip fields; (4) linear villages with strip fields extending through wooded areas; (5) villages built around a central green with rationalized fields; and (6) villages built along a street with rationalized fields. The more diffuse settlements (types 1, 2, and 4) are found in alpine zones. The more nucleated settlements (types 3, 5, and 6) are found in lowland areas. Urban settlements are primarily riverine, nucleated, and, originally, walled. These features derive from the early modern period of town formation (1350–1650) in central Europe when waterways were used as transport routes and there was a high level of political and military insecurity. The most important regional centers—Innsbruck (Tirol), Salzburg (Salzburg), Linz (Upper Austria), Villach and Klagenfurt (Carinthia), Eisenstadt (Burgenland), Graz (Steiermark), and Saint Pölten and Wiener Neustadt (Lower Austria)—are of this type. Vienna, with 20 percent of the national population, is a world-class metropolis and a center for elite entertainments and tourism. It was originally a Roman frontier fortress (Vindobona, A.D. 140) that declined in the post-Roman period only to revive with the building of Saint Stephan's Cathedral in the twelfth century. It was a center of commerce in the early modern period, when it enjoyed staple rights over traffic up and down the Danube. Economic development stagnated in the seventeenth and eighteenth centur-

ies as the Habsburg dynasty transformed the city into a ceremonial and administrative center for the empire. The industrial transformation of the metropolis began late (1820s) and proceeded at a leisurely pace. The razing of the city's walls in 1857 and the development of the broad Ring Boulevard around the central district heralded the beginning of modern city government and planning. By the mid-1890s, all but two of the current twenty-three districts had been annexed from previously autonomous suburbs and the population had swollen to its historic high of 2 million people, two-thirds of whom had been born elsewhere and migrated to the city for industrial employment.

Economy

Subsistence and Commercial Activities. Eighty-five percent of Austrians subsist by selling their labor for wages. However, 10 percent of the population in 1982 maintained a self-sufficient agricultural subsistence. The remaining 5 percent represent various professions who subsist on a fee-for-service basis. Among wage earners, more than half are salaried, white-collar employees in the commercial sector or government service. The blue-collar workers, four in ten of whom are certified as skilled, earn an hourly wage based on a 35- to 40-hour work week. All workers and employees work under contract standards established by the federal government and modified to suit the requirements of specific sectors and industries. All wage earners are currently guaranteed four weeks of paid vacation per year, with additional weeks added with seniority. An extensive program of federally administered benefits (health and unemployment insurance, pensions, general relief, family assistance, housing support, retraining programs, and continuing education) is funded through a gradual and progressive income tax. These taxes tend to level the net incomes of wage earners dramatically.

Industrial Arts. Specialty metals, food processing, chemicals (especially petrochemicals), machine tools, and microelectronics are currently the basis for the greatest industrial-sector growth. Major exports include winter-sports articles, dairy products, and construction materials (lumber and concrete). Real-estate transactions are important to the urban regional economies. Tourism is also an important source of regional income, especially in Vienna and the Tirol.

Division of Labor. A person's work life begins around age 15 and lasts through the early 60s. Retirement is a respected state, made all the more palatable by high pension payments. During a person's work life, promotions to higher pay and responsibility are age-related, although one can find fast-track promotions in young industries and government. Two-fifths of working-age women are employed outside the home. Among urban households of three persons or more, more than 75 percent of adult women are wage earners. In the rural areas, women are more likely to work at home. In two-income households, women continue to perform the traditional household-maintenance and child-care roles.

Land Tenure. In the alpine zones, land tenure is held within family corporations under the leadership of a single person, usually the senior male. As the elevation drops, land is rented for varying periods of time from a titleholder who may reside elsewhere. In lowland regions, land tends to be held by corporations, many of which are wholly owned within families, but with leadership shared among a number of persons.

Kinship, Marriage, and Family

Kinship. The most important kinship group is the bilateral *Familie*. The group tends to be coterminous with the household in both urban and rural zones. Relations between lineal relatives, especially parents and their married children or siblings, is recognized with the cover term *Grossfamilie*. These extended family ties are activated through frequent visiting. Families are embedded within a wider bilateral kindred, the *Verwandschaft*. This grouping is activated for life-cycle events.

Marriage. Marriages are monogamous. The age of marriage in urban centers coincides with the establishment of a career track (early twenties), but many delay marriage until their thirties. In alpine zones, the European late-marriage pattern can be found. The decision to marry signifies an intention to have children, since cohabitation without marriage, even within one's parents' house, is tolerated. The Roman Catholic practice of permanent marriage between sexually chaste partners remains prevalent among the rural population. According to state law, divorce can be initiated by either husband or wife, and remarriage is permitted. Marriages tie two extended families together. As soon as possible after the marriage, the couple establishes a neolocal residence within close proximity to one of the families, most frequently the wife's family. After the birth of children, the mother returns to wage earning after a maximum two years of paid leave. Close kin are employed for preschool child care.

Inheritance. Where land tenure is held within the family under the leadership of a single individual (alpine practice), the ideology of inheritance specifies that the entire estate should go to the firstborn male offspring. In the absence of that heir, the next oldest child inherits. In all other situations, landed or not, inheritance ideology tends to be bilateral and partible.

Socialization. Weaning from the breast occurs within 3 to 6 months. There is strong pressure toward early toilet training, which is often completed by the end of the child's second year. Grandparents play an important role in early childhood development. Disciplinary styles differ between the parents, with the father establishing a harsher, more physical approach, and the mother a more patient and verbal one. Preschool activities begin in the child's third year and regular kindergarten/elementary school in the fifth year. All of these institutions are state-supported. Primary school occupies the years 6 through 10 and emphasizes basic social, reading, writing, and arithmetic skills. Secondary school proceeds from ages 10 through 14. At age 10, the child is tested and tracked into either a continuing elementary school, a basic high school (Hauptschule), or a college-preparatory high school (Gymnasium). Education continues through the mandatory fifteenth year in either vocational schools, teacher-training institutes, apprenticeships, or continuing college-preparatory schools. The wage market relies on the school system for credential certification. Thus, educational decisions are among the most important an Austrian will make.

Sociopolitical Organization

Social Organization. The class structure in Austria has both formal and informal principles. There are five named classes and an all-but-invisible underclass. The named classes are "Bauern" (farmers, especially those with land tenure), "Arbeiter" (workers, especially skilled workers), "Kleinbürger" (bureaucrats, artisans, small-property holders, and shopkeepers), "Grossbürger" (wealthy property owners, industrialists, successful artists, and intellectuals), and "Adelsstand" (nobility with inherited wealth and land). This last class is in decline because public use of one's noble title is now illegal. Families belong to classes; individuals belong to families. Class affiliation is determined by the control of wealth and property or, in lieu of wealth, by educational achievement and the prestige of the position that one's credentials can command. Since real increases in wealth are all but impossible, achieving a higher educational level than one's parents is one of the few paths to social mobility. People tend to socialize, educate, and marry within classes and localities, producing closed, class-based, localized networks that are often activated to solve problems.

Political Organization. Austria is a parliamentary democracy. Representatives are selected for its bicameral legislature from lists prepared by the political parties. The majority party in Parliament or a coalition of parties then names the government ministers. These ministers establish policy, propose laws, and govern the republic on a day-to-day basis. A largely ceremonial official, the federal president, is elected by direct popular vote. Each province has a legislature and a governorship that retain much control over the implementation of federal law. Currently there are four political parties represented in the federal and provincial legislatures: the Social Democrats (Sozialistische Partei Österreichs), the traditional party of working-class interests; the Christian Democrats (Österreichische Volkspartei), the party of clerical, commercial, and industrial interests; the German Nationalists (Freiheitliche Partei Österreichs), who call themselves "liberals" but bear no relation in platform or rhetoric to contemporary European liberal parties; and the Green Party (Österreichische Grünen), which represents the environmentalist movement in Austria. A coalition of Christian and Social Democrats has frequently formed the government since the formation of the Second Republic (1955). The Social Democrats enjoyed a majority government from 1971 to 1983. A Communist party also exists and held seats in Parliament in the 1950s and 1960s but is no longer an important political movement. National Socialism is illegal, but at least one fascist underground group operates in the country.

Social Control. The centralized bureaucracy established under the old empire continues to maintain the most publicly visible institutions of social control. Hardly anything of importance to Austrians can take place without a tax stamp, license, or permit. Conformity to group values is established by gossip within tightly maintained kindreds and networks of acquaintances.

Conflict. The Austrian legal system is Napoleonic. Courts and police have sweeping powers to investigate conflicts. The accused must prove innocence by impeaching government evidence. Violent crimes are reported, but they appear to occur less frequently than in other advanced industrial societies. However, property crimes and white-collar crime, especially embezzlement and corruption, are common. Conflicts also occur between the majority group and resident minorities. Former guest workers from Greece, Yugoslavia, and Turkey, who now reside in Vienna, are often the subject of hate graffiti, racist language, and discrimination in employment and housing. Anti-Semitic and anti-Gypsy sentiment is quite common in private discourse and the public media. Private conflicts and alienation are among the biggest social problems Austrians face. Rates of alcoholism, suicide, and absenteeism are among the highest in European societies.

Religion and Expressive Culture

Religious Beliefs and Practices. Since the Counter-Reformation, Roman Catholicism has dominated Austrian religious belief. Although Eastern Orthodox, Protestants, Jews, Muslims, and Buddhists exist in Austria, they have no power to influence the interpretation of public morality to the extent that the Roman Catholics can. Although church and state are officially separate, the Christian Democratic party represents the interests of the Roman Catholic church in political affairs. In rural zones, this Catholicism can be very conservative. Passion plays with anti-Semitic themes, Latin liturgy, and antimodern ideologies predominate. In urban zones, religious practice is generally sporadic, often limited to life-cycle events.

Arts. In painting, literature, music, architecture, and theater, Austria has produced a significant number of Europe's masters. These artists are celebrated, often deified, in specialized museums, theaters, and concert halls in all of the regional centers, but especially Vienna and Salzburg. Two themes predominate in Austrian arts: an elaborately developed and sophisticated agro-romanticism that glorifies the rural landscape, and an introspective, highly psychologized celebration of modern metropolitan life. These themes coincide with the polarities of Austrian national consciousness: provincialism and cosmopolitanism.

Medicine. In the nineteenth century, Austrian, especially Viennese, medicine was in the vanguard of the development of modern, industrial medical science. Popular beliefs about health, however, retain a much older, humoral character. Much emphasis is placed on the good and ill effects of winds (fresh air, the alpine _Förn_), on the balance of hot and cold meals, and on the natural movements of the body. Homeopathic alternatives to school medicine are so popular that these cures are included in the national health system.

Death and Afterlife. Debilitating disease is feared more than death itself. Death imagery is very important in folk songs, betraying a lighthearted fatalism. Cemeteries play an important role in community life and are visited around 1 November each year. Evergreen wreaths symbolizing resurrection to eternal life are placed on graves.

Bibliography

Cole, John W., and Eric R. Wolf (1974). _The Hidden Frontier: Ecology and Ethnicity in an Alpine Valley._ New York: Academic Press.

Honigmann, John (1963). "The Dynamics of Drinking in an Austrian Village." _Ethnology_ 2:157–169.

Naroll, Raoul, and Frada Naroll (1962). "Social Development of a Tyrolese Village." _Anthropological Quarterly_ 35:103–120.

Ringel, Erwin (1984). _Die österreichische Seele: 10 Reden über Medizin, Politik, Kunst und Religion._ Vienna: Hermann Böhlaus Nachf.

Rotenberg, Robert (1992). _Time and Order in Metropolitan Vienna._ Washington, D.C.: Smithsonian Institution Press.

ROBERT ROTENBERG

Auvergnats

ETHNONYM: Arvernes

Orientation

Identification. The Auvergne is both a historical province in France and one of twenty-two administrative regions created in 1972. The name "Auvergne" derives from the "Arvernes," the Celtic peoples of Gaul who occupied this region during Roman times. Today, the Auvergne is officially composed of the four departments of Allier, Cantal, Haute-Loire, and Puy-de-Dôme. Regional cultural affiliation is sometimes also ascribed to the departments of Aveyron, Corrèze, Lot, and Lozère.

Location. Auvergne is located in the center of France, primarily on the Massif Central, a huge plateau. It covers an area of 26,012.89 square kilometers. Its regional capital, Clermont-Ferrand, is situated at approximately 45° N and 3° E. The climate varies from humid and windy with cold winters in the west to less humid and warmer weather in the east. The average elevation is 850 meters, but the highest mountains in the region, found in Cantal, surpass 1,000 meters. There are ancient volcanoes in both Cantal and Puy-de-Dôme.

Demography. The population of the Auvergne region was 1,334,400 in 1986. There is also a large population of Auvergnats living outside of the region, particularly in Paris. The density of the population is 51 persons per square kilometer. The population of Clermont-Ferrand was 601,900 in 1986. Although historically rural, the region has become increasingly urbanized since the turn of the century; the urban population surpassed the rural population during the 1960s.

Linguistic Affiliation. The Auvergne was a linguistic frontier between northern and southern dialects (the "langue d'oïl" and the "langue d'oc"). French is now the official language spoken among Auvergnats. Except for the very young, many people are bilingual in French and a local dialect (or patois).

History and Cultural Relations

Because of its location on a high plateau, with a mountainous terrain, many parts of the Auvergne remained isolated, marginal, and poor until the twentieth century. It was inhabited early in history, and there is evidence of heavy population during the Neolithic period. The Gergovie Plateau, near Clermont-Ferrand, was the site of the famous victory by the Arverne (and now French) folk hero Vercingetorix over Julius Caesar in 52 B.C., although the region was later conquered by the Romans. The region's history has been marked by its location as a transitional zone between northern and southern France and by the contrasts between the important political and religious center of Clermont-Ferrand and a countryside inhabited largely by peasants. Auvergnats are among many regional groups in the pluralist society of France. There is an intense regional consciousness among Auvergnats, but there have not been militant regional movements in the Auvergne as in other parts of France. The Auvergnats in Paris have their own newspaper, L'Auvergnat de Paris, which attests to the strength of social ties among urban migrants from the region.

Economy

Subsistence and Commercial Activities.   The region depends upon agriculture, industry, and tourism. Agriculture varies from mixed farming and vine growing in the lowlands to dairy farming and cattle raising in the mountains. Cheese making continues to be important to the agricultural economy (especially Saint Nectaire le Cantal cheeses). The Michelin tire company, based in Clermont-Ferrand, dominates the industrial economy. Tourism has long been important in the region, owing to thermalism and mineral waters in such towns as La Bourboule, Vichy, and Le Mont Dore. Today, winter sports and camping are being developed.

Industrial Arts.   In the past Auvergnats participated in several artisanal industries, which are now declining. Lace making was important in the regions of Le Puy, Aurillac, and Craponne. Thiers has long been a center for cutlery; and Ambert is known for its artisanal papermaking industry.

Trade.   Supermarkets and shopping centers dominate in urbanized areas. In towns and villages, however, small specialty shops (bakeries, butcher shops, groceries, etc.) are common. Open-air fairs and markets (foires) operate on a calendrical cycle, and regional centers specialize in certain types of markets (e.g., cheese, livestock, etc.). Agricultural fairs are becoming less common but remain vital in the southern portion of the region. Traveling vendors and merchants are common in more remote areas. Auvergnats participate in worldwide markets and, as French citizens, are incorporated into the European Community.

Division of Labor.   As in the rest of France, the Auvergne has both class-based and gender-based divisions of labor. The sexual division of labor in rural Auvergne varies among local regions, but women are primarily responsible for household labor and child rearing, and men for farm labor.

Land Tenure.   Auvergne is characterized by smallholding farms, with farm ownership in the hands of owner-farmers. Up until the early twentieth century, however, sharecropping was common in the region. A process of regrouping scattered holdings (le remembrement) has been encouraged by the government in recent years.

Kinship, Marriage, and Family

Kinship.   Auvergnats, like other French people, have a bilateral kinship system, with patriarchal overtones. The Ego-centered kindred is the basic descent group. A notion of the patrimony (le patrimoine) as a symbol of the family as an economic, cultural, and social unit is important.

Marriage.   Marriage in the Auvergne involves two ceremonies: a civil one at the mayor's office, and a religious one at the church. A preference for patrilocal residence predominated in the past, although this has declined with both urbanization and the depopulation of farm villages (so that any child is now encouraged to bring a spouse to settle on the farm). As in the rest of France, divorce rates have risen during the postwar period.

Domestic Unit.   La maison (sometimes known historically as le mas) is the most common term for the domestic unit, and connotes reference to the family as household. The less inclusive ménage refers to the nuclear family unit. Nuclear family households predominate throughout the region, although extended (stem-type) family households of two or three generations exist in the countryside. In eastern sections of the Auvergne, family communities were common (particularly among peasants) up until the eighteenth century. Neighboring Auvergnat households traditionally gathered for nightly veillées, which included storytelling and handiwork, until quite recently.

Inheritance.   Although equal inheritance is legally mandated by the French civil code, Auvergnat farmers have attempted to keep their holdings intact through various informal methods of impartible inheritance. Commonly, the "heir" will monetarily "pay off" the inheritances of siblings through going into debt. Primogeniture is preferred, although this is difficult to achieve, and younger sons and daughters often take over farms.

Socialization.   Auvergnat children commonly enter French public or Catholic schools at the age of 3, and the minimal school-leaving age is 16. Family-based socialization instills a strong sense of regional identity. Peer groups, the media, the educational system, and the family compete as agents in the socialization of the youth.

Sociopolitical Organization

Social Organization.   Auvergnats are tied to the French state through a complex bureaucratic infrastructure, yet the primacy of Auvergnat regional identity is strong (particularly among rural inhabitants of the region). There are 1,308 communes in Auvergne, which constitute the smallest administrative units in France and which represent the level at which most social life occurs. There is both urban-rural and class-based social differentiation in the Auvergne. Auvergnats of rural origin who migrate to urban centers often remain in the region and retain close ties to native village and family life.

Political Organization.   France's Fifth Republic is governed by an executive branch, shared by the elected president and the appointed prime minister (and his cabinet), and a legislative branch, consisting of the National Assembly and the Senate. Since 1982, Auvergne has had a regional president and council, as part of decentralizing efforts in France; before that, there was a regional prefect, but more central control over policy-making. France has a multiparty political system.

Social Control.   The French state has a court system and police to enforce social control. Other state institutions, such as education and social services, also operate to perpetuate an orderly society. At the local level in Auvergne, there is both resistance to state forms of social control and pressure to conform to familial and community-based norms.

Conflict.   During World War II, Auvergne was the home of the Vichy government and part of occupied German territory, although the Resistance was strong in southern portions of the region. All of France, including Auvergne, underwent a traumatic period of internal conflict during May 1968, when workers and students launched a series of protests.

Religion and Expressive Culture

Religious Beliefs and Practices.   Roman Catholicism is the major religion among Auvergnats, and pockets of the region are extremely devout. The Diocese of Clermont-Ferrand has a long and important history. Several Romanesque churches are found in the Auvergne, notably at Saint Nectaire and Orcival. Each commune and parish has its own patron saint and holds an annual patron saint festival. Easter (Pâques) and All Saints' Day (Toussaint) are the two most important religious dates, when Auvergnats from throughout the region return to their family homes in rural parishes. Auvergnat funerals are also times for large gatherings of kin and neighbors from far afield. For children, the celebration of First Communion at age 11 constitutes a traditional family feast as well as a religious occasion. Vestiges of ancient Celtic sites and beliefs are found throughout northern Auvergne.

Arts.   The traditional Auvergnat dance of *la bourrée* is now performed by folklore groups throughout the region and less formally at local gatherings. Verbal arts of storytelling and punning are also part of Auvergnat expressive culture.

Medicine.   France has a national health-care system, and there are both public and private hospitals. Country doctors and nurses who regularly make house calls are still common in rural Auvergne. Various folk healers (*guérisseurs*), each specializing in particular types of illness, are also consulted (although their activities are officially illegal).

Bibliography

Fel, André (1962). *Les hautes terres du Massif Central (Traditional paysanne et économie agricole)*. Clermont-Ferrand: Publications de la Faculté des Lettres et Sciences Humaines de Clermont-Ferrand.

Fel, André (1977). "Petite culture, 1750–1850." In *Themes in the Historical Geography of France*, edited by Hugh D. Clout, 215–247. London: Academic Press.

Institut National de la Statistique et des Études Économiques (1987). *Annuaire statistique de la France*. Paris: INSEE.

Manry, André-Georges (1974). *Histoire de l'Auvergne*. Toulouse: Privat.

Prival, Marc, et al. (1987). *Vie rurale en Auvergne: Scènes de la vie quotidienne*. Roanne: Éditions Horvath.

DEBORAH E. REED-DANAHAY

Aveyronnais

ETHNONYM: Rouergats

Orientation

Identification.   The Aveyron is one of ninety-five departments comprising the French republic. Predominantly rural and agricultural, it is one of the biggest of the French departments, with about half the area of New Jersey. It corresponds almost exactly to the province of the Rouergue, one of the smallest and most isolated in pre-Revolution France and one of the few left intact when the departments were created as administrative units under Napoleon. Like some larger French regions or former provinces (e.g., Brittany, Alsace, Provence) and a few other individual departments, the Rouergue/Aveyron has maintained a specific and widely recognized sociocultural identity within modern France.

Location.   Landlocked and far from national boundaries, the Aveyron is located in the west/center of southern France, on the edges of several distinctive regions: the mountainous Massif Central to its east and north, the southwestern plains to its west, the Mediterranean Midi to its south. Its long history of isolation is due in part to its formidable geographic zones. The north Aveyron lies in the Aubrac Mountain range, the south is cut through by the steep gorges of the Tarn River, and the eastern flank is lined with dry and sterile limestone plateaus (the Causses), all inhibiting easy communications within and beyond the Rouergue/Aveyron through much of its history. In the interior is the Ségala region, a well-watered and heavily forested area of high plateaus, rolling hills, and extremely acidic soils. Most of the department's territory is at an elevation of 500 to 800 meters, though descending much lower in the river valleys cutting across the department, and ascending considerably higher on some of the Causses and especially in the Aubrac (up to a 1,400-meter peak). In most of the department, the climate is humid and temperate.

Demography.   In 1886, the Aveyron's population reached its historic maximum of 416,000 (1886 French population: 39 million). During the following decades, large numbers of Aveyronnais (especially from the mountainous north) migrated, mainly to Paris but also to southern cities (Toulouse, Montpellier), the Argentine pampas, and San Francisco. Like other rural areas in France, the Aveyron suffered severe population loss as a result of World War I. During the period of rapid economic growth in France following World War II, great waves of migrants again left the Aveyron, moving predominantly to Paris. By 1975, the department's population had fallen to 278,000 (1975 French population: 52.6 million) where it has since stabilized. The Aveyronnais community in Paris is a coherent and highly visible one, organized into some seventy-five mutual-aid societies (*amicales*) by community or canton of origin. Parisian Aveyronnais are concentrated in the café or café-supply business (controlling about 70 percent of Parisian cafés) and in the lower echelons of the civil service (postal workers, police, etc.). They maintain close ties with the "homeland," to which many return for vacations and retirement.

Linguistic Affiliation.   As elsewhere in France south of the Loire River, dialects of langue d'oc were historically spoken in the Rouergue/Aveyron. These dialects are linguistically closer to modern Spanish or Italian than to French (descended from the langue d'oïl dialects, spoken north of the Loire). In general, the langue d'oc dialects are strictly oral and vary from village to village, but by convention they are grouped into dialect families, roughly corresponding to large pre-Revolution provinces. The dialects (patois) spoken in the north Aveyron are part of the Auvergnat (northern Massif Central) Family, while those spoken in the rest of the department belong to the Languedocian (western Midi) Family. Throughout the 19th century, the French state vigorously attempted to eradicate local patois and replace them with French as a language of national unity, but in most of rural Aveyron, French has become the primary language spoken at home only since World War II. In general, Aveyronnais born in this century speak fluent French, and those born since 1950 speak it as a first language, but most also understand a patois and many (especially older people) often prefer to use the latter. French will undoubtedly fully replace patois within the next generation or two, but the Aveyron will be one of the last areas of France to abandon its local languages for everyday use, more than a century after the state mandate to do so.

History and Cultural Relations

The Rouergue/Aveyron has a long history as an extremely poor hinterland. Its origins are usually traced to the Rutènes, a Celtic people who had established control over much of modern-day Aveyron by the time of their first contact with the Romans in 121 B.C. (Natives of the capital city of Rodez are still referred to as "Rutenois.") Conquered by Caesar's armies in 52 B.C., the area was part of the Gallo-Roman province of Aquitain for the next five centuries, becoming Christianized near the end of this period. Two constants emerge from the subsequent millennium and a half of Rouergat history. First, from the Gallo-Roman era to the modern French republics, the Rouergue/Aveyron has been a distant and generally neglected possession of a succession of regimes: Visigoth, Merovingian, Carolingian, Count of Toulouse, and the kings of France. It has been profoundly marked in myriad ways by the Roman, Toulousan, and French civilizations of which it has been a part, but it has been equally marked by its peripheral status to all of these. Second, the Catholic church has been a constantly powerful force shaping Rouergat history and identity. The counts of Rouergue (first established under Charlemagne) were in chronic conflict with the bishops of Rodez, before and after both became direct vassals of the king of France in 1270. During the twelfth century, much of the Rouergat wilderness was cleared and many agricultural inno-

vations were introduced by the great Cistercian abbeys established in the area. The Rouergue remained a calm Roman Catholic island in the storms raging around the Albigeois heresies just to its southwest and, later, those just to its east around the Reformation. Much later, the French Revolution went relatively unfelt in the Aveyron, until the requirement that priests swear their allegiance to the new constitution prompted popular counterrevolutionary uprisings (1791). During the nineteenth and twentieth centuries, the Aveyron has remained a poor and relatively isolated backwater, marked by devout Catholicism and political conservatism, as well as by selective or belated participation in many modern French institutions. By such measures as infant mortality and illiteracy rates, nineteenth-century Aveyron chronically lagged behind French averages. The great French railroad lines built during the nineteenth century, like the royal waterways and highways of the Ancien Régime and the auto routes of the twentieth century, bypassed the Aveyron. For much of the modern period, the Aveyronnais have been infamous among French administrators for their skills at draft dodging, tax evasion, and manipulation of state agents, as well as their astute use of state institutions (e.g., the judicial apparatus) to settle local scores. During the twentieth century, the Aveyron has served as a labor pool for urban France (especially Paris). Although remaining a rural, agricultural area in postindustrial France, the Aveyron has largely caught up with French averages in most measures of standards of living, particularly since the 1950s. Habits of using, abusing, and ignoring the institutions emanating from distant centers of state power remain strong.

There exists a well-recognized Aveyronnais/Rouergat stereotype in France, largely internalized by Aveyronnais themselves but perfectly consistent with their unambiguously French identity. Aveyronnais are taken to be hard-working, tight-fisted, devoutly Catholic and politically conservative, fiercely loyal to their homeland, neither as ebullient as southerners (from the Midi) nor as reserved as northerners. Their strongest image in the national imagination is as the archetypical provincial in Paris, tending café or working behind the window at the post office.

Settlements

The Aveyron is comprised of nearly 300 townships classified as rural (populations under 2,000), only six centers with more than 5,000 inhabitants, and no cities of national importance. The capital and largest city is Rodez, an administrative center with a 1982 population of 24,000. Two manufacturing centers, Decazeville in the west (coal and steel) and Millau in the east (leather tanning and glove making), achieved some importance in the nineteenth century, but they have long since declined. Rural townships typically are comprised of a small clustered settlement, or bourg, and a number of outlying isolated farms and small hamlets. In some rural areas (especially the Aubrac Mountains and Tarn Valley), many of the homes are owned by migrants or their descendants and are used only for vacations or retirement.

Economy

The Aveyronnais economy is almost exclusively agricultural. Until the twentieth century, most Aveyronnais were subsistence farmers, scraping a meager living from their poor soil and hostile environment. Rye, chestnuts, and (from the mid-nineteenth century) potatoes were the staples in most of the department. The local economy was largely autarkic, with poorly developed markets and little money in circulation. Today, the economy remains predominantly agricultural, but it is thoroughly integrated into national markets. About one-third of the Aveyronnais labor force is employed in production agriculture (compared to less than one-tenth in France as a whole). Most farms are small, family-owned operations engaged in the intensive livestock production that represents over 90 percent of Aveyronnais agricultural goods sold. The Aveyron is France's largest producer of sheep, most of them raised for the milk needed to make Roquefort cheese in the southeastern Aveyronnais village of Roquefort. The single most important category of farm production is dairy products and beef, accounting for about 40 percent of marketed agricultural goods. Most farms produce enough fodder for their herds (although few sell cereals or forage), and many also raise labor-intensive specialty crops under contract to agribusiness firms (e.g., gherkins, strawberries, tobacco, hybrid seed corn). Although cattle and sheep have long been raised by those (increasingly numerous) Aveyronnais farmers sufficiently prosperous to participate in a market economy, neither beef nor mutton figure in the local diet. Virtually all farm and many nonfarm households produce for home consumption the array of pork and poultry foods (e.g., dried and fresh sausage, cured ham, pâtés, foie gras, _confit_ [meat preserved in fat]) for which the region is renowned. The local diet, based on pork and poultry fats, is distinguishable both from the butter-and-cream diets in northern France and olive-oil regimes to the south. In general, those areas of the Aveyron that are ill-adapted to farm mechanization (e.g., Tarn Valley, Aubrac Mountains) or are only marginally productive even with modern chemical and mechanical technologies (e.g., the Causses) have been largely depopulated and abandoned as farmland. Elsewhere (especially the Ségala), intensive agriculture requiring dedicated skilled labor and relatively little land thrives. With the shift to lucrative specialty production, the Aveyronnais economy requires and can sustain a variety of agriculture-related activities. Although about 70 percent of the Aveyronnais labor force now works outside of production agriculture, the overwhelming majority is employed in jobs relating to farm inputs, outputs, or the various human services (e.g., education, health, housing) required by a prosperous farm population. Other economic activities are virtually absent from the department. Attempts have been made to develop a tourist industry, but the area is too remote and inaccessible to attract other than its migrant native sons and daughters. Some remnants remain of the leatherworking industry in Millau and the coal and steel center around Decazeville, but these industries are virtually moribund. With the exception of the cartel of Roquefort cheese firms (the Aveyron's single largest employer), the food-processing industry is weakly developed.

Kinship, Marriage, and Family

Kinship. The key unit among rural Aveyronnais farmers is the _ostal_ or "house," a farm unit associated with an ongoing patriline (designated by a family name) and a fixed location in space (designated by a place name). Kinship is figured bilaterally, but the core of the ostal is an unbroken, single-stranded father-to-son line. In general, the eldest son carries on the line, inheriting the farm and fathering its next heir. Other children are distanced from the line. They may move away from the farm, keeping the family name but losing identity with its named place. Alternatively, they may stay but must remain unmarried, becoming collaterals rather than ascendants to the line. In this system, more emphasis is placed on descent than on affinal ties. The key relationship is between father and eldest son. The mother–eldest son tie is also important: an in-marrying woman, permanently alien to the line, establishes herself within it as mother to its heir, her eldest son, a relationship she is expected to carefully develop and defend in turn against the demands of his own wife, her daughter-in-law.

Marriage. An ostal heir is expected to marry the daughter of an ostal of equal status to his. The bride, bringing a dowry of cash or movable goods, joins the ostal household of her husband and his parents. In the absence of a male heir an heiress is designated; she is normally expected to marry a younger son from a socially superior ostal, who also brings a dowry and moves into the household of his wife and parents. Otherwise, daughters and younger sons are expected to marry someone of roughly equivalent social status, do not receive dowries, and set up households separate from the parents of either. Divorce is not tolerated and premature widowhood of an in-marrying spouse is problematic. If childless, she or he may be sent away with her or his dowry. A widowed in-marrying spouse with small children is expected to marry the brother- or sister-in-law who will replace the deceased as heir to the ostal. If the children are nearly grown, the widow or widower may temporarily take over the ostal until the legitimate heir is able to do so.

Domestic Unit. The ostal household ideally takes a stem family form: an older couple, their eldest son and heir with his wife and children, and their unmarried daughters and younger sons. This pattern, requiring some measure of prosperity, has become more frequent, at least in some areas of the Aveyron, as the local economy has moved away from meager subsistence levels. Nonostal households generally take a nuclear family form.

Inheritance. The Aveyron, in a region of southwestern and central France where impartible inheritance was practiced historically, stands out today as a department in which this practice persists most strongly, despite its illegality since the promulgation of the Napoleonic Code nearly two centuries ago. Generally, farms are passed intact from father to eldest son. Farm value is routinely underassessed, and the share legally due to daughters and younger sons frequently remains an unpaid and unexpected promise. Recourse through the court system is generally considered an unattractive alternative to the social pressures and internalized values underpinning the "rights of the eldest" (_droit de l'ainesse_). The incidence of male primogeniture inheritance, like that of stem family households, has increased with growing prosperity.

Sociopolitical Organization

Modern France is a highly centralized nation, with most political power and socially dominant groups concentrated in Paris. Although there is some social and political fluidity, class consciousness is strong and the weight of the centralized bureaucracy heavy.

Social Organization. The Aveyronnais have an acute sense of social stratification, generally perceiving the world as organized in a hierarchical mode, manageable by astute appeal to higher-ups. Social distinctions were once land-based: landless laborers, smallholders/artisans, full-time landholding peasants, prosperous peasants (*pagès*), landed gentry (urban bourgeoisie or petty nobility). Under current conditions, landless agricultural laborers and the landed gentry have all but disappeared, as have material distinctions among the intermediate groups. Nonetheless, fine grades of social difference based on property ownership, education level, income, and style are noted, reproduced, and capitalized upon.

Political Organization. As everywhere in France, each township is administered by a town council popularly elected every six years and headed by a mayor chosen by the council from among its members. A departmental legislature, composed of popularly elected representatives from each of the forty-three cantons and headed by a president chosen by this body, manages departmental affairs. Formal powers at both these levels are severely constrained under the French constitution. The chief executive of the department is the prefect, appointed by the French minister of the interior. In national elections, the Aveyronnais vote is generally heavily weighted toward the center right, and in local elections toward those with the highest perceived social status, understood as implying best-placed contacts.

Religion and Expressive Culture

Religious Beliefs and Practices. The Rouergue/Aveyron has long stood out as one of the most devoutly Catholic areas of France by such measures as church attendance, participation in religious pilgrimages, percentage of schoolchildren enrolled in Catholic schools, number of priests per capita, and percentage of population joining convents or the priesthood. As virtually everywhere in France, there has been a decline among all of these indicators over the last thirty years, but the Aveyron figures remain much higher than national averages.

Arts. There once existed a lively oral tradition of stories, sayings, and songs in the patois, generally centered on wily or foolish peasants or animals. Although this tradition has not altogether disappeared from everyday life, it has been increasingly codified as folklore and relegated to performance by the several urban folklore societies organized especially in Rodez and Paris.

Medicine. Aveyronnais make ample use of bioscientific medicine (reimbursable under the French national health insurance plan), readily combining it with the use of healers who unofficially practice herbal medicine or the laying on of hands throughout the countryside. Some maladies are considered more treatable by one system or the other, but for many ailments it is considered prudent to try both.

Bibliography

Béteille, Roger (1978). *Rouergue: Terre d'exode.* Paris: Hachette.

Engalbert, Henri, ed. (1979). *Histoire du Rouergue.* Toulouse: Privat.

Groger, Lisa (1981). "Of Men and Machines: Co-operation among French Family Farmers." *Ethnology* 20:163–76.

Rogers, Susan Carol (1985). "Gender Stratification in Southwestern France: The Myth of Male Dominance Revisited." *Anthropology* 2:65–86.

Rogers, Susan Carol (1991). *French Trajectories: Shaping Modern Times in Rural Aveyron.* Princeton: Princeton University Press.

SUSAN CAROL ROGERS

Azoreans

ETHNONYMS: Ilhéus (oceanic yokels), Insular Portuguese

Orientation

Identification. Discovery of the uninhabited archipelago of the Azores was a starting point for Portugal's fifteenth-century overseas empire; five centuries later Portuguese culture continues to dominate its economic, social, and political life. The Azores are named for a seabird (*açor*), displayed on the regional flag beneath an arc of nine stars representing the archipelago's inhabited islands: São Miguel, Terceira, Faial, Pico, São Jorge, Santa Maria, Graciosa, Flores, and Corvo. Most islanders continue to think of themselves as Portuguese. Some push (clandestinely) for independence and some suggest becoming America's fifty-first state.

Location. The nine islands of the Azores straddle the Mid-Atlantic Ridge between 36° and 39° N and 24° and 31° W, some 3,200 kilometers east of New York, and about 1,300 kilometers west of Portugal. Proximity to the Gulf Stream moderates a climate characterized by narrow temperature range, ample precipitation, and dense mists. A prevailing anticyclone (high-pressure) system, which deflects storm fronts, engenders weather stability. A diverse ground cover of indigenous and imported flora is uniformly verdant. Periodic volcanic activity has endowed the land with natural attractions.

Demography. Soon after discovery, crop and stock raising were introduced as members of Portugal's underclass and *donatários* (grantee/landowner class with royal connections) began to settle the islands. The still-pervasive class system originated at that time. Italian, German, and English merchants, Spanish priests, a scattering of Moors and Blacks (slaves), baptized Jews (Conversos), and Flemish peoples came later. The Azore population is around 240,000 and declining. The three major ports are also population centers: Ponta Delgada (22,000), Angra do Heroísmo (14,000), and Horta (7,500). Azoreans emigrate to find employment, during the seventeenth and eighteenth centuries to Brazil, more recently to Canada and the United States.

Linguistic Affiliation. The language of the Azores is Standard European Portuguese (SEP). SEP follows Romance

Language Family conventions, is spoken by continental elites, and is classified as inflective, synthetic, and stress-timed (Brazilian Portuguese is syllable-timed). SEP is used by the media and literati and overlies Azorean regional "folk" speech. Distinctive accents and intonations often mark social status in the class-stratified society.

History and Cultural Relations

Settlement began around 1440 on the eastern islands under the absentee proprietorship of explorer Prince Henry, infante of Portugal, also known as the Navigator. São Miguel and Terceira, in the central island group, soon led in agriculture, producing exportable cash crops (wheat, dyer's woad, oranges, flax, wines and brandies) by the end of the century. Abundant harvests and strategic location made the Azores an important focus of Atlantic maritime trade well into the eighteenth century. During the seventeenth century, Terceira—then the center of Portuguese authority—led in population and prestige, a historical legacy manifest in its persistent interisland rivalry with the Michaelese. After eighteenth-century penetration by American shipping, tourist, and whaling interests, the port of Horta (Faial) became the archipelago's main distribution center and a vital nexus of Atlantic commerce. Telegraphy brought cable stations to Horta and Ponta Delgada, linking the Azores to an international communications network. In 1939 transatlantic flights by Pan American Airlines' "Yankee Clipper" stopped at Horta en route to Lisbon and Marseilles, enhancing Horta's already cosmopolitan image. Today Horta's marina attracts yachters from Europe and the Americas, and the port has a considerable tourist presence. World War II construction of major airports at Lajes (now an American base) and on Santa Maria and the advent of transoceanic planes ended the clipper-ship era. Despite glistening waterfront buildings, busy harbors, and sailboard resorts, the visitors to the Azores see themselves stepping back in time. A country way of life persists: the people hand-cultivate, creaking windmills grind maize, there are tiny walled gardens everywhere, the pigpen is located just outside the kitchen, and black-shrouded widows abound. Also, the presence of the Catholic church is pervasive and remains inextricably linked to state interests.

Settlements

Typically each island has a major perimeter road from which secondary roads—some barely passable—lead into a mountainous interior or down to coastal sites. Settlements follow the road, and cultivated fields and pastures are located behind a strip of contiguous houses. The few small interior villages (each about 500 people) are found at intersections of the roads; dwellings outline a central area of tilled fields, parish church, mill, and café or tiny shop cluster near the main crossroads. In larger settlements (1,000–3,500 people), administrative and commercial sites (café, bus/taxi, hotel, market, bank, _farmácia_, post office) circle a central _praça_, often next to the island's port of entry. At _festa_ time, parades, music, and feasting fill the streets and strings of lights identify parish neighborhoods. Rural farmsteads are built of stone and have whitewashed stucco exteriors, with structural features brightly outlined in red or black. Broad eaves, low-pitched roofs of russet pantile, and a large wedge-shaped chimney are designed to ventilate the interior oven work-

space. Outside is a small open barn with a cruciform frame under thatch for drying maize. Urban doors and windows are framed by black basalt in fifteenth-century Manueline (Romanesque) style of heavy masonry construction of black and white lava stone. Multistoried townhouses—residues of the colonial era—have wrought-iron balconies, ornamental shutters, and painted facades.

Economy

Subsistence and Commercial Activities. The Azore economy is basically one of household subsistence. Islanders engage in crop, dairy, and stock farming or fish for their livelihood; industrial workers (food processing, textiles) represent only 4 percent of the workforce. Service jobs (in sales, health, tourism) relate to the urban sector or to government employment (civil service and public works). Much of the total land area, primarily hill and upland terrain, is in pasturage. Limited arable acreage is planted with staple crops (wheat, maize, white potatoes, vegetables, and fodder), orchard trees, or vineyards on Terceira, Graciosa, São Miguel, and Pico. Dairy products (meat, milk, cheese) are exported in significant quantities.

Industrial Arts. _Azulejos_ (glazed ornamental tiles), Moorish in origin and a former handicraft product, are manufactured locally. Cottage workshops produce needlepoint, embroidered linens, handwoven rugs, bedspreads, counterpanes, pillows, and decorative items of feathers, paper, and fish scales. Many of these creations are sold in local shops. Cachalot (whalebone) carving was important until the mid-twentieth century; one workshop remains on the island of Pico.

Trade. The supermarket (_supermercado_) has arrived in major population centers; a daily open market for home-grown produce is found in most villages, as is the miller. Wines are produced and distributed locally. Portugal is the Azores' major trading partner.

Division of Labor. Traditional sex roles still persist. Women care for children, run the household, and work in farming operations and cottage industries. Men farm, fish, and provide labor for associated commercial activities. They also dominate the urban service sector (roadworkers, bus and taxi drivers). In a society where male emigration remains the norm, it is not unusual for rural women to lead lives of hard agricultural labor (plowing, hauling loads, and harvesting).

Land Tenure. Nearly half of all acreage is in absentee ownership. Land has been fragmented over time into noncontiguous walled plots, as in _curraletas_ used for viniculture. Sharecropping and absentee ownership remain fairly common. Many small farms are privately owned or rented, but pasturage is frequently shared. On Corvo, pasture land above 350 meters is communal, grazed by herds in common ownership; below, a public/private ownership combination exists. Limited access to land has long been a major incentive for emigration.

Kinship

Kin Groups and Descent. Azoreans retain the family structure and living arrangements of traditional peasant culture. The nuclear family core is extended by generation, by collateral and spiritual kin. Shared and proximate dwellings indicate ubiquity of close kin. Naming patterns reflect bilateral descent: two surnames are given to each child, the mother's first, then the father's. Male emigration strengthens bonds of kinship among women. Residential proximity to a bride's kin is preferred. Residues of patriarchy, historically a class phenomenon, are observable in the social standing and commercial prominence of original donatário families (e.g., Bettencourt, Silveira, Souza).

Kinship Terminology.   Kin terminology is formally Eskimo in type, although cousin (*primo*) terms may be extended to include friends and in-laws. Traditional respect for elders is implicit in the important role of *padrinho/a* (godparent).

Marriage and Family

Marriage.   Village or island endogamy has been customary. Girls are protected by close surveillance until an arranged marriage. Cousin marriages are not uncommon. Postmarital residence with or near the bride's or groom's parents is customary. Padrinhos traditionally attend the couple at the sacrament of marriage. Because of absent men and husbands, spinsters and "living widows" (*viúvas dos vivos*) are critical to family and property maintenance. When the Azorean government gained regional autonomy in 1976, it assigned spouses equal rights and duties for the support and education of children. Job opportunities and fertility control for women, better schooling, improved communications with the outside world, and the loosening hold of the church have also expanded choice for men as well as women. Divorce is still uncommon.

Domestic Unit.   "Family members" are those who share a domicile and contribute to its survival. As few as two to more than a dozen people may constitute a family, depending on how the nuclear core is extended. A domestic unit is, in effect, a subsistence (usually farming) unit, with labor shared according to traditional sex roles. If children opt to leave school at age 12, they normally remain in the household and are employed locally—girls in craft workshops and boys in farming or trade apprenticeship—until marriage.

Inheritance.   Property is inherited without regard to gender. An unmarried daughter, the usual caretaker of aging parents, may be designated the major heir and is the likely legatee of the parental home. Upon her death, the home reverts to the family line.

Socialization.   Child care has been the overwhelming responsibility of domestic women living in the household (mother, cohabiting sisters, aunts, grandmothers) and of female kin living in close proximity. Church and family exercise strict control over major rites of passage, but secular education and widening access to European-American culture are loosening many traditional ties. Vestiges of the old ways remain, such as debutante daughters of prominent families and rigid surveillance of adolescents.

Sociopolitical Organization

Social Organization.   The Azores remain a two-class society, although the advent of regionalization and university-level institutions is weakening ascriptive and patronizing features of the social hierarchy. Continental Portugal remains the wellspring of high (literary) culture, as reflected in museums, libraries, the theater, and Manueline architecture. Folk culture is manifest in the aesthetics of the festa and its traditional music, dancing, costumes, and food. Social stratification is marked linguistically.

Political Organization.   Since 1976 the Azores have been designated an "autonomous region" (*região*) within greater Portugal, and are administered under the constitution of the Portuguese republic. Autonomy is limited in two ways: Portugal's sovereignty may not be compromised, and regionally based political parties are prohibited. Governance is by a regional assembly made up of freely elected deputies who choose its presiding officer. A Lisbon-appointed minister of the republic names the president of the regional government. Nine governmental secretariats are divided among cities (Ponta Delgada, Angra, Horta) of the three Azorean districts. Local officials are elected at the level of the municipality (*município, concelho*) and the precinct (*freguesia*). The archipelago participates in, and may benefit from, international agreements having direct local impact (e.g., revenues from the American military presence at Lajes).

Social Control.   Portugal very effectively controls the Azores from afar. Interpersonal conflict is held in check by the parish church and by village gossip. Conflict at any level has traditionally been suppressed rather than openly resolved.

Conflict.   During centuries of cultural and geographic isolation, warfare rarely occurred in the Azores. Internal conflict was largely avoided by restraining freedom of expression and promoting illiteracy. Limited autonomy has lent some support to underlying political dissent.

Religion and Expressive Culture

Religious Beliefs.   Catholicism is pervasive in Portuguese insular society and, through the agency of the parish churches and their patron saints, the Catholic church is an accessory to affairs of state. The Azorean publicly marks his or her faith by ceremonial display and by ritual performances (*festas*). Folk superstition typically penetrates the tenets of state-sponsored religion.

Religious Practitioners.   The parish priest is the spiritual and liturgical leader of his flock, local agent of the church hierarchy, and earthly representative of divine intercession. He is assisted in his healing mission by removers of the evil eye, midwives, folk curers, herbalists, and, importantly, by the *romeiros* (pilgrims).

Ceremonies.   The liturgical calendar is replete with ceremonies for subsistence events, patron saints, and Christmas and Easter rites, the last culminating on São Miguel island in the week-long Senhor Santo Cristo festa and the Espírito Santo (Holy Ghost) feasts, which are held from April through June. The penitential journeys of groups of pilgrims (*ranchos dos romeiros*) during the seven weeks of Lent are uniquely Azorean. Romeiros, a group from each freguesia, visit island churches dedicated to the Virgin Mary (Nossa Senhora). Membership is open to men in good moral standing and spiritual health and willing to submit to specified terms of obedience. Romeiros are identified by their wooden staffs and by their dress; they move as a unit, chanting, singing, and praying.

Arts.   Crafts not directly designed for household use (e.g., pottery, rush mats, embroidered items, wicker basketry) have a religious dimension (e.g., azulejos—glazed ornamental blue-and-white tiles—display scenes of religious devotion and are widely used in churches). The living arts, instrumental music from a twelve-stringed _violão_, dances such as the _chamarrita_, and ballads (_cantigas_) are all prominent in the festa.

Medicine. Government-run district hospitals are gradually replacing small dispersed clinics operated under religious auspices (_misericórdia_). Outlying clinics now service mainly maternity cases. Rural folk curing has its counterpart in the urban _farmácia_ where professionals diagnose, prescribe, and dispense medication. Deficient diet and sanitation, heavy smoking (among males), alcohol abuse, environmental stress, lack of education, and poverty account for the bulk of islander health problems. Dentistry is virtually nonexistent.

Death and Afterlife. Beliefs are grounded in Catholic theology. Salvation is for true believers. Protracted mourning by black-draped widows and bereaved males with black armbands has been the norm; however, males are much likelier to remarry. Funerals are formal ceremonial occasions, and well-tended village cemeteries display elaborate accoutrements.

Bibliography

Bryans, Robin (1962). _The Azores._ London: Faber & Faber.

Cortes-Rodrigues, Armando (1974). _Voz do longe._ Vol. 2. Ponta Delgada: Edicão do Instituto Cultural de Ponta Delgada.

Duncan, T. Bentley (1972). _Atlantic Islands: Madeira, the Azores, and the Cape Verdes in Seventeenth Century Commerce and Navigation._ Chicago: University of Chicago Press.

Laytano, Dante de (1987). _Arquipelago dos Açores._ Porto Alegro: Escola Superior de Teologia e Espiritualidade Franciscana, Nova Dimensão.

Ludtke, Jean (1989). _Atlantic Peeks: An Ethnographic Guide to the Portuguese-Speaking Atlantic Islands._ Hanover, Mass.: Christopher.

Rogers, Francis Millet (1979). _Atlantic Islanders of the Azores and Madeiras._ North Quincy, Mass.: Christopher.

JEAN LUDTKE

Balearics

ETHNONYMS: none

Balearics are residents of the Balearic Isles (in Spanish, Islas Baleares) located about 80 to 300 kilometers off the east coast of Spain. The Balearic Isles are an archipelago composed of an eastern group of islands including Majorca (Mallorca), Minorca (Menorca), and Cabrera and a western group including Ibiza and Formentera. The total land area is 5,014 square kilometers. The islands are a province of Spain with a semiautonomous government. In 1982, Balearics numbered 669,101. Culturally, the Balearics are classified within the Països Catalan tradition.

See Catalans (Països Catalans)

Basques

ETHNONYMS: Eskualdunak, Euskaldunak, Vascos

Orientation

Identification. Basques inhabit the area of southwestern Europe where the western spur of the Pyrenees meets the Cantabrian seacoast. Their territory straddles the French-Spanish frontier, providing a distinction between Spanish Basques and French Basques. There are four traditional regions (Bizkaia, Gipuzkoa, Nafarroa, Araba) on the Spanish side and three (Lapurdi, Behe-Nafarroa, and Zuberoa) on the French side. Basques refer to their homeland as "Euskal-Herria" (land of the Basques) or "Euskadi" (country of the Basques). While the seven regions have not been unified for nearly a millennium, the Basques remain one of Europe's most distinctive ethnic groups.

Location. The Basque country is located between 41° to 43° N and 0° to 3° W. It contains 20,747 square kilometers, of which 17,682 square kilometers are on the Spanish side of the frontier. The Basque country contains three ecological zones. The northern zone is comprised of the Cantabrian seacoast and interior foothills. It has a maritime climate and is one of the wettest regions in Europe. The ridges of the Pyrenees constitute a central zone with an alpine climate. The southern zone, or about two-thirds of the Basque country, is in the rain shadow of the Pyrenees and has a continental climate.

Demography. In 1975 the population was 2,871,717, of which only 229,383 persons resided on the French side. Population density varies greatly by region. Highly urbanized Bizkaia has 533 persons per square kilometer, while rural Behe-Nafarroa has only 22. There are an estimated 828,000 Basque speakers. Basque language proficiency is distributed unevenly, being concentrated primarily in the northern and central ecological zones. It is also more pronounced in rural and fishing communities than in the urban centers. In recent years there has been a vigorous campaign by Basque nationalists to encourage Basque language acquisition. It has met with considerable (though not total) success. All Basques are fluent in either French or Spanish (some in both), depending on which side of the border they inhabit. Use of the Basque language has declined over the centuries in places where it was spoken previously, and use of French and Spanish has increased because of the influx of non-Basque speakers into the area.

Linguistic Affiliation. Basque is an agglutinative language and employs the Roman alphabet. It is the sole representative of its own language family. Scholars have tried to demonstrate affinities between Basque and languages from disparate parts of the world, particularly languages in the Caucasus Mountains of Russia. Another possibility is that Basque is linked to Ibero, a language spoken throughout the Iberian Peninsula in pre-Roman times.

History and Cultural Relations

The uniqueness of the language underscores the mystery of the origins of the Basques. Some scholars have suggested that they may even be the direct descendants of Cro-Magnons and the Upper Paleolithic cave painters active in southwestern Europe about 15,000 years ago. Until the Middle Ages Basques were an enclaved, pastoralist people, fierce in resisting the intrusions of outsiders and regarded as barbarians by them. Romans, Goths, Franks, and Moors all controlled parts of the Basque Country without ever quite subjugating it. It was a Basque force that attacked Charlemagne's rear guard as it traversed the Pass of Roncesvalles, killing Roland and giving rise to the famous epic *The Song of Roland*. After A.D. 1000 the several Basque regions came increasingly under the influence of emerging European kingdoms and duchies. Subsequently the embryonic states of England, France, and Spain fought for control over the regions, which frequently became pawns in larger power plays. Sovereignty over the various Basque regions shifted according to the fortunes of battle or the whims of marital alliances among Europe's royalty. Basques retained, however, a considerable degree of autonomy in their own affairs, codified in written *fueros* or charters. This relative autonomy was reflected in the custom whereby the monarchs of Castille, upon ascending the throne, were required to travel to the town of Guernica to swear beneath a sacred oak to respect Basque laws. Coastal Basques were Europe's earliest whalers. Their shipbuilding and navigational skills made them Iberia's most noted seafarers. By the early fifteenth century (and possibly earlier) Basques were crossing the Atlantic for whaling and cod fishing off the Labrador coast. Basques crewed the ships of Columbus and Magellan. (The Basque Elcano was the first to circumnavigate the globe.) Basque mariners, mercenaries, merchants, and missionaries swelled the ranks of Spain's colonial elite, providing much of the shipping in the American trade and capital for development of the colonies and becoming major figures in both the civil and ecclesiastical administrations. The French Revolution, with its strong centralist tendencies, destroyed the political autonomy of Lapurdi, Behe-Nafarroa, and Zuberoa. Many of their residents resisted and were sent to the guillotine or to concentration camps. In the nineteenth century Basques fought on the losing side of Spain's two Carlist Wars, relinquishing much of their political autonomy in defeat. This, coupled with the late nineteenth-century

influx of Spanish workers to Basque industries, which threatened to make Basques a minority in their homeland, caused concern. By 1900 a modern Basque nationalist movement had emerged to confront Madrid's policies in the Basque country. The nationalists contested elections when allowed to do so, gaining control of many municipalities and the provincial assemblies of Gipuzkoa and Bizkaia. When the Spanish Civil War erupted in 1936, those two provinces remained loyal to the republic, fielded an army, and elected an autonomous government that issued passports and coined its own currency. Within nine months the Basques were defeated by Franco, many were executed or imprisoned, thousands were exiled, and the Basque government had been removed to Paris. During the Franco years there was systematic repression of Basque culture. Consequently, in the late 1950s disaffected Basque youths founded an organization known as "ETA" (Euskadi ta Azkatasuna, or "Basque Country and Freedom") with the goal of complete independence from Spain. Its opposition to Franco escalated into violence, providing Europe with one of its most virulent terrorist movements. Franco's death in 1975 ushered in an era of democracy in Spain. Mainline Basque nationalists collaborated in the framing of a new constitution that accorded considerable autonomy to the regions.

Settlements

In the northern ecological zone there are major cities such as Bilbo (Bilbao), Donastia (San Sebastian), and Baiona (Bayonne), as well as regional manufacturing centers of considerable importance (Eibar, Mondragon, Irun). There are many coastal fishing villages with 5,000–10,000 inhabitants. The interior foothills have peasant villages ranging from 500 to 3,000 inhabitants. The village usually encompasses a river valley and the surrounding hillsides. The nucleus, with church, school, taverns, town hall, handball court or fronton (jai alai arena), general stores, and offices of a few professionals (doctor, veterinarian, pharmacist, postmaster) is located on the valley floor. The surrounding hillsides contain *baserriak*, or farmsteads (sing., *baserria*), either isolated from one another or clustered into hamlets of ten or twelve dwellings surrounded by their collective landholdings. The dwellings are massive stone structures, often three stories tall. The ground floor is for animal stables, the second floor is living space, while the third is used to store hay and other crops.

Economy

Subsistence and Commercial Activities. Only about 20 percent of the population is engaged in agriculture. In Bizkaia and Gipuzkoa more than 50 percent of the active labor force is employed in industry. Until recently the Basque baserria was a mixed-farming enterprise in which the emphasis was upon self-sufficiency. The farm family grew its own wheat, corn, vegetables, fruits, and nuts and raised poultry, rabbits, pigs, cows, and sheep. Land held in common by the village was an important source of animal pasturage, ferns for animal bedding, limestone for fertilizer, and wood for fuel and building materials. Over the past fifty years there has been increasing commercialization of agriculture. Cropland has been converted either to intensive vegetable growing or fodder production for dairy farming, both to supply urban markets. Agriculture is mechanized, though on a small scale because of the steep terrain. In the central ecological zone there is little permanent settlement. In the summer months shepherds ascend with their flocks and loggers cut hardwood species (oak and beech). In the southern ecological zone agriculture is of the large-estate variety with widely dispersed "agrotowns" surrounded by large holdings. The main crops are the Mediterranean trilogy of wheat, olives, and grapes. Near the Ebro River there is extensive irrigation that permits vegetable growing on a large commercial scale. Basque coastal fishing villages today send their fleets into the Cantabrian and Irish seas for hake, anchovies, and sea bream, and as far as the coasts of western Africa in search of tuna. Some of the vessels are state-of-the-art with mechanical nets, refrigeration, and sonic depth finders and helicopters for finding their quarry.

Industrial Arts. The Basque country is one of Iberia's most industrialized regions. The city of Bilbo (Bilbao) houses many heavy industries, including steel plants and shipbuilding facilities. It is also one of western Europe's major ports for off-loading petroleum from supertankers. Smaller industrial towns specialize in modern consumer goods ranging from plastics to sewing machines. There is also an arms industry. Industrial pollution is a major problem in the Basque country, causing poor air quality in the cities, which is exacerbated by traffic congestion. Most of the rivers are notably polluted.

Trade. While some farmers and fishermen market their products directly in nearby towns and cities, the Basque country now has an efficient network of commercial outlets including supermarkets and department stores.

Division of Labor. There is considerable equality between the sexes. In agriculture women frequently work alongside men at the same tasks. In urban areas women are increasingly employed in industry and services. Domestic chores remain, however, largely the purview of women.

Land Tenure. To be the owner of a farm was socially prestigious and represented economic security in a society in which arable land was at a premium. However, developments over the past fifty years have produced both a glut and a scarcity of land. On the one hand, the inability of peasant agriculture to generate sufficient income to support a twentieth-century life-style has prompted many families simply to abandon agriculture, departing for a city and either letting their baserria fall into disuse or planting it with pines for eventual sale to the paper-pulp industry. On the other hand, many urbanites are now buying or renting baserriak and converting them into chalets—weekend refuges from urban ills.

Kinship

Kin Groups and Descent. The urban Basque family is of the nuclear variety, maintaining its own apartment. In the southern ecological zone the nuclear family also predominates in rural districts. On the baserriak the stem family is the basic social form. Kinship is reckoned bilaterally; there is an Ego-centrically defined kindred but it is important only at the marriage or death of the defining member. Neighbors, usually unrelated, play a key role in rural Basque society. One's _lenbizikoatia_, or "first of the neighborhood," is the household of first recourse in a crisis. The larger _auzoa_, or neighborhood, is the source of social intimacy and support.

Kinship Terminology. Eskimo-type terms are used. Sibling terms differ according to whether the speaker is male or female.

Marriage and Family

Marriage. Basques are monogamous and exercise considerable personal choice in selecting spouses. However, people regard the marriage of the designated male or female heir to the baserria as a household affair. The parents transfer ownership of the farm to the newlyweds as part of the marital arrangements. Small villages tend to be endogamous and cousin marriage is not infrequent, including some unions between first cousins.

Domestic Unit. The heir to the baserria and spouse form a stem-family household with his or her parents. Unmarried siblings of the heir may remain in residence in their natal households until death, but they are subject to the authority of the active male and female heads. The family works the baserria together, with children and the elderly contributing to the lighter tasks as well. In the urban areas the apartment-dwelling nuclear family, possibly with a live-in servant for the affluent, is the domestic unit. It may also contain a spinster aunt or aging parent.

Inheritance. Ownership of the baserria is transferred to a single heir in each generation. In parts of the Basque country custom dictates male primogeniture unless the candidate is blatantly unsuitable. Out-marrying siblings of the heir are provided with dowries. They also share equally in the "personal" wealth of their deceased parents (e.g., money, jewelry, etc.). In urban areas the offspring usually share equally in the estate of the deceased, although the national legal codes favor one recipient with a maximum of one-third of the total.

Socialization. Children are raised by everyone in the household. In the case of affluent urbanites the household may also include a female domestic servant who doubles as a nanny. On the baserriak families emphasize subordination of individual interests to the well-being of the domestic unit. One child is socialized as the heir, and his or her siblings are raised with the understanding that they should leave. This system has made the rural Basque country a seedbed of emigrants.

Sociopolitical Organization

The Basque country is a part of Spain and France, both constitutional democracies.

Social Organization. Basque society is suffused with an egalitarian ethos. The owner of a baserria is extolled as an _etxekojaun_ (lord of the household) and his spouse as _etxekoandria_ (lady of the household). Basque fishermen are similarly proud and independent. The Basque country was largely untouched by western European feudalism, and there is a common belief that every Basque is a noble. There is considerable social mobility, and wealth differences do not automatically determine social status. However, there is an urban Basque plutocracy of factory owners, bankers, and wealthy professionals who relate more to the Spanish and French national elites than to their fellow Basque peasants, shopkeepers, etc. There is a near castelike division between Basques and non-Basques, with the latter constituting much of the lower-class, urban proletariat. Non-Basques are the frequent targets of resentment and discrimination.

Political Organization.   At the municipal level communities are governed by an elected mayor and town council. The three regions in France form, with Bearn, the "Département des Pyrénées Atlantiques" with its seat of government in Pau. Each of the four provinces in Spain has its own popularly elected assembly or *diputación*. Nafarroa now constitutes its own autonomous region within the Spanish state. Gipuzkoa, Bizkaia, and Araba together form the Autonomous Community of Euskadi. This regional government is funded largely by the participating diputaciónes. With its capital in Vitoria (Gasteiz), it has its own popularly elected president, parliament, and ministries. It controls some mass media, the educational system, economic development, and cultural affairs. All foreign relations are handled by Madrid. Basques elect representatives to the Spanish and French parliaments as well.

Social Control.   Social control at the local level is largely through peer pressure. The parish priest exercises moral influence beyond the strictly religious sphere.

Conflict.   The Basque area is heavily policed, particularly on the Spanish side. The Spanish "Guardia Civil" is an omnipresent, largely despised factor in local life. Even political moderates tend to regard their homeland as "occupied," and removal of this force is one of the main demands of Basque nationalists of all persuasions. Clashes between the *guardias* and the ETA have produced more than 600 deaths over the past three decades.

Religion and Expressive Culture

Religious Beliefs.   With very few exceptions Basques are Roman Catholic. Even the smallest village has its own church. There are several major monasteries. Basque Catholicism has strong Jansenistic overtones.

Religious Practitioners.   While possibly the last people in western Europe to convert to Christianity, the Basques have produced such titans of the Catholic church as Saint Ignatius of Loyola and Saint Francis Xavier. There is strong Marist devotion focused on icons of the Virgin Mary housed in several churches. Until recently there were so many religious vocations that Basque priests and nuns regularly staffed Catholic missions in Africa, Asia, and Latin America. Since the Second Vatican Council church attendance and religious vocations have plummeted, prompting the closure of some churches. Formerly Basques believed in witches and legendary supernatural dwellers of mountain caverns and forest fastnesses.

Arts.   Practically every village has its folk-dance group. The *txistu* (flute) and drum, played simultaneously by a single performer, are the distinctive musical instruments. There are *bertsolariak*, or versifiers, capable of spontaneously composing and singing rhymes on any subject. Such performances are a part of every village festival, and regional and national championships are held periodically. In the fine arts Basques have produced several composers of note (Arriaga, Guridi, Ravel), writers (Baroja, Unamuno), painters and sculptors (including the world-famous Eduardo Chillida).

Medicine.   Even the most remote villages have access to modern medical care. Nevertheless, beliefs in the efficacy of certain folk treatments (usually herbal) persist. Some of the older generation still fear the evil eye.

Death and the Afterlife.   A funeral is the most important life ritual in Basque society, triggering a year-long series of ceremonies involving the deceased's household, neighborhood, kindred, and village. Failure to conduct them is felt to compromise the deceased's smooth transition to the afterlife. Otherwise standard Christian beliefs in heaven, purgatory, and hell obtain.

Bibliography

Douglass, William A. (1969). *Death in Murelaga: Funerary Ritual in a Spanish Basque Village*. Seattle: University of Washington Press.

Douglass, William A. (1975). *Echalar and Murelaga: Opportunity and Rural Exodus in Two Spanish Basque Villages*. London: C. Hurst.

Greenwood, Davydd J. (1976). *Unrewarding Wealth: The Commercialization and Collapse of Agriculture in a Spanish Basque Town*. Cambridge: Cambridge University Press.

Ott, Sandra (1981). *The Circle of Mountains: A Basque Shepherding Community*. Oxford: Clarendon Press.

Zulaika, Joseba (1988). *Basque Violence: Metaphor and Sacrament*. Reno: University of Nevada Press.

WILLIAM A. DOUGLASS

Bavarians

ETHNONYMS: none

Orientation

Identification.   The Free State (Freistaat) of Bavaria, the largest state in Germany, is divided into seven regions. Upper and Lower Bavaria and the Upper Palatinate form "Old Bavaria," the original homeland of the Bavarian tribes and the core area of the Grand Duchy of Bavaria. Upper, Middle, and Lower Franconia and Swabia became part of the state after 1803.

Location.   Bavaria is bounded to the northwest by the German state of Hesse, due north by the territory that was the German Democratic Republic (East Germany), to the east by the Czech and Slovak Federative Republic and Austria, to the south by Austria, and to the west by the German state of Baden-Wurttemberg. Its location is 47°16′ by 50°34′ N and 8°58′ by 13°50′ E. The landscape consists of plateaus and moderately sized northern mountain ranges, the alpine foothills (Alpenvorland), and the Alps to the south, culminating in the Zugspitze at 2,963 meters. One-third of the state is forested. The continental climate is generally severe, except for the Main and Danube basins. Average temperatures range from a high of 18° C in July to a low of −2° C in January, while extremes are common (32° C in the summer to −18° C in winter). Spring begins in April, and Bavaria has relatively long periods of frost (from 90 to 150 days, depending on proximity to the Alps). Mountain areas experience cool, wet summers and more precipitation in general, with an annual average in excess of 178 centimeters.

Demography. In 1986, the population of Bavaria was 11,026,490, with 85 percent living in communities of 2,500 or more. In 1900 61.7 percent of the population lived in villages of less than 2,000 inhabitants.

Linguistic Affiliation. High German is the official language of the state. The North or Middle version of the Bavarian dialect is spoken as well, while South Bavarian is spoken in the South Tirol of Italy. Local variations are common: often, the dialect spoken in one village may be difficult to understand in a neighboring village. The nearest related dialects are Franconian and Swabian, spoken by the Franks and Swabians in Bavaria and neighboring German states.

History and Cultural Relations

Bavaria has been populated by Neanderthals, Cro-Magnons, and a number of Mesolithic and Neolithic peoples including the Bandkeramik, Urnfield, Hallstatt, and the Celtic La Tène cultures, the last group being defeated by the Romans in 15 B.C. After the fall of Rome, Bavaria was settled by the Alemanni, the Franks, the Thuringians, and the Baiuvarii, or Bavarians, who settled in the south between A.D. 500 and 800. Bavaria was converted to Christianity in the seventh and eighth centuries, and it was ruled by the Agilofings and then the Franks until Duke Otto of Wittelsbach received the territory from the Holy Roman Emperor Frederick I (Barbarossa) in 1180. The Wittelsbach family ruled until 1918. After centuries of political upheaval, Bavaria was united in 1500, with Munich as its capital. During the Protestant Reformation Bavaria chose Roman Catholicism. By 1638, the end of the Thirty Years' War, the invasion of Swedish and French troops and widespread outbreaks of the bubonic plague had devastated Bavaria. Bavaria sided with Napoleon in 1800, secularized church lands, and annexed Franconia and Swabia in 1803, becoming a kingdom on 1 January 1806. Shortly thereafter, the government established its first constitution, consolidated political power, and instituted much-needed reforms. Munich became a major European cultural center, attaining a population of 600,000 by 1910. The Wittelsbach rulers were generally popular with their subjects; the most unusual, "Mad" King Ludwig II, was deposed in 1886 in part because he almost bankrupted the state to construct several palaces, now popular tourist attractions. Bavaria reluctantly joined the German Empire in 1871, but it managed to retain its own railway and postal services. After World War I, a short-lived socialist revolution was followed by a growing trend toward fascism. Bavaria was occupied by the United States after World War II, drew up a new constitution on 2 December 1946, and officially became a state of the Federal Republic of Germany in 1948.

Originally settled by Bavarians, Franks, and Swabians, more than 2,000,000 East European refugees fled to Bavaria after World War II, increasing the population by 28 percent. Foreign workers migrated to Bavaria during the postwar period of economic expansion, 318,936 of whom (28 percent Turks and 24 percent Yugoslavs) still resided in Bavaria in 1977. While the East European refugees were eventually assimilated, foreign workers seldom were. One recent development has been the formation and success of the neofascist Republican party, an aggressive opponent of foreign workers.

Settlements

Agricultural settlements include isolated scattered farmsteads (Einöden), small clusters of farms (Weiler), and small or larger villages, usually with a church. Barns, dairies, and outbuildings can be found in the center of these rural villages, competing for space with shops and gas stations. "Urban" places, including chartered towns (Städte) or markets (Märkte), are often quite small and sometimes retain a medieval flavor, with fortified walls, castles, stuccoed merchant houses, and elaborate churches. The traditional Bavarian farmhouse is a long, rectangular, stuccoed building combining two-storied living quarters with a barn. External features include intricately carved wooden balconies ablaze with geraniums in the summer, colorfully decorated windows and doors, and whitewashed walls, often with religious murals. Modern housing, in contrast, is functional in design and usually plain.

Economy

Subsistence and Commercial Activities. Bavaria, traditionally an agrarian society, has become highly industrialized, with only 15 percent of the population involved in agriculture by 1970. Farms of 10 hectares or less (50.8 percent of all farms) are often owned by worker-farmers, who leave the bulk of the farm chores to their wives. Only 3.4 percent of the state's output comes from agriculture and forestry products. The principal crops are wheat and barley; oats, potatoes, rye, and sugar beets are also grown. Crops for animal feed, especially field corn, are especially prevalent in the south, where dairying predominates. Milk and dairy products such as cheeses, yogurt, and "Quark" (similar to yogurt) are important exports, although a "butter mountain" and surpluses of powdered milk have resulted from Common Market subsidy programs. Bavarians traditionally eat their main meal at noontime, and it consists of meat (usually pork), starch (noodles, potato dumplings), and a vegetable (often salad). Beer, an integral part of Bavarian culture, is the beverage of choice.

Industrial Arts. In 1986, 42.8 percent of Bavarians were employed in mining, manufacturing, construction, and power. Handicrafts remain important, with more than 800,000 individuals employed as artisans in 1976—68,000 more than in 1956.

Trade. Modern shops, specialty stores, artisan workshops, and open-air produce markets cluster around a town square in the downtown area of most of the larger Bavarian towns and villages, and pedestrian zones (Fussgäangerzone) are prevalent. Tourism produces significant profits, especially in Old Bavaria where Alpine scenery and sports, numerous spas, and popular folk festivals such as Munich's *Oktoberfest* draw millions of tourists annually.

Division of Labor. Traditionally, artisan wives usually tended the shop in addition to managing the household. Both men and women actively worked on the farm, but the jobs alloted to each were usually defined on the basis of gender, with men doing heavy work in the fields while women worked closer to the home. Today, women comprise approximately 40 percent of the workforce.

Land Tenure. Except for a small amount of state-owned land, property is privately owned. Since World War II, the Bavarian government has continued a large-scale program of land consolidation, or *Flurbereinigung*, begun in the nineteenth century, which has facilitated the mechanization of many farming techniques. While the postwar trend has been to expand farm holdings, the average Bavarian farm remains moderately sized and family-run.

Kinship, Marriage, and Family

Kinship. The "traditional" Bavarian farm family was patrilineal, patrilocal, patriarchal, and extended. Bilateral kinship predominates in modern Bavaria, although the wife usually takes the family name of her husband after marriage.

Marriage. Prior to 1800, marriage in Bavaria was relatively pragmatic, often occurring as a result of pregnancy. One illegitimate child was tolerated, but repeated illegitimacy was not. Stringent laws controlling marriage were passed in the 1800s in an attempt to control the sudden population explosion, causing a sudden rise in illegitimate births. Gradually, the excess population was absorbed by newly developing industries, and the laws were rescinded. In 1977, 7.4 percent of births were illegitimate, 1.7 percent fewer than in 1960. Marriage has declined significantly since 1900 in spite of population increase, with some fluctuation in response to wars, recessions, and economic recovery. Conversely, divorces have increased sharply from 435, or 1.2 percent of all marriages, in 1900 to 18,352, or 27.5 percent, in 1986. In 1977 the average age for marriage in Bavaria was 25.9 for single males and 23.1 for single females, a rate relatively stable since 1960.

Domestic Unit. The basic elements of Bavarian family life revolved around a strong conservatism, a deep faith in the Roman Catholic church, a belief in strict discipline, and the ideal of having many children. The family might include the grandparents, retired and living in separate quarters; the active son, his wife, and their unmarried children; renters or tenants; unmarried male and female servants; and widowed or destitute family members. In postwar Bavaria, elderly parents often live in apartments in their children's home or farm.

Inheritance. Beginning in the fifteenth century the government passed a series of laws in Old Bavaria requiring unigeniture, which is still common today. Although all heirs have equal claim to the inheritance, only one may own the farm. Conversely, in Franconia, partible inheritance was customary. As a result, by the 1800s, moderate-sized family farms predominated in Old Bavaria, while large landed estates and extremely small, fragmented farmsteads of less than 1 hectare were common in Franconia. In postwar Bavaria it has been difficult to find anyone willing to take over small holdings.

Socialization. Traditional farm discipline was strict and involved corporal punishment. It was common for children aged 6 or 7 to be sent away as servants, in the case of farm families, or as apprentices, in the case of artisan families. Postwar middle-class Bavarian children do not generally do household chores because of the demands of schoolwork. Rather than relying on corporal punishment, modern Bavarian mothers often try to distract small and unruly children. Children are expected to be quiet and tidy when in their own homes; by the age of 13, most free time is spent with peer groups. Bavaria retains a conservative approach to education, with a tripartite system of elementary school, middle school, and "Gymnasium" (college-preparatory high school). School attendance is 100 percent and most children attend elementary school until age 16, then transfer to trade school and begin apprenticeship. Less than 10 percent (162,708) attend one of Bavaria's eleven universities.

Sociopolitical Organization

Germany, a federal republic, is governed by the Federal Parliament at Bonn. States have important rights and a great deal of autonomy. Federal elections occur every three to four years and representatives are elected by the proportional (*d'Hondtische*) method in districts determined by population size.

Social Organization. Bavaria has a class structure based on socioeconomic status, similar to most West European nations. Traditionally, rural communes were ruled by the "Honorationen," usually the wealthiest landowning peasant or petty noble, the schoolteacher, and the parish priest. In larger towns and cities the council was composed of the artisan elite, often a patriciate, and control was absolute. In smaller communities, political power was more fluid and diffuse and less absolute. Until 1800, the Catholic church controlled much land and property, at times up to 50 percent in southern Bavaria, and played a significant role in the power structure.

Political Organization. Bavaria is divided into seven regions, 71 counties, and 2,051 communes, the smallest of which are combined into 345 administrative unions. The state of Bavaria has an assembly with deputies elected by direct vote every four years. These deputies, in turn, elect a minister president and a cabinet. A senate consisting of appointed officials from various Bavarian associates completes the state-level political organization. State government has been controlled by the conservative Christian-Social Union (CSU) since 1957 and was headed most notably by the flamboyant Franz Josef Strauss for ten years, until his death on 1 October 1988. Regional, county, and communal political units are similar in organization. Each is headed by an official chosen by direct vote (president, *Landrat*, and mayor, respectively), each has a general assembly to which representatives are elected (every four years for the region, every six years for county and commune), with assembly size based on population.

Social Control. Formal controls are similar to those that were established in any Western European democracy, and they include a constitutional court, regular courts at the regional and local level, as well as courts of appeal and a state supreme court. In addition, there are specialized courts for labor, social affairs, finance, and administration. Informally, in all but the largest cities, gossip and an efficient network of "moral guardians," often elderly women, effectively control behavior.

Conflict. Warfare has been common in Bavaria since the Romans fought the La Tène Celts. Important conflicts include battles with the Alemanni, Slavs, and Hungarians; conflicts engendered by eastward colonization; quarrels between various branches of the Wittelsbach family for control; the Peasants' Wars of 1525 and 1706; the Thirty Years' War (1618–1648); the Napoleonic Wars (Bavaria sided with France); the Prussian-Austrian War (Bavaria sided with Austria); the Franco-German War (this time Bavaria sided with Prussia); World War I; the ill-fated socialist revolution of 1919; and World War II. Since World War II Bavaria, as the rest of West Germany, has been committed to peace, postwar economic development, and rapid industrialization.

Religion and Expressive Culture

Religious Beliefs and Practices. Roman Catholicism (69.9 percent of the Bavarian population in 1970) is the religion of Old Bavaria, whereas the Evangelical (Lutheran) church (25.7 percent) predominates in Franconia. Both religions are officially recognized and supported by the state. Bavaria was one of the centers of the Old Catholic movement, a schism resulting from the papacy's stand on infallibility in the 1870s. Religious festivals have always been an integral part of life in Old Bavaria; church dedication, or *Kirchweih*, was especially significant. This three-day harvest festival became so economically disruptive that in 1803 all Kirchweih feasts were required by law to be celebrated within the same three-day period, a practice which continues today. *Fasching*, the Bavarian version of carnival, begins in early January with numerous costume balls and continues to the day before Ash Wednesday. In addition to the regular church holidays such as Easter, Christmas, and Pentecost, the patron saints of the markets, artisan groups, and other organizations were also honored. Even today, Bavaria has fourteen official holidays, more than any other German state. Bavarian Catholics tend to be more regular in church attendance than their Protestant neighbors; however, as in many Roman Catholic countries, a serious shortage of priests has resulted in a growing lay ministry.

Arts. Old Bavaria has experienced a renaissance in all aspects of the folk arts. Bavarian folk costumes, or *Trachten*, are worn increasingly for both formal and informal occasions. The woman's *Dirndl*, a tight-bodiced, full-skirted outfit worn with a contrasting white blouse and apron, is especially popular, as are *Lederhosen*, leather shorts for men. Original folk-music compositions and traditional tunes are played on traditional instruments such as the *Hackbrett*, or chimes, the zither, and the folk harp, or sung by soloists or groups. Folk dancing—especially the *Schuhplattler*, or slapping dance—is also popular, and many communes may have two or more groups devoted to various aspects of folk culture. A lively folk literature consisting of stories and poetry in dialect is regularly featured in local newspapers, books, and television.

Medicine. In addition to their efficient modern medical system Bavarians are interested in herbal medical cures, and herbal teas are available in most local pharmacies. Midwives are common and are trained and licensed by the state.

Death and Afterlife. Bavarians are generally pragmatic about death. They observe the religious death rituals normally found in the Roman Catholic or Protestant liturgy. Death notices are published in the local press by family members, by appropriate voluntary associations, and by the firm where the deceased was currently or formerly employed. In addition to a sequence of memorials held for the first year of death, the deceased is remembered on All Saints' Day on 4 November when family members gather in the cemeteries, clean and decorate the graves, and participate in a religious service.

Bibliography

Bavaria, Government of. State Agency for Statistics and Data Processing (1978). *Gemeindedaten* (Communal Data). Rev. ed. 1982. Munich.

Bavaria, Government of. State Agency for Statistics and Data Processing (1978). *Statistical Yearbook for Bavaria*. Munich.

Bavaria, Government of. State Agency for Statistics and Data Processing (1979). *Kreisdated* (County Data). Rev. ed. 1983. Munich.

Hubensteiner, Benno (1977). *Bayerische Geschichte: Staat und Volk, Kunst und Kuultur*. Munich: Suddeutscher Verlag.

Knauer, Ingobert (n.d.). *Chronik Westerndorf-St. Peter*.

Spindler, Max, ed. (1978). *Bayerische Geschichte im 19 und 20. Jahrhundert: 1800–1970*. Vol. 1, *Staat und Politic*. Vol. 2, *Innere Entwicklung, Gesellschaft, Wirtschaft, Kirche, geistiges Leben*. Munich: C. H. Beck.

PATRICIA R. GIBSON

Belgians

ETHYNONYMS: none

Belgians are citizens of Belgium (Kingdom of Belgium). Belgium occupies 30,540 square kilometers and in 1990 had an estimated population of 9,895,000. Belgium is a pluralistic society with the majority of the population divided along linguistic, cultural, and religious lines into two groups: the Flemings and the Walloons. Belgium also has a sizable foreign population, composed primarily of Italians, Moroccans, Turks, and Spaniards.

See Flemish; Walloons

Bibliography

Kurian, George T. (1990). *Encyclopedia of the First World.* 2 vols. New York: Facts on File.

Worldmark Encyclopedia of the Nations (1988). 7th ed. New York: Worldmark Press.

Bergamasco

ETHNONYMS: none

The Bergamasco are a linguistically defined segment of the population of the northern Italian province of Bergamo, concentrated in the provincial capital (also called Bergamo) and its immediate surroundings. The region was territorially incorporated into the Italian state in the early 1800s, and the Bergamasco themselves are highly integrated into the society, culture, and economy of the larger region. They take pride, however, in retaining their distinct linguistic tradition. The Bergamasco language, part of the Lombard Branch of Gallo-Romance, differs greatly from standard Italian and is distinct from Lombard proper.

Bosnian Muslims

ETHNONYMS: Bošnjaci Muslimani

The Bosnian Muslims of the former Yugoslavia, living in the independent state of Bosnia-Hercegovina, number about 1.8 million, or roughly 8 percent of the total previous Yugoslavian population. They constitute the majority ethnoreligious group in the state (44 percent of its population with Serbs making up 31 percent and Croats 17 percent [1991 census]). Since all three groups share in the same Serbian or Croatian linguistic tradition, the distinctiveness of the Bosnian Muslims is primarily based on religious affiliation (the Serbs are Eastern Orthodox Christians and the Croats are Catholic). There is a further, demographic distinction to be made as well. Although there is strong Muslim representation in the countryside, their presence is markedly high in the cities. There has been some dispersal of Bosnian Muslims to territory beyond the state. This emigration has largely been in response to politicomilitary movements such as the occupation and later annexation of the territory by the Austro-Hungarian Empire, the incorporation of the region into the Kingdom of the Serbs, Croats, and Slovenes in 1918, and the installation of a Communist regime in the years following World War II. Many of these émigrés went to Turkey, although others settled in the United States, particularly in the last emigration wave.

Beginning in the mid- to late fifteenth century, when the Ottoman Empire ruled the region, Islam came to Bosnia. Mass conversions took place, although there is no evidence to support a charge that coercion was involved. However, these conversions were centered within the landowning classes and among the free peasantry, whereas the serfs of the region remained by and large Christian.

Bosnia-Hercegovina is predominantly rural and agricultural, and the Bosnian Muslim population is largely involved in agrarian pursuits. Cereal farming and livestock keeping are the centerpieces of the rural economy. Of those animals raised, sheep are the most important. In this respect, they differ little from their non-Muslim neighbors. Their traditional, patrilocal, extended farm households (*zadruga*) also are of a type common to ethnic groups throughout the Balkans. All household members contribute to their collective economic well-being, with the bulk of the heavy agricultural labor and livestock care falling to the males. In the cities, Bosnian Muslims are heavily represented in craft production and tend to dominate the professions and civil-service posts.

Kinship is reckoned patrilineally, but in daily life this emphasis has few applications. Traditionally, the tie among brothers, and perhaps first cousins as well, was more important, as from this pool of kin the cooperative group of the zadruga was formed. The establishment of fictive kin ties through sponsorship roles is also limited; the only occasion for which a sponsor is recruited is the "first haircut" rite of passage for male children. The family generally chooses the sponsor from outside of the Muslim community, so that this ritual provides the occasion for forming alliances with non-Muslim neighbors.

Ideally, marriage among Bosnian Muslims is endogamous. When a marriage does occur between a Bosnian Muslim and an "outsider," that outsider is generally a Muslim of some other ethnic group. In rural areas, marriage to a non-Muslim is extremely uncommon, although it has increased in frequency in the urban areas. Polygyny, though practiced prior to its prohibition by state law, was rare.

In religious matters, Bosnian Muslim practice is similar in most particulars to that of Turkish Muslims. Even after the establishment of the Communist government in the years after World War II, authorities tolerated Bosnian Muslim religious observance and institutions. This toleration extended to Islamic schools, which were allowed to continue to operate, but only in addition to, rather than as a replacement for, the compulsory state educational system.

Bibliography

Cole, John W., and Sam Beck (1981). *Ethnicity and Nationality in Eastern Europe.* Amsterdam: University of Amsterdam.

Lockwood, William G. (1975). *European Moslems: Economy and Ethnicity in Western Bosnia.* New York: Academic Press.

Smajlovic, Ahmed (1980). "Muslims in Yugoslavia." *Journal of the Institute of Muslim Minority Affairs* 2:132–144.

NANCY E. GRATTON

Bretons

ETHNONYMS: Breizhiz, Bretoned

Orientation

Identification. Brittany is the westernmost region (formerly called a province) of France comprising the four departments (large administrative units in France, roughly equivalent to U.S. states) of Côtes-du-Nord, Ille-et-Vilaine, Finistère, and Morbihan. The Breton population is predominantly of Celtic descent.

Location. Brittany is effectively a large peninsula, bounded on three sides by water: the English Channel to the north and the Atlantic Ocean to the west and south. The peninsula is 160 kilometers wide at its eastern boundary and 90 kilometers wide at the west; it is 215 kilometers long and has 2,800 kilometers of coastline. Numerous islands are associated with the Breton mainland both historically and culturally: they are located on all three sides of the peninsula and contribute an additional 700 kilometers of coastline. Although transected by the 47th parallel (the same as Quebec in Canada), Brittany enjoys a relatively mild climate due to the Gulf Stream that courses around the peninsula. Winter is moderate with little or no snow or ice. Summer is cool, with temperatures ranging between 4.4 and 18° C. Rain falls throughout the year (on average 104 centimeters), and land and sea breezes are nearly always present. The peninsula is in general of low elevation, its highest point reaching only 384 meters in the Monts d'Arrée in the northwest. Although low, the interior lands are not generally flat but consist of gently rolling slopes and small hills. Undulating cultivated fields enclosed by dense boundary-marking hedges (_bocages_) are typical of the landscapes offered in interior Brittany. Moorland (_landes_) is also extensive in the north-central and northwestern sectors. The coast is marked by numerous inlets and estuaries, rugged cliffs, and imposing outcroppings of rocks and crags along the northern and western sides; the south in general affords easier access to the ocean and to many fine beaches. Bretons have for generations expressed the contrast between the interior and the coast with the epithets _armor,_ "the sea," and _argoat,_ "the forest" (reflecting an age when the interior was heavily wooded).

Demography. Historically one of the most densely populated regions of France, Brittany has, through high losses in human life suffered during the two world wars and through emigration, dwindled from 6.5 percent (1.83 million) of the French population in 1801 to 4.98 percent (2.7 million) in 1982, and the population continues gradually to decrease. Bretons constitute a unique ethnolinguistic constellation within the territorial boundaries of France, but they are linked culturally and historically to the Celts of the British Isles (the Irish, Welsh, and Scots). Originally a farming and maritime population on the whole, Brittany has in the past twenty-five years lost more than half of its farming families and many of its fishing families to cities in Brittany or elsewhere in France (especially to Paris)—or, to a lesser extent, to other countries. The toll of emigration has been only partially offset in recent years by immigrant workers originating chiefly from Mediterranean countries.

Linguistic Affiliation. The Breton language belongs to the Brythonic Branch of the Celtic Family of languages. It is thus closely related to Cornish (now extinct) and to Welsh, and more distantly related to the Celtic languages in the Goidelic Branch—Irish Gaelic, Scots Gaelic, and Manx. It is estimated that there are 500,000–600,000 speakers of Breton in Brittany; probably all Breton speakers nowadays also know French.

History and Cultural Relations

The presence of this originally insular Celtic population on the Continent is accounted for by their migrations from the British Isles that took place between the third and fifth centuries A.D., apparently set off by the military and territorial pressures exerted by advancing groups of Angles and Saxons. Their settlement in Brittany was permanent, and Bretons managed for a time (ninth–tenth centuries) to create an independent state, but they were subsequently besieged by both Frankish (the future French) and Norman invaders, which reduced the amount of territory under their control. In 1488 Breton forces were definitively defeated in battle by the French, and in 1532 Brittany was officially annexed to the French state. However, throughout the ancien régime, Brittany retained its own parliament and administrative autonomy. Because of these facts and the sheer physical distance of Brittany from Paris, the Breton "province" was able to retain its distinctive Celtic culture and language, particularly in nonurban areas, which meant most of the vast inland territories of the province. The majority of the Breton people did not assimilate linguistically and culturally into the French nation until the nineteenth century, with the imposition of the military draft and obligatory public education, the creation of a network of highways and railways, and the development of industry. World War I greatly accelerated the assimilation process through the patriotic rallying of the populace and through the disproportionate loss of lives to the war effort (12 percent of Bretons were killed in World War I, though they represented only 6.5 percent of the total French population at that time). The interwar years saw the development of a significant movement for Breton autonomy; for some Bretons this meant also a return to the Breton language and traditional cultural values that they felt had been seriously threatened, if not destroyed, by the French. The movement for political autonomy from France is not so strong today, but there continues to be significant agitation among the people for the development of higher levels of cultural, linguistic, and economic self-determination.

Most Bretons perceive themselves as constituting a distinct ethnic or cultural group within France, at least historically. Divisions within the Breton population are chiefly along class and political lines, though tensions at times are manifested between Bretons and non-Breton immigrant groups in urban areas. Many Bretons also identify with the wider Celtic community; cultural and intellectual exchanges between Brittany and Wales, Ireland, and Scotland have been occurring for a very long time.

Settlements

Small hamlets and dispersed farmsteads characterized the settlement pattern in rural Brittany for centuries. Larger agglomerations of population were found in the parish headquarters—the *plou* (in Latin, *plebs,* "people"), which, although based on a church, were by no means limited to religious activities, but served economic and social functions as well. The area covered by a plou could vary widely—between roughly 10 and 100 square kilometers. As the population grew, the plous were subdivided into segments (*treviou*), which in turn would grow into new parishes. The inheritance of this settlement and naming system is still very much in evidence in modern Brittany, where place names beginning in "Plou-" and "Tre-" are abundant (especially in the northwestern regions). The traditional rural house is rectangular, constructed of granite, with a roof of thatch or slate whose gables at each end are topped by a chimney; older houses have but one or two rooms, and appended structures, such as a stable (which would share a wall with the house), add to the impression of size. The traditional style is evident in many new houses throughout Brittany, though today they may be of cement, are whitewashed, and are far more spacious. Most of the major urban agglomerations in Brittany are found strung along or with access to the coast, the most important of which are (proceeding counterclockwise from the northeast) Saint Malo, Saint Brieuc, Morlaix, Brest, Concarneau, Quimper, Lorient, and Vannes. All of these support commercial maritime activities. The only major interior city is Rennes, historically the capital of the province; nowadays it is an industrial center (for the Citroën automobile, printing, and communications industries) and home to one of the two major universities located within Brittany (the other being in the coastal city of Brest).

Economy

Subsistence and Commercial Activities.   Subsistence polyculture was the economic basis for the majority of Bretons living in the interior regions, and fishing and algae gathering for the coastal folk, until the early decades of the twentieth century. Since the two world wars, especially World War II, agriculture has modernized greatly, which has had two important results: first, it has meant the loss of countless small farms and the migration of farming families to the cities; but second, it has also increased the efficiency of agricultural production to the point that Brittany now ranks as the leading agricultural region of France, exporting such products as chicken, pork, fresh and canned vegetables, potatoes, milk, and butter. Fish and crustaceans are also an important economic and culinary resource, as well as a major attraction to tourists. Bretons, too, who in earlier epochs partook but little of marine products, have come to appreciate their own "fruits of the sea." The traditional diet consisted of potatoes, bread, buckwheat crepes, porridge, salt pork, eggs, cider, and milk; relatively little meat or fish was consumed until after World War II. Brittany experienced rapid industrialization after 1960, coming to it later but more intensively than other regions of France. Industries associated with agriculture—canneries, dairies, animal feed producers, slaughterhouses and packing plants, agricultural machinery manufacturers—constitute the largest industrial sector; however, other types of significant industrial activity include mining (of granite, slate, and kaolin), construction (including boats and ships), telecommunications, automobiles, and public works. In spite of considerable industrial growth since over the past thirty years, not all industries have prospered

continuously (e.g., naval construction has markedly declined since 1975), and unemployment rates rose as high as 11 percent in parts of Brittany in the 1980s. A boom in tourism, on the other hand, has spawned a sizable hostelry industry; recent decades have also witnessed a sharp increase in the "secondary residence" building business. Finally, certain Parisian and multinational companies engaged in light industry requiring a sizable labor force have been attracted to Brittany because of the lower salaries accepted by a largely young, nonunionized, female workforce of rural origin.

Industrial Arts.   Woodworking is a traditional Breton craft that has much declined in the wave of machine-turned furniture, yet is still practiced by skilled artisans. Pottery making continues as an important artisanal craft of considerable commercial value.

Trade.   The 1970s brought to Brittany the first supermarket chains, which now flourish throughout the region. Another development has been that of the "commercial centers" where, in addition to food, it is possible to purchase almost any consumer good that can be carted out of the store. These are located on the outskirts of cities such as Rennes, Brest, Quimper, and Lorient, and they draw customers from urban and rural environs alike. Such giant enterprises have threatened, though not entirely eliminated, the family-run specialty shops that used to be the norm. In addition, the tradition of weekly or biweekly open-air markets has remained robust in medium-sized towns.

Division of Labor.   In its days as a rural, strongly Catholic society, male-female division of labor was much as in other premodern agricultural societies, with women having the primary responsibility for food preparation, washing, rearing children, weaving, sewing, etc., while men did the majority of the heavy farmwork and took care of the farm machinery and equipment. With the advent of farm mechanization and the "desertification" of the farm—especially by women—this pattern is no longer so straightforward. Probably a majority of adult women work in the paid labor force at some time in their lives and manage households that have been enhanced with up-to-date services and utilities. Many women have moved into professional and technical spheres of employment. Nevertheless, shopping, cooking, and child rearing are much more likely to be done by women than by men, while mechanical and heavy industrial work are still within the male province.

Land Tenure.   In the Middle Ages, the *domaine congéable* was developed in Brittany whereby land was held by one owner, while the buildings, orchards, tools, livestock, etc. were owned by the occupant. This system gradually was replaced by private (individual or family) ownership of the complete farm. The fragmentation of holdings through the partible inheritance system (also a problem elsewhere in France) has over the generations reduced many fields to such small dimensions that they are unworkable in this age of mechanized agriculture. Many families therefore have sold their parcels to larger, wealthier farmers or to agribusinesses. Yet private ownership of a house and plot of land (for a garden) remains a goal for many Bretons.

Kinship, Marriage, and Family

Kinship. Lineage is traced cognatically, but the naming system is patronymic. Women used to retain their patronyms after marriage, a practice that has been largely supplanted in this century by the French vironymic system. Fictive kinship in the form of godparent-godchild relations was a very important part of the social fabric for a long time; often the godparent would in fact be real kin—an unmarried aunt or uncle, for example. The extended family—consisting of three generations and often collateral kinfolk—was the basic social unit in the countryside, but this has been broken up through the emigration of rural families to the cities or to other regions of France. Nuclear families are now in general the rule.

Marriage. The marriage ceremony remains an important celebration for the individual and the family, and most couples choose to have both the civil and the church ceremonies performed (only the former is strictly necessary). In traditional rural Brittany marriages were the occasion for days-long revelry, with hundreds of people invited to partake in the feasting and games. It was not unusual for multiple marriages to take place—that is, two or more sisters would marry two or more brothers. The levirate was also practiced. Postmarital residence could be either uxori- or virolocal; nowadays it is chiefly neolocal. Young couples tend to have their children early in the marriage. Through birth control practices, couples can limit the size of their families to the desired two or three children (in contrast with past generations of couples who were pressured by the church to produce as many offspring as possible). Divorce is fully legal but still stigmatized.

Domestic Unit. The basic unit is now the nuclear family, though this may expand as needed to accommodate elderly or invalid relatives.

Inheritance. Bilateral partible inheritance has long been customary in Brittany, though generally only one child would inherit the farm (whether it was the oldest or the youngest varied locally). The remaining siblings were recompensed with other property or goods. The female's equal right of inheritance has, through the centuries, been one of the distinctive features of Breton culture vis-à-vis the French (and other non-Celtic Europeans).

Socialization. Although corporal punishment of children is not unknown, Bretons have for long relied on verbal admonishment and instruction through a rich repertoire of proverbs and aphorisms. Appeal to Christian models of behavior and, in earlier days, the inculcation of a fear of hell and the wrath of God were also regularly deployed in the socialization process.

Sociopolitical Organization

Brittany, formerly a province under the ancien régime, today is qualified as a "region" within the republic of France; it is sometimes grouped with other western-lying departments under the generic title of "l'Ouest" (the West). Administratively, it consists of the four departments noted earlier (a fifth department, Loire-Atlantique, was recently reassigned to another region). Each department has delegates elected to the National Assembly under a multiple-party system that represents Communist, Christian democratic, socialist, and right-wing viewpoints. Departments also have _préfets_ (chief executive officers) who are appointed by the central government and are not necessarily of Breton origin.

Social Organization. The traditional social organization revolved around the extended family as the basic unit of kinship and subsistence; however, local groupings of families into hamlets and plous was another important organizational component in which people could provide material and psychological support for one another through mutual cooperative efforts (e.g., at harvest time, at birth and death). Vertical class divisions also organized people and activities, more stringently in the past than now, into peasant, bourgeois, aristocrat, religious, and secular classes.

Political Organization. Implementation of national policies at the regional level is carried out through the French system of departmental, arrondissement, and cantonal divisions (these are in decreasing order of jurisdiction). There is also a regional council with elected representatives empowered to make some decisions independent of the central government. Local matters are considered at the level of the commune, which is presided over by a mayor and municipal councillors (elected positions).

Social Control. The Catholic church historically played a key role in social control (and in reproduction); its influence has steadily diminished in the present century. On an informal level, gossip—within the neighborhood or village—remains a powerful tool of social control. At the formal level of control and conflict resolution, the French legal system—based on the Napoleonic Code—has been in effect since 1804.

Conflict. Breton soil has been the site of much armed conflict throughout its history as Bretons early on fought Frankish and Norse invaders and attempted to gain or maintain sovereignty and territorial integrity; from the eleventh century until annexation of Brittany to France in 1532, innumerable bloody confrontations—on both land and sea—took place as English and French forces vied for Breton territory. Internal conflict has also erupted intermittently, notably following the French Revolution, when Republicans and Royalists were pitted against one another. The 1930s witnessed the rise of syndicalism and the workers' assertion of their rights vis-à-vis employers and unfavorable economic policies. Brittany was occupied by the Germans during World War II; the civilian population suffered considerable losses, and internal conflict again arose here (as elsewhere in France) between collaborationists and _résistants_. Post–World War II years have witnessed protests and demonstrations against the central government's economic policies regarding French regions, against nuclear power plants in Brittany, and in favor of greater economic, cultural, and linguistic autonomy.

Religion and Expressive Culture

Religious Beliefs and Practices. The vast majority of Bretons are of the Catholic faith, though practice of religion (regular attendance at mass, confession, etc.) has waned throughout this century, particularly among men. However, baptism, marriage, and funeral rites within the Catholic church are still pervasive. Historically Bretons have been noted for their deep religiosity, their profusion of saints (most are unique to Brittany) and chapels, their religious festivals—such as the _pardons_—and their pilgrimages. Pardons, marked by singing and dancing as well as religious observances, are still much in evidence today, though the religious underpinnings of these celebrations have been undermined by commercialism and tourism. A salient festival, known as *la grande troménie*, still takes place in western Brittany every six years, in which participants walk 12 kilometers bearing saints' icons, visiting the chapels and sacred spots believed to be inhabited by the saints within the parish.

Arts.   Brittany's visual arts consist of many elements: centuries of architectural styles applied to both secular and religious structures (the Roman and Gothic influences are manifest, in addition to the Breton refinement of the tall, pointed spire so typical of its churches); statuary that is perhaps most memorably displayed in the magnificent calvaries (which depict scenes from the gospels with stone statues) and ossuaries that are the companions to many churches; centuries-old traditions of painting and tapestry; and a rich complex of artisanal crafts. Traditional music of Brittany focuses on two wind instruments—the *biniou* (a small bagpipe) and the oboelike *bombarde*—which are typically paired together in performances. Troops of biniou players are also popular. The Celtic harp has been reintroduced in recent decades; and the accordion has also been a popular instrument in this century. Literary production in the Breton language has seen a great upward surge in diversity and quality since the 1920s following centuries of neglect, which was a result of the castigation and repression of the spoken Breton language by the French and by Breton authorities representing their policies.

Medicine.   Traditional Breton medicine drew on homemade herbal remedies; but there was also reliance on a person called a *diskonter*, who could dispel illnesses or disorders with special incantations (handed down from generation to generation within certain families). Today Breton medicine is almost completely in the hands of highly trained medical specialists in the national health system.

Death and Afterlife.   Bretons tend to prepare for death—ensuring well in advance that their cemetery plot or place in the family vault is secured and selecting their funerary garb. Cremation is seldom practiced. Many superstitions accompany appropriate conduct when a close relative has died: for example, the doors and windows of the deceased's house should be left open to permit the soul (thought to assume the shape of an insect) to leave easily; mirrors should be turned to face the wall. Relatives accompany the deceased to the church, where a mass is said prior to burial, after which the family returns home for a ceremonial meal. In the first year following a person's death, a number of services will be held in the deceased's name to assist the soul in its journey to the *anaon* (the world beyond); such at least was the traditional belief and practice. The legendary death figure is Ankou, represented as a skeleton with a scythe, often riding a wooden cart. Tradition has it that the sound of his cart creaking portends the death of someone in the neighborhood. In popular belief of times past, hell (*ifern*) was conceptualized as a glacial place rather than as an inferno, seen in references to *ifern yen* ("cold hell") in fifteenth- to seventeenth-century liturgical literature.

Bibliography

Badone, Ellen (1989). *The Appointed Hour: Death, Worldview, and Social Change in Brittany*. Berkeley: University of California Press.

Bonneton, Christine, ed. (1979). *Bretagne: Ecologie, économie, art, littérature, langue, histoire, traditions populaires*. Le Puy: C. Bonneton.

Delumeau, Jean, directeur (1969). *Histoire de la Bretagne*. Toulouse: Privat.

Meynier, Andre (1984). *Atlas et géographie de la Bretagne*. Rev. ed. Lausanne: Flammarion.

Segalen, Martine (1985). *Quinze générations de Bas-Bretons: Parenté et société dans le pays bigouden Sud, 1720–1980*. Paris: Presses Universitaires de France.

LENORA A. TIMM

Bulgarian Gypsies

ETHNONYMS: Horahane, Roma, Tsigani

Orientation

Identification.   Bulgarian Gypsies are an ethnic group with strong historical ties to other European Gypsy groups. They have played significant economic and cultural roles in Bulgarian society since their arrival at least 600 years ago. In the 1970s, as part of the socialist government's assimilation campaign, the ethnic category "Gypsy" was abolished, and the word has begun to disappear from print. Despite the official denial of the existence of Gypsies, they are a growing population with a complex relationship to the socialist government. With the current retreat from one-party domination and the demand for democracy, it will be interesting to follow the fate of the Gypsies. Long-standing discrimination is not likely to disappear.

Location.   Bulgarian Gypsies live throughout the country in both rural and urban areas. Their population is centered in cities with the largest concentrations in Sliven (over 30,000 Gypsies), Sofia, and Pazardzik. A number of Gypsy groups have been sedentary in Bulgaria for centuries, while others have been forced to settle more recently. The abolition of nomadism has been a goal of virtually every European government: an 1886 Bulgarian decree prohibited nomadism and the entry of Gypsies from abroad. Gypsies prefer to live in their own neighborhoods, but since the 1950s the socialist government has implemented a policy of integrated resettlement of Sofia Gypsies, tearing down many old neighborhoods and assigning housing in new apartment complexes. Many mourn the passing of the old neighborhood and extended family life, while others eagerly claim their right to live interspersed among Bulgarians. Although the entire extended family rarely lives together in a new apartment, they still gather frequently.

Demography. Reliable population figures for Bulgarian Gypsies are impossible to assemble because no census data on ethnic groups has been published since World War II. Foreign scholars estimate that there are 260,000 to 450,000 Gypsies among a total population of 9 million Bulgarians, representing 2 to 5 percent of the population. The Gypsy birthrate is significantly higher than the Bulgarian birthrate; families of 4–6 children are common among Gypsies, whereas the Bulgarian average is 1.5 children.

Linguistic Affiliation. A large majority of Bulgarian Gypsies speak Romani, a member of the Indic Branch of the Indo-Aryan Language Group, and many also speak Turkish. The Kopanari, a subgroup living mainly in northern Bulgaria, speak Romanian. All Gypsies speak (and most read and write) Bulgarian, since education up to the eighth grade is compulsory. Romani has a rich oral tradition of songs, tales, and expressions, but it is not taught in the schools.

History and Cultural Relations

Gypsies entered the Balkans in approximately the eleventh century from their homeland in India. They were well established in large numbers throughout the Balkans by the fourteenth century, some settling and others remaining nomadic. Initial curiosity about Gypsies by Balkan peoples and governments eventually gave way to hatred and discrimination. In the Romanian kingdom they were serfs until the nineteenth century. Nineteenth-century sources document a distinct economic niche for Gypsies while underscoring their separateness, their exoticism as a culture, and the persecution they suffered. In the twentieth century, approximately half a million European Gypsies perished at the hands of the Nazis. Bulgarian scholars emphasize that Gypsies lived in misery during the Ottoman period due to the oppressive "Turkish yoke" and the Muslim religion. They claim that since the 1944 socialist revolution, Gypsies have become "cultured, advanced, and educated," that they are equal citizens of Bulgaria, and that prejudice is gone and assimilation is occurring (Marinov 1962, 267–270; Georgieva 1966, 43–44). Western scholars, however, claim that Gypsy ethnicity is thriving and adapting in creative ways to the pressures of assimilation (Silverman 1986).

Economy

Bulgarian Gypsies have not until recently been involved in growing their own food; they were not allowed to own land and instead developed service occupations such as fortunetelling, music, horse dealing, bear keeping, entertainment, animal training, acrobatics, blacksmithing, coppersmithing, tinsmithing, woodworking, sieve making, comb making, basket weaving, shoemaking, and seasonal agricultural work. Many of these occupations continue today, in addition to middleman peddling, black market peddling, and the almost ubiquitous wage labor. In wage labor, Gypsies occupy a low-status economic niche: unskilled factory jobs are common, as are agricultural jobs on cooperative farms, street cleaning, and railroad cleaning. With universal education, Gypsies are beginning to assume professional roles as teachers, clerks,

lawyers, journalists, and government officials. Music has continuously provided Gypsies with a viable economic niche in Bulgaria, both in the private and government realms. Gypsies have a virtual monopoly of some instruments, namely *zurna* (oboe) and *tupan* (two-headed drum). Whatever instrument they play, Gypsies learn the repertoire of the local peasants in order to be indispensable at weddings, baptisms, housewarmings, saints' day festivals, etc. The past twenty years have witnessed a grossly inflated market for modern folk music in Bulgaria. Gypsies have played a central role in creating this contemporary "wedding music," which boasts star performers. Adaptability is the key to Gypsy occupations, whether in the private or in the state-sponsored sphere. When working a government job, Gypsies often mold the job to their own family's needs. Some see this adaptation of jobs as a subversion of the Bulgarian work ethic, which stresses pride and devotion to the nation. Gypsies often change and recombine occupations, so a typical person may have 3–4 sources of income. Gypsies are economically flexible within the centralized socialist economy. They manage to keep the benefits of socialism without giving up the independence of the free market.

Kinship

Kinship is reckoned bilaterally with more attachment to the patrilineal side due to patrilocal residence after marriage. Personal names depict kin relations for one or two generations. Muslim names were forcibly changed to Slavic names in the 1970s as part of the government assimilation program. Official Slavic names, however, are rarely, if ever, used.

Marriage and Family

Family life is the basis of social interaction. Marrying and even socializing with non-Gypsies is avoided. Marriages are sometimes arranged by the parents, with the involvement of the bride and groom. Marital age is typically young, between 16 and 21. Elopements often occur. Divorce used to be rare but in the last twenty years it has become increasingly common. Marriage and divorce are sanctioned through ritual, and official documents are often avoided. Extended patrilineal patrilocal families were common until the 1960s, but they have been supplemented by nuclear or vertically extended families (three generations).

Sociopolitical Organization

Leadership within the group comes from powerful elders, usually men but sometimes women. These elders may refer to themselves as "kings" or "queens" (to non-Gypsies) but their power is not hereditary. Rather, it is determined by their reputations. Social control is enforced by public opinion, for example, through the threat of withdrawing sociability. Conflict between Gypsies is settled within the group through mediation or through a council of elders. Gypsies rarely seek help from the Bulgarian government because they generally do not receive fair treatment. Recently, political awareness has grown among intellectual Gypsies who are starting to lobby for ethnic rights.

Religion and Expressive Culture

The large majority of Bulgarian Gypsies are Muslims (Horahane), and a smaller percentage are Eastern Orthodox Christians. Gypsies do not tend to be devout followers of any one institutional religion but rather practice an eclectic folk religion that combines Muslim, Christian, and pre-Christian customs. Since the 1970s the socialist government has clamped down on Islamic worship, closing mosques and prohibiting circumcision, the speaking of Turkish, and the wearing of Muslim ethnic dress. Many of these practices continue in private realms. Gypsies are known for their musical ability, especially their talent for improvisation and their huge repertoire of in-group music and music for outsiders. Gypsy weddings and soldier send-off celebrations are community-wide events where the culture's music, food, and family values are displayed.

Bibliography

Crowe, David, and John Kolsti (1991). *The Gypsies of Eastern Europe*. Arkmonk, N.Y.: M. E. Sharpe.

Georgieva, Ivanichka (1966). "Izsledvanija vurhu bita i kultura na Bulgarskite Tsigani v Sliven." *Izvestija na Etnografskija Institut i Muzej* 9:25–47.

Marinov, Vasil (1962). "Nabljudenija vurhu bita na Tsigani v Bulgaria." *Izvestija na Etnografskija Institut i Muzej* 5: 227–275.

Silverman, Carol (1986). "Bulgarian Gypsies: Adaptation in a Socialist Context." *Nomadic Peoples* 21–22 (special issue):51–62.

Soulis, George C. (1961). *The Gypsies in the Byzantine Empire and the Balkans in the Late Middle Ages*. Dumbarton Oaks Papers, no. 15. Washington, D.C.

CAROL SILVERMAN

Bulgarians

ETHNONYMS: Bulgarini, Bulgars

Orientation

Identification. Bulgaria is identified variously on the basis of geographical, cultural, and political factors as part of eastern Europe, southeastern Europe, the Balkans, the Slavic countries, the South Slavic countries, and, until recently, the Communist bloc. The most likely origin of the name "Bulgarian" is from the Turkic verb meaning "to mix," reflecting the mixture of various Turkic tribes that invaded the region and established the first Bulgarian polity.

Location. Bulgaria is located on the eastern part of the Balkan Peninsula, between 41°14' and 44°13' N and 22°21' and 28°36' E. It is bordered by Romania to the north, Yugoslavia to the west, Greece to the southwest and south, Turkey to the southeast, and the Black Sea to the east. The country has a varied topography consisting of mountains, foothills, and plains. The major feature is the Balkan mountain chain, which runs across the center of the country in an east-west direction, turning northward in the west. The Danubian Plain lies to the north of the Balkans; and the upper Thracian Plain, to the south. Bulgaria abuts the Rhodope, Rila, and Pirin massif, located to the south and southwest. The topography has a strong influence on the climate, dividing the country into two climatic zones. In the north the climate is eastern European continental, with hot summers and cold winters. The Balkan range shields the south from cold winter winds, producing a modified Mediterranean climate with milder winters and hot dry summers.

Demography. In 1988 the population of the country was 8,973,600. Approximately 85 percent are ethnically Bulgarian. There is much concern about the low birthrate among Bulgarians, which has dropped from one of the highest in Europe in the 1870s to the current level, which barely exceeds the rate necessary to sustain existing population levels. This dynamic has led to an increase in the average age of the population. The other major demographic shift has been in the urban component of the population, which has grown from only 20 percent in 1900 to 66 percent in 1988.

Linguistic Affiliation. Bulgarian is classified as a South Slavic language and is written with the Cyrillic alphabet. However, the contemporary grammar and vocabulary show diverse influences, especially Turkish. There are various regional dialects in the country, with the major difference being between eastern and western variants. Other languages in border regions—such as Serbian in the northwest, Macedonian in the southwest, and Romanian in the north-central area—are increasingly influential. Regional dialects are becoming less pronounced as a result of national standardization in education and the rising importance of national media, especially television.

History and Cultural Relations

The Bulgarian lands have been the domain of diverse cultures, including Thracian, Greek, Roman, and Byzantine. Contemporary Bulgarians, however, trace their origins to Slavs who came from the area north of the Carpathians between the fifth and sixth centuries and the subsequent incursion of Turkic tribes from central Asia in the seventh century. The latter are referred to as "Bulgars" or "proto-Bulgarians," and it is from this group that the Bulgarians got their name. Although the "proto-Bulgarians" quickly dominated the region politically, they adopted the customs of the Slavic settlers, which then formed the basis of Bulgarian culture.

Bulgaria's fortunes vis-à-vis numerous hostile neighbors rose and fell over the subsequent years. The most significant event was the fall to Ottoman domination in 1396. Ottoman dominion lasted nearly 500 years and had a significant impact on Bulgarian language, culture, and economic development. The sizable Turkish minority in Bulgaria and the strained relations between Bulgarians and Turks at both the individual and national levels are, in part, consequences of this period. Likewise, the stereotypical good relations between Bulgarians and Russians that epitomized the socialist era can also be traced back to the Ottoman period, since it was the Russian army that liberated Bulgaria from Ottoman control in 1877.

Besides the Turkish minority, which accounts for approximately 10 percent of the population of Bulgaria, Gypsies are the only other sizable group with which Bulgarians interact regularly. The latter are marginalized and stigmatized as a rule; traditionally they have lived separately in distinct neighborhoods, although they are becoming more integrated residentially with Bulgarians. Some large cities also **have** groups of guest workers and students. The largest group of foreign workers are Vietnamese who were sent to work in Bulgaria for five-year periods in exchange for Bulgarian products exported to Vietnam. The contractual arrangement between the two countries was recently terminated and most Vietnamese are expected to return to Vietnam in the early 1990s. Students come primarily from the Middle East and Africa. For the most part relations between these foreigners and Bulgarians take place in the formal context of work or school. Outside of these contexts, relations are minimal and sometimes strained.

Settlements

The location of original settlements in the area was determined by defensive concerns. As settlements expanded, the presence of water and gentle terrain became dominant factors as well, and larger settlements grew up along rivers and in the foothills at the edges of the fertile plains. Contemporary villages are distributed along important travel routes connecting larger towns. In most of the country villages are concentrated settlements with houses in close proximity to each other around a village square. This area of habitation is surrounded by the land that villagers cultivate. Because of migration and demographic changes, many smaller villages have lost their population base and are basically hamlets. As their current population is primarily elderly, their long-term survival is questionable. Larger villages are faring better as a result of governmental migration restrictions, economic development, and closer integration with nearby urban settlements.

Traditional village houses were constructed of wood and plastered with mud. They were small, one-story constructions with one to three rooms. A similar style of house was also constructed from mud bricks or stone and plaster. While some examples of these houses are still evident in contemporary villages, the predominant model is a two-story house with several rooms made of brick and finished with a stucco-type plaster. Urban areas have the same type of constructions, but since the 1950s the large, multistory, concrete apartment building, usually in groups forming a complex, has come to dominate the urban housing scene.

Economy

Subsistence and Commercial Activities. Traditional subsistence was structured around agriculture and herding. The relative importance of these two activities varied regionally: agriculture dominated the plains; sheep- and goatherding typified the mountain regions; and a more balanced combination of both characterized intermediate zones. These resources were augmented by small-scale commodity production and the sale of excess agricultural products. Commercial agricultural production characterized a few areas, such as the Rose Valley, which is famous for the production of rose oil. Elsewhere, the level of commercial production was inhibited by the small size of holdings, which were often barely sufficient for subsistence purposes and typically widely dispersed.

Reciprocal labor sharing was an important element of the subsistence strategy, and some individuals from agriculturally poorer regions migrated seasonally to work in the plains. The crop base varied regionally but usually combined grain, fruit, and vegetable production.

The agricultural situation changed radically with the collectivization of land in the 1950s. Villagers then started working for the cooperative farm and raising additional crops and animals for their own use on small personal plots granted by the cooperative for subsistence purposes. Since the 1960s the development of industrial enterprises and the possibility of commuting to work in towns has turned many villagers into nonagricultural workers who continue to acquire some subsistence needs from their personal plots.

Industrial Arts. Bulgarians traditionally practiced many trades, often in addition to agricultural work. Wood- and metalworkers provided villagers with such necessities as building materials, furniture, horse/donkey carts, and wine barrels. Textile crafts were perhaps the most important, including spinning, weaving, knitting, and sewing. The major products were clothing and household textiles such as bed covers and rugs. Particular designs and colors of clothing distinguished different regions of the country. While all households were involved in domestic textile production, some regions developed significant woolen and braid industries during the Ottoman period. Today textile industries are again a major component of the national economy. Other major sectors of contemporary industry include machine building, metalworking, and food processing. Chemical and electronic industries are important growth sectors.

Trade. After liberation from Ottoman control Bulgarians began exporting agricultural products—primarily foodstuffs—to Germany, Austria, Great Britain, and other western European countries. The sale of foodstuffs to Germany increased significantly in the context of World War II. After the war the nature of trade shifted radically. Bulgaria became part of the Council for Mutual Economic Assistance, and trade—now state-controlled—shifted to the other members of this Communist economic alliance, especially the Soviet Union. With increasing industrialization the profile of exports also shifted to include a balance of agricultural and industrial products. The major imports were fuels, raw materials, and machinery. In the 1970s trade with Western Europe began to develop again on a small scale, and since 1989 there has been a major attempt to establish economic connections with developed capitalist countries.

Division of Labor. In the agricultural subsistence economy labor was divided on the basis of sex and age. Women took care of most domestic activities, including cooking, cleaning, spinning, and weaving. Sewing was done by both men and women, but outer garments were often made by village tailors who were men. In the fields women hoed while men plowed and sowed, but everybody helped in the harvest. Both men and women took care of the animals, with men tending to horses and butchering. Children were primarily responsible for pasturing animals and collecting water. In the socialist era both men and women moved increasingly into wage labor. This has softened the rigidity of the sexual division of labor, but many of the same divisions are operative in the personal plot production and domestic activity of villagers.

Land Tenure.   In Ottoman times land was held by the sultan, who granted rights to collect tribute or tax to Ottoman lords. After liberation most land was divided up among Bulgarian cultivators, but villages retained some areas of pasture and forest as communal property. Schools and churches also had associated lands for their support. After World War II, the controlling Communist government pursued a policy of collectivization. Villagers retained a small "personal plot" of land for their own subsistence use, but the government took control of most land amenable to an economy of scale through village cooperatives. Following collectivization, the trend was toward increasing the size of agricultural production units, first by consolidating cooperatives and subsequently by integrating several cooperatives into large administrative units called agroindustrial complexes. This trend began to wane in the mid-1980s, and with the decline of Communist party influence since 1989, there has been strong official support for reprivatization of agricultural production.

Kinship

Kin Groups and Descent.   Bulgarians trace kinship bilaterally and the major kin group is the kindred. Close relatives are always members of one's kindred, but the importance of more distant relatives is shaped significantly by such factors as geographical distance, frequency of interaction, and interdependence in informal economic activities. Affinal relations between families of married couples are valued and fictive kin relations like godparenthood are of continuing importance.

Kinship Terminology.   The designation of kin follows the Eskimo system with some refinements, such as additional terms for many affinal relations.

Marriage and Family

Marriage.   Marriage was nearly universal and usually occurred when the man and woman were in their early twenties. Village endogamy was common, though marriage of individuals from neighboring villages was also frequent. Spouses met in the context of village life, and village work bees were major occasions for courtship. Spouse selection was based on mutual attraction, and while relatives made their feelings known, they rarely forced a couple to marry against their will. Women were expected to bring a dowry, which commonly consisted of furniture, clothing, and household textiles. Some textiles were given as gifts to wedding guests, and the remainder used by the new couple. Postmarital residence was patrilocal, with the bride going to live in the house of the groom. Divorce was viewed negatively and rarely occurred. Widows and widowers could remarry but only each other. Today marriage is still nearly universal but separation, divorce, and remarriage are fairly common. Also, as there are more contexts for interaction across localities, spouses are more likely to come from more distant locations than in the past, and neolocal residence is not uncommon. The civil ceremony has replaced the religious one, but the remainder of festivities of the traditional wedding, such as the feasts and gift giving, have been retained, if not expanded.

Domestic Unit.   Bulgaria is well known for the historical importance of large patrilocally extended households known as *zadrugas*, typically consisting of a couple, several married sons, and their families. This pattern was disappearing by the turn of the century, and since that time the three-generation stem family has predominated in rural areas. Nuclear family households are also very common, sometimes cooperating economically with related households. In urban areas the nuclear family model is the predominant domestic form, though it is not uncommon to find an elderly parent living with one of his or her children.

Inheritance.   Partible inheritance was legally and socially prescribed. Traditionally, daughters often received less than sons and sometimes forfeited their patrimony or gave it to a favorite brother. Brothers inherited equally, but in the case of stem families the son who stayed at home to take care of his parents received more, usually in the form of the house and other buildings. This son was typically the youngest.

Socialization.   Traditionally the household and the village provided the major context for socialization of children into adults. Children learned by observation and experience. With a reduction in the number of children per couple and the increasing role of socialist education, the process has changed. Parents indulge their children and do not encourage independence, perhaps in opposition to socialist education, which until recently stressed political ideology and commitment.

Sociopolitical Organization

Social Organization.   Village social organization was built around the household and the network of connections between households based on kin relations and socioeconomic cooperation. Connections with neighbors were particularly significant in this network. In the presocialist era neighborhoods were the basis of labor-sharing groups and informal socializing. After collectivization, cooperative brigades were also organized on the basis of neighborhood. Social stratification was minimal as the vast majority of village households were smallholding proprietors. The major social divisions were between agriculturalists, the village artisans, and the intelligentsia; the last group included the mayor, the doctor, the priest, and schoolteachers. The few households with larger landholdings had higher status, but this situation was reversed after World War II when large holdings were expropriated and wealth became a target of punitive political action. Subsequently, the advantages and power associated with political positions controlled by the Communist party were the primary basis of village differentiation. Other associations important in the village in the Socialist era were the Communist Youth League and the Fatherland Front.

Political Organization.   The Ottomans allowed villages to administer much of their own affairs, usually through a council of household heads. In the years following independence, the state administered local villages by appointing mayors who maintained law and order and acted as local judges. Since World War II, the Communist party has dominated local political organization through the appointment of mayors and party secretaries who follow the directions of higher party organs. In addition to the village leaders there is a local Communist party organization of all village party members and a village council with appointed representatives from each neighborhood. There is also an Agrarian party organization in most villages, though until 1989 it followed Communist party policy. In 1988 multicandidate elections for local administrators were held. In 1990 the constitutionally guaranteed political monopoly of the Communist party was abolished and a multiparty national parliament was democratically elected. Multiparty local elections were held in 1991.

Social Control. Traditionally the mayor, the village policeman, and the priest were the main forces of social control. Gossip and the threat of ostracism, however, were more important and ensured that formal sanctions were seldom needed. Major conflicts usually involved disputes between two parties to a financial transaction or disputes between siblings over the division of the inheritance. Such disputes divided not only the families involved but other related families as well. Even after the conflict was legally resolved, the family units often remained estranged. With collectivization the inheritance of land became less important, though the division of other resources sometimes still causes conflicts. Most conflicts are resolved by the village leaders.

Conflict. Bulgarians do not have any major conflicts with other groups, although relations with Gypsies and Turks are sometimes strained. Gypsies are stereotyped as lazy and dishonest, so they are obvious scapegoats when there is theft in the community or problems at places where they work. Conflicts with Turks can be traced in large part to the government's attempt to assimilate them by restricting the use of the Turkish language and forcing Turks to change their names to Bulgarian names. Such conflicts are primarily restricted to those regions where Turks predominate.

Religion and Expressive Culture

Religious Beliefs. The majority of Bulgarians are adherents of the Eastern Orthodox church, whose beliefs they combine with non-Christian ideas about forces of evil such as the evil eye and bad fortune. There are also several thousand Protestants of various affiliations, approximately 3,500 Jews, and a group of Bulgarian Muslims called Pomaks. A large segment of Bulgarians are not religious at all. This number increased during the Communist regime as a result of state-sponsored atheism, but even before World War II many villagers were not devoutly religious.

Religious Practitioners. Traditionally, certain older women in villages had reputations for preventing or countering evil forces, while the Eastern Orthodox priest was considered to be the major intermediary with God and the forces of good.

Ceremonies. The most important religious ceremonies (in addition to regular church services and religious holidays) were christenings, weddings, the blessing of a new house, and funerals. The Communist government provided civil replacements for weddings, funerals, and christenings, though some Bulgarians continued to have religious rituals performed as well.

Arts. Folklore is an important element of traditional and contemporary Bulgarian culture. Folk songs are varied and many of them are connected to the struggle against Ottoman control. After the liberation they served as the basis for subsequent compositions. Singing was an important social activity, as work groups and drinking parties would often erupt into song. Folk dancing likewise served important social functions, and regular dances in the spring and summer brought together much of the village at the village square. Such singing and dancing continues in the contemporary context, though with somewhat less frequency. The Communist gov-

ernment promoted folklore as a symbol of Bulgarian identity and sponsored numerous professional folklore ensembles and amateur festivals. Many villages and towns have amateur folk ensembles who perform in these festivals. Larger villages and towns also have amateur drama and choral clubs that perform for the village. Textile arts were also of traditional importance, especially the weaving of intricately patterned cloth and rugs. Contemporary Bulgarians have achieved excellence in many art forms, and some of their artists, such as opera singers, have gained worldwide recognition.

Medicine. Treatment for illness traditionally included a variety of possibilities: religious actions, such as drinking holy water and kissing icons; non-Christian magical incantations believed to counter or exorcise evil forces; herbal treatments using local plants and their products (such as garlic, wine, and brandy); and consulting a physician. Traditionally the last option was the last resort, but in contemporary Bulgaria it is more often the first response to sickness, though often in combination with folk treatments.

Death and Afterlife. Ideas about the afterlife are extensive, though many Bulgarians deny believing them. Traditionally, bodies had to be buried within twenty-four hours. At death the soul is believed to begin a forty-day journey to the other world. Many necessities for this journey and subsequent life, such as lighted candles, food, wine, clothing, and money, are buried with the corpse or laid on the grave. These supplies are replenished by relatives of the deceased in rituals conducted at the grave site on significant anniversaries of the death, including three days, forty days, six months, and one year. In addition there are several days in the Eastern Orthodox religious calendar devoted to the dead when everyone goes to the graveyard to light candles, lay out food, and pour wine on the graves of their relatives. The Communist government promoted civil funerals to replace religious ones and developed an annual civil ceremony at graveyards for honoring the dead. Bulgarians participated in both, and even in civil ceremonies much of the religious ritual was retained.

See also Bulgarian Gypsies; Pomaks

Bibliography

Crampton, R. J. (1987). *A Short History of Modern Bulgaria.* Cambridge: Cambridge University Press.

McIntyre, Robert J. (1988). *Bulgaria: Politics, Economics, and Society.* London: Pinter.

Markov, Georgi (1984). *The Truth That Killed.* Translated by Liliana Brisby. New York: Ticknor & Fields.

Sanders, Irwin (1948). *Balkan Village.* Lexington: University of Kentucky Press.

Silverman, Carol (1983). "The Politics of Folklore in Bulgaria." *Anthropological Quarterly* 56:55–61.

Whitaker, Roger (1979). "Continuity and Change in Two Bulgarian Communities: A Sociological Profile." *Slavic Review* 38:259–271.

GERALD W. CREED

Burgundians

ETHNONYM: Bourguignons

Orientation

Identification. More than language, culture, government, or topography, history and economy define Burgundy. Burgundy's exact limits have fluctuated considerably, although they have centered on a corridor drawn south from Dijon to Mâcon (roughly the Saône River valley), and westward, overland, to the great bend of the Loire River at Digoin. Modern Burgundy is comprised of four departments (Côte d'Or, Yonne, Nièvre, Saône-et-Loire). This is essentially the territory that was controlled by the Aedui, a Celtic polity that played an important role two millennia ago at the time of the Roman conquest of Gaul. Along the southeast-facing slopes of the Saône River valley, Pinot and chardonnay grapes are grown, making this region's name synonymous with wines of world renown. These vines were planted at least two millennia ago by the Gallo-Roman descendants of the region's Iron Age inhabitants. The region derives its name from neither the Celts nor the Romans but from the Germanic Burgundian kings, who ruled the area from their seat in the Rhône corridor until the mid-sixth century.

Location. Burgundy is located between 46° and 48° N and 3° and 6° E. Two principal river valleys, those of the Saône and the central Loire, have long figured in the historical gography and the economy of the region. Together with rivers that rise in Burgundy (particularly the Yonne and the Seine), passages between highlands and plateaus have connected the Atlantic Ocean, the Mediterranean Sea, the English Channel, and the North Sea, rendering the region a primary western European zone of passage since at least 40,000 B.P. The complex geology of Burgundy, with major rock facies of sedimentary, igneous, and metamorphic origin, ensures an abundance of natural resources: coal, oil, precious metals, naturally radioactive deposits, and a variety of rich soils. North of the Loire and west of the Saône, the Morvan Mountains rise nearly 1,000 meters above sea level. This mountain range is the first obstacle that the westerlies, bringing moisture from the Atlantic Ocean, encounter in France. Characteristically moist, the Morvan is in contrast to the Rhône-Saône river corridor, which acts as a conduit for warm, dry Mediterranean winds. The collision of these two air masses over Burgundy ensures unsettled, sometimes extreme weather conditions and widely variable seasons.

Demography. Burgundy has approximately 2 million inhabitants, about a quarter of whom live in and around the six largest cities (Dijon, Chalon-sur-Saône, Nevers, Auxerre, Mâcon, Le Creusot). Only Dijon and its suburbs exceed 200,000 inhabitants. Somewhat over a quarter of Burgundy's population is considered rural, living in villages or on isolated farms; another quarter of the population lives in towns of a few thousand placed amid farmlands and vineyards. In sum, the region's inhabitants are distributed evenly across the landscape, in what is termed log-normal distribution. The population of Burgundy grew slowly in the first half of the nineteenth century, stabilizing around 1850. After that date, the rural population decreased steadily as a casualty of urban growth caused by industrialization. In many rural areas, half the population was lost between 1850 and 1950. Today, rural residence is enjoying considerable renewed popularity in the form of second or retirement homes, although this obviously does not reflect an increase in numbers of agriculturalists. On the whole, the rural population in Burgundy is markedly older than the urban population, especially in areas of reduced agricultural potential (e.g., Morvan) where population decline has been steep for more than a century.

Linguistic Affiliation. Burgundians speak French, although a characteristic regional dialect is reported from at least the twelfth century; a sonorous Burgundian *r* contrasts with the Parisian uvular *r*. Morvandeau and Brionno-Charolais, distinctive patois (dialects) with a sizable vocabulary unintelligible to most Francophones, are still spoken; numerous other dialects of French are common in the region.

History and Cultural Relations

Earliest traces of human activity in Burgundy date from more than 100,000 years ago; archaeology yields evidence of a considerable hunting (reindeer, horses) and gathering population during the predominantly glacial late Pleistocene (40,000–12,000 B.P.). After the glaciers retreated, the population developed the mixed farming, horticulture, and husbandry still characteristic of the region today. Earliest literary records, Greek accounts dating from the fifth century B.C.E., indicate that the Celtic Aedui and their clients held the bulk of what is now Burgundy, engaging in commercial trade, industrial manufacture (especially ironworking), and agriculture. About the time of the Roman conquest in 52 B.C.E. viticulture was introduced. Christianity was well established in Burgundy by the fourth century. After the collapse of Roman hegemony, Burgundy was ruled by the Germanic Burgunds (A.D. 466–534) and the Frankish Merovingians (A.D. 534–731), although the latter's control was never absolute and regional authority was periodically reasserted. After the Saracens (Muslim Arabs) sacked Autun in 731, Carolingians held sway until A.D. 955. Control was reasserted by the Capetian dukes, who, along with those of Valois, held sway over Burgundy and then all of France by the fourteenth century. Burgundy continues to play an important role in national politics: President François Mitterrand began his political career as a deputy from Nièvre.

Economy

Subsistence and Commercial Activities. Burgundy's climatic and topographic variety supports viticulture (primarily along the hills south of Dijon and on the west side of the Saône River valley), stock raising (in the Charolais, Autunois, lower Morvan), silviculture (Morvan), and cereal and other crops (e.g., mustard, sunflowers) throughout the region but especially Côte d'Or. The Saône River and the Canal du Centre handle heavy barge traffic, moving goods out of and through the area. Wine, liqueur, and mustard production are centered on rail lines through Dijon and to the south, while trucks move beef, eggs, and other farm products in southwestern Burgundy.

Industrial Arts. An area of considerable historic and contemporary industrial activity is that of Le Creusot/Montceau-les-Mines, which a century ago was known for the extraction of oil and coal that fed huge foundries, and now for the manufacture of sophisticated industrial ceramics. Variety also characterizes the industrial sector: the "company town" of Gueugnon (pop. 10,456) in Saône-et-Loire is internationally known for cold-rolled stainless steel production and is home to a hat-manufacturing company; 16 kilometers south, past farms raising Charolais beef cattle, the Loire River town of Digoin (pop. 11,341) produces a substantial portion of the country's dinnerware.

Division of Labor and Land Tenure. The presence of women has always been important in agricultural enterprises, where besides traditional household duties women undertake nearly every task on the farm except fieldwork. In recent years they have even sold stock at the weekly cattle market in Sainte Christophe-en-Brionnais, long a bastion of exclusively male activity. Since the beginning of the rural exodus in the last century, women have joined the industrial and commercial workforce in increasing numbers. Many farm families partake of both worlds: family members cooperate to keep up with farm duties while maintaining industrial or commercial jobs in nearby towns. The presence of small industrial towns in an otherwise rural landscape underscores the marked heterogeneity of Burgundy and the variety of economic and social options it generates. Although few landless farm laborers remain, as a dual result of agricultural mechanization and the lure of higher-paying industrial jobs, the agricultural population has stabilized in the past few decades, thanks both to government farm subsidies and to effective competition by French agriculturalists in the international marketplace. This favorable economic climate has enabled many farms to keep operating and remain in the family, although in less desirable agricultural areas (e.g., Morvan highlands) the visitor is struck by the number of abandoned dwellings. Rarely, however, is the land out of production, even in these areas; it is rented (or purchased) and often farmed collectively by relatives from a nearby farmstead.

Kinship, Marriage, and Family

Kinship is reckoned bilaterally, monogamy is the only legal marital relation, and among farm families patrilocal residence is often practiced. Overall, inheritance is equitable within the senior surviving generation. Inheritance of the farm is usually by the eldest male sibling, but on occasion (absence or inappropriateness of senior male siblings) younger sons or daughters inherit and (in the latter case) marriages are uxorilocal. The size of farm families has been greatly reduced in this century for two reasons: the toll on three successive generations of war (the Prussian War of 1870, and World Wars I and II) and industrialization. No longer is a large familial workforce either necessary or desirable, and birth spacing and control is clearly practiced, despite the nominal Roman Catholicism of the French population (overall French population growth rate is 1.7 percent). Having children is considered highly desirable in the society as a whole, and, if not indulged, children are certainly given as many advantages as the family can afford. Christenings are as important for designating godparents as for celebrating a new member of the community.

Sociopolitical Organization

France is a parliamentary democracy, governed for a seven-year term by a president whose party has constructed a majority coalition. The primary political parties represent rightist, centrist, socialist, and communist interests, all of which enjoy considerable support in Burgundy. In general, industrial and highland agricultural areas support candidates to the left of center, while small towns and business communities vote more conservatively. Burgundy is considered an administrative unit only on certain issues (e.g., environment, tourism); more important are the hierarchical departmental, prefectural, cantonal, and communal divisions that both mirror and crosscut geographic, economic, and cultural differences. Politics are of central interest to French people in general and to heterogeneous Burgundians in particular, and political matters are a perennial subject of conversation in cafés and on the street.

Social Control and Conflict. A national police, the Gendarmerie Nationale, patrols the highways and rural areas, while municipalities have their own peacekeeping forces. As in many industrialized nations, France has had to combat increasing social disruption as old values and structures disappear and are replaced with an alienated, mobile urban population. Although rural areas of Burgundy remain remarkably free of such disruption, inhabitants are much more alert to such dangers than they were only a few years ago. Rural Burgundians prefer to control tense situations socially rather than by overt conflict, and gossip is a potent community weapon. The court in which the meaning of an act and its ramifications are considered, and moral judgment is passed, is the café.

Religion and Expressive Culture

Religious Beliefs and Practices. Although most Burgundians are nominal Catholics, church attendance, especially in rural areas, is limited to women, children, and the elderly. Most rural men await the end of mass at the café, and even at a funeral they stand hatless outside the church and pass by the bier only just before the coffin is carried out of the sanctuary and to the cemetery. Participation in weddings and christenings is more representative. Burgundy, like many rural areas, harbors little-discussed non-Christian beliefs relating to features of the landscape and the seasons. Burgundy has for centuries been attractive to a variety of religious orders; the important monastery of Cluny was founded in A.D. 910. More recently, the main Buddhist temple in the West and the European home of the Dalai Lama has been built in southern Burgundy.

Arts. Rural artisans continue to manufacture sabots (wooden shoes), _vielles_ (musical instruments like the hurdy-gurdy), and other crafts both for the tourist trade and their own use. Continuing interest by young and old alike (since at least the nineteenth century) in folklore societies has kept many Burgundian traditions vibrant and has contributed greatly to community and regional pride.

Bibliography

Aldrich, Robert (1984). _Economy and Society in Burgundy since 1850._ New York: St. Martin's Press.

Bonnamour, Jacqueline (1966). *Le Morvan: La terre et les hommes*. Paris: Presses Universitaires de France.

Chaume, Maurice (1925–1937). *Les origines du Duché de Bourgogne*. 2 vols. Dijon.

Commeaux, Charles (1977). *Histoire des Bourguignons*. Dossiers de l'Histoire. Paris: Éditions Fernand Nathan.

Crumley, Carole L., and William H. Marquardt, eds. (1987). *Regional Dynamics: Burgundian Landscapes in Historical Perspective*. San Diego: Academic Press.

Gras, Christian, and Georges Livet, eds. (1977). *Régions et régionalisme en France du XVIIIe siècle à nos jours*. Paris: Presses Universitaires de France.

van Gennep, Arnold (1934). *Le folklore de la Bourgogne (Côte d'Or)*. Contributions au Folklore des Provinces de France, no. 1. Paris: Librairie Orientale et Américaine.

CAROLE L. CRUMLEY

Calabrese

ETHNONYM: Calabrians

Orientation

Identification.   The Calabrese are a geographically and, to a degree, culturally defined people of the classic latifundia region of southern Italy.

Location.   Calabria lies between 38° and 39° N and approximately 16° E, constituting the "toe" of the Italian "boot." It has coasts bordering on the Tyrrhenian and Ionian seas. The island of Sicily lies just off to the west, across the Strait of Messina. The region consists of three provinces, with provincial capitals at Cosenza, Catanzaro, and Reggio Calabria. The terrain is predominantly hilly, with some mountains. The climate is typically Mediterranean, with hot, dry summers and mild, humid winters. Mean annual rainfall varies from 60 to 120 centimeters. Summers are a time of drought, and what rain does occur falls in short, heavy showers that wash away the soil and damage the crops. Most of the soils are poor—thin and highly porous. The farmlands are confined to the clayey regions. Forested areas of the region have been dramatically reduced over the years, especially recently, because of overgrazing and overcropping, resulting in much soil erosion.

Demography.   According to a 1981 census, Calabria's population is 2,061,182. Person-to-land ratios are extremely low throughout most of the region, because of the wide dispersal of settlement centers. The population has been steadily declining over the last several decades, largely because of the out-migration of residents. Overall mortality rates have declined, but infant mortality rates remain quite high relative to the rest of Italy. As is the case for much of western Europe, Calabria is experiencing a demographic shift toward an older population, which is exacerbated by the fact that most out-migrants are drawn from the younger segment of the adult population.

Linguistic Affiliation.   The Neapolitan-Calabrian dialect predominates in Calabria, although there are communities of Calabrian-Albanian speakers as well. Although the two languages are linguistically distinct, they are both Indo-European languages. The former belongs to the Gallo-Romance Family, the latter to the Albanian.

History and Cultural Relations

The archaeological record discloses a long and rich history of habitation for the region; Neolithic, Copper Age, and Bronze Age sites are abundant. Earliest records mentioning the region refer to it as "Bruttia," a name retained until the Byzantine period. Few monuments of the Roman occupation remain, but during that time Christianity was introduced to the region. Byzantine control of all of the south, including Calabria, continued for centuries after the establishment of the Holy Roman Empire. It was broken by the arrival of the Normans in the eleventh century. Prior to this, during the tenth century, was a time when monastic settlements were established in great numbers throughout the region, particularly those devoted to Saint Basil of Caesarea. Napoleon's conquest of the south inaugurated the "French Decade" at the turn of the nineteenth century, and during this period feudalism was abolished, although changes in the law had little effect on local practice. Large estates owned by absentee landlords remained the norm. Still, during this time the partition of municipal commons (called "domains") for public sale began. The last half of the nineteenth century saw the start of heavy emigration, as the land became less and less able to support the people, and disease and natural disasters took their toll. Agriculture was in crisis, and efforts by the Italian state were confounded by countervailing actions on the part of the traditional landholding families of the region. The volatility of the social and economic situation of the period was increased with the introduction of anarchism and socialism, and during years of crop failure riots were common. The years between the two world wars saw a concerted movement toward land occupations, which were ultimately legitimated by the state government. This broke the traditional pattern of the feudal estates, as many of the newly occupied properties were even then run on collective lines. In the years immediately following World War II, the Italian government embarked upon the largest regional development program known to Western Europe, specifically intended to address the reality that the south lagged behind the north in industry and infrastructure. Calabria, however, received little benefit from this new effort to improve infrastructure and to develop industry.

Settlements

Calabria is characterized by the form of settlement known as "agrotown": large, isolated towns centrally situated in a much more extensive territory made up of agricultural lands. The concentration of people in these centers is great: approximately 80 percent of the regional population is town-based, with less than 20 percent living in dispersed settlements across the countryside. Average settlement populations are between 2,000 and 8,000, and some are as large as 20,000 to 40,000. This settlement pattern derives from Roman times and was designed to facilitate defense in times of war or invasion. Most of the townspeople are landless, having only their manual labor to sell to the farmers of the surrounding area.

While urban in size and physical layout, these settlements are strongly focused on the rural, agricultural world, whose laborers they shelter and whose products they consume.

Economy

The crops grown in the region are typical of Mediterranean extensive-farming communities. The principal crop is wheat, olives and grapes are also important, and citrus and cotton are grown as well. There is little industrialization. Traditional Calabrian farming was, and in many places still is, done on the basis of leasehold access to a portion of an absentee landlord's property. Leases are commonly issued on a multiyear basis, and the tenant is responsible for managing the operation, hiring the necessary labor, and providing his own seed and tools. Multiyear leases are contracted on the basis of the landlord receiving a portion of the proceeds of the harvest, usually wholly in cash and often representing as much as three-fourths of the total product. One-year leases are also common, though less favored by tenants. Women's participation in agricultural labor is and traditionally has been marginal. Merchants and artisans reside in the towns, and the overwhelming influence of the estates upon the orientation and conduct of town life has diminished somewhat. Very few employment alternatives are available locally, other than in farming. For this reason, and because smallhold farming is unsuitable in all but a few parts of the region, there has long been a high rate of out-migration of youth and men to the industrial north, other European countries, and the United States. These workers usually send back a portion of their wages to support the families they have left behind. Because of this, there has been a process of "feminization" of local town populations, and often a change in local conceptions of "men's work"—often the men simply are not there to do it, so women must take over. Thus, although there is a long tradition of women's avoidance of the "public" sphere, such avoidance is today followed less assiduously.

Kinship

The hard facts of economic life in Calabria have had implications for the structure of the local kin group. Unlike in the north, where the patrilinear extended family is the form most commonly associated with farming communities, in the south the nuclear family is largely detached from any broader kinship unit. Ties beyond the nuclear family are also difficult to maintain because of the high degree of mobility required when farm laborers must circulate through the region in search of temporary or seasonal employment, or when individuals must leave the area entirely to find factory work.

Marriage and Family

Marriage. Marriage is celebrated within the Catholic church, and matches are often arranged. A woman is expected to be chaste before marriage, and courtship is carried out under the watchful eye of the family and community. Long courtships are common, and age at marriage is generally in the mid-twenties for women and late twenties or early thirties for men. Marriage is expected to be for life, and divorce is not an option.

Domestic Unit. The household consists, as a rule, of the nuclear family. Families tend to have many children, though high infant mortality rates keep families small. The widowed parent of either the husband or wife may, for economic reasons, move in. When this occurs, it is generally the case that a widowed mother will move in with her married son, while a widowed father will live with a married daughter. This is intended to avoid conflicts with regard to household authority, but in practice such arrangements are rife with tension—particularly between mother-in-law and daughter-in-law. It is generally understood that these arrangements, when they occur, are far less than ideal. In practice, although the domestic unit consists of the husband-wife pair plus their children, the residential unit is quite frequently a female-headed family, as husbands are gone for much of the year to work in the north or out of the country.

Inheritance. Those who have real property are a small minority of the population, but among them land tends to pass to sons rather than daughters. A daughter's inheritance, if there is to be one, usually passes to her as a marriage settlement, in the form of household goods.

Socialization. The mother is the primary care giver for young children and often remains their sole adult focus until they reach maturity. Older daughters are expected to help care for their younger siblings as soon as they are competent to do so. Free schooling is available and is mandatory for the first few years, after which usually only the boys—and only a small percentage of those—go on to higher levels of education.

Sociopolitical Organization

The population centers provide an administrative link between the region and the national polity, politically integrating Calabria into the Italian state. Traditionally, because of the economic focus of the town upon the needs of the estates, local leadership was drawn from the landowning families, if they were resident in town, or from the numbers of the leasehold masters of the estates. Like much of southern Italy, the region was historically plagued by bandits, against whose depredations the estate guards were expected to defend. However, this arrangement often resulted in the abuse of authority by the guards themselves, who then became an extortionate and violent class. The strongly held social value of individualism makes it difficult for individuals to operate in groups larger than the family, but on occasions that require the recruitment of outside help—to conduct official business, secure a job, or the like—such transactions are frequently couched in the terms of a patron-client relationship.

Social Control. Local police enforce the official law in the community, and courts mete out punishment. However, informal sanctions also play a major role in ensuring that individuals comply with local norms and standards of behavior. Gossip is a powerful means of social control and is most frequently concerned with allegations regarding the honor or virtue (or lack of same) of an offending individual or family.

Religion and Expressive Culture

Religious Beliefs. Calabrians are Roman Catholic, but their religious beliefs depart, sometimes quite radically, from the formal tenets of Catholicism in particular and Christianity in general. There is a strong faith in a distant, all-powerful God, but this deity is seen to have little interest in or concern for humanity. The focus of religious expression is, therefore, upon a mediator—some saint or supernatural entity that can be importuned to intercede on behalf of humans. In Calabrian beliefs, the Madonna is the most important intercessionary figure among a myriad of saints—but within the term "Madonna" are implicit a great variety of entities, not all (or perhaps any) having much to do with traditional Christian beliefs. Her intercession is sought for help in all sorts of matters, from finding a husband to ensuring the fertility of one's fields or livestock. The retention of superstition and pre-Christian beliefs is evident also in the still strongly held belief in both good and bad (but usually bad) magic—particularly the concept of the "evil eye."

Religious Practitioners. Formal religious practice, through the church, is led by priests. Magicoreligious practice outside the formal structure of the church is the province mainly of women. However, this status is attributed—not achieved or inherited. Essentially, a witch is a witch because people say she is one, and such accusations tend to be reserved for the anomalous or marginal people in the community—people who are, for example, possessed of greater-than-usual economic success, or who fail to live up to local expectations of behavior.

Ceremonies. The most important ceremonial occasions are the feasts of local patron saints and the feasts of the liturgical calendar devoted to the Madonna. Bonfires, processions, and fireworks all form characteristic parts of such celebrations. The seven sacraments of the Church (baptism, confirmation, confession, Communion, marriage, ordination, extreme unction) are honored, and both Christmas and Easter are important religious holiday periods.

Medicine. Calabria is a poor and unhealthy region. Malaria is common in many areas, particularly along the coast. Modern medical care is not well distributed throughout the population, and a strong reliance on traditional curing techniques that combine the use of poultices and infusions and beliefs in magical interventions remains. Prayer, or the lighting of votive candles, is one frequently tried avenue to healing.

Bibliography

Arlacchi, P. (1983). *Mafia, Peasants, and Great Estates: Society in Traditional Calabria*. Cambridge: Cambridge University Press.

Berkowitz, Susan G. (1984). "Familism, Kinship, and Sex Roles in Southern Italy: Contradictory Ideals and Real Contradictions." *Anthropological Quarterly* 57:83–92.

Chubb, Judith (1982). *Patronage, Power, and Poverty in Southern Italy*. Cambridge: Cambridge University Press.

Cornelisen, Ann (1977). *Women of the Shadows*. New York: Random House.

King, Russell, Jill Mortimer, and Alan Strachan (1984). "Return Migration and Tertiary Development." *Anthropological Quarterly* 57:112–124.

Moss, Leonard W. (1974). "The Passing of Traditional Peasant Society in the South." In *Modern Italy: A Topical History since 1861*, edited by E. R. Tannenbaum and Emiliana P. Noether, 147–170. New York: New York University Press.

NANCY E. GRATTON

Canarians

ETHNONYMS: Canary Islanders, Guanches

Orientation

Identification. The Canary Islands were known in the past as the Fortunatae Insulae and Hesperis. There is some disagreement on the origin of the name "Canaries," but generally it is thought to come from the Latin word *canis*, because of the large number of dogs that lived in the islands. Since their conquest by Spain in the fifteenth century, the islands have belonged to Spain, and since 1982 they have been an autonomous community in the Spanish state.

Location. The archipelago is located between 27° and 29° N and 13° and 18° W, and it belongs to the Macaronesian region, which also includes Cape Verde, Madeira, and the Azores. The islands are of volcanic origin, though at one time some believed that they formed part of the submerged continent of Atlantis. There are seven main islands (Tenerife, La Gomera, El Hierro, La Palma, Gran Canaria, Fuerteventura, and Lanzarote) and several smaller islands with a total area of 7,541 square kilometers, spread over an ocean surface of 100,000 square kilometers off the coast of northwest Africa. The climate is characterized by alternating subtropical anticyclones, which produce a stable weather pattern with few storms. The prevailing climate is determined by the trade winds, which produce mild temperatures, although on occasion the islands experience the effects of Saharan and polar winds. The annual average temperature is 20° C on the coast. Despite the steady climate, the islands have a complex ecology, with various microclimates found even on the same island.

Demography. The Canarian population numbered more than 1,600,000 in 1990. The core population consists of people descended from indigenous inhabitants and the Spanish conquerors. To this basic nucleus later European immigrants were added, mainly from Portugal, Italy, Belgium, Ireland, England, and France. The demographic evolution of the islands is linked strongly to their economic history and emigration to America. Canarian emigrants settled in several South American countries and the United States, but mainly in Cuba and, more recently, in Venezuela, where people of Canarian origin number more than 500,000. In these countries Canarians are called *isleños* (islanders).

Linguistic Affiliation. Canarians speak Spanish, but the pronunciation is considerably different than Castilian Spanish. The lexicon includes words taken from the indigenous languages—especially place names and names of individuals—as well as Portuguese and English.

History and Cultural Relations

The islands were colonized by Berber groups from northwest Africa. The indigenous inhabitants were called *guanches*, although this label correctly applies only to Tenerife. After being conquered by the Spanish in the fifteenth century, the natives were assimilated quickly. The Canarians today are a homogeneous and well-defined ethnic group who stress their differences from the Spanish, whom they call *peninsulares* or, more pejoratively, *godos*. The islands were of major strategic importance during European expansion and their harbors were of value in the trading routes between Europe and America. Since 1852 the islands have had free ports that serve to increase the volume of commercial traffic. Although historic movements for independence have existed, the desire for political sovereignty generally takes the form of a desire for political autonomy. After the democratization of Spain in 1977, the Canary Islands received autonomous status in 1982. In recent times, conflicts over political and economic power in the archipelago have been continuous between Gran Canaria and Tenerife, the most important islands. All national political parties are represented throughout the islands, although the local parties have strong support and demonstrate the strong insular identities that characterize Canarian society.

Settlements

Indigenous settlements were usually located in ravines, which provided caves for habitation. After the Spanish conquest, settlers went to the windward sides where water was more abundant and the soil more fertile. Pirate incursions from the fifteenth through the eighteenth centuries required that the main villages be located inland. During the eighteenth century, an economic crisis and the necessity of increasing agricultural lands led to the clearing of large areas of forest and to the dispersal of settlements. More agricultural land was needed to feed the local population and to provide products for export. In the cities, and especially in the ports, a powerful commercial class composed of the families of old settlers and

European immigrants began to emerge. At the beginning of the twentieth century, the growing of bananas, tomatoes, and potatoes for export to Europe increased. More recently, since the 1960s, the Canarian economy has been orientated toward tourism, causing wholesale urbanization on much of the coastal land formerly used for agriculture. At the same time, the local population moved inland. Also, during the last twenty years a strong internal migratory movement has led to the depopulation of the peripheral islands and an overpopulation of Gran Canaria and Tenerife, mainly in the capitals where trade and industry are important.

Economy

Subsistence and Commercial Activities. The indigenous inhabitants had a subsistence economy based on agriculture and pastoralism. With the arrival of European settlers most of the population began to work in agriculture for export. At the same time, subsistence agriculture remained important as a source of food such as cereal grains, maize, and potatoes. In the cities and villages, people made agricultural implements, textiles, etc. for sale. Today, much land formerly given to subsistence agriculture is being abandoned as farmers seek work in the tourism and construction sectors. Nevertheless, several traditional crops persist through part-time agriculture in which reciprocal work is very important.

Industrial Arts. Many traditional industries have disappeared in the last few decades. Those still surviving include textile production by women, mainly silk, embroidery, and *calados* (openwork). Pottery, basketry, and other types of handicrafts formerly linked to agriculture and household needs survive as part of the tourist trade.

Trade. The economic history of the islands has been linked to international trade owing to the position of the islands in the commercial routes between Europe and America. The most productive crops were always for export, with the actual crops grown changing in response to demands from the European countries. The first important crop was sugarcane but it failed as an export crop because of competition from sugarcane exported from the Antilles. Sugarcane was replaced by wine, which was exported to Europe and America until the eighteenth century. In the nineteenth century, cochineal insect cultivation for the production of dyes was widespread, but when anilines (synthetic organic dyes) were discovered cochineal production was discontinued. During the first decades of the twentieth century, bananas, tomatoes, and potatoes were the major crops for export. More recently, flowers and green vegetables exported to Europe have become important.

Limited local industrial development has always necessitated a dependence on imported manufactures. Since 1852 the Canary Islands have had a free-port system that has favored the open character of the islands' economy, but this system has also led to economic dependence and the growing influence of British trade. Until 1936 the British owned many local businesses, banks, insurance companies, etc. At the same time, they began banana export and created the first tourist facilities. After World War I, the Canary Islands lost their place in the international banana market and slowly became part of the Spanish economy. Actually, a special economic arrangement recognizes some commercial peculiarities of the islands in spite of their integration in the European Community.

Division of Labor. Socioeconomic changes during the last thirty years have brought women into the labor market. Traditionally, women were confined to agriculture and to the household. Cooking and child rearing continue to be primarily female activities, but in urban areas men play a larger role in domestic tasks. Until the 1960s, most Canarians worked in agriculture, but today more than 80 percent of the working population is linked, in some way, to tourism. Native peoples also hold some positions in the island and state governments, though Spaniards hold most of these positions. Similarly, most of the executive positions in the major tourist companies are held by Spaniards and other Europeans.

Land Tenure. Immediately following the Spanish conquest, the lands were redistributed through a system (*repartimientos*) that gave large tracts to those involved in the military expeditions. Therefore, until the nineteenth century, only a few families owned agricultural land. Following the medieval system of "shared property," the peasants worked the land, paying their rent with a part of the crops, mainly cereals. Beginning in 1812 many peasants gained control of land, leading to the development of many small- and medium-sized farms. During the 1980s there were more than 70,000 farms, each with more than 6 square kilometers of land. The more profitable ones are mainly on the coast and grow crops for export. Farms devoted to local trade are located in the midlands and highlands.

Kinship, Marriage, and Family

Kinship. Kinship is traced bilaterally. Kin relations also extend to the descendants of relatives and to godsons. Kin terms follow the Eskimo system, with much use of terms for fictive kin.

Marriage. Historically, local and insular intermarriage was common, especially in the interior. The heavy maritime traffic on the coast reduced the incidence of endogamous marriage in the harbor cities. Marriages were formed between families of similar social status. Marriages between people of different social status or with an important difference in age were prevented by public defamation of the couple. The incest taboo extended to first cousins. Postmarital residence is neolocal and uxorilocal. The role of the mother-in-law is considerable. One popular saying also states that "if you marry a daughter you gain a son, but if you marry a son you lose both." Wedding ceremonies mainly follow the Catholic rite, but civil marriages have increased in number in recent years. Wedding celebrations take place in public establishments, and this practice has popularized the use of "wedding lists" in businesses with gifts given at marriage.

Domestic Unit. The nuclear family is the most common form, although in rural areas three-generation stem families are still found.

Inheritance. Inheritance is legally regulated. In rural areas the house and lands are divided in equal parts among heirs. Domestic items are inherited by the unmarried daughter who lived with the parents until their deaths. Among shepherds, livestock is inherited by the youngest son.

Socialization. Formal education is required for all children between 5 and 16 years of age. In the cities children also attend kindergarten at age 4.

Sociopolitical Organization

Social Organization. In the past, networks of bilateral kin in the village associations linked individuals of different social classes through religious and/or work ties (*hermandades* and *cofradías*). Neighboring associations often organize several social activities. Also important are the Carnival associations, in which men and women of all ages take part.

Political Organization. The Canary Islands are divided into two provinces in the Spanish political system, with the entire archipelago forming an autonomous community. Political activity centers on the political parties. The provinces take part in the Spanish parliament and senate. The Canarian parliament is elected by insular electoral districts, and this parliament elects the Canarian government. The government of each island is the *cabildo*, a traditional institution that also has a role in relations with the state government. Actually, cabildos have lost some of their importance as government institutions, but they are still important in the coordination of insular investments. Traditionally, political clients were significant, and through this system wealthy men had a large network of social and political contacts.

Social Control. Deferential behavior in relation to elders is especially important. A son must ask for his father's blessing as a sign of respect and submission. Inappropriate behaviors, mainly those associated with drunkenness, may lead to ostracism and a loss of public respect.

Conflict. Disputes about boundaries or properties were the most common conflicts in the rural areas. Different types of conflicts between bordering villages were also frequent, although they were generally expressed in the fiestas and sport competitions.

Religion and Expressive Culture

Religious Beliefs and Practices. Canarians are mostly Catholics. Devotion to the Virgins is considerable. Each island has a virgin as patron saint and islands make periodic pilgrimages to their sanctuaries. These pilgrimages are also important demonstrations of each island's identity; each village also celebrates its patron saint's day. The church continues to play a major role in organizing this festival, although the event becomes more secular in nature each year. Baptism, marriage, and death are celebrated following the Catholic rite. In recent years, small groups have begun following other Christian rites. Although the state claims to be nondenominational, religious education is common in both public and private schools.

Religious Practitioners. In the past the Catholic church occupied an important place not only in the religious sphere but also in the social and economic aspects of Canarian society. The loss of church lands and the secularization of public life have now weakened its influence in these areas. Priests receive a subvention from the state, but they also receive gifts and donations from the people.

Arts. Traditional arts focused mainly on the manufacture of domestic implements. Religious painting and sculpture were common until the nineteenth century. In the twentieth century, painting inspired by the indigenous culture and traditional rural life has been a noteworthy development.

Medicine. The National Health Institute and private medicine provide services to the entire population. In the country and peripheral areas of the cities people often go to folk healers who rely on a variety of local plants. Although physicians enjoy a high social status, the healer (*curandero*) enjoys some recognition for curing certain diseases. For example, for afflictions called *mal de ojo* (evil eye)—thought to affect mainly children and domestic animals—*insolación* (sunstroke), and herpes, people go to the healer, believing the source of the affliction can be removed from the body.

Death and Afterlife. Beliefs about life after death follow Catholic tradition. Death is publicly commemorated, and family and community take part in funerals. Traditionally, when a person died, the relatives—especially the women—mourned for one year after the death. Regularly, one month later and one year later people celebrated the death in order to perpetuate the memory of the deceased and to ensure rest for his or her spirit. All Souls' Day is commemorated by almost the entire population, all of whom go to the cemeteries to bring flowers and to clean the tombs.

Bibliography

Afonso, Leoncio (1984). *Geografía de Canarias*. Tenerife: Interinsular Canaria.

Fernández Armesto, Felipe (1982). *The Canary Islands after the Conquest: The Making of a Colonial Society in the Early Sixteenth Century*. Oxford: Clarendon Press.

Galván Tudela, Alberto (1987). *Islas Canarias: Una aproximación antropológico-social*. Barcelona: Anthropos.

Mercer, John (1980). *The Canary Islanders: Their Prehistory, Conquest, and Survival*. London: Rex Collings.

FERNANDO ESTEVEZ

Cape Verdeans

ETHNONYMS: In New England: Black Portuguese, Brava, Crioul

Orientation

Identification. Most Cape Verdeans dwell in their native Cape Verde Islands off the coast of West Africa. Diaspora settlements, however, are located around the world. "Cape Verde" refers to the green color of the islands that sailors first saw after traveling south from European shores. "Black Portuguese" refers to the Cape Verdeans who settled in New England; they are distinct from other black Portuguese-speaking people from the islands of the Portuguese empire (principally Azoreans) who often settled in the same New England neighborhoods where Cape Verdeans lived. "Crioul" refers to the language the Cape Verdeans speak. In New England the term "Crioulo" also refers to their distinctive life-style.

Location. The archipelagoes of ten larger islands of Cape Verde, of which nine are inhabited, and numerous uninhabited islets are located between 17°13′ and 14°48′ N and 22°40′ and 25°22′ W, about 455 kilometers from the West African coast. Good tradewinds, desirable natural resources of fresh water and salt, and good currents helped make Cape Verde a port of trade in the sixteenth century. Its strategic geopolitical and military position continues to make it a desirable base of operations between Europe and Africa. Its climate is tied to that of the Sahel region of Africa and therefore is dry, with low average rainfall, at 25–30 centimeters annually. Drought is common.

Demography. In 1988 the population estimate for Cape Verde was 357,478 (295,703 in the 1980 census). Population density is 89 persons per square kilometer, with a population growth of 0.92 percent (urbanites were 31.5 percent of the total population in 1988). In 1985 the total labor force was 81,700, and life expectancy was 63 years. In 1988 infant mortality was estimated at 65 per 1,000. The majority ethnic group is *mestico*, or people of mixed racial heritage, whose skin color ranges from white to black. Cape Verdean settlements of up to 50,000 people can be found in New England, especially in and around Boston (Massachusetts), New Bedford (Massachusetts), and Providence (Rhode Island). There are also settlements in Rotterdam, the Netherlands; in France; in the West African states that formerly were Portuguese colonies (São Tome, Principe, Guinea-Bissau, Angola, Mozambique, and Senegal); and in Portugal.

Linguistic Affiliation. The Cape Verdeans speak Portuguese, the official language, as their contact language. Crioulo, however, is their everyday language. It has a Portuguese morphology and an African phonetic system; lexical items derive from both.

History and Cultural Relations

The Cape Verdeans were born of west European colonialism and African slavery. Most likely the islands were used by African and Arab fishing folk and sailors as seasonal bases and as safe ports and provisioning points. They were not discovered and claimed until 1460 when Antonio di Noli and Diogo Gomes assumed control over the Windward Islands (Sotavento) in the name of King Alfonso V of Portugal. Two years later, Diogo Alfonso sighted the Leeward Islands (Barlavento). From then on settlers arrived from Algarve and the Madeira Islands and from the Iberian Peninsula. The largest numbers of these settlers were political exiles, adventurers, and criminals, as well as Portuguese administrators and clergy. The mixing of slaves with these settlers created Luso- (or Portuguese-) African and Afro-Portuguese ethnic groups such as Ladinos, *mesticos*, and *tangomaus*, on the one hand, and *degredados, feitors*, and *lançados*, on the other hand (see below for further discussion of terms).

Since its settlement in the fifteenth century, Cape Verde was closely linked with the region of Africa now called Guinea-Bissau. The slave-trade economy linked the islands with Africa, western Europe, and the New World in the sixteenth century. During the seventeenth century, slaving increased, although the role of Portuguese vessels declined. By the eighteenth century, whaling had become a crucial aspect of Cape Verdean development and often the only means of escape from drought and abject poverty for the men. This business created a link with New England, whose whaling industry was famous. Contact with New England provided opportunities for Cape Verdeans to settle in North America. Furthermore, American interests kept slaving alive. The "African Squadron" was created in the 1850s to prevent continued American involvement in West African slave trading.

In 1884–1885 the Berlin Congress confirmed the territorial claims that separated Portuguese and French colonies. In 1870 Guinea-Bissau was separated from Cape Verde for the first time. This division gave Portugal greater administrative control over both regions. The abolition of the Portuguese monarchy in 1910 and the seizure of power by Fascists in 1926 changed little for the islanders. In 1963 Portugal claimed Cape Verde as an "overseas province." It was no longer a colony.

Decolonization in Africa also generated an armed national liberation struggle in Cape Verde, led by the PAIGC, the African Party for the Independence of Guinea-Bissau and Cape Verde. PAIGC was founded in 1956 in Guinea-Bissau, having its origins in an earlier clandestine group founded by Henri Labery and the nationalist leader and revolutionary philosopher Amilcar Cabral. Military confrontations between Portugal and PAIGC marked the 1960s, forcing the Portuguese government in 1971 and 1972 to revise the Portuguese constitution and to pass the Overseas Organic Law, thus giving Portugal's overseas provinces even more autonomy. Despite the assassination of Cabral on 20 January 1973, the PAIGC under the leadership of Aristides Pereira formed a new state, which by October 1973 had received diplomatic recognition from countries around the globe. In April 1974, the Portuguese Armed Forces Movement successfully overthrew the Fascist regime and negotiated full independence. On 30 June 1975, a general election was held for representatives to the Cape Verdean People's National Assembly, an act that represented the independence of Cape Verde. The Republic of Cape Verde officially declared its independence on 5 July 1975, although maintaining a unity of state with Guinea-Bissau. In 1980, a coup d'etat split PAIGC and divided the state into its geographically distinct parts. Cape Verde became an independent country, separate from Guinea-Bissau.

Settlements

Initial settlement through land grants destined the majority of Cape Verdeans to varying states of poverty, destitution, and dependence. The island of Santiago was divided between Diogo Gomes and its codiscoverer, Antonio di Noli; their families retained rights over the island for 130 years. While initial settlement took place upon discovery, it was through slavery that the islands became populated. The first capital was Ribeira Grande (now known as Cidade Velha), abandoned with the economic decline and the self-liberation of slaves on Santiago. Praia, on the island of Santiago, became the capital. Slaves (domestic servants and plantation workers) escaped into the interior, especially on Santiago. They es-

tablished communities that traded with white settlers. In the mid-nineteenth century freed slaves became small peasants on marginal land and landless laborers. Famines ravaged the population in 1770, 1830, and a generation later. Each time between 40 and 50 percent of the population perished. At the turn of the twentieth century, another drought struck with accompanying famine, killing 25 percent of the population.

The first settlements were created on Santiago in 1462. Sugar plantations were planned, modeled after those of the island of Madeira. Santiago residents were granted exclusive rights to the slave trade along the section of the Guinea coast nearest to the island because their lands were unable to produce sugar for the export market. Portuguese colonial landlords and merchants on the African mainland prevented Cape Verdean economic expansion. Cape Verdean smuggling developed as an important social and economic activity in response to this trade restriction.

Lançado merchants were active along the Guinea coast. Initially they were primarily Jews and then increasingly mulattoes. They also settled along the Gambia River and in Sierra Leone.

Piracy and attacks by foreign flotillas destroyed coastal towns, forcing many of those who survived to flee and settle in the interior.

Droughts shaped Cape Verdean settlement patterns, forcing people to move to areas of relative plenty. Furna, a town on Brava, was created in such a fashion. Droughts forced peasants into cities to obtain alms or public relief, creating shantytowns. Droughts also were responsible for long-term labor migration, following the extension of the Portuguese Empire. For example, Cape Verdean men and women went to the notorious labor camps in the cacao plantations of São Tome and Principe.

Sharecropping patterns have changed little since emancipation from slavery and, since independence in 1975, have been defined by absentee landlordism. In practice, though no longer by law, civil authorities usually reinforced traditional patterns of race and class differentiation. The black or mulatto peasant or laborer was as vulnerable to brutality from the police, under the direction of the administrator, as from the landlords. About 90 percent of the Cape Verdeans work as peasants, laborers, or fishers.

Economy

Subsistence and Commercial Activities. As a socialist country, Cape Verde maintains a mixed economy. State-operated concerns such as the Empresa Publica de Bastecimento (Public Supply Company) or the Sociedade para a Comercializacão e Apoio ao Pesca Artesanal (Society for Fish Purchasing and Marketing) must turn a profit. Remittances from immigrant communities and the substantial aid packages put together by Cape Verde's aid partners have provided crucial economic support for Cape Verdeans. Remittances have played a central role in sustaining household economies since the establishment of diaspora communities. The central government maintains a hands-off policy regarding private investments. Agriculture has been virtually ignored, requiring the importation of most of the islands' food. In rural areas, agricultural production consists almost exclusively of maize, beans, sugarcane, and bananas, although drought has steadily decreased output. Five percent of all production is produced by 29 percent of the working population.

Industrial Arts. Cape Verdeans use natural resources to fashion ornaments and household implements. For example, men carve coconut shells and sperm-whale teeth into a variety of decorative and utilitarian items. Women weave *panos,* strips of cotton cloth of West African texture and designs, which were originally woven on simple Mandingo strip looms. Cape Verdean weavers added indigo dye and wove elaborate Moorish or Portuguese designs in contrasting white thread. Pano production, for export as well as local use, involves local cotton growing, dying, spinning, and weaving. The indigo plant and *Urzella* lichen produce blue dyes, used in the production of panos, which also have become an important export item.

Trade. The slave trade in Cape Verde started in the sixteenth century, intensified between 1475 and 1575, declined in the early nineteenth century, and ended in the third quarter of the nineteenth century. Slaves were replaced by *contratados,* or contract labor. The export of labor, through contract or immigration, continued to be important well into the twentieth century. During the slaving period, metals, textiles, beads, spices, silver coins for jewelry making, wine, and brandy were traded through the port of Santiago to the Guinea coast. In addition to slaves, Africa exported ivory and beeswax. The "triangular trade" refers to trading relations that tied together New England colonies, the West Indies, and western Africa. Slave trade stimulated other trade in Cape Verdean goods, including animals, salt, and textiles. Panos and indigo dyes were important export items. The abolition of slavery in the middle of the nineteenth century stimulated the market-driven production of palm and coconut products. In the twentieth century, Cape Verde has had to import food because it lacks sufficient water for irrigation.

Division of Labor. Patriarchy has shaped Cape Verdean society. Women bear the brunt of an economy unable to sustain nuclear-family households. Over the centuries, men have had to go in search of work at sea or in America, Europe, or Africa. Women traditionally carried the burden of sustaining the household, often made up of many children, including illegitimate offspring of wealthier men of the region.

Land Tenure. Plantation agriculture resulted in latifundia. Land grants were made in the early sixteenth century by the Portuguese crown to the first settlers and inherited through primogeniture norms, which were broken often. In 1864, the universal primogeniture rule was abolished. For the most part, landownership among Cape Verdeans was severely limited. With the abolition of slavery, freed slaves became sharecroppers on the land of their former owners, paying as much as one-half of their crop to landlords until independence in 1975. Tenant farmers and sharecroppers were dependent on merchant-moneylender-landlords. Black and mulatto peasants were particularly subject to their coercive brutality, often backed up by local authorities who continued to enforce traditional discriminatory race and class relations.

Emigrants have played an important role in land tenure on the islands. Cape Verdeans living abroad maintain ownership of land inherited from their families and often return

from the United States or France to retire. Such people have significant economic and political power.

Kinship

Kin Groups and Descent. Cape Verdean kinship is bilateral with a patrilineal preference. The more favored ancestry derives from the white colonial population rather than the African, though the latter is by far the more important demographic factor. Fictive kin practices include godparenthood, or *compadrio.* When slaves were freed, often a compadrio relationship was maintained between master and freed slave. Illegitimacy is a common feature in Cape Verdean history. Often, *lançados* (illegal traders and merchants) were illegitimate offspring (*filhos de fora*) who used their patrilineal kin networks to ply their trade. Genealogies are used primarily to identify others as descendants of slaves or oneself as a descendant of Europeans.

Marriage and Family

Marriage. Marriage relations focus on race as a central organizing feature. Marriage ideally occurs between social and economic equals, as defined by skin color and racial heritage. Premarital sexual relations for women are considered a dishonor, no matter the race of the sex partner. For men, an active sex life is an expected element of "manhood" and knows no racial bounds. Men are supposed to marry within or above their class and within or lighter than their color. The different islands traditionally had slight variations in marriage customs. In Brava and Fogo, the preference for first-cousin marriage was a strategy for maintaining resources within a family and therefore was practiced among the wealthy. Preferential first-cousin marriages also ensured racial purity. While marriage norms discouraged racial, class, and kindred exogamy, everyday life gave people opportunities to rebel against or reject such norms. Among Protestants, religion—rather than race or class—defined status, allowing the expansion of mixed marriages. Finally, economic means could transcend all other barriers to marriage. Wealthy men of color found white and "aristocratic" marriage partners. Remittances from immigrant family members enabled traditionally impoverished people and people of color to move into higher status categories.

Domestic Unit. Stem families are common and reflect the poverty under which many Cape Verdeans subsist. The size of a household unit depends on the number of children. Matrifocal households are common, a phenomenon related to a poverty that forces men to seek work elsewhere.

Inheritance. Traditionally, land was inherited on the basis of primogeniture, a norm that continues with exceptions in Santiago. In Fogo, the preference for marriages between first cousins in the landlord class has kept landholdings among wealthy families.

Socialization. Children are very much loved and live within a wide network of family relations that tie together individuals spread out over many parts of the world. Adults teach children class and race consciousness to help them function properly in Cape Verdean society. Rites of passage related to Roman Catholic traditions prevail.

Sociopolitical Organization

Social Organization. Traditional patterns of cooperative labor, *juntamao*, have given way to cooperative associations for production. Divisions of social organization based on slavery and race have blended with class divisions. Miscegenation was an important historical factor and remains the rule. Mulattoes in Cape Verde make up specialized strata within racially and class-stratified society. Skin color and other physical characteristics remain a central organizing principle in society. The hegemony of machismo defines gender relations.

Political Organization. The Republic of Cape Verde constitution defines the state as democratic and revolutionary nationalist. Its objectives include "the construction of a society free from the exploitation of man by man." By definition, the African Party for the Independence of Cape Verde (the PAICV) is the "leading political force in the society and in the state." The PAICV is the successor political party to the PAIGC, the African Party for the Independence of Guinea-Bissau and Cape Verde (discussed earlier in this essay). In 1974, after armed struggle against Portugal, the new Republic of Guinea-Bissau gained independence. On 5 July 1975, the Cape Verde Islands won their independence as the Republic of Cape Verde. The two republics of Guinea-Bissau and Cape Verde were united for five years, until their separation in November 1980. With the liberation of Cape Verde from Portuguese colonialism, the legitimacy of the state has increased. The state continues to penetrate further into the lives of even the most remote communities. The Cape Verdean People's National Assembly (ANP) is made up of elected deputies from around the country. Party membership is not necessary. A list of deputies is generated through a consultative process at the level of villages and workplace meetings. The ANP has the power to legislate in its meetings twice each year. In practice, however, the ANP is primarily a ratifying body. The president and the prime minister have the formal powers of government in their hands. Nonetheless, the ANP represents an important democratic element in the formal political structure of Cape Verde society. It is the focus of popular elections and debate regarding legislation.

Social Control. Local social structures, based on class and race, maintain social conformity. Self-government has been difficult at times because of passive political participation, which is a legacy of centuries of authoritarian political regimes. In recent times, youth have mobilized politically through the JAAC—CV (Juventude Africana Amilcar Cabral—Cabo Verde, or Amilcar Cabral's African Youth of Cape Verde). Women are organized through the OMCV (Organização das Mulheres de Cabo Verde, or Cape Verdean Women's Organization). Both organizations reflect the democratic centralism of PAICV. Another mass organization is the UNTC—CS (União Nacional dos Trabalhadores de Cabo Verde—Central Sindical or National Union of Cape Verdean Workers—Central Union), the federation of trade unions. Organizations for mass mobilization, such as JAAC—CV and OMCV, are expanding the ability for people to obtain greater justice at the local level.

Religion and Expressive Culture

Religious Beliefs. Cape Verdeans are overwhelmingly Roman Catholic. In the early 1900s the Protestant Church of the Nazarene and the Sabbatarians had successful conversion drives. Each was able to build a church and translate the Gospels into Crioulo. Only 2 percent of the population is not Roman Catholic. Patron-saint festivals are commonly observed through the incorporation of non-Catholic activities. In the 1960s, *rebelados*, remote São Tiago peasants, rejected the authority of the Portuguese Catholic missionaries and began to perform their own baptism and marriage rituals. These people also are referred to as *badius*, descendants of runaway slaves, and are less assimilated than other groups into Portuguese and Cape Verdean national culture. (More recently, "badius" has become an ethnic term referring to the people of Santiago.) In one annual festival, or *festa*, in honor of Fogo's patron, Saint Philip, men, women, and children from the poorer classes parade down to the beach early in the morning, led by five horsemen invited as honored guests. Saint John's and Saint Peter's day festivals on the islands of São Vicente and Santo Antão include the performance of the *coladera*, a procession dance accompanied by drums and whistles. During the *canta-reis*, a festa to welcome the new year, musicians serenade neighborhoods by moving from house to house. They are invited in to eat *canjoa* (chicken and rice soup) and *gufongo* (cake made from corn meal) and drink grog (sugarcane alcohol). Another festa, the *tabanca*, is identified with slave folk traditions that at various times in Cape Verdean history have symbolized resistance to the colonial regime and support of Africanisms. Tabancas include singing, drumming, dancing, processions, and possession. Tabancas are religious celebrations associated with the badius. The badius are the "backward" people of Santiago who represent the opposite of being Portuguese. In this sense, the term represents the essence and disdained characteristics of Cape Verdean identity. Tabancas were discouraged at times when Cape Verdean identity was suppressed and encouraged when pride in Cape Verdean identity was being expressed. Belief in magic and witchcraft practices can be traced from both Portuguese and African roots.

Religious Practitioners. Roman Catholicism has penetrated all levels of Cape Verdean society, and religious practices reflect class and racial segmentation. Conversion efforts were extensive among slaves, and even today peasants distinguish between foreign missionaries and local priests (*padres de terra*). Local clergy hardly test the power of local elites. The Church of the Nazarene has attracted individuals who are unhappy with the corrupt Catholic clergy and desire upward mobility through hard work. Folk religious practices are most noticeably related to rites and acts of rebellion. The tabancas include the selection of a king and queen and represent the rejection of state authority. Rebelados have continued to reject the penetration of state authority.

Arts. Expressive and aesthetic traditions are maintained through cyclical ritual events that include the playing of music, singing, and dancing. Contemporary music styles assimilate appropriate themes and forms from these traditions to create popular art, acceptable in metropolitan life and in the diaspora. Pan-African traditions have increasingly tied together the various populations who identify themselves as Crioulo.

Medicine. Modern medical practices are increasingly available to the population as a whole, complementing traditional healing arts.

Death and Afterlife. Illness and death are significant occasions for social gatherings in the households of the afflicted. Friends and relatives participate in visits that may occur over a period of months. Hosts must provide refreshments for people of all stations in society. Mourning falls mainly to women, who participate more in the visitation practices, which in more well-to-do families take place in the _sala_, a ritual chamber also used for guests.

Bibliography

Beck, Sam (1991). _Manny Almeida's Ringside Lounge: The Cape Verdean Struggle for the Neighborhood._ Providence, R.I.: GAVEA-Brown.

Foy, Colm (1988). _Cape Verde: Politics, Economics, and Society._ London and New York: Pinter.

Machado, Deirdre Meintel (1981). "Cape Verdean Americans." In _Hidden Minorities: The Persistence of Ethnicity in American Life,_ edited by Joan Rollins. Washington, D.C.: University Press of America.

Meintel, Deirdre (1984). _Race, Culture, and Portuguese Colonialism in Cabo Verde._ Foreign and Comparative Studies/African Series, no. 41. Syracuse, N.Y.: Maxwell School of Citizenship and Public Affairs, Syracuse University.

Nunes, Maria Luisa (1982). _A Portuguese Colonial in America: Belmira Nunes Lopes. The Autobiography of a Cape Verdean-American._ Pittsburgh, Pa.: Latin American Literary Review Press.

SAM BECK

Castilians

ETHNONYMS: none

Orientation

Identification. Castilians are the people of Castile, the interior lands of the Meseta, the central plateau of Spain, traditionally a region of rural smallholdings and the historic seat of what eventually became the Spanish kingdom. The name "Castile" derives from the great many frontier castles to be found in the region.

Location. There are two officially recognized regional units that bear the name "Castile" (Castile-and-Leon, and Castile–La Mancha), but historically and ethnographically, "Castile" refers to the tablelands (Meseta) of interior Spain, divided by the Sierra de Guadarrama, which runs east-west across the center of the region. Annual rainfall is scanty, averaging 70 centimeters, and most of it falls in the spring and winter. In late spring and early summer, thundershowers are common, but they bear inadequate moisture and often bring hail, which damages local crops. At one time, all of Spain was heavily forested in pine. Of the much-reduced forest lands of today, most are to be found in Castile. Other than these woodlands, the Castilian terrain is either scrub-covered or under cultivation. Soils are poor to mediocre, and the principal water courses (running east-west) are the Duero and Tagus rivers.

Demography. Reliable population figures specific to Castile are not readily ascertainable, but one may roughly estimate that of the 1986 total population of Spain (38,700,000), three-fourths live in the Castilian region. This number is misleading, however, for Castile is a predominantly rural smallholding region, where average population densities are low but are offset by the fact that the region also contains massive urban concentrations in cities such as Madrid, Toledo, and Valladolid. Throughout the region, the demographic trend has been toward the depopulation of the rural sector as its residents migrate toward urban centers or abroad.

Linguistic Affiliation. Of the six recognized Spanish dialects (Andalucian, Aragonese, Asturian, Castilian, Leonese, and Valencian) Castilian is the official one. Indeed, the linguistic designation "Spanish" refers specifically to the Castilian dialect—much to the discontent of many other Spanish (but non-Castilian) speakers. More than 28,000,000 speakers of the language are estimated in Spain alone, although not all of these speakers reside in the historic region of Castile. Castilian, along with the other five Spanish dialects, is a member of the North Central Ibero-Romance Family, and it displays strong lexical similarities (greater than 80 percent) with Portuguese, Catalan, and Italian. Less closely related, but still quite similar (greater than 70 percent lexical similarity) are French, Rheto-Romance, Sardinian, and Romanian.

History and Cultural Relations

Originally populated by Iberian and later Iberoceltic peoples, Castile was for a time ruled by Rome and, later, the Moors. For a time it was governed by counts under the supremacy of Asturias and Leon; it was later annexed by Sancho of Navarre (1026–1035), who gave Castile to his son Ferdinand I in 1033. Leon was united to Castile in 1037, separated in 1065, and reunited under Alfonso VI in 1072, who also annexed Galicia. Afterward, Castile and Leon were separated but were finally reunited under Ferdinand III in 1230, when he conquered large parts of southern Spain from the Moors. Other noted kings were Alfonso X and Pedro the Cruel.

Isabella of Castile married Ferdinand of Aragon in 1469, and became queen of Castile in 1474. Ferdinand became king of Aragon in 1479, from which time Castile and Aragon were united. Under Ferdinand and Isabella, not only was the Spanish territory consolidated, but authority was finally centralized in the hands of a single royal government, and Castile became the regional seat of that authority. Prior to this centralization, the independence of feudal nobles meant that the territory was riven with lawlessness and disorder. By legislating property and personal rights and stripping the nobility and the great crusading orders of much of their former independence and power, Ferdinand and Isabella gained great support among the populace. The ruling pair acquired from the pope the right to nominate all the higher ecclesiastical officers in Spain, and they used that right to reform the church by filling its offices with men of unquestioned orthodoxy and unwavering loyalty to the crown. Thus the church became an extension of royal power.

The Inquisition, begun in 1478 under the control of the monarchy, was directed from Castile to root out heresy and crush what remained of Muslim religious practice, often bloodily. The Inquisition soon developed an independence and momentum of its own, and by 1492 it had far exceeded its original purpose of ensuring that Moors and Jews were expelled from the country. In 1609, Philip III ordered the expulsion of the Moriscos (descendants of Christianized Moors) as well. As a result, when Charles II took the throne in 1665, he inherited a country that had been stripped of nearly all of its tradespeople and artisans. Agriculture declined; arts and literature degenerated.

In 1700, the death of King Charles II of Spain opened the door to dispute over who should be his successor. France favored Charles II's own choice, Philip of Anjou (grandson of Louis XIV), of the Bourbons. But France's adversaries of the time were less pleased with this choice, and they formed a "Grand Alliance" in an attempt to wrest control from the French favorite. Thus began the Wars of Spanish Succession, which raged throughout Europe until 1713–1714, ending with the Peace of Utrecht and leaving Philip V on the throne.

In 1808, Napoleon's brother Joseph succeeded to the throne. His efforts to modernize Spanish institutions led to a backlash against liberalism. By this time the populace consisted of wealthy noble, ecclesiastic, and military groups on the one hand and poor agriculturalists on the other. Because crafts and trade had been largely the province of the original Jewish and Moorish peoples in Spain, when they were suppressed and later expelled from the region there was no powerful or progressive middle class to serve as a source of reformist sentiment, so that such movements became concentrated in the military and among the intellectuals. In 1822, the crown reacted against liberal pressures, and Ferdinand VII acted against the wishes of his own people to secure the assistance of other European powers in controlling his now rebellious colonies in the Americas. Ferdinand set aside established laws of succession and transmitted the throne to Isabella II in 1833, sparking the Carlist Wars (1833–1840), in which supporters of his brother Charles challenged her succession. In 1868, a revolution drove Isabella from the throne, and the period that followed was a confused succession of contenders—each briefly securing, then losing, control over the country.

In 1870, the throne was offered to Leopold of Hohenzollern-Sigmaringen. This move incited a diplomatic crisis in Europe as a whole, and for the French in particular, precipitating the outbreak of the Franco-Prussian War. Still unable to settle their problems of government within the country, the Spanish offered the throne to Prince Amadeo of Savoy, but he abdicated in frustrated discouragement three years later. Then a brief period of republican rule ensued, which lasted until 1875, when Alfonso XII assumed the crown and restored peace to the nation. When he died in 1885, he was succeeded by his posthumous son, Alfonso XIII. Until Alfonso was declared of age in 1902, however, Maria Cristina (widow of Alfonso XII) served as regent.

The last of Spain's colonial holdings in the Americas broke out into open revolt, beginning with the island of Cuba in 1895. U.S. intervention resulted in the loss by Spain of not only Cuba but also Puerto Rico, the Philippines, and Guam, which resulted in the impoverishment of the Spanish economy. A coup d'etat in 1923 established General Primo de Rivera as chief minister of the Spanish cabinet with dictatorial powers, and he managed to enforce a period of quiescence, though one could hardly call it peace, until 1931, when revolution broke out.

Alfonso XIII fled Spain in 1931, and a republican constitution provided for the confiscation of church property, the suppression of religious instruction in the schools, and the expulsion of all religious orders. The attacks on the church, intended to destroy a major source of the monarchy's power and influence, were resented by the largely pious population. This policy, as well as plans for land reform and an attempt to curb the power of the military, alienated the three most powerful traditional elements of Spanish society. The "Popular Front," composed of leftists (including Communists and Socialists), won the elections in 1936. The disgruntled military reacted by revolting, initiating the Spanish Civil War in 1936, aided by arms, planes, and artillery from Germany and Italy. The Soviets aided the Republican side against the Fascist "Nationals," but the Nationalists, under General Francisco Franco, emerged victorious in 1939.

The Franco regime remained nominally neutral but actively favored the Axis powers during World War II, so in the postwar years there was no incentive for the Allied powers to provide economic development aid to Spain. Thus Spain was left out of the Marshall Plan for aid to Europe. These postwar years are known in Castile as the "years of hunger," when the economy was so devastated that even the dogs and cats disappeared from Spanish streets—they either starved to death or were eaten. Although Franco continued in power (he was made acting head of state for life), Spain was in theory still a monarchy.

By 1950, economic recovery was slow at best, and the government's efforts at social and economic reform simply meant a greater intrusion of the state into the lives of individuals, minor industrial development of the urban centers, and the introduction of foreign firms. This meant that the rural areas benefited little from development, except for Franco's public-works schemes. Agriculture remained largely unchanged, and people from predominantly rural areas, including Castile, were forced to emigrate to the major cities and foreign countries. In 1973, Franco made Adm. Louis Carrero Blanco prime minister in the hope that Blanco would continue his policies after the end of Franco's rule. However, Basque terrorists assassinated the admiral six months after his appointment. The admiral was replaced by Carlos Arias Navarro (Arias). Franco's death, in November 1975, returned power to the crown. King Juan Carlos selected Adolfo Suarez as prime minister, inaugurating a period of massive reform, both political and economic. A new Spanish constitution was passed in 1978 and was hailed as the most liberal constitution in Western Europe. It defined Spain as a parliamentary monarchy with no official religion and prescribed a limited role for the armed forces, the abolition of the death penalty, and an extension of suffrage. But although political reform earned the government a great deal of popular support, resentment and dissatisfaction grew among the military. When Suarez resigned the premiership in 1981, and before his successor was sworn in a month later, this dissatisfaction was vented in a rightist coup attempt which, although foiled, persuaded the government to take steps to appease the military. Since that time, the country has attempted greater economic development, particularly of its agriculture, and has moved toward greater provincial autonomy.

Settlements

Although there are a number of large urban centers in the region, Castile is essentially rural, characterized by small towns and villages that are tied closely to a mixed agricultural, vinicultural, and forestal economy. Nonurban settlements are called _pueblos_. Small or large, the pueblo is a nucleated settlement, consisting of a central plaza surrounded by shops and (in the larger towns) municipal buildings, themselves surrounded by residential structures. At one side of the plaza is the town church, with its tall belfry that (characteristically) harbors the large nest of a crane. The oldest houses in Castilian villages often combine dwelling, stable, and barn, constructed with separate entrances for the residential and livestock portions. On the residential side, the upper floor consists of bedrooms and perhaps an attic space. The traditional Castilian kitchen has as its center a _chimenea_—an open-hearthed fireplace, around which are hung great cooking pots. Many village homes lack running water, but every settlement has a public fountain. The houses of the more well-to-do are frequently constructed of stone, although stucco is a frequently encountered building material.

Economy

Subsistence and Commercial Activities. Although smallhold farming is the linchpin of the regional economy, it is rare for an individual or household to live off agricultural income alone. Income provided by the family farm is augmented by small-scale animal and poultry husbandry, by public-works employment, and by individual enterprises such as beekeeping, shopkeeping, and other such supplementary economic pursuits. On the farms, alternate-year dry-farming/fallow rotations are customary. Barley and wheat are the important cash crops and are harvested in the summer. Grapes are commonly grown and are harvested in October. Even in those parts of the region not important for wine production, a farm will generally have small grape arbors, from whose fruit a household will press its own wine. Sugar beets, introduced as a cash crop about fifty years ago, provide a winter harvest. Other common crops, grown for local consumption rather than for sale, are melons, pumpkins, carob beans, lentils, and chickpeas. Traditional farming methods—using a chisel-point plow, handsowing, weeding by hand-held hoe, and harvesting by scythe—have only slowly been replaced by mechanized means. Chemical fertilizers have slowly replaced manure since the early to mid-1950s. Animals are raised both for fieldwork and for food. Oxen, once the most important draft animals, have largely been replaced by mules. Sheep husbandry was once the heart of the Castilian economy, and in the eighteenth century huge flocks, raised for their wool, were common. Today, however, the number of sheep has declined drastically, and they are mostly raised for their meat,

which is an important component of the local diet. Of all animals raised for food, the pig is most important, and nearly every family raises one or two. Commercial swine herds began to be established in the 1960s, as did commercial poultry production. Large-scale cattle-raising operations exist in some parts of the region, where pasturage makes it possible. A very important nonagricultural product is pine resin, from which tar, turpentine, and other resin derivatives are made. Forestry-based industries have always been under strict state control, and they can only be carried out in compliance with the regulations of the local forest district office. Even when trees are on privately held property, there are strictly enforced rules regarding the start and end of tapping season, which trees may be cut, and whether or not new forests may be opened up for exploitation.

Industrial Arts. There are few industries in rural Castile. Sawmills and the production of pine-resin derivatives are two such enterprises. In the past, local artisans crafted the tools, utensils, and other consumer goods used by the villagers of Castile, but today the people are more likely to depend upon the stores of the neighboring towns or cities to provide such items.

Trade. Items produced regionally for export to the rest of the country and beyond Spain's borders include pine-resin products, meat, dairy, and poultry products, cereals, and, in some areas, wine and sugar beets.

Division of Labor. In Castile, the division of labor according to sex is best understood according to the distinction between the public and private spheres—to males belongs the world of paid labor, to females the domestic tasks. This division is not complete, however, for it is crosscut by considerations of class and by the demands of the household farm. Generally speaking, in poorer households, a woman may need to seek paid employment in order to supplement the otherwise inadequate cash income of her husband. In any case, the heavy work of farming and all specialized agricultural and forestal jobs are the province of men. The task of threshing wheat falls to the male youths of the farm household. While economic necessity may force a woman to take on paid domestic work or seek employment in a local shop without seriously damaging her reputation, there is no such mitigating circumstance to justify a man's assumption of "woman's work"—a man who does so is simply not considered a "real" man.

Land Tenure. Agricultural land is privately owned, in smallholdings. The pine forests are owned by the _communidad_, a group of neighboring villages. This form of organization derives from medieval times, when clusters of villages and hamlets were under the authority of a ruling lord who maintained his seat in a nearby city. These affiliated settlements held large tracts of land, much of it forested, in common under the dominion of the lord. Although the individual settlements eventually achieved politically independent status as _municipios_ in the sixteenth century, their confederation in the communidads remained in place with regard to forests and pasture lands. Today, the primary role of the communidad is to apportion the income realized from commonly held lands and to regulate the use of such lands in order to protect future income. For the pine forests, this means that the rights to harvest the trees or their resin—but not the property rights to the land itself—are periodically allocated by communidad authorities.

Kinship

Kinship is reckoned bilaterally. Fictive kinship in the form of godparenthood is of social and ritual importance, but as godparents tend to be chosen from within the bilaterally determined consanguinal kin circle (grandparents, aunts, or uncles) it does not usually result in the extension of kin-based rights and obligations beyond the preexisting family group. The single most important kin group is the nuclear family. The term *pariente* (kinsman) refers to all consanguineal relatives, but family loyalty tends largely to focus on one's siblings and parents. This loyalty, however, is frequently contradicted by disputes, particularly over inheritance.

Marriage and Family

Marriage.   Marriage is a milestone in the lives of individuals and for the community. Young village girls will pray to the saints to bring them husbands, and fiestas are occasions for girls to flirt with the boys they favor. For males, it is only upon marriage that full adult status is achieved. It is nearly unheard of for a male to marry prior to the completion of his national military service, and couples do not care to marry before achieving at least a minimal degree of independence, so that couples tend to postpone marriage until about the age of twenty-five. There is strong social pressure for individuals to marry within their own socioeconomic class. When exceptions occur, they usually involve a male of higher class and status marrying "beneath" his station—rarely the other way around. Marriages between first cousins can and do occur, but they require special church dispensation. Parents exercise a great deal of control in the selection of their children's prospective spouses, but they do not arrange the actual match. Rather, a young man and woman will develop an interest in one another, and should they desire marriage the young man will formally request that the woman's parents consider him as a formal suitor. Upon the acquiescence of the woman's parents, the couple may begin holding hands in public, and they are invited to social occasions together. Propriety is carefully maintained during courtship, for not only the reputation of the couple but also that of their respective families may be damaged by scandal. A young woman is expected to be modest and, above all, chaste before marriage. Upon becoming formally engaged, the bride-to-be begins to prepare her trousseau of linen and clothing, all finely embroidered by the young woman, or handed down to her by her mother. In much of Castile, the groom pays a small sum (traditionally not to exceed 10 percent of his fortune, now often a token sum). Until relatively recently, marriages throughout Spain were recognized only when consecrated by the church, but with the introduction of laws allowing religious choice in the 1960s, civil ceremonies became permissible. Still it remains rare for a couple to marry outside of the church in most of Castile. The ceremony is held in the parish church of the bride. During the ceremony, a white veil is held over the bride's head and the groom's shoulders, to symbolize the submissive role a proper wife should adopt toward her husband. Spiritual sponsors (godparents) stand with the bride and groom at the ceremony. These traditionally were the father of the bride and the mother of the groom, but they now may be aunts and uncles or influential friends. There are strong prohibitions against adultery and divorce.

Domestic Unit.   A new domestic unit is established with marriage, and it is expected that a couple will live apart from the parents of either spouse. However, the parents of the new bride usually will provide substantial assistance in the purchase or building of the new home, so that the couple generally takes up residence in the vicinity of the bride's parents.

Inheritance.   Inheritance is bilateral—each child can expect to inherit an equal share of each parent's property.

Socialization.   Child rearing is a mother's responsibility. The relation between father and child is distant, and it remains so between father and son throughout their lives. Concern for the good name of oneself and one's family in the face of possible gossip or censure is very high.

Sociopolitical Organization

Social Organization.   There are three broad social classes represented in the region: a small upper class consisting of families descending from the old nobility, wealthy industrialists, and high government officials; a small middle class of professionals, government functionaries, and the clergy; and a predominantly agricultural working class. The first two categories are largely urban—in the villages, most residents share similar opportunities and access to resources, at least in principle, so that an egalitarian ethic is the rule. Informal authority is conceded to a villager on the basis of age, economic success, or other personal qualities. Castilian village society is highly individualistic, with weak, limited institutional venues for cooperative action. One such institution is the *cofradia*, or lay religious society, which is dedicated to the veneration of a specific saint and cooperates in the planning of Lenten ceremonies and processions.

Social Control and Conflict.   In the villages, the strongest mechanism for social control is the fear of loss of reputation. While municipal authorities can and do enforce public law, behaviors are kept in check informally through the fear of incurring the disapprobation of one's neighbors, of inciting gossip and scandal.

Religion and Expressive Culture

Religious Beliefs.   Within predominantly Catholic Spain, Castile has the reputation of being one of the most religiously conservative regions. Church attendance by both men and women is generally high on Sundays and holy days of obligation, although it is usually only women who attend daily services. Religious belief and practice assume a rather personalized character in Castile as elsewhere in Spain, and cofradias (Catholic lay brotherhoods and sisterhoods devoted to particular saints) are important to community and ritual life. In 1967, the passage of the Religious Liberty Law granted rights of free worship for non-Catholics throughout Spain, but the country and the region of Castile remain strongly Catholic.

Religious Practitioners.   The village priest has traditionally exercised a great deal of authority over his congregation regarding questions of the faith and secular affairs, but this control appears to be somewhat on the wane.

Ceremonies. Within the liturgical calendar of the Catholic church, the most important ceremonial occasions are Christmas and Easter, as well as the feast day for the patron saint of the village, when nearly everyone will attend mass regardless of their usual level of church attendance during the rest of the year. But much of Castilian ceremonial life, although tied to the religious calendar, has a strong secular flavor as well. The patron saint's feast day is the occasion for a village-wide fiesta, planned by village officials and involving soccer matches, bullfights, dances, band concerts, and fireworks. A parade of _gigantes_ (giants) and _cabezudos_ (big heads) marches through the streets of the village, headed by a band playing spirited tunes. The gigantes are 3-meter-tall effigies of Ferdinand and Isabella made of huge papier-mâché heads over long robes that conceal the man carrying them. Cabezudos are papier-mâché heads depicting historical, ethnic, and fantasy caricatures and also are worn by men. Life-cycle events (baptism, marriage, funerals) involve churchly ritual.

Arts. Castile possesses a long and brilliant artistic heritage—a result in part of its historic role as the seat of the Spanish court, with its provision of royal patronage. Today Castilian participation in the arts remains vital and ranges through the various musical genres (today including everything from rock to opera), the visual arts and architecture, film, theater, literature, and bullfighting. Outside of Spain, the most famous of Castile's literary figures is Cervantes. But this great productivity in the arts retains little ethnic specificity, unlike the distinctive regional flavor of works produced by Andalusians, for example, or Catalans. This universality, too, may be the result of Castile's heritage as the seat of Spanish government, and the cosmopolitanism of its courtly, and later governmental, patrons. Except locally—and for certain ceremonial practices, such as the processions of the big heads and giants—Castilian artistic production has come to draw on influences originating throughout the Spanish culture as a whole, and/or to participate in the larger, international sphere, rather than to celebrate or reaffirm regional or folk themes.

Medicine. Modern medical care and facilities are available and used throughout Castile, as is the case for nearly all of Spain. Folk medical practices have, as a result, largely been lost. While in the more remote, rural areas there may still be some reliance on herbal remedies, and while it is still not uncommon to find people seeking the intervention of one or another saint in the case of illness or injury, such practices and beliefs are secondary to modern medical treatment.

Death and the Afterlife. Mortuary belief and practice are conducted within the general context of Catholicism. The priest officiates over funerals and also confers the sacrament of extreme unction. The body of the deceased is interred after an appropriate mass has been said. Friends and close relatives of the bereaved are expected to provide support, beginning with their willingness to keep vigil over the corpse until burial. The body is carried in its coffin to the church in which a burial mass is said, then to the ceremony for burial, which traditionally is attended only by men. Throughout Castile, the family of the deceased traditionally hosted a funeral banquet, but this practice has fallen into disuse. The hiring of paid mourners and the distribution of food to the poor in conjunction with burials are two other traditional customs that now

are encountered less frequently. A widow is expected to assume black mourning clothing, or at least a black head scarf.

Bibliography

Aceves, Joseph (1971). _Social Change in a Spanish Village._ Cambridge, Mass.: Schenkman.

Hooper, John (1986). _The Spaniards: A Portrait of the New Spain._ New York: Viking.

Kenny, Michael (1961). _A Spanish Tapestry: Town and Country in Old Castile._ London: Cohen & West.

NANCY E. GRATTON

Catalans (Països Catalans)

ETHNONYM: Catalonians

Orientation

Identification. Catalans can be defined by participation in the historical polity of Catalonia, which occupies the northwest Mediterranean coast and eastern Pyrenees. Some areas of the formerly independent political unit now form separate regions in contemporary Spain and France: Valencia, the Balearics, and Rosselló (Pyrénées Orientales). Andorra constitutes an independent state. Together these are known as the "Països Catalans" (Catalan countries). The traditional primary language of the polity is Catalan, a Romance language, although most inhabitants are bilingual (in Spanish or French). In the contemporary Països Catalans—after two centuries of industrial development and immigration—language, residence, cultural traits (food, arts, etc.), heritage, and political affiliation are complex and ambivalent markers of ethnic, class, and national membership.

Location. Catalonia is located between 40° and 42° N and 0° and 3° E. Rosselló lies at about 42° N and between 1° and 4° E. Valencia falls between 38° and 40° N and 2° W and 1° E. The Balearic Islands lie between 38° and 40° N and between 1° and 4° E. The total land surface is 69,032 square kilometers; in Spain, the Països Catalans occupy 13 percent of the land surface while in France, Rosselló occupies less than 1 percent of the land surface. The countryside is predominantly mountainous, dropping from the Pyrenees (above 3,000 meters) and the Iberian system to the Mediterranean coast. The most important rivers, the Ebre (Ebro) and Xúquer (Júcar), originate outside the Països Catalans, while the rest of the hydrographic network consists of small, intermittent rivers that flood periodically. The climate is Mediterranean, characterized by a season in which heat and dryness coincide from June to September, with strong rains in September/October and April/May. The eastern and southern regions are extremely arid (less than 30 centimeters precipitation per year).

Demography.   Regional populations of the Països Catalans are: Catalonia, 6,079,903 (1987); Valencia, 2,918,714 (1987); Balearics, 671,233 (1987); Roselló, 349,100 (1986); and Andorra, 49,976 (1986). Catalans constitute 28 percent of the population of Spain; Catalans in France, by contrast, represent less than 1 percent of the national population. Population density averages 176 persons per square kilometer, and the population is stable. Approximately 9,000,000 speak Catalan; almost all are bilingual. Immigrants account for the majority of Spanish or French monolinguals.

Linguistic Affiliation.   Catalan is a Romance language derived from Latin and written with the Roman alphabet. It has 7 vowels and 27 consonants. Dialects are associated with the historical divisions previously cited, including Valencian, Mallorquí, Menorquí, and Eivissenc.

History and Cultural Relations

Settlement in Catalonia antedates historical records, with Paleolithic and Neolithic remains. Successive immigrations have included Celts, Iberians, Phoenicians, Greeks, Romans (who established a capital in Tarragona in the first century B.C.E.), Jews, Visigoths, Arabs, and Gypsies. Barcelona was reconquered from the Arabs in 801 and became capital of the Frankish county of Catalonia. Catalonia became independent about 988, uniting with the Kingdom of Aragon in the twelfth century. Balears and Valencia were reconquered from Arab domination in the thirteenth century. The Catalan-Aragonese empire also extended into Sardinia, Naples, Sicily, and Greece as its mercantile society and culture flourished. At the end of the fifteenth century, its population neared 700,000. In 1469, King Ferdinand of Aragon and Catalonia wed queen Isabella of Castile and Leon, uniting the two kingdoms that became the foundation of Spain. For centuries thereafter, Catalans struggled to preserve political and cultural autonomy as the Mediterranean region lost power to Atlantic states. Bids for independence were defeated by the central state in 1640–1659 (at which time Roselló was incorporated into France) and in the early eighteenth century. Nonetheless, the subsequent growth of trade with Spain's New World colonies and of industry, especially textiles, gave Catalonia new economic power in the nineteenth century. In the twentieth century, a rich Catalonia has attracted immigrants from the rest of Spain while seeking to redefine its relationship to the centralized state. Under the Second Spanish Republic (1931–1939), especially during the Spanish Civil War of 1936–1939, Catalans sought new forms of autonomous government; Franco's victory brought an intense repression of the polity, its culture, and its language. Under the Spanish democratic regime (1977–), the Països Catalans have regained autonomy within the reorganized state, and a revitalization of Catalan language and culture has been evident in Spain, with repercussions as well in France.

Settlements

Catalans have been urban for millennia. Major cities include Barcelona (with a metropolitan area of 3,000,000), Valencia, Palma de Mallorca, Tarragona, Perpinyà (Perpignan), Lleida, and Girona. All tend to be based on Roman models, although they have undergone extensive development subsequently, especially in the past century. Cities tend to be centered on civil, Catholic church, and commercial activities, which form a core network rather than occupying a single central space. The urban landscape is extremely dense, as is typical of the Mediterranean. Residences, long associated with professional quarters and workplaces, are now more often separated from work and tend to reflect class-linked variations on a shared pattern of multistory apartment buildings. The rural Països Catalans center on the *mas*, an agricultural household production unit, with dispersed populations in the north and larger villages in the south. Northern houses consist of extended-family dwellings above barns and storage areas, developed on a Roman pattern; southern houses are simpler but encompass wide variations. Since the industrial era, rural areas have been invaded from urban centers and, in the past twenty years, by intensive tourism, both internal and external.

Economy

Subsistence and Commercial Activities.   Roughly 10 percent of the active population of the Països Catalans is engaged in agriculture, with 45 percent in industry and 45 percent in service. The last is the most productive sector (60 percent of the net product), mainly because of international tourism.

Agricultural production is dominated by arboriculture: citrus, grapes, and olives, all of which are now highly industrialized in production. The need for irrigation constrains other crops, although rice is characteristic of Valencian agriculture and cuisine. The typical production unit is a *horta* (*huerta*), a small, single-family irrigated garden of less than one hectare. These gardens produce domestic foodstuffs as well as flowers and specialties for urban markets. Domestic animals may include cattle, pigs, and sheep, but milk and meat products are generally industrialized. Fishing, despite a long economic and cultural tradition, has largely disappeared.

The Països Catalans lack natural energy resources for industry; growth relied on imported fuels until the construction of nuclear reactors. Cottage industries in the eighteenth century gave way to family-controlled urban factories and rural mill towns (*colònies*) in the nineteenth. Textiles were the foundation of growth; chemicals, leather, construction materials, automobiles, and appliances have also been important, organized as government or multinational corporations. Commerce and finance were linked to industrial growth, especially in the development of a petite bourgeoisie (shopkeeper and small merchant) infrastructure.

Division of Labor.   This follows gender and class. Women of rural and working-class households participate actively in the production process; middle-class and upper-class women have been less incorporated into the labor market than in similar developed areas. Class division has been a source of conflict for centuries.

Land Tenure.   The Països Catalans are typified by small and medium landholdings; even among the bourgeoisie, money tends to be heavily invested in land, both rural and urban.

Kinship, Marriage, and Family

Kin Groups and Descent.   Traditional Catalan kinship is based on the stem family and a designated heir, generally an elder male. This pattern has been increasingly nuclearized in cities, although ties across generations remain strong. Descent is bilateral; kinship terminology is equivalent to the rest of Latin Europe with an emphasis on the nuclear family and designation of generational and affinal distance.

Marriage.   Catalans are monogamous, following Catholic tradition. Civil marriage has been permitted in Spain since 1968, divorce since the 1980s. Both were available earlier in France. There are no marriage rules beyond minimal Catholic exogamy, although land and economic interests have shaped marriages in rural areas as well as among urban elites. In rural traditions, the inheriting couple resides with the heir's family. Neolocal residence is more common in the city, although economic limitations on space may preclude it.

Domestic Unit.   Coresidence of the productive unit has been a cultural ideal, and the unit may include grandparents, siblings and families, children and spouses; this is more common in the countryside than in cities. The past three decades have seen a dramatic rupture in domestic relations throughout the Països Catalans.

Inheritance.   In Catalan customary law, two-thirds of the property was given to the designated heir, and the rest was divided equally among all surviving children, including the heir, constituting the dowry or a professional stake for other siblings. After 1555, three-quarters was allotted to the heir. Customary law may still be invoked, but generally equipartite division seems to dominate, at least in cities.

Socialization.   Children are raised primarily by mothers with help of other female kin or servants. Fathers have variable but limited involvement. Schooling was dominated by the Roman Catholic church until the establishment of post-Franco governments, which have greatly expanded all youth services.

Sociopolitical Organization

The Països Catalans today encompass regions in Spain and France and the independent state of Andorra.

Social Organization.   Catalan society, since the Middle Ages, has been divided into socioeconomic groups based on occupation, descent, wealth, and prestige markers (education, cultural goods). Medieval and early modern categories of nobility, clergy, merchants, and artisans have given way since the nineteenth century to modern capitalist divisions. Successive waves of modern immigrants have been incorporated as workers with marked social and cultural discrimination. Conflict has been intense and often violent.

Political Organization.   The Països Catalans now comprise three autonomous Spanish regions and eight provinces—Catalunya (four provinces), the Comunitat Valenciana (three), Illes Balears (one)—as well as a French department and the Principat of Andorra, administered by _sindics_ representing its joint rulers, the bishop of the Seu d'Urgell and the president of France. Local administration is heavily fragmented. Municipal and autonomous governments ("Generalitats" in Catalonia and Valencia, the "Consell" in Balears) have been elected by universal suffrage in Spain since 1977. France has a longer tradition, but in Andorra voting citizens account for only 25 percent of the population. Spain and France have party systems in which class

and nationalist interests are debated. Services are distributed among all levels of government. Taxes are paid to municipal governments and to the state, which redistributes part of them: the Spanish national budget is 25 percent for local administrations, 10 percent for autonomous regions, and 65 percent for national services. Països Catalan citizens also vote for European parliament members and participate in Common Market programs.

Social Control.   Values of authority, tradition, and the importance of appearance are inculcated through school, home, and church. Formal systems of control include police, prisons, and the army, organs of the national state against which Catalan governments have attempted to construct their own agencies. Conflict between Catalonia and the central state, as well as internal class conflicts, have been recurrent themes of Catalan history.

Religion and Expressive Culture

Religious Beliefs and Practices.   For centuries, the Roman Catholic church has provided the dominant belief system, while also being an important actor in Catalan society. This identification of the Catholic church and Catalan culture has been weakened by industrialization, secularism, and cultural contact. Most Catalans are Catholic by baptism and observe other Catholic life-cycle rites, but many do not practice regularly. Only one-third of those in Spanish Catalonia identified themselves as Catholic in 1988. Jews lived in the area until their expulsion in the early modern period; synagogues and mosques are now found in Barcelona and other metropolitan centers as a result of recent immigration. There are also active Protestant and evangelical communities, the latter including many Gypsies. Religious leaders are generally specialized males, but Catalonia also has many men and women in religious orders in schools and charity work as well as monasteries and convents.

Ceremonies.   The religiously based calendar, now secularized and politicized, includes: New Year's Day (January 1); Reis (Epiphany and distribution of gifts, January 6); Carnestoltes (Carnivals); Pasqua Florida (Easter); Pasqua Granada (Pentecost); Sant Jordi (feast of Saint George, the patron saint, April 23); a group of primarily summer festivals of fire and fireworks—Sant Josep (feast of Saint Joseph, or "Falles" in Valencia, March 19), Sant Antoni (feast of Saint Anthony, June 13, in Balears), Sant Joan (feast of Saint John, June 24) and Sant Pere (feast of Saint Peter, June 29); Dia dels Difunts (Day of the Dead, November 2); and Nadal (Christmas, December 25). Sunday is the general weekly holiday. Saints and apparitions of the Virgin Mary figure in regional and local cycles as well as folklore, legend, toponyms, and personal names.

Arts.   Catalan culture is one of the richest in Europe, traceable to the artistic, architectural, and literary golden age in the Middle Ages and early modern period. Urban, elite, and educated culture has coexisted with folk traditions to the present. Urban culture declined in the seventeenth and eighteenth centuries, but it revived in the nineteenth century with the growth of industrial wealth. Catalan expression, however, was limited by Francoist repression. Well-known figures from the Països Catalans, important in development of local and international culture, include: Ramon Llull, Ausiàs Marc, and Ramon Muntaner in early writings; Salvador Espriu, Vincente Blasco Ibáñez, and Llorenç Villalonga in contemporary literature; Salvador Dalí, Joan Miró, and Pablo Picasso (formative period) in painting; Antoni Gaudí, Aristides Maillol, and Josep Lluís Sert in architecture and plastic arts; and Pablo Casals and Montserrat Caballé in music. Folk traditions of note include music and dancing, especially the *sardana*, a Mediterranean circle dance that has become a national symbol; gastronomy and wine; ceramics; and various forms of textile design.

Bibliography

Elliott, J. H. (1963). *The Revolt of the Catalans: A Study in the Decline of Spain (1598–1640)*. Cambridge: Cambridge University Press.

Gran enciclopedia catalana (1968–1980). 15 vols. Barcelona: Editorial Gran, Enciclopedia Catalana. 2nd ed. forthcoming.

Hansen, Edward (1977). *Rural Catalonia under the Franco Regime: The Fate of Rural Culture since the Spanish Civil War.* Cambridge: Cambridge University Press.

McDonogh, Gary (1986). *Good Families of Barcelona: A Social History of Power in the Industrial Era.* Princeton: Princeton University Press.

Vilar, Pierre (1962). *La Catalogne dans l'Espagne moderne.* Paris: S.E.V.P.E.N.

Woolard, Kathryn A. (1989). *Double Talk: Bilingualism and the Politics of Ethnicity in Catalonia.* Stanford: Stanford University Press.

CARLES CARRERAS AND GARY W. McDONOGH

Cornish

ETHNONYM: Kernow

Orientation

Cornwall, the southwesternmost county of England, was so long isolated from the rest of the country by virtue of its geography that its linguistic and cultural traditions developed under a unique set of pressures and influences. The name "Cornwall" refers to the geographic entity, while "Cornish" is the name of the indigenous language—a Brythonic dialect of the Celtic Family, related to Welsh. At its height it is estimated that there were no more than 30,000 native Cornish speakers, restricted to the geographic confines of the Cornish peninsula. As early as the tenth and eleventh centuries, the effects of Anglicization were strongly noticeable, and the Cornish tongue soon came to be thought of as the speech of the uneducated, unlike the situation in Wales where the in-

digenous tongue retained some cachet as a language of poetry and of erudition. The language became extinct in the vernacular with the death of the last fluent native speaker in 1777, but it has profited in this century from a Cornish cultural revival, and it has begun to be taught in the schools. For all Cornish speakers of today, however, English is the first language.

Cornwall is technically a peninsula, but the landmass is almost completely separated from the remainder of the country by the River Tamar, and it boasts the longest coastline of all the English counties.

History and Cultural Relations

The archaeological record shows that the Cornish peninsula was inhabited as long ago as the Paleolithic period, but the evidence of these earliest inhabitants is scanty. The first substantial archaeological sites date to the Mesolithic period and suggest a hunting and gathering population. This life-style was supplanted during the Neolithic period by the more sedentary practices of farming and animal husbandry, and it is to this period that the first monumental construction in the region belongs. The Cornish landscape is dotted with a great many "quoits" (also called dolmens and cromlechs) that are believed to have been chamber tombs. These distinctive structures consist of large upright stones topped by a large flat stone. Later arrivals to the area (approximately 1800 B.C.) were the "Beaker folk," who migrated from the European continent and brought with them a particular style of pottery and more elaborate burial practices. More important, these newcomers introduced mining and smelting to the area, beginning Cornwall's long association with tin mining that continues to this day. It is, however, with the arrival of the Celts from their homelands in eastern Europe, in the final centuries B.C., that we find the beginnings of what was to become the Cornish language. These Celtic settlers are also the likely source of the nonnucleated pattern of settlement that characterized Cornwall for most of its history.

The Roman invasion of Britain appears to have had little practical impact on the inhabitants of Cornwall. No Roman towns have been found further west than Exeter, so it seems contact must have been limited to trading and tax-collecting visits. However, the arrival of the Romans marked the beginning of Cornwall's economic and political incorporation into the larger entity of England as part of the Roman Empire. When Roman rule ended in the fifth century A.D., the trajectory of Cornish development once again diverged from that of the rest of England: each area faced invasion, but while the interlopers in eastern and southeastern England were of Germanic descent, in Cornwall the invaders were settlers from Ireland. Anglo-Saxon influences eventually did expand westward, but it was not until near the end of the tenth century that Cornwall was wholly incorporated in the political rubric of the newly united kingdom of England, and its county border was set at the Tamar. Never again would Cornwall or the Cornish people regain political independence. It is to this period that the Arthurian legend—originally a tale of a strong Cornish king who would free his people from English rule—may be dated. Arthurian sites include the River Camel, from which comes Camelot, and most importantly the castle of Tintagel, where Arthur is said to have been born.

Economy

The Cornish economy was traditionally associated with farming and animal husbandry (specifically, sheep farming), tin and copper mining, and the exploitation of the resources of the sea—a trilogy of pursuits that remains today, with the recent addition of tourism. Cornish agriculture traditionally focused on wheat, with some rye being sown in the poorer soils. Potatoes and some vegetables grown for the larger English market have become important, but Cornwall remains somewhat disadvantaged in terms of access to efficient transport for its goods. In upland areas, sheep raising and dairying have taken on greater importance. Maritime pursuits remain important to the Cornish economy as well, although the days of the legendary Cornish pirates, smugglers, and "wreckers" (who plundered the cargoes of ships that foundered on the rocky coast) are now past. The latter illicit activities once provided an important source of income for the coastal dwellers of Cornwall.

Sociopolitical Organization

The Cornish are, of course, integrated into the larger English polity, but the 1950s brought the formation of the Sons of Cornwall (Mebyon Kernow), a group dedicated to the preservation of Cornish customs and linguistic traditions, but also strongly committed to the concept of a domestically self-governing Cornwall. While the impact of this group has been rather small on the national level, its participation in and influence on local politics has been great in recent times.

Religion and Expressive Culture

The Cornish today are largely Wesleyan Methodist, although other denominations are represented among the population as well. But in the rich folklore and customary practices among the people, one can still find references to pre-Christian beliefs of pagan Celtic origin. The process of Christianization, however, began as early as the second century and was well established by around A.D. 600. The Celtic church enjoyed a certain independence from the practice of Anglo-Saxon "coreligionists" until well into the eighth century. Cornwall was not, however, exempt from the religious strife that plagued Britain, and the clash between Catholic and Protestant forces led Cornwall into direct, and ultimately futile, confrontation with the crown in the 1500s. The ultimate triumph of Protestantism in England eventually made itself felt even in this former bastion of Catholicism. Cornish cultural revival efforts have led to a resurgence of interest in, and performance of, the traditional "mystery plays," a Christian-era tradition dramatizing the lives of local saints.

Bibliography

Halliday, F. E., ed. (1969). *Carew's Survey of Cornwall, 1602.* London.

Hatcher, J. (1970). *Rural Economy and Society in the Duchy of Cornwall.* Cambridge: Cambridge University Press.

Soulsby, I. (1986). *A History of Cornwall.* Chichester, U.K.: Phillimore.

NANCY E. GRATTON

Corsicans

ETHNONYMS: les Corses (French), i Corsi (Corsican)

Orientation

Identification.   Corsicans are the native inhabitants of the Mediterranean island of Corsica, now part of France. Corsicans consider themselves a distinct ethnic group, a claim which is vigorously promoted by the Corsican nationalist movement.

Location.   Corsica lies in the central Mediterranean Sea, 168 kilometers from Provence but only 81 kilometers from Tuscany, and separated from the Italian island of Sardinia to the south only by the 11-kilometer-wide straits of Bonifacio. Corsica is the most mountainous island of the Mediterranean. Its topography has a rugged beauty but poor soils: 40 percent of the land area is covered by the *maquis,* or *macchia,* a form of vegetation that signals land degradation in the Mediterranean region; 20 percent is covered by forests; and 25 percent is suitable for pasture. Only a small (and declining) portion of the island is cultivated. The lowland plains are the only highly productive agricultural areas; yet until the postwar era, these were malarial and little used. The Corsican landscape is characterized by three altitudinal zones: coastal, dominated by the low bushes of the maquis with a few oak and olive forests; mountain, where forests of chestnut, evergreens, oak, and beech are common; and subalpine, dominated by pine forests to the tree line, above which may be found natural pasture. Unlike most of the Mediterranean islands, Corsica receives abundant precipitation, averaging 88 centimeters per year, most of which falls in the winter. In locales above 1,000 meters, precipitation normally falls in the form of snow from December until April.

Demography.   The present population of Corsica is 240,000 inhabitants, and its population density, only 28 persons per square kilometer, is one of the lowest in Europe. Since the turn of the century, Corsica has been steadily depleted of her people, and today the majority of all Corsicans (one-half to two-thirds, according to different estimates) live outside of Corsica, with Marseille being the largest Corsican town. Of the 360 communes on the island, 316 have a natural population decrease (deaths outnumbering births) because of the exodus of the island's youth. Unemployment and underemployment are blamed for the high emigration levels, although the lack of higher education on the island is also an important factor. The economic consequences of this demographic decline are great, thus further contributing to the downward spiral of underdevelopment. During the 1960s, the island's population was boosted by the repatriation of French colonials from Algeria, and now 10 percent of Corsica's population are such "Pieds Noirs" immigrants. Immigration since then has included large numbers of North Africans, who do primarily low-status, menial jobs, as well as continental French, employed especially in high-status positions. Of the 240,000 island residents, only 166,600 (69.4 percent) are of Corsican origin (of whom 86 percent are island-born); 33,600 (14 percent) are of continental French origin; and 39,800 (16.6 percent) are of foreign origin.

Linguistic Affiliation.   Standard French is the official language in Corsica, and it is the language of education, the media, the workplace, the government, and upward mobility. The local language, however, is Corsican (Corsu), which is spoken as a native tongue by decreasing numbers of inhabitants (despite the efforts of nationalists to revive the language). Corsican is of the Latin Family of languages and closest to the rural dialects of Tuscany, but it has no standard form and varies greatly.

History and Cultural Relations

Invaded and colonized through the centuries by Phoenicians, Greeks, Carthaginians, Romans, Vandals, Byzantines, Ostrogoths, Lombards, Saracens, Tuscans, Genoese, Spaniards, English, and French, the original inhabitants of Corsica are known today only by their megalithic monuments. For the early seafaring empires of the Mediterranean, the islands were important stopping places in their commercial and military sea routes; of these groups, the Romans were the most influential rulers and provided the longest period of peace the island has known in historic times. From the Romans, the pastoral Corsicans inherited the olive tree, the vine, new cereal crops, irrigation, the Latin language, and, eventually, Christianity, as well as a number of ports and towns along the coast. But the Vandal and other invasions of the Dark Ages destroyed most of the Roman settlements and pushed the islanders inland, away from the coasts, which remained abandoned until modern times. In 1077 the pope gave Corsica to the bishop of Pisa, ushering in a half-millennia of conflict and competition between the European powers of Pisa, Genoa, Aragon, and France for control over the island. Throughout the seventeenth century, Genoa ruled unchallenged; however, the coasts were subject to virtually constant raids by pirates from northern Africa and Turkey, attacks which did not cease until the nineteenth century. The eighteenth century was marked by local rebellions, which weakened foreign domination, and by struggles between France, England, and Genoa for sovereignty. In 1755, Corsican nationalists declared independence, driving the Genoese to take refuge in the fortified coastal cities. In 1768 Genoa ceded the island to France, which defeated the nationalists, but the movement reemerged during the French Revolution, and Corsicans again declared their independence in 1793. The eighteenth century closed with skirmishes between nationalists, sometimes supported by the British, and the Napoleonic army, whose victory finally ensured that Corsica remained within French control. Since then, Corsicans have worked and fought along with France, in her civil service, military, colonies, and wars. Initially this peace encouraged a period of development and dynamism in the island: small-scale industrialization began and the population grew to its highest levels ever, about 280,000–300,000. By the close of the last century, however, the trend was already slowing and reversing: competition from France's north African colonies undermined Corsican agricultural exports, industries began to close, and emigration accelerated. The combined effects of emigration and losses suffered during the two world wars brought the population level to its lowest point in modern times, about 150,000 in 1954. The postwar eradication of malaria in Corsica, endemic in the coastal areas at least since the Christian era, signaled Corsica's transformation into a

modern society. Corsican modernization has been characterized by the underdevelopment and withering of traditional resources, especially agriculture; the widespread emigration of Corsicans; the immigration of Pieds Noirs colonists, followed by Sardinian and then North African laborers; the founding of a new, large-scale coastal agricultural industry, largely by the Pieds Noirs, with French government financing and North African labor; the development of a mass-tourism industry; and the growing importance of economic aid from the central French government in pensions, welfare, subsidies, etc. These developments have caused disillusionment and bitterness among many Corsicans, leading to the rise of a militant and occasionally violent nationalist movement. Beyond the general pattern, the turbulent history of the island has left the stamp of heterogeneity on Corsican culture: each part of the island evolved particular cultural patterns as a result of the various local experiences of subjection and local methods of accommodating and resisting the dominators.

Settlements

Today, the greater part of Corsica's population (54 percent) is concentrated in the two main cities, Ajaccio and Bastia; 80 percent of the island's 360 communes have less than 500 inhabitants, 60 percent less than 200. The interior highlands most clearly show the effects of the Corsican exodus; many villages are left with only a few individuals as permanent residents. These inland villages also have the oldest populations, with one-third of Corsica's elderly (60 years and older). Formerly, the majority of Corsicans were concentrated in the rural villages of the interior.

In the interior, dressed-stone multistory buildings cluster on the hillsides in nucleated villages; often these stand today pristine and well maintained, as the emigrant villagers residing in distant cities return only during holidays to their ancestral homes. A few old fortified coastal cities of densely built housing laced by narrow medieval streets remain home to a dwindling population of traditional urbanites descended from the colonists of earlier eras. In the main cities of Ajaccio and Bastia, and along the rest of the coastal areas, modern housing and hotel developments predominate.

Economy

Subsistence and Commercial Activities.   Subsistence-oriented production, although the mainstay of traditional Corsica, varied widely from region to region in the degree of dependence upon agriculture, pastoralism, and other types of primary production. Most areas practiced mixed agropastoralism, incorporating the ecosystems of different elevations for transhumance and to produce different crops; agriculture was clearly dominant in only two regions. The northeast was unusual because agriculture and livestock raising, especially pigs, were overshadowed by the importance of the chestnut forests; the nuts were ground into flour or used as fodder. The abundance of this resource allowed for one of the highest population densities of rural Europe in earlier times. Many of the coastal areas were abandoned as permanent sites for residences and for most agriculture and were used primarily as winter pasture by transhumant shepherds from higher elevations. In some of the more mountainous regions transhumant pastoralism was of paramount importance, agriculture being a more marginal and supplementary occupation. Fishing, combined with agriculture, was of basic importance only on the Cap Corse Peninsula. Today, traditional agriculture has been virtually abandoned and pastoralism has declined severely. Modern, large-scale agriculture is profitable only in the formerly abandoned lowland plains of the coastal areas.

The collapse of the traditional economy has created severe employment problems for Corsicans, leading to high levels of emigration. The new large-scale, coastal agriculture is dominated by non-Corsicans (Pieds Noirs owners and North African laborers), thus doing nothing to combat the problems of unemployment and emigration of Corsicans. The export orientation of modern agriculture and the decline of pastoralism have led to increased dependency on food imports.

Industrial Arts.   The major industry on the island is tourism, which is growing rapidly: tourism generates revenues double that of agriculture and triple that of building and public works, the next-largest sector. However, tourism is dominated by national and international capital, employment is seasonal and dominated by non-Corsicans (43 percent French and 29 percent foreign), and most of the goods and food required by the tourists must be imported; thus, few Corsicans benefit from the tourism boom that brings millions of visitors annually to the island. There is almost no other industry, except construction and public works; Corsica is almost completely dependent on imports.

Trade.   Corsica exports mainly wine and small amounts of citrus fruits, wood, cork, and other products; the percentage of exports to imports in 1979 was only 22 percent. Symbolic of the economic dependence of the island on the central state is the fact that the single largest employer in Corsica is the state.

Division of Labor.   The traditional division of labor was based on the intersecting principles of gender, social status, and age. The social status of the *signori*, the upper class, was marked by their withdrawal from manual labor; for the women of this strata, this implied seclusion within the home to a greater or lesser degree. Among the peasants, however, everyone worked. Under normal circumstances, with a balanced family grouping, the division of labor by gender was well defined and exclusive; only under exceptional circumstances would an individual undertake tasks assigned to the opposite sex. Women's responsibilities included domestic work; food preparation; care of the young, the elderly, and the ill; gardening; fetching water; supervising the ripening of the cheeses; harvesting or collecting olives, chestnuts, wild fruits, and wood. Men were responsible for most of the agricultural tasks, herding, woodcutting, hunting, and defense. The allocation of specialized occupations varied regionally. In the highly stratified villages of the south, for example, the shepherds comprised the lowest social class, segregated from the other villagers; in the more egalitarian villages of the northeast this hierarchy of occupations was generational within the family, with the landowning peasant father being in charge of agriculture and his sons herding until their inheritance of the land allowed them to take over the agricultural tasks. In the more pastoral regions, however, shepherding was a high-status occupation.

Land Tenure.   Although a small portion of the land in Corsica is considered state-owned, most is either privately owned or owned by the village communities. The ratio of private to communal lands varies greatly, some regions having primarily private landholdings and others primarily communal. The traditional pattern was typically to hold pasture lands in common and agricultural lands in private ownership.

Kinship, Marriage, and Family

Kinship.   The symbol of kinship is blood: the blood that is shared by kin, the blood that may be shed for kin. Blood ties are considered supreme and unbreakable; for example, a woman's closest ties are to her brothers, and later to her sons. Extended family ties are very important as the basis for political strength, and traditionally alliances were cemented by ties of marriage. Large kin groups were also economically important, particularly in areas characterized by communal ownership of land, where wealth depended on the number of people bringing in income from diverse sources. Kinship continues to be an important resource for emigrants, who depend on kin for assistance in the initial stages of the move and who maintain village ties and assist, in turn, those who may follow.

Marriage.   Marriage was traditionally arranged by the families; the bride and groom normally had little or no say in the choice of spouse. Parental consent could be circumvented by a variety of stratagems: the couple could run away together for a few days, thus compromising the woman's (and her family's) honor and forcing the parents to choose between the marriage and a vendetta; or the couple could announce publicly their intention to marry and allow the community to judge whether to sanction the union; or a man could try to force a marriage by abducting a reluctant young woman. These alternatives always carried the risk of embroiling both families in a vendetta if unsuccessful. Village endogamy was preferred, although *pieve* endogamy (i.e., marriage within a group of villages) was also practiced. Residence on marriage was normally patrilocal; unmarried adults usually lived with siblings.

Domestic Unit.   The family is a fundamental social unit in Corsican society. The individual is subordinate to the family in many ways and the strong sense of individualism in this culture is directed toward fulfilling familial roles and responsibilities. The father or eldest brother is the authority figurehead, although the eldest woman also wields considerable power over her sons and daughters-in-law. The symbol of the family is the house, the place of trust and secrecy.

Inheritance.   Traditionally, the general principle was that women received dowries and men inherited wealth from their natal families, but this was not a strict rule: it was modified by many other considerations, including marital status and residency, and varied throughout the island as well. Today, village property, especially in the mountainous areas, often is not divided and is inherited jointly, to ensure that those who wish to remain in the natal village will retain use rights to the family property. After several generations of emigration, sale of village property may become impossible, as this requires consent of all inheritors and their descendants.

Sociopolitical Organization

Social Organization.   The traditional Corsican village was more than an aggregate of families, more than physical geographic boundaries: it was a social unit of overlapping kin ties, maintained by preferential village endogamy; an economic unit that could ensure subsistence of its members through access to communal lands; and a moral entity characterized by strong social control and conformity of its members—that is, it was a corporate group with well-defined collective rights and responsibilities. The most important intervillage unit was the pieve, a grouping of villages which (typically) shared the same valley and was defined in terms of the limits of marriage exchange; this traditional social organization today is reflected in the boundaries of the French cantons.

Political Organization.   Corsica was annexed to France in 1769, and was made a department in 1789 at the request of the inhabitants. The island's 360 communes are organized into 62 cantons. It is the local village and island politics, however, which most excite people's passions, because of their long tradition of effective local self-government. Also, in this society where the village community is the most important social unit, the mayor is a man of great importance and wields significant power through his control of community property. The mayor is an elected representative, the head of the *partitu* with the greatest local support. The partitu (sometimes glossed as "clan") is an unstable alliance of families, kin groups, or other local political groupings. These political subgroups support one or another of the leaders according to a variety of criteria, including kinship, clientism, sentiment, loyalty to alliances, services promised or received, etc.; voting as a block, they can use their electoral support to lobby for privileges and services and to enhance their position within the community. Corsican municipal politics, therefore, are nonideological; ideas or principles are far less important than power itself (a variation of "might makes right"). Although one of the few means by which families are unified at the subvillage level, this system—characterized by polarization and instability and by passionate and sometimes violent election campaigns that involve all kinds of strategies and coercion—also intensifies intravillage conflict and factionalism. The partitu has not lost relevance in modern Corsica, and in fact it has expanded its traditional role as mediator between the local community and the outside world: today, for example, partitu leaders use their ability to obtain social benefits such as pensions and welfare from the state as a major advantage with which to bargain for political support.

Social Control and Conflict.   Traditionally, the lives of individuals living in the small, insular villages of the island were subject to very strong social control by the community, especially in terms of the pervasive cultural value of "honor." Gossip was the principal mechanism by which the community evaluated and judged the behavior of individuals and families; in extreme cases the vendetta, or blood feud, was employed to defend the family honor or enact justice or vengeance. A vendetta is usually between families, with responsibilities and limits defined in terms of degree of kinship distance from the perpetrator and victim; vendetta violence, however, varies considerably in intensity and frequency by region. State control and justice has traditionally been ineffective against indigenous forms of informal control, although today the vendetta is gradually losing prestige and it is becoming more and more acceptable to seek justice through the state legal system.

Religion and Expressive Culture

Religious Beliefs.   The majority of Corsicans are Roman Catholic, although previously (as late as World War II in some cases) beliefs in spirits, sorcerers, prophecy, and magic were also common. Women have traditionally been responsible for the religious life of the family, both in the Christian church and as the practitioners of the non-Christian beliefs.

Arts.   The most famous of the Corsican arts are verbal: song, chant, improvised poetry, lament, and story. These traditional skills have declined dramatically in the face of modernization and emigration, although there has been a minor renaissance in recent times, partly in conjunction with the new nationalist mood.

Bibliography

Bonneton, Christine, ed. (1984). *Corse.* Encyclopédies Régionales.

Caisson, M., C. Casanova, F. J. Casta, J. Defranceschi, F. Ettori, M. Giacomo-Marcellesi, J. C. Leca, F. Pomponi, and G. Ravis-Giordani (1978). *Pieve e Paesi: Communautés rurales corses.* Paris: Éditions du Centre National de la Recherche Scientifique.

Carrington, Dorothy (1971). *Granite Island: A Portrait of Corsica.* Longmans. Reprint. 1984. London: Penguin Books.

Holway, Bradley (1978). "Adaptation, Class, and Politics in Rural Corsica." Ph.D. dissertation, McGill University, Montreal.

Ravis-Giordani, Georges (1983). *Bergers corses: Les communautés villageoises du Niolu.* Aix-en-Provence: Edisud.

Renucci, Janine (1987). *La Corse.* Que sais-je? Paris: Presses Universitaires de France.

L. M. EDELSWARD

Cretans

ETHNONYMS: Krites (formal), Kritiki (demotic), Kritiči (dialect)

Orientation

Identification.   The Cretans, overwhelmingly Greek Orthodox Christians, speak dialect forms of Modern Greek and inhabit the island of Crete, which is midway between the

Greek mainland and Libya. Unofficially, the country dwellers are divided into plains folk (*kambites* or *katomerites*) and mountain dwellers (*aorites* or *anomerites*).

Location. Crete is located between 34° and 36° N and 23° and 27° E. There is a rainy season from October through March, with hot summer days at around 26° to 38° C at midday. Winter snows fall in the more mountainous areas; the Messara Plain, with relatively high winter rainfall and a dry summer, is especially fertile, but many areas of higher ground are rocky and deforested.

Demography. In 1981 the official population of Crete was 502,165. The three largest towns accounted for 32 percent of this figure (Iraklio, 101,634; Khania, 47,388; Rethimno, 17,736). While most rural communities have suffered continual demographic depletion since the early 1960s, mostly through emigration to West Germany and to Athens and Iraklio, a few highland communities on Psiloritis have actually increased in size because this trend has been offset by a high birthrate. Jewish communities in the main towns, small before World War II, were destroyed by the Germans; a small Catholic presence survives in Iraklio. The Armenian population, much of it composed of Asia Minor refugees, largely departed for Soviet Armenia in the late 1940s. There are a few Jehovah's Witnesses. Among the Greek Orthodox is a significant though scattered number of Old Calendrists (Paleoimeroloyites) who reject the adoption of the Gregorian calendar and celebrate religious holidays accordingly. No Muslims are left; after the compulsory population exchanges that followed the Treaty of Lausanne (1923), the significant but already depleted Muslim population (which had been about 36 percent of a total population of 279,165 in 1881) departed and was replaced by a far greater number of Orthodox Christian refugees from Asia Minor; this population increased by about 15 percent between 1913 and 1928, as against 20 percent in the previous thirty-two years. The refugees, although formally assimilated into the larger population, still retain a discernible identity and are treated by some indigenous Cretans with dislike.

Linguistic Affiliation. An early form of Greek appears in the later fifteenth century B.C., using the Linear B syllabary. Some pre-Hellenic toponyms still persist. Greek inscriptions appear again in the Archaic period and suggest the persistence of a pre-Dorian (Eteocretan) population until as late as the third century B.C. Some scholars believe that the modern Cretan dialects betray evidence of Doric derivation. While Cretan is clearly closer to Cypriot or Dodecanesian than to standard Greek, which it influenced through its literary renaissance under Venetian rule, it has retained a number of archaic syntactic forms and has borrowed heavily from the lexical stocks of both Venetian (Italian) and Turkish. City dwellers speak a more standardized form of Greek, and the local dialects, having no formal status in the educational system or the media, are increasingly yielding to social pressure and official indifference. The Greek alphabet, used even for dialect publications (mostly of folklore or local literature), does not represent all local phonological features successfully.

History and Cultural Relations

Neolithic remains from Knossos date back to about 6000 B.C. After the collapse of the Bronze Age Minoan civilization, during which Greek was introduced in the fifteenth century B.C., the Dorian invasions—which appear not to have eradicated the preexisting local culture entirely—were followed by a cultural efflorescence that continued into Roman (from 67 B.C.) and early Byzantine times. Muslim Saracen invaders, who came from Spain by way of Egypt in about A.D. 823, may have presided over the development of the Cretan dialects into roughly their present form. They were driven out by the Byzantine Emperor Nikiforos Fokas in 961. Alexios Comnenon I allegedly brought twelve noble families (*arkhondopouli*) from Byzantium to repopulate the ravaged island. Some of their names still survive, as do surnames of Venetian settlers who arrived after the collapse of the short-lived (1204–1210) Genoese occupation. The Venetian period was one of great cultural revival, with Italian-influenced literature and art incorporating local verse traditions and Byzantine iconography; after the collapse of most of the island in 1645–1646 and of Iraklio (Candia) in 1669, refugees carried this literary culture to the Ionian Islands. The Turkish period was marked by bloody revolts and fierce repression. In 1898 Crete, under the joint supervision of Britain, France, Italy, and Russia, became a semiautonomous protectorate, and in 1913 it was united with Greece. The 1941–1944 German occupation was extremely harsh and revived the traditional Cretan values of warlike independence. Despite the prominence of Cretan politicians in national life, Cretans have felt excluded from the centers of political power in the larger national entity. They have been strongly antimonarchist and prosocialist, the latter tendency being only slightly offset by powerful liberal and right-wing political patronage in the rural areas. Despite sporadic separatism in the past, Crete now appears solidly embedded in the national political structure, although cultural and political hostility to Athens persists. The more isolated mountain dwellers' tradition of especially active resistance to authority may account for some distinctive local cultural forms, some of which suggest links with much earlier periods.

Settlements

Rural communities range in population from less than 100 to several thousands. Some small but spatially distinct villages are absorbed into larger communities for purposes of local government and church affairs. Most villages are constructed on a cluster pattern, often around a church and plaza, although the excellent road system has induced an increasing tendency toward the development of areas along the roads, or "ribbon development," often leading to the absorption of smaller subsettlements (*metokhia*). Houses, commonly grouped in patrigroup-based neighborhoods, often have small adjoining vegetable gardens; terraces, formerly used for grain cultivation and now mostly given over to grazing, rise above many mountain villages. Plains dwellers have direct access to fields in adjacent areas; many highland pastoralists who have turned to agricultural pursuits have purchased lands in the more depopulated, lower-lying villages. Village houses used to be single-story, with a single room to house the entire family at night; these have been replaced largely by two-story concrete structures. Many urban dwellers live in apartments, while others—mostly in Khania and Rethimno—inhabit refurbished houses of Turkish and Venetian date. Front balconies on all kinds of dwellings provide a view of surrounding social activity and a place to entertain less formal visitors.

Economy

Subsistence and Commercial Activities. Rural Crete is predominantly agricultural, with transhumant pastoralism (now being sedentarized) among the mountain villagers who rent winter pasturage in the coastal areas to the north and northeast. Goat- and sheepherding are common and increasingly commercial pastoral activities. Cattle are now rare, but pigs and chickens are raised for food and mules and donkeys remain an important mode of transporting produce and people over short distances. Major crops include vines (for wine, table grapes, and raisins) and olives; the latter increasingly predominate because of their greater ease of cultivation and high yield. Little grain has been grown, especially since government subsidies to certain areas since 1964 have discouraged further investment. Fruit production includes bananas, pears, and citrus (mostly oranges); the avocado has recently been introduced and seems destined mostly for export. In the fertile Messara Plain, huge tomato-growing greenhouse nurseries have proliferated, providing wages for poorer villagers from all over the island. Carobs are an important item, and some tobacco is grown (especially in areas populated by Asia Minor refugees). Coastal communities are extensively engaged in fishing; the Asia Minor refugees introduced nighttime fishing with decoy lights.

Industrial Arts. Urban occupations include an extensive carpentry tradition; metalworking and boot making, once important, have decayed. Until about 1960, Rethimno was a major producer of soap, utilizing the large resources of olive oil from the rural hinterland. Today there is an extensive cottage industry in some (mostly mountain) villages producing woven goods for the tourist trade, and tourism is also the major source of income for the coastal towns and villages near archaeological sites.

Trade. Small all-purpose stores predominate in the villages; in the towns, supermarkets are threatening their survival. Itinerant vendors, often Gypsies from the Greek mainland, provide cheap goods and also work as metalworkers and chair makers, but they are treated with contempt. The village woven goods, produced by women at home, are distributed to tourist markets by wholesalers from the home villages. Produce is distributed through cooperatives and markets.

Division of Labor. There is a strong sense of sexual division. Men tend the flocks and engage in political life; women may work in the fields, but growing "embourgoisement" reduces this involvement in fieldwork and tends to close them up at home. Women do all domestic chores, including cooking (although men may roast meat on certain occasions). In the towns, women may take on domestic labor in the tourist sector. Both sexes tend shops, even the male-only coffeehouses.

Land Tenure. Cretans of both sexes inherit land from both parents in a system of equal, partible inheritance. Some lands belong to monasteries. Urban dwellers mostly own some ancestral village property, which they either tend themselves or work on a fifty-fifty sharecropping basis (*simisako*) with local kin. Land tenure in the towns is largely through recent purchase or inheritance, and renting of houses and apartments is common.

Kinship

Kin Groups and Descent. Although Cretans formally adhere to the officially and ecclesiastically sanctioned kinship mode of the cognatic kindred, mountain village men emphasize segmentary, agnatic loyalties at times of crisis or during municipal (and sometimes parliamentary) elections. Households are nuclear in both town and country, sometimes with the addition of a widowed (grand)parent.

Kinship Terminology. Cretans commonly use the standard Greek system, which is essentially the same as the English, except that the term for daughter's husband is the same as sister's husband but different than wife's brother, and the term for sister's husband is the same as brother's wife but different than husband's sister. Contrary to the Greek system, however, Cretans use separate group terms for agnatic loyalties. The terms *kouniadhos* (male) and *kouniadha* (female) are sometimes used as reciprocals in remoter villages for sister's husband and wife's brother and brother's wife and husband's sister as well as for cousins of any kind. This usage appears to be derived from a tendency to large-lineage endogamy (and, in the case of men, the solidarity of those who collaborate to raid others' flocks).

Marriage and Family

Marriage. Marriage is monogamous, and divorce is strongly disapproved. In the villages, couples sleep together from the time of engagement, and they may await pregnancy before proceeding to the church ceremony. There is a strong preference for village and large-lineage endogamy, but this preference must be set against strict incest rules that formerly precluded marriage between third cousins (although the church's restriction extended only to second cousins). In the villages of western and central Crete, residence is in a house provided by the groom's father and furnished by the bride's family; in eastern Crete and in virtually all urban areas, residence is uxorilocal. Couples usually assume independent residence at marriage. Abduction and elopement remain common, especially in the rural areas.

Domestic Unit. The nuclear family is almost universally the residence unit throughout Crete.

Inheritance. Flock animals are mostly passed from father to sons. Land is divided equally among all children of both sexes, although daughters may receive an additional amount as dowry. Division of the parental property is often done by lot, usually at the death of the parent in question, except for dowry lands for daughters (who receive them at marriage). In the towns, the legal requirements of equal partible inheritance may render small properties practically worthless, especially when many of the coheirs have emigrated, and agreements to sell in order to divide the income are common in such cases. The youngest son often receives the parental house in the mountain villages of central and western Crete.

Socialization. Children are raised in the mountain villages to be aggressive and teasing and to defend their personal integrity against all comers. Sexual segregation is encouraged rather than enforced in the earliest school-going years. Grandparents, aunts, uncles, and family friends provide a demonstratively affectionate counterpoint to occasional displays of paternal strictness. Mild corporal punishment is common, but unfulfilled threats are far more frequent.

Sociopolitical Organization

Crete is an integral part of the administrative structure of the Hellenic republic. The four prefectures (_nomi_) are divided into districts (_eparkhies_), in which communities (_kinotites_) each comprise a single village with smaller residential units occasionally attached; larger units are called demes (_dhimi_).

Social Organization. Household autonomy is strong. Patrigroups, at various levels, engage in feuding and raiding in the Milopotamos district. Patronage is endemic, with powerful political leaders protecting those who engage in such activities. An egalitarian social ethos does not prevent the emergence of extremely strong local patrigroups; in Sfakia (southwestern Crete), the sharp discrimination between upper (_kalosiri_) and lower (_kakosiri_) shepherds is based on wealth and social reputation. In the highland villages, most pastoralists affect to despise full-time agriculturalists as unmanly, although there is an increasing perception that sheepherding is a rough life that lacks the economic and social advantages of an educated existence. Civil-service jobs are much coveted. Urban merchants engage in patronage based on mutual advantage with village suppliers, but the encroachment of nonlocal entrepreneurs is gradually undercutting this system. A cosmopolitan urban "aristocracy" has largely yielded to new wealth from land speculation and tourism. Lower clergy often serve in their home villages. Cretan policemen, who comprise a high percentage of the Greek force, are largely drawn from the rural population but may not serve in their home communities.

Political Organization. The kinotites (communities) have some autonomy in day-to-day government, with elected mayors and councils. In an increasing proportion of villages, the voting follows national party lines, although agnatic loyalties remain fierce in the western and central mountain communities and kinship, spiritual kinship, and neighborhood ties continue to influence choices elsewhere. Village councils are responsible for purely local road building and municipal improvement; other services, including major roads, electricity, water, and health and police services are furnished by the state, which is also responsible for tax collection and market regulation. The village priest often mediates in disputes; in general, mediation by intimates is preferred to police intervention. Law courts are located in district and prefecture capitals, and they often seem more concerned with drawing conflict away from its original locus and reaching an acceptable settlement than with precise attributions of guilt.

Social Control. Gossip is a powerful factor, reinforced by the power of envy symbolized by the evil eye. Public ridicule is rare but effective; the fear of feuding is also a strong deterrent.

Conflict. Many rural Cretan men carry knives and often also guns, but they avoid quarreling except where others—including women—can be expected to exercise restraint. Most quarrels arise from bride theft, animal raiding, politics, or insults against manhood, household, and patrigroup; married women may echo their husbands' quarrels among themselves. Feuding is endemic, and in extreme cases only a marriage alliance can stop it. Men who do not avenge the slaying of close agnates are despised. The police usually attempt to intervene using the traditional idiom of reconciliation (_sasmos_) wherever possible, in order to obtain longer-lasting (because socially sanctioned) results.

Religion and Expressive Culture

Orthodox Christianity accounts for the overwhelming majority of religious affiliations. Religion and ethnicity are often identified, so that pre-1924 "Turks" were often Greek-speaking Muslims.

Religious Beliefs. Many Cretans are vociferously anticlerical, acknowledging the existence of a higher power but despising the (especially higher) clergy and accusing them of venality. Despite their skepticism, Cretans do seem to recognize a wide range of ambiguous supernaturals in official doctrine.

Religious Practitioners. The priests and a dwindling number of monastics of both sexes are recruited largely from the local population. Women are given custodial tasks around the church but are barred from the inner sanctum. Committees of local people oversee the daily management of church affairs. Nonecclesiastical rituals such as curing of evil eye and other ailments are conducted by informal local experts, who receive gifts rather than money for their services.

Ceremonies. In most rural and urban communities, the most important ceremonies are those of the Easter cycle and the local saint's day. Christmas and Epiphany are also important, as are the commemorative ceremonies of the state; Independence Day (March 25) coincides with the Feast of the Annunciation.

Arts. Crete is famous for its music and dance, and for its woven goods. Some village artists and wood-carvers have achieved local fame. There is a lively tradition of informal assonant distich (_mandinadha_) contests, to which improvisatory skills are central.

Medicine. Despite official opposition, local practitioners (_praktiki_) continue to do bonesetting, and evil-eye curers seem concerned with primarily psychosomatic conditions.

Death and Afterlife. Funerals, although conducted by the priest, also give women in some villages the opportunity to express their grief through improvised keening verses (_miroloya_). Memorial services are held at statutory increasing intervals after death, and they also may be accompanied by female keening. The death of an unmarried person is celebrated with wedding symbolism; the death of the old is often treated as "less serious." Interment is preceded by a wake. Despite Christian teaching, a vague notion of "Hades" (_Adhis_) persists.

Bibliography

Allbaugh, Leland G. (1953). _Crete: A Case Study of an Underdeveloped Area._ Princeton, N.J.: Princeton University Press.

Burgel, Guy (1965). _Pobia: Étude géographique d'un village crétois._ Athens: Centre des Sciences Sociales d'Athènes.

Greger, Sonia (1988). *Village on the Plateau: Magoulas—A Mountain Village in Crete.* Studley, Warwickshire: Brewin.

Herzfeld, Michael (1985). *The Poetics of Manhood: Contest and Identity in a Cretan Mountain Village.* Princeton, N.J.: Princeton University Press.

MICHAEL HERZFELD

Croats

ETHNONYMS: Croatians, Hrvati

Orientation

Identification. Croatians are a Slavic people. They began to form as a distinct group in the seventh century as part of a process completed during the modern national integration in the nineteenth and twentieth centuries. At various times, the Croatian name has been used not only for the contemporary Croats but also for two other Slavic tribes (in the vicinity of Krakow, Poland, and in northeast Bohemia). It was used for the first time as a personal name (Horóathos, Horúathos) in the second to third centuries in Tanais on the river Don and on some historic monuments (Trpimir, dux Chroatorum; Branimir, dux Cruatorum) from the ninth century. Science has not yet solved the question of the origin and meaning of the name "Croat(ian)."

Location. Croatia encompasses 56,538 square kilometers and is located between 42° 23′ and 46° 32′ N and 13° 30′ and 19° 26′ E. The north plain—the biggest, most populated, and economically most active part of the country—is separated from the coastal part in the south (east coast of the Adriatic Sea) by the central mountainous region. Considering its location, Croatia is a Pannonian and Adriatic region, at the juncture of the central Danubian Plain and the Mediterranean. The climate in the north is continental, in the central region mountainous, and in the south Mediterranean.

Demography. The majority of Croats (3.5 million) lives in Croatia itself; an additional million live in Bosnia and Herzegovina, Serbia, and Slovenia. It is estimated that Croatian emigrants in western Europe, the Americas, Australia, and New Zealand number more than 3 million. Although the number of live births exceeded by 3 percent the number of deceased persons between the censuses of 1971 and 1981, there were 100,000 fewer Croatians because they identified themselves as Yugoslavs.

Linguistic Affiliation. The Croatian language is a South Slavic language and encompasses three major dialects (Štokavian, Čakavian, and Kajkavian). Literary Croatian, developed since the twelfth century on a South Štokavian base (with some influence of other dialects) was accepted in the first half of the nineteenth century as the national language. Since then it has been standardized and has become the uniform means of communication in professional, scientific, and artistic expression. The alphabet is Latin (twenty-five consonants and five vowels). In the past, Slavic alphabets were employed, including *glagoljica,* which was used in some areas around the Adriatic until the nineteenth century.

Settlements

The percentage of rural population by residence has always been very high, with significant differences between geographic regions, ranging in the 1980s from a high of about 70 percent in the central region to a low of 40 percent in southern Croatia. Traditionally, there were wide differences among different settlements in the house style and interior design. Today, however, there is a tendency toward uniformity. Settlements are either clustered (mainly in the north and south) or dispersed (mainly in the hinterland of the south and central regions). Clustered settlements are either compact and centered on a square or stripped into perpendicular streets. In the south, houses are made of stone, with roofs of reed (the oldest tradition), stone slabs, or convex tiles (the newest tradition). They are usually two-story buildings along the coast and one-story buildings in the coastal hinterland. Elsewhere, the material is wood (oak logs or trimmed wooden planks), clay mixed with chaff, or more recently brick (at first adobe) and concrete. The roofs are covered either with shingles, thatch, or flat tiles (the most recent tradition). Houses were one-story buildings.

History and Cultural Relations

After settling into today's homeland in the seventh century, Croatians organized a state. From the beginning of the twelfth century, after the demise of the national royal dynasty, the Croatian state unified with Hungary (linked by the same ruler); after 1527, the Austrian royal family of Habsburg ruled Croatia. With the consolidation of the Republic of Venice on a large section of Croatian coast (only the Republic of Dubrovnik kept its independence) and with the Turkish conquests since the fifteenth century, Croatian lands were divided and to a certain extent the ethnic structure was changed (emigration of Croatians and immigration of Balkan and central European peoples). Subsequently, Croatian history has been marked by a struggle for national and cultural survival, for maintenance of state independence, and for territorial integrity. Following the disintegration of the Austro-Hungarian monarchy in World War I the Croatians removed themselves from it, proclaimed independence, and joined the new South Slav state (the Kingdom of Serbs, Croatians, and Slovenes, renamed the Kingdom of Yugoslavia in 1929). After the liberation struggle in World War II and socialist revolution, Croatia became a federal state (Socialist Republic of Croatia) in the Socialist Federal Republic of Yugoslavia. In 1991, following the fall of Communist rule and a bloody civil war, Croatia became an independent state, the Republic of Croatia.

In the course of developments since the mid-nineteenth century, Croatia has lived through political, social, and economic change. Since the time of Christianization in the early centuries after settling the region, Croatians have belonged to the Western-European cultural milieu. The organizational foundation of the contemporary scientific and artistic life is a branchlike system consisting of institutions of higher education (e.g., University of Zagreb since 1669; universities in

Split, Osijek, and Rijeka); scientific institutions (e.g., the Yugoslav Academy of Sciences and Arts since 1867, renamed the Croatian Academy of Sciences and Arts in 1991; the Archive of Croatia and the National University Library in Zagreb); museums, galleries, and theaters (e.g., the central Croatian National Theater in Zagreb); and academies of arts. The cultural life is expressed also in literary and fine arts, films, and radio and television programs.

Economy

Subsistence and Commercial Activities. Somewhat less than half of the population of Croatia is economically active (working outside the home). About 45 percent of the active population is employed in the service sector, 35 percent in industry and 20 percent in agriculture. Eighty-five percent of the agricultural activity is on small peasant farms and 15 percent on state farms. Until 1990, peasant farms were limited by law to 15 hectares (of cultivable surface) and therefore, although it is widely mechanized, agricultural production is not very profitable. The predominant agricultural products are maize, wheat, milk, and meat. The production of wine and fruits is also important, while production of industrial plants (flax, hemp, sunflowers, etc.) is less significant. Almost all agricultural products are used by the domestic population; only a small part of the produce (meat, maize, tobacco, and wine) is exported.

Industrial Arts. The dominant industries are shipbuilding, textiles, and food processing. Less important are the chemical and timber industries. The industrial sector of the Croatian economy creates 50 percent of the gross national product (GNP) while employing one-third of the working population. In the 1960s and 1970s big industrial enterprises were developed in Croatia, while in the 1980s smaller ones, especially in electronics, metalworking, and plastics, also emerged there. The problems faced by industry are insufficient energy (most oil is imported), and the need to import chemical products, raw materials, and industrial machinery.

Trade. About 10 percent of the Croatian working population employed in trade creates about 17 percent of the Croatian GNP. Large state enterprises (stores, supermarkets, specialized shops) dominate this sector. Recently, small specialized private shops (fruit and vegetable stores, stores for other food products and textiles) have been emerging.

Division of Labor. Traditionally, women were assigned domestic tasks (cleaning, cooking, tending babies, etc.) but also shared some agricultural tasks, which otherwise were dominated by men. Today, women are still occupied by household and family work, but women also comprise one-third of the work force. They are most frequently employed in education and medicine, where they outnumber men, and also in tourism and trade.

Kinship, Marriage, and Family

Kinship. Descent is traced patrilineally and the social emphasis on father's lineage is reflected in more elaborated terminology for father's relatives. Kin groups were based traditionally on patrilocal residence and patrimony, which was jointly owned and managed by a father and his married sons (_zadruga_). Matrilineal kin was less important in social practice and lived at a distance. Further patrilineal kin often inhabited the same hamlet or nearby villages. The zadruga system disappeared by the early twentieth century, and because of migrations and intensive urbanization, patrilineal kin groups are presently more dispersed, with their interaction mostly limited to yearly or life-cycle rituals, while in everyday practice one's mother's and father's relatives have equally important roles. Post-World War II family law gave a married woman the opportunity to keep her maiden name or hyphenate it with her husband's surname. This practice indicates a shift toward bilaterality. Children, however, rarely receive other than their father's surname. Inheritance of parental property also has become largely bilateral.

Marriage. Marriages are monogamous. In the past, they were arranged by corporate kin groups and parents. Marriage partners were sought from neighboring hamlets and villages (regional endogamy). Residence was traditionally patrilocal. As a consequence of rural-urban migrations as well as education and employment of women, ambilocal residence has become predominant, while neolocality is the ideal for young couples. The divorce rate is constantly rising (177 per 1,000 marriages in 1988), peaking in the city of Zagreb, where every third marriage ends in divorce. Divorces are "no-fault," by agreement, with laws mainly oriented toward the protection of the rights of children.

Domestic Unit. The domestic unit is that group of people who sleep and eat "under one roof" and who jointly manage family (_obitelj_) resources. The structure of this group has changed from the zadruga type to three-generational stem family (parents with children and one or two grandparents), nuclear family (parents with children), and even smaller "fragmented" types of domestic unit. While the three-generational family is still common in rural areas, the average number of persons in domestic units in Croatia is hardly above three. Less than half of the domestic units have a nuclear family structure, whereas others include single persons (16 percent), childless couples (24.6 percent), mothers with children (8.4 percent) and fathers with children (1.5 percent). The reasons of such fragmentation, besides divorce, are labor migration, a drop in the fertility rate, and a decrease in contracted marriages.

Inheritance. Traditionally, sons inherited equal shares of patrimony, while daughters married out with dowries in land, cattle, or money. Presently property is divided equally among all children, often allotted to them gradually during the parents' life, in order to help the children establish their own households. Remaining property is divided equally upon the parents' death. However, cases of daughters who fight for their share in court against their brothers are not infrequent.

Socialization. Children are raised by parents or grandparents. Great emphasis is placed on achievement through education as it is the main means of climbing the social ladder. For this reason children are often excused from assuming early responsibilities in domestic and productive spheres. Socioeconomic opportunities are limited, and parents sacrifice their labor and money to support their children for a long time, frequently into adulthood.

Sociopolitical Organization

Social Organization. Since the socialist revolution of 1945, no social classes have been officially recognized, but there are distinguishable social strata. The class of large land-owners and industrialists was discredited after World War II, making wealth only a minor marker of social class. Instead, occupations associated with education and with access to power (as in the case of the bureaucratic elite) have become a major basis of social stratification. Differences in the standard of living and in subjective evaluations of status exist between the agricultural and industrial population, that is, between the rural and urban populations. Since the 1970s the difference has been diminishing because of secondary urbanization of rural settlements, on the one hand, and deteriorating quality of life in the cities, on the other. A trend toward stratification on the basis of wealth has developed, since the sector of private artisans, entrepreneurs, merchants, services, and professions is gaining strength again. Considerable social mobility is secured through the educational system, which is open to everyone. Yet, many social routes are also open through informal personal networks and loyalties, such as those based on familism and localism.

Political Organization. From 1945 to 1991, Croatia was one of six federal republics that made up the Socialist Federal Republic of Yugoslavia. After the death of Marshall Tito in 1980, it elected a delegate to the board of the "Presidency"—the collective head of the Yugoslavian state—and a number of delegates to the Federal Assembly, the supreme body of government. As a federal state within Yugoslavia, Croatia had its own government, of which the parliament (Sabor) and the president of its executive council were the supreme bodies. A multiparty political system was reestablished in 1990. The nationalist Croatian Democratic Union (HDZ) won the parliamentary elections that year, taking the majority of seats in the Sabor and having its leader indirectly elected president of Croatia. The new government declared the independence of Croatia in October 1991, amid civil war and aggression from Serbia. Regional and political reform is pending. Croatia is still divided into 115 communes (općina), each comprising a number of villages and hamlets. Their population varies in size and density. Communes are clustered into 10 municipalities, each with a major urban center. The division reflects historical, cultural, economic, and administrative divisions so that regional identity and loyalty remains strong. A significant portion of rural-urban migration takes place within municipalities, oriented toward regional urban centers. Each općina has an assembly and its executive council and president. There are also boards which take care of schools, health services, public roads, and the local economy; offices for tax collection, vital statistics, and urban planning; and courts and police. An općina center also has secondary schools and religious establishments.

Social Control. Under the former system, a strong mechanism of social control, both institutionalized and ideological, was the League of Communists, which, although formally separate from the state, exerted influence at all levels of social organization. Preceding the elections of 1990, there was a proliferation of alternative movements (ecological movements, initiatives for democratic reform, new women's movements, agitation for human rights, etc.), creating considerable social impact and causing a concomitant weakening of the ideological grip of the league. In 1990, the league was renamed the Socialist party and became oppositional after the elections. A number of other movements were transformed into political parties at the same time. Informally, gossip and personal alliances on the basis of kinship and common local origin remain strong means of social control.

Conflict. Dominant values regarding conflict and warfare are ambivalent, because of the complex history of Croatia: historical border areas (the mountainous zone) emphasize fighting for freedom and undefeatable frontierspeople, while areas of historical feudal states with a tightly controlled population place more value on passive resistance, mediation, clever avoidance of imposed duties, and outwitting opponents in inconspicuous ways. Under the Yugoslav system, courts were formally independent from the legislative and executive branches of government, but politics had influenced them greatly nevertheless. Courts were organized on five levels: communal, regional, state, federal, and supreme courts. In addition to regular courts, there were mediating agencies of different kinds, for business conflicts (e.g., "Social Defense of Self-Management") or for private matters (e.g., obligatory counseling with a social worker before divorce). Reform of the judicial system is pending.

Religion and Expressive Culture

Religious Beliefs and Practices. Croatians are mainly Roman Catholic, with small percentages of Uniates (Eastern Orthodox Christians, recognizing the pope), Protestants, and Muslims. Some pre-Christian elements have been integrated into Christian beliefs and practices. Other influences on Croatian religious beliefs and practices have come from European and Near Eastern cultures, from rural and urban traditions alike, resulting in an amalgam of different heritages. Sacred and religious aspects of traditional culture were neglected during the Socialist period because religion was relegated solely to the private sphere of life. The first post-Communist government is reintroducing the Catholic church into public life in many conspicuous ways.

In traditional culture, there had been many beliefs connected with the dead, as well as many beliefs in fairies, vampires (who disturb their relatives by sucking their blood), witches (demonic women), mythic female beings who determine the fate of children, or others who choke people during sleep. There is still a widespread belief in the evil eye, in the power of casting spells over people or over their property, and in various protective magical acts. Traditionally, people paid special respect to animals to which they attributed supernatural properties (e.g., snake as a house protector). Such beliefs have disappeared or are slowly fading away, but they have been transmitted through and persist in myths, legends, tales, and poems.

Ceremonies. Ceremonies and rituals can be divided into several types—annual celebrations associated with church holy days, life-cycle events, and work rituals (the last group is connected with harvest, building of a house, etc.). The most prominent among calendrical rituals are those of Christmas Eve—*badnjak*, the burning of the yule log, an older tradition; the decoration of a Christmas tree, a newer tradition; and all sorts of practices linked to the cult of the deceased—and *koleda*, men's processions during the period between Christmas and New Year's. Mardi Gras carnival celebrations featuring processions and burning of a straw effigy have been revived recently thanks to the mass media and tourist agencies. In spring, in addition to Easter celebrations (including coloring of eggs), there used to be various village processions (on St. George's Day, First of May, Ascension Day, Whitsuntide, etc.) and bonfires (especially on St. John's Day in June). Those processions and bonfires were apotropaic rituals meant for the protection of people, fields, and cattle and for promoting fertility. There were also new rituals created in the Socialist period, such as celebrations of Workers' Day on 1 May and of International Women's Day on 8 March. Both were canceled in 1991. Among life-cycle rituals, most important are those centering on birth, marriage, and death. Today some new ones have emerged (e.g., the day of graduation, especially in cities), while the old ones have an impoverished repertoire. A wedding traditionally has been the most important family and community event. It once consisted of a complex of ritual events such as solemn carrying over of the bride's trousseau, humorous negotiations over false brides when the wedding party arrived at the bride's house, and symbolic acts by the bride upon arrival at bridegroom's home (holding a male child in her lap, sweeping the floor, starting the fire on the hearth, etc). Death gave rise to numerous beliefs, most important being the belief in life after death, marked by feasting ceremonies and loud laments for the deceased (*naricanje*).

Arts. A wide variety of folk music is found among Croatians. Specific features are exhibited in tonal relationships of tunes and instrumental melodies. The musical styles range from a rather old, narrow-intervals style (in which the intervals in the tonal ranges are sometimes narrower than the intervals between the twelve equal semitones in an octave), in central and south Croatia, to a widespread contemporary style called "in bass" singing, in eastern Croatia. Folk music is interwoven with all kinds of everyday and festive activities (especially working songs, weddings, and spring processions). Today, its main function is entertainment. The main instruments used to accompany the singing are cordophones and aerophones. Dances differ as much as do tunes and instruments. Today they are almost restored to their pre-World War II forms, thanks to their revival on stage; forms include the couple dance, a closed circle dance (*drmeš*), and circles and lines. Artistic expression can be found on decorative clothes, wood carving, pottery, pictures painted on glass, metalwork, and even egg painting. Oral literature is dominated by epic poetry. Among lyric poetry, the Dalmatian ballads are noteworthy (Adriatic coast). The earliest records of oral literature are from the sixteenth century and point to a wide variety of genres. Croatian art also includes church architecture, frescoes, reliefs, and decorated facades and balconies.

In the twentieth century, painting, sculpture, and music have exploded in various styles. Architecture suffered under the planned socialist economy.

Medicine. Folk medicine was imbued with magic, but it was also rational, especially in the identification, preparation, and use of medicinal herbs. The pharmaceutical industry has incorporated some of this folk knowledge in the production of herbal drugs.

See also Dalmatians

Bibliography

Erlich, Vera Stein (1966). *Family in Transition*. Princeton: Princeton University Press.

Gavazzi, Milovan (1939). *Godina dana hrvatskih narodnih običaja* (Yearly cycle of Croatian folk customs). Zagreb: Matica Hrvatska.

Historical Maps of Croatia from the Penguin Atlas of World History (1992). Zagreb: Croatian Information Centre.

"Hrvati" (Croats) (1988). In *Enciklopedija Jugoslavije*, edited by Jakov Sirotković. Vol. 5, 1–151. Zagreb: Jugoslavenski Leksikografski Zavod.

Grupković, D., ed. (1989). *Statistički kalendar Jugoslavije* (The statistical calendar of Yugoslavia). Vol. 35. Belgrade: Savezni Zavod za Statistiku.

Grupković, D., ed. (1990). *Statistički godišnjak Jugoslavije* (The statistical yearbook of Yugoslavia). Vol. 37. Belgrade: Savezni Zavod za Statistiku.

Šeparović, Zvonimir (1992). *Documenta Croatica*. Zagreb: Croatian Society of Victimology.

JASNA ČAPO, JAKOV GELO, TRPIMIR MACAN, AND OLGA SUPEK

Cyclades

ETHNONYMS: none

Orientation

Identification. The Cyclades are a group of Aegean Islands whose name derives from the fact that they form a circle (*kíklos*) around the ancient sacred island of Delos.

Location. The Cyclades lie in the Aegean Sea to the south and west of the Greek mainland. They are the peaks of a range of submerged mountains, separated by deep channels from the islands to the south and east. Precipitation in the Cyclades falls mainly in the winter, beginning in November and tapering off by the end of March. Little or no rain falls in the summer. During the period 1971–1980, the island of Naxos had an average of 41 centimeters of rain, the largest amount falling during January, February, and March. As a whole, the Cyclades are rather dry; only the meteorologic station at Athens reported less rainfall during this period. Winters nonetheless tend to be chilly and damp, with an occasional snowfall. Temperatures in the summer are moderated by the proximity of the sea. The average temperature reported at Naxos during July and August for 1971–1980 was 25° C, with highs of about 32° C. Temperatures may fall as low as 6° C in the winter. The average annual temperature was 18° C. The mild summer temperatures make the islands attractive to city dwellers fleeing the heat. However, the summer also brings the fierce summer wind, the *meltémi*, which can make sea travel unpleasant during this time.

Demography. There are some forty-four islands in all, some tiny and uninhabited, others with numerous villages and flourishing main towns. The island with the largest population is Syros, with 19,668 inhabitants (1981 census). The largest island in terms of landmass is Naxos, which has an area of 428 square kilometers. The Cyclades as a whole have an area of 2,527 square kilometers, which is about 1.9 percent of the land area of Greece. The total population of the islands is 88,458, less than 1 percent of the population of Greece. The number of inhabitants per square kilometer is 34.4. Thirty-seven percent of the inhabitants live in urban (population more than 10,000) or semiurban (population 2,000–10,000) areas, the rest in rural areas (communities of under 2,000). In general, the populations of the coastal settlements of the islands have increased, while those of the interior communities have declined.

Linguistic Affiliation. Although the history of the Cyclades has been one of constantly mixing populations of migrants, conquerors, and refugees, the present-day population is basically ethnic Greek. There is a certain sense of island cultural distinctiveness, however, because throughout their history the Cyclades have been both connected and isolated by the sea, serving in their connectedness as way stations along trade routes and routes of conquest, open to a multitude of cultural influences, and in their isolation as places of political exile. The present-day inhabitants of the Cyclades speak modern Greek, with a variety of local dialects among and within the islands. Albanian has been reported only for the island of Andros. Some of the islands are visited by large groups of Gypsies (*Tsigánes*), but they are not permanent residents.

History and Cultural Relations

It is difficult to generalize about the Cyclades as a whole, for each island has to some extent experienced its own unique history. Although visited by Paleolithic peoples seeking obsidian and other stone, the Cyclades seem to have been first inhabited in the late Neolithic (c. 5000 B.C.), and they were probably settled by peoples arriving from the Greek mainland. The islands flourished during the Bronze Age, despite the occasional destruction of some settlements by earthquakes. Although subject to the cultural influences of other areas (particularly Mycenean and Minoan influences) and to periodic invasions and/or waves of immigration, the islands developed a distinctive Bronze Age culture with a now well-recognized Cycladic art, perhaps most clearly represented in the characteristic Cycladic marble figurines. In the eleventh century B.C., at the end of the Bronze Age, the Cyclades underwent a decline in population, but by the ninth to eighth centuries B.C. their population began to grow again, and new settlements were established. In the classical period some islands were the home of independent city-states. From the eighth century B.C. the island of Delos was an important holy place for Ionian Greeks; during Hellenistic times it was an international merchant community as well, and it continued to flourish into Roman times. Ravaged by Mithridates of Pontus in A.D. 88, it fell into decline, and then eventually into oblivion with the arrival of Christianity. After the Romans, the Cyclades became part of the Byzantine Empire. It is uncertain exactly when Christianity came to the islands, but it may have been sometime in the late fourth or fifth century. By the late eleventh century the Byzantine Empire was no longer able to protect its Cycladic holdings effectively, and they were subject to raids by both Italians and Turks. Following the Fourth Crusade and the division of the Byzantine Empire between the Venetians and the Crusaders, many of the islands fell into Venetian hands. It was during this period that the islands acquired their Catholic populations. During the centuries of Venetian rule, the islands gradually declined, their populations ravaged by the depradations of pirates, by struggles among the local rulers, and by the Venetian rulers' conflicts with both Turks and Greeks. When Constantinople fell to the Turks in 1453, the position of the islanders became even more difficult. One by one, the islands were ceded to the Ottomans, with Tinos, the last to capitulate, surrendering to a Turkish fleet in 1714. After the Greek War of Independence from Turkey (1821–1829), the Cyclades became part of the newly formed nation of Greece. The population at this time appears to have been increased by Greek refugees from areas still under Turkish rule. The Cyclades probably reached the peak of their population in the nineteenth century, declining somewhat in the early twentieth century and then dropping precipitously through out-migration after World War II.

Settlements

In general, the Cyclades are steep and rocky, though some islands have stretches of coastal and interior plains. Although many of the islands appear to have had forests in ancient times, land clearing, shipbuilding, animal grazing, and the use of wood for fuel and house building have taken their toll, and today the islands are severely deforested and suffer from erosion by water and wind. Since prehistoric times, settlement seems to have followed a general pattern of nucleated villages (with some variation according to land tenure and kinship systems), the location being determined by the need for protection, shelter, and/or proximity to water and cultivable land. Each village is surrounded by cultivated fields, though some fields may be at a considerable distance from the village. Houses today are built of concrete block or reinforced concrete, but in the past houses were constructed of local stone, usually plastered inside and out, and whitewashed. Roofs were made of branches covered with packed earth or clay, or sometimes flat stone. On some islands pitched tile roofs are also found, though these are less characteristic of the Cyclades as a whole. Although "mosaic" floors are the norm today, one can still see the occasional traditional packed-earth floors in village homes. Aside from rafters, wood is rarely used in buildings except for shutters and trim (which may be painted in bright colors). There is generally one main town on each island, and this town today is often the port (though there may also be smaller secondary ports as well). In the past, villages were clustered for defense against frequent raids by pirates and Turks, and the main towns themselves (such as the port town of Naxos) were fortified or were situated inland for protection (as the now-deserted town of Exobourgos on Tinos). In some towns and villages remains of such fortifications with their thick exterior walls and small windows may still be seen. Nowadays, the nucleated village settlement pattern is being broken somewhat by the building of summer "country" houses, which may be located in fields outside the villages.

Economy

Subsistence and Commercial Activities. The major form of subsistence, in the past at least, has been agriculture, though fishing, trading, and commercial activities have also been important. Basic Mediterranean crops—olives, grapes, wheat, barley, fruit, and garden vegetables—have been cultivated, some since the Bronze Age. In addition there are specialty crops, which may vary by island. (On the island of Tinos, for example, silkworms used to be grown; Thera has had a history of wine making; Syros is noted for its dairying.) Goats and sheep are also raised on the islands, and sometimes cattle. There are also fishing communities. Agriculture follows a basic yearly round determined by the Mediterranean climate. Plowing for planting is done in the fall, after the first rains have softened the ground, winter crops are planted, and grain is harvested in early to midsummer. Some irrigation is practiced, particularly for garden vegetables, but dry farming is the rule for other crops. Fields are plowed periodically during the growing season with a shallow plow in order to prevent moisture loss from the soil. Not all islanders, nor even all villagers, own land, and even those who do may also work at other occupations or businesses in addition to farming. Several of the islands have marble quarries dating back to the Bronze Age. The marble of Paros and Naxos is particularly well known, and marble working is a craft with a long tradition. In the past, farmers grew more of their own food than they do today, particularly in the more isolated villages.

Trade. Trade with the outside world and migration have a long history in the islands. The inhabitants of the Cyclades have exported both their products and their labor, particularly as seamen, domestic workers, and construction workers. Both permanent and temporary migration have been practiced. Before the Greek defeat in Asia Minor in 1922 ("the Catastrophe"), a common destination of migrants was Istanbul (or "the City," as many Greeks continue to call it). Since then, the primary destination for migrants from the Cyclades has been Athens. Although out-migration seems to have slowed somewhat in recent years, the post–World War II movement to Athens has resulted in severe depopulation and the virtual abandonment of some of the smaller rural villages. Much of the more marginal agricultural land is no longer cultivated. Better agricultural land, however, continues to be worked in many areas, with new plantings of crops such as olives and grapevines, which require only periodic attention and seasonal labor. Greenhouse agriculture continues to be profitable. Recently, out-migration has lessened somewhat. This slowing of migration reflects the generally increasing affluence of the islands, mostly a result of tourism. On some of the islands, towns have actually grown in population, reflecting the increase in both foreign tourism and summer travel by urban Greeks. On these islands, new businesses have been opened, and greater opportunities for employment (for example, working in construction or in hotels and restaurants) are available now locally.

Kinship, Marriage, and Family

Kin Groups. Patterns of sociability within island communities are structured around gender, kinship and spiritual kinship, friendship, neighborliness, and (especially in larger towns) social class. Kinship is important in mutual aid, at ritual events, and in arranging for migration. At the same time, loyalty to one's immediate family (whether natal or marital) takes precedence over other kinship ties, and bitter conflicts can occur among relatives, especially over matters of inheritance. In addition, politics may also determine male patterns of sociability, and politics and factionalism may determine who frequents individual coffeehouses.

Spiritual kinship also plays an important role in island life, as it does elsewhere in Greece, offering the possibility of creating new economic, social, and political ties. Spiritual kinship is established through baptismal and wedding sponsorship, and those so related refer to each other as *koumbáros* (male) or *koumbára* (female). A godparent is *nonós* (male) or *noná* (female).

Kinship Terminology. Kinship, as elsewhere in Greece, is formally bilateral, with the bilaterality reflected in terms for consanguineal kin that follow a western European pattern of distinguishing lineal from collateral relatives, sex, and generation (Eskimo-type terminology). Terms for affinal kin distinguish relatives who have married into one's own family and members of the family into which one has married.

Domestic Unit. In general, island households tend to consist of married couples and their children. Although more extended forms of residential units (for example, those containing the parent of one of the spouses) are not unknown, they are not the norm, and the patterns of patrilocal residence noted elsewhere in Greece are rare. There is, however, a tendency toward matrilocal neighborhoods. Each family owns its own land or other means of subsistence. Marriage is negotiated between families, though it is becoming more and more common for young people to take the initiative in choosing their own partners. Part of the negotiation is the arrangement of the dowry, to be given by the young woman's parents. Although dowry was legally abolished by the recent Socialist government, it is still an important social institution. It is common in the islands for a dowry to consist of a house, though other property (such as land) may also be given. Neolocal residence after marriage is preferred, though young people may live temporarily with one or the other set of parents.

Separation by gender is a striking feature of island—and particularly village—life. Men's and women's tasks, use of space, and sociability are in many respects distinct, with the men's world centered on work and the coffeehouse (*kafenío*) and the women's on the home, neighborhood, and religious activities. There is a close symbolic association of the woman with the house. Not only do most of a woman's tasks revolve around the house, but its order and cleanliness reflect her character and diligence, and her position as *nikokirá* (mistress of the house) is a source of power and influence. Houses may be passed on (through the dowry system) in the female line. Naming also reflects a sense of distinct paternal and maternal lines. The firstborn female is named after her mother's mother; the second, after her father's. First sons are generally given their paternal grandfather's name; second sons, that of their mother's father. Although women take their husband's last names at marriage, they do not take a female form of the husband's first name (as is the practice in some other areas of Greece). Women are responsible for the spiritual welfare of their families, tending the household icons, observing mourning rituals for the dead, and making vows and pilgrimages on behalf of family members.

Socialization. Children are raised in the household of their parents, usually with frequent help from other relatives, particularly grandmothers. Children also tend other children and form play groups. Verbal threats of a sometimes drastic nature are frequently employed in disciplining children—a common example is *tha fas ksílo,* "you'll eat wood"—but physical punishment is unusual. Young children are expected to be shy with strangers, and this is considered normal. Boys are given considerably more freedom than girls, who are expected to stay closer to home and to help with household chores.

Inheritance. Inheritance is equal among all children, by Greek law and by custom. A daughter's dowry counts as her portion of the inheritance. If the youngest child remains at home and cares for the aging parents, she or he is entitled to the family house and a somewhat larger portion of the inheritance when the parents die.

Social and Political Organization

The Cyclades are part of the state of modern Greece. They belong to the geographic region known as the Aegean Islands, which also includes the Dodecanese, Lesvos, Samos, and Chios. The Cyclades themselves form a separate administrative unit or department (*nomós*), containing eight eparchies, eight municipalities, and 109 communities (*kinóites*), each of which generally is comprised of one or more villages. The town of Ermoupolis on the island of Syros is the capital of the nomós. Greece is a parliamentary democracy and, as Greek citizens, the inhabitants of the Cyclades participate in democratic political processes of the region and nation. Each community elects its own officials, as well as voting for regional and national candidates. Many migrants remain registered to vote in their home communities and return there on election day to cast their ballots. The Cyclades can perhaps best be described as "middle of the road" with respect to political affiliation. In the 1985 national parliamentary elections, for example, 45.39 percent of the islanders voted for the Conservative party, Nea Dimocratia, and 48.12 percent for the main Socialist party, PASOK. (The rest voted for various leftist parties.) In elections in the summer of 1989, the vote shifted to 49.09 percent for Nea Dimocratia and 41.18 percent for PASOK.

Religion and Expressive Culture

Religious Beliefs. The majority of islanders are of the Greek (Eastern) Orthodox faith, though the Cyclades also have a large Catholic minority, the result of long years of Italian rule. Because the islands' Catholic populations are descended—in part, at least—from the Venetians who once ruled the island, religious differences are sometimes exacerbated by class differences.

Beliefs in magic, ghosts, and other spirits are still to be found among at least some islanders. The most widespread and enduring belief, however, is the belief in the evil eye (*máti*). As elsewhere in Greece, no baby is ever seen without its blue bead, medallion, or other object to protect it from the harmful glance of those who have the "eye," and certain individuals are believed to have the knowledge and skill to diagnose and counter the eye's ill effects.

The islands of the Cyclades derive their name from a holy place, the ancient sacred island of Delos, which once drew pilgrims and visitors from around the ancient world. Today, while the ruins of this ancient glory still attract foreign visitors, other islands such as Mykonos, Naxos, and Thera have also become notable tourist attractions. In addition, the Cyclades are the home of such important contemporary holy places as the Church of the Annunciation of Tinos and the Church of the Hundred Gates at Paros, popular destinations for Greek pilgrims, especially on major holy days. In general, the islands are becoming increasingly attractive to both tourists and urban Greeks who are drawn by the Cyclades's rugged scenery, picturesque towns and villages, and cultural diversity.

Ceremonies. The liturgical calendar structures the ritual year with its sequences of saints' days and other holy days. In addition, the life-cycle rites of baptism, marriage, and death are important familial and community ceremonial events. Each village has its particular saint's day, which is celebrated with a church service, visiting and eating at village houses, and eating, music, and dancing at the village tavernas. As elsewhere in Greece, one celebrates name days (the day of the saint for whom one is named) rather than birthdays. In recent years, these village saints' days (*paniyíria*) have tended to become somewhat commercialized. They are advertised to townspeople and tourists, and sometimes the village even charges admission. The major religious holiday of the Greek Orthodox liturgical cycle is Easter. Preceded by the long period of Lent (*Sarakostí*), it is a time of intense activity in the island villages. Houses are cleaned and whitewashed, special Easter sweets are baked, and animals are slaughtered for the Easter feast. Many villagers who have migrated to Athens return to their native villages for the holiday. The climax of Easter services comes at midnight on Saturday, when the church bells ring to proclaim the resurrection and the congregants join in a procession around the village in celebration. Afterward, families return to their homes to break their fast with a large meal, and there follow several days of celebration in the houses and tavernas.

Death and Afterlife. Although conventions of mourning such as the wearing of black are less scrupulously observed by a younger generation, death continues to be commemorated with a long mourning period (usually three years) marked by periodic memorial services (*mnimósina*). At the end of this period, it is the custom on at least some of the islands to disinter the bones and place them in an ossuary, at which time the formal mourning period ends.

Bibliography

Barber, R. L. N. (1987). *The Cyclades in the Bronze Age.* Iowa City: University of Iowa Press.

Bent, James Theodore (1884). *The Cyclades, or Life among the Insular Greeks.* Reprint. 1965. Chicago: Argonaut.

Dimen, Muriel, and Ernestine Friedl, eds. (1976). *Regional Variation in Modern Greece and Cyprus: Toward a Perspective on the Ethnography of Modern Greece.* Annals of the New York Academy of Sciences, 268. New York.

Kolodny, Emile Y. (1974). _La Population des Îles de la Grèce._ 2 vols. Aix-en-Provence: Edisud.

JILL DUBISCH

Cypriots

ETHNONYM: Kypriotes

Orientation

Identification. Cypriots are the inhabitants of the island of Cyprus, an independent republic since 1960. Two principal ethnic groups—Turkish and Greek—form the majority populations on Cyprus; there are small numbers of Armenians and Maronites as well.

Location. Cyprus, the third-largest island of the Mediterranean, has an area of 9,251 square kilometers. It lies 64 kilometers south of Turkey and 96 kilometers west of Syria. The northern and southwestern portions of the island, roughly two-thirds of its area, are composed of hilly and mountainous terrain, while the remaining third is relatively flat. Of the total landmass, 49.6 percent is suitable for farming. The climate is typically Mediterranean, with low annual precipitation (50 centimeters, average) and frequent summer droughts. Temperatures fall to mean winter averages of 7° to 13° C, and rise to summer averages of 29° to 35° C. Water resources are scant—rivers are shallow and short, and they dry up during the summer. There are few fish in the coastal waters, and the only large wild animal indigenous to the island is the mouflon (wild sheep), and it is nearly extinct today. Other native fauna include hares, foxes, hedgehogs, and numerous species of birds.

Demography. Population estimates for the island are somewhat confused. In 1970 there were 628,000 Cypriots, with approximately 82 percent of Greek extraction and 18 percent of Turkish descent. At that time, Greek Cypriot communities accounted for 97 percent of the land area of the island, and Turkish Cypriot communities controlled 3 percent. However, beginning in the mid-1970s, as the Turkish communities sought independence, there have been successive waves of emigrants—principally to Greece and the United Kingdom, although also to the United States, Canada, Australia, and South Africa. When, as a result of the Turkish independence movement of the early 1960s, a territory comprising 37 percent of the country was occupied by Turkey in the north, there were large-scale displacements of the population—some 180,000 Greek Cypriot refugees fled south during the occupation period—and a fresh incursion of settlers from the Turkish mainland, further confusing the demographic picture. The economic disruption resulting from the political problems of the island during the 1970s and 1980s has also touched off new waves of emigration, as people have sought more secure working opportunities. In 1990, the over-all population was estimated at 708,000 (78 percent Greek and 18.7 percent Turkish).

Linguistic Affiliation. Both Turkish and Greek are official languages on Cyprus, with Greek having far more speakers. English is used as a second language by most Greek and Turkish speakers.

History and Cultural Relations

The archaeological record discloses settlement along the southern coast of Cyprus prior to 6000 B.C. Bronze Age cultures actively traded with Crete, Anatolia, Syria, and Egypt, and early records indicate that the island was an important source of copper. At around 1200 B.C., the first Greek immigrants are thought to have begun arriving from the Peloponnesos, with the major influx occurring between 1100 and 700 B.C. These new immigrants firmly established the Greek language on the island and founded six city-kingdoms. The Phoenicians established a colony in 800 B.C., and aboriginal inhabitants had a kingdom as well. Beginning in the early 700s B.C., the island came under the domination of the Assyrians, who ruled for about 150 years, during which time the arts—particularly poetry, bronzework, and ironwork—flourished. The Egyptians followed the Assyrians and ruled until the Cypriots allied themselves with Persia in 525 B.C. However, during the next 200 years, the island strongly supported and identified with the Attic revolts against Persia, and finally it came under direct Greek rule in 323 B.C. The Romans annexed Cyprus in 58 B.C., and it was during the Roman period that Christianity was introduced to the island. When the Roman Empire split, in A.D. 395, Cypriot Christians were subject to the Byzantine Empire, but in 488 the church was granted autocephalous status. There were periods of insecurity, as the island was periodically subject to frequent Arab raids, but these were lessened first by treaties and later by the Byzantine accession, in 965, to complete control of Cyprus. When the governor of Cyprus rebelled against the Byzantine Empire in the late 1100s, the crusading forces of King Richard I seized the island and later sold it to the dispossessed king of Jerusalem. Thus began a long feudal period, as the new ruler granted lands on the island to his supporters. Because of its location and the loyalties of its rulers, the island also then became a staging area for further crusades. Control of the island was contested, first lost to Genoa, and later ceded to Venice, and then the island fell to a Turkish invasion in 1571. It is from the ensuing three-century period of Ottoman rule that most of the present Turkish Cypriot minority can be traced. Muslim settlers were brought to the island, the feudal system was dismantled, and all remnants of the Latin church were suppressed in favor of the Eastern Orthodox version. The Ottomans relied upon the archbishop of Cyprus to collect taxes and impose order, which contributed to rebellions by the Turkish settlers in the 1700s and 1800s. In 1878, the Cyprus Convention established British administration of the island while retaining Turkish sovereignty, so that the British could establish a base from which to protect the Ottoman Empire's possessions from possible Russian incursion. However, during World War I the British and their former Turkish allies found themselves on opposing sides, and the British annexed the island, eventually declaring it a crown colony in 1925. The Greek population was at first amenable to British annexation, hoping that this would eventually lead to *enosis* (union with Greece). However, the strong minority population of Turks was equally adamant in its desire for *taksim* (separation), and since that time these two competing drives have led to political agitation and violence. The years between 1947 and 1959 were marked by demonstrations, bombings, and other such violence, as enosis and taksim factions vied with one another and also against movements toward self-government. Finally, with United Nations involvement, Greece and Turkey settled the issue by establishing independent republic status for Cyprus, which would not allow the partition of the island nor political or economic union with any other state. The new constitution provided for a sharing of administrative, executive, and judicial functions between the two ethnic communities, but its implementation was problematic and caused more violence. In 1964, the United Nations intervened, sending a UN peacekeeping force to control the situation. Nevertheless, conflict between the two Cypriot populations increased, troops from both Greece and Turkey were smuggled in, and throughout the period there were frequent threats of invasion by one or the other of the two larger nations. In 1974, following an assassination attempt against the Cypriot president on the part of Greece, Turkish forces invaded the island, eventually succeeding in occupying 37 percent of the island. In 1983, the Turkish Cypriot representative on the island declared the independent Turkish Republic of Northern Cyprus, but this independent status has remained unrecognized by all nations other than Turkey. The self-proclaimed Turkish Republic covers 3,400 square kilometers and in 1990 had an estimated population of 171,000, 99 percent of whom are Turks.

Settlements

Cyprus is, and has traditionally been, largely agricultural and rural in orientation. For historic and economic reasons, there are few coastal settlements—the island was often plagued by pirates, and the lack of fish meant that there was little economic incentive for settling on the coast. Houses in the villages are two- to four-room structures of sun-dried mud brick or stone, with long, flat roofs also made of mud. Village settlements were and remain ethnically exclusive, although in the cities such strict divisions necessarily broke down. Nonetheless, even in the cities, there tends to be a marked division into ethnically homogeneous enclaves. Some 40 percent of the population lived in the cities as of 1970, and that ratio has been steadily increasing.

Economy

Although agriculture is the principal economic activity on Cyprus, it is inefficient and incapable of providing full employment even for the small village populations. Principal crops are wheat, barley, and citrus fruits, grown on small, scattered plots. Livestock are kept, particularly sheep and goats. The Greek Cypriots raise pigs. Industry is limited on Cyprus and focuses on copper and iron pyrite mining. Petroleum refining, the manufacture of cement and asbestos products, and electricity are currently being developed, as are light manufacturing enterprises. The Turkish Cypriot sector is today nearly completely divorced from that of the Greeks, and it has had greater difficulties in development. The tourist trade, which had been of great importance to the economy since 1960, suffered greatly during the period of the Turkish

land occupations, but it has been recovering rapidly in the Greek Cypriot portion of the island.

Agricultural labor is considered an exclusively male activity, and, except in times of necessity, a "proper" woman will avoid such work. Land is privately owned and is cultivated by its owner. The scattered, piecemeal nature of farm plots directly derives from the fact that a man's property has traditionally been divided up among his heirs, rather than kept together as a shared family patrimony.

Kinship

The Greek Cypriots reckon kinship bilaterally, but kinship ties beyond the nuclear family or the three-generation-deep household are unimportant. The relationship between godchild and godparent is expected to be a close one and to endure throughout the lifetimes of its members. Ceremonial kinship establishes a *koumbari* relationship; individuals who stand in ceremonial kinship to one another are prohibited from marriage to one another. Among Turkish Cypriots, kinship is reckoned patrilineally.

Marriage and Family

Marriage. The family is the fundamental social unit of Greek Cypriot society, and its importance is reflected in the practice of arranged marriages. Engagements of two to eight years are common, and marriages must be celebrated in the church. The Greek Cypriot bride brings a dowry, which constitutes her portion of the familial inheritance; among Turkish Cypriots, the dowry does not occur. In the countryside, there is a strong tendency toward village endogamy. The church prohibits marriage between second cousins or more closely related blood kin, and tradition prohibits marriage between individuals sharing in a koumbari relationship, as mentioned earlier. Divorce is neither socially nor religiously countenanced.

Domestic Unit. The household is usually composed of a single nuclear family, although it can include the parents of either husband or wife as well, and sometimes it also includes newly married offspring of the core husband-wife pair, depending on a number of circumstances, mostly economic. The household is patriarchal—that is, its oldest male member has the strongest voice in the ordering of familial affairs. There is a strong emphasis on family honor, and each individual member is held to represent that honor. Women of the household are thought to embody the most important potential threat to that honor—particularly in the possibility that they may comport themselves immodestly. Consequently, the males of the household act as the public family spokesmen and work and live in the more public sphere, while the women are expected to confine themselves as far as possible to the domestic sphere.

Inheritance. The estate of an individual is shared equally by all his or her offspring. However, daughters receive their portion in the form of a dowry, and land tends to pass to sons.

Socialization. Child rearing during the early years of life is the province of the mother and other female members of the household old enough to lend a hand. The family is the focus of all social values, the most important being the principles of (family) loyalty, honor, and shame. This emphasis on familial honor is shared by Turkish Cypriots, who also highly value principles of discipline, religiosity, propriety, and hospitality. A child's formal education begins at age 5, when he or she begins six years of compulsory elementary education. The educational systems of the Turkish and Greek sectors are segregated and separately administered. Secondary education extends to vocational and technical training, much of which is offered free, but there is no university on Cyprus. Students wishing to pursue education at the university level go abroad, most commonly to Greece, Turkey, Britain, or the United States.

Sociopolitical Organization

Social Organization. In the Greek Cypriot communities, individual families and the relations established between families on the basis of friendship or ceremonial kinship ties provide the framework for organized action. Leadership beyond the family level is achieved by establishing a reputation for reliability, wisdom, strength, success in business, and honor.

Political Organization. The Republic of Cyprus, formed in 1960, adopted a constitution that provided for the election of a president (chosen from the Greek Cypriot community) and a vice president (chosen from the Turkish Cypriots), each to serve five-year terms; a cabinet; and an elected house of representatives. The ethnic composition of the last two bodies was to be regulated by constitutional provisions as well, reflecting the majority position of Greek ethnics in the general populace. The events of the 1970s and 1980s have produced a number of changes, particularly the declaration of the independent Turkish Republic of Northern Cyprus in 1983. The most apparent change in the recognized constitutional government has been an increase in the number of governmental positions held by ethnic Greeks. Local government officials are either appointed (district officers) or elected (mayors, council members).

Social Control. Both the Greek and Turkish communities have a formal police body, and a UN civil police force acts as liaison between the two. Roman law forms the basis for the formal Cypriot justice system; community courts are still in use in Turkish communities, although the government officially abolished them in 1964.

Conflict. Cyprus has had a turbulent history over the last three decades, with ethnic separatism often leading to violence. The UN has been involved with the republic, in mediating and peacekeeping roles, since the 1959 Zurich-London agreements that led to the republic's formation. Because of the breakdown in relations between the Turkish and Greek communities beginning in the early 1960s, the UN has had to maintain a continuous presence on the island since 1963.

Religion and Expressive Culture

Religious Beliefs. The Turkish Cypriots are Sunni Muslims, while Greek Cypriots are practitioners in the Orthodox Church of Cyprus. The Orthodox Church of Cyprus is a part of the Eastern Orthodox Church, but it was granted autocephalous status in A.D. 488. The Greek church emphasizes the mysteries of faith and the performance of ritual. The veneration of icons is a strong characteristic of the faith. Turkish Cypriot beliefs are also devoutly held, but they place greater emphasis on "works" than do precepts of the Greek church.

Fasting, almsgiving, and the making of a pilgrimage to Mecca are all important, as is true throughout Muslim society. There are a few Maronite Catholics from Syria, Roman Catholics, and Anglicans on Cyprus as well. The small Armenian population participates in the Armenian (Gregorian) Apostolic Church.

Religious Practitioners. In the Orthodox Church of Cyprus, the highest spiritual authority is held by the archbishop, who, during the Ottoman Empire, was also made responsible for the secular well-being of the faithful and given the title of _ethnarch_. The spiritual leader for the Muslim community is called the _mufti_.

Ceremonies. Within the Orthodox Greek communities, ritual expression accompanies the seven sacraments of baptism, confirmation, confession, Communion, marriage, ordination, and extreme unction. Easter is the most important of the ceremonial occasions on the liturgical calendar. For the Turks, Ramadan is of special importance.

Arts. There is a strong respect for the arts in Cypriot culture, and cultural support is provided through both individuals and the government. Theater, writing, painting, and sculpture are strongly encouraged.

Bibliography

Attalides, Michael A. (1976). "Forms of Peasant Incorporation in Cyprus during the Last Century." In _Regional Variation in Modern Greece and Cyprus: Toward a Perspective on the Ethnography of Modern Greece_, edited by Muriel Dimen and Ernestine Friedl. Annals of the New York Academy of Sciences 268:363–378. New York.

Attalides, Michael A. (1977). _Cyprus Reviewed_. Nicosia: Jus Cypri Association.

Durrell, Lawrence (1957). _Bitter Lemons_. New York: E. P. Dutton.

Ertekun, N. M. (1984). _The Cyprus Dispute and the Birth of the Turkish Republic of Northern Cyprus_. Oxford: Oxford University Press.

King, Russell, and Sarah Ladbury (1982). "The Cultural Construction of Political Reality: Greek and Turkish Cyprus since 1974." _Anthropological Quarterly_ 55:1–16.

Loizos, Peter (1981). _The Heart Grown Bitter: A Chronicle of Cypriot War Refugees_. Cambridge: Cambridge University Press.

NANCY E. GRATTON

Czechs

ETHNONYMS: Češi or Čechové (plural), Čech (singular), referring to people whose native language is Czech and, more specifically, to those native to or residing in Bohemia (Čechy); Moravané (plural), Moravan (singular), referring to the Czech-speaking population native to or residing in Moravia (Morava)

Orientation

Identification. Czechs constitute 94.2 percent (1986) of the population of the Czech Republic (Česká republica, hereafter CR), which is federated with the Slovak Republic (SR) in the Czech and Slovak Federative Republic (Česká a Slovenská Federativní Republika, or CSFR).

Location. CR is bounded by Poland on the north, Germany on the north and west, Austria on the south, and the Slovak Republic on the east. The geographic location of CR is between 12°05′ and 18°51′ E and 51°03′ and 48°33′ N; the area is 78,864 square kilometers. Historically, CR consists of Bohemia, the largest province, in the west; Moravia, to the east of it; and the part of Silesia just below the northern Moravian border with Poland. Bohemia is ringed by low mountain ranges, with the highest peak (Sněžka) reaching an altitude of 1,602 meters. The southern half of Bohemia's interior is an elevated plateau; in the northern half, the distinguishing feature is the plain along the Labe (Elbe) River. The dominant feature of Moravia is the basin of the Morava River separating the Bohemian massif from the westernmost extension of the Carpathian Mountains in SR. The climate of CR is predominantly continental, with some influence of oceanic weather systems. Summers are warm, winters cold. The average temperature in Prague, the capital, varies from a high of 19.9° C in July to a low of −0.8° C in January, with an annual average of 9.7° C. The average precipitation is around 70 centimeters per year, with the summer months being the wettest. The higher elevations along the border receive more moisture than the interior. The main Bohemian river, the Labe, is joined by the Vltava (Moldau) about 32 kilometers north of Prague and empties into the North Sea north of Hamburg. The Morava, which flows from the north, marks the boundary in southern Moravia between CR and SR, and some 50 kilometers farther south it empties into the Danube.

Demography. Historically, CR has been a land of small towns (10,000 to 30,000 inhabitants), their distribution reflecting the pattern of medieval settlement and growth. The relatively early industrialization of the area has increased the concentration of population in cities at the expense of rural areas. While the rural exodus continues to the present day, the inhabitants of metropolitan areas, especially Prague, tend to buy or build summer cottages in the country and to spend much of their free time away from the city, especially during the summer. The years immediately following World War II were marked by high population mobility. The border regions, inhabited from the thirteenth century on by a high proportion of German-speaking people, were resettled by Czechs after World War II when more than 2.5 million Bohemian and Moravian Germans were transferred from the country or chose to leave. The population of CR is 10,365,000 (1989 estimate), with a population density of 131 per square kilometer (1988 estimate). Of this total, 94.2 percent are Czechs and 3.9 percent Slovaks, with the remainder divided among several ethnic minorities (0.7 percent Polish, 0.5 percent German, with several other groups represented). Prague is the largest city and capital, as well as the federal capital, with a population of 1,206,098 (as of the end of 1987). Brno, the second-largest city and unofficial capital of Moravia, has a population of about 400,000.

Linguistic Affiliation. As a West Slavic language, Czech is a member of the Indo-European Language Family. It is most closely related to Slovak, with which it is mutually intelligible. Spoken Czech is differentiated into regional dialects still to be heard in Moravia and several marginal areas of Bohemia, but interdialects—especially Common Czech—have been replacing local and regional dialects at an increasing rate. Literary Czech is the form of the language used in writing and formal communication. Czech makes use of the Latin (Roman) alphabet supplemented by several diacritical marks.

History and Cultural Relations

After the fall of the Great Moravian Empire at the beginning of the tenth century, much of today's Slovak Republic was incorporated into the Hungarian state, while Prague developed as the center of what was to become the Bohemian Kingdom. The crowning of the first Bohemian king took place in 1085 and the title became hereditary in 1198. The peak of medieval civilization was attained during the second half of the fourteenth century; the first university in central Europe was established in Prague in 1348. The beginning of the fifteenth century was marked by the teachings of Jan Hus, a Czech religious reformer, and, after his death at the stake in Constance in 1415, by wars against the propapal King Sigismund. When the Bohemian throne became vacant in 1526, a member of the Habsburg dynasty was elected Bohemian king. Less than a century later, in 1620, when the Czech estates were defeated in the battle of White Mountain (Bílá Hora) near Prague, the Bohemian Kingdom lost its independence and its provinces were declared the hereditary property of the Habsburg family. Wholesale emigration—resulting from forcible re-Catholicization, the effects of the Thirty Years' War (1618–1648), and epidemics of plague and other diseases—reduced the population of Bohemia by about one-half and that of Moravia by about one-fourth. A period referred to as "the darkness" (temno) ensued, and it was not until the end of the eighteenth century that the Czech national revival began. Independence for the Czechs arrived in 1918 with the breakup of the Austro-Hungarian Empire. The Czechoslovak Republic, which resulted from the political reorganization of Europe in the aftermath of World War I, included not only the historic Bohemian Kingdom (Bohemia, Moravia, and a part of Silesia) but also Slovakia and Carpathian Ruthenia in the extreme east. The new republic lasted a mere twenty years. Following the infamous Munich Agreement of 1938, Bohemia and Moravia lost over a third of their combined area to Germany. On 15 March 1939 Germany annexed the remainder and declared it a protectorate, thus effectively ending the independent existence of the Czechoslovak Republic. (Slovakia became a nominally independent state under the protection of the Third Reich.) Czechoslovakia was reestablished in 1945, though without Carpathian Ruthenia, which was ceded to the USSR. The majority of the population wished to continue the democratic tradition of the interwar period and hoped to establish the country as a bridge between West and East. However, in February 1948 the Communists took over the government, and Czechoslovakia became part of the cultural, economic, and political orbit of the Soviet Union. On 1 January 1969, four months after the Warsaw Pact armies put a stop to attempts to create "socialism with a human face," the federalization of the Czechoslovak Socialist Republic into the Czech Socialist Republic and the Slovak Socialist Republic took place. The transformation of Czechoslovakia from a rigid Communist country into a democracy began in November 1989 and was accomplished bloodlessly with remarkable speed. One of Czechoslovakia's best-known dissidents, the playwright Václav Havel, became president on 29 December 1989.

The Czechs have always considered themselves as belonging culturally to western Europe, and no more so than after they were incorporated into the sphere of Soviet influence in the late 1940s. Because they constitute the westernmost Slavic outpost, surrounded as they are by speakers of German, and because of the memory of official Germanization during much of the eighteenth century as well as forcible Germanization during World War II, the potential for ethnic tension between Czechs and Germans has always existed. In prewar Czechoslovakia (1918–1939), the attitude of the Czechs toward the much less urbanized Slovaks was patronizing. After World War II, the relationship between the two peoples continued to be asymmetrical until 1969, when the federalization of the country helped to bring about a measure of dynamic balance between them. Ethnic tensions resurfaced in 1990 as a result of Slovak expectations of a greater degree of autonomy.

Economy

Subsistence and Commercial Activities. Before World War II, agriculture, commerce, and industry were for the most part in private hands. After the Communist takeover in 1948, commerce and industry were completely nationalized, and virtually all agricultural production came to be based on unified agricultural cooperatives (1,025 in 1987) and state farms (166 in 1987). The cooperatives employed about four times as many workers as the state farms. Because of a fairly high level of mechanization, the total number of persons engaged in agriculture is about one-fourth of those employed in industry.

Industrial Arts. During the nineteenth century, Bohemia became the industrial heart of the Austro-Hungarian Empire. It was known not only for its heavy industry but also for a long and distinguished tradition of ceramic, glass, and textile manufacture.

Trade. Until the introduction of socialism after World War II, the economy was to a considerable extent capitalistic. After 1948, all commerce was managed and controlled by the state. The inefficiency of central planning was compensated for by a "second economy"—obtaining goods or services in short supply by barter or by paying someone willing to perform a service on a private basis. Relying on acquaintances to get things done (networking) was widespread. Privatization of business and industry began in 1990, but it is

likely to proceed slowly. A vigorous economy may take years to reestablish.

Division of Labor. Women have made significant strides since World War II in terms of education, employment opportunities, and participation in public life, and they have benefited from social legislation. However, some of the discriminatory practices and behaviors found in many parts of the world exist in CR as well—in particular, the disproportionately large number of women in the lower half of the pay scale and the excessive demands on employed women to do far more than their share of child-rearing and household tasks.

Land Tenure. Since the late 1940s, the vast majority of land has been publicly owned. The few exceptions include small gardens, adjacent to family dwellings or on the outskirts of large towns, and small plots (on the order of half a hectare) that members of unified agricultural cooperatives are allowed to hold for family use.

Kinship, Marriage, and Family

Kinship. For the Czechs, the effective kin group is limited to the closest relatives. Most people consider collateral relatives beyond uncles, aunts, and first cousins to be rather distant and are likely to see them only at weddings or funerals. Descent is bilateral, with family names patronymic. Kinship terminology is of the Eskimo type, emphasizing both lineal descent and generation membership.

Marriage. For much of this century the selection of a spouse and the decision to marry has rested with the young couple. Before World War II, education and economic standing of the prospective bride and groom were of considerable importance. Men did not usually marry until they completed their education and were launched in their careers, typically in their late twenties or early thirties; women at marriage were for the most part in their early or mid-twenties. In 1986, the average age of individuals marrying for the first time was much lower: 35.7 percent of women were below 20 years of age, 51.9 percent of women and 58.4 percent of men between 20 and 24, and 23.8 percent of men between 25 and 29. Wedding celebrations rarely exceed one day. The most desired postmarital residence is neolocal; however, housing shortages in big cities since World War II have made that goal difficult to attain. Divorce, relatively rare at the beginning of the century, is now quite common: there were 2.2 divorces per 100 marriages in 1919, but 37 per 100 in 1987. The two-child family is the ideal, although childless families among career-oriented spouses are not uncommon. The number of legally approved abortions per 100 births amounted to 62.4 in 1986.

Domestic Unit. The nuclear family has long been the typical domestic group, especially in the cities.

Inheritance. Inheritances in former times helped perpetuate differences between the rich and poor. Under socialism, the importance of inheritance diminished. Nevertheless, most parents make every effort to help their children become comfortable.

Socialization. Until World War II, middle-class women as a rule did not hold a job but stayed home to manage the household and take care of children. At present, with women accounting for 46.3 percent (1987) of those employed in the national economy, small children not cared for by mothers on generous maternity leave are enrolled in nurseries or are in the care of relatives, especially grandmothers. Mothers tend to exercise more authority over children than do fathers. Parents tend more to criticize than to praise their children. Czechs place a high value on education and on academic titles. In terms of values, children are brought up to be egalitarian, individualistic, personally orderly, pragmatic, rational, hardworking (for one's own benefit), peaceful, present-oriented, and materialistic.

Sociopolitical Organization

Social Organization. The traditional tripartite social structure—a sizable working class including the peasants, the middle class, and a relatively small upper class—gave way during Communism to a "classless" society with two distinct classes: privileged members of the higher echelons of the Communist party and the rest of the population. Material benefits also accrued to successful artists and to those who performed valuable services or distributed goods in short supply.

Political Organization. Between 1918 and 1939, political life was characterized by a large number of rival political parties. Between 1948 and 1990, there were only three, all part of the National Front, but the Communist party had a monopoly on power. The free national election in June of 1990 was again characterized by the rivalry of a large number of political parties. The republic as a whole (CSFR) has two legislative houses—the Chamber of Nations and the Chamber of the People. The highest administrative organs of CR are the Czech National Council, the government of CR, the supreme court, the office of the prosecutor general, and the defense council. Administration on the level of the region (kraj), district (okres), and community (obec) continues to be in the hands of the respective national councils, but some administrative changes are under consideration.

Social Control. Conformity with the law is maintained by a police force and a strict and efficient court system. Since the end of 1989, political dissent is again tolerated. A tradition of strong bureaucracy, inherited from Austro-Hungarian times, continues unabated.

Conflict. The Czechs view their history as a series of conflicts with the surrounding German-speaking population. The most recent expressions of this conflict were the German occupation of the area from 1939 to 1945 and the removal of the great majority of Germans after World War II.

Religion and Expressive Culture

Religious Beliefs and Practices. Christianity was introduced to the area during the ninth century by both German and Byzantine missions. By the time the bishopric of Prague was established in 973, Latin had replaced Old Church Slavic as the liturgical language. A serious breach with Rome occurred during the early part of the fifteenth century as a result of the reformational movement inspired by Jan Hus. His "Protestant" legacy became an important aspect of Czech national heritage, having been further reinforced by the efforts at forcible re-Catholicization of the population during the Counter-Reformation and the association of Catholicism with the Habsburg rule. The history of Bohemia accounts in

large measure for the nature of post–World War I religious sentiments: the generally lukewarm Catholicism among the Czechs (but less so in Moravia); the fairly devout Protestantism represented by several sects; the establishment of the Czechoslovak Church (a splinter from Roman Catholicism) in 1920; and the rise of agnosticism and atheism. Many urban Czech Catholics went to church only to be baptized and married, and eventually they received their last rites and were buried by a priest. The attitude toward religion was rational rather than emotional. Relations among the members of various religious organizations were marked by tolerance. After 1948 the Communist government became hostile to organized religion and discouraged religious beliefs and observances by a variety of means, including intimidation and persecution. While the relations between the state and the Roman Catholic church were adversarial between 1948 and 1989, there was some resurgence of religious commitment in recent years, especially among young people. Nominally, at least, the country is predominantly Roman Catholic, but reliable figures concerning religious preference have not been available since the end of the last war. Christmas is the only religious holiday officially recognized, even though observances have in part been secularized. While Jan Hus is regarded as a national hero who laid down his life in defense of the truth, St. Wenceslaus (Václav), murdered around 930, is considered the country's patron saint.

Arts. The Czechs have a long and rich tradition in the arts, both folk and elite. Music is the most popular of the arts. There is a great deal of truth in the saying "Co Čech, to muzikant" (Every Czech is a musician). In literature, lyric poetry has surpassed in quality both prose and dramatic writing.

Medicine. Use of medicinal plants, based on empirical evidence gained over centuries, for the most part was replaced by use of synthetic drugs during the course of the first half of this century. In general, Czech medicine has followed the course of Western medicine and at present is keeping up with modern advances. Health care, including hospitalization and drugs, is available free or at nominal cost. Health spas are numerous and popular.

Bibliography

Nyrop, Richard F., ed. (1982). *Czechoslovakia: A Country Study*. 2nd ed. Washington, D.C.: United States Government.

Paul, David W. (1981). *Czechoslovakia: Profile of a Socialist Republic at the Crossroads of Europe*. Boulder, Colo.: Westview Press.

Salzmann, Zdenek, and Vladimír Scheufler (1986). *Komárov: A Czech Farming Village*. Enl. ed. Prospect Heights, Ill.: Waveland Press.

Statistická ročenka Československé Socialistické Republiky (Statistical yearbook of the Czechoslovak Socialist Republic). Prague and Bratislava: SNTL and ALFA. [Appears annually, now with an adjusted title.]

ZDENEK SALZMANN

Dalmatians

ETHNONYM: Dalmatinci

Orientation

Identification. Dalmatia is a region within the Republic of Croatia, formerly part of the Socialist Federative Republic of Yugoslavia. Although its population is predominantly Croatian, Dalmatia is included on the basis of its strong historical ties to other parts of Europe by way of the Mediterranean Sea. The term "Dalmatian" is derived from the name of the Illyrian tribe Delmatea, which inhabited the region in the first century B.C.

Location. Dalmatia lies on the rugged eastern coast of the Adriatic and is the southwesternmost region of Croatia. It stretches about 400 kilometers from the Bay of Kvarner to the Bay of Boka Kotorska in Montenegro, is up to 70 kilometers wide, and includes an archipelago of about 600 islands along the coast. Geographically the area can be divided into the islands, the coastal belt, and the hinterland. The entire area of Dalmatia covers 12,043 square kilometers. On its easternmost borders, running from north to south, are the irregular mountains of the Dinaric range, whose highest peak is Dinara (1,913 meters). Dalmatia is known for its karst topography, composed mainly of limestone, which easily erodes and dissolves in rainwater. Flowing along underground cracks, the water continues to widen and deepen these crevices until they become underground caves. When such a cave becomes large enough and the roof extends close to the surface, it then collapses, producing a depression or a sinkhole called a _dolina_. Larger depressions are called _polje_. These depressions often contain alluvial soil and usually constitute the only cultivable land in this region. The landscape can be pictured as vast areas of glistening and eroded limestone punctuated by many patches of green oasis. The Dalmatian climate is Mediterranean. The summers are very dry with scorching temperatures; however, in winter there is ample rainfall.

Demography. In 1981 the population of Dalmatia was estimated at 888,926 (78.3 percent Croatians, 11.5 percent Serbians, 6.2 percent ethnically unspecified Yugoslavs, and 4 percent others). The population density averages 64 persons per square kilometer. Differences in the population density between the islands, the coast, and the hinterland are remarkable. For example, the population density of the island of Lastovo is 18 persons per square kilometer, whereas the coastal urban center of Split has a population density of 275 persons per square kilometer. The uneven population density is related to areas of low fertility and high out-migration. Rough and unfertile terrain makes it hard to eke out a living, and this hardship is further accentuated by underdevelopment of industry. These factors force many people to look for wage labor elsewhere.

Linguistic Affiliation. Dalmatians speak regional dialects of the Croatian language (Ikavica, Jekavica, Čakavica). On some islands and parts of the coast mixtures of Croatian and Italian are found (e.g., Talijanština, or Croatian-Italian creole), attesting to the long influence of Venetian rule.

History and Cultural Relations

Dalmatia's position on the fringe of the Balkan peninsula has given it a tempestuous history and has made it the scene of many migrations, wars, and conquests. For millennia, Dalmatia has provided a link between the cultures of the East and the West. The first traces of humankind in Dalmatia date back 5,000–6,000 years, when archaeological evidence indicates that the people living here had links with other Mediterranean areas. The first historically recorded inhabitants of Dalmatia were the Illyrians, an Indo-European people who ruled the northwestern part of the Balkan peninsula. Many traces of their stone-piled grave sites (_gomila_) and fortified towns, surrounded by connecting circles of dry-stone walls, still stand today on the summits of the steep hills on both sides of the mountain chains that stretch down the coast. The Illyrians were not strong enough to stand up against the culturally more advanced, better organized, and materially stronger states of Greece and Rome, whose rulers became very interested in their opposite shores along the Adriatic. The Greeks spread up the coast from the fourth century B.C. and founded their colonies on both the mainland and islands: Issa (Vis), Pharos (Hvar), Corcyra Melaina (Korčula), Epidaurum (Cavtat), Iadera (Zadar), Tragurion (Trogir), and Salonia (Solin). During this time, the first vineyards were planted, olive groves cultivated, and southern fruit and vegetables grown. However, the Illyrian tribes did not relinquish their autonomy easily and continued to oppose Greek rule until the Roman conquest in the first century A.D. With the coming of the Romans, the whole coastal region began to develop rapidly. The conquerors organized administration, justice, and trade on the Roman model and built new towns in accordance with Roman city planning. With the building of new towns the Roman Empire began expanding into the hinterland toward the Dinaric range, as well as into the southern edges of the Pannonian Plain. Then, hard pressed by the barbarians, the Roman frontier fortifications on the Danube cracked, marking the disintegration of an empire already decaying from within. The Avars with their Slav allies pressed down into the Balkans, destroying what Rome had built over the centuries. But the Avar Kingdom soon disintegrated and the Avars disappeared from the Balkans, leaving their dead empire to the Slavs, who became Christianized and formed several small medieval states on the eastern shores of the Adriatic: Duklja, Zahumlje, and Croatia. Croatians settled the greatest part of the coast, where they remain to this day. The Franciscan, Dominican, and Benedictine orders had a great effect on cultural development, to which schools, various libraries, and archives still bear witness. City administrators began to appoint public notaries and draft city statutes in the course of the twelfth and thirteenth centuries. During the Renaissance, Dalmatia was a treasury of architecture, art, and literature. Venetian rule over Dalmatia (1420–1797) was established when the Croatian King Ladislav of Naples ceded part of the country to the Venetian republic. Warfare against the Turks also marked this period. (Ragusa [Dubrovnik], however, maintained its independent city-republic for centuries by skillful maneuvering and trade between the East and the West, until it was subjugated by Napoleon in 1808.) After the defeat of Kosovo (1389) and the fall of Constantinople (1453), Serbia, Bosnia and Herzegovina, and Albania gradually fell under Muslim Turkish domination. Dalmatia seemed likely to be the next victim. To avert this fate, a Croatian knight, Peter Kruzić, formed a corps of guerrillas called _uskoci_ (fugitives) at his stronghold of Klis (near Split) and was able to keep the Turks at bay for a time. However, from 1515 to 1540 Dalmatia was left to its own resources and almost the whole area—except the coastal cities and the islands—fell to the Turks. During later wars, Dalmatia's frontier with Turkey was continually changing, until 1718 when Dalmatia again came under Venice's dominion. Venice, however, was taken by the French and given to Austria. In 1805 Austria had to cede Dalmatia to Napoleon. In 1815, after the fall of Napoleon, Dalmatia was assigned to Austria again, following the Congress of Vienna. It remained part of the Austro-Hungarian Empire until 1918. After World War I Dalmatia, as well as the rest of Croatia, along with Slovenia and Serbia made up the Kingdom of Yugoslavia. However, Zadar and four islands were given to Italy. At the end of World War II, in 1945, this remainder of Dalmatia also became part of Yugoslavia.

Settlements

Coastal and island villages are nucleated (*zbijeni*). While those on the coast are adjacent to the sea, island villages are on both the interior and coastal areas. In the hinterland, they are more dispersed (*razbijeni*) and often located on the very fringe of fertile alluvial depressions.

Economy

Subsistence and Commercial Activities. Only about 20 percent of Dalmatia is utilized agriculturally, and most of this is on a subsistence level. In the hinterland, the arable regions consist mainly of karst depressions (polje). However, the potential of much of this land is lost to drought and poor drainage. Crops that have a summer growing season (e.g., corn, wheat, millet, tobacco, and grapes) are planted on these small scattered plots of land. Throughout the coastal belt and the islands, patches of fertile land on the hilly slopes are terraced with rock walls to form level plots (*podove* or *pristave*). The coastal and island soil is not suitable for cultivation of cereal grains, but it favors olives, figs, cherries, and above all grapes. Fishing is developed along the Dalmatian coast and the islands, especially in areas with good connections to the hinterland (e.g., Split, Šibenik, Zadar). Fishing is largely a subsistence activity since only about 15 percent of all fishermen are considered commercial. The most important type of fishing is seasonal (*periodički ribolov*), occurring at certain times of the year and in specific locations. Dalmatian men are historically famous for their seafaring capabilities and many today are employed by domestic and foreign vessels as navigators and ship captains. Animal husbandry is also limited to the subsistence level because there is very little grazing land available. Tourism is the newest and the most lucrative commercial activity. The picturesque coastline, the romantic islands, and the ancient cities, along with a mild Mediterranean climate, make Dalmatia one of the most frequented summer tourist areas in Europe.

Industrial Arts. The shipbuilding industry is the most developed commercial activity in Dalmatia, and a major shipbuilding yard is located in Split. Dalmatia has abundant reserves of limestone, and more than one-third of Yugoslavia's cement output comes from Split. Rich deposits of bauxite are exploited by the aluminum foundry near Šibenik. The rivers, except for a few kilometers of the Krka and Neretva, are unsuitable for navigation, but their precipitous falls make them natural sources of hydroelectric power.

Trade. Throughout the hinterland are well-established weekly markets (*pazari*) dating back to the Greek occupation. Here peasants sell their homegrown produce, crafts, and livestock.

Division of Labor. People living in Dalmatia, like other regions of Croatia and the Balkan peninsula, have traditionally maintained a strict division of labor. Women were in charge of the domestic sphere, whereas men were in charge of the public sphere. However, with the high rate of out-migration of able-bodied men (up to 20 percent in the underdeveloped regions of the hinterland), women are being employed as semiskilled and skilled factory workers (especially in the textile industry) and are in charge of the entire agricultural cycle as well as domestic work.

Land Tenure. Because of the scarcity of fertile land, landownership is held in high esteem. In the present context, despite the high rates of out-migration, property values have been escalating because of the influx of foreign currency. The most common family form that has existed in Dalmatia as in the rest of the Balkans has been the *zadruga*. The zadruga is a corporate family unit under which all holdings (e.g., property, livestock, land) are held communally. Although the traditional zadruga institutionally dissolved around World War I, a very strong patrilineal and patrilocal agnatic group with traditional structural principles of household composition has persisted over time.

Kinship

Kin Groups and Descent. There is regional differentiation in kinship because Dalmatia has been a meeting ground between the tribal Balkan kin-group types and the Western form of nuclear family organization. Because of this intermediacy, residential kin groups in the hinterland villages are still three-generational while the urban families are often nuclear. Descent is traced bilaterally, but patrilaterality is stressed in some regions. Fictive kinship through godparenthood (*kumstvo*) is significant in some regions.

Kinship Terminology. Kinship terms follow the Indo-European pattern with some stress on patrilineality.

Marriage and Family

Marriage. Although traditionally marriages were arranged, today there is greater individual freedom of choice. Marriages are monogamous, and village exogamy is prevalent in the hinterland. In the past, "bride stealing" (*otmica*) was practiced in some parts of the hinterland. One form of bride stealing—with the consent of the bride, sometimes to avoid dowry—still occurs in some areas and is known as *umicanje* (*umakniti se*, meaning "to remove"). Village exogamy is predominant in the hinterland. On the islands, village endogamy is common. Residence is patrilocal, matrilocal, or neolocal. The last form is necessarily prevalent when a couple moves from the village into the city; nevertheless, couples are strongly tied to their natal households not only economically but also psychologically. Traditionally, divorce was rare, but it is becoming more frequent in the urban centers.

Domestic Unit. The people who cook and eat meals around the same hearth and under the same roof (in the same house or *kuća*) are considered a family (*obitelj, porodica*). The household is frequently made up of grandparents, parents, and children. Sometimes this may also include patrilateral uncles or brothers, along with their wives and children.

Inheritance. Traditionally land was owned and inherited patrilineally. All sons inherited an equal share of the land, while daughters would marry out without a dowry in land. In some cases, however, a piece of land might be given to the daughter as part of her dowry if there were no inheriting sons. In modern times, however, daughters have a legal right to inherit an equal share as do their brothers, but in most cases they forgo their share in respect of custom.

Socialization. Most children are raised in three-generational households. Child care is divided between mothers and grandparents, who carry most of the burden because of the increased number of women in the work force. Socialization creates a sense of intergenerational dependency. Parents live for their children, and children believe that they should care for their aged parents.

Sociopolitical Organization

Social Organization. Dalmatia traditionally was organized on the basis of residence. The Dinaric or hinterland dwellers who were not in immediate contact with the Adriatic Sea were referred to as Vlachs (Vlaji). Traditionally they were tribal and were considered backward and hot-tempered by their coastal counterparts, known as Boduli. Further regional distinction is supported by various dialects, traditional costumes, rituals, and differentiation between village dwellers (seljaci) and city dwellers (gradjani). Strong patron-client relationships still persist throughout Dalmatia.

Political Organization. A region within the Republic of Croatia, which was formerly one of six Yugoslav republics, Dalmatia has twenty-three counties (općine). These counties are further divided into "community organizations" (mjesne zajednice), which are further divided into villages (sela).

Social Control and Conflict. Social control as well as prestige and authority are determined on the basis of sex and age, maleness and seniority being the dominant principles. The virginity and sexual morality of women are stressed and reinforced through the assignment of honor and shame. Social control also is exerted through gossip. Historically, conflict is noted on several levels: interpersonal, interfamilial, intervillage, interregional, and interethnic.

Religion and Expressive Culture

Religious Beliefs and Practices. Catholicism is the primary religion of Dalmatia, followed by Eastern Orthodoxy, and a small minority of Muslims who are mostly immigrants from other Balkan regions. Religious beliefs and practices are representations of syncretism between Christian and pagan forms. Religious beliefs and practices were not commonly expressed in this part of the world for many years because open expression of religious beliefs was not completely sanctioned in the Yugoslav communist context. However, in 1992 the newly independent Croatian government restored freedom of religious expression. Dalmatians staunchly believe in various supernatural beings. These include witches, fairies, and most commonly vampires (vukodlak). Women commonly tell fortunes by reading the patterns in the grounds remaining in the cups after drinking Turkish coffee.

Ceremonies. There are specific rituals exhibiting male chivalry that are exclusively found in Dalmatia. The most famous is a game called alka. Various rituals are related to the Christian church calendar. Both Catholics and Eastern Orthodox Christians observe (služe) a patron saint's day (slava) or a name day (imendan).

Arts. In Dalmatia there are several musical instruments; however, the most famous is a one-stringed viol (gusle), which accompanies epic or heroic singing done by men. Another is the mandolinlike lira, which is more prevalent on the islands. Both men and women, traditionally gender-segregated, sing ganga and ojkavica. Both of these pieces are composed by women or men in a decameter and are sung a cappella. Circle dances (kola) are common throughout Dalmatia; however, their steps and costumes vary regionally. Various forms of carving on both wood and rock date back several centuries and can be found throughout the region. Dalmatia also has one of the richest representations of different architectural types in the world.

Medicine. In the folk system, illness is commonly attributed to hot/cold imbalance, generally believed to be caused by cold drafts. For most ailments folk practitioners recommend that patients "sweat out the evil" (da iznoje zlo) by covering themselves up with several heavy layers of blankets. Western medicine is widespread.

Death and Afterlife. Death is considered a transitory period between life on earth and the everlasting life in heaven. After death the soul can either go to hell, purgatory, or heaven, depending on one's earthly sins. After death, the body is kept overnight in the house and in an elaborate procession carried to the church the following day. A form of chanting (naricanje, nabrajanje) commonly starts immediately after the person dies and lasts through the next day when the person is buried. After the church ceremony the body is buried in an elaborately built grave that generally stands above the ground. Widowed women wear black until their death. If they happen to remarry, which is very unlikely, they abandon this custom.

See also Croats

Bibliography

Davis, J. (1977). _People of the Mediterranean: An Essay in Comparative Social Anthropology._ London: Routledge & Kegan Paul.

Davis, James C. (1986). _Rise from Want._ Philadelphia: University of Pennsylvania Press.

Fortis, Alberto (1774). _Viaggio in Dalmazia._ Venice. Croatian translation. 1984. _Put po Dalmaciji._ Zagreb: Globus.

Hammel, Eugene A. (1968). _Alternative Social Structures and Ritual Relations in the Balkans._ Englewood Cliffs, N.J.: Prentice-Hall.

Kadić, Ante (1976). "The Democratic Spirit of the Poljica Commune." In _Communal Families in the Balkans: The Zadruga,_ edited by Robert F. Byrnes, 201–214. Notre Dame, Ind.: University of Notre Dame Press.

Tomasevich, Jozo (1976). "The Tomasevich Extended Family on the Peninsula Pelješac." In *Communal Families in the Balkans: The Zadruga*, edited by Robert F. Byrnes, 187–200. Notre Dame, Ind.: University of Notre Dame Press.

Simić, Andrei (1983). "Machismo and Cryptomatriarchy: Power, Affect, and Authority in the Contemporary Yugoslav Family." *Ethos* 11:66–86.

MARIA B. OLUJIĆ

Danes

ETHNONYMS: Scandinavians (includes Faroese, Finns, Icelanders, Norwegians, and Swedes)

Orientation

Identification.   The Danes live in the country of Denmark and Danish is their national language. The state-affiliated church is Protestant, historically a branch of the Lutheran church. Danes outside of Denmark, particularly in the United States, tend to become highly assimilated, with almost no development of ethnic neighborhoods or enclaves. The term "Dane" (Danish "Dansker"), as the name of people living in what is now Denmark, can be traced to the early Middle Ages when the Old Nordic term "Danir" was in use. Between the ninth and eleventh centuries, Old English chronicles referred loosely to all Scandinavians who invaded England as Danes (Dena).

To comprehend Danish national character in our time it is necessary to look back to Denmark of the eighteenth century. At that time, Danish cultural distinctiveness was not really evident on manorial estates or in towns. Aristocrats and burghers each lived in terms of Europe-wide cultural norms that tended to blur and diminish their uniqueness as Danes. A national identity was to be found, however, in the way of life of the majority of the population who lived on farms and in villages. The roots of a Danish identity reach deeply into peasant culture.

Location.   Geographically, Denmark is the most northerly extension of the West European Plain, which projects into Scandinavia as the peninsula of Jutland. Jutland points northward toward Norway and Sweden. Denmark also includes several hundred islands. On the largest island, Zealand, the capital city of Copenhagen lies within view of Malmö on the southern shore of Sweden. Copenhagen is located on "The Sound" (Øresund), which narrowly separates Denmark from Sweden and which provides valuable, strategic shipping links between the North Atlantic and the Baltic Sea.

Demography.   Denmark has a population of 5.1 million. Probably because they number so few and live in propinquity with other nations, many Danes speak a second language. German was the most popular before World War II, but now it is English.

Linguistic Affiliation.   Like most Europeans, the Danes speak an Indo-European language. The three most widely distributed branches of this family are the Romance languages, the Slavic languages, and the Germanic languages. Danish is a Germanic language, and thus it is less distantly related to German and Dutch than it is to other European languages such as French or Russian. However, it has its closest ties to neighboring Scandinavian languages. The oldest known example of a Scandinavian language is a Gothic translation of parts of the Bible surviving from the fourth century. The modern Scandinavian languages in addition to Danish are Norwegian, which many Danes can understand, as well as Swedish, Icelandic, and Faroese. Although Finns share in Scandinavian culture and a minority of Finns speak Swedish as their family tongue, the Finnish language as such is non–Indo-European.

History and Cultural Relations

Denmark was formerly a large nation. To the south, its territory included Holstein and Schleswig, which were conquered by Germany in 1864. (Part of Schleswig was returned to Denmark through a referendum held after World War I.) To the northeast, it included the provinces of Scania, Halland, and Blekinge, which became the southernmost provinces of Sweden in 1660. Until 1814 Norway and Denmark were united under the Danish crown. Westward to the Atlantic Ocean, the Kingdom of Denmark includes the Faroe Islands and Greenland. Iceland acquired independent nation status after World War I, subject only to a personal union under the Danish crown. It became completely independent of Denmark in 1944.

Denmark is an industrialized, urbanized nation with virtually universal literacy. Danes are full participants in the international culture of the modern world. Denmark is a member of the European Community (Common Market). A century ago, most were peasants in what was then an impoverished developing nation. They were similar in culture to peasant villagers in neighboring Germany to the south and in Sweden and Norway to the north. Like the rest of Europe, however, the lives of some Danes of the nineteenth century, as well as of earlier times, were not shaped by peasant culture. Those who belonged to the ruling class lived on large estates, followed customs shared by aristocrats throughout Europe, and spoke either French or German in addition to Danish. They looked to the royal court of the king of Denmark for cultural leadership. Townspeople were also different in many aspects of culture, since they lived from crafts, merchandising, and service occupations rather than agriculture. In the seventeenth and eighteenth centuries, German was widely spoken in Danish towns, but by the nineteenth century most spoke Danish as their family language. Culturally, they were influenced by town life in other parts of western Europe, particularly in Germany, since many artisans spent a year or more working abroad before returning to Denmark as journeymen. No comparable custom united Danish townswomen with women in other parts of Europe.

Economy

Subsistence and Commercial Activities.   Denmark today relies upon a diversified economy based primarily on service industries, trade, and manufacturing. Less than 10 percent of the population engages in agriculture, fishing, and forestry. Danish agriculture is known for its cooperatives, particularly in the production of butter, cheese, eggs, bacon, and ham. Danish beer and *snaps* (aquavit) have acquired an international market. The fishing industry supplies markets in Europe beyond Denmark. In American stores one is most likely to encounter Danish marinated herring. From industrial enterprises products of modern design are shipped throughout the world, particularly Danish furniture, ceramics, and plastics. The Danes pioneered in producing furniture that was functional as well as handsome. They have designed chairs in response to studies of spinal biomechanics and have created tables to serve multiple purposes, such as those that convert to desks or collapse for storage against a wall in small apartments. For purposes of international trade, the Danes also have designed furniture to be shipped in disassembled, compact forms that make handling easy and save some shipping costs. The Danish merchant marine, growing out of their own interisland maritime needs, includes large shipping companies, such as the Maersk Lines, that constitute an important source of revenue for the nation. In collaboration with Sweden and Norway, Denmark also operates the Scandinavian Airline System (SAS) for international travel. Taxes are heavy in order to provide citizens with a wide range of welfare benefits that include excellent child care and school opportunities, extensive health benefits, and exceptional housing and care for the aged. Workers live very well by international standards. Although housing is in short supply, most Danes can afford small houses or apartments, dress well, and drive their own automobiles.

Land Tenure and Division of Labor. In historic Denmark, peasants lived in a form of village settlement, known as the open field system, in which communalism was central. The village territory was divided into two or three large fields, in each of which every landholder possessed scattered plots. The unit of work was not the individual plot, however, but the large field. Because fields were worked as units, it was essential that villagers agree on the nature and timing of many of their activities. Meeting in a dwelling or at a central place in the village, they followed old customs for village decision making that were common throughout Denmark. Schedules were agreed upon and implemented. Although cattle were individually owned, they were brought together daily to form single village herds, which grazed on the village common or on stubble left after fields were harvested. It was the custom for villagers to help individuals who fell sick. As a community, they supervised the use of communal facilities such as the meadow, commons, square, pond, hay field, and church. They cooperated in much of what they did, and a communal spirit was the product. By the nineteenth century, major agricultural reforms had changed the old peasant community. The chief reform was to abolish the common system by parceling out the village land. They also consolidated scattered holdings so that each villager ended up owning fields located more or less in one place. Individual management replaced communalism. Gradually, some landowners moved their farmsteads away from the village, resulting in a scattered settlement pattern of villages with interspersed farmsteads. Less fertile soils in western Jutland were settled by farmers who established isolated farmsteads rather than villages. During the nineteenth century, many other changes took place in association with these basic changes in land tenure and the division of labor. Yet, a sense of communalism persisted. Villages continued to manage their affairs by convening meetings of landowners. "Folk high schools," introduced by N. F. S. Grundtvig (1783–1872) and now found throughout Scandinavia, raised the level of education and prepared ordinary people for participation in democratic government. Toward the end of the nineteenth century and during the first decades of the twentieth, communalism reasserted itself as Danish farmers distinguished themselves by their ability to submit individual wishes to group decisions and to form voluntary common-interest associations. The successful creation of farming cooperatives across the nation became one of the foundations of the modernization of Danish agriculture. Meanwhile, the government of the nation shifted to that of a democratic, constitutional monarchy.

Kinship, Marriage, and Family

Kinship. Danish kinship nomenclature was and is bifurcate-collateral in type, differing from English primarily in that uncles, aunts, and grandparents are terminologically distinguished as father's side or mother's side, and blood relatives are always distinguished from relatives by marriage. For example, Danes distinguish father's brother from mother's brother and mother's mother from father's mother. They trace descent bilaterally, but a patrilineal emphasis was visible in the inheritance of property primarily through the male line until recent times, when gender became less determinative. Aristocrats also demonstrate their patrilineal emphasis in the inheritance of family names through the male line. Peasants did not get family names until late in the nineteenth century. Until then, one simply got the name of one's father. Thus Peter Rasmussen was the son of Rasmus Andersen, who in turn was the son of Anders Jensen, and so on. Daughters took the last names of their fathers or husbands.

Marriage. Women married into the circumstances of their grooms, whether landed or landless. Property owners tended to arrange marriages for their sons and daughters so that the young couple could have a farm of their own. Marriage was neolocal insofar as newlyweds usually set up housekeeping on their own. A patrilocal quality was imparted, however, by the tendency to settle in the community of the groom's family or even to take over the farm of the groom's parents. Divorce was difficult to obtain legally and was strongly censured by village opinion and church morality. Adultery in the village was regarded as highly reprehensible. Unmarried mothers were ostracized. A woman encountered no difficulty, however, if a pregnancy occurred before marriage but in betrothal, especially when a gold ring had been given to the young woman. Many couples hitherto only casually joined saved the situation when a pregnancy occurred by announcing that they were engaged. Premarital sexual activity was, in fact, common, and young men in many villages were permitted to sleep over in the bed of a young woman in the custom called night courting. Village customs thus set the stage for the sexual freedom and independence of both women and men that is characteristic of Denmark today.

Family. Traditionally, the Danes practiced monogamy. They lived in nuclear families that became stem families when old parents were cared for by an inheriting son. Today, many children are born to parents united in consensual unions. Single-parent families are common. One-fourth of all marriages terminate in divorce. The stem family has become obsolete as retired parents are provided with good care by the welfare system.

Inheritance.   Primogeniture was formerly the rule. Younger sons acquired farms by purchase or partial inheritance, worked as landless laborers residing in small cottages, or migrated to town to find work or enter a trade. Beginning in the nineteenth century, many of these younger sons and daughters migrated to the United States, particularly to Michigan and Wisconsin. Inheritance today no longer discriminates consistently on the basis of birth order and gender.

Socialization.   The Danes characteristically welcomed the birth of both boys and girls. In traditional village life, children's play was permitted, but it was unsupervised and unsupported. Children created their own toys. Even in the nineteenth century, most boys and girls went to school enough to become literate. From earliest childhood, however, they were expected to contribute to the work of the family by tending lifestock such as flocks of fowl, carrying water, and helping adults at their work. Consistent with an ethic of village communalism—though the principle is long extinct in its historical form—children today still are taught to control and suppress aggression. The censorship of movies in recent decades did not permit the showing of violence but made no objection to films showing sexually explicit scenes as long as nobody was maimed or killed. The Danish child is encouraged to be dependent on his or her mother more than is true for an American child. The principal form of discipline is guilt. The mother lets the child know how hurt she is and how bad she feels because of his or her behavior. Adult Danes thus show a psychiatric vulnerability to any loss of dependency through death, separation, or divorce. They also tend to be obedient citizens.

Sociopolitical Organization

Social Organization.   Class divisions are muted now in a country with a strong egalitarian ethic. Ethnic minorities have changed the character of the nation somewhat in recent decades. Early in the century, Polish migrant workers settled in some areas of the nation, and since World War II foreign workers from as far away as southern Europe and the Middle East have become permanent residents. Contemporary families tend to isolate themselves from one another. Attitudes surviving from an older communalism and from socialization practices result, however, in acquiescence to democratic forms of governing at every level. They also persist in the widespread activities of voluntary associations, which stem from the mutual-assistance societies and the cooperative movement of the late nineteenth century. The societies were forerunners of social insurance.

Political Organization.   Denmark became a constitutional monarchy in 1848. Universal suffrage is practiced. Now ruled by a unicameral legislature, the government is headed by a prime minister. Recently a bourgeois coalition has formed the government. Previously, leadership was most often in the hands of the Social Democrats.

Social Control.   The Danes have some continental (Napoleonic) aspects in their legal system—for example, judges who are career civil servants and the use of lay judges. They

also include some common-law (English) aspects, such as criminal jury trials. On the whole, they are closer to common law, because they mainly follow an accusatorial rather than an inquisitorial system. The courts are strong and untainted, backed by a humane penal system and police who do not carry guns.

Conflict.   Nonviolence is the essence of the Danish polity, reflecting continuities with a history of communalism. At all levels, governmental and nongovernmental, disputes are resolved through the highly developed art of compromise. The Danes pioneered in the global expansion of the Swedish institution of the ombudsman. Appointed by parliament, the ombudsman is empowered to investigate governmental activity but may not compel the implementation of his recommendations other than through reasoned persuasion or publicity.

Religion and Expressive Culture

Religious Beliefs and Practices.   The village church with its state salaried priest united each community for the Sunday church service. The confirmation ritual was a high point in the life of each boy and girl, serving as a rite of passage into adult status. In the twentieth century the Danes became increasingly secularized. Although confirmation is still important, state-supported churches today are usually almost empty for Sunday services.

Arts.   The fine arts and classical music receive state support and are highly appreciated in educated circles. The Danes are best known for their success in modern design. At the same time, they preserve an affection for folk songs and folk culture in a society that values its peasant heritage. The nation maintains an unusually fine system of folk museums, including parks containing authentic, renovated buildings salvaged from premodern times.

Medicine.   In the old days, villagers tended to circumvent medical doctors by going directly to apothecaries for diagnosis and treatment. They also had recourse to village healers (known as clever or wise men and women or as sorcerers). Much that healers did was based upon standard medical practice of the time, including herbs, cupping, and bleeding, but they also utilized amulets and other magical practices. Bonesetters and midwives were also part of the historic health-care scene. Only midwives survive at present in a country that supports state-of-the-art medical facilities and personnel.

Death and Afterlife.   Traditional Danish beliefs paralleled those of other north European Protestant peoples. They feared hell and strived to be worthy of heaven—some with anguish, but many with little obvious concern.

Bibliography

Anderson, Barbara G. (1990). *First Fieldwork: The Misadventures of an Anthropologist.* Prospect Heights, Ill.: Waveland Press.

Anderson, Robert T. (1975). *Denmark: Success of a Developing Nation.* Cambridge, Mass.: Schenkman.

Anderson, Robert T., and Barbara G. Anderson (1964). *The Vanishing Village: A Danish Maritime Community.* Seattle: University of Washington Press.

Anderson, Stanley V. (1967). *The Nordic Council: A Study of Scandinavian Regionalism*. Seattle: University of Washington Press.

Hansen, Judith Friedman (1980). *We Are a Little Land: Cultural Assumptions in Danish Everyday Life*. New York: Arno Press.

ROBERT ANDERSON AND STANLEY ANDERSON

Dutch

ETHNONYMS: Dutchmen, Dutchwomen; Hollanders (in a narrow definition for the people of the provinces of North and South Holland, in colloquial language for all Dutch); further differentiated according to provincial affiliation: Brabander, Drentenaar, Fries, Groninger, Limburger, Zeeuw

Orientation

Identification. The origin of the name "Dutch" is supposed to be a corruption of the word "Duits" referring to the Germanic origin of the Dutch. The word "Netherlands" probably stems from the Rhineland. Since the twelfth century the lower Rhine basin north of Cologne has been referred to as "netherland" (lowland) in contrast to the "overland" (highland) south of Cologne.

Location. The Netherlands is situated between 50° and 54° N and 3° and 7° E. The Netherlands is bordered by the North Sea to the north and the west, Germany to the east, and Belgium to the south. The West Frisian Islands—Texel, Vlieland, Terschelling, Ameland, Schiermonnikoog, and Rottumeroog—are situated north of the Frisian coast. The climate is maritime: wet, with mild winters and cool summers. The Netherlands consists of low-lying land, part of which (in the west and north) is below sea level. This makes water management a crucial strategy. The fight against the water has resulted in programs of land reclamation, dike construction, and drainage of marshlands, generating such amazing infrastructural achievements as the Zuider Zee Works, the Deltaworks, and the canalization of the big rivers. The Netherlands is comprised of three geographic regions: the zones of large-scale agriculture in the north, the regions of mixed agricultural-recreational use in the east and south, and the highly urbanized areas in the west. The Netherlands still possesses overseas territories, which consist of a number of islands in the Caribbean, collectively called "the Dutch Antilles": the Leeward Islands of Aruba, Curaçao, and Bonaire north of the Venezuelan coast; and the Windward Islands of Saba, Saint Eustacius, and Sint Maarten 900 kilometers farther north. The total population of the Dutch Antilles amounts to 250,000 people of multiethnic origin.

Demography. In 1991 the Dutch population was 15 million and the population density was about 440 persons per square kilometer, which makes the Netherlands one of the most densely populated countries in the world. Up to 1970 there was rapid population growth (more than 1 percent per year), declining to less than 0.6 percent in 1990. The declining growth rate was caused by an unexpectedly rapid decrease of the marital fertility rate since the 1960s, when modern contraceptive devices became available. Coupled with a low death rate, the decreasing birthrate results in an aging population. While the natural growth is decreasing, immigration is increasing and 4.3 percent of the population is of non-Dutch origin, especially with an Antillian, Surinamese, South Moluccan, and Mediterranean background.

Linguistic Affiliation. Dutch is a member of the Germanic Language Group (Western Continental) and is related to Afrikaans, German, Yiddish, Frisian, English, and Luxembourgeois. It is spoken in Europe by about 16–17 million people spread over the kingdom of the Netherlands and the northern half of Belgium. Outside the continent of Europe it is spoken in Indonesia by the Dutch who live there and in the Dutch Antilles. Cape Dutch (Afrikaans), spoken in the Union of South Africa, has developed into an independent language. In the course of the state-building process, High Dutch, originally the language of the province of Holland, gradually was adopted as the language of daily intercourse by all the provinces. A peculiar position is occupied by Frisian in the province of Friesland, which is separated from the Dutch dialects by a sharp linguistic boundary line.

History and Cultural Relations

Julius Caesar found the country peopled by tribes of Germanic stock. By the end of the third century the Franks swarmed over the Rhine and took possession of the whole of the southern and central Netherlands. In A.D. 843 the Verdun treaty assigned the central part of the Frankonian Empire (comprising the whole of the later Netherlands) to what was to become Germany. Up to the fourteenth century the history of the Netherlands was the history of the various feudal states into which the Frankonian Empire was gradually divided. Cities played an important part in the development of the Netherlands. The eleventh to the thirteenth centuries were rich in municipal charters granting the citizens considerable rights, counteracting the privileges of the feudal lords. The most powerful and flourishing were the cities of Flanders. They formed the central market and exchange of the world's commerce. In the north a number of "free cities" were established—Dordrecht, Leyden, Haarlem, Delft, Vlaardingen, Rotterdam, Amsterdam—to equal the Flemish cities in power.

In the fifteenth century the Netherlands fell under the dominion of the house of Burgundy. When the sole heiress of the Burgundian possessions, Mary, married Maximilian of Austria in 1477, the long domination of the Roman Catholic house of Habsburg began, bringing the Netherlands into the huge and incongruous collection of states that the wars and marriages of the Habsburgs had brought together. The Netherlands, prosperous under the Burgundy rule, had to make large financial sacrifices to pay for the many wars of the emperor. Opposition emerged in the cities. As a result, the burghers of the cities, the lower gentry, and the nobility united under the leadership of the Prince of Orange (William the Silent) to fight Habsburg domination. This uprising resulted in the separation of the seven northern provinces of the Netherlands from the south (which was to become Belgium). Each developed into distinct political, religious, social, and economic units. Enacted in the Protestant Union of Utrecht in 1579, the northern provinces formed a republic under the legislation of the State-General (the board of representatives of the provinces) and the reign of the stadtholder, William of Orange, who became the symbol of political unity. In 1673 the seven provinces voted to make the stadtholderate hereditary in the house of Orange. William—born the third William in the house of Orange—attempted to centralize and consolidate his government, put down the feudal liberties in the provinces, and free himself from constitutional checks. He was unable, however, to establish absolute monarchy, and the United Provinces remained a decentralized patrician republic until 1795. Married in 1677 to Mary, the king of England's niece, William became king of England in 1689. In the aftermath of the French Revolution liberalism made its entry. Rebellious citizens, aided by French troops, overthrew the stadtholder. From 1795 to 1814 the Netherlands was under French rule. Liberalism, however, turned out to be a disappointment for the Dutch citizens. In 1814, freed from the French, they returned the house of Orange. The Netherlands became a monarchy, though a constitutional one. It was not until the nineteenth century that modernization started—later and more gradually than elsewhere in western Europe. Also in the nineteenth century, the cultural differences between the various ideological and political groups were institutionalized, generating separate organizations for each group in almost every area of life. This development of parallel organizations ("pillars") is called "pillarization." The pluralistic society that developed after 1917 had its origin in this "pillarized" structure.

During World War I the Netherlands kept its neutrality, nonetheless suffering from the economic crises caused by the war. World War II brought German occupation from 1940 to 1945. The postwar reconstruction of the Netherlands generated the modern Dutch industrial welfare state. Processes of European integration led to increasing cooperation with other European states: the Netherlands joined the European Economic Community (EEC)—the Common Market—in 1957. After World War II the Dutch had to cope with their colonies' struggle for independence. Decolonization did not take a peaceful course. The proclamation of the Republic of Indonesia, which was the former Dutch East Indies, provoked military intervention by the colonial authorities. Under international pressure, however, the Dutch government agreed to transfer sovereignty to the young Indonesian republic. In 1962 the Netherlands had to cede New Guinea to Indonesia; and in 1975 Suriname gained independence. The Dutch Antilles are still part of the kingdom.

Settlements

The Dutch population is irregularly spread over the territory. The three provinces in the west (North and South Holland and Utrecht, collectively known as "Randstad Holland") are highly urbanized and most densely populated: almost half of the population lives there. The north (the provinces of Groningen, Friesland, Drente, Overijssel, and South Flevoland) has a rural and relatively small population. The provinces in the east (Gelderland) and south (Limburg, North Brabant, and Zeeland) show a mixed pattern of urban-rural settlements.

Economy

Subsistence and Commercial Activities.   Dutch agriculture is highly commercialized and specialized. The cities have been a market for the country's agrarian products from the twelfth century onward. After the Agrarian Crisis of 1880 the Dutch farmers specialized in labor-intensive horticulture and dairy farming. Intensive fertilization, agrarian training and research, reorganization of small farms, land consolidation, and Common Market agreements increased productivity.

Industrial Arts.   Throughout its history, Dutch industry has depended heavily on the importation of raw materials to supply its major industries: the production of foodstuffs and stimulants, which developed when raw material was imported from the colonies; the nineteenth-century clothing- and footwear-manufacturing and metal industries; and the primary twentieth-century industry, the production of petrochemicals. There is today an increasing number of mergers between both national and multinational enterprises. After the emergence of modern industry in the mid-nineteenth century, the significance of agriculture for the national product diminished steadily, while the significance of the secondary sector increased until it fell behind the growing services sector after 1960.

Trade.   The small size and the spacial position of the Netherlands (especially the location at waterways strategic for maritime and inland shipping) are of enduring significance for the international economic relations of the country. Where the waterways meet, the big seaports have risen; in fact, Amsterdam and Rotterdam's Europoort is the world's largest harbor. Traditionally the Dutch have been traders and merchants. Since the fifteenth century the Netherlands has been a seagoing nation, owing their affluence to the exploitation of overseas provinces and to a prospering trade. The seventeenth and eighteenth centuries were characterized by commercial capitalism: as the trade center of the world the Netherlands maintained and even increased its wealth by trade and the trade-related industries. This era has become known as the "Golden Age."

Division of Labor.   The Dutch labor force consists of 7 million people, with only 38.8 percent being female. Despite the growth of the female work force since the 1960s, labor participation of married women has remained considerably lower in the Netherlands than in other European countries. During the 1960s the Dutch population could not meet the growing demands for labor because the work force was overskilled. Consequently, the Dutch labor market in the 1990s is characterized by a large number of jobless people and at the same time a large number of foreign workers who are employed in the lower-paid and lower-skill jobs.

Land Tenure.   In about 1500 the east and south (the sandy soil regions) were characterized by traditional village communities structured according to the peasant model. Peasants formed the majority of the agrarian population until the mid-nineteenth century, dwelling on very small and unspecialized family farms. Alternative work outside agriculture was lacking. Specialization in cash crops and cattle breeding was impossible because of capital shortage. The peasant family was almost self-sufficient and productivity was low. In the west and north (the clay soil regions) agriculture developed according to the farmer model. In these areas feudalism never gained a foothold. In Holland the polders (land reclaimed from the sea) provided the people with land acquired in ownership or in leasehold on businesslike conditions. Village communities were of no significance in these areas; the farmers lived dispersed over the land on their own farmsteads. They produced for a market, and their enterprises were capital-intensive. After the agrarian crises, modernization led to production increase.

Kinship, Marriage, and Family

Kin Groups and Descent.   Dutch kinship is bilateral with a patrilateral kinship preference. Until recently, this descent pattern was reflected in the custom of adopting the husband's name after marriage. This practice is changing with women's emancipation.

Kinship Terminology.   Kin terms follow the Eskimo system.

Marriage and Family

Marriage.   In preindustrial society, marriage was possible only after acquiring economic independence. The rural population and urban craftsmen used to marry at a later age. The choice of a marriage partner followed endogamous preference. People married within the same occupational sector or social group, the same religious or political pillar, or at least the same village or age group. Maintaining and increasing wealth were crucial motives in arranging marriages among the aristocracy and freeholding farmers. Among urban craftsmen there was more opportunity for individual choice than among the propertied classes. Romantic love was the basis of marriage more often among the urban population than among the rural.

Domestic Unit.   The nuclear family is a typical Dutch phenomenon. The Dutch even have a special word for it: _gezin._ The stem family has never been of any significance in the Netherlands, not even in the rural areas. Since the nineteenth century the concept of the nuclear family has been invested with strong moral feelings. State policy was aimed at fostering and protecting the nuclear family; extramarital relations were condemned as deviant and antisocial. After World War II, several factors—including the emancipation of women, a decline in the number of household members, and an increase in the number of single-member households—resulted in more people living together without marriage, more children being born outside marriage, and more marriages ending in divorce.

Inheritance.   In Dutch rural society it was common that one of the children, usually the oldest son, inherited the patrimony. Impartible inheritance was both customary and legally mandated. Among the urban bourgeoisie—where money, not land, was involved—the children were more equally treated when it came to inheritance. The bourgeois pattern has become the prevailing standard in modern society.

Socialization.   As early as the seventeenth century, the urban middle classes began to treat children not as small adults but as members of a different age group, with their own wants and needs. This attitude became standard in the nineteenth century, partly because of the increasing use of contraceptive measures, which resulted in a decreasing birthrate within the nuclear family and a consequent increase in the time and attention that could be spent on individual children. A number of factors contributed to this concern with keeping the family size small. One powerful incentive was the high cost of raising the next generation. A good education and dowry had come to be considered necessary expenses. Moreover, providing loving care for a child required an enormous effort that could not be bestowed on an unlimited number of offspring. This attitude first emerged among the urban middle classes, who increasingly did not require married women to work outside the home. Thus, middle-class women were able to give much attention to their domestic and maternal tasks. The life cycle of children changed: the interval between puberty and marriage was recognized as a special stage in life.

Sociopolitical Organization

Social Organization.   Although the standard of living is high, it is lower than in some neighboring countries. The burden of taxation is heavy, making considerable collective expenditures possible and resulting in an excellent set of social services. The media, labor unions, public organizations, associations, and club life are defined by the typical Dutch phenomenon of pillarization. Dutch society is characterized by complex social stratification, based on partly converging and partly conflicting criteria. As far as political and economic power relations are concerned, tokens of nineteenth-century class society can still be found in modern Dutch society. However, regional, religious, ethnic affiliation, and life-style factors modify social and economic class differences. The Netherlands is famous for tolerance toward ethnic minorities. Since World War II, Dutch society has developed into a multiethnic society. The persistent flood of allochthonous people, coupled with a growing unemployment rate, however, causes more and more tension and conflict.

Political Organization.   In the nineteenth century parliamentary democracy emerged. The monarch, subject to the constitution, is head of state. The Dutch Lower Chamber is constituted by direct elections by all enfranchised Dutch citizens, while the Dutch Upper Chamber is elected by the provincial states. A political breakthrough happened in 1918 when general elections were established; from that time on the seats in the Lower Chamber were held by representatives of political parties. Dutch political life is characterized by a large number of small political parties competing for votes. Since 1900, when party politics emerged, an average of eleven parties have been represented in parliament each term. The most important movements in Dutch political life have been liberalism, denominationalism, and socialism.

Social Control.   During the Dutch republic (sixteenth to nineteenth centuries) Dutch village life was relatively unrestricted by the central government. Within the village community, however, mechanisms of social control operated. Social mobility was low and social stratification kept people in their places. Consolidation of property formed an important consideration in marriage arrangements. There were almost no illegitimate children. When a girl got pregnant, strong social pressure was exerted on her to marry, especially in Protestant areas. The authority of the older generation was respected. The moral demands of diligence and austerity were internalized and determined the attitude toward life of both young and old. Calvinism, especially north of the big rivers, intensified this propensity as well as the rejection of amusement and diversion. Although city life was less restrained, Dutch mentality, characterized by a strong sense of values, put a check on urban allure. Thus, the image of the Dutch people as tidy, diligent, and hard-working citizens does have historical roots. Since the 1960s, however, the image of the Dutch has changed. The Netherlands has made headlines as the country of the Provo movement (the organized provocative behavior of young people against the authorities, which manifested itself especially in Amsterdam in 1965–1967), insubordinate bishops, long-haired soldiers with their own trade union, and permissiveness in drug use and pornography. The country is famous for its high rate of petty crime, blurred standards, squatting, and civil disobedience—phenomena that the international press has labeled "the Dutch disease."

Conflict.   At home the Netherlands has witnessed a peaceful development through the ages. In political and social life, physical violence was the exception. The pillarized society was characterized by a pacific policy at home. Violence was applied in the process of colonization and in colonial wars abroad. In the twentieth century the situation has reversed: the Netherlands has tried to take a strictly neutral position in external armed conflict (World War I and World War II); at home pacification relations have given way to occasionally violent conflicts between social and ethnic groups, between generations, and between pressure groups.

Religion and Expressive Culture

Religious Beliefs.   The conflict between Roman Catholicism and Calvinism since the Reformation has fundamentally influenced the nature of Dutch society, creating its unique pillarized character. The basic organizational principle in many spheres, at the local as well as national level, is religious, not economic, affiliation. Although this pillarization has begun to erode, it is still quite evident, especially in rural communities where it colors all social relations. Although the Netherlands is characterized by secularization, other more informal ways of expressing religious feelings have emerged.

Religious Practitioners.   Parish priests and parsons have always had an important impact on Dutch mentality, political conviction, and voting behavior. Even people's private lives were ruled by standards of behavior set by the clergy. Ecclesiastical directives influenced the development of taboos on sexual activities and social contact between persons of different social classes. For Catholics the rules were dictated by the pope but translated and mediated by the clergy, with adaptations to local culture. The Protestants did not rely on religious mediators as heavily as did the Catholics, as their religious experience did not lie in the community but in the heart of the individual. Compared to their Catholic counterparts, the parsons were weak and their power limited.

Ceremonies.   Since the fifteenth century Dutch popular culture has increasingly been put under pressure by the bourgeois elite. The tales, riddles, rhymes, feasts, and rituals were suppressed to give way to high culture. Popular culture provided not only diversion and amusement but also an outlet for social tensions and instability, complaints of social abuses, and expression of religious feelings. The Catholic church tried to absorb these elements of popular culture into official religion; Protestantism, however, went on the offensive against popular culture.

Arts.   Art blossomed in the seventeenth century (i.e., the Golden Age). Many Dutch painters from that period have become famous: for example, Rembrandt van Rijn, Jan Vermeer, Frans Hals, Pieter de Hooch, and Jacob van Ruisdael. Because rich burghers and merchants, not the church and court, were the most important patrons of the artists, the art of painting became specialized. Some painters painted only landscapes, others painted exclusively portraits or still lifes. As far as music is concerned, the composer and organist Jan Pieterszoon Sweelinck became well known for his organ playing. Since the seventeenth century, Dutch art has aroused relatively modest international attention, aside from a small number of celebrities such as the painters van Gogh, Mondrian, and Appel. Cultural life is traditionally focused on the big cities, where large orchestras, theater companies, and museums of regional significance have been established in the twentieth century.

Medicine.   In the Netherlands a modern pharmaceutical industry of international significance has developed. Big concerns have concentrated their research activities in the Netherlands. This has led to a widespread penetration of medical standards and medical consumption, resulting in a "medicalization" of everyday life that has come to be such a public-health problem that alternative medicine has recently taken root.

Death and Afterlife.   In the twentieth century compulsory institutionalized mourning has lost much of its force, while the personal side of mourning has been accentuated and privatized. Funerals characterized by public display have given way to cremations in private. As religious beliefs have declined, the dominant standard of bereavement behavior has become more informal and individualized, making higher demands on self-regulation and self-restraint. As far as dying is concerned, the ritual and rigid regime of silence has relaxed, and more informal and varied codes of behavior- and emotion-management have spread.

Bibliography

Boissevain, J., and J. Verrips, eds. (1989). *Dutch Dilemmas: Anthropologists Look at the Netherlands.* Assen and Maastricht: Van Gorcum.

Diederiks, H. A., et al. (1987). *Van agrarische samenleving naar verzorgingsstaat: De modernisering van West-Europa sinds de 15de eeuw.* Groningen: Wolters-Noordhoff.

Goudsblom, J. (1967). *Dutch Society.* New York: Random House.

Schama, S. (1987). *The Embarrassment of Riches: An Interpretation of Dutch Culture in the Golden Age.* New York: Knopf.

Sinner, L. (1973). *De wortels van de Nederlandse politiek: De*

42 _politieke partijen sinds 1848_. Amsterdam: Wetenschappelijke Uitgeverij.

Wouters, C. (1990). _Van minnen en sterven: Informalisering van de omgangsvormen rond sex en dood_. Amsterdam: Bert Bakker.

HEIDI DAHLES

English

ETHNONYM: Engl

Orientation

Identification. England, unlike Scotland, Wales, or Northern Ireland, does not constitutionally exist, and thus it has no separate rights, administration, or official statistics. The Church of England is its main distinctive institution. The English maintain their separate identity in sports (soccer, cricket, and rugby) and heritage; this is manifest in the monarchy, aristocracy, and associated pageantry, parliament, pride in their country, and love for their local community (with the local pub being an integrating institution). English poetry, literature, and art is also distinctive. With the decrease of specialized industry, an increase in mass marketing, and greater population mobility, English distinctiveness is threatened. However, measures such as restoration and protection of city centers, the countryside, and historic buildings—along with the movement for greater control and participation in local affairs—help counter the trend toward homogeneity.

Location. England constitutes the largest land area and highest population density of any of the four units of the United Kingdom. It is also the most intensely industrialized region. Located off the northwest coast of continental Europe, it is bounded on the north by Scotland and on the west by Wales. It is located approximately between 49°56′ and 55°49′ N and 1°50′ E and 5°46′ W (not including the Channel Islands). Geographically, England constitutes 130,863 square kilometers or 53 percent of the land area of the United Kingdom and is divided into the uplands and lowlands. Following a line joining the mouths of the Tees and Exe rivers, the uplands in the northwest are characterized by rocky and mountainous areas while the lowlands of the southeast contain gentle rolling country with some hills. For the United Kingdom as a whole, the terrain is 30 percent arable, 50 percent meadow and pasture, 12 percent waste or urban, 7 percent forest, and 1 percent inland water. The climate is variable and mild for its latitudes. Rainfall for the south is 90 centimeters, with the southwest receiving 105 to 158 centimeters per year, while the extreme east gets 63 centimeters. The mean temperature for England in July is 16° C; in January and February it is 5° C. However, the north is slightly colder than the south; winter in the north averages 70 days of frost while the south averages 13.

Demography. The English number 46,168,120 (1989 estimate), 81.5 percent of the population of the United Kingdom. They have maintained their relative proportion of the United Kingdom population, but the proportion of younger and older people has increased because the birthrate declined between 1921 and 1942 and then increased after World War II. The population is primarily urban and suburban. In 1921, more than 40 percent of the people lived in the six great conurbations that center on London. After World War II, there was movement from the inner cities to the suburban fringes and beyond, with the inner cities showing a marked decrease. However, English population density is among the highest in the world, averaging 840 persons per square mile in 1981 for England and Wales and rising to 12,600 for the greater London area.

Linguistic Affiliation. The English language is of the Indo-European Family. Its parent tongue is the West Germanic Group of Proto-Indo-European. The closest related languages are German, Netherlandic, and Frisian. There is considerable dialectical variation, the most distinctive being in Lancashire, Cornwall, and parts of East London. Radio, television, and transportation are causing these differences to diminish, with the style of the southeast becoming the standard. However, there is no difference in literary style between the various regions.

History and Cultural Relations

Early English history is marked by immigration. Although not the first, the Celts began arriving around 2,500 to 3,000 years ago. England became part of the Roman Empire in A.D. 43. After the Roman withdrawal in A.D. 410, waves of Jutes, Angles, and Saxons arrived and established control, in spite of Danish incursions from the eighth through the eleventh centuries. By the fifth century A.D., the term "English"—"Angelcynn," meaning "angel kin"—was applied to the Teutonic inhabitants collectively. By the eleventh century, the term included the Celtic and Scandinavian elements and all natives of England, except for the Normans, who remained separate for several generations after their conquest in 1066. The signing of the Magna Carta in 1215 guaranteed the rights of rule by law, a point of pride for the English. In 1301, Edward of Caernarvon, son of King Edward I of England, was created Prince of Wales. The Hundred Years' War (1338–1453) resulted in the claim to large parts of France being lost, and the War of the Roses (1455–1485) led to the Tudor monarchy, which in turn led to a distinctively flourishing English civilization. In 1534, religious independence from the pope was established. Under Queen Elizabeth I, England became a major naval power and its colonies and trade expanded. In 1603, James VI of Scotland succeeded to the throne of England as King James I, and the island of Britain was united under one royal family. After a civil war (1642–

1649), a republic under Oliver Cromwell was established, but the monarchy was restored in 1688, confirming the sovereignty of the English Parliament and the English Bill of Rights. By increasing colonial holdings and industrial power in the eighteenth century, the United Kingdom became a world power. Although victorious in both world wars, the country lost its position of world leadership, but it continued its industrial growth. During the postwar period, the Labor party governments passed some socialist legislation nationalizing some industries and expanding social security; but the Thatcher government reversed that trend and increased the role of private enterprise.

Since the Norman Conquest in 1066, a relatively homogeneous population has been maintained. However, England has been a haven for refugees ranging from the Huguenots in the seventeenth century to persecuted Jews in the twentieth. Starting in the 1950s, population homogeneity has been challenged by the immigration of West Indians and South Asians. As of 1989, they comprise about 4 percent of England's population (2 percent of the United Kingdom's population). Laws curbing immigration and prohibiting racial discrimination have been enacted, but racial tensions are present, especially in the inner urban centers of London and West Midlands where 60 percent of the immigrants reside.

Settlements

About 90 percent of England's population is urban or suburban, and less than 3 percent of its people are engaged in agriculture. Thus, there is a structure of towns, villages, and cities where one sees scattered groups of high-density residence patterns. In spite of the large urban sprawl, England has extensive tracts of farms with smaller villages engulfed by trees, copses, hedgerows, and fields. Settlement patterns are classed into seven categories: conurbations, cities, boroughs, towns, villages, hamlets, and farms. Conurbations refer to the large complexes of densely populated urban areas with a complex of suburbs and towns surrounding or within a large city. A city is a large important borough. A borough is a town possessing a municipal corporation with special privileges conferred by royal charter (a city can have boroughs within it). A town can be incorporated or not incorporated within a conurbation, but either way it is a small cluster of buildings, which has an independent government with greater powers of rating (taxation), paving, and sanitation than those of a village. The village is smaller than a town and has less independence, and a hamlet is smaller still, often without a church. An examination of settlement patterns of towns, villages, and hamlets reveals a great variety of planned or unplanned settlements, with buildings at regular or random intervals. They can be clustered around a center, with its own structure of roads or lanes, or linear, along the sides of a road or field. Farmsteads generally comprise the farming family.

Economy

Subsistence and Commercial Activities.   For planning purposes, England is divided into eight regions, but it can be grouped into four divisions comprising the north, Midlands, southeast, and southwest. The north contains about one-third of the total land area and one-third of the population. Although there is some dairy and grazing livestock production, the division is highly industrial, comprising 35 percent of England's manufacturing labor force (43 percent of England's total work force in manufacturing). Most cities are near coal fields. Old, stable industries have declined, leading to unemployment. Emigration from the region has been high, although the region continues to have a slight population increase. The Midlands has about half of its workers employed in manufacturing industries, making automobiles, metal goods, and related products. About 3 percent of them work in coal and iron ore fields and 1.5 percent in mixed farming. It is common to find villages that specialize (locks and keys in Willenhall, needles and hooks in Ridditch, and so on). In the southeast, more than 60 percent of the labor force is in service industries such as construction and public administration, 32 percent in manufacturing, and less than 2 percent in agriculture. Electrical equipment, machinery, paper, printing, and publishing are the leading industries. The southwest has a lower population. Dairy farming is prominent and manufacturing employs 32 percent of the labor force. Many people retire there and tourism is important. However, unemployment is also high. In essence, England has been going through a long process of change. In the nineteenth century, the north, which was previously underdeveloped and backward, became the powerhouse or "workshop of the world." As the United Kingdom lost its prominence in the world economy, the north also lost its importance and power shifted to the southeast.

Industrial Arts.   Service industries employ about half of England's work force, while a third of the workers are in manufacturing and engineering. The remainder are in agriculture, construction, mining, and energy.

Trade.   Three types of trade take place in English communities. The traditional institution is the central market, which is often covered but open. It has stalls that sell everything from fish to clothes. Within neighborhoods there are clusters of specialty shops which usually comprise a grocer, butcher, newsstand, appliance store, and sweet shop. Since 1970, chain enterprises in fast food and groceries have developed and expanded.

Division of Labor.   There is a hierarchy and division of labor with limited mobility. In manufacturing, jobs are specialized according to skill and hierarchy of class is maintained where bosses have authority over subordinates. Division of labor according to gender is diminishing in the workplace as well as the domestic sphere. Class consciousness is decreasing, with the upwardly mobile young urban professional (Yuppie) becoming a dominant role model.

Land Tenure.   Land in England is privately owned.

Kinship, Marriage, and Family

Kinship.   The most important kin group is the extended family, which generally includes all known relatives. Although descent is not strictly lineal, the family name is traced patrilineally. However, relationship through the female line is acknowledged informally. If he has no male heir, a son may incorporate the name of his mother's family as his family name in a hyphenated form. Kin relationships are strongly influenced by distance, stage of life, and closeness of relationship. In practice, the mother-daughter relationship dominates and it is around the wife's mother that much family activity is determined. Other members of the kin group are included if they live nearby. However, neighbors are very important in providing companionship and social support, and these friendships are often maintained after a person has moved away.

Marriage. The emphasis on marital status has decreased in the last decade. Self-esteem and status are now determined by a career, whereas previously they centered on having a spouse and children. Today people often delay marriage and children until their career aspirations stabilize. Generally marriages are by the choice of the male and female. Abortion is legal and divorce is acceptable; both have increased in the postwar era.

Domestic Unit. The nuclear family is the most prevalent domestic unit. It consists of the mother, father, and juvenile children. During times when housing was scarce, it was common for a newly married couple to live with the wife's family. Among the landed gentry residence for the eldest son was patrilocal while other offspring resided elsewhere.

Inheritance. Traditionally, inheritance was through the male line. The aristocracy maintained its wealth by a system of primogeniture, where the estate went to the eldest son. Other sons had to serve in the army, the church, or business, or vanish into obscurity or poverty. Now, inheritance is according to the wishes of the owner of the resources. He or she dictates the inheritance by a will or testament. If there is no will, it is probated in a court.

Socialization. Parents, peers, and media are three primary influences for socialization. Parents discipline, but corporal punishment is not acceptable. Evaluation by one's peers is important for English children. Television, videos, rock music, advertising, and other forms of popular media culture exert a strong influence on children.

Sociopolitical Organization

England is a constitutional monarchy. There is no written constitution, and so statutes, common law, and practice guide governance. The monarch is the chief of state and controls the executive branch. The prime minister is the head of the government and has a cabinet. The legislative section is a bicameral Parliament composed of a House of Commons and a House of Lords; primary power lies with the House of Commons. There is also a court system, with the House of Lords being the highest level.

Social Organization. In English society, the aristocracy, "new society," middle class, and working class are the primary units. The landed aristocracy is the only aristocracy. Alongside the aristocracy is the new society, the self-made rich. In the nineteenth century, wealth did not buy power, because it was concentrated in the aristocracy. However, the aristocracy has lost its monopoly on power. At present, most Britons see themselves as belonging either to the middle or working class. What makes a person claim membership to one of these two classes varies; economic affluence and occupation are not consistent indicators. Also, the middle class is fragmenting with each group defining itself in opposition to other groups.

Political Organization. Under the central government, the country is divided into municipalities, counties, and parliamentary constituencies. In 1974, the conurbations were detached from existing counties and designated as metropolitan counties.

Social Control. The court system, sense of tradition, public opinion, and mass media all work together to promote conformity and resolve conflicts in English society.

Conflict. Since England has not suffered from invasions since the Norman Conquest, there is no focused animosity against any particular group, although some resentment toward the Germans exists as a result of the two world wars. Internal conflicts have been primarily with Northern Ireland. They started in 1968 with demonstrations by Catholics who charged that they were discriminated against in voting rights, housing, and employment. Violence and terrorism has intensified between the Irish Republican Army (which is outlawed), Protestant groups, police, and British troops. Racial tensions between the white English community and the West Indians and South Asians have developed recently, but they have not resulted in ongoing terrorism and violence.

Religion and Expressive Culture

Religious Beliefs and Practices. Although England is a secular country, about one-half of the population is baptized in the Anglican church; however, only 10 million are communicant members. Roman Catholics number 6 million, and the rest belong to nonconformist free churches such as Methodist or Baptist. Except for some areas of Irish settlements in the northwest, religious tolerance persists.

The Church of England traces its history back to the arrival of Christians in Britain during the second century. It has preserved much of the tradition of medieval Catholicism while holding on to the fundamentals of the Reformation. It broke with the Roman papacy during the reign of Henry VIII (1509–1547). The church has gone through persecution and was also influenced by the Puritans. Nevertheless, it has maintained an episcopal form of government, with the monarchy acting as the secular head of the English church and the Archbishop of Canterbury having spiritual prominence.

Arts. England has a strong and distinctive tradition in literature, theater, and architecture. In literature, writers tend to focus on their particular region, while in plays they are more likely to deal with England as a whole. In architecture, the English have borrowed from other cultures, but they have transformed the concepts into a characteristically English style. England has also become a leader in popular culture with musical groups that have captured international prominence. London is the theater center for the English-speaking world.

Medicine. England's national health service provides quality care. However, the system has declined somewhat under the Thatcher government and private practice has increased.

Death and Afterlife. In the Anglican church, exactly what happens at death is a mystery. However, Anglicans believe that the individual "is received by God into his arms," which is taken to mean the person passes into a timeless and spaceless relationship with God, unlike that which is experienced in this life. Funerals are conducted by a priest or minister a day or two after death.

Bibliography

Bonfield, Lloyd, Richard M. Smith, and Keith Wrightson, eds. (1986). *The World We Have Gained*. Oxford: Basil Blackwell.

Helweg, Arthur W. (1986). *Sikhs in England*. 2nd ed. Delhi: Oxford University Press.

Newby, Howard (1979). *Social Change in Rural England*. Madison: University of Wisconsin Press.

Noble, Trevor (1981). *Structure and Change in Modern Britain*. London: Batsford Academic and Educational.

Priestley, J. B. (1934). *English Journey*. New York and London: Harper Brothers.

Sampson, Anthony (1983). *The Changing Anatomy of Britain*. New York: Random House.

United Kingdom, Government of. Central Office of Information (1989). *Britain 1989: An Official Handbook*. London: Her Majesty's Stationery Office.

Young, Michael, and Peter Willmott (1957). *Family and Kinship in East London*. Baltimore: Penguin.

ARTHUR W. HELWEG

Faroe Islanders

ETHNONYM: Føroyingar

Orientation

Identification. The Faroe Islands are a culturally distinct, monoethnic, internally self-governing dependency of Denmark.

Location. Comprising seventeen inhabited islands and several islets, the Faroes lie between 62°24' and 61°20' N and 7°41' and 6°15' W. The land is mountainous and treeless, with rocky outcroppings seaming upland reaches of moor, meadow, and fen. Settlements lie amid hayfields along the shores of fjords or sandy bays. Elsewhere, the land ends in sea cliffs up to 600 meters high. The highest point on the islands is 882 meters. The average temperature ranges from 2.6° C in January to 10.7° C in July and August. The average yearly precipitation is 159 centimeters. Winter storms are frequent.

Demography. The Faroese population is 46,313. (1986 figures are used here and throughout.) The live birthrate is 17.1 per thousand; the death rate is 8.0 per thousand. Tórshavn, the capital and by far the largest town, has 13,905 inhabitants. Eight other townships, including Tórshavn's suburbs, have more than 1,000 inhabitants.

Linguistic Affiliation. Faroese is a linguistically conservative descendant of Old West Scandinavian akin to Icelandic and the western dialects of Norwegian. Having passed out of written use in the sixteenth century, it was given an orthography resembling that of Icelandic in 1846 and has been the primary official language since 1948. Danish is taught in the schools and may be used for many official purposes but is rarely spoken.

History and Cultural Relations

Occupied by Norse settlers in the early ninth century, the Faroes were Christianized and made subject to the Norwegian crown in the early eleventh century. At the time of the Reformation (ca. 1535–1540), which took place peacefully, the Dano-Norwegian king appropriated the extensive holdings of the Catholic church; most became tenant farms. In 1557, the Faroese bishopric was reduced to a deanery. In the early seventeenth century the islands' governance was shifted from Bergen to Copenhagen. From 1709 through 1855 all trade with the Faroes was in the hands of a Copenhagen-based royal monopoly, whose store in Tórshavn was the islands' only commercial establishment. In 1816, the Faroes were made a Danish province (*amt*), and their ancient high court, the Løgting, was abolished. Reconstituted as an advisory assembly in 1852–1854, it eventually acquired legislative powers. The introduction of free trade in 1856 led to the growth of an export fishing industry and the rise of a native intelligentsia and middle class. A cultural revitalization movement that gained widespread support in the 1890s soon entailed the growth of political separatism. Following an amicable British occupation during World War II and an inconclusive referendum on full independence in 1946, the Faroes were made internally self-governing in 1948. Varied and extensive relations with foreign, chiefly Scandinavian, countries are maintained by individuals and numerous official or semi-official institutions, mostly in Tórshavn. The Faroes acquired a radio station in 1957 and a television station in 1984.

Settlements

Until the nineteenth century, Faroese villages consisted of one or more loosely agglomerated hamlets. The industrialization of the fishery after 1880 spurred the growth of Tórshavn and a few distant-water fishing ports, while the most isolated villages began to dwindle in size. The revival of the inshore fishery since the 1950s has enlivened a number of small and medium-sized villages (roughly 250–800 inhabitants). Dwellings were formerly built of fieldstone, with sod roofs and tarred wooden siding. In the early twentieth century, most were sided and roofed with gaily painted corrugated metal. Since World War II, most construction has been in poured concrete, also painted. Today's densely populated settlements take several forms, but except for Tórshavn and to some extent the larger towns, they have no well-defined centers.

Economy

Subsistence and Commercial Activities. The Faroese economy has always had a monolithic export sector and a diversified internal one. Formerly, the principal export was wool; subsistence pursuits included fishing, fowling, sealing, pilot whaling, digging peat, keeping milk cows, raising hay, and—until potatoes became popular around 1830—raising barley. Today, most villagers raise potatoes and own a few sheep; some fish inshore for domestic needs or supplementary income. Pilot whaling provides an important and prized source of meat and fat. The principal export is fish. Fish and fish products regularly account for about 95 percent of Faroese exports by value; and fishing and fish processing, which employ about a fifth of the working population, account for 24 percent of the gross domestic product. The next largest categories are government services (19 percent), commerce (14 percent), shipyards and other industry (11 percent), transportation and communication (8 percent), and construction (8 percent). The GNP is about 5.6 billion krónur, or about $12,000 per person, and is growing at a real annual rate of 4.3 percent.

Industrial Arts. In addition to a fishing fleet, which includes 270 vessels of over 20 gross tons, there are three shipyards and numerous firms engaged in construction, road building, food processing, and so forth.

Trade. The Faroes depend heavily on imported food, petroleum products, machinery, manufactured goods, raw materials, etc. About half their imports come from Denmark, and a quarter from Norway, Sweden, the United Kingdom (U.K.), and western Germany. About a fifth of the Faroes' exports go to Denmark, and over half to the United States, the U.K., and Germany. The balance of trade is perennially negative. The larger towns and especially Tórshavn have many wholesale firms and specialized stores; the villages have small general stores selling foodstuffs, clothing, and household wares.

Division of Labor. A strong sexual division of labor is only gradually weakening. Women performed household tasks and, for example, some chores in haying and digging peat. Men performed outdoor tasks and helped to card and spin wool in the winter. Women, who began to work in fish processing in the nineteenth century, today also work as clerks, nurses, teachers, etc.

Land Tenure. Lands may be either leasehold or freehold. About half the land in the Faroes is leasehold (*kongsjørð*), owned by the state. The approximately 300 leaseholds are impartible and inherited by male primogeniture. Freeholdings (*óðalsjørð*) may be divided by sale and inheritance. All land is divided between outfield (*hagi*) and infield (*bøur*). Tenancy or ownership of a stretch of outfield confers rights to a proportional stretch of infield, and, for example, to certain fowling privileges. The outfield is used for summer pasturage. The infield is used for crops and winter pasturage. A stone wall separates infield and outfield. Large sections of outfield are similarly divided, but the infield is unfenced. The village is set in the infield.

Kinship, Marriage, and Family

Kin Groups and Descent. Descent is traced bilaterally. An agnatic bias is expressed in the terms *ætt* or, colloquially, *fólk*, a patriline of indefinite depth often associated with an ancestral homestead. An ancient system of patronymics was formally set aside in 1832 in favor of surnames passed from father to child and husband to wife, but it survives informally in a modified form. A person is said to be *hjá* ("of," "at the home of") his or her father, except that a married woman may be hjá to either her father or her husband. In informal usage, a person is often identified by reference to his or her natal homestead. There are no corporate kin groups larger than the nuclear family.

Kinship Terminology. Most kinship terms are (or may be) descriptive—for example, *pápabeiggi* (father's brother), *mammubeiggi* (mother's brother), *beiggjakona* (brother's wife), etc. All first cousins are called *systkinabørn* (sing. *systkinabarn*, sibling's child). The terminology is thus bifurcate-collateral in distinguishing all uncles and aunts, and Eskimo in lumping all first cousins together. Grandparents are called *omma* (grandmother) or *abbi* (grandfather), and depending on the sex of the speaker a grandchild is called *ommubarn/-dóttir/-sonur* (grandmother's child/daughter/son) or *abbabarn/-dóttir/-sonur* (grandfather's child/daughter/son). First-degree affines may be identified by combining a pair of nuclear terms, or by prefixing *ver-* to one of them (e.g., *versystir, konusystir,* sister-in-law); but the term *svágur* covers wife's brother, sister's husband, and daughter's husband (the last of these may also be called *mágur*). Within the nuclear family, a married couple is a *hjún*, siblings are *systkin*, and a father and son together are *feðar*.

Marriage. Marriage is generally neolocal (occasionally patrilocal). Divorce is very rare.

Domestic Unit. The domestic unit is the nuclear family.

Inheritance. Except for leaseholds, inheritance is generally equal among male and female heirs.

Socialization. Children are allowed considerable freedom. Depending on their ages, children are looked after by their mothers or by an older (female) relative, or play in roughly age- and sex-segregated groups. Sibling rivalry is discouraged. Corporal punishment is virtually unheard of. Schooling begins at age 7.

Sociopolitical Organization

Social Organization. There was formerly a fairly marked distinction between tenant farmers and freeholders. (There were also many servants on the larger, leasehold estates, and a few paupers.) Society's upper ranks were swelled in the late nineteenth century by wholesale merchants and shipowners; however, continued economic growth, occupational diversification, and a strong egalitarian ideology have forestalled any clear class distinctions.

Political Organization. Since 1948, local legislative authority has been vested in the Løgting, a democratically elected body of (at present) thirty-two members. The Løgting elects its own foreman, the Løgmaður, who chairs a three-member executive council (the Landsstýri) and is in effect the Faroes' prime minister. Governments are formed by coalitions among the Løgting members, who represent the several political parties (at present seven). The Faroes are divided administratively into 6 counties (*sýslur*), 50 townships (*kommunar*), and 108 villages or hamlets (*bygdir*). The counties are exclusively administrative units, whose chief official, the sheriff (*syslumaður*), is, among other things, a policeman. Townships are governed by elected councils. Party affiliation has little importance in township politics outside Tórshavn and the larger towns. Meanwhile, on the Danish side of things, the queen is the head of state, and the Faroes elect two members of the Danish parliament. Danish interests in the Faroes are overseen by the Ríkisumboðsmaður (in Danish, Rigsombudsmand), an ex officio nonvoting member of the Løgting. The Faroese króna is defined as equal to the Danish krone, although Faroese control their own taxes, customs regulations, and so forth. Foreign affairs are the sole responsibility of the Danish government (in consultation with the Faroese). Because of the threat to the fisheries, the Faroes refused to follow Denmark into the Common Market in 1973, and in 1977 the Faroes joined the other North Atlantic fishing nations in establishing their own 320-kilometer economic zone. In both cases, special accommodations were worked out with Danish and foreign governments. Membership in NATO, which maintains a radar facility near Tórshavn, continues to be a sore point.

Social Control. Formal social control is exercised by the police and the court in Tórshavn, with the Danish supreme court serving as a court of last appeal. Most social controls are informally yet effectively exercised through gossip and humorously slighting anecdotes, nicknames, and songs.

Conflict. Conflict is avoided as much as possible, open altercation being considered scandalous.

Religion and Expressive Culture

Religious Beliefs. The Faroes form a subdiocese of 13 parishes within the established Danish Lutheran Church. Some 85–90 percent of Faroese are Lutheran, perhaps 10 percent are Plymouth Brethren, and the rest belong to a scattering of evangelical sects or to a small Catholic congregation in Tórshavn. Despite a strong evangelical strain within the Lutheran church, the bulk of the population is only moderately observant. The principal supernatural is the Christian God. Traditional beliefs in such semisupernaturals as trolls and sea sprites have largely disappeared, although *huldufólk* (a gray, elvish people of the outfields) and *vættrar* (rock sprites) are still believed in to some extent.

Religious Practitioners. Religious practitioners include the Lutheran priesthood and lay readers; the ministers, missionaries, and more active members of the Lutheran and other evangelical groups; and the Catholic priest and a few nuns, who are all foreign.

Ceremonies. The old holiday season running from Christmas to Lent traditionally featured weekly communal dances. (Traditional Faroese dance, in which people link arms and chant heroic and lighter ballads, is the last survival of a style common in medieval Europe. Today it is most actively preserved by private dance clubs.) Other festive times, still recognized but no longer celebrated as energetically as formerly, include Christmas, New Year's, Shrove Tuesday, and Midsummer Eve. The slaughter of a school of pilot whales (*grindadráp*) traditionally offers an occasion for festivity. A number of occupational ceremonies (parties for fishing crews, groups of milkmaids, etc.) passed away because of the advent of a cash economy and, since they involved drinking, because they offended temperance advocates. Significant moments in individual life cycles—baptisms, weddings, funerals, and some birthdays and anniversaries—are celebrated with meals for family and friends. Dancing is customary at wedding parties. The national holiday, Ólavsøka (July 29), marking the opening of the parliamentary session, features processions, sporting events, dances, and exhibitions, and it draws large crowds to Tórshavn. Several regional holidays are patterned after it.

Arts. The vital Faroese literary scene is centered in Tórshavn, as is a smaller but no less lively scene in painting and sculpture. Several rock bands are the most visible producers of popular-culture artifacts.

Medicine. Medical services are provided by general practitioners in each county, small hospitals in Klaksvík and Tvøroyri, and a large central hospital in Tórshavn. Medical, dental, ambulance, and apothecary services are supported by a comprehensive national health program. Additional care may be obtained in Denmark.

Death and the Afterlife. Except to some extent among evangelicals, death and afterlife are secondary if not exactly minor concerns in popular belief and practice. Faroese believe that a person's soul leaves the body at death. A good person's soul joins God in heaven, while a bad person's goes to hell. The body is buried in a simple ceremony in a graveyard or churchyard on the outskirts of the village.

Bibliography

Danmarks Statistik. *Statistisk Årbog.* Copenhagen: Danmarks Statistik.

Føroya Landsstýri and Ríkisumboðsmaðurin í Føroyum. *Ársfragreiðing fyri Føroyar.* Tórshavn: Føroya Landsstýri and Rísumboðsmaðurin í Føroyum.

Joensen, Jóan Pauli (1978). "Føroysk Fólkamentan: Bókmentir og Gransking." *Fróðskaparrit* 26:114–149.

Joensen, Jóan Pauli (1980). *Färöisk Folkkultur.* Lund: LiberLäromedel.

Nielsen, Niels, et al., eds. (1968). *J. P. Trap, Danmark.* Vol. 13, *Færøerne.* 5th ed. Copenhagen: G. E. C. Gads.

Wylie, Jonathan (1987). *The Faroe Islands: Interpretations of History.* Lexington: University Press of Kentucky.

JONATHAN WYLIE

Finns

ETHNONYMS: Karelians or Karjalaiset, Suomalaiset, Tavastians or Hämäläiset

Orientation

Identification. Finns constitute the majority of the citizens of the Republic of Finland, which has a Swedish-speaking minority as well as Saami (Lapp) and Gypsy minorities.

Location. Finland is located approximately between 60° and 70° N and 20° and 32° E and is bordered on the east by Russia, on the south by the Gulf of Finland and Estonia, on the west by the Gulf of Bothnia and Sweden, and on the north and northwest by Norway. Four physiographic-biotic regions divide the country. An archipelagic belt embraces the southwestern coastal waters and the Åland Islands. A narrow coastal plain of low relief and clay soils, historically the area of densest rural settlement and mixed farming production, extends between the Russian and Swedish borders. A large interior plateau contains dense forests, thousands of lakes and peat bogs, and rocky infertile soils associated with a glacially modified landscape containing numerous drumlins and eskers. This interior lake and forest district lies north and east of the coastal plain toward the Russian border. Beyond the Arctic Circle, forests give way to barren fells, extensive bogs, some rugged mountains approaching 1,300 meters, and the large rivers of Lapland. Continental weather systems produce harsh cold winters lasting up to seven months in the interior eastern and northern districts. Annual fluctuation in daylight is great, and long summer days permit farming far to the north. The climate in southern and western Finland is moderated by the warm waters of the Gulf Stream and the North Atlantic Drift Current, where more than half of the 60–70 centimeters of annual precipitation falls as rain. Maximum summer temperatures may be as high as 35° C with a mean July reading of 13–17° C. Minimum winter temperatures fall below −30° C with mean February readings of −3° to −14° C.

Demography. In 1987 the population of Finland was about 4,937,000, 95 percent of whom were ethnically and linguistically Finnish. High mortality from wars and famine dampened Finland's population growth between the sixteenth and late nineteenth centuries. Over the past century falling birthrates and heavy emigration have perpetuated a very low population growth. Dramatic internal migration accompanied Finland's economic transformation between the 1950s and mid-1970s, when agriculture and the forestry industry were rapidly mechanized. At that time many young people left the rural areas of eastern and northeastern Finland to work in the urban industrialized south. While 75 percent of the Finnish population lived in rural areas just prior to World War II, by the early 1980s 60 percent of Finns were urban dwellers. Other substantial Finnish populations live in Russia, the United States, Canada, and Sweden, and smaller numbers have settled in Australia, South Africa, and Latin America.

Linguistic Affiliation. Finnish belongs to the family of far-flung Finno-Ugric languages in northeastern Europe, Russia, and western Siberia, including Saami (Lapp) and Hungarian. The languages most closely related to Finnish are Estonian, Votish, Livonian, Vepsian, and the closely allied Karelian dialects of the Balto-Finnic Branch. Although Finnish was established as a written language as early as the sixteenth century, its official status in Finland did not become equivalent to Swedish until after the Language Ordinance of 1863. Finnish is a euphonious language with a wealth of vowels and diphthongs, and its vocabulary has many Germanic and Slavic loanwords.

History and Cultural Relations

Human habitation in Finland dates to the early postglacial period in the late eighth century B.C., long before Finno-Ugric migrations into the area from the east. Earlier evidence indicated that the ancestors of the Finns migrated into southwestern Finland from Estonia as recently as the first century A.D. during the early Roman Iron Age. Recent research, including paleoecological evidence of agricultural grain pollens dating to the second millennium B.C., suggests a much earlier proto-Finnish presence. By the beginning of the Bronze Age, around 1200 B.C., these proto-Finnish or Finnic tribes were geographically divided. Those in southwestern Finland were heavily influenced by Scandinavian cultures, while those in the interior and eastern districts had ties with peoples of the Volga region. A series of crusades by the expanding Swedish Kingdom between the 1150s and 1293 was the vehicle for spreading the Roman Catholic church into Finland. By the time of the Lutheran Reformation in the early sixteenth century, the Swedish crown had strong control of colonial Finland, and a modified estate system forced Finnish peasants to participate in the wars of their Swedish lords. The destruction of Finnish settlements and crops, as well as large population losses, resulted from conflicts between the Swedish and Russian empires. By the mid-eighteenth century strong Finnish separatist movements were growing. Russia finally conquered Finland during the Napoleonic Wars of 1808–1809, annexing it as an autonomous grand duchy. The nineteenth century was a period of coalescence of Finnish national consciousness in scientific thought, politics, art, and literature, as exemplified by Elias Lönnrot's 1835 compilation of Finnish and Karelian rune songs in the famous Finnish epic poem, the _Kalevala_. This movement served as a counterpoint to a growing Russification of Finnish institutions, and Finland declared its independence immediately after the Russian Revolution of 1917. However, like Russia the new Finnish state was immediately embroiled in a civil war, the result of growing class tension between property owners (the counterrevolutionary "White" forces) and landless farm, forest, and factory workers (the "Red" forces) who wanted a socialist state. The scars from that strife had not entirely healed when Finland was united by its conflicts with the Soviet Union during World War II. Finland surrendered several eastern territories amounting to 10 percent of its area, and 420,000 Karelian Finns in those ceded areas chose to migrate across the newly formed national boundaries to Finland, requiring a massive resettlement and rural land-reform program. After World War II the Finnish parliamentary state actively pursued an official policy of neutrality combined with expanded trade and cultural contacts with the Soviet Union, a political adaptation known as the Paasikivi-Kekkonen Line.

Swedish is the second official language of Finland and is spoken by about 6 percent of the population. Living primarily in the southwestern part of the country, Swedish colonists and Swedish-speaking Finns had for centuries been the source of a ruling elite. Swedish was the language of commerce, the courts, and education, and Finnish was regarded as a peasant language until the nationalist movement of the nineteenth century advanced Finnish as an official, written, and cultural language of the majority. Political tensions arising from this ethnolinguistic division have largely faded as the Swedish-speaking minority declines in size and assimilates through frequent marriage with Finnish speakers. By contrast, Finland's 4,400 Saami or Lapps have largely avoided assimilation into the cultural mainstream, having been displaced from the southern part of the country by northward colonizing Finns over the past 2,000 years. Separateness is now reinforced as much by the economic marginality and limited educational opportunities in Finnish Lapland as by cultural-linguistic enclavement. Gypsies have lived in Finland since the sixteenth century and, perhaps, have endured the greatest prejudice of any minority. They number between 5,000 and 6,000, and in recent decades government measures have attempted to improve their economic situation and mitigate overt discrimination.

Settlements

With the rise of permanent agricultural settlements in the fertile plains of western and southern Finland in the Middle Ages, communal ownership and management practices were employed so that an entire hamlet, including fifteen to twenty closely spaced farms, assumed joint ownership of fields, forests, and pastures. Land reforms in the eighteenth and nineteenth centuries broke down the communal villages, but the newly created individual farmsteads retained a modified courtyard arrangement with dwelling units, sauna or bathhouse, grain and food storage buildings, livestock barns, and hay sheds enclosing an inner yard. Wooden domestic architecture displayed a high level of woodworking skill and embellishment, with two-storied houses marking prosperous farms. However, in the eastern and interior areas of Finland agricultural settlement occurred at a later date, and it was characterized by a more flexible system of landownership and farmstead organization. The persistence of "burn-beating" cultivation (poltta kaskea, kaskiviljelys), a form of pioneer extensive farming of the conifer forests, involved mobile populations and a dispersed pattern of settlement. Remote individual farms or extended dual-family holdings were won from the forest, often along favored glacial esker ridges or "home hills" (harju, vaara). While these historical patterns of settlement affect the present rural landscape, six of every ten Finns now live in urban areas. The largest cities are greater Helsinki, with 950,000 people in the 1980s, and Tampere and Turku, each with a population of 250,000. The majority of Finnish residential dwellings of all types have been constructed since World War II, many of them consisting of apartment-house complexes in the large cities. Social and emotional adjustment to this urban landscape has been problematic for many recently uprooted migrants from the countryside.

Economy

Subsistence and Commercial Activities.   Livestock raising was a major element in the Finnish peasant economy, but always in combination with activities such as fishing, hunting, tar production, and peddling. Wood as a commercial product did not become part of the farming economy until liberalized marketing policies, improved sawmilling techniques, and foreign demand for wood products converged in the late nineteenth century. The precariousness of crop cultivation in Finland, coupled with the emergence of new international markets for butter during the Russian colonial period (1808–1917), intensified production based on dairy cattle. Gradually, cultivated grasses replaced grains and wild hay as a source of cattle pasturage and fodder, and after the turn of the century farmers began establishing cooperative dairies (osuusmeijerit). The general shift toward commercial agriculture coincided with the decline of the old burn-beating system. Nonetheless, many farm families in northern and eastern Finland maintained an essentially subsistence orientation into the 1950s. Increased mechanization and specialization in farm production (dairy cattle, hogs, or grains) since the 1960s has occurred as the Finnish labor force has moved into manufacturing and service industries. Less than 11 percent of the labor force is now involved in agriculture and forestry. However, the rural economy is still based on modest-sized family-owned farms where marketing of timber from privately owned forest tracts is an important means of financing agricultural operations. Milk is prominent in the diet as a beverage and as the basic ingredient in a variety of curdled, soured, or cultured milk products; in broths used for soups, stews, and puddings; and in regional specialty dishes such as "cheese bread" (juustoleipa). There are notable differences between western and eastern Finland in bread making and in the manner of souring milk.

Industrial Arts.   Handicraft and artisan traditions were well developed, and some have survived the conversion to industrial manufacturing. Men specialized in making furniture, harnesses, and wooden vessels or "bushels" (vakka) and in various kinds of metalwork. The sheath knife (puukko) was a versatile men's tool, and it continues to symbolize maleness in recreational hunting and fishing contexts. Women specialized in textiles and lace making. The woven woolen wall rug (ryijy) has become a particularly popular art form in Finnish homes, emblematic of a family's patrimony.

Trade.   By the Middle Ages local markets and fairs were important in the Finnish economy, the latter often held in the vicinity of churches and associated with saints' days or other aspects of the religious calendar. Furs and naval stores comprised a large share of the export trade at that time, much of it destined for the cities of the Hanseatic League. German and Swedish merchants were prominent in Finland's early Baltic port cities. After the mid-nineteenth century Finland's foreign trade shifted toward Saint Petersburg and Russian markets with lumber, paper, and agricultural products becoming the chief exports. Since World War II, forest products have remained crucial to Finland's export economy, but these are now complemented by sophisticated metal, electronics, engineering, and chemical products. In recent years Finland's trade with countries in the European Community has expanded and is reinforced by its membership in the European Free Trade Association.

Division of Labor. The rural economy positions women as the primary cattle tenders and men as field and forest workers. On the one hand, being a good *emäntä* (or farm wife) involves a deft balance of cow care, child care, food processing, meal preparations, arduous cleaning chores in both cowshed and house, and ritual displays of hospitality for visiting neighbors, friends, and relatives. Men, on the other hand, are symbolically and practically associated with the outdoor domain, preparing and maintaining pastures and hayfields, cutting wood, coordinating labor with other farms, and operating and maintaining machinery. However, a decline in availability of work crews of kin and friends and a concomitant increase in mechanization have contributed to some convergence in male and female work roles. A complicating factor is that young Finnish women have left the countryside in greater numbers than men in recent years. Existing farms have aging personnel and few assisting family members, and some farmers are forced into bachelorhood.

Land Tenure. Historically in western Finland it was customary for a farm to be passed on to the eldest son, or possibly to the eldest daughter's husband. In eastern Finland a pattern of dividing land among all adult male family members prevailed. Such regional patterns have largely faded, and intergenerational transfers of land have become highly variable throughout Finland. Despite a bias toward patrilineal transmission, farms can be inherited by sons or daughters, oldest or youngest offspring, or they can be divided or jointly held by multiple heirs. However, at the beginning of the twentieth century a landless proletariat comprised half of Finland's rural population. A major agrarian reform was the Crofters' Law of 1918, serving to create holdings for landless rural poor and unfavorably situated tenant farmers. The latter reform also served to redistribute land to ex-servicemen and Karelian refugees in the wake of World War II.

Kinship

Kin Groups and Descent. Finnish kinship is basically bilateral, thus creating overlapping personal kindreds (*sukulaiset*) derived from one's father's and mother's relatives.

Kinship Terminology. Kin terms conform to the Eskimo system in Ego's generation. In the first ascending generation, terminology is lineal for females and bifurcate-collateral for males.

Marriage and Family

Marriage. Endogamous tendencies characterized marriage in Finnish rural society, with mates frequently chosen from the same village, parish, or rural commune. This tendency was most pronounced in the eastern districts among large Karelian joint families and those of the same background and status. Night courting and bundling rituals achieved a high degree of elaboration among the youth of southwestern Finland. Originally, bilocal marriages began with engagement and leave-taking (*läksiäiset*) ceremonies at the bride's home and ended with wedding rites (*häät*) held at the groom's home. Under church influence these were replaced by unilocal weddings staged at the bride's home. In recent years community and regional endogamy has declined. In the strict sense marriage rates have also declined, as cohabitation has become more common in urban areas. However, the latter pattern preserves some of the "trial marriage" aspects of earlier times when weddings were performed to finalize a marriage after a woman had conceived a child.

Domestic Unit. Historically, joint families were common in the eastern Karelian area where a founding couple, their adult male children, and the latter's in-marrying wives formed multiple-family farm households that were among the largest (20–50 persons) in Scandinavia. Elsewhere in Finland it has been common for only one child to remain on the parents' farmstead, and smaller stem and nuclear families have prevailed. Overall, family size has become smaller under the impact of urbanization, dropping from an average of 3.6 persons in 1950 to 2.7 by 1975.

Inheritance. A common historical pattern was for a son to take over a farm and care for his parents in their old age. As suggested previously (see under "Land Tenure"), the custom of patrilineal transmission is changing, perhaps as differential migration to cities alters the sex ratios of rural areas. In many cases, relinquishing coheirs (usually siblings who move away) must be compensated for their shares in a farm by the remaining heir, and often this is done with timber income from a farm's forest tracts.

Socialization. Gritty perseverance (*sisu*), personal autonomy and independence, and respect for the autonomy of others are central themes in Finnish child training and the Finnish personality.

Sociopolitical Organization

Social Organization. Prior to the nineteenth century Finnish society was divided into peasants (*talonpojat*), burghers, clergy, and nobility. Subsequent economic change fostered the wane of the clergy and nobility and an expansion of entrepreneurial and working classes. In recent decades considerable social mobility and an egalitarian ethos have emerged with increasing economic prosperity, progressive social welfare, an open educational system, and consensus politics. While Finns themselves may not always recognize clear economic class divisions, they are likely to be conscious of status attached to educational and honorific titles and to political-party affiliations. From an external view, the currently unfolding class system includes: farmers; working class (nonrural manual laborers); petite bourgeoisie (shopowners, small entrepreneurs); lower middle class (lower-income service sector); upper middle class (higher-income white-collar professionals); and upper class (corporate owners and managers).

Political Organization. The administrative district or commune (*maalaiskunta*) is a locale embodying a sense of community and self-identification for its residents. It often coincides with the historically deeper church parish, and it is a local unit of self-government that generally collects taxes, regulates economic affairs, and maintains public order. Every four years a communal council is elected to manage local affairs. Much of a council's work is implemented by a communal board comprised of members appointed to reflect the council's political-party composition. With as many as a dozen political parties in Finland, *kunta* government is sometimes represented by opposing coalitions of socialist and non-socialist party interests.

Social Control.   The institution of a village-governing alderman was part of the authoritarian moral environment in the dense rural settlements of southern and western Finland. Village fight groups and fights (*kylätappelut*) were ritualized conflicts, sometimes associated with weddings, which integrated communities via rivalry relationships. In the sparsely settled eastern interior, social life was more individualistic and social control less formal. In contemporary Finnish society, independent courts and centrally organized police forces maintain public order.

Conflict.   Finland's historical position as a frontier of colonization, military incursion, and subordination to external contesting empires is part of the Finnish collective conscience. Strategic victories by Finnish troops against invading Soviet forces during the "Winter War" of 1939–1940 are symbolically integral to the lore and identity of many Finns. By contrast, the "reign of terror" following Finland's civil war of 1917–1918 profoundly polarized the Finnish middle classes and working classes, with the latter remaining especially alienated and embittered.

Religion and Expressive Culture

Religious Beliefs.   Traditional Finnish conceptions of the supernatural had much in common with those of other Balto-Finnic peoples. The creation of the world was associated with the culture hero Väinämöinen, and the cosmos was layered into an underworld of the dead, a middle world of the living, and a sky-heaven supported by a giant pillar. Supernatural beings or deities included a god of the sky (Ilmarinen), a rain-giving god (Ukko), who was converted to a supreme or universal god under Christian influence, and other spirits of nature such as Tapio, a forest guardian of game. Many old features of Finnish-Karelian religion were preserved within the Russian Orthodox faith, which currently includes about 56,000 members in Finland. However, Lutheranism, which contributed to an erosion of native Finnish religion, embraces 90 percent of the population. Revivalist movements, like Laestadianism, have flourished within the context of the Lutheran church.

Religious Practitioners.   Prior to Christian and medieval Scandinavian influence, Finnish religion was embedded in shamanism with practitioners mediating between the present world and the altered consciousness of the upper and nether realms of the universe. Traces of this tradition, perhaps, survive in the divinatory practices of the seer or *tietäjä*. Evangelical Lutheran clergy, elected by local parish members, are the prominent religious specialists in contemporary society.

Ceremonies.   Bear ceremonialism was part of the Finns' ancient hunting traditions. Ritual slaying, feasting, and returning the skull and bones of a bear to the earth were fundamental to sending the animal's soul back to its original home and, thereby, facilitating its reincarnation. Ceremonies to promote farming and livestock became associated with holidays and the cult of the saints in the Christian calendar. Lutheran church life-cycle rites surrounding baptism, confirmation, marriage, and death remain significant for most Finns.

Arts.   Finnish culture is known for its rune song (folk poetry) traditions, which were synthesized in the epic *Kalevala*, a powerful symbol of national identity and source of artistic inspiration. In recent decades, innovative functionalist movements have distinguished Finnish architecture and the design of furniture, ceramics, glass, and textiles.

Medicine.   As a symbol of cleansing and purity, the sauna was a focus of therapeutic and curing activity as well as ritualized social bathing. It was common to give birth in saunas prior to the availability of hospitals in this century, and cupping and bloodletting were performed there. Generally, the sauna is still seen as a remedy for pain and sickness.

Death and Afterlife.   Living and dead kin formed a close unity in traditional Finnish and Karelian belief, and death was viewed largely as transfer to a new residence. The complex rituals accompanying death were orchestrated by women who arranged the wake, washed and shrouded the body, and sometimes sang laments to send the deceased, along with food and implements, to the place of the family ancestors. Memorial feasts were held six weeks and one year after death. Those who passed on to the realm of the dead (a place known as Manala or Tuonela) remained a profound moral force among living descendants. Days set aside for commemorating the dead were eventually adapted to a Christian calendar under Roman Catholic and Russian Orthodox influence.

Bibliography

Engman, Max, and David Kirby, eds. (1989). *Finland: People, Nation, State*. London: Hurst & Co.

Jarvenpa, Robert (1988). "Agrarian Ecology, Sexual Organization of Labor, and Decision Making in Northeastern Finland." In *The Social Implications of Agrarian Change in Northern and Eastern Finland*, edited by Tim Ingold, 76–90. Helsinki: Finnish Anthropological Society.

Lander, Patricia Slade (1976). *In the Shadow of the Factory: Social Change in a Finnish Community*. Cambridge, Mass.: Schenkman.

Pentikäinen, Juha Y. (1989). *Kalevala Mythology*. Bloomington: Indiana University Press.

Sarmela, Matti (1969). *Reciprocity Systems of the Rural Society in the Finnish-Karelian Culture Area*. FF Communications, no. 207. Helsinki: Suomalainen Tiedeakatemia.

Siikala, Anna-Leens (1987). "Finnic Religions." In *The Encyclopedia of Religion*, edited by Mircea Eliade. Vol. 5, 323–330. New York: Macmillan.

Solsten, Eric, and Sandra W. Meditz, eds. (1990). *Finland: A Country Study*. Washington, D.C.: Federal Research Division, Library of Congress.

Talve, Ilmar (1980). *Suomen Kansankulttuuri* (Finnish folk culture). Helsinki: Suomalaisen Kirjallisuuden Seura.

Vuorela, Toivo (1964). *The Finno-Ugric Peoples*. Indiana University Uralic and Altaic Series, no. 39. Bloomington: Indiana University Publications.

ROBERT JARVENPA

Flemish

ETHNONYMS: Flamencos (Spanish), Flandres (French), Flemings, French-Flemish, Northern Belgians, Southern Dutch, Vlaamingen (Dutch), Vlamisch (German)

Orientation

Identification. The Flemish are an admixture of the original Celtic inhabitants of the region, Roman invaders and settlers in this remote outpost of the empire, and Salian Franks, who invaded the Roman empire in the fifth century. The name "Vlaanderen," Flanders, derives from a Carolingian district, Pagus Flandrensis, of the eighth century. Today, the Flemish are the ethnic majority in the kingdom of Belgium and an ethnic minority in France.

Location. For the most part, the Flemish people are culturally integrated into the nation of Belgium, playing an equal role in national politics and social life. Belgium, located at 51° N and 4° E, southwest of the Netherlands, northeast of France, and northwest of Germany and Luxembourg, is comprised of Flanders and Wallonia, the French-speaking area of the country, separated by a linguistic border that runs east-west. Flanders is the northern region, composed of low-lying and coastal areas bordering the North Sea and reaching inland to the hills of Brabant. Some Flemish live in the northeast regions of France, in an area known as French-Flanders. Others have migrated to Africa and the New World. Political and religious divisions have through the centuries divided a people previously united by a common language and cultural traditions into distinct national ethnicities: the Dutch, the French-Flemish, and the Belgian Flemish.

Demography. The population of Belgium in 1990 was roughly 9,868,000 divided into 58 percent Flemish, 32 percent Walloon, with the remaining 10 percent a mixture of German speakers, Jews, Muslims, and others. The number of Flemish in France and elsewhere is unknown.

Linguistic Affiliation. The Flemish speak numerous dialects of Flemish Dutch, called Vlaams, which is distinct from the Dutch spoken in the Netherlands (Nederlands). Regional dialect differences are characterized by vowel and consonant changes, distinct word differences, and unique expressions that refer metaphorically to regional history. An identification of language use with culture is not possible; however, French-speaking Flemish in both France and Belgium retain traits specific to Flemish culture. In France, where the use of regional dialects has been actively discouraged and proscribed in the schools, the Flemish have developed an ethnic political movement that emphasizes the use of the Flemish language at home, practice of Flemish art forms, and training in traditional industrial skills and work patterns.

History and Cultural Relations

The original Celtic tribes of the North Sea coastal regions became part of the Roman Empire when they were conquered in 57 B.C. by the armies of Julius Caesar. (The name "Belgium" derives from the original inhabitants of the region, labeled the Gallia Belgica by the Romans.) During this time, the inhabitants of southern Belgium were heavily influenced by Latin culture, giving rise to Latinate cultural traditions and the use of a Latin language. In the north, the cultural influence of Rome was weaker. The invasion of Salian Franks in the fifth century abruptly interrupted the period of Latin influence and established a Germanic Frankish kingdom, which included the use of a Germanic language. The linguistic border that crosses Belgium is believed to mark the extent of Frankish influence. In the ninth century, Charlemagne united independent Frankish regions into a vast kingdom, of which Flanders was a central part. In the division of Charlemagne's kingdom upon his death, Flanders came under the control of his son, Lothair, comprising Lotharingia. Weak governments under Lothair and his successors resulted in a process of fragmentation that gave rise to the feudal period, extending from the ninth to the twelfth centuries (A.D. 862–1128), during which distinct principalities, counties, and duchies were established. The county of Flanders, the duchy of Brabant, and the bishopric of Liege were three of the most politically dominant. In spite of political, organizational, and language divisions, similar cultural traditions and a prosperous textile industry led to a degree of political cooperation between districts. From 1128 to 1278, the authority of nobles was challenged by the growing political power of city-dwelling burghers who gained political and military control of transportation and trade. During the Burgundian period, 1384–1482, a series of noble marriages and alliances unified the smaller principalities while preserving and extending citizen authority and the relative economic autonomy of cities. During the fifteenth and sixteenth centuries, under a balance of power between nobles and free citizens, Flemish cities established a trade association in London and became central to trans-European trade, as members of the German Hanse. This period, considered the golden age of Flemish culture, produced great works of art and music. However, the process of consolidation into yet larger political bodies was not favorable for the Flemish. When Flanders became part of the kingdom governed by the Spanish Habsburgs (1506–1700), the people became subject to authoritarian structures foreign to developing cultural traditions. The rule of the Spanish proved disastrous for the Flemish people; during the years of the Spanish Inquisition, many were tortured or killed for religious and political dissent. In an attempt to end Spanish rule, the region went to war against Spain, resulting in the separation of the northern from the southern Flemish, the creation of the independent nation of Holland comprised of liberated northern provinces, and the continued subjugation of the "Spanish Netherlands." The Flemish and the French-speaking Walloons continued to live under the Spanish until the War of Spanish Succession, 1700–1713, when the territories passed to the Austrian Habsburgs. During this period, French became the dominant language for social and political life; the Flemish became marginalized as a national identity grew. In 1794, Napoleon conquered and annexed the Flemish and Walloon territories for France. After his defeat in 1815, the Treaty of Vienna assigned these areas to the new kingdom of the Netherlands, under the rule of King William I. However, the years of economic and political separation between the Dutch and the Flemish, the years of a common fate with Wallonia, and the quite different economic and political positions of the Dutch and the Belgians in a world economy proved to be stronger political factors than a common heritage in a more distant past. Belgians—both

Walloons and Flemish—revolted against the Dutch in 1830, proclaiming Belgium as an independent nation. In 1831, they elected Prince Leopold of Saxe-Coburg-Gotha as king, defined their government as a constitutional monarchy, and instituted a bicameral parliament with democratic representation. Although Flemish leaders were an integral part of Belgian independence efforts, the Flemish played a minority role in national politics until the early 1900s, because of the predominance of French language and culture during the period of French and Austrian control. In 1914, Germany invaded Belgium. Many of the battles of World War I were fought in Flanders, which sustained enormous damage in both urban and rural areas and suffered great loss of life. Again, in 1940, Germany invaded. In an attempt to avoid the devastation it had suffered in World War I, the king quickly surrendered to the Germans. The strategy was ineffective and deadly. Belgian Jews and Gypsies were exported and killed by the Nazis. Many Flemish and Walloons were conscripted and sent to work in German factories and labor camps. The nation was occupied and became one of the most embattled fronts of the war, in both Wallonia and Flanders. In 1944, Belgium was liberated by Canadian, Australian, and American forces. The postwar period was a time of rebuilding, but it was also internally divisive and disruptive for the Belgian people. German collaborators were punished, and the king was forced to give up his rule to his son. Partly because of the favoritism shown by the Germans for the Flemish during the war, ethnic tensions between Flemish and Walloon increased. Also, Belgian colonial holdings in Africa were lost either through civil unrest or the granting of independence to restive former colonies. During the 1960s and 1970s, ethnic divisiveness in Belgium was largely resolved with the creation of independent Flemish and Walloon assemblies, which each have authority over cultural, social, political, and regional administrative affairs of their respective groups. At this time Flemish was recognized as an official state language. The Flemish regions also gained in relative economic importance, while Wallonia experienced a decline in the heavy industries—notably in steel and coal. Flanders's importance rose as well in international trade, high-tech manufacturing, industrial agriculture, tourism, and fishing. Today, the Flemish enjoy full political and social equality with the Walloons.

Settlements

Early settlement sites were located along natural waterways and on protected coastal bays. Larger settlements grew up at trading points, located on natural overland and water transportation routes. The human hand has greatly altered the Flemish landscape, by building canals, by dredging and straightening natural rivers, and by creating dikes and stabilizing sand dunes to create dry land out of marsh and to reclaim coastal floodplains. Walled cities are the hallmark of Flemish settlements, but villages, manorial estates, religious complexes, and farms are also significant. Dwellings and public buildings are made of local brick and cut limestone. Few buildings are constructed of wood, because of its scarcity, but early structures include half-wood upper stories, half-timbered buildings with brick infilling, and wooden roofs. Flemish "art cities," including Bruges, Ghent, and Antwerp, are noted for their skillfully carved stone and brick buildings. Stone and brick masonry, slatework, lead-pipe forming, and

other building trades were highly developed industrial arts from the twelfth to the eighteenth centuries, as is evident today in the finely constructed bridges, churches, city and guild halls, stockmarkets, and municipal markets. Residences dating from the seventeenth and eighteenth centuries were often built in a distinctly Flemish "stepped-gable" style, the echoes of which are reflected in more recent architecture. To this day, residences are "human-scale," building up rather than out. Residents often make space available on the ground floor for business activities: hence, the ubiquitous *winkelshuis*, "shop house," or *handelshuis*, "business residence."

Economy

Subsistence and Commercial Activities.   Today, Flanders has primarily an industrial and postindustrial economy, depending on the service and tourist industries. In recent years, economic activity in Flanders has expanded in final-step manufacturing, electronics, computer technology, and industrial agriculture. The economy has contracted in heavy industry, such as steel manufacture and boat building. The North Sea cities are commercial fishing centers, supporting large-scale fish processing. Several coastal cities are important ports for industrial production, raw materials, and agricultural produce. The fertile, flat land remains an agro-industrial center. Farmers grow vegetables, fruit, animal feed, forage, and grains, which in turn support large commercial baking, meat-processing, vegetable-oil extraction, commercial fiber-processing, and vegetable- and fruit-canning enterprises.

Industrial Arts.   The Flemish are noted for small-scale artisanal production of foods and luxury goods. Chocolate, lace, tapestry, glass, and pottery are notable. Early Flemish dominance was based on the production and finishing of cotton, linen, and woolen cloth.

Trade.   Flemish social values and cultural institutions are rooted in protoindustrial and industrial production for trade. The rise of early trade networks established Flemish municipal independence from an overarching feudal system and helped to install a system of government by a council of citizen representatives. Flemish cities established and joined trade associations that supported and facilitated trading relationships throughout Europe. Today, the Flemish character and culture are heavily influenced by traditions of trade, both on a large and small scale. The existence and persistence of the *zelfstandigen*, or independent self-employed business families, serves to define the Flemish people as independent economic actors.

Division of Labor.   In Belgium, occupational specialization is based on knowledge, training, and ability, but access to education and job training is limited by social class, ethnicity, gender, and economic status. Access to some occupations is facilitated only through family connections or kinship ties. In bicultural Brussels, some occupations are thought to be restricted ethnically, with the Flemish dominating many of the working-class occupations. Work is divided along gender and age lines in business, in the family, and in the household, as well, although not so strictly in practice as in widely held gender ideologies. For women, work in small firms and commercial enterprises is overlain so completely on domestic gender roles that household and business-related tasks are often difficult to distinguish: for example, wives of business owners receive visitors in the home as wives, and they also "help" their husbands as unpaid receptionists, office assistants, and business administrators in household-based firms.

Land Tenure. Land is owned legally by individuals or by corporate groups, such as business investors or religious orders. Ownership is enforced by the legal system, based on written records of ownership through purchase or inheritance. Rights to use and allocate the use of land and other property are held solely by the legal owner(s). Businesses and business profits are owned solely by the individuals or legal entities that have invested either property or money—but not labor, energy, or time—into those concerns.

Kinship

Kin Groups and Descent. Kinship is recognized bilaterally by family naming practices, but with an emphasis on the patriline. Upon marriage, the family names from both husband and wife are combined into a "household" name by which the nuclear family it creates is known; thus Geert DeJonge (the groom) and Kristin Vandeputte (the bride) create the family DeJonge-Vandeputte, but only the wife (and the business they operate, if any) adopts the combined last name. The children from this couple are given the family name DeJonge, unless the wife's family name is of high social rank.

Kinship Terminology. Most kin terms are based on descent/ascent and collateral relationships, and they are distinguished by gender: _moeder, vader, grootmoeder, grootvader_ (mother, father, grandmother, grandfather); _dochter, zoon_ (daughter, son); _zuster, broer_ (sister, brother); _tante, oom_ (aunt, uncle); _neef, nicht_ (nephew, niece). Other kin terms are ascriptive, denoting a social, fictive kinship that echoes genealogical kinship but indicates specific social responsibilities and duties, such as _meter, peter_ (godmother, godfather).

Marriage and Family

Marriage. Marriage unites an adult male and female into an economic unit ideally distinct from the natal families of each. Marriages are arranged by the bride and groom themselves, but with family influence. The economic aspects of marriage are not often explicitly expressed (people prefer to say they marry because they love one another or they wish to raise children together), but marriage is clearly an economic partnership between spouses and between their natal families. Notably, _zelfstandige_ (self-employed) couples and farmers work together in income-producing enterprises. Compatibility in work, the willingness to divide labor, and a shared work ethic are important reasons to marry a particular spouse when anticipating this work in adulthood. Men and women typically marry for the first time in their teens or early twenties, and they begin childbearing soon thereafter. Families of two to four children are the norm. Second and subsequent marriages are common following the death of, or separation from, one's first spouse. Legal divorce is increasingly common, but it is considered a misfortune particularly for children and wives who depend economically on husbands. Coworking couples will find it expedient not to divorce when marital difficulties arise because divorce can have a detrimental effect on business. In such cases, couples will remain married but live apart, creating social-sexual alliances with

others. There are few institutions that cater to the single adult. Subtle social sanctions are brought to bear on adults who remain single past the middle thirties without a legitimate reason, such as entry into the priesthood. Extramarital alliances, both purely sexual as well as those that result in children, are common for both men and women, but they are not often maintained openly. Wealthy Flemish men and women may maintain semipermanent liaisons for years. A secondary common-law spouse is not uncommon.

Domestic Unit. The nuclear family, composed of husband, wife, and their children, is the ideal family form. Coresident extended families are not common. Unmarried adults will commonly live with aged parents until marriage. Married couples establish new households when they wed, or shortly thereafter. Often in "business families," whose members work in the same trade, several nuclear families of kin will live in adjacent housing, next to or above the workspace. Old people who can no longer care for themselves are often cared for in old-age homes run by religious orders, sociopolitical unions, or insurance organizations. There are similar institutions for the mentally and physically disabled and the mentally ill. In recent years, young unmarried adults have begun to live apart from parents in shared housing. Alternative households and unmarried cohabitation are still uncommon.

Inheritance. Inheritance is strictly partible and is governed by state laws. A property owner's estate is to be divided equally between legitimate heirs. If a spouse survives, he or she is entitled to use rights to the home the couple previously shared. Business property is handled as the personal property of the owner and willed separately in ways that often result in the disinheritance of individuals who invest years of labor in the business.

Socialization. Children are allowed carefree childhoods, without major work responsibilities. Creative, imaginative play is encouraged. Children are much loved and spoiled. Older relatives and neighbors and older children are charged with care of little ones, teaching them a rich children's culture of play songs and rhymes as well as good behavior, which is defined as showing respect for elders, keeping quiet, following instructions well, and being resourceful. Willful and stubborn behavior on the part of children is tolerated and even admired as the first sign of a strong and independent character. Few children work, but the children of business owners often work part-time as "helpers" at as early as 8 years old. This experience is viewed as good preparation for following in a family trade. Flemish children are formally educated in schools, with the majority enrolled in private Catholic schools. After elementary grades, children are then either expressly guided to or given a choice between a trade-oriented education, a liberal education, professional training, or business training. An apprenticeship system survives in the half-time work-study programs of some vocational schools, but students still reside at their parents' home.

Sociopolitical Organization

Social Organization. The Flemish are socially divided into distinct social groupings defined by family pedigree and history, nobility, family business history, language use, personal occupation, and visible wealth. Both men and women try to "marry up" or marry within their social level. Gender is an important social divider; women typically do not receive as much from their natal families in terms of business training or education as men do. Women are expected to join their husband's family, fate, and fortune upon marriage. Because a woman's social status as a wife is therefore more significant to her social position in adulthood than her status as a daughter, courtship and marriage constitutes an important social-ranking process for women.

Political Organization. Both small communities and large cities are directed politically by *raden,* elected bodies of representatives from distinct districts. As mandated by law, all adults must vote. Representatives from Flemish districts are elected to the Flemish regional assemblies and to the parliament. These representatives make law and defend the interests of the Flemish in formulating national policy. Belgium is a constitutional monarchy, with a king at its head. The king has primarily symbolic power as the most important unifying force in the nation. Kingship is inherited through the male line and devolves only to males. The Flemish in France are not recognized officially as a political or ethnic body within the nation of France. Their participation in French political life is viewed as regional, rather than ethnic, participation.

Social Control. Conflicts inherent in Flemish culture are those that center on control over private property and conflicting interpretations of private versus public interest. State social control is accomplished by means of a judicial system that interprets the laws enacted by legislators and enforced by state and local police. Cultural mechanisms of social control consist of social sanctions, public and private censure of nonconforming behavior, and effective socialization of children and young adults. Violence against the person is not tolerated, with one exception. Stiff legal penalties are levied for crimes against unrelated persons, but the state allows intrafamily violence to continue by a policy of nonintervention in nuclear-family affairs. Spouse and child abuse, as well as mistreatment of the elderly, are problems in all social classes.

Conflict. In recent years, social conflicts have arisen and divided the Flemish over social policy issues such as abortion, which has divided the nation of Belgium in ways that crosscut social-class, ethnic, and religious differences. The Flemish people do not present a unified view on the basic question of whether abortion should be a legally protected right or a crime, nor on how it should be defined by law or handled in the courts. Such policy issues have been addressed in the past by face-to-face meetings among legislators, religious leaders, the king, and cabinet advisers, in which compromise positions have been reached and made law. National-level conflict exists between the Walloons and the Flemish centering on the dynamics of economic change in the nation of Belgium. In France, conflict over issues of ethnic and regional autonomy continue to simmer and, on occasion, boil over.

Religion and Expressive Culture

Religious Beliefs. The Flemish are overwhelmingly Roman Catholic. Membership in the Catholic church is the norm, regardless of personal religious belief. Although nearly everyone is baptized and learns Catholic doctrine in catechism classes or Catholic school, many Flemish people are not practicing Catholics or are active nonbelievers. Leaving the church in an official act of excommunication, however,

creates myriad social difficulties, because many social services are linked with the parish or other church institutions. Flanders has a small Protestant community composed of Flemish converts to Jehovah's Witnesses, the Mormon church, and other Christian sects. In addition, there is an active, large, and dynamic Jewish community, particularly in Brussels, Antwerp, and the coastal area; an ephemeral surviving Gypsy community; and a growing community of Muslims in Brussels. "Flemish" Jews and Muslims have not adopted the culture of their neighbors, and they continue to practice their faiths in separate ethnic communities. However, Belgian religious minorities often speak the language of the region in which they live and participate in Belgian social and political life.

Religious Practitioners. Priests and nuns organize most religious functions. Lay religious leaders are active in parish associations and participate in the organization of religious ceremonies and church services. The Freemasons also comprise an important quasireligious group in Flemish culture, establishing ties of brotherhood that crosscut social, religious, and ethnic differences. Freemasons have been influential in liberal party politics and in the process of defining a middle-class Flemish political interest.

Ceremonies. Baptism, first communion, and confirmation mark the child's entry into the Catholic family and community. There are no official rituals marking entry into adulthood—except perhaps graduation from school, military service (for men), and marriage. The Flemish celebrate many days in the Catholic religious calendar that mark events in Christ's life. Also, there are a series of folk processions, rooted in historic events and legend, often using masks and papier-mâché "giants" (e.g., the Kattestoet in Ghent). Other ceremonies mark religious miracles, such as the Procession of the Holy Blood in Bruges, or are more purely commercial, on the order of street theater, combining spectacle with romantic reformulations of history.

Arts. Flemish literature, painting, sculpture, music, and dance are highly developed arts, comprising Flemish regional and ethnic styles, as well as participating in widespread European art movements. Early Flemish literature, written in local dialect, is linked with the growth in political importance of the Flemish population, depicting folk heroes that personify the political and social character of the Flemish. More recent literature is often nihilistic or surreal, influenced by the damage inflicted by both world wars on the Flemish psyche. Many of the great early works of Flemish musical composition are liturgical pieces for voice and organ, for example Orlando de Lassus's Gregorian compositions. The exceptional works of the Flemish primitives—including Memling, Bosch, and the Van Eycks—and the numerous Flemish masters, such as Rubens, were commissioned by noble patrons throughout Europe. More recent Flemish painting and sculpture often highlight the pleasures and pains of rural life, but others, such as works by Ensor, depict urban decadence and cultural decay. Folk arts, notably street singing, folk opera, and marionette and hand puppetry, have revived in recent years as part of the folk movement. Antwerp has a tradition of puppet theater that often crosses into the realm of political and social critique. In the plastic arts, tapestry and lace manufacture have evolved from early products of cottage industry into domestic crafts. Today, lace is simultaneously a fine art, a hobby craft, and a tourist art; and many varieties of lace are available for sale, collection, and display.

Medicine. Modern medical care is provided in state-run hospitals and clinics and is also available through private doctors and health practitioners. The scientific model of medicine is widely accepted, but health maintenance often involves folk beliefs regarding the use of herbs, mineral and saltwater baths, and the use of certain foods as preventative cures. Many Flemish also believe in the curative value of Oriental medical treatments, such as acupuncture. Devout Catholics often pray for divine assistance with health problems, posting placards of thanks to the Virgin Mary in churches. Many Flemish people avoid dental care, with a resulting loss of teeth from decay.

Death and Afterlife. Beliefs about death and an afterlife are shaped by Catholic doctrine. Funerals are sad and frequently private events, shared only by the deceased's family, close friends, and neighbors. The death of a child is a particularly sad and private event. Public displays of grief are not common. Graves, located on church grounds or nearby, are cared for by the survivors of the deceased. National graveyards of the fallen of World Wars I and II, located in northern Flanders, are maintained by the nations whose dead are buried there. For the Flemish, these vast graveyards are monuments to sacrifice and freedom, symbolic of a national and Flemish resolve to work for international peace and political compromise.

Bibliography

De Meeus, A. (1962). _History of the Belgians._ Translated by G. Gordon. New York: Praeger.

Goris, Jan Albert (1945). _Belgium._ Berkeley: University of California Press.

Huggett, F. E. (1969). _Modern Belgium._ New York: Praeger.

Lijphart, Arend, ed. (1981). _Conflict and Coexistence in Belgium: The Dynamics of a Culturally Divided Society._ Berkeley: University of California Press, Institute of International Studies.

Pirenne, Henri (1915). _Early Democracies in the Low Countries: Urban Society and Political Conflict in the Middle Ages and the Renaissance._ Translated by J. V. Saunders. New York: Harper & Row.

Riley, R. C. (1989). _Belgium._ World Bibliographic Series, edited by R. G. Neville, vol. 104. Oxford: Clio Press.

Van Houtte, J. A. (1977). _An Economic History of the Low Countries, 800–1800._ New York: St. Martin's Press.

MERIELLE K. FLOOD

French

ETHNONYMS: none

The French are citizens of France (the French republic). Including the island of Corsica, France occupies 549,183 square kilometers and in 1990 had an estimated population of 56,184,000. About 10 percent of the population is composed of immigrants and workers from Italy, Spain, Portugal, and other European nations and refugees from former French colonies in Southeast Asia and Africa. French is the language of France and about 90 percent of the people are Roman Catholics, with a large Muslim population made up mainly of immigrants from northern Africa, especially Algeria. A strong Parisian-centered government and centralized authority began to emerge in the tenth century, and in the twentieth century mass communication has strengthened French nationalism at the expense of the regional cultures. Still, though, there are viable regional cultures and marked linguistic variations. Among the major regional cultures are the Alsatians in the east; the Corsicans on the Mediterranean island of Corsica; the Bretons in the northwest; the Burgundians, Auvergnats, and Aveyronnais in central France; and Aquitaine, Occitans, Provencal, and the Basques in the south.

See also Alsatians; Aquitaine; Auvergnats; Aveyronnais; Basques; Bretons; Burgundians; Jurassians; Occitans; Provencal; Walloons

Bibliography

Kurian, George T. (1990). _Encyclopedia of the First World._ 2 vols. New York: Facts on File.

Worldmark Encyclopedia of the Nations (1988). 7th ed. New York: Worldmark Press.

Frisians

ETHNONYM: Frysk

Orientation

Identification. The Frisians are a linguistic and cultural minority of the Netherlands (with some pockets of Frisian speakers living in Germany as well).

Location. The majority of Frisians live in Friesland, a province in the north of the Netherlands that is bordered on the south by the Zuider Zee (IJsselmeer) and on the east and north by the North Sea. Most of Friesland lies below sea level, subject to storms and flooding through much of the year. The soil is mixed: sand, clay, and peat. The coastal _terp_ region, so-called for the mounds (_terpen_) built by early inhabitants to raise their dwelling sites above the flood line, is essentially sandy soil. To the east, two ecological zones can be distinguished: the "low middle" area of flat wetlands formed by the silting-in of old riverbeds; and the marshy forest area in the southeast.

Demography. Frisian speakers today number approximately 730,000, with about 400,000 living in Friesland Province, 300,000 living elsewhere in the Netherlands, and the remainder living in Germany, Denmark, and North America.

Linguistic Affiliation. Frisian is a member of the North Sea Branch of the Western Germanic Family of Indo-European languages and bears strong linguistic resemblance to both English and Dutch. Most speakers are bilingual in Dutch. There are three dialects: West, Eastern, and Northern Frisian. Frisian has an official orthography in the Netherlands.

History and Cultural Relations

Frisian mythology holds that an Indian prince, Friso by name, was drafted into the Macedonian army of Alexander the Great, deserted from that army, and sailed north from Greece with his brothers in the fourth century B.C. to eventually make landfall in Friesland. There is archaeological and historical evidence that a proto-Frisian culture developed on the coast between 400 and 200 B.C. and that the construction of terpen was well under way by 200 B.C. By 12 B.C., Roman records tell of Frisians assisting the ships of Roman invasionary forces in the region. The Frisians entered into trade with Rome's legions, providing them with hides. The alliance with Rome, however, was uneasy, and between A.D. 25 and 70 the Frisians rebelled openly against Roman demands for tribute. The Romans were finally forced to retreat from the region by A.D. 70. The years A.D. 700–900 were the time of greatest Frisian influence in the area, because of their extensive involvement in seafaring trade, but Frankish expansion (in the early 800s) soon reduced the territory under Frisian influence. The Franks brought Christianity as well as political control to Friesland, though conversion of the Frisians did not come easy. Between the twelfth and thirteenth century, however, Christendom was securely established, though not without undergoing syncretization with indigenous beliefs—a phenomenon common throughout the Germanic territories. By the medieval era, the scattered homesteads of Frisian families began to give way to nucleated village settlements each centered on a small church built on high ground. The inland areas were characterized by smallhold farms, with more extensive landholdings along the coast. However, a classic feudal system never developed in Friesland. Much of Frisian cultural identity today can be directly attributed to the strong and successful tradition of independence maintained throughout the period of Saxon domination during the fourteenth and fifteenth centuries, when the slogan "Free and Frisian, without Tax or Excise" was the rallying cry for rebellion against foreign rule. In 1579, with the Treaty of Utrecht, Friesland became part of "the Seven United Provinces," which included Holland, Zeeland, Groningen, Overijssel, Gelderland, Utrecht, and Friesland, and from which the modern nation of the Netherlands is derived. Within this union, there was provision for a great deal of regional autonomy, which again contributed to the preservation of a distinctly Frisian identity. Of all the united provinces, Holland assumed an ascendancy

early on because of its great success in shipping and mercantilism. This ascendancy was partly responsible for the introduction of the highly influential Dutch Calvinist sect in Friesland. In 1795, the French occupied much of Friesland, bringing with it the ideals that informed the French Revolution (liberty, equality, and fraternity) and the Napoleonic Code. But the Frisians never cared for foreign rule, however "enlightened," and threw their support behind William V of Orange-Nassau. In 1813 the kingdom of the Netherlands, including Friesland, was formed, and prospects for absolute political autonomy for the province were ended. Early in World War II, the Netherlands was occupied by the Nazis, and Frieslanders were active in the Dutch Resistance, although there were some few who, as in the Netherlands as a whole, collaborated with their occupiers. The tales of heroic Frisian resistance against Nazi occupation provide the newest episodes in their long-standing tradition of independence from foreign rule.

Settlements

Settlement of Friesland depended upon protecting its low-lying lands from inundation by sea floods. The "Golden Hoop" of dikes that today extends along the whole of the Frisian **coast** was begun as long ago as A.D. 1000. The earliest Frisian **settlements** were built on mounds of refuse covered with clay, and drainage windmills were constructed to pump water out of sodden fields. The inland portion of Friesland is still dotted with scattered farming homesteads, although nucleated village settlements became common beginning in the medieval period. A group of villages forms a *gemeente,* or community, which is similar to, but not identical with, the concept of the Anglo-American county. (The gemeente was originally a cooperative unit, rather than an administrative one.) The classic Frisian homestead is called "head-neck-body"—a series of articulated structures in which the family quarters are contained in the smallish "head," connected to the larger "body" (the barn), by a narrower and shorter section (the "neck") that contains the kitchen, milk cellar, and churn room. The living quarters include a parlor, reserved for formal use (e.g., Sunday visits), as well as a larger, plainer room for day-to-day family use. Traditional, but rarely used today, is the "bed-cupboard" that opened off the living area and was precisely what the name suggests: a sort of closet containing a bed. Hearths, and sometimes internal walls as well, were tiled. Barns were traditionally built of wattle and daub, but brick is the more common material today. Thatching for barn roofs remains in use, but house roofs are usually tiled. Barn roofs were traditionally finished off with decorative gables, a practice that is rapidly dying out. In the "heather villages" of old, where the peat workers lived, dwellings (called *spitkeat*) were semi-subterranean constructions of turf and planking, covered over with a peaked thatch roof.

Economy

Subsistence and Commercial Activities. The Frisian economy centers on agriculture and dairying—the Frisian dairy breed is famous the world over. Inland farms are smallholds, worked by the families that own them. Even in the coastal regions where larger holdings were once common, farming was done on a smaller, family scale on leased lots. In the forested area, livestock takes precedence, while the open lands have emphasized crop production since the introduction of chemical fertilizer and mechanized traction. The weekly livestock market in Tjouwert is an important economic as well as social occasion. In the seventeenth century, peat working became an important economic pursuit as well, when demand for cheap fuel increased because of the introduction of industrialization throughout the Netherlands. Although peat is no longer the marketable item it once was, its exploitation had a number of important effects upon Friesland: reduction of arable land, the building of canals throughout the region for the inland shipping of peat, and the expansion of the inland shipping industry itself. The tourist industry is well developed, catering to vacationers from Holland, as well as from the rest of Europe. Frisian towns were and are trade and crafts centers.

Industrial Arts. Frisian industry includes clock making, tile working, building construction, and the production of dairy products. A traditional craft, distinctive to Friesland, is the carving and painting of *ulebuorden* or "owl boards"—barn gables that were once a standard part of barn construction but are no longer so common.

Trade. From very early on in the history of the Frisian people, trade was an important aspect of the economy. The location of Friesland made the Frisians admirably placed for participation in a trading network that extended from Brittany to Scandinavia, and their seafaring skills gave them a great deal of influence within that network. Early Frisian trade goods were furs and hides. Later on, agricultural produce was added. With the introduction of money, which dates back to Roman times, Frisian trade gave place to commerce. Peat was an important commercial item during the seventeenth and eighteenth centuries.

Division of Labor. Except for the association of women with the domestic arts, there is no strict division of labor by sex. Both male and female family members participate in the work of the family farm, and in the towns women participate in merchant and craft activities along with the men.

Land Tenure. Land is privately owned, and it can be bought, sold, or leased.

Kinship

Kin Groups and Descent. Kinship is reckoned bilaterally, with a patrilineal bias.

Kinship Terminology. Frisian kinship terminology is of the Eskimo type. Naming practices prior to the French occupation of the early 1800s consisted of the simple reversal, from one generation to the next, of "first" and "last" names. Thus, the son of Hans Koek would be named Koek Hans, and the grandson would be Hans Koek once again. The French introduced permanent, or patrilineally heritable, family names, and at that time people either registered the names they currently held (often with a suffix), took geographic referents as the family name (the name of their town, for example), or registered their occupation (Weaver, for instance, or Farmer). A special relation exists between neighbors, entailing obligation of mutual assistance, and is marked by a specific term of address ("neighbor-man" or "neighbor-woman") used as a preface to the addressee's surname.

Marriage and Family

Marriage. Weddings were once very elaborate celebrations, and were traditionally performed by a priest. Today, however, civil weddings are as common as church ones. Marriages also used to be finalized when the bride and groom were still quite young—in their middle teens, or shortly after concluding elementary school. Today, however, the average age at marriage is higher, partly reflecting an increased interest in higher education prior to "settling down." Sex prior to marriage is relatively common, though a certain amount of discretion is expected of the parties involved, and "homing," or living together out of wedlock, has a long tradition despite the disapproval of the church. Divorce is as common in Friesland as in the rest of the Netherlands.

Domestic Unit. Although the "ideal typical" Frisian family configuration is the nuclear family, single-parent families, independent spinster or bachelor households, and any of the variety of other household arrangements to be found in the Netherlands—and, indeed, European society as a whole—have their counterparts in Friesland.

Inheritance. Heritable property is passed on at the discretion of its owner, although there is a distinct bias that favors a son inheriting from his father.

Socialization. In the face-to-face community of the Frisian village, socialization is not the specific province of any one person or institution. Parents are the primary care givers and socializers of the very young, but once a child is old enough to be out and about in the village, other villagers and the child's own peers contribute much to his or her socialization as well. The school and the church are the two principal socializing institutions outside the family, and the public school provides formal instruction in the Frisian language. The much larger Christian school provides instruction only in Dutch, however. Friesland has no university of its own.

Sociopolitical Organization

Social Organization. There is a basic distinction between rural and town-based Frisians, with greater status accorded to the town dwellers. Communalism, necessitated by the demands of the environment (i.e., the need to build and maintain the extensive system of canals, dikes, and drainage ditches), is reinforced by the concept of *buorreplicht* (neighbor's duty)—a part of Frisian folk law that appears in the *Lex Frisionum* of Charlemagne—which requires that neighbors provide assistance to one another when the occasion demands it. By extension, neighbors are expected to attend one another's life-cycle events (weddings, funerals, etc). Neighbor relations, rather than kinship ties, are the principal vehicle for the formation of larger cooperative groups in Frisian society.

Political Organization. Modern Frisian political organization derives from the thirty gemeenten, or countylike communities, and the "Eleven"—the Frisian cities established as independent of county governance during medieval times. Decisions requiring action or imposing obligations on the Frisian people as a whole are made by forty-one appointed representatives (one for each county and one for each of the cities). The highest-ranking official in Friesland is also appointed—that is the queen's commissioner, who acts as a liaison between the province and the federal government.

Social Control.   Frisian folk law was laid down in written form as part of Charlemagne's *Lex Frisionum* in A.D. 801–802, and it provides the formal means for the adjudication and mediation of conflicts within Frisian society. Informal mechanisms of social control are those common to many village communities: gossip, joking, ridicule, and other expressions of public disapproval for an individual's social transgressions.

Conflict.   Friesland is but one province within the larger national entity of the Netherlands, and thus it does not have autonomy in relating to other nation-states. While enjoying a great deal of provincial autonomy within the Netherlands, it is subject to the national government's policy decisions concerning foreign relations, alliances, and disputes.

Religion and Expressive Culture

Religious Beliefs.   Christianity came early to Friesland with the dominion of the Franks in the eighth and ninth centuries, but it did not succeed in completely eradicating indigenous tradition. Pre-Christian beliefs, called *byleauwe,* are derived from the larger Germanic folk tradition, and they retain some currency especially in rural areas and the forested region. These folk beliefs, modifying and being modified by the newer Christian faith, now consist of an interwoven tapestry of folktales and superstitions regarding supernatural beings such as devils, spooks, and ghosts; "white ladies" who lived underground and kidnapped travelers in the night; a more beneficent category of female spirits who provided help to travelers in distress; and elves, witches, wizards, and trolls. Belief in oracles and predictive visions were common in the relatively recent past. Predominantly, Frisians are Protestant: 85 percent are members of the Calvinist Dutch Reformed or Reformed churches, with another 5 percent being Mennonites.

Ceremonies.   Many traditional ceremonial occasions—such as the start of Lent (Mardi Gras) and Palm Sunday—have become exclusively religious observances, with little community celebration. Easter, however, remains a major community celebration, marked by special family meals, egghunt competitions, and the like. Queen's Day, a national observance, is celebrated on 30 April with parades and festivals. St. Martin's Day, once associated with the church and the spirits of the deceased, is now a children's holiday. As is true throughout the Netherlands, the holiday of Saint Nicholas (*Sinterklaes*) is celebrated on 5 December. It marks the arrival of Saint Nicholas and his assistant, Black Peter, who travel to the Netherlands in a boat from Spain and bring sweets for the children of the village. Presents are exchanged between friends and family members on this day as well. Christmas, however, is strictly a church observance.

Arts.   Traditional Frisian folk arts include tile making, elaborate embroidery, and the uleubuorden, the ornately decorated gables that once graced the traditional Frisian barns and have now become purely aesthetic productions. Friesland has a long tradition of excellence in the literary and visual arts as well.

Death and Afterlife.   Frisian attitudes toward death are characterized by a markedly practical acceptance of its inevitability. The obligation of performing funerary tasks once fell to the neighbors of the deceased as one of the obligations of buorreplicht, but more recently they have been assumed by burial associations. The deceased traditionally was wrapped in a white shroud but is now more commonly dressed in everyday clothing. The body is carried to the cemetery in a horse-drawn hearse, followed by the family and neighbors of the deceased in a procession on foot. Although beliefs in the afterlife are largely consistent with Christian teachings, some elements of Frisian funerary practice reflect non- or pre-Christian influences. For example, the funeral procession, according to tradition, ought to follow a winding path in order to disorient the spirit of the dead person and thus frustrate its efforts to return to the home it knew in life. Similarly, the coffin is carried around the cemetery three times before being brought in for interment.

Bibliography

Kalma, J. J. (1977). *Friesland toen en nu.* The Hague: Boekencentrum.

Mahmood, Cynthia Keppley (1989). *Frisian and Free: Study of an Ethnic Minority of the Netherlands.* Prospect Heights, Ill.: Waveland Press.

Van der Plank, P. H. (1985). "Ethnicité dans une province périphérique: La Frise." *Recherches Sociologiques* 15:129–141.

Wittermans, Tamme (1967). "The Frisians: An Ethnic Group in the Netherlands." *Sociology and Social Research* 52:88–100.

NANCY E. GRATTON

Friuli

ETHNONYMS: Friulano, Friulans, Friulians, Priulians

Orientation

Identification.   The Friuli are speakers of a Rhaeto-Romance language, Friulan, who live in the north of Italy, on the border of Austria and Slovenia.

Location.   Friuli-Venezia-Giulia, the autonomous region of Italy in which Friulan speakers live, is bounded on the west by the Dolomite Alps, on the north by the Carnic Alps, on the east by the Julian Alps, and on the south by the Adriatic Sea. This territory, with an area of 7,900 square kilometers, has a total population of in excess of 1,232,000. Of this number, perhaps a little over half are Friulan speakers, most of whom live in the province of Friuli, between the Livenza and Timavo rivers. The environment is favorable to agriculture, with its high, reliable annual rainfall and fertile soils.

Demography.   The total number of Friulan speakers today is on the order of 600,000, and most of these live in the province of Friuli. Within that province, Friulan speakers constitute the majority, but they share that territory with speakers of Venetian, Slovene, and German.

Linguistic Affiliation. Friulan is a Rhaeto-Romance language, related to but distinct from Ladin and Romansh. It was derived from vulgar Latin some time after the fall of the Roman Empire. Its exact relationship to Ladin remains a matter of some linguistic debate. Many scholars have tended to treat Friulan as a Ladin dialect, but scholars today generally agree that it is a separate language. Friulan displays significant Germanic and Venetian influences. The earliest evidence of a Friuli written form are books that were written about 1150. Some attempts are currently under way to use Friulan as a literary language. The Friuli use both their own language and Italian in their everyday discourse. In some Friuli parishes, historical factors have resulted in a trilingual situation, the third language being a German dialect. In these areas, the three languages are used diatypically, which is to say that speakers select among their language options according to situational factors: Italian is used for church or school occasions, as the principal written form, and to speak to or in the presence of outsiders; Friulan is used within the community among acquaintances and friends as a "locally public" language; and German is reserved for use in the home or in private conversation among close friends.

History and Cultural Relations

There is little known of the Friuli prior to Roman times. The region's Latin name, when it was the home of the Tenth Roman Legion, was Patria Fori Julii, from which the name "Friuli" derives. Its early history was extremely turbulent, as it was conquered by the Huns, by Charlemagne, by the Lombards, and by the Magyars. In the mid-900s it had become a sovereign state under the aegis of King Henry IV of Germany. In the mid-1700s this sovereign status was dissolved because of internal dissension, and in 1797 Napoleon occupied the region. The Friuli parliament, established in 942, met for the last time in 1805. From 1814 to 1866, Friuli became a part of Austria. When the kingdom of Italy was proclaimed in 1866, however, Friuli voted to join it. In the early 1900s, Friuli once again but only briefly became a part of Austria, to be returned to Italy in 1919 with the collapse of the Hapsburg Empire and the Treaty of Saint Germain. After World War II, portions of traditional Friuli territory were lost to Yugoslavia, while the major part of the region remained in Italy's hands.

Settlements

The Friuli live in both rural and urban settlements. Rural settlements are small, agriculturally oriented villages; the towns and cities have an industrial focus.

Economy

Economic activity in Friuli is varied, although the region has never been a wealthy one. In the countryside, farming and animal husbandry are of great importance. Industrial activity centers on the urban areas, and individual cities are often associated with specialized products or services. Udine, for example, is associated with textiles; Monfalcone on the Adriatic coast serves maritime industries. Wood-based industries—

sawmills, furniture manufacturing, and the like—have been significant economic pursuits since the 1500s. Friuli is also well known throughout Italy for the toys, basketry, and knives produced in the north of the province. The region also supports mining (of lead and tin), quarrying (marble), and factories for the production of paper, cement, clocks, clothing, and a variety of other products. Both men and women are represented in the work force, but there is a strong bias associating domestically related work with women. Real property, including land, tends to be passed from father to son.

Kinship, Marriage, and Family

Kinship is reckoned bilaterally, but with a strong patrilineal emphasis. Surnames are passed from the father to his children, and a husband's name is assumed by a wife upon her marriage. The Friuli are monogamous. Marriage is proscribed between first cousins, whether the relation is reckoned matrilineally or patrilineally. Divorce is prohibited. Neolocal postmarital residence is the general rule, with the new household usually, but not always, established in the home village of the husband. The ideal typical household consists of the nuclear family, but in this as in postmarital residence, economic or personal factors result in variations on the general rule. Child rearing, as a domestically oriented task, falls primarily to the mother.

Sociopolitical Organization

While fully a part of Italy, Friuli has long considered itself united and deserving of regional autonomy—the demand for which made itself felt strongly in the post–World War II years. In 1963, Friuli-Venezia-Giulia achieved recognition as the Fourth Region of Italy, with its own regional council. At that time, Trieste was made the capital, against the wishes of Friuli nationalists who would have preferred the selection of Udine, their historic seat, and setting off a movement to remove Friuli from the Fourth Region and to establish a fully autonomous Friulian administrative unit, free of the perceived dominance of Trieste and Venezia-Giulia. In conjunction with this effort, there have been movements to establish a university at Udine and the teaching of Friulan in the schools, as well as renewed interest in matters of local history, folklore, and other elements of Friuli culture. Politically, Friuli is predominantly Christian Democrat. The Friuli participate fully in local politics but have yet to make much of an impact in general elections, even within the region.

Religion and Expressive Culture

Friuli is a Catholic region and is subject to the principles, laws, and ethos espoused by that church. Recent studies have focused on the historical conflict between church and folk beliefs, as they are reflected in the records of Inquisition trials for heresy and witchcraft during the sixteenth and seventeenth centuries. These studies present evidence of an indigenous agrarian cult that relied upon rituals intended to promote or defend the fertility of the soil and the success of crops.

In the field of the arts, Friuli was noted for its own vigorous literary style throughout the fourteenth through eighteenth centuries, distinct from the more formal style employed elsewhere in Italy. This productivity suffered when, in the eighteenth century, Friulan lost status as a language and was treated as a form of rustic speech. In the nineteenth century, a renewed European interest in vernaculars brought back the work of Friulan poets and prose writers in a kind of renaissance. While Friulan has never achieved recognition as an official language in Italy, there have been writers, particularly poets, working in the language throughout this century. Other expressions of Friuli folk culture are to be found in local theater and folk dancing.

Bibliography

Ginzberg, Carlo (1980). *The Cheese and the Worms: The Cosmos of a Sixteenth-Century Miller.* Translated by John Tedeschi and Anne Tedeschi. Baltimore: Johns Hopkins University Press.

Ginzberg, Carlo (1983). *The Night Battles: Witchcraft and Agrarian Cults in the Sixteenth and Seventeenth Centuries.* Translated by John Tedeschi and Anne Tedeschi. London: Routledge & Kegan Paul.

Gregor, D. B. (1975). *Friulan Language and Literature.* New York: Oleander Press.

Holmes, Douglas R. (1989). *Cultural Disenchantments: Worker Peasantries in Northeast Italy.* Princeton: Princeton University Press.

NANCY E. GRATTON

Gaels (Irish)

ETHNONYMS: Celts, Gaedhils, Irish countrymen and countrywomen, Kelts

Orientation

Identification. The Gaelic language (Gaedhilge) is a primary cultural marker of Gaels living on the Atlantic fringe of Ireland, distinguishing them from the English-speaking Irish of Ulster and the Irish republic in general.

Location. Apart from Iceland, the Gaelic enclaves represent the westernmost culture of the Old World. They are found along the south and west coasts of the republic, and these pockets, called "Gaeltachts," have had a special protected status since 1956. They are located in seven discontinuous areas: western Donegal, western Mayo, western Galway, the Aran Islands, western Kerry, western Cork, and southwestern Waterford. Only in these areas is Gaelic still widely spoken, though English is learned in school and also used. They are completely rural areas, and their economic development is tightly regulated; indeed, the frequency of Atlantic gales and the poor soil make farm improvement especially difficult. The number of primarily Gaelic speakers has steadily declined since the great potato famine of 1845–1848, and since then the boundary of their habitat has correspondingly been retreating westward. Although a century ago they covered the western half of the island of Ireland, today Gaelic enclaves are found discontinuously between 51°40' and 55°20' N and 7°30' and 10°30' W.

Demography. In 1981 1,018,413 Gaelic speakers were claimed for the Republic of Ireland (including 72,774 in the Gaeltachts), perhaps 20,000 in Northern Ireland, and a few thousand more who had settled in England, Australia, or North America. The number of Gaelic speakers (1,018,413) —which is 31.6 percent of the total population of the republic—does not come close to expressing the reality, since most of the self-identified "Irish speakers" are English speakers who learned some Irish in school. The number of speakers has really been declining for some centuries. Thus for example in the entire island in 1851 there were 319,602 speakers of Gaelic only, plus 1,204,684 bilingual in Gaelic and English. By 1901 these figures had dropped to 20,953 monoglots and 620,189 bilinguals. This trend has continued until recent times. However, the decline in numbers of Gaelic speakers cannot be explained simply by general population decline in the country. The closely related phenomena of population decline, high rates of underemployment, overseas emigration, the rural incidence of anomie, and the creation of the "Congested Districts Board" in 1891 must be considered together, as they apply in particular to what later became categorized as the Gaeltachts. In these areas the government has since 1891 made modest attempts to improve living conditions in what were recognized to be the poorest, least arable, and least developed parts of the country; but despite the board's activities and the creation of Roinn na Gaeltachta in 1956 to promote welfare in the Gaeltachts, the introduction of better housing, cooperative dairies, and certain welfare facilities has done nothing to hold the population in these areas. Typically today they contain an "old" population of widows, widowers, and other elderly people who have never married. While there are, of course, some young people too, many have moved to the Dublin area on the other side of the country or gone overseas. With national unemployment throughout Ireland (and Ulster) at 18 percent in 1989—and higher in the Gaeltachts—no reversal of this demographic trend is in sight.

Linguistic Affiliation. Gaelic, Irish, or Erse is an ancient language of the Indo-European Family. It is not closely related to the neighboring English but instead is one of the languages forming the small subfamily of modern Celtic, a relic of the ancient Celtic that reached in pre-Roman times from Britain and Iberia as far as Asia Minor. The modern Celtic languages, in addition to Irish, are Scottish Gaelic (also called Erse), Welsh, Breton or Armoric, Cornish (extinct in 1777), and Manx (virtually extinct by 1990). Most of them have an ancient literature. Two other important languages that had disappeared by about the fifth century A.D. were Gaulish and British. All Celtic languages have certain non-Indo-European features, such as positioning of the verb at the beginning of the sentence, which are otherwise known to us from Berber and Ancient Egyptian. Gaelic currently has the status of "first official language" in the Republic of Ireland, and because of urban migration the largest pocket of Gaelic speakers today is in Dublin County.

History and Cultural Relations

The long history of Gaelic speakers in Ireland has been marked by the production of noble epic poetry but also by the depredations of Viking marauders and later by the suppression of the language by English soldiers and settlers in the country. Parallel with this military suppression of the Irish peasantry was the outlawing of the Gaelic tongue, which inevitably led to the "hedge schools" of the seventeenth and eighteenth centuries, so called because they had to meet in secret behind hedges. Irish literature and classical learning were both imparted in Gaelic. By the nineteenth century, village schools teaching in English were becoming widespread. The founding of the nationalistic Gaelic League in 1893 put the Gaelic language into a new light: from then on it was promoted (by urbanized, English-speaking Irish) as the language of what would one day become the Irish Free State (formed in 1922); and the literary revival of Gaelic that the league initiated has marked the twentieth century. But those in the Gaeltachts found little comfort in being patronized by city intellectuals, and otherwise they saw no real extension for the utility of Gaelic.

Settlements

Villages are small, usually with 100–200 inhabitants, and consist of dispersed farmsteads, each surrounded by a few acres of farmland (or "townland"). There are four important centers of interaction in a Gaelic village: the pub or pubs; the post office or store (if there is one); the space outside the church; and the crossroads, which was the traditional place for dancing, gossip, and interaction among the young people on a summer's evening. The main farmhouse is usually next to another building that houses cattle, horses, donkeys, and farm implements. This latter building may be a relatively new structure, or else the ancestral home of the family that they have recently relinquished to their animals. Prehistoric and medieval stone buildings (_clocháin_) have sometimes been preserved in this manner. The traditional Gaelic home is a long one-storied cottage divided into three rooms, its long axis roughly oriented east-west. The west room has a special position in Irish folklore, for it is where the aging parent or parents traditionally live out their last years amid family mementos before "going west." The middle room, the largest, is the general living and dining room, and also serves as the kitchen. It has two external doors, on the north and the south sides of the house. The small eastern room is a bedroom, but in the more northerly Gaeltachts it is common for the living room to have a protrusion or "outshot," which also can contain a bed. The cottages are sturdily built of cut stone, with wooden rafters supporting a thatched roof. The kitchen fire provides the only heat, and so peat (the usual fuel) is burning

there fairly constantly. An adjustable iron pot hanger (_croch_) hangs over it to support a pot or kettle; the smoke escapes up a chimney.

Economy

Subsistence and Commercial Activities. A mixed subsistence economy prevails throughout the Gaeltachts, with some farm surplus being produced for sale to neighbors or in local markets. Since these areas are near the coasts, ocean fishing used to be a prominent activity. Its importance has diminished considerably, partly because of the risks to older men that would come from going out in frail boats, but partly too because recent commercial trawling by both Irish and European Community boats has largely destroyed the breeding grounds on the sea bottom. The remaining boatmen today are more likely to put to sea to take a group of tourists for an outing. Other aspects of the traditional mixed economy are still observable, however. Cows and poultry are kept for domestic needs; goats or pigs are sometimes found. Horses and donkeys are used in all Gaeltachts to pull the carts and implements used in farmwork and dairying. Oats and potatoes are important crops, along with hay for winter feed, and some wheat, rye, and barley are also grown for bread. Timber is extremely scarce, requiring the reuse of old rafters and even the collection of driftwood. The common heating and cooking fuel is peat cut from the local bogs and dried for a month or more before being brought home. Cooking stoves using canned gas are now common. Sundry farm products are sold, privately or through cooperatives. There are also two major sources bringing money in from beyond the Gaeltacht: tourism, and numerous government subsidies. Since many villagers claim to be unemployed they can obtain unemployment benefits ("the dole"); others receive old-age pensions from age 66 on. There are small financial incentives given for speaking Gaelic in the home or for supporting an incapacitated family member. In addition to these sources, many families receive cash remissions from relatives overseas, especially in Massachusetts, Chicago, and New York. Of these various sources, the provision of meals and accommodation ("country teas" and "farm holidays") to tourists (high-school students, urban Irish, and English and Americans) are among the most remunerative today.

Industrial Arts. There are very few towns in the Gaeltachts and virtually no industrialization. Boats, carts, and houses used to be made by Gaelic villagers. Now few have the skills or the need, as cars slowly replace carts and contractors build modern houses for the people. In earlier times coastal villages had large fishing vessels, but by the present century most fishermen only had small four-man canoes (called _curragh_ in the north, _naomhóg_ farther south). There were no shipbuilding yards for these vessels, which were built by the boatmen themselves and are still repaired by them. Small seaports no doubt used once to have a thriving shipbuilding and repairing industry for larger vessels.

Trade. A large village may often serve as a shopping center for a Gaeltacht, and a small town always exists somewhere nearby, perhaps an hour's bus ride away. Here a handful of shops, nearly as many pubs, a government office or two, and perhaps a weekly market supply the basic needs of the rural community.

Division of Labor. With little perceptible class differentiations among the Gaelic peasantry, division of labor along lines of gender and age is normal. Men do the fishing, dairying, and farmwork, and they cut and cart the peat, until at 60 or 70 they become too old for all this and have to rely on their sons. Women do the housework and may also handle the dairying and the feeding of domestic animals. They are largely responsible for bringing up the children. The entire family has to go into the fields in July or August to turn the hay repeatedly and then stack it. Children are normally at school, but they are given chores to perform around the house or farm and may work hard during the summer vacation.

Land Tenure. About 6 percent of Ireland is allocated to the Gaeltachts, and they are home to about 10,000 small farmers. These areas, however, contain some of the worst farmland in the country. It has been estimated that about 80 percent of the Gaeltacht land is mountainside, bog, or marshland, good only for grazing sheep or digging out peat: the good arable land is in the central and eastern parts of the country. Land tenure is intimately linked with the arranging of marriages and with migration. In the present century marriages are still often arranged, but the small farmer can reasonably give his land to just one son: any other sons have to go elsewhere for work, emigrate overseas, or join the priesthood. But the one son who stays on the farm of his ancestors inherits everything at his marriage. Generally, a formal contract is drawn up by a solicitor in which the old farmer agrees to transfer ownership of land, home, and livestock to his son upon the latter's marriage. This contract then becomes a key part of the young man's marriage arrangements and also takes the place of a will. The money may be used to help support the old farmer and his wife in their retirement in the west room, or it may become the dowry with which one of their daughters is married off. All too often nowadays, though, no suitable girl willing to marry a young farmer is available, and so he goes through life remaining unmarried while he toils on the land and supports his aging parents. As long as the father does not legally hand the property over to his son, the latter will remain there in a web of obligations and delayed expectations.

Kinship

Kin Groups and Descent. In Gaelic culture, *clann* has a different meaning than the Scottish clan and the common anthropological term. The Irish clann traces descent through both males and females; thus, a clann is the entirety of all persons descended from the clann progenitor (regardless of whom those persons may have married). This means that an individual will belong to several clanns simultaneously: his or her father's one or more clanns, plus his or her mother's. The clann is not necessarily exogamous. There are other categories of kin that overlap with the clann. A person has a body of known relatives recognized as his or her kindred ("my people," *mo mhuintir*). A smaller kinship group is made up of those people considered relatives "by blood" (*gaolta*). Membership in these groupings corresponds to a very different system of naming than the Christian-name-plus-surname pattern of Anglo-Saxon lands. A person's descent is actually named, going back to one, two, or three patrilineal ancestors. There are also surnames, but the well-known *O'* of so many Irish names occurs less often in Gaelic: *O'* means "son of."

Women instead carry the term *Ní*, "daughter of." Neither of these terms is used in a surname except on very formal occasions.

Kinship Terminology. The Gaelic kinship system uses bifurcate-collateral terminology, which is very different from the English system so widespread in Ireland.

Marriage and Family

Marriage. A woman's marriage traditionally centered on finding a young man who stood to inherit a farm and then paying a dowry to his parents. Even today, arranged marriages along these lines still occur. It has also long been thought desirable, however, for a farmer's daughter to marry someone with a shop in a nearby town; in this way the woman can hope for a somewhat easier life than if she marries into another farm. At the same time her family can expect little favors from the shop that she helps to run, while her in-laws can expect some fresh farm produce whenever her relatives come to town. This tendency of girls to move to the towns in marriage—or even to migrate to Dublin, Liverpool, or London to work as chambermaids or in other service occupations—has contributed to the steady depopulation of the Gaeltachts during the past century. Since World War II, the tendency for both male and female youths to migrate has been enhanced by the ease of air travel and the knowledge that they can find well-paid jobs in Massachusetts or Chicago. Nowadays everyone seems to have at least one relative in the United States.

Domestic Unit. Six types of household can be found in the Gaeltachts: (1) single-person households; (2) joint-sibling households, with unmarried or widowed brothers or sisters living together; (3) widow/widower households, including married or unmarried children; (4) *nepotal households,* defined by Fox as "households consisting of an uncle/aunt with his/her married/unmarried nephew/niece"; (5) extended households, consisting of father and mother with their unmarried children, one married child with spouse, and perhaps grandchildren; (6) nuclear households, made up of parents with their dependent children. In each case the household is viewed as a family and is a labor unit.

Inheritance. A young man whose father owns land and livestock can hope to inherit these at the time of his marriage, rather than at his father's death. A marriage contract thus often replaces a will. If there are more sons, only one will have hopes of getting the small farm, since the land cannot usually be divided among several sons.

Socialization. All children get an informal education in daily activities by helping their parents around the home or on the farm. Gaeltacht children nowadays are usually educated at village schools provided by local government authorities. The average school-leaving age is 16, and after that boys tend to work on the farm, at least for a while. Girls are likely to emigrate sooner than their brothers. A few of these young people attend universities or theological colleges, in preparation for careers that will almost certainly keep them away from their home villages.

Sociopolitical Organization

Social Organization. Gaelic villages are usually acephalous entities with a tendency toward exogamy.

Political Organization. Ireland is a sovereign, independent, democratic republic. At the national level is an elected president (An Uachtarán), a partially elected senate (Seanad Éireann), and the Assembly (the Dáil Éireann) in Dublin, which has 166 representatives (*teachta dala*) elected by universal adult suffrage and proportional representation; in the Assembly the Gaeltachts are represented through their several parliamentary constituencies. Of the two major parties, Fianna Fail draws most support in the Gaeltachts because of its pro-Gaelic policies, and it forms the current government. At the local level are twenty-seven county councils in the republic, made up of elected members.

Social Control. The formal authorities in Irish villages are police constables (*gardai*). Gaeltacht villages do not have elected mayors, and the moral leader of a community is likely to be the parish priest. His threat of supernatural sanctions for wrongdoing is taken very seriously. Gossip and public opprobrium are also strong forces of social control. Not long ago, another powerful deterrent was the fear of what the fairies might do to one at night. Even now, one of the worst things one can ever say about a neighbor is to hint that he or she is in league with the Devil and thus is an agent of evil powers.

Conflict. Incidence of crime in the Gaeltachts is generally very low, rarely involving more than occasional petty theft or drunk and disorderly behavior. The people of the Gaeltachts are not directly involved with the current strife in Northern Ireland.

Religion and Expressive Culture

Religious Beliefs. The religion in the Gaeltachts is generally Roman Catholicism, and in most of them Protestant churches account for less than 5 percent of believers. Vestiges of ancient pre-Christian practice and belief are nonetheless still to be observed (for example, in some annual festivals).

With Roman Catholicism so widespread, the usual Christian beliefs in the Trinity are universal. But in Gaelic belief the Trinity that people acknowledge is less often the orthodox triad of Father, Son, and Holy Ghost than the distinctly Irish one of Jesus, Mary, and Joseph—with Mary being the dominant figure in the Holy Family. A lively cult of saints is also found everywhere, many of them distinctively Irish ones. Saint Patrick (Pádraig) was the semimythical bearer of Christian civilization to the pagan Irish. Rich legend surrounds all of the Irish saints and dozens of other Christian saints. Clearly many minor gods, goddesses, and other spirits of pagan times were incorporated into Christian faith during the Middle Ages, to such an extent that much of the idiosyncrasy of Irish Catholicism can be traced by a folklorist back to pagan custom and belief. Some of the ancient cults have been kept alive in innocent-looking folk customs and a huge corpus of epic poetry. On the borderline of Christian belief is the Devil ("Black Nick" or "Old Nick," as he is usually called), a powerful presence still active in the world. He takes the form of a black dog, a cat, or an anthropomorphic figure with tail and cloven feet. The Devil, like a more powerful form of the fairies, is potentially harmful, causing some disease, crop failure, or other disasters. He even possesses selected humans, thereby making them into his agents. People hope they have a guardian angel who will protect them from the advances of the Devil; otherwise they must rely on rosaries and Christian

prayer. People also commonly have a personal saint, chosen not so much on the basis of his or her history as on whether the saint is known to be a powerful intercessor with God. Other beings of the supernatural world are the fairies or elves, the cobbler (*leipreachán*), and the vindictive female ghost or banshee (*bean sídhe*, "the white woman"). In addition many people believe in ghosts, the wandering souls of the dead (*taidhbhsí*).

Religious Practitioners. Pagan practitioners of healing and witchcraft are no longer to be found, and the parish priest is now the ubiquitous spiritual shepherd of his flock. While a few of these men are from the Gaeltachts themselves, most of them are from other parts of Ireland: they were trained at Maynooth College and learned Gaelic for the ministry. Mass is now commonly said in Gaelic in the Gaeltacht communities.

Ceremonies. Christenings, weddings, and funerals are religious rites celebrated by the parish priest at his church. But beyond these life-cycle ceremonies are others marking the annual cycle, many of them grounded in pre-Christian antiquity. The Gaelic annual cycle includes: Saint Brighid's Day, 1 February; Shrove Tuesday (just before Lent); Chalk Sunday (the first Sunday of Lent); Lent; Saint Patrick's Day; Easter; May Day, 1 May; Midsummer, 23 June; Michaelmas, 29 September; Samhain (Halloween or All Souls' Day), 31 October–1 November; Christmas; Saint Stephen's Day, 26 December. As elsewhere throughout modern Europe, many of these calendrical observances are becoming past memories.

Arts. The traditional arts of the Gaeltacht are music, storytelling, and poetry, all still very much alive. The pride of many communities today is the local teller of folktales (*seanchaí*) or the singer of mythical epics (*scéalai*). Their skills are usually heard in the pubs, shebeens (*scíbíni*), and nighttime dance parties (*ceilidh*), essential scenes for community interaction. The tourist trade has brought forth several other arts, among them pottery and knitting, which might seem traditional to the culture but in fact are not.

Medicine. Ireland is divided into a large number of "Dispensary Districts," each with at least one doctor and some nurses on duty. Thus the government makes modern health care available in the Gaeltachts, as elsewhere, and for those of low income it is free. There are also some "herb doctors," unlicensed and untrained folk healers who practice their craft in Gaelic villages, making use of various herbs as well as talismans and charms. Theirs is of course a traditional lore in these areas, specific to the flora of the Atlantic fringe.

Death and Afterlife. Christian burial is universally practiced in hallowed ground in the Gaeltachts, but it is preceded by the distinctive Irish institution of a wake. The principal realms of the other world in Christian thought are heaven, purgatory, and hell. People see heaven as a calm and peaceful place where the dead are reunited with friends and relatives; thus, people look forward to this afterlife, and the thought of it makes present troubles easier to bear. Despite much skepticism about the existence of hell, many Gaels do see it as a place of fire and punishment that will engulf evildoers. Purgatory is often seen in the folk eschatology as a part of this world, not the afterlife.

See also Tory Islanders

Bibliography

Arensberg, Conrad M., and Solon T. Kimball (1968). *Family and Community in Ireland.* 2nd ed. Cambridge, Mass.: Harvard University Press.

Brody, Hugh (1973). *Inishkillane: Change and Decline in the West of Ireland.* London: Allen Lane, Penguin Press.

Cresswell, Robert (1969). *Une communauté rurale de l'Irlande.* Paris: Institut de l'Ethnologie, Musée de l'Homme.

Danaher, Kevin (1972). *The Year in Ireland.* Cork: Mercier Press.

Evans, E. Estyn (1957). *Irish Folk Ways.* London: Routledge & Kegan Paul.

Fox, Robin (1978). *The Tory Islanders: A People of the Celtic Fringe.* Cambridge: Cambridge University Press.

Freeman, T. W. (1960). *Ireland: A General and Regional Geography.* 2nd ed. London: Methuen & Co.

Gregory, Augusta (1970). *Visions and Beliefs in the West of Ireland Collected and Arranged by Lady Gregory: With Two Essays and Notes by W. B. Yeats.* London: Colin Smythe. [Several other editions.]

Mac Gobhan, Mici (1962). *The Hard Road to Klondike.* Translated by Valentin Iremonger. London: Routledge & Kegan Paul.

Messenger, John (1969). *Inis Beag, Isle of Ireland.* New York: Holt, Rinehart & Winston.

Ó Crohan, Tomás (1934). *The Islandman.* Translated by Robin Flower. New York: Charles Scribner's Sons. [Several later editions.]

O'Sullivan, Maurice (1933). *Twenty Years A-growing.* Translated by Moya Llewelyn Davies and George Thomson. New York: Viking Press. [Several later editions.]

Sayers, Peig (1973). *Peig: The Autobiography of Peig Sayers of the Great Blasket Island.* Translated by Bryan MacMahon. Dublin: Talbot Press. [Several later editions.]

Scheper-Hughes, Nancy (1979). *Saints, Scholars, and Schizophrenics—Mental Illness in Rural Ireland.* Berkeley: University of California Press.

PAUL HOCKINGS

Gagauz

ETHNONYMS: none

The Gagauz are a Greek Orthodox group believed to be descended from the Oghuz tribes. The Gagauz are today found mainly in Moldova, Ukraine, and Kazakhstan (173,000 in 1979); Bulgaria (12,000 estimated in 1982); Greece (perhaps as many as 30,000); and Romania.

See Gagauz in Volume 6.

Bibliography

Svanberg, Ingvar (1984). "The Turkish-Speaking Ethnic Groups in Europe." *Europa Ethnica* 5:65–73.

Galicians

ETHNONYMS: Galego, Gallego

Orientation

Identification.   The people of Galicia in Spain (*o pobo galego* in Galician) inhabit the northwestern corner of the Iberian Peninsula, directly north of Portugal. They speak Castilian Spanish and Galician, the latter a Romance language that is parent to modern Portuguese. They are predominantly Roman Catholic. The name "Galicia" is derived from the name for the people in the region when the Romans arrived in the second century B.C.E., the *gallatae*, but there is disagreement about the ethnic source of the people, with many celebrating a Celtic origin.

Location.   Galicia lies between 42° and 44° N and 7° and 9° W. The 29,434 square kilometers in the region take the form of a rough square bounded by the Bay of Biscay (Sea of Cantabria) to the north, the Atlantic Ocean to the west, the River Miño separating Galicia from Portugal to the south, and the mountain ranges of León and Asturias to the east. The coasts of Galicia are indented with drowned estuaries (*rías*). About 80 percent of the region lies above 300 meters, with the highest ranges (some with peaks over 1,800 meters) forming an effective eastern barrier between Galicia and the rest of Spain.

Galicia has a mild climate, averaging between 7.2° and 18.9° C through the year. Frequent rain, drizzle (*calabobos*), and heavy mists (*brétemas*) contribute to the 76 to 203 centimeters of rain that falls over an average of 150 days per year.

Galicia's isolation has led to the region's being one of the few in Europe where the original postglacial mammalian fauna remain virtually intact. Of the 500–600 wolves left in Iberia today, for example, most are in Galicia.

Demography.   In 1980 the population of Galicia was estimated at approximately 3 million inhabitants (about 424 per square kilometer), with a growth rate of less than 1 percent per year. The urban areas account for about 30 percent of the total population. Galicia is the sixth most populated of the fourteen regions of Spain, with about 7.5 percent of the country's inhabitants.

Linguistic Affiliation. Nearly every Galician uses Castilian Spanish, but about 80 percent of the population also speaks Galician (_galego_), which, along with Castilian, is taught in the grade schools and studied in the university. The use of Galician has rapidly expanded since the region became autonomous. Historically, Galician was one of the principal and mutually comprehensible Hispano-Romance dialects spoken in the northern third of the Iberian Peninsula. When the Christian reconquest of Spain began (by the tenth century), speakers of each of these dialects gradually moved south. The central Castilian-dominated swath gradually grew broader, cutting off the southward expansion of the dialects of Leonese, Navarro-Aragonese, and Catalan, with a substantial strip in the west populated by speakers of Galician. In the twelfth and thirteenth century, Portugal began to take shape and finally was separated from Galicia at the River Miño, leaving the two languages to develop independently.

History and Cultural Relations

The Iberians migrated to Spain in the third millennium B.C.E., probably from the eastern Mediterranean, likely encountering the Basques in the peninsula. They lived in small tribal groups, isolated from one another by geography, and each with a distinct regional and political identity. When the Celts crossed the Pyrenees into Spain (sixth century B.C.E.), their cultural influence, which included gender equality, ultimately triumphed. Augustus romanized the Iberians in 19 B.C.E., cutting up the peninsula into a series of provinces. Galicia as a kingdom was founded by the Germanic Suevi in 409 after the Visigoths drove them into the peninsula. The Visigoths defeated the Suevi in 585. Early in the eighth century armies from North Africa began their invasion of Spain, initiating the Moorish epoch, which lasted until 1492 when Ferdinand and Isabella triumphed over Boabdil at Granada. Early in this period, the shrine of Saint James was established at Santiago de Compostela (813), with Saint James subsequently becoming the symbolic commander and Spain's patron saint in the reconquest struggle after the battle of Clavijo (844). Pilgrims flocked to the shrine from throughout Europe, bringing the region into contact with the Christendom of France and Italy for the first time. In the fifteenth century Ferdinand and Isabella unified Spain, and Galicia began to be considered an underprivileged, conservative province, remote from the Castilian center to the south; even the fact that Francisco Franco was born in Galicia and returned for frequent visits did notably little to change this attitude. A strong sense of autonomy now pervades the region, however, and Galicia is developing considerable self-esteem through its language, industry, and rising tourist business.

Settlements

Outside the major cities, most of Galicia's population is spread in some 29,000 hamlets and tiny settlements called _aldeas_ with an average population of 80 people. The cultural focus of each village is the church, which draws upon perhaps a dozen family groups that work together and are often related. In the mountain villages, a small oval house with a thatched roof (_choza_ or _palloza gallega_) can still be seen occasionally. In the aldeas, the houses are generally single-family dwellings made up of slabs of gray granite hewn from Galician bedrock. The animals frequently live on the ground floor or in an adjoining enclosure. Almost all village houses have their own _hórreo_, a rodent-proof granary (built on stilts) for storing maize and potatoes. In the cities, the older buildings are constructed of granite, while the new multistoried apartment houses are typically constructed of poured concrete or bricks faced with stone or concrete.

Economy

Subsistence and Commercial Activities. Old shipbuilding, tanning, and sawmill industries have declined, leaving fishing and agricultural crops to dominate the Galician economy. The small farms (_minifundios_) produce maize, potatoes, turnips, cabbages, small green peppers, apples, pears, and grapes. Although tractors are common, plowing on some farms is still done with a single blade or pointed prod pulled by oxen; heavy wooden-wheeled carts (_carros chiriones_, "screeching carts") are still seen. Harvesting is frequently by hand. A textile industry has produced income in the region, as have petrochemical and automobile factories. Tungsten, tin, zinc, and antimony are mined. Tourism is also growing, with the beaches of the various estuaries on the Atlantic coast (the Rías Atlas and Rías Bajas) being particularly attractive.

Emigration is the traditional way of alleviating land pressure and keeping the region's problems within manageable proportions; these days, however, greater prosperity is causing fewer than an estimated 10,000 per year to leave for Latin America and Europe, compared with the 230,000 who emigrated to Latin America between 1911 and 1915. In Buenos Aires, so many Galicians have immigrated that all people who have immigrated from Spain in the last century are called _gallegos_. There are Galician communities in all the big towns of Spain, France, Germany, and Switzerland. The Galicians' capacity for hard work is matched only by their ability to save. The strategy is to save as quickly as possible for a rapid return to Galicia. Some of the savings brought back by migrants go into land, but much more is invested in houses and in food and drink businesses.

Trade. Small stores, café-bars, street vendors, and open-air markets are found throughout Galicia. Homegrown produce or other homemade products are brought (usually by women and not infrequently on their heads) to the markets to sell or to supply other merchants.

Division of Labor. In 1980, 46 percent of the region's labor force (1,175,400 persons) was engaged in agriculture, 16.3 percent in industry, 8 percent in construction, and 27.1 percent in services; 2.6 percent of the available labor force was unemployed.

In Galicia, more than 75 percent of the women work for pay, generally sharing the same jobs as the men. Both women and men work the farms, tend the animals, sell fish, run café-bars and markets, and serve as heads of households. The traditional home tasks are also assigned to women, but men will tend babies and do housework.

Land Tenure. Nearly everyone owns land in Galicia, but it is precious little; most plots are from 1 to 2.5 hectares. There are few examples of large landholding such as in the south. "Galicians never use handkerchiefs; they till them" is a frequent assertion, reflecting the scarcity and dimensions of the landholdings.

Kinship, Marriage, and Family

Kin Groups and Descent. Galician descent is generally patrilineal, with children taking their father's family name and appending their mother's. The wife, however, does not add her husband's name to her own, retaining her own name throughout her life. She may choose to use her husband's name after his death so that she is known as "[her name], widow of [husband's name]."

Kinship Terminology. The Galician kinship system is much like that found in the United States. Cousins are distinguished from brothers and sisters, but all cousins are placed in the same category. Aunts and uncles are distinguished from parents and labeled separately according to gender. No other relatives are referred to by the same terms used for members of the nuclear family.

Marriage and Family. Galician marriages are monogamous, and there is considerable freedom in the choice of marriage partners, although social pressures function to keep the economic classes fairly rigid. The nuclear family is usual. Only 10 percent of households could be termed extended or joint. As long as both elderly parents are alive, they tend to stay in their homes. After a spouse dies, the widower may move to the home of a married child, but widows who are accustomed to the daily tasks of running a household generally try to reside alone rather than rely on their children. Also, among adults in Galicia with older children, it is rare to find a couple without most of their children residing either permanently or temporarily away from the village.

Inheritance. The surviving spouse is the automatic heir to the deceased spouse's property, and all children regardless of gender, age, or place of residence divide the property of both parents equally. Because longevity is a feature of Galician society, late inheritance of property forces most children, even those with wealthy parents, to be on their own for long periods. Young women may remain at home to care for their aged parents in return for some advantage when the property is divided.

Sociopolitical Organization

After forty years under the dictatorship of Francisco Franco (1936–1975), Spain is now a parliamentary monarchy with a king as the head of state and a president as head of the government.

Political Organization. Galicia is an autonomous region of Spain and is governed by the Xunta de Galicia (the Galician Assembly). The region is divided into four provinces (La Coruña, Lugo, Orense, and Pontevedra), each with its own governing body. There are further administrative divisions for the municipalities and the hamlets. In 1992, Spain will be admitted to full partnership in the European Community (EC).

Religion and Expressive Culture

Religious Beliefs and Practices. Roman Catholicism is overwhelmingly the central religious force in Galician society, although men tend to be less obviously religious than women. Catholic churches, cathedrals, monasteries, and various types of shrines, including distinctive high stone crosses (cruceiros), dot the landscape. Mormons and Jehovah's Witnesses are actively proselytizing in the region, but they are gaining only a smattering of converts.

The beliefs of most Galicians are infused with a vigorous strain of supernaturalism. Ceremonies connected with these beliefs are frequently celebrated simultaneously with traditional Catholic ceremonies. Fig-symbol amulets, scapulars, and objects to ward off the evil eye, for example, are often sold close to the church where a religious rite is being celebrated. Various types of people are commonly believed to have supernatural powers: meigas (who provide love and curing potions), barajeras (who cast out evil and foretell the future), and brujas (who are believed to cause harm). A common saying is Eu non creo nas bruxas, ¡pero habel-as hainas!, or "I don't believe in brujas, but they exist!"

A considerable number of sites in Galicia have profound religious significance. For example, the Galicians, other Spaniards, and a vast number of Europeans consider Santiago de Compostela, in the La Coruña Province, to be one of the great spiritual centers of the world, ranking equally with Jerusalem and Rome. Early in the Christian reconquest, the bones of Saint James were believed to be uncovered in the area (in 813). Saint James (Santiago) subsequently was ensconced as the rallying figure in the ultimately successful wars against the Moors. A vast number of faith-promoting Saint James stories permeate the beliefs of Galicia, and the symbols of Saint James (cockle shells and the distinctive cross of Saint James) are ubiquitous.

Ceremonies. Saint's day celebrations, popular religious excursions (romerías), night festivals on the eve of a religious festival (verbenas), and the whole traditional calendar of Catholic observances provide rhythm to the lives of Galicians. A considerable number of nonreligious observances are threaded through the calendar of observances—for example, the "Disembarking of the Vikings" at Catoira, which vigorously reenacts the attack of a marauding Viking fleet in the tenth century.

Throughout Galicia a great number of varying charms, incantations, rites, and sympathetic actions are performed at each step in the life cycle.

Medicine. In case of illness, the usual Galician pattern is to consult a medical doctor first. If the illness does not subside, then the person doubts that the illness is medical and may consult a healer (curandero or curandera) who can cure with herbs or other nonmedical remedies.

Arts and Crafts. Galicia is famous for its folk dance groups, which are accompanied by the skirl of Galician bagpipes (gaitas). Various vocal and instrumental groups (some even cranking medieval hurdy-gurdies) sing and play popular Galician music. Thriving groups of artisans produce works in silver and gold, ceramics, fine porcelain, jet (azabache), lace, wood, and stone.

Galician literature today maintains characteristics developed during the Middle Ages; it is largely a literature of lyrical poetry. Notable Galician writers include Rosalía de Castro, who expressed the deep nostalgia (_morriña_) of nineteenth-century emigrants; Manuel Curros Enríquez, whose poems exalt the regionalist spirit of Galicia; and Valle-Inclán, noted for his elegant poetic prose.

Regional Foods. Galician restaurateurs command considerable respect in Spain. The estuaries produce shellfish of all kinds, from the famous cockleshells of Saint James to lobsters, mussels, shrimps, oysters, clams, and crabs. _Caldo gallego_ is a broth of turnips, cabbage or greens, and white beans. At most bars and at all sorts of outdoor celebrations, there are roast sardines, octopus, squid, little green peppers (the famous _pimientos de Padrón_), and _churros_ (doughnutlike tubes of fried pastry). Many of the cheeses are traditionally in the shape of breasts (called _tetillas_). A strong liquor called _aguardiente_ or _orujo_ is served burned (_queimada_) with lemon peel and sugar.

Bibliography

Buechler, Hans, and J.-M. Buechler (1981). _Carmen: The Autobiography of a Spanish Galician Woman._ Cambridge, Mass.: Schenkman.

Fraguas, Antonio (1988). _Romarías e Santuarios._ Vigo: Galaxia.

Lisón Tolosana, Carmelo (1971). _Antropología cultural de Galicia._ Madrid: Akal/Universitaria.

Mariño Ferro, Xosé Ramón (1985). _Cultura popular._ Santiago de Compostela: Museo do Pobo Galego.

EUGENE VALENTINE AND KRISTIN B. VALENTINE

Germans

ETHNONYMS: Alemanes (Spanish), Allemands (French), Deutschen (German)

Orientation

Identification. The Germans are a cultural group united by a common language and a common political heritage. In the past, the term "German" could rightly be applied to many of those now regarded as Dutch, Swiss, or Austrian. These peoples developed separate identities as their lands split politically from a broader German area. Other regional identities—for example, Bavarian, Prussian, Saxon, and Swabian—were largely subordinated to a common German identity in the course of a nationalist movement that began during the Napoleonic Wars and led to the founding of the German Reich in 1871. Today's Germans include especially the citizens of the newly reunited Federal Republic of Germany, though enclaves of ethnic Germans persist in parts of eastern Europe, Ukraine, and Russia.

Location. Germany fits roughly between 47° and 55° N and 6° and 15° E. Prior to World War II, however, Germany included other surrounding territories and extended eastward into what is now Poland and the western regions of the former Soviet Union. The German terrain rises from the northern coastal plain to the Bavarian Alps in the south. The Rhine, Weser, Elbe, and Oder rivers run toward the north or northwest, emptying into the North and Baltic seas and draining northern, central, and southwestern Germany. The Danube has its source in the Black Forest and then runs eastward, draining southern Germany and emptying eventually into the Black Sea. Germany has a temperate seasonal climate with moderate to heavy rainfall.

Demography. Following normal modern European patterns, Germany's population rose from about 25 million in 1815 to 67 million in 1914, despite the loss of more than 3 million emigrants. The population continued to rise in the first half of this century, though this trend was hindered by heavy losses in the two world wars. When World War II ended, approximately 7 million ethnic Germans left Eastern Europe and resettled in Germany. An additional 3 million East Germans fled to West Germany before the construction of the Berlin Wall in 1961. The current population of Germany is estimated to be about 78,000,000, with 61,500,000 residing in the western Länder, or federal states, and 16,500,000 in the new states of former East Germany. In 1986 West Germany's growth rate was slightly negative and East Germany's nearly zero. The population is, however, augmented by more than 4.5 million foreign workers and a new wave of immigrants from eastern Europe. Since antiquity, Germany's largest settlements have been located along the river valleys and the northern coast. Today, three-quarters of the population occupies urban settlements in these areas. Nevertheless, less than half of about 100 independently administered cities in Germany have a population of more than 200,000, and only three cities—Berlin, Hamburg, and Munich—have more than a million inhabitants.

Linguistic Affiliation. German belongs to the Germanic Branch of the Indo-European Family of languages. The major German dialect groups are High and Low German, the languages of the southern highlands and the northern lowlands, respectively. Low German dialects, in many ways similar to Dutch, were spoken around the mouth of the Rhine and on the northern coast but are now less widespread. High German dialects may be divided into Middle and Upper categories, which, again, correspond to geographic regions. The modern standard is descended largely from East Middle High German and was shaped in part by the Lutheran Bible and by the language of officialdom in the emerging bureaucracies of the early modern period. The standard was firmly established with political unification in the late nineteenth century, and twentieth-century migrations have further contributed to dialect leveling. Nevertheless, local and regional dialects have survived and in some places have reasserted themselves.

History and Cultural Relations

German-speaking peoples first entered the historical record when tribal groups migrating southward reached the Roman frontiers along the Rhine and the Danube. Some crossed over and merged with southern or western European populations; others stayed behind to farm or to build on the outposts abandoned by Rome. In the Middle Ages, the area now known as Germany presented a variegated sociogeographic landscape, characterized by both peasant agriculture and riverine and coastal commerce. Rival royal and noble houses sought to establish administrative bases through expanding their domains, controlling clerical appointments, or, by the thirteenth century, colonizing the eastern marches. As the struggles among emperors, popes, and nobles continued, many cities enjoyed political autonomy and prosperity. Urban manufacture and commerce suffered during the religious wars, when the German princes tried to co-opt the church administration and consolidate their territories. Conflicts beginning with the Protestant Reformation culminated in the Thirty Years' War, which devastated central Europe economically and fragmented it politically. By 1648 Germany was divided into more than 300 small principalities. France's revolutionary army struck the first blow for centralization by bringing western Germany under direct French rule and organizing the rest of Germany into a handful of tributary states. On the eve of Napoleon's defeat, Germany spawned a nationalist movement that in many ways anticipated similar movements in eastern Europe and the third world. Because of its famous army and the industrial strength of its newly acquired Rhine Province, Prussia prevailed over Austria in the struggle for intra-German hegemony. Germany was united in 1871 under a partially liberalized but still largely autocratic Prussian regime. Germany's bid for global hegemony failed in World War I and again under Hitler in World War II. In 1949 the zones occupied by the French, British, and Americans combined to form the Federal Republic of Germany (West Germany), and later that same year the Soviet zone became the German Democratic Republic (East Germany). The two German states persisted as Western and Soviet client states until 1989, when reform in the Soviet Union contributed to the fall of the East German regime. The new German currency union was formed on 1 July 1990, and political unification followed on 3 October.

Economy

Industry and Trade.   The tradition of urban handicrafts and riverine commerce, large and readily available coal deposits, and economic and political union all contributed to the dramatically successful industrialization of the Rhine-Ruhr region and the Elbe River valley in the latter half of the nineteenth century. Following World War II, West Germany again emerged as one of the strongest economies of the West European industrial core. East Germany's socialist economy was successful by Eastern bloc standards, but it crumbled when it was incorporated into the West German market. In the last decade of the twentieth century, the new federal states of the east face wholesale rebuilding. Germans describe their economy as a "social market," where the welfare state ameliorates the extreme effects of competitive private enterprise. Automobiles, aircraft, chemicals, machine tools, and optical and electronic equipment are among the most important products of Germany's export-oriented economy. German industry is distinguished by long-range planning; cooperation between private enterprise, government, banks, and unions; and a highly skilled work force. In the postwar period, West Germany has traded primarily with European Community partners and NATO allies, but the reunited Germany is renewing traditional trade relationships with eastern Europe and the peoples of the former Soviet Union.

Agriculture and Land Tenure.   In Germany, the reform of feudal land tenure was not completed until the late nineteenth century. East of the Elbe, where Prussian nobles had managed large estates, reform resulted in the creation of a landless rural proletariat. Peasants of the highly subdivided southwest were often forced to migrate either to the cities or overseas, though some became owners of small farms. The free northern peasantry was most successful in making the transition from feudal obligations to private ownership, though here too expropriation and consolidation were common. The Nazis espoused an agrarian ideology, but the trend toward industrialization and rural depopulation continued. The southwestern and northern zones now lie in former West Germany, where 5 percent of the work force is employed on privately owned farms averaging just 16 hectares. Under the now defunct East German regime, the Prussian estates were transformed into large-scale, state-run agricultural enterprises, which employed 11 percent of the work force. In both regions, further reduction in agricultural production may be anticipated, since the state subsidies that sustained it have been withdrawn or are under attack.

Division of Labor.   Germany's work force includes laborers, entrepreneurs, clerical workers and other employees, managers and administrators, and professionals. Class membership is determined partly through education and individual ability and partly through family background. German labor is represented by well-organized and aggressive unions, which, however, often cooperate with capital and the state in long-range economic planning. German women are accorded equality in the workplace de jure, though equal pay, child care, maternity benefits, and abortion are still subjects of debate and shifting legislation.

Kinship, Marriage, and Family

Kinship.   The Germans trace descent bilaterally and employ an Eskimo kinship terminology. Many of the standard kin terms are recognizable as English cognates, though there is some variation by dialect.

Marriage and Domestic Unit.   Today's marriages are individualistic "love matches" but similarities in class, ethnicity, and religious affiliation are often considerations in these matches. The household is based on the nuclear family, which joins occasionally with members of a wider kindred in the course of the annual festive cycle. Divorce is a legally codified dissolution of marriage; Germans resort to divorce in about three out of ten cases. Since recent legislation protects the rights of unwed mothers and their offspring, many Germans are forgoing or postponing marriage: in 1987 an estimated 40 percent of West German couples under 35 were unwed.

Inheritance.   Rights to private property and legal inheritance, guaranteed by the Basic Law of the Federal Republic of Germany, are typically exercised within the nuclear family or the wider kindred. Now that East Germany is subject to West German law, the courts will be busy resolving the conflicting claims to property resulting from a half-century of expropriation under the Nazi and Socialist party regimes.

Socialization. Germany's school system differs from state to state, but in most cases students are split between vocational and university preparatory tracks. The vocational track includes nine years of school and further part-time vocational training, with a paid apprenticeship. The university preparatory track requires attendance at the humanistic *Gymnasium* and successful completion of the *Abitur,* a university entrance examination. Germany has a highly differentiated system of higher education, including sixty-two universities and technical colleges in former West Germany and fifty-four in former East Germany.

Sociopolitical Organization

Social Organization. Modern German voluntary associations, or *Vereine,* first appeared among the bourgeoisie during the Enlightenment but spread throughout the population as laws governing free assembly in the various German states were liberalized in the course of the nineteenth century. Prior to 1848, voluntary associations were typically both nationalist and republican in orientation. After the founding of the Reich, they split into politically opposed bourgeois, Catholic, and working-class blocs. Under the Third Reich, Germany's dense network of voluntary associations was co-opted by the Nazi party. East Germany's Socialist Unity party pursued a similar strategy but, again, with less success. The Basic Law of the Federal Republic of Germany guarantees German citizens the right to free assembly, and voluntary associations are correspondingly numerous. Today, club life helps shape the local festive calendar and is an important constituent of local identities and status relations. Many local associations belong to umbrella organizations and thus help integrate members into social networks beyond the community.

Political Organization. The Federal Republic of Germany has succeeded in realizing many of the liberal reforms first proposed at the Frankfurt Parliament of 1848 and first attempted during the Weimar Republic (1919–1933). Germany is now a parliamentary democracy, where public authority is divided among federal, state, and local governments. In federal elections held every four years, all citizens who are 18 or older are entitled to cast votes for candidates and parties, which form the *Bundestag,* or parliament, on the basis of vote distribution. The majority party or coalition then elects the head of the government. Similarly, states and local communities elect parliaments or councils and executives to govern in their constitutionally guaranteed spheres. Each state government also appoints three to five representatives to serve on the *Bundesrat,* or federal council, an upper house that must approve all legislation affecting the states. Germany's most important political parties are: the Christian Democratic Union and its corresponding Bavarian party, the Christian Social Union; the Social Democratic party; the Free Democratic party; the Greens; and the Party of Democratic Socialism, the successor to the East German Socialist Unity party. In the latter 1980s, the right-wing Republican party gained some seats in local and regional councils, but after the fall of the East German regime their constituency dwindled. The first free all-German national election since 1932 was held on 2 December 1990 and resulted in the confirmation of the ruling Christian Democratic/Free Democratic coalition.

Germany's free press produces hundreds of daily newspapers with a total circulation of 25 to 30 million. Post, telephone, and telegraph facilities are federally owned and managed. Radio and television stations are "corporations under public law," which are run by autonomous bodies and monitored by political parties in proportion to their representation in state and federal parliaments. These measures are intended to prevent the media from being manipulated for propaganda purposes, as they were by the Nazis and, with somewhat less success, by the former East German government. As of 1973, East Germans had legal access to West German television broadcasts, which contributed in no small measure to undermining the legitimacy of the Socialist regime.

Social Control. It has often been noted that German society still retains a small-town ethos, which arose in the early modern period under conditions of political and economic particularism. Indeed, many Germans adhere to standards of *Bürgerlichkeit,* or civic morality, that lend a certain neatness and formality to behavior in everyday life. Public standards are further enforced by a strong emphasis on the rule of law. This is, perhaps, in part a legacy of Germany's bureaucratic tradition and in part a response to the criminal activities of the Hitler regime. Today, Germany is regulated by a larger body of legislation than exists in either Britain or France.

Religion and Expressive Culture

Religious Beliefs and Practices. The Germans have been predominantly Christian since the early Middle Ages. A large German-Jewish minority was driven out or destroyed by the Nazi regime between 1933 and 1945; it is represented today by a returning community of perhaps 100,000. Approximately 56 percent of all Germans are Protestant and 37 percent Roman Catholic. Protestant populations are concentrated in the northern, central, and eastern regions, and Catholics predominate in the south and in the Rhineland. Since the eighteenth century many Germans have opted for secular alternatives to religion, including rationalism, romanticism, nationalism, socialism, and, most recently, consumerism or environmentalism.

Ceremonies. Germany's festive calendar includes a cycle of Christian holidays, which are observed especially but not exclusively by Catholics. In October, many towns celebrate harvest festivals that combine regional traditions with modern tourist attractions. Carnival, or *Fastnacht,* is celebrated throughout Germany but especially in the Rhineland and the south. The carnival season begins on 11 November and ends on Mardi Gras with parades and "fools' assemblies" organized by local voluntary associations.

Arts. Germans have made major contributions to all of the typically Western fine arts, especially music. The folk traditions of Germany's various provinces declined with industrialization and urbanization, but some are still maintained as expressions of local patriotism or in connection with the promotion of tourism. A distinctively German cinema had its origins in the Weimar Republic and was revived in West Germany after the war. Postwar themes in German literature and cinema include especially the Nazi past, the Westernized or Socialist present, and resulting problems of German identity.

Medicine. Germans were among the leaders in the development of both Western biomedicine and national health insurance. Biomedical health care in Germany is extensive and high-quality. Alongside biomedicine there is a strong German tradition of naturopathic medicine, including especially water cures at spas of various kinds. Water cures have been opposed by some members of the West German biomedical establishment but are regularly subsidized by statutory West German health insurance agencies.

See also Austrians; German Swiss; Silesians

Bibliography

Applegate, Celia (1990). *A Nation of Provincials: The German Idea of Heimat.* Berkeley: University of California Press.

Ardagh, John (1987). *Germany and the Germans: An Anatomy of Society Today.* New York: Harper & Row.

Craig, Gordon (1982). *The Germans.* New York: Meridian.

Lowie, Robert H. (1954). *Toward Understanding Germany.* Chicago: University of Chicago Press.

Peukert, Detlev (1987). *Inside Nazi Germany: Conformity, Opposition, and Racism in Everyday Life.* London: B. T. Batsford.

Spindler, George (1973). *Burgbach: Urbanization and Identity in a German Village.* New York: Holt, Rinehart & Winston.

Walker, Mack (1971). *German Home Towns.* Ithaca, N.Y.: Cornell University Press.

JOHN R. EIDSON

German Swiss

ETHNONYMS: Deutschen Schweiz, Schweiz, Swiss, Tütsch Schweiz

Orientation

Identification. The German Swiss are the linguistic majority in nineteen of Switzerland's twenty-six cantons and half-cantons. They call their country "Schweiz," which comes from the canton of Schwyz. They are generally either Roman Catholic or Protestant.

Location. Switzerland is located between 46° and 48° N and 6° and 10.5° E. It is a small country of 41,295 square kilometers. The German Swiss occupy central, north, east, and a third of the south of Switzerland's land area. The west is French-speaking, while the southeast is either Italian- or Romansh-speaking. The geography of Switzerland is divided into three areas: the Alps, the Mitteland, and the Jura. The Alps are the mountainous spine of Europe forming the southern portion of Switzerland, while the Mitteland is a plateau between them and the Jura Mountains, which form the

northern frontier along with the Rhine River. The German Swiss live principally in the Alps and the plateau.

Demography. The population of Switzerland in 1982 was 6.5 million with 5.5 million of that figure being Swiss. German Swiss comprise 65 percent of the total population, and they represent 73.5 percent of the native Swiss. The population density is 153 persons per square kilometer, ranging from 9,868 persons per square kilometer in Geneva to 1.3 persons per square kilometer in Fieschental, in the canton of Valais. The population is growing at a rate of 40,000 persons per year or less than 1 percent per year. The three largest cities in Switzerland—Zurich (369,000), Basel (182,000), and Bern (149,000)—are in German Swiss cantons. Switzerland as a whole has become an industrialized urban nation with a large net internal migration from the mountain areas to the plateau (with 26 percent of the country's total population migrating in 1850, decreasing to 15 percent by 1950, but still comprising a significant amount). This is particularly true for German Switzerland. The urban population has shifted toward German Swiss cities, with Geneva and Lausanne both being larger than Zurich in 1850 and rating fourth and fifth in overall population size today.

Since 1976, German Switzerland has had a decreasing population. The reasons include reduced marriage rate, lower number of births, increase in childless marriages, unwed cohabitation, and postponement of births. The largest demographic problem in German Switzerland is considered to be the alien or foreign-worker problem (*Auslander Probleme*). Over 1 million non-Swiss work in the Swiss economy. This wave of immigrants is a post–World War II phenomenon. Most were, or are, unskilled workers who do the menial labor the Swiss refuse to do.

Linguistic Affiliation. Swiss German (Schweizerdeutsch, Schwyzertütsch, or Schwyzerdütsch) represents a wide range of local and regional dialects that are derived from the Old Allemmanic, a West Germanic language. Most are classified as High Allemmanic, with exceptions such as Basel (Low Allemmanic) or Samnuan (Tirolean). The number of dialects has been estimated to be in the hundreds, but they are generally mutually intelligible, with rare exceptions—such as dialects spoken in the most remote valleys. High German, *Hoch-Sprache* or *Schriftdeutsch*, is taught in schools and used as the written language. Strangers are addressed in High German, and for the German Swiss it constitutes their true second language.

History and Cultural Relations

The German Swiss trace their ancestry to a Celtic tribe called the Helvetti, who were defeated by Rome in 58 B.C. This is suggested by the Latin name for the Swiss Confederation, "Confoederatio Helvetica." Romanized for centuries, the fall of the western Roman Empire in the fifth century A.D. brought Germanic tribes (Allemani and Burgundians) into Switzerland. These tribes were, in turn, conquered by the Franks, with the area of Switzerland becoming part of Charlemagne's eighth-century Holy Roman Empire. Under the vestiges of this polity during the Middle Ages, the Swiss lived under various duchies until 1291, the founding date of the first Swiss Confederation. Formed by the three German Swiss "forest cantons" of Uri, Schwyz, and Unterwalden, the nucleus of modern Switzerland was born as a defense league against the

Hapsburg emperors. From this time until 1515, Swiss militarism enlarged the Swiss Confederation and fostered an export of mercenary soldiers primarily from the poor, mountain cantons. At the Battle of Marignano, Francis I of France forever punctured the bubble of Swiss invincibility with a crushing defeat wherein Swiss fought Swiss. During this period, Bern was ascendant, being the largest and most dominant of the thirteen cantons. During the Reformation, Geneva replaced Bern in international importance, being the home to Calvin and Voltaire. Napoleon occupied Switzerland in 1798, dissolving the old Swiss Confederation to form the Helvetian Republic with six more cantons. In 1815, the Congress of Vienna added Geneva, Valais, and Neuchâtel to a reconstituted neutral Switzerland. Only Jura (established in 1979) is of twentieth-century origin, being formed out of the German Swiss canton of Bern. Switzerland remains politically neutral today and is the home of the International Red Cross. German Swiss Bern is the capital of the modern Swiss Confederation.

Settlements

German Switzerland is a modern economic landscape of cities, towns, and villages. Urbanism is a feature of the plateau, while the mountains remain the domain of villages. Towns are found throughout the German Swiss area, being concentrated along the larger valley floors and plateau. The pre–World War II agricultural villages of the mountain areas are generally a thing of the past. Many villages of this type have shifted to tourism as their principal economic endeavor. Villages have post offices, *Gasthofs* (guest houses), churches, and houses with barns. Chalets and field buildings are found outside the alpine villages. Villages and towns are located on avalanche-free slopes. Tree lines and barriers are maintained to prevent avalanches. In the major valleys, villages and towns are along principal automobile routes or rail lines. Less and less construction of houses is of wood. Modern homes are brick or block, even in the most remote areas. The older homes in the mountain and foreland areas are wooden with shingled or tiled roofs. These houses have carved gables, other ornamentations and inscriptions. Regional styles differentiated the carved Bernese farmhouse from the rock-roofed, inscribed Valais home. With the advent of stone or masonry construction, these embellishments have all but disappeared on modern homes. The exceptions are chalets built by urban dwellers as vacation homes, which imitate the older rustic forms. Towns and cities are characterized by a center with older buildings. The newer homes, apartments, malls, and industrial buildings lie on the periphery. The train station or *Bahnhof* is still a central focus in the larger towns and cities.

Economy

Subsistence and Commercial Activities. The mountainous landscape of much of German Switzerland makes over a quarter of its land area unproductive for agriculture. Even before the addition of more modern agricultural aids, there was rarely little more than subsistence farming in the mountain areas. The agro-pastoralism of pre–twentieth century Switzerland gave rise to much that is considered "Swiss"—community, cooperative labor, frugality, provincialism—peasant values born out of a unique adaptation to a harsh environment. The shift away from agriculture is reflected in a comparison of 1860 and 1980 agricultural population percentages: 43.6 versus 6.2, for the German Swiss cantons. Nonetheless, Switzerland as a whole produces more than half its food. This output comes principally from the plateau, while the Rhone Valley is a major fruit and vineyard area. Stock farming is the most important part of agriculture, which results in two-fifths of the arable land being devoted to pasture, alpine or otherwise. As a result of this emphasis, milk and its by-products—especially cheeses—form the major agricultural export. Swiss wines are rarely exported and there are heavy subsidies for this and other agricultural products provided by the government.

Industrial products are four-fifths of the commercial output of Switzerland. The bulk of this is centered in German Switzerland at Zurich, Winterthur, Basel, and Oerlikon. The major products are chemicals and pharmaceuticals (Basel), with engineering, armaments, and optical products manufactured at the other centers.

Banking and insurance are major industries with principal centers in the German Swiss areas. Swiss industry is depauperate in raw materials and energy, with the exception of electricity. As a result, Swiss industry competes in foreign markets on the basis of quality rather than price. Because of its reliance on world markets, Swiss industry emphasizes English as the language of world commerce. As a rule, most German Swiss engaged in commerce are bilingual in English rather than any of the national languages.

Division of Labor. German Switzerland emphasizes a traditional division of labor by sex. As in all Western countries, this division has been modified with women playing roles in all elements of Swiss society. Increasingly, women work outside the home, particularly in the urbanized cantons of the plateau. In the more conservative mountain cantons, the traditional roles were more varied as cooperative labor was necessitated by subsistence agricultural practices. Today, with men of these cantons involved in trade, the woman's roles have centered on the home or jobs in tourist-related fields, such as hostelry. Women work as nurses, teachers, and shopkeepers in rural areas and are part of industry, notably watchmaking and electronics in the urban zones. Young German Swiss are encouraged to follow the pattern of a *Welschlandjahr*, a period of apprenticeship or domestic service outside German Switzerland. Both sexes participate in this practice.

Land Tenure. Land is a limited commodity in German Switzerland as it is in the whole country. Dense population in the plateau and continued emigration from the mountain areas has increased property values throughout. Maintenance of property rights through inheritance predominates. In the rural areas, land has passed to developments or otherwise is not used for agriculture. "Alp rights," or access to pastures, are sold to urban dwellers to build chalets or homes for vacations. Decentralization of industry has produced industrial plants in smaller towns throughout the plateau and even the alpine foreland. Housing access, particularly in urban areas like Zurich, has led to unrest among younger German Swiss. While not necessarily a "landless" stratum, they represent a result of changes in land tenure and usage in modern German Switzerland. Property can be owned by non-Swiss, but it is controlled both by federal and cantonal regulations to limit foreign penetration.

Kinship

Kin Groups and Descent.   Descent is bilateral with a very slight emphasis upon the male side. Men never use the wife's maiden name, but women may include it in a hyphenated form after marriage. No attempt is made to distinguish patrilateral or matrilateral kin. A distinction is made between female and male first cousins. No distinction exists for more distant cousins, although distant relatives are considered to be of the *Stamm* or kin group. Fictive kin, such as godparents, have a specific role in religious ceremonies in Catholic areas. Affinal kin terms are noted in normal speech. Neither fictive nor affinal designations connote any special reinforcement of obligations within kin groups today.

Marriage and Family

Marriage.   Marriages are monogamous. Prohibitions on first-cousin marriage exist in Catholic cantons of German Switzerland. Neolocal residence is favored today, but newly married couples often reside with either the man's or woman's family. This practice reflects less on the role of kin ties than on the availability of housing or land. Under Swiss law, married women have some of their premarital privileges proscribed or limited. A married woman needs her husband's permission to seek employment, to run for political office, or to open a bank account. Marriage ages have fallen to younger levels in rural and urban settings. Marriage in the mid-twenties for both sexes is common. In rural areas, there is a high level of endogamy to, for example, a specific valley. This practice is less prevalent today with out-migration to cities becoming more common. German Swiss tend to be endogamous to their language group as a whole. In 1960, a total of 51,800 German-French households were recorded. Divorce is more common in non-Catholic areas.

Domestic Unit.   The nuclear family is the minimal family unit. In Catholic cantons, it can number between six and seven persons with fewer members in the urban, non-Catholic cantons. Family size has dropped since 1970 with the falling birthrate, and three or more children are increasingly rare. Men no longer exert the same control over their children as in pre-industrial days, although they are recognized as the family head.

Inheritance.   Inheritance is both partible (equal divisions among children) and impartible. In rural areas, Swiss law requires agricultural operations to be inherited intact, if one of the male heirs who is capable of managing it makes the request. If an heir dies childless, the estate is divided among siblings and does not go to the surviving spouse. Landholdings within rural valleys do promote a certain level of endogamy as the joint inheritance of the partners provides for a certain security. Again, this is less important with the decreased importance of agriculture for subsistence.

Socialization.   Infants are reared by both parents and any relatives who are household members. Children live at home during schooling, until trade school or college age. The interest in children is strong at the commune level. Each canton is responsible for its educational program and, until recently, has seen considerable diversity in educational philosophy. For instance, the obligatory schooling is nine years, seven primary and two secondary. The Federal Maturity Certificate awarded after completion of upper-level secondary schooling

at age 19 or 20 is recognized as qualification for entry into other sectors of higher education. Schooling acts as a primary agent in socialization and reflects the accepted standards of the community and nation as a whole. All Swiss males between the ages of 20 and 50—German or otherwise—are required to serve in the military. The importance of the military service in Swiss socialization is more appreciated today after its integrative role during two world wars, which produced great tensions between German Swiss and non-German Swiss. Many scholars credit the military with modeling the ethos of modern Switzerland. Still, socialization begins with family and continues through community (schooling, religion, service). Religion's socializing role is more important in Catholic areas of German Switzerland.

Sociopolitical Organization

Switzerland is a federal, constitutional democracy termed the Swiss Confederation (*Schweizerische Eidgenossenschaft*). Its head is a president chosen for one year from the Federal Council (Bundesrat) of seven members who serve four-year terms. These are elected by the 200-seat Federal Assembly (*Bundesversammlung*) composed of representatives of the twenty-six cantons and half-cantons.

Social Organization.   The German Swiss, by virtue of sheer numbers, have more influence than the non-German Swiss within the Swiss Confederation. All Swiss citizens, German or otherwise, consider themselves equal. No social classes exist within German Swiss society. Status is achieved rather than ascribed. If there is a tiering of German Swiss society, it is not recognized as such, although the farmer or peasant is unofficially recognized as the lower rung of the economic ladder. By extension, then, the industrialist, being more economically successful, holds a higher position. Few Swiss, German or otherwise, would publicly validate this hierarchy. The foreign worker or Auslander is the true lower class—isolated and often shunned.

Stereotypes exist, with the German Swiss temperament characterized as orderly, practical, little given to abstractions, capable of intense commitment to work, scrupulously honest, blunt and plain-spoken, solid, unswerving, and implacable in the application of rules. Among the German Swiss, the most extreme form of this stereotype is applied to the residents of the alpine cantons. These hillfolk turn the negative aspects of the stereotype into virtues by emphasizing hard work, communal spirit, and religious conviction over what they perceive to be the lesser virtues of the city dwellers. Social mobility is based mainly on education and acquired wealth.

Political Organization.   The smallest and most important administrative structure is the commune or *Gemeinde*. There are more than 3,000 of these independent bodies that raise taxes and maintain municipal councils. The German Swiss's first loyalty is to the Gemeinde. The next highest order is the canton, and then the Swiss Confederation. Under the 1874 constitution, no Swiss can be denied residence anywhere within the confederation unless he becomes an "undesirable" because of criminal activity. German Swiss have voting rights in the canton of residence. Bern is the federal capital of the Swiss government. The structure of Swiss federalism is predicated on initiative and referendum. To call a referendum, 30,000 signatures are required. For an initiative (proposed legislation), 100,000 signatures are needed. Any Swiss, age

20 or older, can initiate the process. Female suffrage came last to German Switzerland, with Appenzell being the last canton to grant it, although women were given the right to vote in federal elections in 1971.

Social Control. A shared value system exerts the greatest social control in German Switzerland. This value system has been erected on foundations of the values of the past. Order and continuity are prized in social life. Still, control is not overt but discrete. Peer presence as much as overt pressure operates throughout German Swiss society. The German Swiss is rarely outside the community of his or her peers because of the small size of the country itself. Self-control is taught early by the family and reinforced throughout all stages of the German Swiss's life.

Religion and Expressive Culture

Religious Beliefs. German Switzerland is equally divided between Protestant (44.4 percent, 1980) and Catholic (47.6 percent, 1980). Religious divisions within the German Swiss reflect those of the confederation as a whole. These divisions have been a major source of internal tensions since the Reformation. The canton of Bern is over 75 percent Protestant, while the alpine zone is Catholic. Religion plays a structural role in countering the linguistic pluralism within German Switzerland itself and the confederation. Greater tensions exist between German Swiss Protestants and Catholics than between the German Swiss and French Swiss. Political affiliations crosscut these dimensions and tend to offset religious differences today. Alpine areas of German Switzerland have customs that relate to supernatural beliefs outside the traditional religions. In the mountains, natural forces are viewed as generally malevolent or, at best, neutral. These forces manifest themselves in avalanches, landslides, mists, or storms. The *Föhn*, a warm, gusty wind blowing from the Alps and creating sudden temperature reversals, has been associated with madness. These beliefs are fading in the Alps today.

Ceremonies. Each canton and commune has ceremonies unique to it. To the non-Swiss visitor, German Switzerland must appear, at times, to be on some continual form of vacation. There are festivals to herald the coming spring, harvest festivals, major and minor religious days, founder's days, and the Swiss National Day, 1 August. The most famous carnival is the Baseler Fastnacht, a 48-hour festival with grotesque masks and garb and parades.

Arts. German Switzerland was particularly rich in folk arts. Today there is a renewed interest in this heritage. Many of the skills in native woodcrafts have disappeared, as the winterbound peasant farmer is essentially a thing of the past. Tourism and nostalgia have promoted activity in carving, weaving, embroidery, and traditional dressmaking (*Frauentracht*) among both urban and alpine German Swiss. Much of this craftwork is done at a cottage-industry level with commercial sale as the ultimate objective. The federal government encourages this activity, and authorized craft outlets (*Heimattwerke*) are found in the large cities. The arts and customs of dance and song have survived less affected by social and economic changes. Yodeling, which originated in ancient times, persists, and alp horns are played. The German Swiss hold a strong place in the literature, music, and art of modern Western culture. In particular, they have merged architecture and

engineering into structural art, most notably with the bridges of Robert Maillart, Othman Ammann, and Christian Menn.

Bibliography

Friedl, John (1974). *Kippel: A Changing Village in the Alps.* New York: Holt, Rinehart & Winston.

Herold, J. Christopher (1948). *The Swiss without Halos.* Westport, Conn.: Greenwood Press.

Imhof, Eduart, ed. (1965–1978). *Atlas der Schweiz.* Wabern-Bern: Verlag der Eidgenössischen Landes Topographie.

Kennan, George F. (1989). "The Last Wise Man: Sketches from a Life." *Atlantic Monthly* 263(4):51–52.

Luck, J. Murray, ed. (1978). *Modern Switzerland.* Palo Alto, Calif.: Society of Promotion of Science and Scholarship.

McRae, Kenneth D. (1983). *Conflict and Compromise in Multilingual Societies: Switzerland.* Waterloo, Ontario: Wilfrid Laurier University Press.

Suter, Marc R. (1976). *Switzerland, from Earliest Times to the Roman Conquest.* London: Thames & Hudson.

ERVAN G. GARRISON

Gitanos

ETHNONYMS: none

Orientation

Identification. "Gitanos," the term that almost all Gypsies of Spain use to identify themselves, is also the word that non-Gypsy Spaniards use. Gitanos are monolingual Spanish speakers, and although some claim that an identifiable physical type exists, Gitanos are in fact phenotypically indistinguishable from other Spaniards. They are overwhelmingly sedentary, not nomadic. They derive their name (as do Gypsies, Gitans, Tsiganes, and Zigeuners) from the misnomer "Egyptian." The term originated with the erroneous notion, dating back to western Europe's early modern period, that "Gypsies" originally came from Egypt. Gitanos probably account for well over 99 percent of the Gypsy populations in Spain. They should be distinguished from Spain's tiny minority of Indic-speaking people, who are also glossed in English as "Gypsies." (The latter, whom both Gitanos and non-Gitano Spaniards call "Húngaros," or "Gitano-Húngaros," call themselves "Rom.") Gitanos rarely intermarry with Spain's Romany-speaking Gypsies even when they live in the same quarter, and they have many more social and economic relations with non-Gypsy Spaniards than they do with the Rom.

Demography.   No reliable censuses of Gitanos in Spain exist today, although estimates vary from 100,00 to 300,000 persons. Earlier censuses are referred to in the historical record, but only one approximation to a census, a national prison roster, has actually been found. This roster, which is considered to have comprised almost all the Gypsies in Spain, is a 1749 listing of some 9,000 Gypsy prisoners who were rounded up and incarcerated for three months under Philip VI: if correct, it would show that Gitanos in the mid-eighteenth century constituted about 0.2 percent of the Spanish population. While the relative proportion of Gitanos to non-Gitanos has doubled and perhaps quintupled since the mid-eighteenth century, the present Gitano incidence is still estimated as ranging from at most about 0.5 to 1 percent of the total Spanish population.

Linguistic Affiliation.   Gitanos in Spain, like Gypsies in many other countries, are monolingual speakers of the language of their own country—in this case, Spanish. In the past Gitanos spoke Caló, a speech form characterized by Spanish grammar but containing words of Indic origin. It is not known when Caló emerged, but its lexical items show it to have been derived from a language akin to Romany (Romanés), the language of the present-day Rom. Caló was entirely distinct from Germanía, or "thieves' slang," of Spain, and although it penetrated Germanía, the reverse did not occur to any great extent. By the mid-nineteenth century, the different local variants of Caló together constituted some 2,000 lexical items, and Gitanos could still communicate without being understood by outsiders. Today, Caló is no longer a living speech code, although isolated lexical items may be widespread in the speech of some Gitanos. One interesting aspect of Caló has been the attention given to it by non-Gypsy aficionados of Gypsy culture. In the nineteenth century as well as today, non-Gypsies have taught themselves to speak, and even compose poetry, in Caló. In the present climate of Gitano consciousness-raising, both Gitanos and non-Gitanos engaged in Gypsy politics have learned to speak a form of Caló (largely from written sources), have organized classes to teach Gitanos Caló, and have composed political verse in it. Caló has contributed words to spoken Iberian Spanish, and it has found a small place in the Spanish dictionaries.

History and Cultural Relations

The earliest records of people who are believed to have been the first Gypsies to enter Spain are several scattered documents of safe conduct, or "passports," from the early fifteenth century. These documents refer to the "Princes and Counts of Little Egypt," and place these people in the north and northeast of Spain, where they had probably arrived after crossing the Pyrenees from France. (There is no evidence to support a popular notion that they entered Spain from North Africa.)

From the first national law about Gypsies in 1499 to the last in 1783, all Spanish decrees about Gitanos had the single goal of assimilation (only the very early laws decreed banishment for the unassimilated). To achieve this end, the laws ordered the dispersal of Gitano barrios in the cities, the separation of children from parents and their simultaneous enrollment in schools (even when schools hardly existed), with other coercive measures. Beyond everything, however,

were the continuing directives attempting to compel Gitanos to participate in wage labor. These laws, which failed repeatedly, were also repeatedly reissued over three centuries. In 1783, in the last national law that was directed at Gitanos, Charles III's government abrogated all previous laws about Gypsies, decreed "benevolently" that Gitanos could now enter many professions (but not those of innkeepers or livestock traders), and once again ordered that they become wage laborers. The law also successfully enacted directives that had previously failed, and it forbade the use of the word "Gitano" or the then-common euphemism "Nuevos Castellanos" (New Castilians). The principal result was that Gitanos effectively disappeared from national law. This gap in the data remained until the mid-twentieth century, when Spaniards in the social services began to form associations to address the Gypsy situation.

From the 1960s on, the Catholic church and lay social-service organizations began to concern themselves with what they called the *problemática gitana,* "the Gypsy question," a trenchant expression more powerful than *el problema gitano,* "the Gypsy problem." Today, government agencies and voluntary associations still attempt to assimilate Gitanos by bringing them into wage labor. Gitanos are no longer depicted as being noxious and dangerous to the state but instead as being disadvantaged by centuries of prejudice, a people who need help to *promocionarse,* to "modernize." Brutal laws to coerce wage labor have now become social work programs for job training and other kinds of "development." A change may finally occur, even though Gitanos continue to control their own work. In the last ten years almost all Gitano children for the first time have been registered in schools. This powerful acculturating institution may eventually lead to the kind of assimilation that authorities have aimed at since the late fifteenth century. (See under "Economy.")

Although Gitanos have never constituted more than 1 percent of the total Spanish population, they have regularly come to represent part of the romantic image of Spain. Even today, travel posters and airline advertisements still portray Spain as a mosaic of bullfights, castles, and Gypsies. While romanticizing Gitanos as exotic "Others" began in the early seventeenth century with Cervantes's *La Gitanilla,* it was George Borrow's adventurous travel books of the mid-nineteenth century that popularized Gitanos for the European and American public. Gitanos became the subject of nineteenth-century novels and operas (by Mérimée and Bizet); of travel accounts (by Hans Christian Andersen, George Henry Borrow, Théophile Gautier); of an entire genre of nineteenth-century *costumbrismo* plays about the Spanish lower classes; and of numerous paintings. Like Gypsies elsewhere, Gitanos have historically been the object of elite and artistic interest in subordinate minorities. Often depicted as idealized noble savages and sometimes as depraved beings, Gitanos have embodied the fantasies of both non-Gypsy critics and champions of Spain.

Settlements

Virtually all Gitanos are now sedentary, and some proportion were sedentary at least as early as the first third of the seventeenth century. We know this because of the many laws and regulations extending from 1633 through 1783 that attempted to force Gitanos to leave the Gypsy quarters, or _gitanerías_, and disperse themselves among the general population. We also know about early sedentarization from seventeenth- and eighteenth-century documents that variously describe Gitanos as nomadic, seminomadic, and entirely sedentary. We do not know, however, what proportion of Gitanos were sedentary or nomadic in any period before the late twentieth century, why or how sedentarization began earlier among Gypsies in Spain than among Gypsies elsewhere in western Europe, nor why the process was so extensive in Spain. In the past Gitanos earned their living in cities or in metropolitan centers of the countryside, such as livestock fairs. Today almost all Gitanos are urban residents, and those few who live in villages are engaged in trades (and are mostly self-employed) rather than agriculture.

Economy

Gitanos belong to a great range of economic classes and engage in many kinds of work. One of the most distinctive features of the ways they have earned a living, both historically and now, has been their avoidance of proletarianization—that is, their resistance to losing control over the organization, schedules, and products of their own work.

Data about Gitanos' work in the past is derived principally from laws and official correspondence dating from the late fifteenth to the late eighteenth centuries. These laws were repressive attempts to assimilate Gitanos by turning them into wage laborers. Authorities assumed, almost certainly correctly, that if Gitanos became wage laborers dependent upon their employers, they would, like other Spaniards, be easier to control and supervise. Despite innumerable repressive laws and regulations directed specifically at Gitanos, however, they continued to avoid proletarianization. From the sixteenth through the eighteenth centuries, they worked in the livestock trade (an occupation that continued into the early 1940s), as traveling livestock shearers, as traveling entertainers, and as operators of inns, some of which appear to have been way stations along smuggling routes. Although the data are sparse for the nineteenth and early twentieth centuries, it appears that Gitanos continued to remain self-employed throughout this period.

Today Gitanos still generally control the way they earn a living. Women and men work; so do children except when they are in school. Time analyses show that Gitanos work fewer hours than their non-Gitano neighbors to maintain the household. Gitanos work in the scrap trade; in the discount-clothing and household-goods trades, where they sell on different days in different open-air municipal markets; in well-paid, short-term harvesting (which, although salaried, is similar to self-employment in that they control their own work schedules); as self-employed painters and whitewashers; and in a medley of other occupations. Their work organization is still characterized by the same features that characterized their work historically: a minimal overhead and a mobile place of business (such as selling in a variety of municipal markets rather than owning a shop); quick turnover of stock; income derived from multiple sources; a changing clientele; exchanges carried out in cash (including, today, transactions that involve more than $5,000); work that is labor-intensive, not capital-intensive; and revenues unencumbered by taxes. Gitanos have been highly successful, in other words, in exploiting the informal economy—an economy that in Spain is not hidden or "underground" but has been calculated as constituting as much as one-third of the present gross domestic product.

Kinship, Marriage, and Family

Kinship.   There is little evidence of organized kinship beyond the nuclear family, and Gitano kinship terms are the same as those of other Spaniards. Some clusters, or adhesions, exist of grandparents and one or two of their married children and young grandchildren who work together and pool certain resources. These family clusters, however, are largely divided into separate, nuclear-family households, and they are not very different from non-Gypsy extended families in urban Spain. Close kin visit one another regularly, and friendship is almost always embedded in kinship.

Marriage.   Marriages are still arranged for adult children if the bride can be found to be a virgin, if the parents of the potential spouses are on speaking terms, and if the marrying partners agree. Other Gitanos elope, especially if the bride cannot pass a virginity test, one of the few distinctly Gitano practices. Eloping couples return to their kin after about a month. Newly married couples tend to live for the first year with the groom's parents. Close kin, including first cousins, marry. After disputes, arranging marriages is one of the few important events that convene Gitanos beyond the level of elementary families. Links between brothers and other male kin related through either mother or father (links, that is, between the fathers of the marrying couple) are likely to erode, and arranging marriages builds alliances between such males.

Sociopolitical Organization

Social Organization.   As it is difficult to find _a_ group or _the_ group among Gitanos, so it is difficult to find neat patterns of elaborate social organization, ideas, or traditions. Because Gitanos do very few things together, because they avoid continuity and instead celebrate impermanence, they conserve few customs. They do have a tradition within flamenco (concentrated among Andalusians), a sometimes-practiced virginity test for brides, and a special involvement with recently dead kin. Apart from these practices, however, their well-known, distinctive exuberance and dash is invested in personal interaction, especially with other Gitanos, not in material objects or in "tradition." Gitanos, in fact, may be characterized as anticonservative. The way they treat custom is the way they treat material goods. As they discard and change "custom," so they consume and repurchase costly and ordinary possessions much more rapidly than their non-Gitano neighbors. Their lavish dispensation of their material inventory is not profligate (no more than, say, a Kwakiutl potlatch) but instead is part of a larger pattern of avoiding permanence and structure. Against the background of few ongoing economic groups or religious systems (or even a cuisine), of politics based on avoiding mobilization, and of a fluctuating interchange of allies and foes, what remains predictable is the unpredictable. The systematic configuration or pattern among Gitanos is one of avoiding patterns—but with ebullience and verve. Their resistance to continuity and structure is a living example that demonstrates how the range of variation in human societies extends from the maximally to the minimally organized. The fact that social groups can successfully exist without intricate internal organization is an important contribution that the study of Gitanos makes to social research in general.

Political Organization. The most characteristic feature of Gitano political organization is the absence of proper groups. Gitanos rarely act together to achieve a common end; they rarely mobilize around issues of "Gypsyness" or to gain access to resources or power. For this reason, Gitanos are best described as a cultural minority rather than as an ethnic group. Gitanos are egalitarian, and there are no statuses or offices endowing anyone with authority. There are some instances of powerful individuals who can exercise control in neighborhood disagreements and whose occasional authority originates in their personal qualities, not in office. These men organize themselves in fluctuating bilateral kindreds with a heavy sprinkling of their own male kin. Such kindreds have sometimes been mistakenly called lineages and clans by the popular press. The data from anthropologists who have studied Gypsies, however, show an undisputed absence of unilineal corporate descent groups among Gitanos, as well as a kinship profile typical of Spain and western Europe.

In contrast to the low level of political mobilization among Gitanos themselves, many non-Gitanos in Spain organize themselves around issues concerning Gitanos. Every medium-size and large city in Spain has at least one, and often several, such organizations. This is not a new phenomenon. Since the sixteenth century, elites in Spain have organized and reproduced themselves around the tasks of regulating marginal peoples, including Gitanos. Today, government and social-work agencies have established more than 200 offices to carry out aid-to-Gypsies programs. While these associations provide social services, they also attempt to change the Gitanos' low commitment to the institutions and values of the dominant society. In addition, a few organizations provide legal aid to defend Gitanos against local authorities. These authorities, responding to shop owners threatened by competition in an inflationary economy, prohibit Gitano street selling in areas outside public markets.

Conflict and Social Control. While Gitanos rarely work together beyond the level of a few closely related nuclear families, rarely act in concert for political ends, and rarely even congregate except for life-cycle events, there is one activity that does convene people. These are disputes. Disputes, which occur over large and small issues, do not divide people; rather, they routinely bring together kin and nonkin. There are no feuds, for although the same types of fights are reenacted recurrently, participants fluctuate and rotate as friends and enemies change places. Feuds in the Gitano context would be impossible: structuring fights into allies and foes would grind their society to a halt. (There are exceptions, of course; extreme physical force, which is unusual, can lead to permanent separations.) Disputes also delimit the moral community (Gitanos do not fight with non-Gitanos). Thus, by serving first as a locus of assemblage beyond the small family, and second as a definer of the group boundary, quarrels produce and reproduce the connections and activities of local Gitano societies.

Quarrels and fights are also a mode of communication. More than just a locus of assemblage, they conjoin people in intimate, face-to-face relations unregulated by hierarchy, age, or gender. Among Gitanos, however, these intensely intimate interactions are not fleeting escapes from the ordinary constraints of daily social life, nor are they restricted to special events, such as rituals, pilgrimages, rebellions, and other passionate social dramas. They are, instead, secular and quotidian. This ordinary secularity is merely to be expected since sociopolitical organization is so loosely structured and egalitarian. Nevertheless, although disputes are a daily event, they remain a principal focus of the Gitano culture and a topic of steadfast, enthusiastic interest.

Religion and Expressive Culture

Religion. Gitanos are Roman Catholics who participate in four of the church's sacraments (baptism, marriage, First Communion, and extreme unction), but they are not assiduous churchgoers. They rarely go to folk healers, and they participate fully in Spain's state-supported medical system. Gitanos have a special involvement with recently dead kin, visit their graves frequently, and spend a great deal more money than non-Gitanos of equivalent economic classes in adorning grave sites.

Arts. Flamenco is a cluster of related music and dance forms that originated in Andalusia, southern Spain. In the popular imagination, it is strongly associated with Gitanos, though there are both Gitano and non-Gitano traditions, and as yet no one is sure of flamenco's origins. In the musical tradition, the oldest Gitano songs appear to be a group of unaccompanied verses relating to prison life and other privations of the late eighteenth and early nineteenth centuries. Gitano flamenco artists have remained among the most well-known of Spanish performers.

Bibliography

Clavería Lizano, Carlos (1962). "Notas sobre el Gitano español." In *STRENAE: Estudios de filología e historia dedicados al Profesor Manuel García Blanco*, 109–119. Serie de Filosofía y Letras, 16. Salamanca: Acta Salamanticensia.

Gómez Alfaro, Antonio (1990). *Notas sobre el expediente de 1749 de Carlos III*. Ph.D. dissertation, Faculty of Law, Universidad Complutense de Madrid.

Kaprow, Miriam Lee (1982). "Resisting Respectability: Gypsies in Saragossa." *Urban Anthropology* 11:399–431.

Quintana, Bertha B., and Lois G. Floyd (1976). *Qué Gitano: Gypsies of Southern Spain*. New York: Holt, Rinehart & Winston. Reprint. 1986. Prospect Heights, Ill.: Waveland.

Sánchez Ortega, María Helena (1977). *Los Gitanos españoles: El periodo borbónico*. Madrid: Castellote Editor.

San Román, Teresa (1986). "Los Gitanos y las exclusas de la marginación." In *Entre la marginación y el racismo: reflexiones sobre la vida de los Gitanos*, edited by Teresa San Román, 232–239. Madrid: Alianza Editorial.

Volland, Anita (1990). "*Carceleras*: Gitano Prison Songs in the 18th Century." In *100 Years of Gypsy Studies*, edited by Matt T. Salo, 251–266. Cheverly, Md.: Gypsy Lore Society.

MIRIAM LEE KAPROW

Greeks

ETHNONYMS: Ellines, Hellenes

Orientation

Identification. Greeks constitute an ethnic group of great longevity, tracing their origins to the first appearance of complex society in southeastern Europe. A common sense of culture, language, and religion signified by the term "Greek" (Hellene) developed in antiquity and has endured, with changes, to the present. Greek identity today emphasizes early Greek civilization, the Christian traditions of the Byzantine Empire, and the concerns of the modern Greek nation established in 1831. Throughout Greek history, members of other groups were periodically assimilated as Greeks, while Greeks themselves migrated in a worldwide diaspora. The ethnic Greeks now residing outside the Hellenic republic equal those within. This article, however, is restricted to the latter.

Location. The southernmost extremity of the Balkan Peninsula, Greece is located between 34° and 41° N and 19° and 29° E. It contains 15,000 kilometers of coastline and over 2,000 islands fanning into the Mediterranean Sea. The total land surface is 131,947 square kilometers, of which 80 percent is hilly or mountainous with only scattered valleys and plains. Nine geographical regions are generally recognized. Macedonia, Epirus, and Thrace form Greece's northern border with Albania, Macedonia (that section of what was Yugoslavia that is now seeking recognition as a separate nation), Bulgaria, and Turkey. The southern mainland includes Thessaly, central Greece, and the Peloponnesos. The Ionian Islands to the west of the mainland, the Aegean Islands (including the Cyclades and Dodecanese) to the east, and Crete to the south constitute the major island regions. The climate varies from Mediterranean to central European with generally hot, dry summers and cool, wet winters.

Demography. The 1991 Greek census recorded 10,042,956 citizens, of whom 96 percent were ethnic Greeks. There were also small numbers of Jews, Turks, Slavo-Macedonians, Gypsies, Albanians, Pomaks, Armenians, Lebanese, Filipinos, Pakistanis, North Africans, recent refugees from eastern Europe, and transhumant shepherd groups, including Koutsovlachs, Aromani, and Sarakatsani. The national population has increased greatly from its 1831 level of 750,000, because of territorial accretion, the immigration of Greeks from outside Greece, and a rate of natural increase annually averaging 1.5 percent prior to 1900 and 1 percent thereafter. This growth was countered, however, by massive emigration to North America, northern Europe, Australia, and other locations throughout the nineteenth and twentieth centuries. The once sizable Turkish, Bulgarian, and Serbian populations living within current Greek boundaries also fell to minimal levels after several treaties and population exchanges around the time of World War I.

Linguistic Affiliation. The primary language of Greece is Greek, an Indo-European language first attested around 1400 B.C. Modern Greek has two major forms: _katharevousa_, a formal, archaizing style devised by Greek nationalist Adam-antis Korais in the early nineteenth century; and _dimotiki_, the language of ordinary conversation, which has regional variations. Many Greeks mix these forms according to demands of context and meaning, and the choice of one or the other for schooling and public discourse has been a political issue. Hellenic Orthodox church services are conducted in yet another Greek variant, _koine_, the language of the New Testament. While 97 percent of Greek citizens speak Greek as their primary language, there are small groups who also speak Turkish, Slavo-Macedonian, Albanian, Vlach (a Romanian dialect), Pomak (a Bulgarian dialect), and Romany.

History and Cultural Relations

The ancient origins of the Greek people remain obscure and controversial, particularly as regards the relative importance of conquering invasions, external influence, and indigenous development. Most now agree that by 2000 B.C. Greek speakers inhabited the southern mainland, at the same time that non-Greek Cretans developed Minoan civilization. Mycenean society, arising in the Peloponnesos around 1600 B.C., spread Greek language and culture to the Aegean Islands, Crete, Cyprus, and the Anatolian coast through both conquest and colonization. By the rise of the classical city-states in the seventh to eighth centuries B.C., Greek identity was firmly in place throughout these regions as well as Greek colonies near the Black Sea, southern Italy, Sicily, and North Africa. The Macedonian kings, Philip II and his son, Alexander the Great, spoke Greek and embraced Greek culture. They conquered and united Greek lands and built an empire stretching to India and Egypt during the fourth century B.C. These Hellenistic kingdoms quickly crumbled, and Greek dominions gradually fell to the Roman Empire during the first and second centuries B.C. Greeks lived as a conquered but valued cultural group under the Romans. After this empire split in A.D. 330, the eastern half, centered in Constantinople and unified by the new religion of Christianity, quickly evolved into the Byzantine Empire, in which Greeks controlled much of the eastern Mediterranean world for over one thousand years. The Venetian-led Fourth Crusade seized Constantinople in 1204, reducing the Byzantine Empire to a much smaller territory, established Frankish feudal principalities in much of what is now Greece. Both Byzantine and Frankish holdings eventually fell to the advancing Ottoman Empire, which conquered Constantinople in 1453. The Ottoman Turks treated Greeks as a distinct ethnic group, forcing them to pay taxes and often work on Turkish estates but allowing them to keep both identity and religion. Inspired by nationalistic ideals, and supported by England, France, and Russia, the Greek War of Independence (1821–1829) against the Turks produced the modern nation of Greece in 1831. The original nation contained only the southern mainland and some Aegean islands, but it gradually expanded through successive wars and treaties with the Turks and other neighbors. Nevertheless, attempts to gain the predominantly Greek areas of Constantinople, the western coast of Anatolia, and Cyprus were not successful. Compulsory population exchanges after World War I removed most Greeks from the first two areas, as well as most Turks and other non-Greeks from Greece.

Settlements

Greeks have been very mobile throughout their history. Areas of population concentration have shifted, and villages have come and gone with transitions from one period to another. Since establishment of the Greek nation, there has been much movement from upland, interior villages to lowland and coastal ones. Hundreds of new villages have been founded in the process. There has also been increasing migration from all villages to a few large cities. Greece became over 50 percent urbanized in the late 1960s. Metropolitan Athens now houses nearly one-third of the national population. Villages, which now average 500 inhabitants, can be compact clusters around a central square, linear strings along a road, or even sometimes scattered housing dispersed over a region. Market towns, ranging between 1,000 and 10,000 residents, are intermediaries between various regions and such major cities as greater Athens, Thessaloniki, Patras, Iraklion, and Volos.

Economy

Subsistence and Commercial Activities. Under the Ottomans, most Greeks were peasants or craftsmen. At the end of this period, however, a few shippers and merchants rose to power and wealth by mediating between the expanding capitalist economies of western Europe and the Ottomans. After independence, Greece entered a fully "marketized" economy from a largely dependent position. Feudal estates were replaced by small family-farming operations. While an elite class continued, their wealth did not foster national economic development. Greece remains at the bottom of European Community economic indicators. Subsistence agriculture of grain, olives, and vines has given way to cash cropping of these and other produce such as cotton, tobacco, and fresh fruits. The difficulties inherent in farming on mountainous terrain have led many to seek urban or foreign employment. By 1990, less than one-third of the Greek population were farmers.

Industrial Arts. Greece is one of the least industrialized European nations. While carpentry, metalworking, and similar shops exist in all Greek towns, other industry is heavily concentrated in Athens, Thessaloniki, and a few other cities. Work is often organized along family lines, and in 1990, 85 percent of Greek manufacturing units had less than ten employees. The most important industries are food, beverage, and tobacco processing, with textile, clothing, metallurgical, chemical, and shipbuilding operations following.

Trade. At independence, Greeks exported currants and other produce to northern Europe, importing metal goods, coffee, sugar, grain, and dried fish in return. While trade has since increased greatly, it remains heavily weighted against Greece and toward its current trading partners—Germany, Italy, France, the United States, Japan, and Saudi Arabia. Greece now exports textiles, tobacco, produce, ores, cement, and chemicals while importing food, oil, cars, electronic items, and other consumer goods. Partially offsetting this unfavorable balance are receipts from shipping and tourism and remittances from Greeks abroad. Greece initiated membership in the European Community in 1962, becoming a full member in 1981.

Division of Labor. Despite the importance of women's productive work in farming, household maintenance, and familial businesses, wage labor outside the family has been male-dominated until recently. At present, many Greek women work for wages only until they marry, and only 30 percent of wage earners are women. Of the total labor force in 1990, less than 29 percent were in agriculture, about 30 percent in manufacturing, and the rest in the service sector. Emigration to find work abroad has generally kept Greek unemployment rates under 5 percent.

Land Tenure. At independence, prime agricultural lands were controlled by Turkish (and a few Greek) overlords and by Hellenic Orthodox monasteries. The new government established a series of land reforms, whereby large estates were distributed to poor and landless peasants during the nineteenth century. The practice of bilateral partible inheritance has since led to considerable farm fragmentation, whereby familial holdings average 3 hectares scattered in several different plots.

Kinship

Kin Groups and Descent. The relatives who share a household are a basic unit of economic cooperation and collective identity. Extending outward from the household, loose networks of both consanguineal and affinal kin provide social support. This bilateral kindred is often referred to as a *soi*, although this term has an agnatic bias in certain regions. Marriage connects family lines, as does ritual kinship. Those chosen as wedding sponsors or godparents stand in a special relationship to the entire kindred.

Kinship Terminology. Greek terminology follows a cognatic (or Eskimo) pattern. The gender of cousins is denoted by different endings, and in some regions more distant cousins are distinguished from first cousins. There also exist special terms for men married to two sisters and women married to two brothers. The terms for bride and groom broadly refer to people married by various members of one's family.

Marriage and Family

Marriage. Greeks exhibit higher marriage and lower divorce rates than northern Europeans. Marriage is monogamous, and it is forbidden between first cousins by the Hellenic Orthodox Church. Civil marriage outside the church has only recently been allowed. Divorce is permitted by both law and religion, and, since 1982, it can be granted through common consent. Marriages were commonly arranged by parents until the last few decades. Both families take an active interest in the groom's potential inheritance and the bride's dowry. Men and women generally marry in their mid- to late twenties. Postmarital residence is normally neolocal with respect to the actual house or apartment, although some couples reside temporarily with either the bride's or groom's parents. With respect to the village or neighborhood where a new rural couple resides, however, postmarital residence tends toward virilocality on the mainland and uxorilocality in the islands. The urban pattern is more complex, although much uxorilocality occurs in Athens.

Domestic Unit. The nuclear family household is statistically the most common, although stem families and other combinations of close kin also form households, as a result of economic need, recent migration, and variations during the life cycle. Elderly parents often reside with an adult child toward the end of their lives. House or apartment ownership is a major familial goal, and considerable resources are directed toward this. Greece ranks at the top of the European Community in per capita construction of dwellings.

Inheritance. By both custom and law, all children inherit equally from their parents. Daughters generally receive their share as dowry when they marry, and sons receive theirs when the parents retire or die. Dowries consist of land, houses, livestock, money, a trousseau, furnishings, and, more recently, apartments, household appliances, education, and a car. Significant dowry inflation has occurred during the last few decades, a circumstance favoring female inheritance over male. A 1983 law correspondingly limited the use of the dowry. Whether called a wedding gift or dowry, however, the practice of providing daughters with much of their inheritance at marriage continues.

Socialization. Parents assume primary responsibility for raising children, assisted by many members of the kindred. Godparents also look after a child's material and spiritual welfare. Most children are minimally disciplined during early childhood; later they are actively trained into their proper roles through example, admonition, teasing, and comforting designed to teach such traits as wariness, cleverness, family loyalty, verbal proficiency, and honorable behavior. Nine years of formal education are both free and compulsory. A full 82 percent of Greek children complete twelve years of secondary education, and another 17 percent attend university.

Sociopolitical Organization

Social Organization. Kinship, ritual kinship, local connections, and patronage shape Greek social relations. People operate through networks of known and trusted others, extending their relationships outward through these. Status accrues from a combination of honorable behavior, material wealth, and education. Social stratification varies between city and countryside. In rural areas, large landowners, professionals, and merchants are at the top; farmers, small shopkeepers, and skilled workers in the middle; and landless farm workers at the bottom. In cities, bankers, merchants, shipowners, industrialists, wealthy professionals, and bureaucrats compose the upper stratum; executives, civil servants, shopkeepers, office workers, and skilled workers the middle; and unskilled workers the bottom. In both cases, the middle class is the majority, and there is considerable opportunity for upward social mobility.

Political Organization. The modern Greek state, initially established as a monarchy guided by northern European nations, has emerged as a republic with a unicameral legislature headed by a prime minister as head of government and a president as ceremonial head of state. Public officials are elected by universal adult suffrage. For the last two decades, two main political parties have alternated control of the government: the conservative Nea Dimokratia party, and the Socialist PASOK party. The political system is highly centralized, with considerable power residing in national ministries and offices. The nation contains approximately 50 *nomoi* (districts), each divided into eparchies (provinces), *demoi* (municipalities), and *koinotites* (communities). Local officials, elected on the basis of patronage and personality as well as political party, oversee regional affairs.

Social Control. Struggle and competition among different families is a major theme of Greek life. Familial conflicts emerge over land, flocks, political office, and a variety of local affairs. Insults, ridicule, feuds, and even theft sometimes result. The formal legal system is based on codified Roman civil law, with a network of civil, criminal, and administrative courts. Towns have a corps of city police, while rural regions have a gendarmerie modeled on the French system.

Conflict. Greece has a standing army and universal male conscription. Turkey is perceived as the greatest threat to national security, and the Turkish occupation of Cyprus since 1974 has caused considerable regional tension. Greece's relations with its northern neighbors, stable for some time, have recently become more tenuous as the Eastern bloc dissolves into separate ethnically based nationalities and the boundaries established after World War I are called into question. On a broader level, Greece's strategic location involves it in various international struggles. A member of NATO since 1952, Greece generally has been aligned with the West.

Religion and Expressive Culture

Religious Beliefs. Over 97 percent of Greece's population belongs to the Hellenic Orthodox church, a branch of Eastern Orthodoxy. Since the Byzantine Empire, and particularly after the schism between eastern and western Christianity in 1054, Eastern Orthodoxy has been part of Greek ethnic identity. Proselytization by other religions is legally forbidden. There are only small numbers of Muslims, Roman Catholics, other Christians, and Jews. The formal theology of Eastern Orthodoxy is often mixed with informal beliefs in fate, the devil, and other supernatural forces.

Religious Practitioners. During the last few centuries, various nationally based Eastern Orthodox churches separated from the patriarch of Constantinople, among them the Hellenic Orthodox church, established in 1833. Each of these fifteen autocephalous churches runs its own affairs, while recognizing the historical and spiritual importance of the patriarch. Except for a few regions, the Hellenic Orthodox church is governed by the Holy Synod convened by the bishop of Athens. The church hierarchy includes bishops of the approximately 90 dioceses, as well as monks and nuns. While these clergy are celibate, priests may marry. Most priests have families, and many continue to practice a trade or farm in addition to performing their religious duties. Members of the local community voluntarily maintain the church building and assist with weekly services.

Ceremonies. The Sunday liturgy is the most significant weekly ritual of the Hellenic Orthodox church. There are also twelve annual Great Feasts, of which Easter and the Holy Week preceding it are the most important. Other rituals mark various points in the life cycle, particularly birth, marriage, and death. Baptism and confirmation of infants are performed simultaneously, and infants can then receive communion.

Arts. Displays of ancient and Byzantine art in museums, public archaeological sites, and reproductions permeate the

Greek landscape, attracting tourists and symbolizing Greek identity. Contemporary artistic expression draws from folk, religious, and international traditions in varying ways. Weaving, knitting, embroidery, carving, metalworking, and pottery remain active crafts in most regions. Dancing demonstrates individual and group identity and is an integral part of most celebrations. Contemporary composers work with the instruments and motifs of folk music, particularly the more urban bouzouki, as well as the clarinet, *santouri* (dulcimer), violin, lute, and drums. Contemporary literature, film, and theater echo pan-European styles, and Greece counts two Nobel laureates among its modern authors, George Seferis and Odysseus Elytis. Television and cinema, both foreign and domestic, are prevalent and very popular.

Medicine.   Scientific medicine is well developed and accepted. Hospitals and clinics exist in most towns, and the National Health Service sends doctors to more remote areas. Hospital births have largely replaced the use of midwives. Abortions performed by both doctors and lay practitioners are a major means of birth control and may equal live births in number. The belief that illness stems from emotional, moral, and social causes coexists with the formal medical system. Folk healers, generally women, are sometimes called to use divination, spells, and herbal remedies against both sickness and such forces as the evil eye.

Death and Afterlife.   Death practices follow Hellenic Orthodox ritual modified by other beliefs, regional traditions, and contemporary circumstances. Upon death, a person's soul is thought to leave the body: at first it remains near the house, but gradually it moves farther away, until finally, after a year's time, it reaches God, who pronounces judgment and consigns the soul to paradise or hell. The body is buried within twenty-four hours of death with ceremonies at both house and local church led by the priest and female mourners who sing ritual laments. Important rituals are performed at the grave both forty days and one year after the death. After several years, the bones generally are exhumed from the ground and placed in a community ossuary.

See also Cretans; Cyclades; Cypriots; Greek-Speaking Jews of Greece; Ionians; Macedonians; Mount Athos; Peloponnesians; Pontic; Sarakatsani; Tsakonians

Bibliography

Campbell, John (1964). *Honour, Family, and Patronage: A Study of Institutions and Moral Values of a Greek Mountain Community*. Oxford: Clarendon Press.

Danforth, Loring M. (1989). *Firewalking and Religious Healing: The Anastenaria of Greece and the American Firewalking Movement*. Princeton: Princeton University Press.

Dimen, Muriel, and Ernestine Friedl, eds. (1976). *Regional Variation in Modern Greece and Cyprus: Toward a Perspective on the Ethnography of Greece*. New York: Annals of the New York Academy of Science.

Friedl, Ernestine (1962). *Vasilika: A Village in Modern Greece*. New York: Holt, Rinehart & Winston.

Herzfeld, Michael (1985). *The Poetics of Manhood: Contest and Identity in a Cretan Mountain Village*. Princeton: Princeton University Press.

Hirschon, Renee (1989). *Heirs of the Greek Catastrophe: The Social Life of Asia Minor Refugees in Piraeus*. Oxford: Clarendon Press.

SUSAN BUCK SUTTON

Greek-Speaking Jews of Greece

ETHNONYMS: Griegos, Romaniotes

Orientation

Identification.   The Greek-speaking Jews of Greece are the so-called remnants of Byzantine Jewry. Today they reside primarily in the northwestern corner of Greece, in the city of Ioannina, capital of the province of Epirus. These people are thought to have retained cultural traditions that date to Byzantium, with influences from the Sephardic and Italian Jews as well as the Ottoman Muslims. Their language, traditional culture, and liturgical rites are distinct, however, from those of the Sephardic Jews found in other commercial centers of the country. Because the majority of the scholarship on Greek Jewry focuses on the Sephardic, Judeo-Spanish-speaking Jews, this community with its special history and unique cultural expressions is virtually overlooked.

Location.   As noted above, the Greek-speaking Jews of Greece are concentrated in the city of Ioannina in northwestern Greece. Before World War II, small family groupings were found in the surrounding villages of Paramithia, Margaritaria, Filiates, Pogoni, and Vostina and the cities of Arta and Prevesa, as well as in Albania. Immigrant communities exist in Athens, Jerusalem, and New York City.

Demography.   Reports from travelers in the Balkans in the early nineteenth century recorded the total population of Ioannina as about 40,000 inhabitants, of which approximately 2,000 were Jews. By 1883, that figure had risen to 3,334 with reports of Jewish populations in the mountain town of Pogoni and the port of Prevesa. At the turn of the century, Ioannina had shrunk to 20,000 with the departure of Ottoman troops; at that time the Jewish population numbered 4,000–5,000 individuals. The first three decades of the twentieth century were marked by Jewish emigration from Ioannina because of political, economic, and religious pressures. By 1928, the Jewish population had decreased to 2,000. Fifteen years later, on 25 March 1943, approximately 1,800 Jews were deported by the Nazis to Auschwitz. At the close of the war about 200 Jews returned to Ioannina from the death camps, the Greek Resistance, and hiding places in the villages. In 1983, approximately 57 Jews remained in Ioannina.

Linguistic Affiliation.   The Greek-speaking Jews speak a regional dialect of Greek with some Hebrew words integrated into their speech. Records of Judeo-Greek, written in Hebrew script, exist. From 1904 to the outbreak of World War II, young people were instructed in French and Hebrew at schools administered by the Alliance Israelite Universelle. Because community members living in New York emigrated in the early decades of the twentieth century, remnants of Turkish words are found in their language.

History and Cultural Relations

Jews have resided in the Greek Peninsula and islands since classical times. Archaeological remains reveal the existence of ancient synagogues in scattered locations. The peripatetic Spanish rabbi, Benjamin of Tudela, found Jews in many coastal locations on his journey around the Mediterranean. With the influx of Sephardic Jews from the Iberian Peninsula in the late fifteenth century, a phenomenon of reverse assimilation took place. In language, traditional culture, and rite, most of the existing Jews of Greece took on the attributes of the newcomers. Evidence remains of the persistence of Greek-speaking enclaves in the names of synagogues in Salonika and Istanbul. Oral tradition places the Jews of Ioannina at the fall of the Second Temple (70 C.E.). Written documents, however, date their presence to the fourteenth century. The Byzantine Golden Bulls of Andronicus II reaffirmed the rights of the Jews of Ioannina. Under 400 years of Ottoman rule, the Jews in Ioannina prospered and the community grew, with new populations coming from Spain and Sicily. With the entry of Ioannina into the modern state of Greece in 1913, certain restrictions were placed on the Jews, such as moving the market day to Saturday and not allowing store openings on Sunday. The religious Jews emigrated to Jerusalem at this time. Others seeking better economic opportunities emigrated to Athens and New York. The community literally was decimated during the years of World War II. Many of the survivors who returned emigrated to other Greek cities or to other countries very quickly. Others who had served in the Communist wartime resistance movement were persecuted. Over the past forty years, the community has been reduced to its present size of approximately fifty individuals.

Settlements

Settlements are essentially urban. Ioannina remains a major provincial capital of governmental, military, and commercial importance. Traditionally, the Jewish community centered on the synagogue and the marketplace. Distinct Jewish neighborhoods, both inside and outside the Byzantine walled city (_kastro_), were established but were by no means exclusively Jewish. Jewish homes were often distinguished by the presence of a frame for the _sukkah_, constructed in the fall festival of Sukkot, and a wood-burning oven for the preparation of kosher meals and the baking of Sabbath bread. Up to World War II families established shops and homes in the smaller towns of the region. They returned to Ioannina for major holiday celebrations and their children were often sent there for schooling. Young men from Ioannina trained to read the Torah would also be sent to some of these settlements for holiday celebrations.

Economy

The Greek-speaking Jews were primarily engaged as merchants. Many were in the textile business, selling ready-made fabrics, manufacturing textiles, and thread. A noted home industry of the Jewish women was the production of card-woven garters (_kaltsodetes_), for the stockings of Greek Christian men's traditional dress, as well as silk culture. Other Jewish businesses included that of butcher or animal factor, small goods or haberdashery shops, and brokerages for property or wholesale goods. A few members of the community were employed as professionals such as doctors, teachers, and lawyers. Today, Jewish shops sell household goods, furniture, clothing, and fabrics. One man repairs tin utensils for the villagers. Two young men run an electric repair shop. One man, educated in the United States, teaches at the University of Ioannina.

Kinship, Marriage, and Family

Kinship. The Jews of Ioannina are historically extended families with a patriarchal authority structure and patrilineal inheritance of surnames. In the past, nicknames were used extensively to distinguish between family members; they frequently supplanted surnames. Kinship is reckoned bilaterally.

Marriage. Traditionally, marriages were arranged through a system of matchmakers. This pattern is still practiced regularly in the late twentieth century, with partners coming from other cities in Greece. Intermarriage with Greek Christians is a common occurrence. Postmarital residence is usually in the home or, more recently, in the city of the husband's family. Today, the couple usually lives alone in a furnished apartment, which is part of the wife's dowry.

Domestic Unit. The domestic unit is often a nuclear family, although widowed parents will live with the family or in an adjacent apartment. There are two or three children in the average family. Before World War II, marriage between first cousins was a common practice.

Sociopolitical Organization

The synagogue and the Jewish communal offices are the centers of the community. Most members of the community live in close proximity to each other in a communally owned apartment house, which was built in the 1960s, and in neighboring homes. They are thus in daily contact with each other. Interaction on the business level is with both Jews and Christians. Generally, few members of the Jewish community have in-depth social contact with the Christians. As in other Jewish communities, self-help societies (_hevrot_) traditionally were active in Ioannina, including the society for poor brides, the society for the poor, and the burial society. Only the last is still in existence today. Other Jewish affiliation is with the KIS, the central Jewish organization in Athens, which monitors all community affairs in the country and provides financial assistance.

Religion and Expressive Culture

Religion. The Greek-speaking Jews of Greece are traditional Jews. Originally, the community had two synagogues with attached chapels or _minyans_ for smaller numbers of worshipers. The one located outside of the kastro was destroyed in the bombing during World War II. Holidays and life-cycle rituals were practiced in a manner peculiar to the community. These celebrations included Irtaman, a carnival-like celebration on the first day of the Jewish month of Adar, and the Purim Katan (small Purim), called the Siciliano, which was brought to the city by immigrants from Sicily. Homes were scrupulously kosher and several wealthier homes had built-in *mikvahs* (ritual baths). Religious practice is minimal now because of the reduced numbers of the community. The synagogue is cleaned and opened for major holidays, when a rabbi from Athens or Salonika is brought in to lead services. The laws of kosher practice are rarely followed, neither the eating of kosher meats nor the separation of milk and meat. The young people are sent to summer camp and annual seminars sponsored by KIS to learn about the Jewish traditions and to meet other Jewish youths.

Arts.   The most evident characteristic of the traditional expressive culture of the Greek-speaking Jews is the use of the Greek language in songs in popular settings and for festival and life-cycle celebrations. Songs at weddings are sung in demotic Greek. Two traditional songs sung in the home after the Passover seder, "One Goat" (Had Gadya) and "Who Knows One?" (Echod Mi Yodea), are also sung in Greek.

Bibliography

Attal, Robert (1984). *Les Juifs de Grèce: Bibliographie.* Jerusalem: Institute Ben-Zvi.

Bowman, Steven B. (1984). *The Jews of Byzantium, 1204–1453.* University: University of Alabama Press.

Matsas, Iosef M. (1953). *Yiannotika Evraika Tragoudia.* Ioannina: Ekthosis Eperotikes Estias.

Mazur, Belle D. (1935). *Studies on Jewry in Greece.* Vol. 1. Athens: Printing Office "Hestia."

ANNETTE B. FROMM

Gypsies and Caravan Dwellers in the Netherlands

ETHNONYMS: Buitenlandse Zigeuners (foreign Gypsies), Nederlandse Zigeuners (Dutch Gypsies), Woonwagenbewoners (caravan dwellers)

Orientation

Identification.   Gypsies and caravan dwellers, often seen by the Dutch population as members of one and the same group, have been in an isolated position since the nineteenth century. They are distinct from the general population in terms of their way of life and housing (a caravan). The most important difference between the two groups is that most car-

avan dwellers are indigenous Dutch, whereas Gypsies came from elsewhere. For different reasons both groups chose a mobile life-style during the nineteenth and twentieth centuries. The Dutch Gypsies can be divided into Sinti (82 percent) and Roma (18 percent). The Sinti, coming from Germany, France, and Belgium, entered the Netherlands in the first half of the nineteenth century. The Roma (mostly Lowara) arrived around 1900 from Romania and Hungary. They left these countries about 1860 and before coming to the Netherlands first traveled through Germany, France, and Scandinavia. Both groups settled more or less permanently and obtained Dutch citizenship. Apart from these Dutch Gypsies we can distinguish the so-called foreign Gypsies, who left Eastern Europe from 1960 on and stayed for some time in Italy and France. From there small groups annually roamed throughout Western Europe, also visiting the Netherlands. Because they were considered unwanted aliens everywhere, the Dutch government decided in 1978 to legalize a limited number.

Demography.   There are about 800 foreign Gypsies living in the Netherlands. The number of Dutch Gypsies is estimated at 2,700, 90 percent of whom live on caravan sites. The total number of caravan dwellers is about 20,000.

History and Cultural Relations

The history of Dutch Gypsies can be divided into three periods. The first period, from 1420 to about 1750, began when a small group of wandering people appeared in the Netherlands. They said they were pilgrims from "Little Egypt" and were soon called *Egyptenaren* (Egyptians) and *heidens* (heathens). In the beginning they were received reasonably hospitably. This attitude changed around 1500 when government policy toward them became increasingly repressive. They were accused of being spies for the Turks and were prohibited from dwelling in the Netherlands, as well as in surrounding countries. Heidens caught by the authorities were to be punished and banned. Their sheer presence was enough for persecution. This policy was also motivated by accusations that they troubled the population by begging, stealing, and fraud. Toward the end of the seventeenth century the persecution intensified, resulting in their being driven to criminal acts. By then the authorities had become overtly violent and in some provinces a reward was offered for every heiden, dead or alive. As a reaction to their outlaw status, the Gypsies formed gangs and their crimes became more and more serious. This escalation of violence ended in an attempt at extermination. Those who escaped went into hiding or fled to surrounding countries, such as Germany and France.

The second period, from 1750 to 1868, was one during which the authorities were convinced that there were no longer any heidens living in the Netherlands and therefore did not maintain any specific policy regarding them. The negative image of the group, however, was kept alive by diverse sources and the memory of the "stealing and murdering heidens" remained.

The third period, from 1868 to the present, began when Hungarian coppersmiths (also called Kaldarash) and Bosnian bear leaders (Ursari) and their families entered the country in 1868 and the government reacted negatively. The foreigners were immediately "recognized" as heidens, a term soon replaced by the new label "Zigeuners" (Gypsies). The

Kaldarash and Ursari were thought to possess the same vices as their presumed predecessors, the heidens. The stereotypes of the authorities were so deeply rooted that, although the Hungarian coppersmiths and Bosnian bear leaders were self-sufficient and appreciated by the population for their skills and services, the central government defined them as unwanted aliens. The military police, among whose duties was the guarding of the borders, was instructed to remove all Zigeuners as soon as possible. Most of the Kaldarash and Ursari were, however, only passing through, on their way to the United States. After the turn of the century they appeared only sporadically. From 1900 onward their place was taken by the Lowara, a subgroup of the Kaldarash, who had changed their profession to horse dealing and who had managed to obtain German, French, and Norwegian passports. The Lowara were not immediately "recognized" as Gypsies, since they did not conform to the dominating "Hungarian image." Although they earned enough money through horse dealing, the central authorities nevertheless looked upon them as parasites. Contrary to the Kaldarash and Ursari, the horse dealers settled in the Netherlands and succeeded in obtaining a firm footing with the cooperation of municipal authorities. After some time (around 1930) the "Hungarian image" faded in importance and the Lowara were definitely regarded as Gypsies. At the same time a fourth group, the Sinti, specialists in music and other forms of amusement, were also labeled as Gypsies. They appeared to have been living for generations in the Netherlands already, but up to that time they were not regarded as Gypsies.

In the 1930s the anti-Gypsy policy was intensified and many Lowara and Sinti were registered as such. This made it easy for the Dutch authorities to pick them up during World War II and deliver them to the Nazis. Because of their presumed race, 245 of them were finally sent to Auschwitz. Only 30 of them survived. Together with family members who managed to go into hiding they returned to the caravan sites after the war and tried to continue their way of life. This became more and more difficult as the government encouraged a sedentary life-style and discouraged free traveling. Moreover, the recollection of the cooperation of Dutch authorities at the time of the Nazi raids in 1944 greatly increased their isolation from Dutch society.

We know very little about the history of Dutch caravan dwellers. People began to live in caravans for the first time around 1880. Some of them did so because that type of dwelling made it easier to practice their ambulant professions, such as basket making, knife grinding, and chair mending; others ended up in caravans because of a housing shortage. In general they traveled within a limited region. During the twentieth century they have become a distinct subcultural group in the lower strata of Dutch society.

Settlements

In the past, almost all caravan dwellers and Dutch Gypsies lived in so-called *woonwagenkampen* (caravan camps), mostly in immobile caravans. Only in the summer did some of them use a smaller mobile caravan and leave the sites for some time. A minority of Dutch Gypsies also lived in houses. The foreign Gypsies used to live in caravans and tents, but after their legalization they were placed in houses in ten municipalities throughout the country.

After the war the concept of integration gained increasing acceptance among government officials. The opportunity to travel was minimized and the majority of Gypsies and caravan dwellers found themselves, socially and economically, living on "a dead-end street."

Traveling nowadays has only a symbolic function for them. The option of a caravan is obviously discouraged. Only the children of caravan dwellers can officially get a new permit to live in a caravan. But the reality is that they can find a house in a certain municipality or neighborhood more readily than an official site in a caravan camp. In the long run the goal of the government is sedentary housing. This is best illustrated by its policy toward foreign Gypsies, who were put up in houses from the moment of their legalization in 1978.

Economy

In contrast to the negative stereotype of Gypsies, the history of the Kaldarash, Ursari, Lowara, and Sinti in the Netherlands makes it clear that they fulfilled a useful economic function and in general were able to provide for their livelihood. The Kaldarash were praised for their skill in mending copper and tin objects, especially kettles. They not only worked for the rural population, but also received orders from local shopkeepers and industry. In the twentieth century they worked for bakers and dairy factories. They did not have a monopoly position in their trade; their nomadic life-style was too unpredictable. Nevertheless they were successful until World War II. The Ursari earned a good living by their performances. They taught their bears, and sometimes monkeys, to dance and do all kinds of tricks. These activities were especially appreciated by the rural population, because it was a welcome distraction from their monotonous daily life. This can be deduced from the sometimes impressive wealth of the Ursari and also from letters sent by local authorities who pleaded in their support against the accusations of the central government. Because of a ban on performances with bears during the Nazi occupation, the Ursari exchanged them in the 1930s for monkeys and street organs.

The history of the Kaldarash and Lowara in the Netherlands shows that the prevalent opinion that Gypsies hold on to traditional and outdated professions is false. It is likely that as a result of the diminishing demand for the services of coppersmiths at the end of the nineteenth century many Kaldarash shifted to the horse trade. In the following decades they became known as Lowara. This is an illuminating example of economic adaptation, as this market was booming in western Europe and remained important until World War II. The Lowara more or less controlled the trade in cobs at the Dutch horse fairs and made an important contribution to this economic sector. The Sinti were mainly show people and concentrated on juggling, acrobatics, music, and dancing. In the course of the twentieth century many felt forced to restrict themselves to music and became popular musicians in cafés, pubs, and restaurants. Apart from this they traded in violins, which they also made and repaired.

After World War II, the Dutch Gypsies—both caravan dwellers and foreign Gypsies—did not occupy a stable position in the labor market, but they remained adaptable. However, because they were discouraged from traveling, they did not succeed in increasing their job opportunities. At present about 90 percent of the three groups receive social-security benefits. They try to supplement this income by all kinds of small-scale activities, such as selling automobiles, peddling, playing music, etc.

Kinship, Marriage, and Family

Until recently Gypsies used to live as extended families and therefore retained especially strong extended-family ties. Social-security benefits have made them more independent, however, and they have begun to adopt a nuclear family structure. In addition to these family connections there also exist among the Roma work and travel units, which are more or less flexible economic entities, called *kumpanias*. They can include part of a family or a caravan camp.

With respect to marriage we know that only 5 percent of the Dutch Gypsies have married a non-Gypsy. The older generation in particular stresses the importance of endogamy.

Sociopolitical Organization

Social Organization. The position of Gypsies and caravan dwellers in the Netherlands can only be understood in the light of the role of the Dutch judicial authorities in the last century, when they had the authority to label widely different groups as deviant. Thus the necessary conditions for the label of "Gypsy" were: traveling as a family, an overtly nomadic lifestyle, and a foreign origin. Begging and a poor appearance were of secondary importance. Around the turn of the century the call for jurisdiction to restrict the number of people living in caravans, foreigners as well as natives, became stronger. This led to the *Woonwagenwet* (Caravan Act) in 1918. The dominant idea behind this legislation was that caravan dwellers were antisocial, refused to work, and bothered the inhabitants of the country. The only difference between the Dutch caravan dwellers and the Gypsies was that the former were considered a domestic problem, the latter a problem that concerned aliens. Because of the institutionalization of the policy toward aliens around 1930, all groups that fulfilled these conditions were considered undesirable. Because the nomadic way of life was seen as outspoken antisocial behavior, the government emphasized the alleged indecent and immoral aspects of such groups. Cohabitation by adults was easily associated with unbridled sexuality, and it was assumed that their children would come to no good and continue the deviant life-style of their parents. This view corresponded with the general stigmatizing of so-called antisocials, who in the twentieth century faced constant attempts to "civilize" them.

During World War II this attitude reached its peak. The Dutch call for special camps to resocialize caravan dwellers was welcomed by the Nazis. Because of their racial ideas, however, they differentiated between antisocials and Gypsies. Consequently, the latter group was sent to a concentration camp, while the others escaped this fate.

Political Organization. Gypsies are not really integrated into the formal system of Dutch society. Even among themselves, they generally form alliances only on an informal basis. In the fight for the legalization of foreign Gypsies, however, they founded the pressure group Vereniging Rom (1977). Later followed the Vereniging Lau Mazirel (1982), the Internationaal Romano Comité (1986), and the Landelijke Vereniging Sinti (1989). The caravan dwellers have set up two organizations: Landelijk Platform Woonwagenbewoners en Zigeuners and Landelijk Overleg Woonwagenvrouwen.

Religion. No anthropological field research has been done in the Netherlands on the cultural aspects of Gypsies and caravan dwellers. We only have some information about their religious beliefs. Dutch Gypsies in general adopted the religion of the region where they settled. Almost all of them became Roman Catholics. About one-third recently converted to the Pentecostal church, spreading from France, whose influence among European Gypsies is increasing. A separate "Gypsy mission" has been founded with its own organization, journal (*Leven en Licht*), and meetings. Among the foreign Gypsies we can discern Muslim and Eastern Orthodox beliefs. The Dutch caravan dwellers are predominantly Roman Catholic.

Bibliography

Cottaar, Annemarie, Leo Lucassen, and Wim Willems (1988). "Een zwerver verdwaald: Balans en perspectief van het onderzoek naar Zigeuners en Woonwagenbewoners in Nederland." In *Zigeuners in Nederland: Cultuur, geschiedenis en beleid*, edited by P. Hovens and R. Dahler, 113–144. Nijmegen and Rijswijk.

Lucassen, Leo (1990). *En men noemde hen Zigeuners. De geschiedenis van Zigeuners in Nederland: 1750–1944.* Amsterdam: Stichting beheer IISG: SDV Uitgeverij.

Overbekking, Annet Hahn, and René Geerts (1987). *Nederlandse Zigeuners en burgermaatschappij: Een eeuwigdurend schaakspel.* Nijmegen.

Willems, Wim, and Leo Lucassen (1990). *Ongewenste vreemdelingen. Buitenlandse Zigeuners en de Nederlandse overheid: 1969–1989.* Leiden: SDV Uitgeverij.

WIM WILLEMS AND LEO LUCASSEN

Highland Scots

ETHNONYMS: Celts, Celtic, Highlander, Scots, Scottish, and sometimes Scotch. West coast islanders sometimes refer to themselves and others by island names, such as a Lewis man, a Barra woman.

Middle English "Scottes," Old English "Scottas," Late Latin "Scotus" are references to Gaelic people from northern Ireland who settled in Scotland about A.D. 500.

Orientation

Identification and Location. The Highlands of Scotland include the lands north of a line from the town of Inverness on the northeast running south and west to a point 56° N and 5° W in Scotland, encompassing the shires of Caithness, Sutherland, Ross and Cromarty, Inverness, and Argyll, as well as the islands making up the Inner and Outer Hebrides. Geographically, this area is characterized by rolling rock-faced hills and scattered lakes and rivers, interspersed with land covered by a thin layer of peaty soil. Temperatures along the coasts are fairly consistent (4.4° to 13° C) with colder temperatures inland. In mid-June, daylight may extend to midnight; in mid-December, there is daylight for only a few hours.

Demography. The 1981 census reported a population of 200,000, an increase of 14.3 percent over the previous decade. There was also a slight increase in population from 1951 to 1971. These figures indicate a change in what had been a steady decline in population beginning in the mid-1700s. These increases are the result of gains in the number of people in the urban and burgh populations, which have offset losses in rural areas.

Linguistic Affiliation. Historically, the early settlers spoke Gaelic. English has been the official language since 1754, but there remain some local dialect variations of Gaelic spoken in a few areas of the west coast, Argyll, Sutherland, Skye, and the Western Isles. Recent attempts to renew interest in written and spoken Gaelic have been undertaken, including Gaelic programming on BBC-Scotland.

History and Cultural Relations

The division of Scotland into two cultural areas, the Highlands and the Lowlands, can be traced to the works of early writers who romanticized rural life in northern Scotland. Anthropological research, which began in the 1950s, accepted this distinction, and most of the ethnographic data have been collected in small rural communities.

The history of the Highlands has been characterized by a number of events that have led to the present-day conditions. There has been a steady deforestation of the Highlands since 1700. The clan system was broken up following the 1715 and 1745 conflicts with England. An increase in population, coupled with declining resources, placed great hardships on the people throughout the eighteenth century. The nineteenth century proved even more calamitous. In the Hebrides, for example, the cheviot was introduced in 1810; the kelp industry diminished after 1821; the potato blight occurred in 1828; and the herring disappeared in 1830. The cheviot, a species of sheep able to withstand severe winter conditions, replaced people who were cleared from the land beginning in 1828. The years 1846 and 1847 witnessed the potato famine throughout the Highlands. The policy of the government was that the laird was responsible for the welfare of the people living on estates. In 1883 the Napier Commission redefined the responsibility of government, an action which eventually led to the government's becoming the largest landholder in the Highlands and thus having greater responsibility for the social and economic needs of the residents. The 1886 Crofter Act gave lands to individuals and established the crofting system.

Settlements

Inverness is the largest city, with a population of 57,000 in 1981. On the east coast, the town of Wick is the largest remaining sea-fishing port. On the west coast, Kyle of Lochalsh, Ullapool, Mallaig, and Stornaway have active fish sales and harbor facilities. The settlement pattern in these communities focuses on the harbor. Houses are close together and there are few streets. Another settlement pattern is associated with crofting. Crofting was established with the 1886 Crofting Act. The croft is a 0.4- to 2-hectare parcel of land, on which the crofter has the right to build a house. In addition, the crofter enjoys common rights to grazing land and access to peat as a source of fuel. Crofting has largely disappeared, and crofts today are often holiday homes used only during the summer months, with the grazing rights given or rented to others. The majority of crofting townships are located along the coast at an elevation lower than 75 meters. This pattern reflects the dual adaptation of crofting-fishing. Croft houses are usually one-story dwellings arranged in a scattered or lineal pattern with wide separation between dwellings. The crofting community might contain a post office and a small shop. The most recent housing and settlement pattern is attached flats built by the Forestry Commission to house employees engaged in reforestation efforts.

Economy

Work Cycles in Crofting. While the Highland Scots have a somewhat mixed economy, most of the literature focuses on crofting and fishing. The intensity of participation in these activities is partially determined by seasonal changes. In crofting communities agricultural work requires interhousehold cooperation for tilling, planting, and peat cutting from March to April. Potatoes and oats are the main agricultural products. Harvesting of oats is in August; potatoes in October. Intense and extended cooperation is required in April or May when lambing takes place.

Work Cycles in Fishing. Fishing has had a differential impact on local economies, either as a food source or wage labor. In the Outer Hebrides, agriculture has never provided enough for self-sufficiency, and incomes have been supplemented by exporting cattle or by fishing. During the summer months, herring is available fresh; for the winter, salt herring is purchased. In the nineteenth and the early twentieth century, crofters worked on foreign-owned boats engaged in commercial herring fishing. The crofter-fishermen, and sometimes women, would follow the migrating herring north to Shetland and then down the east coast to East Anglia in England. In other locations (e.g., Skye) there was very little fishing by crofters. Since World War II some Highland Scots have obtained grants and loans, along with training, to become commercial fishermen. They are found at the major ports on both the east and west coasts. Smaller boats are sometimes used by the crofter-fishermen to catch lobsters, which can provide a cash income. There has been some attempt to develop small fish-processing factories that employ local labor. In general, since the turn of the twentieth century there has been a decline in the numbers of crofter-fishermen. ʹ̇hose areas that have specialized in fishing the population as either remained constant or has increased.

ʹm.   Another contribution to local economies is ᴜrism. The clearances of the eighteenth and nineteenth centuries were not only responsible for the depopulation of the Highlands; they also introduced tourism. Deer and salmon, once a source of food, attracted and continue to attract outsiders who are willing to pay for the rights to hunt and fish these animals. The pheasant was even introduced in the middle of the nineteenth century as a sport bird. Hunting and fishing do provide employment for gamekeepers and gillies, along with temporary work for beaters who drive the game to waiting hunters. Poaching of deer, salmon, and sea trout may provide some illegal income for Highlanders. But the major source of tourist income comes during the summer months. These temporary visitors require housing, camping sites, food, and other services that employ local labor and younger workers from other parts of Great Britain. When the migrant labor and the tourists leave at the end of the summer, public entertainments, such as galas and dances, disappear.

Industrial Arts.   Knitting, weaving, and craft work for export provide income for some Highlanders. This is largely a home industry.

Division of Labor.   In crofting communities, male/female distinctions in labor vary by activity and historical time period. In the Hebrides, during the herring days, the most significant group of wage earners were the "herring girls," women who followed the herring fleet, gutting and packing the fish. On Lewis, when the men were away fishing, the croft and home were operated by women. In traditional activities such as peat gathering, men cut the peat blocks while women lifted them into creels and took them to where they were stacked. In Glen Fhraoich, the household was democratic in principle, but two major activity domains existed. The women's domain included the interior of the house, the "green" and the "byre." The area between the house and the byre, which contained the peat pile, henhouse, and clothesline were also included in her domain. The men's domain encompassed the wider croft area, the fields, peat bogs, and common grazing area. In addition, men were the only wage laborers. This same pattern was observed on Lewis, except that the men's domain included the fishing boat as well. Decisions involving major purchases were joint unless one partner relinquished his/her authority. In crofting, the household is the economic unit, and regardless of the number of people in the household, there is only one male and one female in charge. Armstrong found that women in Kilmory worked in the fish factory, shops, or in activities associated with tourism. With the decline of the male-dominated fishing industry, the role of women has become increasingly important. On Barra, Valee found decreasing differences in the sexual division of labor. In the study of Kinlochleven, an industrial community, there were fewer and lower-paying jobs for females than for males.

Outside the household, the division of labor is rooted in occupational differences. On Harris, this distinction is sometimes marked by language. Crofters or fishermen speak Gaelic; professionals speak English. In Kintyre there is casual labor including road work, forestry, and seasonal services to tourists. On Islay the major occupations are working in the distillery, limestone quarrying, and farm and estate work. The historical trend has been away from employment in agriculture. For the Highlands, including Orkney and Shetland, between 1871 and 1971 the proportion of agricultural workers declined from 40.5 percent of the work force to 9.9 percent.

Development.   In 1965, the Highlands were designated a development area, and the Highlands and Islands Development Board was established to increase industrial production, alleviate unemployment, and stem out-migration. Grants have been given to maintain crofting and develop local industries. Another development scheme has been the reforestation of certain areas of the Highlands. Although forestry accounts for just over 2 percent of the total employment, it is four times more important to the Highlands than to the United Kingdom as a whole. The oil industry has contributed to some local commercial, service, and construction industries. A major theoretical dispute related to the role of development has emerged in the recent literature on the Highlands. One observation is that the Highlands are simply underdeveloped and have had a history of boom-and-bust cycles since 1700. Others suggest that the Highlands are part of a larger capitalistic economy, and "traditionalism" is an adaptive response to that economy, not some form of vestigial survival from a past state of peasantry. Condry observes that characteristics associated with "traditional" Highlands culture were "modern" practices of the past, and he suggests that such "modern" practices of the present will become absorbed into future "traditionalism."

Kinship, Marriage, and Family

Kin Groups and Descent.   While descent is bilateral, there is an emphasis upon patrilateral kin in actual practice. The household is the organizational unit of descent and consists of an unbroken line of males.

Kinship Terminology.   Kinship terminology differs depending on whether English or Gaelic is used. Gaelic has fewer terms than English (e.g., English "uncle" is "mother's brother" in Gaelic). Naming of children usually follows the tradition of "turn and turn about": one spouse chooses a name for one child; the other spouse selects the name of the next child.

Marriage.   The selection of spouses depends upon demographic possibilities and economic conditions. Where there are inheritance considerations, marriages are often postponed until the person is over the age of 30 or until after the death of parents. Marriages are sometimes postponed if there is a shortage of housing. If women have migrated from an area, the remaining men may face a shortage of eligible women that necessitates their going outside the community for wives. The overall pattern seems to be a shift from community endogamy to exogamy. There are few reports on nuptial rituals. However, one study reported that wedding gifts tend to be lavish and are publicly displayed. Weddings are usually held in hotels, and guests are transported to the wedding and the postnuptial celebration by bus.

Domestic Unit. The household is the organizational unit of kinship, and much of crofting life can be understood in reference to problems related to the formation of households. Spinsters, for example, are explained as those reluctant to give away inherited property and the power associated with that property when they marry. Property is a consideration prior to marriage, especially among crofters where extended families may occupy the croft. Under these conditions, the person who moves into the croft of their spouse is subservient to the spouse's parents until they die. In noncroft settings the pattern is neolocality. Regardless of the economic base, the function of marriage is to produce children, and the household is established for this purpose.

Family. The boundaries of "family" are determined by propinquity. Kin living nearby are included as family; those who have moved away, even if they are closer kin, are not. The household is the smallest unit with which one identifies and through which one is identified. The attributes of the male head of the household characterize all members of that household. Thus, if the male is viewed as clever, all members of the household are viewed as clever. The household consists of the male head, his wife, their children, and, if only daughters, the eldest's husband. Adult siblings have equal rights to remain in the household, but each is expected to contribute to the household. Outside the household, emotions are rarely publicly expressed. However, members of the household engage in intimate joking relationships. The structure of the household can produce conflict. In disputes between wife and mother, husband is expected to support his wife. In households where there is a wife and sister-in-law and the wife is the female head of house by virtue of her marriage, the sister-in-law may feel proprietary rights because she was a member of the household first. Beyond the household are more inclusive identifiers. From less to more inclusive are the household, the croft, the township, the glen (demarcated by a steep hill dividing townships), and the parish.

Inheritance. In croft systems, propinquity and sex are determinates of inheritance. The eldest and remaining son usually inherits the croft. When there is only a daughter, her husband becomes the head of the household after his father-in-law dies, and his sons will inherit.

Sociopolitical Organization

Social Organization. The clan was a historical political group with a hereditary chief who controlled lands in common. Consanguine links between members was either demonstrated or stipulated. The clan system was abolished in 1746 after the battle of Culloden. Today the term "clan" is used to designate all the descendants of a particular person, usually cognates.

In general, few distinctions in social status are found. Where a laird is present in a community, he is recognized as a leader. A laird is the traditional landowner. The factor, the man who manages land for the laird, is usually respected because of his role in mediating relationships between laird and crofters. High status or prestige may vary by institutional ar-

rangement. Religious prestige is highest for ministers, missionaries, and lay elders. Cultural prestige is awarded to bards, musicians, and "Gaelic scholars." Political-communal prestige is associated with "good" works such as participation in local committees. In Gaelic-speaking communities this category is usually occupied by "outsiders" whose work is done in English—for example, the schoolteacher(s), the local doctor, and the nurse(s). Prestige distinctions are governed by Calvinistic virtues, which, if pursued, will result in high standing in the bank and the community. Display of wealth is considered immoral and there is a marked absence of distinctions in housing, food, and clothing. Vocatively, social distinctions are often reflected in terms of address. Professionals (most often outsiders) are addressed by formal title (e.g., Mr., Mrs., Dr.). Persons from the community are addressed by first name.

Political Organization. The principal units of local government are either the town or the county councils, which are made up of elected and appointed officials.

Social Control. Leveling seems to be a powerful force in maintaining social similarities. Locals who return to the community with a formal education are often disliked because they showed evidence of a desire to "get ahead." Persons whose peat stacks are not neat will lose prestige. One is expected to carry out business relationships with people one knows and on a personal basis. Outsiders, and agencies outside the community, are viewed as too far away for meaningful interaction.

Alcoholism rates are high for Scotland in general and the Highlands in particular. The islands of Lewis and Harris have an alcoholism rate six times higher than Scotland. They also have the highest admission rates for involutional melancholia in the United Kingdom. The ethic that one does not publicly criticize others takes precedence over drunken behavior, which often leads to a general disregard for the problem at the local level. Very low rates are reported for delinquency.

Conflict. Personal disputes do occur. Darling reports that petty bickering often occurs about precise boundary lines between properties. In households where no will has been left, intense intrafamily conflict may occur.

Religion and Expressive Culture

Religious Beliefs and Practices. Both Catholicism and Protestantism are practiced in the Highlands. Evangelical Protestantism came in the early nineteenth century. It is associated with the breakup of the clan and opposition to the system of laird-appointed ministers of the Church of Scotland. The Free Church broke from the Established Church (Presbyterian) in 1843 over the issue of land reform. It has become the church of the people and has the largest number of adherents. The Church of Scotland has a smaller number of parishioners and tends to be the church of those with official power. On Lewis, the three principal churches are the Free Church of Scotland, the Established Church of Scotland, and the Free Presbyterian Church. The Free Church is the largest, but the Free Presbyterian is perhaps the most influential regarding community sentiment. It espouses the Calvinistic doctrine of self-denial, otherworldly orientation, and the notion of the elect. The elect are those chosen by God. The church offers the greatest single social outlet for women, who otherwise lead a life largely restricted to the household. Women are also a majority in both the Free Church and the Church of Scotland.

Catholic and Protestant communities vary in their involvement in social issues. The Protestants are most active. In Protestant communities the rates of alcoholism and mental disorders are highest.

Medicine.   Medical care is provided by local physicians under the National Health system. For those illnesses or accidents outside the capability of local health-care units, patients are transported to regional or national hospitals. The aging of the population has led to greater demand for Home Help Services and a large percentage of social-service funding is allocated for this government program. Home Help provides services for the aged and infirm who are unable to take care of themselves, and it provides employment for women who might otherwise be ineligible for other support.

Death and Afterlife.   In Catholic Barra, when death is imminent, the priest is called to deliver the last rites, after which the close relatives maintain a constant vigil. After death, the responsibilities for the funeral are assumed by the oldest ablebodied male relative. Women usually volunteer to wash and clothe the body. Some social activities may be curtailed for the period between death and the funeral. Usually this includes the neighborhood of the deceased as well as close family members. Pallbearers are male. The eldest responsible male walks in front of the casket; the eldest responsible female follows the casket. Catholics and Protestants are buried in the same cemetery.

Bibliography

Condry, Edward (1983). *Scottish Ethnography*. Association for Scottish Ethnography, Monograph no. 1. Social Science Research Council. New York.

Ennew, J. (1977). "The Impact of Oil-Related Industry on the Outer Hebrides, with Particular Reference to Stornoway, Isle of Lewis." Ph.D. dissertation, University of Cambridge.

Parman, Susan M. (1972). "Sociocultural Change in a Scottish Crofting Township." Ph.D. dissertation, Rice University, Houston, Tex.

Vallee, F. G. (1954). "Social Structure and Organization in a Hebridean Community: A Study of Social Change." Ph.D. dissertation, London School of Economics.

ED KNIPE

Hungarians

ETHNONYMS: Magyarok, Magyars

Orientation

Identification.   Hungarians are the most populous group in the Finno-Ugric Subfamily of the Ural-Altaic people. They are considered to be the descendants of the Magyar tribes that migrated from the Ural mountain region and that settled in the Carpathian Basin during the ninth century. Hungary (Magyarország) was declared a republic (Magyar Köztársaság) in October 1989.

Location.   A landlocked country since 1920, Hungary is bounded on the north by the Czech and Slovak Federative Republic, on the east by Ukraine and Romania, on the west by Austria, and on the south-southwest by Slovenia, Croatia, and Yugoslavia. The country occupies 93,030 square kilometers or 1 percent of the total land area of Europe. It is located between 45°48′ and 48°35′ N, and 16°05′ and 22°58′ E. To the east of the Danube River lies the Great Hungarian Plain (Alföld) with some of the finest agricultural land in the country. To the west of the river is Transdanubia (Dunántúl). With the exception of low mountains in the north and rolling hills and low mountains in Transdanubia, most of Hungary is flat: 8 percent of its land area lies less than 200 meters above sea level. The country is located in a transitional zone between maritime and continental climates. Most winters are cold, and the summers are hot. The average annual temperature is 8° C in the north and 12° C in the south.

Demography.   In January of 1989 Hungary's population was estimated at 10,590,000 with an ethnic composition of 97.7 percent Magyar, 0.5 percent German, 0.3 percent Slovak, 0.8 percent Gypsy, 0.3 percent Croatian, and 0.4 percent other. The population density averages 114 persons per square kilometer. More than one-fourth of the population is over the age of retirement, which is 55 for women and 60 for men. With a very low birthrate, one of the highest mortality rates in Europe for mature and middle-aged men, and the highest suicide rate in the world, Hungary's population has been decreasing since 1981. Also, in part because of high outmigration from villages, the rural population has declined since World War II. Now 42 percent of the country's population is concentrated in rural settlements, but many Hungarians commute and work in cities. Urban dwellers make up about 58 percent of the population; 20 percent of the total population resides in Budapest, Hungary's capital city.

Linguistic Affiliation.   All the neighboring cultures belong to the Indo-European Family of languages, but Hungarian is a member of the eastern division, the Ugric Group of the Finno-Ugric Language Family. Hungarian is an agglutinative language, without prepositions and auxiliary words; it is characterized by an extensive use of suffixes. It is written in Latin script with additional letters and diacritical marks. This language is spoken by about 10 million people within Hungary and an additional 5 million distributed around the world. From the 5 million about 3.5 million live in the surrounding countries (Romania, the Czech and Slovak Federative Republic, Yugoslavia, Austria, and Ukraine), while the remaining 1.5 million settled in Canada, the United States, and elsewhere. Hungarian is distantly related to Estonian and Finnish.

History and Cultural Relations

The tribal Magyars, Uralo-Altaic nomadic people by origin, entered the Carpathian Basin in 896, led by Árpád, their chieftain. After several military campaigns into western Europe and the Balkans, the Hungarian state was established in 1000 under King Stephen I, who accepted Christianity for the country. This conversion was confirmed by Pope Sylvester II, who symbolized with a gift of a crown Hungary's entry into the European feudal community. The Latin alphabet was introduced, but the original runic script (*rovásírás*) was used for centuries. In the early twelfth century King Coloman "the Scholar" abolished witch hunts and updated all previous laws governing the country's affairs. King Béla III in 1180 ordered record keeping for all official business. A century later, in 1222 King Andreas II issued "the Golden Bull" (Aranybulla), a code that specified both the nation's rights and the king's obligation to uphold the country's laws. A more representative parliamentary system was introduced in 1384. In the thirteenth century Hungary was invaded by Tartars, reducing the population to one-tenth of its former size. After Turks invaded the Balkans, János Hunyadi and Fr. Capistrano won a decisive victory in 1456 at Nándorfehérvár (now Belgrade, Yugoslavia). Christian church bells tolling daily at noon still commemorate this victory. During his reign between 1458 and 1490 Matthias Corvinus, the son of János Hunyadi, built up both the economy and a powerful nation-state, while he introduced the culture of the Renaissance. At that time, the population of Hungary equaled that of England and France (4 million people). After Matthias's death, however, there came a period of feudal anarchy and, for the serfs, destitution and oppression. A peasant revolt in 1514 was crushed by the Magyar nobility. After the peasant war still heavier burdens were imposed on the serfs. Ottoman Turks defeated the weakened country in 1526 at Mohács and occupied the central plains of Hungary for 156 years. Hungary's western and northern regions were ruled by the Austrian Habsburgs. The eastern zone and Transylvania became a semi-independent principality. Thousands of Serbs, Romanians, and others fled from the Turkish-occupied Balkans to this principality. In 1557 the Diet of Torda, Transylvania, enacted a law proclaiming freedom of religion. Finally, in the late 1600s Habsburg forces drove the Turks out of Hungary. Then the Habsburgs took control, reunited the country, and settled thousands of Germans in depopulated areas. Led by Ferenc Rákóczi, Hungarians rose in 1703 against Habsburg colonization but were defeated, with Russian intervention, in 1711. Reform movements culminated in another attempt to obtain freedom in the revolt of 1848–1849, led by Lajos Kossuth, which was ultimately crushed by the Habsburgs with the aid of the Russian czar. War-weakened Austria compromised in 1867. The dual monarchy of Austria-Hungary was established with internally independent Hungary sharing common external services and military. Defeated with the other central powers during World War I, Hungary was forced to sign the Treaty of Trianon at Versailles in 1920. This treaty compelled Hungary to cede 68 percent of its land and 58 percent of its population: Transylvania and Bánát to Romania, Slovakia and Carpatho-Ruthenia to Czechoslovakia, Croatia and

Bácska to Yugoslavia, Port Fiume to Italy, and the western part of the country to equally defeated Austria. After the dissolution of the Austro-Hungarian dual monarchy, Hungary first became a republic in 1918. Then for 131 days in 1919 it had a Communist government, and in 1920 it became and remained for the entire interwar period a constitutional monarchy with Admiral Nicholas Horthy as regent. After regaining some lost territories between 1937 and 1941 with the help of Italy and Germany, Hungary joined the Axis powers in World War II. Soviet troops entered and occupied Hungary and the 1945 Armistice returned the country to its 1937 borders. A year later the country was declared a republic, and free elections were held in 1947. Even though the Smallholders' party won, it was forced out by Communists who were trained in and supported by Moscow. In 1956 there was a popular revolution against repressive Communist rule, which had included punitive measures against private peasants and a forced policy of heavy industrialization. Soviet forces crushed the revolution and made János Kádár the new leader of what was then called the People's Republic of Hungary. Imre Nagy and other leaders of the revolution were executed; tens of thousands died or were deported, and 200,000 people fled the country to the West. In 1963 there was a sweeping amnesty for political prisoners. The New Economic Mechanism, launched in 1968, introduced, among other things, elements of a market economy, and it helped to improve living standards. In the spirit of Soviet glasnost (openness) and perestroika (restructuring), Hungarians started strong movements for democratization in 1987. They removed János Kádár from power and rehabilitated the names of Imre Nagy and others. The ruling Communist party renamed itself, opposition parties were legalized, and freedom of press was extended. Free elections were held in 1990 and more radical political and economic changes are occurring.

Settlements

Geographical conditions influenced the development of regionally varied settlement patterns, along with many historical events, like the long Turkish occupation and Habsburg political and economic domination. In addition to the populous peasant towns, in rural Hungary there is still evidence of *tanyas*, or single isolated farmsteads, regular villages with geometrically designed streets, and irregular streetless villages that were settled by *hads* (agnatic kin groups) and *nagycsaládok* (extended families) in clustered and random style. Until a relatively recent attempt to integrate all buildings and farmyards into one section, in the northern and central parts of the Great Hungarian Plain most villages and boroughs had *kertes*, or *kétbeltelkes* settlements, meaning that the dwellings and farmyards were separated from one another.

Economy

Subsistence and Commercial Activities. Depending on the region, the rural economy was and is currently based on agriculture (including grains, tobacco, flax, peppers, melons, fruits), viniculture, animal husbandry (with a focus on raising cattle, pigs, horses), and forestry. Today, however, men and some women regularly commute between villages and urban industrial and mining centers. Also, light industrial plants were established in rural settlements, where village women work. Most village households, therefore, have wage income both from agriculture and industry. Traditional patterns of group work projects and mutual help (*kaláka*) continue to be visible in such activities as house building and harvesting, as well as weddings, funerals, and other important rites of passage.

Industrial Arts.   Depending on the area, larger settlements had potters, glazed earthenware makers, furrier-embroiderers, fancy honey-cake makers, wood-carvers, and other specialists. In addition to rural craft production, larger cities boasted sophisticated traditions of crafts.

Trade.   Throughout the countryside national fairs are frequently held, and there are weekly markets where villagers sell their produce and livestock. In addition, there are general and specialty stores, and in larger towns there are Western-style supermarkets. In 1973 Hungary joined the General Agreement on Tariffs and Trade. A decade later it was admitted to the International Monetary Fund. The country exports many of its products throughout the world.

Division of Labor.   Traditionally there was a marked sexual and age-group division of labor. In rural Hungary the eldest male was the head of household. Men's special jobs included plowing, reaping, building, and woodwork. Cooking, baking, cleaning, child rearing, weaving, and embroidering were considered the women's domain. Currently, because of out-migration and regular commuting of young and middle-aged men, there is increasing feminization and aging of village populations. Despite the major changes within the structure of agriculture, industry, and services, much of the traditional sexual division of labor remains.

Land Tenure.   Prior to 1945, land was privately owned either in small (often unviably small) plots by peasants or in large estates by aristocrats and wealthy families. In the land reform of 1945, large estates were redistributed among poor families across the country. After 1948 the Communist party and the government attempted to collectivize all agricultural properties and finally succeeded in 1961. As of the 1980s, 93 percent of arable land is cultivated in cooperative or state farms. With changes in property rights imminent, the possibility of increasing amounts of acreage becoming privatized is very likely.

Kinship, Marriage, and Family

Kinship.   In traditional Hungarian society an individual was identified principally by his or her place in a kinship organization. In Hungarian address and reference terms, one does not distinguish between paternal and maternal relatives (or between parallel and cross cousins). Rather, kin from both the father's and mother's side are included in a common class. Kinship is bilaterally reckoned. Traditionally, however, more emphasis was placed on the paternal kin than on the maternal because of the "male-centric" worldview in Hungarian rural society and the economically more beneficial inheritance system to males along the patriline. There is no uniform reckoning or terminology of kinship. Rather, an urban and a rural system coexist in Hungary. The urban system reflects nuclear family organization, and the rural system and its many regional variants depict the traditional extended family organization. Generally, Hungarian kinship terminology is descriptive and sharply distinguishes between affinal kin, consanguineous kin, and fictive kin. In Hungarian, like in other Finno-Ugric languages, there is a systematic differentiation between elder and younger brothers (*báty, öcs*), and between elder and younger sisters (*nővér, hug*). The fictive kinship of godparenthood (*keresztkomaság*) is a highly significant, lifelong alliance.

Marriage.   Even though only the birth of a child transforms a couple into a family, marriage is the emblem of maturity and conveys a status of adulthood, particularly in rural communities. Weddings are very elaborate, opulent affairs. Being unmarried after the age of 20–22 for women and 25–27 for men is negatively sanctioned. Traditional patterns of wife beating continue. Divorces are increasingly common, particularly in urban areas. According to 1987 data, there were 2.8 divorces per 1,000 inhabitants in the country.

Domestic Unit.   Depending upon socioeconomic circumstances, both the nuclear family and various forms of the joint or extended family organization were present even within the same rural settlement in traditional times. Extended families were maintained the longest among some Hungarian subethnic groups, for example among the Palóc, Matyó, and Seklers. While there are still a number of multigenerational families who live under the same roof and share "the same bread" today the most frequent form is the independently residing nuclear family.

Inheritance.   According to an 1840 law, property was to be divided equally among all surviving children regardless of gender. Most often, however, land was either divided equally among sons or the entire land property and the family dwelling were given to the eldest or most capable son. Other sons were given their share in money. Daughters, who of course married out of the paternal household, either gave up their rights to inherit real property or were paid a small sum. Often it was the responsibility of mothers to provide their daughters with proper dowries.

Socialization.   In the past, with a pattern of patrilocal postmarital residence, the mother, older siblings, and the female kin in the paternal household were responsible for the upbringing of children. Independence at an early age, respect for elders, and conformity to local and familial values were stressed. Currently, with the increasingly frequent pattern of neolocal postmarital residence, most rural children are raised by their mothers, maternal natal kin, and the village nursery and elementary schools. Even though today there is strong orientation toward child-centeredness, corporal punishment is still frequent.

Sociopolitical Organization

Political Organization.   In October 1989, Hungary was declared a republic. There are nineteen counties within the country. Hungary is presently undergoing very rapid and radical changes with the development of parliamentary democracy. Potential changes in political, administrative, and state structures are envisioned.

Social Control.   The county and national court systems attempt to resolve conflicts and maintain conformity. At the same time, public opinion, gossip, and tradition are still strong forces in many rural settlements, where often village customs continue to function as a largely self-contained "legal system," independent of the state.

Conflict. The history and cultural relations of the Magyars were laden with internal and external conflicts. Some of these continue into the present. Most explicitly on the domestic scene there is discord between the Magyar and the Gypsy populations, and in the international arena there is considerable friction between Hungary and the governments of Romania and the Czech and Slovak Federative Republic.

Religion and Expressive Culture

Religious Beliefs. Approximately 62 percent of the population is Roman Catholic, 25 percent Protestant, 3 percent Eastern Orthodox, 1 percent Jewish. Some of the practices combine elements of Christian and ancient pagan folk beliefs and customs.

Ceremonies. Some of the most important celebrations of the church calendrical year include namedays (*névnapok*), New Year's Day, Carnival (*Farsang*), the village patron saint's day (*búcsu*), Easter, Whitsuntide, All Saints' Day, and Christmas. In addition, rituals tied to the agricultural calendar include new bread, harvest, and grape-harvest festivals. National holidays commemorate significant historical events.

Arts. There is considerable regional differentiation in Hungarian folk art. Still, most designs are floral, and often even the geometric motifs are turned into monumental and colorful flowers. On furniture, wood carvings, paintings, and pottery patriotic symbols such as heroes of liberty, the national shield of Hungary, and the red, white, and green of the national flag appear. Pentatonic music, *csárdás* dances, and traditional rural architecture are also noteworthy representations of Hungarian art. Of course, urban forms of literature and the plastic arts have consistently represented all significant artistic expressions known throughout Europe.

Medicine. Since the early 1950s, Hungarian medical care has been socialized. Women give birth in hospitals rather than at home, and regional doctors and medical clinics take care of the ill. Among other things, drafts are assumed to cause some infirmities. There are home remedies, such as herbal teas and compresses, that are believed to help various health problems.

Death and Afterlife. A number of ancient beliefs and customs still surround the dying and the dead, as well as the mortuary practices and funerals. It is believed that before leaving for the life hereafter, the deceased's spirit lingers on for a while in or near the body. Elaborate rituals both during the preparation of the body for the coffin and during the funeral procession ensure that the spirit will not cause harm to the living but that it can find its way to the netherworld. Both urban and rural people sometimes consult seers (*halottlátók*), who act as mediators and through whom they communicate with their dead.

Bibliography

Andrew, János (1982). *The Politics of Backwardness in Hungary, 1925–1945.* Princeton: Princeton University Press.

Balassa, Iván, and Gy. Ortutay (1984). *Hungarian Ethnography and Folklore.* Budapest: Corvina.

Bell, Peter (1984). *Peasants in Socialist Transition: Life in a Collectivized Hungarian Village.* Berkeley: University of California.

Dégh, Linda (1989). *Folktales and Society: Storytelling in a Hungarian Peasant Community.* Bloomington: Indiana University.

Fél, Edit, and Tamás Hofer (1969). *Proper Peasants: Traditional Life in a Hungarian Village.* Viking Fund Publications in Anthropology. Chicago: Aldine; Budapest: Corvina.

Ferge, Zsuzsa (1979). *A Society in the Making: Hungarian Social and Societal Policy.* New York: M. E. Sharpe.

Illyés, Gyula (1936). *People of the Puszta.* Budapest: Corvina. Reprint. 1967.

Lukács, John (1988). *Budapest 1900: A Historical Portrait of a City and Its Culture.* New York: Weidenfeld & Nicolson.

Macartney, C. A. (1962). *Hungary: A Short History.* Chicago: Aldine.

Ortutay, Gyula, et al. *Magyar néprajzi lexikon* (The encyclopedia of Hungarian ethnography). 5 vols. Budapest: Akadémiai Kiadó.

Sozan, Michael (1979). *The History of Hungarian Ethnography.* Washington, D.C.: University Press of America.

ÉVA V. HUSEBY-DARVAS

Icelanders

ETHNONYMS: none

Orientation

Identification.   Icelanders speak Icelandic and trace their origins to settlers who came from Norway in the ninth century. According to the Icelandic literary-historic tradition, it was an early settler who gave the island its foreboding name when he was forced to return to Norway because he fished and hunted all summer and failed to lay up hay for his livestock. Today Icelanders enjoy a long life expectancy and one of the highest standards of living in the world.

Location.   Iceland is an island in the North Atlantic Ocean, located between Greenland and Norway, just south of the Arctic Circle. It covers 103,000 square kilometers, of which about 1,000 are cultivated, 20,000 pasture, 12,000 covered by glaciers, and 67,000 covered by lava, sands, and other wastelands. Volcanic activity continues. The Gulf Stream moderates the climate. The average annual temperature in Reykjavik, the capital, is 5° C. January averages −0.4° C and July 11.2° C. Average annual precipitation in Reykjavik is 80.5 centimeters.

Demography.   The total 1983 population was 237,894, about 2.3 persons per square kilometer. There were 128,221 people living in the area of the capital, and 87,106 in Reykjavik itself. There were 211,716 living in towns and villages of more than 200 people, and 26,178 in rural areas.

Linguistic Affiliation.   Icelandic is a Germanic language akin to Norwegian. Some call medieval Icelandic, the language of the Icelandic historic-literary tradition, Old Norse. Icelandic retains the full case structure, and some claim it is virtually unaltered since medieval times, though many modern Icelanders disagree. There are no family names. Everyone has one or two names and is referred to as son or daughter after his or her father. Directories are organized alphabetically by first name.

History and Cultural Relations

A number of medieval Icelandic manuscripts have been preserved. They include a compilation of stories collected just within the living memory of some of the earliest settlers about the settlement itself (the "Book of Settlements"); a grammatical treatise; the family sagas, composed during the thirteenth century about events of earlier periods; the Sturlunga sagas about contemporary thirteenth-century events; lawbooks; biographies of churchmen; other religious writings; and compilations of and commentaries on poetry and mythology. This is a unique record of a stratified society without a state, provided by the people of the society themselves. Romanticized nationalistic treatments of this tradition are common and are related to the ideology of the nineteenth-century Icelandic independence movement. This influence remains in some Scandinavian and other treatments of Icelandic culture and history. While scholars continue to debate the reliability of the documents of the Icelandic literary-historic tradition, most agree about the following history. Iceland was settled by people from Norway beginning in the ninth century. Each nonchieftain belonged to the assembly group of a chieftain. The society was stratified, but there was no state system. In A.D. 930 a General Assembly based on the model of Norwegian assemblies was established. One "law speaker" was elected every three years to memorize the customs and laws and recite one-third of them at each annual meeting of the assembly. He had no executive authority, but he could be consulted on points of law. The chieftains in assembly changed laws and heard cases. The assembly was not a parliamentary structure nor in any way did it resemble a democracy. Under pressure from the king of Norway in 1000, Christianity was adopted as the general religion of the island by arbitration at the meeting of the General Assembly. With Christianity came bishops and, in 1096, a tithe law. Early in the twelfth century the laws were written. A period of strife among chieftains resulted in the concentration of power into the hands of a few families in the thirteenth century, and in 1242 the remaining chieftains surrendered to the king of Norway. In 1380 Norway came under Danish rule, bringing Iceland with it. During the Reformation, in 1550, Catholicism was replaced by Lutheranism. From 1602 until 1787 there was a trade monopoly to prevent Icelanders from trading with British, German, and other fishermen and traders. In 1918 home rule was granted. During World War II, the Germans occupied Denmark and the British occupied Iceland. At the invitation of the British and occupied Iceland, the United States established military bases to free the British for other war tasks. Iceland became an independent republic in 1944. The American bases remain as NATO bases. Their presence is hotly debated in Iceland. Some argue they are Iceland's contribution to NATO while others argue they contradict Iceland's independence. Language, geography, and history place Iceland in the sphere of Scandinavian culture.

Economy

Subsistence and Commercial Activities.   Iceland has always depended on trade. The growing season is too short for any crop but grass, cultivated as feed for cattle and sheep. Fishing and hunting have always supplemented livestock production. The relative place of each component in the economic system has changed over the centuries. Initially, livestock production was important both for domestic consumption and for production of woolen goods for trade with Europe for metal and wood products. Fishing provided additional food, and cod may have been traded commercially since medieval times. During the period of Danish colonial rule, livestock production predominated. As Danish rule weakened toward the end of the nineteenth century, and local capital accumulation became possible, fishing communities grew along the coast and merchants developed foreign markets for fisheries products. Modern Iceland has an industrial economy based on fishing, fish processing, and fish exporting. Icelanders enjoy a high standard of living with 508 cars, 525 telephones, 266 television sets, and 2 physicians per 1,000 inhabitants in 1983.

Industrial Arts.   Iceland's fishing and fish processing industries are among the most innovative and modern in the world. From their trawlers to their line boats and freezing plants, they take advantage of the most modern technology and innovations in all fields from computer science to plastics. Hydroelectric plants provide electricity for an aluminum processing factory.

Trade. The nation exports fish and fish products and imports most of its consumer goods.

Division of Labor. Most Icelandic adults work, including most married women. As in other industrialized countries, the question is not so much one of division of labor as division of rewards such as wages and prestige. Icelandic women are generally paid less than their male counterparts. Women are usually assigned less desirable and less remunerative work in fish processing plants, for example. They are underrepresented on the faculty of the University of Iceland. This overall inequity may be in the process of changing, however. The economics and politics of gender equality have been issues in Icelandic politics for years, but during the 1980s the Women's List, a national political party, had some electoral success in parliamentary elections.

Land Tenure. In medieval Iceland land tenure depended on being able to appeal to sufficient force to prevent others from taking the land one claimed. Chieftains built coalitions of commoners and entered into alliances with other chieftains. Commoners joined chieftains to insure their land claims. One of the contradictions of the period was an economic system based on concepts of landownership and stratification with no state system of governance to enforce it. From the thirteenth century on many landless people worked for wages or rented from the few landowners. This system continued virtually until independence. In independent Iceland land tenure is less important than sea tenure. In 1975 Iceland led the way to the establishment of the international 200-mile (333-kilometer) offshore limit, which resulted in its cod wars with Great Britain. This limited the right to fish within these limits to Icelandic fishermen, thus reserving a rich fishing area for Icelandic use. This has been and remains one of the most important aspects of Icelandic foreign policy.

Kinship, Marriage, and Family

Kinship. The modern kinship terminology is made up of two systems. One is Ego-centered with terms that indicate specific individuals. The second is a set of collective terms that indicate groups of kin. Each of these two systems is divided into two more or less classificatory or descriptive subsystems. Descriptive terms designate individuals by generation, sex, and laterality. Merging terms refer to individuals with others of other positions of the same category. These systems have evolved from similarly complex medieval systems.

Marriage. Documents of the literary-historic tradition record instances of men having multiple mates if not legal wives. Marriage has never been considered as important in Iceland as in some other societies. Since the early nineteenth century when national statistics began to be recorded, from 13 to 36 percent (in 1977) of births have been illegitimate. Illegitimacy has never been a stigma or hindrance. Of the Nordic countries, Iceland has the youngest age at marriage (24.9 years for males, 22.7 years for females). Divorce has always been easy. The rate of divorce in 1977 was 9.12 per thousand married women. Because of the high rate of cohabitation, this figure does not necessarily have the same social meaning as it might in a society with a higher rate of marriage.

Domestic Unit. In 1703 the average household size was 5.6 persons and remained between 6 and 7 until 1901 when it was 6.2. In 1950 it was 3.8 and in 1960 3.9.

Inheritance. There is no kindred-based land inheritance in Iceland. Personal decisions outweigh structural obligations. The historical-literary tradition records cases of contested inheritance, usually resolved by force in medieval times.

Socialization. Modern Icelanders are very aware of issues of child rearing, child welfare, and education, and these issues sometimes become political. Public-health nurses make periodic house checks on newborns to ensure that they are staying on their growth curves and to help mothers with any problems they may encounter. Day care for preschool children is widely available in and near Reykjavik. In less metropolitan areas parents rely more on kin and friends for child care. Some rural and urban households have au pair girls to help with young children.

Sociopolitical Organization

Iceland has been a stratified society without a state and a colony of Denmark, and it is now an independent republic with an elected president as ritual head of state, a multiparty system, a parliament, and a prime minister who is the effective head of state.

Social Organization. Iceland has a strongly egalitarian ideology and the distribution of income is more equal than in most other societies. Differences in economic status, however, have become greater in recent years under conservative economic policies. There are significant differences between male and female remuneration for similar work. There has never been any Icelandic royalty, though some people have been and remain in privileged positions relative to others. These differences are well documented and discussed, and they sometimes become political issues. Almost all workers belong to well-organized unions.

Political Organization. Since its establishment as a republic in 1944, Iceland has never had a majority government. It is governed by a coalition of several parties that range from the Left to the Right in their political rhetoric and policies.

Social Control. The small size of Iceland and its population makes for greater accessibility than in larger, more populous societies. People know each other and know of each other. This closeness operates as a kind of social control and may be characterized as stifling or as close. Icelanders tend to be tolerant and nonfanatical. When someone says "it is not fair," he or she gets an immediate hearing. The response is not "no one said life was fair." Appeal to egalitarian ideals, concepts of justice and fairness, are given weight rather than disregarded. Discussions and debates, like the political parties, tend to be many-sided rather than two-sided.

Conflict. The literary-historic tradition records many instances of conflict in medieval times. Today conflict tends to be verbal and legal rather than physical. Sometimes there are strikes. One definition of chaos is the interruption of normal middle-class patterns of life. There is no military. There is a small police force and coast guard. There is no national guard. When there are strikes, the policemen's union is as likely as any other to be on strike, so they are not used to break strikes. Since most people belong to unions, nonunion workers are not available to break strikes.

Religion and Expressive Culture

Religious Beliefs and Practices.   The Icelandic writer Sigrdur Nordal wrote, "We have been bad pagans for a century and bad Christians for ten." During early times, chieftains were also priests. As in many other primitive societies, their offices were both secular and sacred. After Christianity was introduced, clergy refused to abide by the rule of celibacy, bore arms, and entered feuds. The higher clergy functioned as another kind of chieftain. Most modern Icelanders are confirmed in the Icelandic State Church, a major rite of passage. The clergy have social as well as religious roles. The church is tax-supported, but individuals who do not want to support the church may so indicate on their tax returns and their taxes are used for other purposes. Nonstandard quasireligious movements such as spiritism and folk concepts such as elves and prophetic dreams have some support and go in and out of fashion from time to time.

Arts.   Choral singing may be one of the most popular art forms in Iceland. Rural as well as urban areas support choirs. There is an active theater community, symphony orchestra, new music movement, and visual arts community. There are several art museums, some of which are dedicated to individual artists. There is a small film-making industry. There is a state television station, two state radio stations, and one commercial television station. Icelandic rock-and-roll bands come and go in national and international popularity. One of the problems they must face is whether to perform in the Icelandic language, thus maintaining a strong sense of Icelandic identity but limiting their appeal to the island, or to perform in English (e.g., the Sugarcubes), thus appealing to an international audience but losing some of their national identity. Iceland is a nation of poets and writers. The most internationally known writer is the Nobel Prize winner Halldor Laxness, who has written only in Icelandic. Before he won the Nobel Prize, Icelanders gave him a cool reception because of his challenges to long-held myths of egalitarianism and romantic ideas of independence.

Medicine.   Iceland has a modern and advanced healthcare system. All Icelanders participate in this system, and health care is available to all.

Bibliography

Durrenberger, E. Paul, and Gisli Palsson, eds. (1989). *The Anthropology of Iceland.* Iowa City: University of Iowa Press.

Gelsinger, Bruce E. (1981). *Icelandic Enterprise: Commerce and Economy in the Middle Ages.* Columbia: University of South Carolina Press.

Rich, George W. (1989). "Problems and Prospects in the Study of Icelandic Kinship." In *The Anthropology of Iceland,* edited by E. Paul Durrenberger and Gisli Palsson, 53–118. Iowa City: University of Iowa Press.

Tomasson, Richard F. (1980). *Iceland: The First New Society.* Minneapolis: University of Minnesota Press.

E. PAUL DURRENBERGER

Ionians

ETHNONYMS: Eftanissiotes, Ioniennes

Orientation

Identification and Location.   The Ionian Islands lie off the western coast of Greece in the Ionian Sea, a northern branch of the Mediterranean. The group of islands has been referred to variously as the Septinsular Republic, the Eftanissa or Eptanissa, or the Seven Islands, reflecting the number of large islands in the group. Smaller inhabited islets bring the total number of islands to twenty-four. The main islands are Corfu (Kerkyra), Cephalonia (Kefallinia, Kefalonia), Ithaca (Ithaki), Lefkas (Lefkada), Paxos (Paxi), Zante (Zakinthos), and Kithira. Kithira, while geographically separate at some distance to the south, is culturally similar and shares most of its history with the rest of the islands. Following tradition, Kithira is thus included in the group. Spreading north to south, the islands are actually the tips of a submerged limestone mountain range. The soil is often thin and rocky; exceptions to this include the Lixouri Peninsula of Cephalonia, the broad plain of Zante, and portions of Corfu. The islands receive 90 to 115 centimeters of torrential rains from November through February; the temperature seldom falls below 4.4° C. The hot, dry summer days reach temperatures above 32° C, and there is little precipitation from May through September.

Demography.   The population of the islands is estimated at 120,000. An influx of tourists in the summer doubles or trebles the population in some areas. In areas where many men are employed in the merchant marine, the actual resident population is perhaps 80 percent of the numbers reported in the census. Heavy emigration has resulted in a population pyramid that is both age- and sex-skewed, with a relatively greater proportion of women and elderly.

Linguistic Affiliation.   The Ionians speak a variant of the Greek language that reflects Italian influence in vocabulary and intonation. Greek is an ancient branch of the Indo-European Language Family.

History and Cultural Relations

Archaeological evidence indicates habitation of Corfu as early as 70,000 B.C. Historical mention of the islands begins with Homer; Mycenean colonization of the region took place in the thirteenth century B.C. In the late eighth century B.C., the Corinthians colonized Corfu. The Romans made Corfu a Roman protectorate in 229 B.C., the first Roman possession in Greece. Within forty years, the other major islands in the Ionian group fell to Rome. In A.D. 330, when the Roman capital was shifted to Constantinople (Istanbul), Byzantine rule began. Like other parts of the disintegrating Roman Empire, the Ionian Islands were the site of major political and social upheavals for the next 900 years; wars and invasions were common. Urbanization was spurred by developing industry and commerce and by foreign invasions as people sought protection within city walls. Venetian expansionism and desire for control of Oriental trade led to the fall of Constantinople in 1204, as Venice persuaded the Crusaders to call first at

Constantinople before proceeding to the Holy Land. The Ionian Islands became Venetian possessions; at this time the history of the islands became quite distinct from the rest of Greece, which eventually fell under Turkish rule. Feudalism developed and crystallized during the Venetian period as land and power were concentrated in the hands of Italian and Greek-Italian nobles. Commercialization of agriculture also took place during this period. Particularly affected were Cephalonia and Zakinthos, where the introduction of the profitable currant crop brought sudden wealth to the islands' large landholders. Vigorous export trade spurred the development of a middle class of merchants and skilled artisans. The peasantry, however, remained in poverty and suffered greatly when the market for currants declined periodically. At the end of Venetian rule, the islands passed through the hands of the Russians and the French before British rule began in 1815. Important roads and bridges opening up the rural hinterlands were built during this time. As the British penchant for social order and equality took over, the feudal structure began to disintegrate. By the middle of the nineteenth century, a disillusioned nobility was emigrating, and long-standing clamors for union with the recently formed modern nation of Greece increased. In 1864, Great Britain ceded the islands to Greece. The modern period has been characterized by heavy emigration and expanding tourism. When the Greek economy collapsed with the fall in currant prices at the turn of the twentieth century, opportunities in industrializing America expanded at roughly the same time, and many Ionians were affected. By the second half of this century, Ionians were scattered around the globe, with sizable communities in Australia, Germany, Canada, Zambia, England, and the United States. In the 1960s and 1970s, European and American tourism to the Ionian Islands escalated, bringing needed jobs and cash to the local economies. Corfu has been a center for elite Greek tourism for some time, but as the number of foreign tourists has increased, many Greek tourists have begun to travel to the southern islands as well. The local communities swell in size with the influx of tourists and the seasonal return of migrants.

Settlements

Villages dot the mountainous countryside, with larger settlements as ports and/or marketing and administrative centers. Homes and shops cluster around one or more main village squares or *plateia*. Numerous earthquakes plague the Ionians; in some areas, over 90 percent of the homes and other buildings have been destroyed by quakes in this century. Private homes are generally surrounded by a wall; the yards often overflow with flowers and herbs. In some rural areas, animals such as goats, sheep, chickens, and donkeys are kept in structures attached to the home.

Economy

Subsistence and Commercial Activities; Industrial Arts. In the early 1900s, over 56 percent of the Ionian population was regularly engaged in full-time agriculture; the figure now is estimated at between 10 and 15 percent. Income is likely to be supplemented by migrant remittances and/or short-term employment in construction or seasonal agricultural labor. Agricultural production focuses on olive oil, wine grapes, and wheat. Bees are kept, and honey is produced and sold. Iso-

lated pockets of currant cultivation are still found, particularly on Zante. Cephalonia has been known for centuries as an island of sailors, navigators, and captains, and as many as 70 percent of the men in some villages on that island and on Ithaca are or have been employed in the merchant marine. Migrant remittances and revenue generated through the sale of goods and services to tourists and emigrants returning to the islands during Christmas, Easter, and in the summer stimulate and maintain the local middle class of entrepreneurs. Rapidly increasing tourism has brought relative prosperity to the islands and has begun recently to stem the tide of emigration. Tourist shops proliferate, as do bars, discotheques, restaurants, and hotels in the larger urban areas. Many migrants returning to the islands for the summer open businesses or drive taxis during these months. Cottage industry for the production of local arts and crafts exists as well.

Trade. Small specialty shops with limited types of merchandise predominate in both urban and rural areas; stores carrying like products tend to cluster together. The past glories of the currant trade have vanished, and the Ionians now export human labor as a primary product.

Division of Labor. The male/female dichotomy is particularly evident. The women are associated with production in and around the home, while the men labor in the fields, on ships, or in shops. Increasingly, women are left in charge of family stores while the men of the household seek employment or conduct personal business elsewhere.

Land Tenure. Since Napoleonic times, partible inheritance has been both the ideal and real practice in the Ionian Islands. As the population grew, increasing fragmentation of land plots plagued the islands; the situation has been reversed in modern times through depopulation. While legal records still show numerous owners of small, dispersed plots, actual access to land for those actively engaged in agriculture is greatly facilitated through leases from owners who have emigrated and no longer desire or require the use of agricultural land. Historically, large landowners held sizable fiefs throughout the islands; numerous land redistributions in the twentieth century have made small peasant landholdings more typical.

Kinship, Marriage, and Family

Kinship, Marriage, and Domestic Unit. The nuclear family is the most common social unit among Ionians today, although vertically extended families composed of an elderly couple and one child with his/her family are also found. Horizontal extended or joint families of married brothers with spouses and children are the ideal following the death of both parents, but in reality they are rare. In the twentieth century, residence has changed from a pattern predominated by patrilocality to mixed patrilocal and matrilocal households or neighborhoods, with some neolocality as well. The modern inclusion of a home, apartment, or addition to a home in daughters' dowries has led to the increase in matrilocality, as families build on their own or adjacent properties to provide this element of their daughters' inheritances. Bilateral kindreds are seen at personal and village celebrations. One of the most obvious facets of the nuclear family today is the absence of one or more principal members through migration; some villages have a high percentage of elderly couples who have no children in the village. The kin terminology is Eskimo, like that in the United States; terms in some areas reflect Italian influence. In the past, marriages were arranged by parents; the practice is still common today. An intermediary's advice is often sought; such an individual is expected to have full knowledge of available unmarried individuals, including familial background, familial and personal reputation, and any potential flaws in character. Success at migration is an important characteristic contributing to the relative desirability of a potential spouse. It is increasingly common for individuals to be involved in love matches and to make their own marriage arrangements. Such romances often begin in Athens or elsewhere outside the islands. As a result, an earlier pattern of regional endogamy is changing. Divorce is still rare but has become more common with the introduction of legal civil marriages and divorces in 1980. Divorce is frowned upon, however, and divorced women are unlikely to remarry. Women who have been partners in broken engagements experience similar difficulty in finding a husband. These situations increase the likelihood of a woman's migrating to a city where her past experiences are unknown.

Inheritance. A child's equal portion of the inheritance may take the form of funds for migration or higher education as an alternative to the traditional land and household property. Women receive at least a portion of their inheritance at marriage in the form of a dowry. Household furnishings and land were traditional dowry elements; modern changes include a home or attached rooms and cash. Land is less likely to be included, unless it is located in an area that can be developed for tourism. The division of the inheritance generally takes place at the death of parents.

Sociopolitical Organization

Social Organization. Sex roles are clearly differentiated among Ionians. Women are associated with the private sphere of the home; men circulate in the public arena. Male presentation of self involves a stance of dominance over women and a love of honor or *philotimo*, which includes a willingness to defend familial reputation. Sexual prowess and ability to provide economically for the family are also emphasized. Women wield significant power within the nuclear family; ties between mothers and children are very close. Traditional strict separation of unmarried men and women is giving way in the face of increasing tourism and the spread of urban values to rural areas through returning migrants. Decision making is undertaken by the family as a whole.

Political Organization. Ionians are actively interested in local and national politics; debate on political issues is common among men in particular. Townspeople elect public officials, including a mayor and town committee, to direct affairs. The positions carry prestige but can be difficult in a politically fractious community. Greece is divided administratively into *nomes*, which are further separated into *eparchies*. Lefkas and Zante are nomes; the nome of Cephalonia includes Ithaca as an eparchy. Kithira is now attached to a non-Ionian nome, and the eparchy of Paxos is part of the nome of Corfu. Migrant associations have formed in urban areas in Greece; they have become important and influential political groups in Ionian life.

Social Control. Gossip is the common means of social control; any activity in small communities is easily observed and closely monitored. An individual's and family's reputations are constantly scrutinized and subject to public discourse. The behavior of the women in the family is a common topic of local gossip, as are the economic abilities of the males.

Conflict. A man must be willing and ready to defend the honor of his family; arguments and overt fights occur frequently, and political brinkmanship reigns. A circular court system brings judges to central towns regularly; the most common disputes involve landed property.

Religion and Expressive Culture

Religious Beliefs and Practices. Despite centuries of Catholic rulers, Eastern Orthodoxy remains the primary faith; a number of Catholic churches are found in the urban areas. Also reflecting the Italian influence is the emphasis on processions associated with local saints. Most notable are the celebrations for Saint Spiros on Corfu and Saint Gerasimos on Cephalonia. Personal attachment to individual or local patron saints is a part of the Little Tradition. Village celebrations or *panayiria* are occasions for marked *communitas* and the return of migrants. Christmas, the festivities for the Virgin Mary on 15 August, and Easter Week draw returning migrants as well. A declining belief in the evil eye is found among the elderly in particular, who believe it to cause illness, impotence, sterility, and death. Women and children attend church more frequently than men.

Arts. Traditional music and dance among Ionians reflect the Italian heritage through couples' dances and unusual rhythms; Western influence in modern music and dance is readily apparent in local discotheques. Artisans flourished in the Ionian Islands during the Venetian and British periods, and the architecture in urban areas is visibly Italianate. Clothing has shown European influence among the upper classes since the 1600s.

Medicine. The Ionians have long emphasized education, and students commonly specialize in law or medicine. Access to medical care is facilitated by a national program that installs doctors in small villages throughout the country. An emphasis among the elderly on medical care involving such practices as leeching, cupping, and bleeding is fading.

Death and Afterlife. Women are largely responsible for the care of the dead. Disinterment and placement of the bones in an ossuary is not as common in the Ionian Islands as it is elsewhere in Greece, where a shortage of land exists. It is typical to have a single family burial plot and to bury the dead without embalming and in simple wood coffins. Over time, the bones of the family mix together.

Bibliography

Ansted, D. T. (1863). *The Ionian Islands in the Year 1863.* London: W. H. Allen.

Costa, Janeen Arnold (1988). "The History of Migration and Political Economy in Rural Greece: A Case Study." *Journal of Modern Greek Studies* 6:159–185.

Costa, Janeen Arnold (1988). "Systems Integration and Attitudes toward Greek Rural Life: A Case Study." *Anthropological Quarterly* 61:73–90.

Jervis, Captain Whyte (1863). *The Ionian Islands during the Present Century.* London: Chapman & Hall.

Kirkwall, Viscount (1864). *Four Years in the Ionian Islands: Their Political and Social Condition.* 2 vols. London: Chapman & Hall.

Young, Martin (1973). *Corfu and the Other Ionian Islands.* London: Jonathan Cape.

JANEEN ARNOLD COSTA

Irish

ETHNONYM: Eireanneach

Orientation

Identification and Location. For the Irish and Ireland, identification and location are inextricably linked aspects of self-definition. Ireland, located between 51°30′ and 55°30′ N and 6°00′ and 10°30′ W, is an island 480 by 273 kilometers at its longest and widest (N–S and E–W, respectively). It is separated on the east from Great Britain by the narrow Irish Sea (17 to 192 kilometers wide). To the west is the Atlantic Ocean. The island consists mainly of low-lying land whose central lowlands support rich pastureland, agricultural regions, and a large central peat bog. The rim is mountainous, especially in the west, but elevations are rarely higher than 900 meters. Ireland's geographical location—combining proximity to England with peripherality vis-à-vis Europe—has played the major role in defining its historical experience. This relationship has also made the definition of just who and what is Irish problematic. Centuries of British rule culminated in the division of the island in 1922 into two political entities: the Republic (Free State from 1922 to 1949) of Ireland, comprising twenty-six counties and 70,550 square kilometers, and the Province of Northern Ireland, comprising six counties and remaining part of the United Kingdom. The population of the republic is 95 percent Catholic and that segment identifies itself unambiguously as Irish. Members of the Protestant minority may choose to emphasize their English ancestry, but they typically call themselves "Irish"—or "Anglo-Irish" as they are identified by their Irish Catholic neighbors. In Northern Ireland, however, the situation is more complex. The substantial Catholic minority—whatever their political affiliation—consider themselves ethnically Irish, while the subjective and objective identification of Protestants has been far more fluctuating and context-dependent. At various points, they may identify themselves as "Irish," "Ulster," "Ulster Protestant," or "British." The merging of religious, geographical, and ethnic labels is also applied from

the outside. Irish Catholics may use a variety of such terms to identify their neighbors, and the choice of label nearly always has a political subtext.

Demography. The population of the Republic of Ireland was 3,540,643 in 1986, representing an increase of 97,238 persons since the 1981 census. The population, which began a steep decline during the late 1840s famine, has been increasing since the 1961 census and has now been restored to the level of 1889–90. However, a recent decline in the birthrate and a leap in the emigration rate (at least 72,000 between 1981 and 1986), makes the demographic future uncertain. The high birthrate in the sixties and seventies has made Ireland one of the youngest countries in Europe, and migration to Dublin has made the population far more urban than it had been up until recently (57 percent urban, 43 percent rural), with close to a third of the population living in Dublin County.

Linguistic Affiliation. Although Irish Gaelic is the official language of the republic, the vast majority of people on both sides of the border speak English. Irish is the daily language of only tens of thousands (disputed number) of inhabitants of scattered Gaeltacht zones mainly along the west coast. Irish Gaelic, a Celtic language, has three main dialects and is closely related to Scottish Gaelic. The Goidelic Branch of the Celtic languages also includes Manx (once spoken on the Isle of Man), while the Brythonic Branch is represented by Welsh and Breton. The language issue has played a central part in the ethnic identity issues previously mentioned. Although Irish Gaelic was by the late nineteenth century very much a minority language, proponents of Irish nationalism (Protestant and Catholic) favored the restoration of the "national language" as a critical element in the maintenance of a distinct national identity and culture. Government measures meant to ensure this restoration have gradually relaxed over the decades, however, and despite the persistence of Irish in a few enclaves and a lively Irish-language literary and cultural scene, English is clearly the de facto national language.

History and Cultural Relations

The earliest inhabitants of Ireland were Mesolithic hunter-gatherers whose sites are dated as early as 8980 B.P., but it is the extensive Neolithic settlement that has left a large number of impressive megalithic constructions. The exact origin point of "Celtic culture" in Ireland and its relation to preexisting cultures and/or populations is much disputed. By the first few centuries B.C., however, a clearly Celtic culture was established all over the island, with clear connections to continental Celts. Iron Age Celtic society established a lasting economic, political, social, and cultural framework for Irish society. Unhampered by the Romanization that transformed so much of continental Europe, Ireland's cattle-based chieftaincies remained the basic social unit through the early Christian period, giving Irish Christianity a Celtic construction that would give rise to Roman consternation at various historical junctures. Celtic Ireland was notably rural, and it was the Vikings who established the major port cities that would continue to play an important role in Irish history (e.g., Dublin, Cork, Waterford, Wexford). The English presence began with the twelfth-century Anglo-Norman expedition under the auspices of Henry II, in aid of one side in an internecine struggle in the south. The invaders settled, particularly in the southeast, bringing with them a manorial type of settlement and economy, as well as a new language and culture. The succeeding centuries brought much cultural borrowing between native Irish and Anglo-Norman cultures, particularly in areas distant from the capital. The Cromwellian and Williamite wars of the seventeenth century established Ireland as a fully colonial society, with political rule and most landownership in the hands of English-speaking Protestants, and with a native population of mainly Gaelic-speaking Catholics, the vast majority of whom were poor tenant farmers, seen and described by their overlords in increasingly "primitive" terms. The wars also brought the "plantation" of Northern Ireland, the importation of thousands of mainly Presbyterian Scots who took ownership of small farms and settled in areas from which Catholic Irish had been driven. There was also a very considerable influx of Protestant English into the south. For most Catholic tenants, the central issue through the eighteenth century was local land tenure, and a variety of locally based secret societies—such as the "White Boys"—were active in retaliatory guerrilla raids against landlords, agents, or collaborators. After the failure of the United Irishmen's rebellion in 1798, land tenure as well as cultural and religious identity came more and more to be linked with nationalism. The nineteenth century saw a series of attempts, armed and legislative, to win independence and/or redress land issues, culminating in the Easter Uprising of 1916 and the war of independence that followed. Ireland achieved independence as a Free State with the treaty of 1922, which left the six Protestant-majority counties of Ulster in the United Kingdom. The Free State became Eire, or the Republic of Ireland, in 1949. One faction of the Irish—represented thereafter by the Irish Republican Army (IRA)—refused to accept the legitimacy of the boundary. Within Northern Ireland most Catholics—and a few Protestants—are "nationalists" favoring a "United Ireland." The vast majority of Protestants—and very few Catholics—espouse "Unionism," seeking to remain a part of the United Kingdom. It is difficult to assess what proportion of either population supports the activities of violent paramilitary organizations, which continue to carry out assassinations and bombings. After the bloody reaction to Catholic civil rights demonstrations in Northern Ireland in 1969, the British Army began to maintain a strong and active presence that continues to this day.

In addition to the political developments already described, the eighteenth and nineteenth centuries brought tremendous economic and social upheaval to Ireland. The population increased at a tremendous rate and grew increasingly dependent on the potato for sustenance. The great potato famine of the late 1840s (numerous smaller ones occurred before and after) led to evictions and immigration that vastly increased the flow of Irish to America.

While significant numbers went to England—and, to a lesser extent, Canada and Australia—the large proportion of Irish in America has had a great and lasting impact on both the United States and Ireland. Even since 1973, when Eire joined the European Economic Community, cultural (as opposed to economic) attention has been focused on the United States, to which the current crop of emigrants have once again come.

Settlements

Settlement patterns have of course varied much over time and place. The dominant Celtic pattern seems to have been scattered fort/cattle pen/households (*rath*). Peasant communities following a mixed-cattle, agricultural regime, at least in the west of Ireland, lived in small hamlets (*clachan* or *clibin*), using a commonly held infield for grain and vegetables and an extensive outfield "mountain" for livestock. This pattern was generally eliminated (though there are a few survivals) through landlord intervention by the middle of the nineteenth century. The demise of such traditional patterns was also accelerated by the famine and emigration. The resulting pattern was of more or less dispersed households and farms, or more concentrated but separate rows of dwellings where geography and varying land type made that form appropriate. In either case, however, the "townland" (*baile fearainn*), which corresponds to the common holding of the traditional cluster settlement, may continue to operate as a socially significant "neighborhood" and its inhabitants may even continue to hold common rights to turf (for fuel) in bogs and grazing land on mountains. Elsewhere other agricultural and/or geographical factors made for other settlement types, including dispersed large farms, estate villages, or the street market towns, which mainly developed in the nineteenth century under landlord regimes.

Economy

Subsistence and Commercial Activities. Agriculture, until recently the overwhelming mainstay of the Irish economy, remains important, although a decreasing percentage of the population is engaged in such pursuits. Most arable land is devoted to pasture or hay production, and livestock and livestock products are the most important exports, sold in European and Near Eastern markets. The United States is also a major trading partner. Tourism, greatly promoted in recent decades, provides the single largest item in the country's net earnings. Since the 1960s, attractive conditions have brought many foreign-owned small factories to Ireland, and they along with Irish manufacturing and construction firms now employ around 27.5 percent of the labor force. While the city of Dublin has grown at a great rate, the lack of a large industrial or commercial base there has meant much unemployment. Membership in the European Common Market has benefited agricultural producers through subsidies and opened up new channels for emigration for professionals, but so far has not done much to change the economic peripherality of Ireland. The relative prosperity of the sixties and seventies seems to have been based on borrowed money, leaving Ireland with one of the highest per capita foreign debts in the world. Inflation and high unemployment fueled renewed emigration, mostly to the United States, in the late 1980s. In the west of Ireland, where most anthropological fieldwork has been carried out, small farms—where viable—continue to produce livestock and dairy products sold at marts or through local cooperatives. Much of the extreme west, including Gaeltacht zones, is characterized by underfarmed smallholdings, which support a subsistence crop of potatoes and vegetables, combined in varying degrees with sheep farming (whose economic viability depends on government subsidies). In a few areas small- or medium-scale fishing or rural factory employment adds to the income of such families or provides the total support of younger families. Government welfare and old-age pensions, however, contribute importantly to the maintenance of many households. Where the farm is viable, it absorbs the labor of the entire family. In smaller holding areas, however, younger family members are often engaged in subsidiary income pursuits. Where available, factory jobs are sought by young men and women. Areas of large farms, such as Meath and West Meath, and the city and suburbs of Dublin exhibit different sociocultural patterns, which are only recently being studied by anthropologists.

Land Tenure. Although after the seventeenth century the mainly British landlords held proprietary rights, the Irish tenantry continued to pass on the right to these tenancies as if they were property. Land reforms in the late nineteenth and early twentieth century turned these tenants into peasant proprietors. Common rights were often retained in bogs (for peat fuel) and in extensive mountain pasturelands.

Kinship, Marriage, and Family

Kinship. *Clan* is an Irish word and traditionally referred to the agnatic descendants of a common ancestor (e.g., "the O'Donnells"). Such clans had a hierarchical territorial arrangement in traditional chiefdoms, wherein subgroups and individuals were linked to superiors through cattle clientship and/or tribute and service. The local kin group in this system was called a *fine*. In this way traditional commonage rundale (common land that is distributed among owners in such a way that an individual's holdings are scattered among those of others) was followed by divided inheritance in western Ireland, which gave way, again under landlord action, to enforced undivided inheritance. This continues to be the legal mode today, with the father naming a single son as heir to the farm. The social integrity and relative autonomy of the household farm based on the single heir is a central concern of many influential studies of the culture. However, in some areas at least, the ethos of continuing obligation to and among all siblings makes "stem family" a misleading designation, even for the contemporary rural Irish family.

Marriage. Sibling solidarity before and after marriage is a striking feature of daily life. In the west, in particular, individuals still marry close to home and tend to keep up frequent visiting patterns with siblings. In the extreme case men and women may even remain with their natal households after marriage. Unmarried siblings will very often live together and will frequently be joined by a widowed sibling late in life.

Sociopolitical Organization

Social Organization. Although an increasing share of the population lives in Dublin, rural culture enjoys a disproportionate importance, and many urban dwellers retain ties to the countryside. While an egalitarian ethos prevails in most rural areas, there are large differences in the "objective" class situation of farmers, ranging from large numbers of very small farmers cultivating less than 6 hectares, mainly in the west, to graziers farming hundreds of hectares in the east. The class structure of the cities resembles that of other urban areas in western Europe.

Political Organization. Eire is a parliamentary democracy with a nonexecutive president elected by direct vote. The parliament (Oireachtas) consists of a lower house (An Dail Eireann) elected through proportional representation by a single transferable vote, and an upper house (An Seanad Eireann). The government is headed by a prime minister (An Taoiseach) chosen by An Dail. The two principal political parties, Fine Gael and Fianna Fail, are both centrist in European terms and owe their origins to respective positions on the border question seventy years ago. There are a variety of other parties holding few seats, including the Labor Party and Sinn Fein (the political wing of the IRA). Local government is through the "county council," but recent changes in the structure of taxation have left that body with little real resources and hence little power, making Eire's political system an increasingly centralized one.

Social Control. In rural areas, the local community and kin groups continue to play the most obvious role in daily social control. The Catholic church, especially in the person of the parish priest, typically continues to exercise considerable authority, especially in the rural areas. In these same areas the "legitimacy" of the state to interfere with local practice may be more often questioned.

Conflict. Irish nationalists tend to sum up Ireland's history as "800 years of British oppression and Irish resistance." Academic histories currently debate whether the local uprisings and guerrilla activity of the eighteenth century, the 1798 rebellion, the Fenians of the nineteenth century, and the ongoing "troubles" can best be understood in terms of class, nationalism, or local interests. From any point of view, however, conflict continues to define the Irish experience, historically and currently.

Religion and Expressive Culture

Religious Beliefs and Practices. By any measure, Ireland is a profoundly Catholic country and culture. Weekly mass attendance continues at nearly 90 percent of the population, and the influence of the clergy on all social as well as narrowly religious questions is enormous. Ireland, alone with Malta in Europe, has no legal divorce, and abortion—never legal—has recently been made unconstitutional. The central tenets of the Catholic church are mainly accepted, but various local heterodox usages continue in some areas. Notably, holy well cults are still an important aspect of local practice. There are more than three thousand holy wells listed for Ireland, most of them associated with a Roman Catholic saint and with beliefs about curing, indulgences, honor, prayer, etc. Major pilgrimage points within Ireland (Knock, Croagh Patrick, Station Island, Lady's Island) attract tens of thousands annually, and the Irish are disproportionately represented at Lourdes.

Arts. Language remains perhaps the most important form of expressive culture: from the oral narrative that still characterizes much local Irish life to one of the most vibrant literary traditions in Europe. Although less well-known, there is a lively visual art scene in the urban centers. Music, always important in the folk tradition, has made a great resurgence in recent decades with much creative interaction between folk and rock forms.

Medicine. Although most Irish avail themselves of whatever modern medical facilities are available, many will combine such treatments with propitiation of saints and/or pilgrimages to the above sites.

Death and the Afterlife. For the vast majority of Irish, the rites of the Catholic church are followed scrupulously on the occasion of death. Wakes held in the home of the deceased for two or three days, however, continue to provide a central communal focus to the event in many areas. Appropriation of the powerful act and rites of death has characterized Irish political activity, especially in the twentieth century.

See also Gaels (Irish); Irish Travellers; Northern Irish; Tory Islanders

Bibliography

Arensberg, Conrad (1937). *The Irish Countryman*. New York: Macmillan.

Arensberg, Conrad, and Solon Kimball (1968). *Family and Community in Rural Ireland*. 2nd ed. Cambridge, Mass.: Harvard University Press.

Curtin, C., and T. Wilson (1989). *Ireland from Below: Social Change and Local Communities*. Galway: University College Galway Press.

Fox, Robin (1978). *The Tory Islanders: A People of the Celtic Fringe*. Cambridge: Cambridge University Press.

O'Kelly, Michael P. (1989). *Early Ireland*. Cambridge: Cambridge University Press.

Taylor, Lawrence J. (1989). "Bás InÉirinn: Cultural Constructions of Death in Ireland." *Anthropological Quarterly* 62:175–187.

LAWRENCE J. TAYLOR

Irish Travellers

ETHNONYMS: Itinerants, Tinkers, Travelling People

Orientation

Identification. Irish Travellers are an itinerant ethnic group. Similar itinerant trader, artisan, and entertainer minorities live in many other complex societies around the world. Group members refer to themselves as "Travellers" or as "the Travelling People." The term "tinkers" was once commonly used by members of mainstream Irish society and by some Travellers. It was derived from the occupation of tinsmithing, which many Travellers once practiced; specifically, from the sound of hammer striking metal. Over the years, "tinker" became a pejorative label and is seldom used publicly today. The term "itinerant" was used extensively in the 1960s and 1970s by the government and news media; it has since been replaced by "Travellers" and "the Travelling People."

Location. Irish Travellers live and travel throughout Ireland and in the neighboring British Isles (Northern Ireland, Scotland, Wales, and England). In addition, families who identify themselves as Irish Travellers live in the United States, primarily in southern states, many having emigrated there in the 1800s.

Demography. In 1981 there were 14,821 Travellers or 2,432 Traveller families in the Republic of Ireland. An estimated 1,000 Traveller families live in the British Isles. Travellers comprise a tiny minority in Irish society, approximately 0.5 percent of the population. Nevertheless, it is a fast-growing population with an annual growth rate of 6.7 percent. The age structure of the Traveller population differs dramatically from that of the general Irish population. Nearly 40 percent of Travellers in 1981 were under 10 years of age; over 50 percent were under age 15. This compares to 20 percent and 30 percent, respectively, for non-Travellers. Only 6 percent of Travellers, however, are over the age of 50, compared to 24 percent of non-Travellers. These figures reflect the very high birthrate of Travellers; the median number of children born live to mothers aged 45 and over is 10. They also reflect a high death rate and a low average life expectancy. Alcoholism, related diseases, and alcohol-related accident deaths take a high toll on adult Travellers.

Linguistic Affiliation. Irish Travellers speak English and an argot known as Gammon or Cant (also known as Shelta) that is based on Irish Gaelic but also incorporates English, Romanes (the language of Romany Gypsies), and slang. It is used primarily as a secret language to obscure conversations from outsiders. At one time Travelling People living in Irish-speaking parts of the country undoubtedly spoke Irish, but no longer.

History and Cultural Relations

Travellers are indigenous to Ireland. Although there has been some intermarriage with British Gypsies, Travellers are genetically closest to other Irish people. Nevertheless, they have formed a sufficiently isolated breeding population to have diverged from the Irish population at a number of gene loci. The early history of Ireland's Travelling People is obscure. Being illiterate until recently, they have left no written records of their own. Being poor, they have been largely ignored in the literature of the "Great Tradition." Not all families originated at the same time nor in the same way. Some families date back centuries; others have adopted a traveling lifestyle in recent times. Tinsmiths have formed a distinct group for many centuries; "tinker" and "tynkere" first appear as trade- or surnames in written records during the twelfth century. But as early as the fifth century, these itinerant "whitesmiths"—as well as other artisans and specialists such as tanners, musicians, and bards—traveled the Irish countryside fashioning jewelry, weapons, and horse trappings out of bronze, silver, and gold in exchange for food and lodging. Tinkers were numerous enough in Ireland (and Scotland) by the sixteenth century to have given Romany Gypsies stiff competition when they arrived in the British Isles for the first time. By 1835, when Britain's Poor Inquiry commissioners visited Ireland to collect evidence on the state of the poor, they were told that "wives and families accompany the tinker while he strolls about in search of work, and always beg. They intermarry with one another and form a distinct class." Other Travellers were originally peasants and laborers who voluntarily went on the road to look for work or else were forced into it by eviction or some personal reason—a problem with drink, the birth of an illegitimate child, marriage to a "tinker." Through time, these disparate itinerant people coalesced into a distinct group labeled by outsiders as "tinkers." Today, Travellers are characterized by a growing solidarity and political activism based on their own increased sense of ethnic or group identification as Travelling People.

Some form of social separation from outsiders is fundamental to the preservation of Traveller identity. Interaction between Travellers and other Irish people is typically limited to economic exchanges and brief instrumental encounters with bureaucrats or institutional representatives such as the police, welfare, and hospital personnel. Practices of some Travellers (e.g., keeping unsightly campsites, drinking in public, aggressive selling tactics) reinforce social distance between members of the two groups. But prejudice and discrimination have played a larger role in segregating the two communities. Government proposals to build official campsites for Travellers are invariably rejected by the local community. Most people avoid any interaction with Travellers; very few would consider marrying a Traveller. Since the mid-1960s, the Irish government has attempted to solve what it labeled "the itinerant problem," that is, the existence of Traveller families living on the roadside in tents and wagons without basic amenities such as running water, toilets, and electric lights. The solution was believed to lie in settlement, in placing families on serviced government campsites and in houses from which they could send their children to school, get wage-labor jobs, and learn to live a settled life. Assimilation was the goal. Since then, however, Travellers have become more vocal and politicized. Political action groups have been organized in some cities. Travellers now consider themselves to be an ethnic group with the rights to maintain their own identity and life-style while enjoying the privileges of other citizens.

Settlements

As recently as 1960, 92 percent of Traveller families camped in rural areas in horse-drawn wagons and in tents. Most lived in dispersed groups of one to three families from mid-March until November, when they moved back to their home village or took shelter in abandoned houses in the countryside. When traveling, they seldom remained camped in one place for more than two or three weeks and frequently for only a day or two. By 1971, the number of Traveller families living in horse-drawn wagons and in tents had dropped to 27 percent; and by 1981, to 4 percent. Today most families live in modern trailers or in houses in urban areas. Forty percent live on the roadside or in vacant lots in groups that range in size from a single nuclear family to as many as fifty families on occasion. A quarter live on government "sites" in trailers or small houses built especially for them; most of these campsites accommodate fifteen families. Thirty-six percent now live in public housing estates.

Economy

Subsistence and Commercial Activities. Travellers exploit social (rather than natural) resources, that is, individual customers and client groups within the host society. They are self-employed opportunists who use generalist strategies and spatial mobility to take advantage of marginal economic op-

portunities. Prior to World War II, Travellers moved from one farm and village to the next making and repairing tinware, cleaning chimneys, dealing in donkeys and horses, selling small household wares, and picking crops in exchange for food, clothing, and cash. They also made clothespins, brushes, brooms, and baskets; repaired umbrellas; collected horse hair, feathers, bottles, used clothing, and rags; and exploited the sentiments and fears of the settled population through begging, fortune-telling, and bogus money-making schemes. Occasionally a Traveller family worked for a farmer for an extended period of time. Travellers were welcomed for the useful services they performed and for the news and stories they brought to isolated farms, but they were also regarded with suspicion by the settled community and once their work was done they were encouraged to go. With the introduction of plastics and cheap mass-produced tin and enamelware following World War II, the tinsmith's work became increasingly obsolete. The growing affluence of the Irish population in the 1950s and 1960s also contributed to the demise of their rural-based economy. As farmers bought tractors and farm machinery, such as the beet digger, they no longer needed the agricultural labor and draft animals Travellers had provided. Likewise, the increased ownership of private cars and an expanded rural bus service, which made access to towns and shops easy, eliminated the need for the itinerant peddler. Travellers were thus forced to migrate to urban areas to look for work. In the cities they collected scrap metal and other castoffs, begged, and signed up for government welfare. Today most families earn their livelihood by selling portable consumer goods from roadside stands and door-to-door, by salvaging old cars and selling the parts, and from government assistance.

Division of Labor. Household income is produced by all family members—men and women, young and old. Children traditionally became economically productive at an early age: begging, peddling small items, picking crops, scouting opportunities for other household members, and helping in camp. Today, many attend school for part of their childhood. Older people contribute income through passive employment such as the collection of special welfare benefits. Women have always assumed important economic and domestic responsibilities within Traveller society. In rural areas, they did most of the peddling—bartering small household wares such as needles, scrubbing brushes, combs, and handmade tinware for farm produce and cash. Many also begged, told fortunes, and collected castoffs. Traveller men made tinware, swept chimneys, dealt in horses and donkeys, hired themselves out for farm and repair work, or produced handicrafts (e.g., small tables, brooms). With the move to urban areas in the 1960s and 1970s, women's economic contribution relative to men's initially increased; they begged on city streets and in residential areas, sometimes developing patron-client relationships with Irish homemakers. Their economic importance was also enhanced by the collection of the state children's allowance, which is paid to all Irish mothers. In the cities, women also began acting as cultural brokers, handling most interactions with outsiders (e.g., police, clergy, social workers). Traveller men initially focused on collecting scrap metal and other castoffs and more recently, on selling salvaged car parts and new consumer goods from roadside stands and door-to-door. They also collect unemployment assistance.

Kinship, Marriage, and Family

Kin Groups and Descent.   The basic structural unit as well as the primary unit of production and consumption is the nuclear family. Descent is bilateral with individuals having equal rights and obligations toward both their maternal and paternal kin. The importance of cognatic kinship is reflected in the use of Eskimo kinship terminology; in flexibility and choice in residence patterns, with households alternately affiliating with either the husband's or the wife's kin (although a preference for husband's kin is evident), or with nonkin, or else living on their own; and the absence of corporate kin groups.

Marriage.   Travellers marry at an earlier age than the general Irish population. In the past, most marriages were "matches" or arranged marriages negotiated by the couple's parents, typically between families who traveled in the same counties. Today, in urban areas, individual choice is much more common. But initially with the move to the city, the number of arranged marriages between close kin—first and second cousins—actually increased, as parents responded to the new experience of living in close proximity to Travellers from other parts of the country whom they barely knew.

Domestic Unit.   Traveller families range in size from 1 to 19 persons. The median family size is 6, but 36 percent of Travellers live in families of 10 or more persons.

Sociopolitical Organization

Social Organization.   The composition of groupings larger than the household, whether they are travel and camp clusters or stationary enclaves within cities, is fluid. Cognatic kinship is the fundamental means for association, but at any one time household clusters reflect a variety of individual and situational choices and may even be formed among unrelated households. Group composition and size is continually being renegotiated in response to changing economic opportunities and a host of social concerns: the emergence of personal animosities and the resulting fissioning, visits from distant kin, the need to defend relatives from insult or attack, the desire to affiliate with households of similar or higher economic status, the wish for a change of scene. The actions of police, legislators, and local government employees also play a role. In England in the 1980s, for example, the average camp size for Irish Traveller carpet dealers was 19 households, but it was not uncommon for 30 households to congregate. Such large groupings were a reaction to local authority eviction policies. By traveling and camping in large groups, Irish Travellers made it more difficult for local authorities to evict them and thus ensured themselves a longer and more economically profitable stay. Travellers respond quickly to opportunities for assembly and social engagement. Annual fairs provide distant groups, former associates and neighbors, and members of overlapping kindreds with the opportunity to meet for entertainment, trading, marriage negotiations, and fighting. Life-crisis events—marriages and funerals as well as fights, hospitalization, and imprisonment—are also important opportunities for assembly.

Political Organization.   Travellers have a common identity based on their shared life-style and marginality to settled society, but they lack formal political leaders and superordinate political structures. Indeed, adults—especially men—take great pride in their independence. Respect is paid to the elderly, especially to male heads of large families, and their advice may be sought by kin, but it is not binding.

Conflict and Social Control.   Minor disputes between households are settled through a variety of familiar mechanisms such as joking and ridicule, gossip, and, less often, discussions between the parties involved, sometimes with the help of ad hoc mediators. Serious disputes are settled by fighting or by fissioning (i.e., moving away) and avoidance. Not surprisingly, it is typically the most vulnerable families—the poorest and those least able to mobilize a large number of adult male kin—who move away. Fighting between close relatives and with nonkin is quite common. Lacking formal legal institutions and officers, physical aggression is the Travellers' ultimate mechanism of social control. But fighting also appears to be a basis for social organization. When families come together to defend each other in a major quarrel, they are expressing and reinforcing kin solidarity.

Religion

Religious Beliefs and Practices.   Irish Travellers are Roman Catholics as are most other Irish people. Most are baptized, married, and buried in the church, although few attend mass regularly. Irish Travellers have no unique religious beliefs and lack specialized religious practitioners of their own. Travellers believe in various omens that portend good or bad luck or some specific event. Chattering magpies, for example, presage trouble, flying cranes foretell a meeting with friends, two magpies and a crow hopping about the camp together mean the police are near. Many beliefs were shared with the settled Irish population, while others appear to be unique to Travellers. Today these beliefs are dying out, as is storytelling, which was once an important tradition among Irish Travellers. Around the campfire at night, they often told ghost stories and other tales of supernatural happenings, such as getting mysteriously lost while crossing a familiar field and horses balking on the road when passing the place where someone had died.

Arts.   Tinsmiths were skilled craftsmen who produced a variety of household objects, from buckets, milk containers, cake pans, sieves, funnels, and scoops to decorated lanterns. A few tinsmiths still practice, selling their wares to tourists. Other Travellers were wagon builders who decorated their wagons and carts with wagon art—painted scrolls, horseshoes, grape and leaf motifs. Music is very important to Travellers; social gatherings often include ballad singing and instrument playing. Many adult Travellers, particularly the men, play either the accordion, melodeon, harmonica, tin whistle, or spoons. Some Travellers are skilled folk musicians, interpreting old Irish ballads in new ways and creating new ones.

Death and Afterlife.   It used to be customary for families to abandon, sometimes to burn, the wagon and possessions of a dead relative for fear of the individual's ghost and to avoid bad luck. Travellers still move away after a death to escape both the memory of their loved one and the person's ghost, and most sell or abandon the trailer or wagon the person lived in. Funerals draw especially large crowds of Travellers who often come at considerable expense and from considerable distances to express their respect for the dead and to reinforce group bonds. Such large assemblies reinforce a common identity as Travellers that overrides, at least temporarily, kinship and localized political alliances. These meetings have an emotional intensity that is striking to an outside observer. It is as if what Travellers lack in formal organization or structure they make up for by periodic assembly and intense emotional interaction.

Bibliography

Gmelch, George (1987). _The Irish Tinkers: The Urbanization of an Itinerant People_. Prospect Heights, Ill.: Waveland Press.

Gmelch, Sharon (1986). _Nan: The Life of an Irish Travelling Woman_. New York: W. W. Norton.

Joyce, Nan, and Anna Farmar (1985). _Traveller: An Autobiography_. Dublin: Gill and Macmillan.

Rottman, David, A. Dale Tussing, and Miriam Wiley (1986). _The Population Structure and Living Conditions of Irish Travellers: Results from the 1981 Census of Traveller Families_. Dublin: Economic and Social Research Institute.

SHARON GMELCH

Italians

ETHNONYMS: none

Italians are citizens of Italy (the Republic of Italy). Italy occupies 301,230 square kilometers and in 1990 had an estimated population of 57,657,000. The modern nation of Italy, unified in 1861, is a mix of different regional cultures who, prior to unification, formed a number of distinct political, linguistic, and cultural units. The Tuscan dialect of Italian is the national standard, although regional dialects and languages are still widely spoken and in some areas other languages, such as Sard on Sardinia, are considered official second languages. In addition to the regional cultures—Tuscans, Sicilians, Calabrese, Piemontese, etc.—there are also distinctive national minorities—Austrians, Albanians, Germans, Greeks, French, Slovenes—and linguistic minorities such as the Ladin and Friuli.

See Calabrese; Friuli; Ladin; Piemontese; Piemontese Sinti; Sardinians; Sicilians; Slovensko Roma; Swiss, Italian; Tiroleans; Tuscans; Xoraxané Romá

Bibliography

Kurian, George T. (1990). _Encyclopedia of the First World_. 2 vols. New York: Facts on File.

Worldmark Encyclopedia of the Nations (1988). 7th ed. New York: Worldmark Press.

Jurassians

ETHNONYMS: none

The Jurassians are a French-speaking linguistic minority who live in the Jura region of the otherwise predominantly German-speaking Swiss canton of Bern. The region consists of the districts of Porrentruy, Delémont, Franches Montagnes, Moutier, Courtelary, and Neuveville. The Jura region borders France and has a total French-speaking population of about 1,235,000, constituting about 19 percent of the Swiss population as a whole.

The "Swiss Jura question"—the question of self-determination for Jurassians—has its roots in the early nineteenth century. Beginning in A.D. 1000, when Rudolph III, king of Burgundy, granted the lands of the region to the Catholic bishop of Basel, Jura was a small, independent state. It maintained its autonomous status for hundreds of years. However, when war broke out between France and Austria at the end of the eighteenth century, the Jurassians ultimately voted to become a department of the French republic. When Napoleon I was defeated in 1813, the Treaty of Paris forced France to give back the territories it had gained during the

war, including Jura, and the region once again became a part of the Swiss polity—over the strong protests of the people of Jura themselves.

After their return to Swiss control, the maintenance of a French-speaking identity and the regaining of political autonomy became issues of great importance to the people of Jura, but these issues were complicated by questions of religious orientation. The northern districts (Porrentruy, Delémont, and Franches Montagnes) were, and remain, Catholic. Their cultural identification has been strongly linked to that of France. In the southern districts of Moutier, Courtelary, and Neuveville, which are Protestant, there has been more political and religious sympathy with the canton of Bern, which is also Protestant. Although both northern and southern districts resisted all efforts toward linguistic assimilation into the German-speaking majority of Switzerland, the impetus to Jurassian political autonomy has historically been strongest by far in the districts of the Catholic north.

In the years immediately following World War II, separatist feeling ran high in the north, giving rise to the "Rassemblement Jurassien," a movement dedicated to the formation of an autonomous, French-speaking, pan-Jura canton. Although sharing the dedication to maintaining their French linguistic identity, the Jurassians of the south did not wholeheartedly support separation from the canton of Bern, and so the mostly Protestant oppositionist party, "Les Patriotes Jurassiens," was formed. The issue of Jurassian separatism thus came to polarize the region.

After nearly twenty years of political debate, the Rassemblement Jurassien succeeded in forcing a referendum on the future of Jura in 1965 that dealt specifically with the question of creating a separate canton of Jura. By 1970, the movement for an autonomous Jurassian canton had moved from the sphere of political debate: acts of violent protest against targets symbolizing the Bern regime were committed by the clandestine "Front de Libération Jurassien" with increasing frequency. At last, in 1970, the question of Jurassian autonomy was brought up before the Swiss Federal Council, which appointed a commission to study the problem. The committee recommended approval of cantonal status for Jura. The north-south division within Jura, however, was clearly shown in the results of the vote that was finally taken in 1974: while the Catholic districts voted overwhelmingly in favor of autonomous status, the three southern, Protestant districts opposed the change with a vote of seven to three against. Thus,

although the total vote came out in favor of separation, the margin of victory was slim. These results required a further political decision, for the southern districts were granted the right to decide whether or not to remain a part of Bern's canton or to join with their neighbors to the north. Two votes were taken, in March and then in September of 1975. The results were that eight communes of the southern districts cast their lot with the new canton of Jura, while the remainder retained their membership in the canton of Bern. For the Jurassian separatists this constituted a major victory, but not a complete one—their goal was, and remains, the unification of the entire French-speaking region into a single autonomous whole.

Bibliography

Bassand, Michel, Christian Lalive d'Espinay, and Pierre Thoma (1976). *Un essai de democratie culturelle: Le centre culturel jurassien.* Bern: Herbert Lang.

Clavel, Bernard (1981). *Terres de mémoire: Le Jura.* Paris: J.-P. Delarge.

NANCY E. GRATTON

Kashubians

ETHNONYMS: Cassubians, Kaszubs

Orientation

The people of Kashuby are the westernmost of the Northern Slavs, living today in north central Poland along the left bank of the lower Vistula and along the coast to the west of Gdansk. Their language has two dialects, both heavily Germanized: Kashubian proper, and Slovincian. There are approximately 200,000 Kashubian speakers living in Poland today. Their territory is in relatively high country, with many ponds, lakes, and streams. The soils are poor, principally suited for the growing of wheat. Winters are long and severe, and spring comes late to the region.

Settlements

Kashubian settlements follow no set plan. The most commonly encountered pattern is the "street village": a string of homesteads fronting upon a single roadway, with a church located somewhere along the row. However, there are also likely to be a good many outlying homesteads located at some distance from the roadway but nonetheless sharing in the village life. Houses and other buildings are principally of wood. The oldest are log cabins capped with moss or clay. Brick and mortar are relatively new building materials and still somewhat unusual. Houses are rectangular, with thatched and gabled roofs and 1.8- to 2.1-meter, cross-beamed ceilings. The chimney is located in the rough center of the house. The Kashubians do not employ carving or decoration as part of house

design, except for simple carved boards ornamenting the gables. There are two house types: the oldest kind has its entrance at one of the gabled ends and also includes a veranda within which some of the family's animals may shelter. The second house type has its entrance on one of the long sides, and within the house, one side is often given over to the animals. Most Kashubians have at least a small farm and garden of their own, but the poorest are landless and must live and work on the farms of others. In return for their labor, they receive a cottage on the farm property, as well as payments in cash and kind.

Economy

The Kashubian economy is principally based on peasant farming. Cultivation in the fields generally employs a crop rotation of potatoes, followed by two or more crops of rye, followed by wheat. In addition, the people keep a few horses and cattle, though the scarcity of pasturage limits their numbers. Hogs are universally kept, and geese, chickens, and ducks are very common. Most families also grow a vegetable garden, with peas, carrots, and cabbages. Mushrooms and berries are gathered as well. In villages near ponds or lakes, the community often specializes in fishing for salmon, flounder, eels, and pilchards, according to the season.

Whether the family is principally involved in farming or fishing, the entire family participates in the economic labor of the household. Even young children are pressed into service, tending the geese and hens. Title to property is vested in the head of household, usually male, and passes from father to eldest son or daughter upon marriage, in return for the provision of a lifetime right to lodging, as well as an allowance in cash and gardening rights for the remainder of his life. Property is transferable, but should the farm be sold, any new buyer must take on the responsibility of paying the living allowance of the elderly, should the old head of household remain alive.

Kashubian crafts reflect the self-sufficiency of the peasant farm household; traditionally, almost all the necessary tools, implements, and clothing were produced within the home. Today, such things have become the product of specialists or are likely to be of modern manufacture, but wood carving remains a common male pursuit. Carving in horn is also done, particularly of snuffboxes. Each household also once prided itself on making its own snuff, though this practice is now in decline. Women do elaborate embroidery, as well as weaving, and both men and women may weave baskets. These items are produced now for sale rather than for home consumption.

Kinship, Marriage, and Family

Kashubian marriages are arranged through a matchmaker. Long before marriageable age, a young woman begins to make her bridal outfit and to accumulate her trousseau. Once the match is approved by the couple's parents and the dowry has been fixed, arrangements for the wedding begin. Just after the arrangements are set, the father (if the groom-to-be is the eldest son or inheriting daughter) signs over title to the family farm. Weddings occur in winter, when the demands of the farm are less. The celebration includes wedding breakfasts, church service, dinners, and dancing; traditionally it went on for several days. Premarital sexual relations are known to occur and do not constitute a sufficient reason for marriage, even if a child results from the affair. Divorce is greatly frowned upon.

The household, taken as being established upon the marriage of a young couple, consists of the husband and wife, their children, and the dependent parents from whom the right to the farm was derived.

Kashubians undertake a great many precautions during a woman's pregnancy to ensure the well-being of the newborn, involving the observance of a number of food and behavioral taboos. Newborns spend the first part of their lives tightly swaddled. As they get a bit older, their care falls to elder children for the most part, and young Kashubians are expected to begin helping out around the farm at the time that they attain school age.

Kashubian households are largely independent and self-sufficient. Although subject to the laws of the Polish state, local authority is vested in the individual heads of households. There is little call for group cooperation beyond that of the family, except in the case of religious observances, and in such matters leadership falls to the priest or minister of the local church. Otherwise, it is the individual's reputation for honesty, hard work, and perhaps wit that will persuade others in the village to accept his or her advice or suggestions regarding community action.

Religion and Expressive Culture

Although Kashubians have long been Christians—and both Catholic and Protestant denominations are found in the region—a tradition of far older beliefs is still strong as well. A now-vanished race of giants was traditionally believed to have created the physical landscape. Dwarfs or goblins, thought usually to be helpful but often moved to malice if slighted or spied upon, are blamed for most misfortune. The Devil, or devils, are treated as active, personalized presences in the world. Death and disease, too, are believed to assume personified forms. Individuals are thought to have a number of supernatural capabilities, the most benign being the gift of "second sight." Less benign are those, usually women, who possess the "evil eye" and work spells against their neighbors. _Mora_, or succuba, are usually women who, unintentionally, become the host of a vindictive spirit that slips out of the body while it sleeps, assuming the form of a familiar animal, and sucks the blood of others. To protect against the depredations of the mora, pentagrams are drawn, and windows and doors are kept locked at night. In some villages there is also the belief in werewolves, which can only be men.

Important ceremonial occasions for the Kashubians, other than life-cycle rituals, derive from the liturgical calendar and from the agricultural cycle. Midsummer's Eve is one such occasion, involving processions, bonfires, musicians, and the performance of a village drama. At the end of May, a solemn procession is made to secure blessings for the fields and crops. Christmas is a time for family feasting, but Twelfth Night (Epiphany) is a much larger celebratory event, involving processions, and may have its origins in pre-Christian Carnaval.

Kashubian beliefs in life after death diverge somewhat from the strict teachings of Christianity. After death, the deceased is thought to undergo a formal trial before God and to depart to a heaven or hell that is construed to mean a physical place. Souls are thought to remain in the area known to them in life if there are sins that must be expiated. The relationship between a farmer and his property is considered to be highly personalized; therefore, the eldest son is required to go out and announce the death of the head of household to all the deceased's animals and to the fields. In the house of the deceased, all windows are opened to encourage the soul to escape, and the mirror is covered and the clock is stopped. The funeral ceremony at the church is solemn, as is the burial procession, but these are followed by a lively funeral feast in the village.

Bibliography

Lorentz, Fr., Adam Fischer, and Tadeuxz Lehr-Splawinski (1935). _The Cassubian Civilization_. London: Faber & Faber.

NANCY E. GRATTON

Ladin

ETHNONYMS: Dolomites, Ladinos

The Ladin are a predominantly Catholic, linguistic minority of northeastern alpine Italy. They live in the high valleys of Alto Adige and the Dolomites and number approximately 30,000. Although most Ladin can speak Standard Italian, they have taken great pride as well in maintaining their own language. Classed as a member of the Rhaeto-Romance Family, Ladin was long thought to be one of three dialects (the other two being Friulian and Romansch), but it now is treated as a language in its own right. The use of the term "Ladino" as an ethnonym for "Ladin" is somewhat confusing, since "Ladino" refers as well to the traditional language of Sephardic Jews, from which Ladin is quite distinct. While there is some inferential evidence suggesting that Ladin may have existed in written form as early as the fourteenth century, the earliest documents that have been found date only to the 1700s.

The Ladin are a mountain peasantry who have historically and culturally identified with the German-speaking populations of the part of South Tirol in which they live. Their economy was based originally on the cultivation of fruits and vegetables and on pastoralism. Today the region's economy centers on mining and quarrying, manufacturing, industry, and tourism. In the area of Alto Adige, viticulture also plays an important role.

Prior to World War I, the portion of the southern Tirol occupied by the Ladin was a part of Austria, but after the Treaty of Versailles it was annexed to Italy. The Ladin resisted Mussolini's policies of linguistic assimilation, and after World War II they secured the right to institute instruction in the Ladin language in the schools of some parts of the region. Since the 1960s there have been a number of efforts to foster a Ladin cultural renaissance and to secure a greater degree of political autonomy for the region.

Although there has been a great deal of scholarly attention paid to the Ladin, particularly with regard to their language, there are no full-length works available in the English language.

Bibliography

Bezzola, Reto R. (1979). *Litteratura dals Rumauntschse e Ladins*. Curia: Ligra Ramontscha.

Sabatini, Gianpaolo (1976). *I Ladini: Come nato e come si estingue un popolo*. Florence: Cipriani.

Sulzer, Giuseppe Giorgio (1985). *Dell' origine et della natura dei dialetti comunements chiamanti romanici messia confronto coi dialetti consimili esistenti nel Tirolo*. A. Forni, Sala Bolognese.

Leonese

ETHNONYMS: none

Orientation

Leon is a province of northern Spain, bordered on the north by Asturias, on the south by Zamorra, on the east by Palencia, and on the west by Galicia. Its capital, also called Leon, is located roughly at the center of the province, on the Torio and Bernesga rivers at 42°37' N and 5°30' W. The land is generally mountainous, extending some 9,600 square kilometers, and is largely rural in character. There are extensive woodlands, wastelands, and natural pastures. Except along the several rivers of the province, the soils are generally poor, best suited to the cultivation of cereals. Winters can be cold, and drought in summer is not uncommon—this region does not partake of the Mediterranean climatic influences felt in the more southerly regions of Spain.

The ratio of persons to land in Leon is low, and much of the territory is unsettled and undeveloped today. Over the last several decades, population has increased only slowly, more as a result of a lowered death rate than any rise in birthrates. Migration out of the rural areas also has been a long-standing factor in keeping demographic pressures low.

Leonese is one of the many dialects of Spanish, not sufficiently divergent to be considered a language in its own right.

History and Cultural Relations

The city of Leon was founded as a Roman frontier town, later conquered by the Moors. Very early in the period of the Spanish reconquest—in the eighth to tenth centuries—it, and the countryside surrounding it, regained its independence. During this time, the movement of populations into the area was encouraged by the Spanish kings, through the policy of granting ownership of unoccupied lands to those who took the care and time to clear and cultivate them. In about the middle of the eleventh century this region was united with Castile, only to be separated again in the mid-twelfth century; it was reunited with Castile once more in 1230.

Settlements

In Leon one finds small, nucleated village or town centers, each consisting of residences, local shops, taverns, and a church, as well as an administrative center. The median size of such a village is small—perhaps twenty-five households. Surrounding these settled areas one finds a region of cultivated lands, broken up into a myriad of small plots often less than a hectare each in size; this cultivated zone is itself generally surrounded by uncultivated scrub or woodland. Mud and adobe brick form the principal construction materials. The houses of the village are built as roughly rectangular structures, with each surrounding an open central space that serves as a corral. Set into the front wall are two doors, the smaller one to provide access for people and the larger one to accommodate the passage of a wagon. In the traditional layout, the principal living quarters are set up along the front of the structure, with sleeping rooms on the second floor, while shelter spaces for household animals (cows, sheep, chickens, pigs, and perhaps a donkey or two) run along the two sides. Along the back one finds storage areas for grain and other farm products. At one corner of the structure one once commonly found a kitchen; nowadays the room that serves that function for the household is part of the living area at the front. Where the old kitchen once stood, today one frequently finds a large oven used for baking bread.

Economy

Subsistence and Commercial Activities. The Leonese economy is predominantly agricultural, with grain being the principal crop. Rye and wheat are the most important and are sown on as much of the private land as will support them, as well as on common lands. Barley is sown on the remainder. Animal husbandry is also important—each household keeps cows, oxen, sheep, and goats. These animals are merged with the livestock of other households in the village and pastured together on common lands, with herding responsibilities rotated among households in a system called *vecera*. Households also maintain gardens and keep chickens, turkeys, ducks, and geese, as well as a family pig.

Industrial Arts. There is specialization in the trades (e.g., carpentry, smithing), and shops specialize in the provision of goods and services needed by the community. There is, however, little industrialization outside of major urban areas, and when farm work is not sufficient to employ villagers, some must leave the area to find employment. Traditional cottage industries arise from the processing of flax and the production of linseed and thread.

Division of Labor. Women work in the fields along with the men and are included in all household and farm decision making, but they are excluded from community leadership. Domestic tasks and child rearing are specifically women's work.

Land Tenure. Individuals each hold title to several scattered, small plots, the total area of which rarely exceeds 3 hectares, as a result of an inheritance system that operates on the principle of equal shares to all heirs, women as well as men. These small holdings, in themselves inadequate to support the needs of individual households, are offset by use rights to communal lands, which consist of woodlands, "wastes" or scrublands, and grazing areas.

Kinship, Marriage, and Family

Kinship is reckoned bilaterally, as is descent, but in terms of descent the paternal line is the more significant.

Marriage. Age at first marriage in Leon is generally 18 to 23 for women and 24 to 26 for men. Each of the potential spouses has a say in the match. Traditionally, each of the newlyweds received a marriage portion (*dote*) from their parents, as a sort of advance on their inheritances, but beginning in the late nineteenth century this practice became too great an economic burden, jeopardizing the functioning of the parental households, and thus it no longer occurs. Husband and wife often continue to live in their respective parents' houses, so that they can continue to help on the farm and share in the harvests—otherwise, they would have no land upon which to establish their own farming enterprise. At night, the husband goes to the wife's house to sleep.

Domestic Unit. In Leon, the house itself may contain a number of related nuclear families, usually constituting a sororal or fraternal cooperative group (sisters, their spouses, and their several offspring; or brothers and their spouses and children) or a marital pair and one or more of their married offspring. A widowed parent generally goes to live with a married daughter.

Inheritance. Property rarely passes to the children of the owner prior to his or her death. Rather, use rights to the property, including land, are conferred. Children exercising rights of usufruct are thought to owe their parents part of the grain harvest in return for their land use. Strict equality of inheritance is observed—not only in kind but in quality. Thus, if the family property consists of lands of varying arability, each heir will receive a small part of each type of land. This principle is followed in the case of inherited livestock and household goods as well, whenever possible. The division of all property into equal portions is established in advance, and then the portions are allocated among the heirs by drawing lots. Inheritance of the house itself usually falls to the daughter or son who takes care of the elderly parents prior to their deaths.

Socialization. Early childhood training is the responsibility of the mother, although other female members of the household may participate in the process. Extrafamilial institutions involved in socialization include the school and the church.

Sociopolitical Organization

Each household is independent in the conduct of its internal affairs. Deference in this context is paid to the owner of the house, when decisions must be made regarding joint activities on the farm. However, each adult member of the household, female and male, has a voice. Outside of the household, local sociopolitical organization is dominated by the concept of the *concejo* or council, in which each head of household participates. Meetings held in fall and winter, often in conjunction with feasts, are held in the town meeting hall. In spring and summer, they are often held outside. These councils stand as the guardians of customary law, deciding on such community concerns as the use of common lands. Only men could serve on the councils, and among men, only those who were married and possessed a house and some land in the village itself. Upon admission to the council, the member paid a fee. The system of turn taking—in pasturing the pooled cattle of the villagers, for example—was regulated by the council. Other activities that were the responsibility of the council were the organizing of communal labor to repair roads and maintain boundary markers and to serve in other economic, political, and religious capacities on a turn-taking basis. Such council decisions were optimally achieved by consensus, but leaders and officers existed, chosen by election. Community self-rule of times past was legally displaced in the nineteenth-century imposition of uniform laws throughout the state, and organs responsive to the centralized government (*juntas administrativa*) were established in their place. Yet the council system persists, retaining much of its role as interpreter and enforcer of local customary law.

Religion and Expressive Culture

Spain is a Catholic country, and the influence of the church is strong in Leon. Attendance at weekly mass and at masses celebrated for important events on the liturgical calendar is expected. The bread for the mass traditionally was baked by a different female head of household each week, with one piece held in reserve to be passed on to the woman who would be responsible for the next week's baking.

Beliefs regarding the afterlife are consistent with the teachings of the Catholic church. Traditionally, when a villager or his or her spouse died, all work in the community was prohibited and the council sent two fellow villagers to the household of the deceased in order to sit vigil over the body. The council also provided someone to dig the grave. Attendance at the funeral by villagers was equally enforced, through the assessment of fines. Responsibility for sitting vigil circulated among the households of the village, according to the system of turn taking mentioned earlier with reference to herding duties; however, funeral attendance was a villagewide responsibility.

Bibliography

Behar, Ruth (1986). *Santa Maria del Monte: The Presence of the Past in a Spanish Village.* Princeton: Princeton University Press.

NANCY E. GRATTON

Lowland Scots

ETHNONYMS: Scots, Scottish

Orientation

The Scottish Lowlands are made up of the southern portion of Scotland, the central region, the eastern coast, and most of the northeastern coast. The bulk of Scotland's population (about 80 percent) lives in the Lowlands, particularly in the urban and industrial areas around such major cities as Glasgow and Aberdeen, as well as in the capital city of Edinburgh. Taken as a whole, the Lowlands comprise some 48,648 square kilometers in land area and have a population in excess of 5 million. The climate is generally cool and wet, but there is variation across the region. There are few thunderstorms and little fog. Days are long in summer, short in winter.

Unlike that of the Highlanders, the language of Lowland Scots is not Gaelic but is rather a variant form of English introduced by Germanic settlers in the region as early as the sixth century A.D. The distinctiveness of what is now called "Scots" or Northern English, which was once called "Inglis," is great enough to merit its treatment as a language in its own right, rather than simply a dialect of the official or Standard English of southern Britain. Scots is a language with a long literary tradition, dating back to the 1300s. In the early 1700s English was made the official language, at least with regards to administration, for all of Britain, and Scots suffered a loss of prestige for a time. However, the linguistic tradition remained strong, borne in ballads, verse, and folk songs and preserved in the mid-seventeenth-century poetry of Robert Burns, perhaps the most famous of writers associated with the tongue.

History and Cultural Relations

The Romans arrived in the Scottish Lowlands in A.D. 80 but left few traces of their stay. During the period known as the Dark Ages, four groups emerged in Scotland: the Picts in the north; the Scots (of Irish origin) in the west; the Britons, who were related to the Welsh, in the southwest; and the Angles in the southeast. Linguistically, these groups were distinct from one another: the linguistic tradition of the Angles derived from Low German and Saxon English, the Scots and Britons spoke Gaelic, and the Picts possessed a language of their own. The formation of a unitary nation out of these disparate groups came about as a result of external pressures and the slow growth of Christianity in the region.

The first Scottish king, formally recognized, was Malcolm II (1005–1034), who inherited control of the southwestern portion of Scottish territory and won lands to the southeast through conflicts with England. But through the eleventh and twelfth centuries, rulership was frequently disputed among local leaders, and individual petty kings often sought English alliances to strengthen their causes. By the late thirteenth century, this state of affairs had resulted in increasing English control over the region. King Edward I of England arbitrated among claimants to the Scottish throne and installed John Balliol in that position for a time—though he was later to depose Balliol and assume personal control in 1296. The Treaty of Northhampton, in 1328, confirmed Scottish nationhood.

At about this time the house of Stuart arose, from which line came a succession of Scotland's leadership, nearly ending with Catholic Mary Stuart, who was beheaded in 1587. Her son became James I of England and James VI of Scotland. The last reigning Stuart was James II of England (James VII of Scotland), who was forced to abdicate in 1688, largely because the predominantly Protestant Scots rejected his devout Catholicism.

The year 1707 brought about the formal Act of Union with England, linking the political entities of Scotland and England. While the political fortunes of the two nations have remained joined one to another since that time, the strong sense of a specifically Scottish national identity has never been erased, and to this day there are strong movements aimed at establishing Scottish independence.

Economy

The Lowlands consist of both rural and urban, agricultural and industrial, areas. Within the Lowlands, regional differentiation is marked in part by divergent economic practice. Although the county of Lothian, for example, is predominantly industrial, East Lothian is known as "corn country" and possesses some of the most prosperous farms of the region, while the Borders are associated with sheep husbandry. Glasgow is the industrial heart of the region, with its economy centered on the busy Clyde docks. It is thus difficult to describe some overall Lowland Scots culture, tradition, or economy. Once known for having higher wages and greater economic opportunities than the rest of Great Britain, the area has suffered something of a decline since the middle of this century, and unemployment has led to significant out-migration. Its traditional industries include shipbuilding and coal mining, both of which have grown less prosperous in recent years. Newer industries include electronics. Women working outside the home can be found today in all fields, but in the past they were associated largely with the textile industries and domestic work. In agricultural regions, a greater division of labor by gender was to be found, with women traditionally occupied in hand weeding and reaping with the sickle; culturally they were prescribed from working with horses. In the Scottish Lowlands, as elsewhere in industrialized regions, there is a marked difference in wage levels for men and women, with women often earning substantially less than their male counterparts.

Scotland as a whole has long honored the idea of education and equal access thereto. Public education, once controlled by the churches, came more and more under the control of the state during the nineteenth century. Higher education is highly valued, and the universities of St. Andrews, Edinburgh, and Glasgow are of world renown. It was not until the last decade of the nineteenth century that women were legally granted full-status access to university-level education.

Religion and Expressive Culture

Religious affiliation in Lowlands Scotland is pluralistic, and sissenting churches have included the Secession, Relief, Episcopal, and Roman Catholic churches. The Free Church of Scotland was created in the mid-1800s, and the Catholic church underwent a significant increase during roughly the same period, largely as a result of a major influx of Irish immigrants who fled to Scotland to escape the Irish potato famine. Also during this period, the Secession and Relief churches, which had formed in rebellion against the control of the Crown over the established Church of Scotland, were merged to form the United Presbyterian church. Church affiliation is to some degree linked to socioeconomic position in the Lowlands, with tradespeople predominating within the United Presbyterian church, the "landed gentry" associated most strongly with Episcopalianism, and rural laborers largely belonging to the Church of Scotland. Church influence in daily life was and remains strongest in rural areas as compared to urban ones.

The contribution of Scots to literature and the arts is immense. Lowlanders of world renown include R. L. Stevenson, Walter Scott, A. Conan Doyle, J. M. Barrie, David Hume, and Adam Smith. The Borders are famed as the heartland of minstrels and were the home of Walter Scott. Thomas Carlyle was born in the rural southwest. Burns wrote of the rich agricultural world of East Lothian.

Bibliography

Fraser, W. Hamish, and R. J. Morris, eds. (1988–1991). _People and Society in Scotland: A Social History of Modern Scotland in Three Volumes_. Edinburgh: John Donald Publishers.

NANCY E. GRATTON

Luxembourgeois

ETHNONYM: Luxembourgers

The Luxembourgeois are the citizens of the nation of Luxembourg (Grand Duchy of Luxembourg). Luxembourg is a landlocked nation of 2,586 square kilometers bounded on the south by France, on the west and north by Belgium, and on the east by Germany. In 1990 the estimated population was 369,000. Luxembourgeois are mostly of German, French, Belgian, and Italian ancestry. Today, however, they see themselves as a distinct cultural group. That distinctiveness, however, is based more on their political independence than on marked cultural or linguistic distinctions. French is the language of government while German is the language of business. Recently, there has been a resurgence of interest in learning and speaking Letzeburgeshe (Luxembourgian), a local dialect of German with roots in the Moselle Frankish language once spoken in western Germany. Most Luxembourgeois are Roman Catholics, although there is also a marked Mennonite community.

Luxembourg has a free-market economy based on agriculture (barley, oats, potatoes, clover, rosebushes, grapes for wine making), livestock (pigs and dairy products), tourism, and industry (steel). Luxembourg is a constitutional monarchy governed by the Grand Duke or Duchess, a prime minister, and a Chamber of Deputies.

Bibliography

Kurian, George T. (1990). _Encyclopedia of the First World_. 2 vols. New York: Facts on File.

Madeirans

ETHNONYMS: Insular Portuguese, Madeirense

Orientation

Identification. In about 1419 Portuguese mariners made landfall on the little Atlantic island (42 square kilometers) of Porto Santo (holy haven); 40 kilometers to the southwest they discovered Madeira (isle of timber), the most populous (260,000) and largest (741 square kilometers) island of the Madeiran Archipelago. Portuguese culture, with a strong British overlay, still permeates insular political, economic, and social life. The archipelago includes the uninhabited Ilhas Desertas (Deserta Grande, Châo, Bugio), just offshore southeastern Madeira, and the tiny Ilhas Selvagens (wild islands) 270 kilometers south, on the northern fringe of the Canaries. Madeira owes its resort image to a benign climate, a profusion of scenic marvels, and world-renowned wines.

Location. The Madeiran archipelago lies between 33° and 30° N and 15° and 17° W on the eastern edge of the Atlantic Basin, 978 kilometers southwest of Lisbon. These islands are mountain peaks of seismic origin rising from the abyssal ocean floor; from an ocean depth of 5,000 meters its central massif rises to 1,861 meters (Pico Ruivo). The island's sheer, unapproachable coastline and convoluted terrain create multiple microclimatic and vegetation zones. Southern Madeira is warm (with a mean annual temperature of 18° C) and dry. The north receives heavy precipitation (up to 200 centimeters per year) and functions as an island watershed by virtue of an intricate water-control system (*levadas,* or conduits) dating from the sixteenth century. The high overall population density (440 persons per square kilometer) requires intense utilization of every type of econiche. Porto Santo is warm, dry, and largely flat, with a 7-kilometer-long beach along its southern fringe.

Demography. By 1427 three captain-proprietors (*donatários*) were directing settlement (*povoamento*) of Madeira's southern and northern halves and of Porto Santo. The southern "captaincy," centered on Funchal (named for *funcho,* or fennel, a local aromatic herb), soon outpaced other regions. Today almost half of the island's population of 260,000 inhabitants live in greater Funchal. The original settlers were Portuguese; later genetic admixtures came from occupying pirate forces, British merchants, Spanish priests, and Africans, Moors, and Jews. Until recently most islanders lived in extreme geographical and social isolation. The small stature, darker skin, and inflected speaking of people from Madeira's remote northwest suggest protracted genetic drift. Rural Madeirans inhabit different linguistic, social, and economic worlds than city residents. The prevalence of absentee landholdings and high population density gives rise to frequent emigration, commonly to South America. Porto Santo's population (3,500) is largely composed of retirees, airline personnel, and (permanent) tourists.

Linguistic Affiliation. The language of the Madeiras is Standard European Portuguese (SEP), which follows Romance Language Family conventions (inflective, synthetic, and stress-timed) and is the norm against which internal insular variations are evaluated. The most distinctive pronunciation feature is a characteristic shift of high front "i" (as in English "*see*") to the diphthong "ei" (as in "th*ey*"). A marked contrast between the speech of Madeira's urban elites and rural folk is a strong indicator of social status. English is the lingua franca in Funchal and other tourist centers. A richly diverse lexicon reflects a cosmopolitan cultural ambiance.

History and Cultural Relations

In about 1419 Prince Henry the Navigator incorporated the uninhabited Madeiras into Portugal's overseas territories. To three of his captains he delegated the task of settlement: Zarco and Teixeira in Madeira, Perestrelo in Porto Santo. Funchal's founder, Joâo Gonçalves Zarco, is prominently memorialized in the city. To make Madeira cultivable, forests were burned and mountainside terraces (*poios*) were constructed. Despite harsh terrain, massive soil erosion, and difficult access to water, agriculture remains Madeira's lifeblood. In the late sixteenth century, wine replaced sugar as the island's chief export commodity. Madeira was a nexus of Atlantic trade in the days of sailing ships, and a frequent target for pirate raids. Spain ruled the Madeiras, Azores, and mainland Portugal from 1580 to 1640. In 1660 the British, already influential in island viniculture, signed a commercial treaty with Portugal, and between 1807 and 1814 they occupied Madeira. Their shipping interests opened the island to nineteenth- and twentieth-century British tourism. In the 1950s seaplanes linked Madeira to Portugal and England. Porto Santo's international terminal, a NATO emergency base, opened in 1960; Madeira's opened in 1965. Portugal granted limited local autonomy to the Madeiras in 1940 and regional autonomy in 1976.

Settlements

Major Madeiran settlements lie below 700 meters and on, or accessible to, Madeira's crucial national coastal road (Estrada Nacional 101). EN101's last (1952) link was a tunnel through the rock precipice that is Madeira's north coast. Major EN101 towns average 3,000 to 4,000 inhabitants and range in size from Seixal (900 people), at the east end of the north coast tunnel, to Machico (11,000), landing site of the original settlers. Interior towns (2,000–8,000 residents) lie at the head of *ribeiras* at the edge of mountain heartland, are on main roads, are handicraft centers, and are of historical interest or scenic value. Strip settlements follow a twisting EN101 from Funchal west to Calheta (60 kilometers) along Madeira's populous south coast. In the sparsely settled north, villages cluster in valley bottoms away from the coast or on promontories above the sea. Many small farmsteads remain in remote mountain valleys, their isolation diminished by an ever-expanding island road network. The traditional peasant dwelling is low-lying and dark, with thick stone walls under crawling ivies, not much larger than nearby straw-thatched *palheiros* (cow huts). Pastel stuccoed exteriors with *azulejo* (glazed decorative tile) trim, russet tile roofing, shuttered windows, and multistory units have superseded older half-timbered, ridged-thatch, A-frame rural structures. By contrast, Funchal is an architectural mélange of palatial homes, malls, tessellated plazas, relic colonial buildings, former country estates (*quintas*) incorporated within city limits as museums, and high-rise glass and concrete hotels. The most striking is the Casino Park complex designed by Brazilian Oscar Neimeyer; the most elegant is Reid's, the former Blandy (British) estate, one of Europe's prime resort hotels. The cathedral (_sé_), center of Madeiran spiritual life, blends Moorish, Gothic, Romanesque, and Manueline design elements that echo formative historical forces. In old parts of the city, tiny artisan workshops line narrow cobbled alleys near the old customs house (_alfândega_).

Economy

Subsistence and Commercial Activities. Madeira has a cash economy centered on the export of agricultural commodities (sugar, tropical fruit, wine); internal commerce is heavily dependent on tourism, the major island revenue source. Despite constant emigration, population density is at a level to preclude subsistence on locally produced food; staples (wheat, corn, meat) are imported. Tourism provides service jobs for 25,000 residents. Madeiran handicrafts (_artesanato_)—wicker, embroidery, wood carving, wines—are major export commodities and an important adjunct to tourism.

Industrial Arts. Skilled, manual labor is integral to Madeiran artesanato developed over the years in tiny mountain enclaves. Wickerwork (_obra de vimes_), hand embroidery (_bordados_), tapestry (_tapeçaria_), wood- and wrought-ironwork, porcelains, and viniculture (_vinhos_) are major folk industries founded on artisan tradition. Decorative tiles (_azulejos_) of Moorish provenience are widely used in design.

Trade. Funchal's Mercado dos Lavradores, market center for island produce and some crafts, is the "floating garden" in microcosm and sells fruits of land, sea, and skilled folk labor. Shops for specialty products (e.g., fish markets by the water's edge) are found throughout Madeira, and refreshment stands and cafés line Porto Santo's 7-kilometer beach. Primary trading partners are Portugal, the United States, and European nations.

Division of Labor. Tourism has shifted traditional labor allocations within the peasant household. Some members now commute daily from all parts of the island to service jobs. Women continue to perform the bulk of household chores and child care, for themselves and for urban employers. Men are responsible for poio maintainance, construction, bus and taxi driving, and fishing. Wickerwork and viniculture are largely gender-neutral; women do needlework, men woodwork.

Land Tenure. The term _bemfeitoria_ (improvements) is mnemonic for a sharecropping system. Land and water rights are owned by a landlord. "Improvements" (walls, buildings, walkways, trees), which are reimbursable in event of eviction, are owned by the tenant. The landless 40 percent of farm workers has the lowest priority for water distribution, the sine qua non of land value. One-third to one-half of produce is taken by the proprietor.

Kinship

Kin Groups and Descent. Portuguese administrative practice and religious ideology stress the family as basic kin unit, a tenet historically reinforced in Madeira's isolated uplands by extreme lack of peasant mobility. Kin relationships extend into mutual support networks among women and into cooperative labor pools for locally based farm or cottage industry. Emigrant remittances make manifest enduring kin ties; bilateral descent is culturally underlined by island endogamy. Urban Madeirans follow modern European familial conventions.

Kinship Terminology. Kin terminology is formally Eskimo, subject to generational and collateral extension in domestic groups where elderly female kin customarily remain active. The _padrinho/madrinha_ (godparent) role adds a spiritual dimension to respectful acceptance of the aged.

Marriage and Family

Marriage. Marriage among the tiny population aggregates of remote mountain ravines can be assumed as historically endogamous to the point of inbreeding. Today there are few arranged marriages, and local exogamy and on-island intermarriage among villagers are the norm. The peasant family household has been the core productive unit of Madeira's agricultural economy and now provides labor for its service economy. Access to Funchal and the employment alternatives of tourism have weakened the hold of the church in marital affairs, but even city parishioners remain devout. Divorce is still rare, though philandering and abandonment (by emigration) are not.

Domestic Unit. Outside metropolitan Funchal, the domestic unit remains the basic subsistence unit, and (nuclear) family tasks are allocated by traditional sex roles. Farming and a variety of cottage industries are chief sources of support. At home or workshop, girls acquire needlework skills (embroidery, bordados, and tapestry, tapeçaria), while boys apprentice in viniculture, artisan trades, and construction until marriage.

Inheritance. Inheritance occurs without regard to gender, with slight preference going to the caretaker of elders. Traditional land tenure renders moot many meaningful rights of inheritance.

Socialization. Rural children are raised within a loosely extended family, and their labor is accessory to farm work from an early age. Preautonomy (1976), schooling was minimal: it is now compulsory through primary level (age 11). Further options, mostly vocational in nature, require moving to Funchal or off the islands. The parish church reinforces conformity to values such as the central role of family and respect for authority.

Sociopolitical Organization

Social Organization. In terms of economic, occupational, and legal norms, rural Madeirans have lived as if on a medieval estate; that is, they have endured social and geographic immobility in a virtual caste system. Social inequality was—and, to some extent, still is—validated by adherence to religious orthodoxy. Its tourist-generated wealth, sophisticated ambiance, and educated citizenry make socially complex Funchal a subcultural anomaly within all of insular Portugal. Despite rural-urban interpenetration and growing economic interdependence, patron-client social distinctions remain largely in place.

Political Organization. Since 1976 the Madeiras have been an autonomous region (_região_) within greater Portugal, with their civil affairs administered under Portugal's constitution by a Lisbon-assigned minister of the republic who appoints the president of regional government. A locally elected regional assembly selects from among its deputies a president and presiding officer, who is second to the minister of the republic in political power. Funchal is headquarters for six regional secretariats, one for Porto Santo. Locally based political parties are illegal and expressly forbidden, but they continue to operate clandestinely in Funchal (e.g., FLAMA, Frente de Libertaçâo da Madeira). Widespread popular participation in local governance is inhibited by a long tradition of colonial dependence, by mass ignorance of political procedure, and by the parochialism and debilitation that centuries of choking authoritarianism have created.

Social Control.   Portugal has been imperially proficient at control from afar, abetted on the parish level by the Catholic church and, in Madeira, by de facto British economic control. Conflict at any level has been traditionally suppressed.

Conflict.   Madeira has been a passive participant in European warfare. Rural dwellers remain effectively hostage to basic human rights' suppression. Underlying political dissent is mainly confined to Funchal. Disputes over women, and more recently drugs, account for most interpersonal conflict.

Religion and Expressive Culture

Religious Beliefs.   Although Catholicism is the state religion of Portugal and its insular extensions, on a village level the parish church controls spiritual affairs. The folk publicly mark their faith by ceremonial display and by ritual performance in the *festa*, as does the city dweller.

Religious Practitioners.   The priest is the liturgical leader of his parish, the local agent of the church hierarchy and an earthly representative of divine intercession. The church's healing mission in Funchal has been superseded by modern medical practice and facilities. Outlying clinics with trained midwives have largely replaced rural "granny" healers.

Ceremonies.   Madeira's festivals (festas) are traditional, most of them seasonal, and all are, in some measure, lures for the tourist dollar. The festival year begins in February with Carnaval; in spring there is Funchal's Festa da Flor (flowers) and Bachfest (music); in mid-August, the pilgrimage to the church of Madeira's patron saint (Nossa Senhora do Monte); wine harvest festivals during autumn; and Christmas and year's end festivals in Funchal (Festa de Sâo Silvestre). Local saints are celebrated in parishes all over Madeira. Folk dancers perform at Funchal's larger hotels on a regular schedule.

Arts.   In addition to the crafts (artesanato) listed in Industrial Arts, Madeiran art includes religious design (intricately carved ceilings, balustrades, altars), gilded wood figurines (*talhas douradas*), and monumental architecture in the Manueline tradition. Folk dancers (*danças populares*) in native costume (*trajes*) use indigenous musical instruments (*machête, braguinha, bringuinho*). Tapestry (*tapeçarias*) objects include portraits, local landscapes, floral motifs, and copies of famous paintings. Madeira's most famous tapestry has 7 million stitches and is on permanent display at the Instituto do Bordado, Tapeçarias e Artesanato da Madeira.

Medicine.   Medical and public health practice in Funchal is similar to that of western Europe; rural Madeira and Porto Santo have easy access (e.g., interisland flights with ambulance capability). Folk curers are the rural equivalent of the city pharmacy (*farmácia*), which can diagnose illness, prescribe medication, and keep patient records. Heavy smoking and alcohol abuse account for many islander health problems.

Death and Afterlife.   Beliefs are grounded in Catholic theology. Funerals are an important liturgical event, followed by a prescribed, but no longer protracted, period of mourning and diminishing restrictions on widow remarriage.

Bibliography

Brown, A. Samler (1901). *Madeira and the Canary Islands, with the Azores*. 6th ed. London: Marston.

Bryans, Robin (1959). *Madeira, Pearl of the Atlantic*. London: Robert Hale.

Duncan, T. Bentley (1972). *Atlantic Islands, Madeira, the Azores and the Cape Verdes in the Seventeenth Century: Commerce and Navigation*. Chicago: University of Chicago Press.

Ludtke, Jean (1989). *Atlantic Peeks: Ethnographic Guide to the Portuguese-Speaking Atlantic Islands*. Hanover, Mass.: Christopher Publishing House.

Rogers, Francis Millet (1979). *Atlantic Islanders of the Azores and Madeiras*. North Quincy, Mass.: Christopher Publishing House.

Serstevens, Albert t'. (1966). *Le périple des îles Atlantides: Madère, Açores, Canaries*. Paris: Arthaud.

JEAN LUDTKE

Maltese

ETHNONYM: il-Maltin

Orientation

Identification.   Malta and her sister islands, Gozo and Comino, together with the uninhabited islets of Filfla and Cominotto, make up the Maltese Archipelago.

Location.   The Maltese islands lie midway between Gibraltar and the Lebanon, at almost the exact geographical center of the Mediterranean Sea. Sicily is 93 kilometers to the north, and Tunis just over 320 kilometers to the west. Malta, the largest and southernmost island, is 27 kilometers long and 14.4 kilometers wide, and it covers an area of 247 square kilometers. Gozo is only 14.4 kilometers by 8 kilometers, with an area of 67.6 square kilometers. The little islands of Comino and Cominotto, which lie in the 4.8-kilometer-wide channel separating the two larger islands, together have an area of 2.6 square kilometers. Filfla, a large rock that was used for gunnery practice, lies 4.8 kilometers off the southwest coast of Malta. The climate is typically Mediterranean, with long hot summers and cold wet winters. Average annual precipitation is about 58 centimeters. Temperatures vary from a mean maximum of 31.6° C in July to a mean minimum in January of 9.3° C. In general the sea insulates the islands against extreme temperatures, though July temperatures occasionally rise to around 40° C and can drop to just above freezing in January.

Demography. In 1989 approximately 350,000 persons lived on the islands' 317 square kilometers. This makes the Maltese archipelago, with a population density of 1,104 per square kilometer, one of the world's most thickly populated countries. The birthrate declined sharply following World War II and in 1987 stood at 15.4 live births per 1,000 people. As infant mortality also declined (in 1987 7.3 deaths per 1,000 live births) and net emigration ceased by the mid-1970s, the population has been expanding since the 1960s (population in 1967 was 314,000).

Linguistic Affiliation. Maltese is a Semitic language. It is morphologically related to North African Arabic but draws much of its vocabulary and idiom from Sicilian and, more recently, from English. This interesting and difficult language is spoken by all classes, but it did not become an official language of the law courts until 1934, when it replaced Italian. It has been a written language since the middle of the last century and uses the Latin alphabet. Much of the instruction at the University of Malta and in secondary schools is given in English, which is widely spoken.

History and Cultural Relations

Malta's strategic location and its large sheltered deep-water harbors have influenced its history in no small measure. Malta has belonged to a succession of major Mediterranean powers. Phoenicians, Carthaginians, Greeks, Romans, and Arabs occupied the islands. Following conquest by the Normans in 1070, Malta shared the fate of Sicily and passed successively to the Swabians, Angevins, Aragonese, and Castilians. In 1530 the islands were handed by Emperor Charles V to the Sovereign Military Order of St. John of Jerusalem. This powerful body of wealthy European nobles, dedicated to helping the poor and sick and to waging war on Islam, in their turn were driven from Malta in 1798 by Napoleon. Britain replaced France in 1800 and controlled the islands until the country gained its independence in 1964.

The legacy of its checkered history as a bastion of Christianity and an island fortress is still very much evident: relative prosperity; a high degree of centralization; the power of the Roman Catholic church; an ability to adapt to new economic, political, and cultural influences; and a deep-seated cultural orientation toward Europe.

Settlements

In spite of the intense crowding, there is considerable open land away from the industrial and residential conurbation surrounding Valletta and the harbor area. There are more than fifty villages and towns, which range in size from 1,000 to 15,000 inhabitants.

Until the beginning of the nineteenth century, villages and towns were located on inland hills and around the fortified Grand Harbour. Houses were tightly clustered around enormous churches. This settlement pattern was dictated by the need to shelter from marauding pirates, especially Muslim corsairs, and from the malaria that flourished in the coastal marshes. Since the pacification of the central Mediterranean early in the nineteenth century, seven coastal parishes have been established.

The houses are constructed from limestone blocks, are flat-roofed, and traditionally have been built around a central courtyard. Most of the important associations, shops, and residences were clustered in and around the square in front of the church or in the streets leading to it. Thus, the pattern of residence was concentric, and it also reflected the distribution of economic and political power. Those with the highest status tended to live nearest the church and those with the lowest status farthest away, in little alleys that backed on to open fields or in rural hamlets. Residence in the village center conferred prestige, for the built-up village traditionally was associated with the culture of the town, with "civilization." The periphery of the village was associated with the countryside and agricultural work, which in Malta had low status, being linked with poverty, physically punishing work, and cultural and social deprivation. A Maltese village was thus inward-looking, focusing on the parish church and the intense social, political, economic, and ceremonial life that took place in and around the central square. This concentric pattern has changed since 1964.

Government programs to build new roads and housing, together with rising prosperity, resulted in a building boom. An influx of foreign residents keen on living near the open country and/or in traditional village houses introduced new housing standards. These have radically affected the utilization of social space.

The village periphery, once socially marginal, and the open country, once stigmatized, have become sought-after residential areas. A ring of villas and housing estates encapsulate traditional village centers, many of which have been gentrified by elite outsiders seeking characteristic, rustic houses.

Economy

Subsistence and Commercial Activities. Malta is an industrialized society. In 1987 less than 2.5 percent of the 122,000 gainfully occupied population was employed full-time in agriculture. Five times that amount worked as part-time farmers, reflecting the islands' recent agrarian past. Roughly 33 percent of the working population is employed by the government. The (ex-British naval) dockyard is the largest employer, but there are a growing number of smaller export-oriented manufacturing industries located in small industrial estates throughout the conurbation. Thus, though most people are employed outside the communities in which they live, no one has to travel very far. Tourism has become a major element in the Maltese economy. Between the mid-1960s and 1989, annual tourist arrivals increased from 20,000 to over 800,000. Employment in this sector has increased apace.

Traditionally, the Maltese rural and urban working class diet consisted mainly of bread and vegetable stew (*minestra*), fresh fruit in season, and occasionally meat, often rabbit.

With the growth of prosperity since independence, the diet has become more varied and much richer.

Industrial Arts.   Except for blacksmiths, cabinetmakers, and carpenters, for whose work the demand is declining rapidly, there are few artisans in Malta. In Gozo, however, there is still a lively tradition of female handicraft: weaving, lace making, and, stimulated by tourism, knitting pullovers.

Trade.   Throughout Gozo and especially Malta there are modern stores, (weekly) open-air markets, and a stream of hawkers who sell local and imported household goods, tools, furnishings, and fresh meat, fish, and produce.

Division of Labor.   Until the mid-1960s there was a pronounced gender-based division of labor. Women worked at home and helped in farming, while men worked outside the house. That arrangement has changed markedly. Today most unmarried women work outside the house for wages. Increasingly, women are continuing to work after marriage, and, if helpful relatives are nearby, even after their first children are born.

Land Tenure.   Agricultural land is normally leased under emphyteutic contracts from government, church, or private landowners. Land rents generally were and still are modest, for they were tightly controlled by the British to avoid social exploitation and rural unrest.

Kinship

Kin Groups and Descent.   The Maltese reckon kin relationship equally through males and females. Each person is thus at the center of a wide network of cognates (*qraba*) and affines (*l-imhalltin*). While there are no descent groups, a person feels closest to his blood relatives, the cognates of his own parents, sometimes collectively referred to as one's *razza*. Generally maternal relatives are favored. The institution of godparenthood is well established, though it is less demanding than elsewhere in southern Europe and Latin America.

Kinship Terminology.   Maltese kinship terminology generally resembles the form that is common throughout southwestern Europe. Maternal and paternal kin are addressed and referred to by similar terms, which are extended as a matter of courtesy to affines.

Marriage and Family

Marriage.   There is no rule of village endogamy or exogamy. While postmarital residence ideally is neolocal, the strong tie between mothers and daughters ensures that couples tend to live nearer the wife's parents than those of the husband. However, when the husband's place of work is in his village, as with farmers, shopkeepers, and artisans, the couple will tend to live in the husband's village. Most Maltese now marry in their mid-twenties. Long engagements are common, as couples work for several years to build and furnish their own house. The age at marriage as well as the scale and cost of wedding receptions have increased markedly during the past thirty years. While legal separation is possible, divorce is not recognized by the church. Although the church prohibits contraceptive devices, many are legally obtainable. Abortion, though illegal, is fairly widely practiced.

Domestic Unit.   The prevalent domestic unit is the nuclear family, which may include an aging parent or an unmarried sibling. Generally children continue to live with their parents, even as adults, until they marry.

Inheritance.   Under Maltese law male and female children inherit equally. Dowry, when given, is an anticipated portion of the inheritance. It remains inalienable. The husband obtains management and usufruct rights, but he cannot sell immovable dowry property without his wife's written consent. If she dies without children, the dowry property passes back to her parental family, unless she wills otherwise.

Socialization.   Children are valued and indulged. Although corporal punishment occurs in moments of anger, it is not a common means of discipline. Older persons are generally respected. Children are respectful and often silent in the presence of their father.

Sociopolitical Organization

Social Organization.   Maltese society is stratified. There are a small number of generally landed and comfortably well-off nobles, some of whose patents go back to the Middle Ages. Of the commoners, the professional classes, including the clergy, traditionally were accorded the highest esteem, and peasants the lowest. The considerable wealth acquired by many traders, business owners, contractors, and some politicians since independence has created a new elite. Generally, a rather egalitarian ideology prevails. With the exception of professionals, who are addressed by their titles, people are quick to use first names. In the villages and urban neighborhoods, nicknames are widely used as a term of reference and even address. In spite of a campaign of nation building and class-based political mobilization following World War II, family ties remain the primary focus of allegiance.

Political Organization.   Malta is a republic with a sixty-five-member unicameral parliamentary government elected every five years by means of proportional representation, with single transferable votes from thirteen five-member constituencies. Political control since independence has passed between the Malta Labour party (1971–1987) and the Nationalist party (1962–1971, 1987–). The voting strength of the two parties is almost equal. Administered for centuries as a fortress, the Malta government is still highly centralized. All services are run from Valletta. There are no mayors, headmen, or councillors who represent or administer individual towns or villages.

Social Control.   The country's small scale, large police force, established court system, and powerful church and its citizens' face-to-face knowledge of each other ensure tight social control.

Conflict.   Maltese society is riven with conflict. The corrosive competition between the Nationalist party and the Malta Labour party affects all dimensions of Maltese social life. The middle-of-the-road NP generally has the support of the professional classes, the self-employed, and the church. The Socialist MLP is generally favored by the industrialized working population. Many towns and villages are further divided by rivalry between those supporting different patron saints and parishes. Both national and parochial competition is often accompanied by excessive abuse and even physical violence. At the interpersonal level, the Maltese are very litigious.

Religion and Expressive Culture

Religious Beliefs and Practices.   The principal religion of the Maltese is Roman Catholicism. The Maltese are devout: most men and women attend mass at least once a week. The religious practitioners are the diocesan and regular clergy. Among Roman Catholics, Malta has the highest ratio of priests to laypeople in the world.

The Maltese celebrate the liturgical calendar with great enthusiasm and pomp. Intricate and richly adorned outdoor processions form part of many rituals. For centuries, these have provided the principal entertainment of the population. The most devoutly celebrated rituals are those that take place during Holy Week (Our Lady of Sorrows, Palm Sunday, Maundy Thursday, Good Friday, and Easter). In addition, each parish annually celebrates its patron saint with sacred rituals, joyous outdoor band marches, wild demonstrations, and lavish displays of fireworks, many of which are made by parishioners. Some parishes celebrate two saints in this fashion, thereby generating fierce rivalry.

Arts.   There is a rich tradition of decorative art. There are many part-time sculptors and painters. Traditional extemporaneous competitive singing (_ghana_), which had all but disappeared thirty years ago, is making a modest comeback.

Medicine.   Western medicine has been universally practiced in Malta for centuries.

Death and Afterlife.   The Maltese accept death and, in accord with Roman Catholic teaching regarding afterlife, great fear is associated with it. Funerals are held the day after death. Graves are tended and the dead are celebrated annually on All Souls' Day, 1 November. It is widely believed that the spirits of the dead (_wahxi_) return to haunt the living if the religious arrangements for the repose of their souls have not been faithfully carried out.

Bibliography

Blouet, Brian (1989). _The Story of Malta_. Malta: Progress Press.

Boissevain, Jeremy (1965). _Saints and Fireworks: Religion and Politics in Rural Malta_. London: Athlone Press.

Boissevain, Jeremy (1980). _A Village in Malta_. New York and London: Holt, Rinehart & Winston.

Malta, Government of. Central Office of Statistics (1987). _Annual Abstract of Statistics_. Valletta.

Vassallo, Mario (l979). _From Lordship to Stewardship: Religion and Social Change in Malta_. The Hague: Mouton.

JEREMY BOISSEVAIN

Manx

ETHNONYM: Manks (archaic)

Orientation

Identification.   The Isle of Man is located in the Irish Sea and is politically and legally separate from the United Kingdom. The indigenous Manx population shares the island with populations of Irish, Scots, and English, along with seasonal influxes of tourists.

Location.   The Isle of Man is roughly equidistant from Ireland, Scotland, England, and Wales at approximately 54°25' by 54°05' N and 4°50' by 4°20' W. The island is 21 kilometers wide at its broadest east-west point and 50 kilometers long north to south. Geographically, the Isle of Man has a mountainous interior (the highest elevation is 610 meters) with low-lying coastal plains. The island is part of the larger geographical zone that includes the Highlands of Scotland. The climate is generally mild because of the Gulf Stream. The growing season begins in April and runs through October. The average annual precipitation is 100–127 centimeters, although considerable local variation exists. Average temperatures vary from a high of 15° C in August to 5.5° C in January, the coldest month.

Demography.   The population in the Isle of Man in 1981 was 64,679. At this time, approximately 47,000 individuals (73 percent) listed themselves as Manx, making them the largest ethnic group on the island. The next largest group is the English who number some 17,000 (1986) and represent the fastest-growing population in the island. The total population increased by 16 percent from 1971 to 1981.

Linguistic Affiliation.   The Manx speak English, and in recent years some have revived Manx Gaelic, which virtually had disappeared by 1973 with the death of the last native speaker. Manx is a branch of Goidelic Gaelic, which includes Scottish and Irish. Although there are currently no native speakers of Manx, the linguistic revival has been successful enough so that some families now use Manx in household communication. The Manx prefer using the Latin alphabet for both English and Manx. In recent years, bilingual street signs, place-names, and some publications have appeared.

History and Cultural Relations

The area that is now the Isle of Man was inhabited by hunters and gatherers after the last glaciation, around 9,000 B.C. The rise of agriculture occurred around 4,000 B.C., and later the people developed the use of bronze (c. 2,000 B.C. to 600 B.C.). The Celtic culture developed shortly before the Roman occupation of Britain (55 B.C.). Although the Romans were aware of the Isle of Man, no archaeological evidence exists to show they ever visited the island. The historical period dates to the late fifth to early sixth century A.D. and roughly marks the beginning of the Early Christian period (A.D. 450–800). In the eighth century, Vikings used the island as a staging area for raids against Ireland, and later they conquered the Manx, incorporating the island into various rulers' kingdoms. Many existing institutions, place-names, and linguistic features date from this period. In 1266, the period of Viking dynastic kings ended, and the Scots and the Irish vied for the island, until Edward III defeated the Scots and established the isle as a separate kingdom. The island continued to change hands until 1405, when John Stanley acquired it and began a 300-year dynasty. In 1651, the Manx, led by Illiam Dhone (William Christian) rebelled against the island's rulers, an event that facilitated the island's surrender to Cromwellian forces. The Stanley family was reinstated after the restoration of the monarchy, but the island came under Crown dominion in 1765, when John Murray, then Lord of Man, sold his sovereignty rights.

The Isle of Man remains an ethnically diverse and complicated society. The island has long attracted Irish, English, and Scottish immigrants. Economic hardships following World War II resulted in Tynwald (the Manx government) legislating tax reforms and offering economic incentives to attract the wealthy (known locally as "New Residents") to settle. This legislation has brought economic prosperity, but economic opportunism among New Residents, land speculation, and rising living costs have heightened ethnic tensions. Since the late 1960s, nationalism among the Manx has grown, sometimes resulting in vandalism of New Residents' property.

Settlements

Traditionally, Manx coastal towns and villages developed as farming, fishing, administrative, and religious centers. In addition, isolated farmsteads were established in the interior agricultural lands. Today, the population is predominantly urban, residing in the four principal towns of Douglas-Onchan, Castletown, Ramsey, and Port Saint Mary–Port Erin. Smaller towns are expanded villages serving as parish administrative and economic centers. Ramsey, the largest town in the north, was partially razed to make room for modern dwellings intended for New Residents. Houses are ideally two-storied, thick-walled, wood-frame structures with interior chimneys, stucco exteriors, and tile roofs. Newer construction employs a diversity of modern building materials and can include apartment or condominium dwellings.

Economy

Subsistence and Commercial Activities.   Manx economy has historically been subservient to the rise of English industrial production. Hence, many Manx enterprises have declined. The most stable sectors are fishing, agriculture, and summer tourism. Because of the strategic location, restriction on Manx trade, and lack of viable alternatives, Manx coastal sailors engaged in smuggling in the eighteenth century. The fishing fleet engages in seasonal harvesting (scallops, prawns, herring, and mackerel). In agriculture, the Manx raise lambs, sheep, and dairy cattle and grow grains, potatoes, and other vegetables. The summer tourist trade developed in the nineteenth century and today caters to the working classes of northern England. Associated with the tourist season are a number of motorcycle, bicycle, and car races drawing many thousands of spectators from the United Kingdom and Europe. Tynwald legislation has encouraged the development of a financial sector, involving banking, insurance, and other fiduciary enterprises.

Industrial Arts.   Many people engage in small crafts production, and a thriving antiques trade keeps many people employed in restoration work. Artisans also engage in textile production, painting, woodworking, and sculpting.

Trade.   Each village and town has a shopping district where individual stores and food markets are located. In other areas of the towns, some residents run small commodity shops. At Saint Johns, a livestock auction is held weekly. An open-air market is held on Thursdays in most towns. Open-air markets are also held during festivals and special events.

Division of Labor.   Despite a growing feminist consciousness, the division of labor is based on gender. Women perform household maintenance and familial work, and men perform most occupational work. Fishing, construction, and agriculture tend to be dominated by men, while school teaching, restaurant work, and health care tend to be dominated by women. In addition to the gender division of labor, certain ethnic groups tend to dominate different sectors of the economy. For example, English workers predominate in the financial sector, while Manx engage in agriculture.

Land Tenure.   All land is held privately, except that held by the Manx National Trust, a government agency. In recent years, land speculation and extensive residential development has resulted in rising land values, taxation, and loss of Manx ownership of land. After the razing of Ramsey, many Manx called for limitations on land development, and in response Tynwald has initiated a growth-management plan to control future development. Considerable disagreement surrounds this plan.

Kinship, Marriage, and Family

Kinship.   The Manx reckon descent bilaterally with patrilineal surnames. The most important domestic unit is the nuclear, monogamous family, which is the main unit for socializing offspring and of production and consumption of family resources. Strong ties are maintained with kin groups outside the nuclear family, and frequent visiting and sharing of resources reaffirms recognition and support of consanguineal and affinal kin. Formerly, the Manx were organized in geographically localized patrilineages, although lacking the corporate features of true unilineal descent systems. Today, many Manx can trace descent bilineally to their patrilineage, despite complicated changes in surname spellings and pronunciations. Some can point to ruined ancestral farm houses (tholtan). Tynwald has sponsored genealogical programs to assist people in tracing connections to their original lineages. Manx formal kinship terminology is identical to English kinship terminology. Informally, the Manx use nicknames to distinguish living and dead relatives. Formerly, nicknames were added through patrilineal descent, so a son would earn his own nickname and also be ascribed his father's nickname. This process could be repeated over many generations, so that a man might have eight or more nicknames representing a public display of descent.

Marriage.   Marriage marks an important change of status to adulthood, so the age of marriage is low. Both men and women marry in their early twenties and immediately start a family. Postmarital residence is ideally neolocal, except among agricultural families where the eldest son is expected to reside patrilocally. However, many young couples working in agriculture attempt to relocate to an abode close to the family farm. The choice of marriage partner is at the discretion of young adults. Divorce is becoming increasingly common, and remarriage after a divorce or the death of a spouse is accepted.

Inheritance. Land as a heritable resource ideally has been kept intact in intergenerational transfers, and typically it is given to the oldest son. Other resources, such as houses, money, and belongings, are divided equally between the other male and the female heirs.

Socialization. Children are well disciplined at home and are expected to participate in household chores. However, corporal punishment is not common and is reserved for the gravest disobedience. Young adults are expected to contribute to the household, either through labor or earnings, but in other respects they are allowed considerable latitude in their free-time behavior.

Sociopolitical Organization

Social Organization. The class structure is based on occupational and ethnic divisions. Wage labor tends to be performed by Manx, while professional occupations tend to be filled by ethnic English. Both socially mobile and landless Manx tend to leave, seeking education opportunities elsewhere. Highly educated and trained Manx who return often accept employment below their qualifications. Local Tynwald officials wield power, but they find their power increasingly challenged by members of the growing financial sector.

Political Organization. The Isle of Man is a Crown dependency with political and legal autonomy from the United Kingdom. In actual practice, however, the United Kingdom holds considerable power over the Manx. The island's government, Tynwald, is divided into a bicameral parliamentary body (the House of Keys and the Legislative Council), and an executive branch (the Queen of England as Lord of Man and the resident lieutenant-governor as her representative in the island). No Manx representatives sit in the British Parliament. Tynwald makes laws concerning insular affairs, while the British Home Office maintains jurisdiction over all international affairs. Even in domestic legislation, the Crown holds veto power, although it rarely exercises it. The Isle of Man has been included in the European Community, thus blurring the distinction between domestic and international matters. Below Tynwald, administration is handled by village and town councils. Village boards are locally elected by a complicated process and are responsible for deciding local affairs. Manx political parties reflect British political parties, but also include the Manx National party and the nationalist party, Mec Vannin. Despite the existence of political parties, most Manx prefer nonpartisan elections. Consequently, many candidates successfully run as independents.

Social Control. Tradition and Manx informal communication networks effectively express public opinion and control deviance. In addition, a well-developed court system and police force serve to punish criminal behavior.

Conflict. Despite the ongoing ethnic tensions in the islands, the Manx have avoided becoming embroiled in the ethnic violence in Northern Ireland and Wales. Manx ethnic conflict has been expressed through destruction of property and political opposition. In other areas of conflict, homicide is very rare, but domestic violence and brawling do occur. Summer tourists sometimes fight among themselves, and tourist racing events often result in injuries and fatalities, although these are not considered instances of conflict.

Religion and Expressive Culture

Religious Beliefs and Practices. The principal religion among the Manx is Protestantism, as practiced either by the Church of England or by Wesleyan Methodists. A small but visible enclave of witches practice on the island. In addition, many islanders express belief in Celtic supernatural beings and forces and regularly observe taboos and customs associated with averting misfortune. The most important seasonal holidays include Christmas, Easter, and Tynwald Day (a both secular and sacred midsummer festival). Important religious life ceremonies include baptism, marriage, and death.

Arts. Many Manx make ritual objects, such as straw crosses, for protection against malevolent forces.

Medicine. Modern medicine is available to all. Home cures and medicine are strictly limited to treatment of minor ailments. The witches, however, regularly practice healing rituals among themselves.

Death and Afterlife. The Manx believe in an afterlife as described in Protestant doctrine. Upon death, a wake is held for the corpse, and relatives, neighbors, and friends attend. A wake will last 24 hours and can be mildly boisterous, but not overly so. After the wake, the corpse is buried in the church graveyard in a formal religious ceremony.

Bibliography

Birch, J. W. (1964). *The Isle of Man: A Study in Economic Geography.* Cambridge: University of Bristol.

Isle of Man, Government of (1987). *Digest of Economic and Social Statistics.*

Kermode, D. G. (1979). *Devolution at Work: A Case Study of the Isle of Man.* Westmead: Saxon House.

Kinvig, R. H. (1975). *The Isle of Man: A Social, Cultural, and Political History.* Rutland, Vt.: Charles E. Tuttle.

DAVID GLYN NIXON

Montenegrins

ETHNONYM: Crnogorci

Orientation

Identification. Montenegrins live predominantly in the region currently constituting the Socialist Republic of Montenegro, the smallest republic within modern-day Yugoslavia. Montenegrins speak the Štokavian dialect of Serbo-Croatian and call their republic "Crna Gora," meaning "Black Mountain." Culturally, they are closely related to the Serbs; some authors consider them to be of the same ethnic group. Montenegrins closely identify with the Serbs through common history and culture. Nonetheless, there are some important cultural, economic, and historical differences that distinguish the two groups. This entry focuses on aspects of Montenegrin life, history, and geography that differentiate them from Serbs. In general, however, there is little published research on contemporary Montenegrin culture. The reader should consult the entry under Serbs for additional information.

Location.   Montenegro is located between approximately 42 and 43.5° N and 18.5 and 20.5° E. It is bounded on the northeast and east by Serbia and the autonomous region of Kosovo, on the west and northwest by Bosnia and Herzegovina, and on the south by Albania and the Adriatic Sea. Terrain and climate are highly varied. Mountains rise from the seacoast, reaching inland heights of 2,400 meters in some parts of the republic. Rainfall varies from lows of only a few centimeters per year along the coast to highs of 200 centimeters in some mountainous areas. The growing season in the limited arable areas can last from April to October. Much of the republic is otherwise covered by barren limestone known as the *karst*. Even in areas with abundant rainfall, this geography limits the availability of surface water.

Demography.   The population of the Socialist Republic of Montenegro in 1981 was 584,000. People identifying themselves as ethnically Montenegrin constituted approximately two-thirds of the total population. Serbs make up about 11 percent of the republic's population, and there is a small but significant Muslim minority.

Linguistic Affiliation.   Montenegrins speak a dialect of Serbo-Croatian known as Štokavian (subdialect: Ijekavian), which is a South Slavic language from the Slavic Branch of Indo-European. Nearest related languages are Slovene, Macedonian (both spoken in other Yugoslav republics), and Bulgarian. Like other Orthodox Serbo-Croatian speakers, they traditionally employed the Cyrillic alphabet, although the Latin alphabet is now also widely seen.

History and Cultural Relations

Slavic settlement of the area dates to Slavic migrations of the sixth and seventh centuries. From 1389 and the Serbian defeat at Kosovo until 1516, Montenegro was nominally an independent principality. Montenegro was the last Balkan area to be subjugated by the Ottomans in the late fifteenth century and the first "liberated" when control passed to the Cetinje monastery and the hereditary prince-bishops around 1700, but it was never fully subjugated. Researchers note considerable variation from source to source in these dates, the degree of subjugation, and centers of political power. Montenegro was an independent kingdom for a brief time in the early 1900s before joining the Kingdom of the Serbs, Croats and Slovenes in 1918. Since the end of World War II it has been part of modern-day Yugoslavia.

Montenegrins have traditionally sided with the Serbs, with whom they share many cultural and historical links. This has remained true in the current conflict with Croatia beginning in 1991; during this conflict Montenegrins have supported Serbian guerrilla insurgencies in southern Croatia. At the national level Montenegro supported Serbian attempts to block Croatian ascendancy to the national presidency in the spring of 1991.

Settlements

Settlement patterns vary but most villages are small with populations of less than 1,000. Montenegro is the most sparsely populated republic in the country with only 42 persons per square kilometer in 1981 (as compared to 105 persons in Serbia). The two major village types are clustered and dispersed. Where land is arable, villages tend to be clustered on the borders of the cultivated basins. Elsewhere, the pattern is more one of dispersed family residences.

Nearly all houses traditionally were made of stone using lime mortar. One or two stories was the general rule. Windows are small and, in older houses, it is still possible to see the loopholes used in warding off Turkish attacks or blood feuding. Roofs were traditionally made of tile, straw, or stone, depending on local availability and economics. Since World War II, modern buildings have appeared, but home styles remain based on the old patterns. During the summer months when livestock are pastured on the high mountain grasses, the herders live in smaller summer cabins grouped together into *katuns*. These are typically also made of stone.

Economy

Historically, Montenegrins have been farmers, in the areas where agriculture is possible, and herders elsewhere. Major agricultural products include rye and barley, as well as other cereal crops. In coastal areas, olives, figs, and grapes are also grown. Most important, however, has been the herding of sheep, goats, and cattle based on seasonal movement of flocks.

Subsistence and Commercial Activities.   Although post–World War II modernization has produced some industrialization, Montenegrin industry and agriculture remain underdeveloped and the population poor by Yugoslav standards. In the post–World War II period, Montenegro continued to rank last among the Yugoslav republics in the percentage of its work force employed in industry.

Trade.   In general, external trade was historically of only minimal importance. Because of the isolation generated by centuries of military conflict with the Ottomans and extensive raiding outside of the mountain strongholds, trade links did not develop as they had farther up the Adriatic coast.

Division of Labor.   Sex roles traditionally were well defined and women economically important but of low status.

Land Tenure.   Contemporary landholding laws and patterns are governed by Yugoslav law and mirror those in Serbia. However, according to late nineteenth-century reports, historical distinctions existed in grazing versus farming rights. Whereas arable holdings and their inheritance followed the traditional Serbian pattern, grazing rights were vested in the larger clan and tribal communities.

Kinship

Kin Groups and Descent.   One important point differentiating the Montenegrins from the Serbs is the existence of kin and social groups larger than the lineage. Both clan (*bratstvo*) and tribe (*pleme*) were important economic and social groups. The pleme was composed of several contiguous bratstvo. These larger groups have been important throughout Montenegrin political and economic history. Economically, they defined cooperative labor arrangements. Politically, they formed the basis of the alliances from which political and military power were generated. Fictive kin ties established through godfatherhood and blood brotherhood also figured prominently in kin relations.

Descent is patrilineal, and great emphasis is placed on the perpetuation of male lines.

Kinship Terminology. Kinship terminology is parallel to that used in Serbia. On the first ascending generation, terminology is bifurcate-collateral for males and lineal for females. In general, terms for consanguineal kin are more specific than for affines.

Marriage and Family

Marriage. Traditionally, marriages in Montenegro were almost always arranged by the parents. Family reputation, not love, was the primary factor in selecting a bride. Virginity before marriage was highly valued and in some areas the practice of displaying the bloodied wedding sheets as proof of the bride's chastity was common. Some sources note a pattern of "trial" marriage in which consumation of the union was delayed for a period of up to a year. Marriage was an important way to create bonds of friendship between families and to maintain or improve the family's status in the community. Unlike nearby Bosnia, the practice of *otmica,* or bride capture, was rare in Montenegro. When it did occur, the consent of both families had been quietly prearranged. There was likewise no pattern of bride-price. Although divorced individuals could remarry within the church, the actual incidence of divorce was low until after World War II and the establishment of secular reforms in marriage law. Among the most common causes of divorce were sterility or the failure to bear male offspring, both of which were always seen as the wife's fault. Women could not initiate divorce in the pre-Socialist period. Postmarital residence is typically patrilocal.

Domestic Unit. The basic household and family unit is the patrilocal extended family. Although the most basic term of reference is *kuća,* meaning simply "house," this area was characterized like much of the Balkans by *zadrugas,* large extended-family households.

Inheritance. Inherited property traditionally was divided equally among surviving sons, although a widow was entitled to usufruct. Traditionally, in cases where a man had no sons, property that passed instead to daughters was said to "come on the miraz." By contrast, post–World War II legal codes specify bilateral inheritance, although the laws are still frequently circumvented.

Socialization. Corporal punishment is a common means of discipline. Traditional emphasis on respect for elders, concepts of honor and shame, and conformity to household goals has been eroded in the post–World War II period.

Sociopolitical Organization

The Socialist Federal Republic of Yugoslavia has separate heads of state and government. By 1991, however, the central government had disintegrated and the national Communist party, under its old framework, had been dissolved. In late 1991 Slovenia and Croatia, having declared themselves separate nations, were accepted as such by the European Community. In Montenegro, the old-line Communist government was forced from power by large-scale street demonstrations in January 1989. Montenegro aligned itself with Serbia in the creation of a new Yugoslav federation in May 1992.

Social Organization

Class structure is relatively undifferentiated in rural areas, but as elsewhere in Yugoslavia, the urban elite traditionally have wielded both internal and external political power.

Political Organization. Administrative divisions below the republic level have been reorganized several times since 1945. Below this level, however, the village and other local councils are important to local affairs. Village Council members are locally elected and are responsible for the exercise of federal and republic government policies at the local level; they also determine policy in local affairs. Traditionally, bonds of kinship expressed in clan or tribal affiliations were important to defining political power.

Social Control. Honor, shame, and duty have traditionally been highly important concepts in defining proper behavior. Proper behavior is reinforced through violence, as evidenced by the high incidence of blood feuding, and gossip. Historically, capital punishment was common for a number of offensives, both major and minor by modern standards. In contemporary times, the federal court system has attempted to usurp many of the powers earlier vested in kin groups and less formal clan and tribal courts, but informal settlement of disagreements (often through bloodshed) remains common.

Conflict. Montenegrin history is fraught with conflict, both internal and external. Montenegro fought in seven wars between 1850 and 1918. Revolt against Ottoman rule was continuous, and the area served as a refuge and staging area for revolts elsewhere in the region. Feuding between kin groups was endemic and continues in some areas even today.

Religion and Expressive Culture

Religious Beliefs. Traditionally, Montenegrin beliefs are a syncretic blend of Eastern Orthodox Christianity and pre-Christian practices. Although most people consider themselves Orthodox, there are significant Catholic and Muslim minorities. God (Bog), Saint Elijah, and the one or two patron saints associated with each clan are the most prominent supernatural figures. Other supernatural beings such as vampires, ghosts, and nature spirits often figure prominently in folk epics and stories.

Religious Practitioners. In addition to Eastern Orthodox priests, there were historically large numbers of local "popes," lay priests frequently ignorant of written doctrine and tradition.

Ceremonies. The religious calendar includes all the normal Christian holidays, with Easter being the most important church holiday. Life-cycle ceremonies, particularly those marking birth and death, are also important events. However, two other ceremonies also figure prominently in people's lives. The first is the ceremony establishing godfatherhood or *kumstvo.* The second is the *slava,* or the feast of the clan's (*bratstvo's*) patron saint. Today the slava has lost much of its former functions in promoting kin-group solidarity and reinforcing kin-group boundaries.

Arts. As for the Serbs, the Montenegrin national instrument is the *gusle*—a single-horsehair wooden instrument stroked with a horsehair bow. The most important function of the instrument is to provide accompaniment for the singing of oral epic poetry. This tradition is wholly oral in the sense that, while the formula uses ten-syllable lines, each performance is a unique creation. Texts are not memorized. Common story themes include battles with the Turks, encounters with supernatural beings, the exploits of culture heroes, and the recounting of lineage ancestry.

See also Serbs

Bibliography

Boehm, Christopher (1983). *Montenegrin Social Organization and Values.* New York: AMS Press.

Boehm, Christopher (1984). *Blood Revenge: The Anthropology of Feuding in Montenegro and Other Tribal Societies.* Lawrence: University Press of Kansas.

Denton, William (1877). *Montenegro: Its Land and Their History.* London: Daldy, Isbister & Co.

Durham, Mary E. (1928). *Some Tribal Origins, Laws, and Customs of the Balkans.* London: George Allen & Unwin.

Federal Statistical Office of Yugoslavia (1983). *Statisticki kalendar Jugoslavije* (Statistical pocket book of Yugoslavia). Belgrade.

Partridge, Monica (1964). *Serbo-Croatian: Practical Grammar and Reader.* New York: McGraw-Hill.

RICHARD A. WAGNER

Mount Athos

ETHNONYMS: Athonite Monks, Hagiorites; also terms that designate the monastic brotherhoods to which individual monks belong: e.g., Lavriotes (monks belonging to the Lavra monastery); Philotheites (Philotheou monastery), Vatopedini (Vatopedi monastery), etc.

Orientation

Identification. Mount Athos is an autonomous republic of Eastern Orthodox monks situated on the easternmost peninsula of the Chalkidiki in northeastern Greece. It is also known as the Holy Mountain (in Greek, "Hagion Oros," whence the ethnonym "Hagiorite"). Both names refer to the 2,039-meter mountain at its southern tip. The Holy Mountain is venerated throughout Eastern Orthodox Christianity as a holy land and place of pilgrimage. Its monastic community has played a major role in shaping the theology of Eastern Orthodoxy and in the development of Eastern Orthodox monasticism. Most contemporary Eastern Orthodox theologians and ecclesiastical leaders have passed a novitiate in an Athonite monastery. Aside from the monastic and personal regimen required of monks and the higher levels of education prevalent today among contemporary abbots and Hagiorite leaders, the ethos and values of the Hagiorites in general reflect those of the rural, northern Balkan villages from which most of the monks come.

Location. The Athonite Peninsula, a promontory of about 360 square kilometers, about 8 to 12 kilometers in width, extending approximately 60 kilometers from northwest to southeast, is divided longitudinally by a steep ridge rising at its southern end to the mountain peak.

Demography. Mount Athos is occupied predominantly by Greeks, reflecting the present Greek protectorate, but also by brotherhoods of Bulgarian, Georgian, Romanian, Russian, and Serbian monks. The monastic population, in decline throughout most of the twentieth century, has grown in the last quarter of the century to over 2,000, owing in part to the worldwide revival of conservative religion. The revival on Mount Athos has also benefited from disillusionment with the pace and quality of life in the overpopulated major cities of Greece, nostalgia for the traditions and distinctive cultural identity of the past as Greece has been absorbed into the European Community, the problems of depopulation and economic collapse in rural mountain villages, and the threats that materialism and atheism represent to traditional Eastern Orthodox Christianity in Greece.

Linguistic Affiliation. The major language of Mount Athos is demotic Greek colored with archaisms instilled in monks continuously through the language of the liturgy, the psalmody, and hagiographical readings that accompany the common meals in the refectory. The archaic quality of the language is also partly a result of conscious use of traditional monastic phrases that evoke central symbolic features of monastic life, a sense of unchanged adherence to the tradition of the fathers, and a sense of separation from "the world." As elsewhere in northeastern Greece, it includes an extensive vocabulary of Turkish loanwords. The languages of the other Orthodox ethnic groups are also spoken, with similar monastic and archaizing features.

History and Cultural Relations

As early as the seventh century the Athonite Peninsula, depopulated since the classical age, was settled by hermits, many of them refugees from the Arab conquests of that time or victims of the iconoclasts, who sought to end the veneration of icons, a custom deeply rooted in Byzantine monasticism. The Byzantine emperor Basil I recognized Athos as a territory for male hermit monks in 885, banishing from the territory all resident laymen and shepherds as well as women and female domestic animals. The first monastery, the Megisti Lavra ("the Great Lavra"), was founded by the emperor, Nicephoros Phocas, in 963 as an independent monastery. Its charter was a landmark in the reform of abuses associated with the economic control of monasteries and their lands by secular overseers and local bishops. From the perspective of the abbots, the charter's importance was the reestablishment of their authority, without which the traditional discipline based on submission would break down. During the Latin occupation of Byzantium (1204–1261), when the Holy Mountain was under the jurisdiction of the Latin Kingdom of Salonica, and immediately thereafter, the Athonite monasteries resisted pressure to support union of the Eastern Orthodox and Roman Catholic churches. During the Turkish occupation of Greece, 1453–1822 (the Turkocrateia), the monasteries were impoverished by heavy taxation and loss of outlying endowment properties. In the sixteenth century, the monasteries resisted the Turkish regime's intensified "Islamization" by collecting and copying theological, hagiographical, and liturgical books on a large scale and by training and ordaining priests for outlawed missionary work. This resistance produced hundreds of "neomartyrs," Hagiorites and others, who continue to be commemorated. The Greek revolution brought depopulation, disrupting the continuity of monastic life and oral tradition as monks left to join the "holy war" against the "infidel" Turks. During World War II and the subsequent Greek civil war, the monasteries served as places of refuge for the injured and displaced, including women and children. The monastic republic has been a protectorate of Greece since 1912, when the first Balkan War ended Turkish hegemony there, and is under the ecclesiastical jurisdiction of the Greek Orthodox Ecumenical Patriarchate.

All of the Athonite monasteries, Greek and other, maintain close ties with traditional geographical areas where they have possessed monastic properties, from which they have received patronage, and which are the homelands of many of their present monks. These ties are reflected in architectural styles, styles of hymnody, commemoration of founders and patrons, patterns of pilgrimage, and of course, language. As with the Greek monasteries under the Turkocrateia, the various ethnically defined monasteries have tended to be symbols of nationalism, exploited to promote or preserve cultural identity.

Settlements

Large, fortified monasteries with defensive towers (against piracy) dating from as early as the tenth century dot the Athonite coasts. The oldest monasteries (the Lavra, Iveron, Vatopedi) were built facing toward Byzantium (modern Istanbul), the major source of their patronage, from the northeastern coast, as did the main port of Athos during the Turkocrateia. Most of the monasteries, however, were founded on the southwestern coast because of its more favorable climate, while some (smaller monasteries) were built on arable highland plateaus. In addition to those monks living in the twenty ruling monasteries, many monks live individually in small houses near the monasteries (_kathismata_), taking their meals and attending services in the monastery proper; others live in groups of three or more in farms with chapels (_kellia_, "cells"); others reside in houses or small settlements with chapels (_kalyvia_), where they support themselves in specialties such as icon painting; still others live in subordinate monasteries (_skites_). Hermit monks live in remote places on the peninsula, the most austere in caves overlooking the sea from the cliffs on the southwestern point of the peninsula

(Karoulia). In addition, there are three Hagiorite villages, Saint Anne and New Skiti, both skites, and the capital, Karyes. Located centrally on the ridge, Karyes is occupied mostly by monks serving in the central government or tending the small houses or apartments maintained by most ruling monasteries for their members while on business at the capital. Shops run by monks cater to pilgrims and provide supplies and services needed in the village. The port, Daphni, on the southwest coast, is Athos's main link with the world, consisting mainly of postal, police, and rescue services, a customs inspection station, and dock facilities.

Economy

Subsistence and Commercial Activities.   Historically the economy of the monastic community has depended upon income from profitable farms and other properties (_metochia_) dedicated to the monasteries as endowments by royal or other wealthy patrons. The property acquired in this fashion during the Byzantine period, much of it located in the northern Balkans, was confiscated during the Turkocrateia or in more modern nationalistic confiscation. The pattern continues, however, with many monasteries deriving income from endowment properties in or near Thessaloniki.

Today as in the past the monasteries and the smaller institutions depend on subsistence farming, with maintenance and other services provided when necessary by hired resident lay workers, but otherwise by monks trained in the requisite specialties (masonry, carpentry, shoemaking, tailoring, etc.). Some monks and kellia support themselves or contribute to the economy of their ruling monasteries by such traditional arts as icon painting and wood carving. The monasteries also harvest and package for sale herbs, hazelnuts, tea (especially herbal and linden teas), incense used in the church services, and other products.

Extensive chestnut forests on the central ridge provide the monasteries with building materials, as they always have, and increasingly in today's income-based economy, supply Greece with much-needed hardwood. Lumbering is managed by outside syndicates employing local lay workers and, in the past decade, increasingly sophisticated equipment. The monasteries practice a method of clear-cutting, harvesting yearly on a twenty-year cycle about one-twentieth of the timberland, a practice that has drawn protest from those concerned to preserve the unique Athonite ecosystem.

Land Tenure.   All land on Mount Athos is allotted to one of the twenty ruling monasteries, which grant to monks or small brotherhoods nonheritable short-term or lifetime leases of kathismata, kellia, or other properties.

Sociopolitical Organization

Social Organization.   In accord with the classic monastic social structure—that is, the cenobitic (common-life) monastery—housing, meals, clothing, and observance of liturgy and other services are governed by a central rule that applies to all monks alike, and monks relinquish control of personal possessions. The abbot is a patriarch who serves for life, the absolute authority and spiritual father of the brotherhood (whose members are usually referred to as fathers). The superior is assisted by a council of elders. Some "idiorhythmic" monasteries also survive on Mount Athos. In these, internal regulations are determined by a council of superiors, members for life, who also determine what monks shall be admitted to that council. A board of two or three monks elected for one-year terms is head of the council and the monastery. Monks in idiorhythmic monasteries may be paid for their services, retain control of their personal property, earn money from outside sources or through personal skills such as icon painting, and eat in their own apartments according to their own schedules. Accommodations are the common property of the monastery. Attendance at services, observance of fasts and festal periods, work assignments, and schedules of work are all according to the central rule and the decision of the board of elders. Skites also may be either cenobitic or idiorhythmic. Athonite law devalues idiorhythmism as an anomalous condition necessitated by extreme economic or other difficulties; it allows monasteries to convert to cenobitism but not to idiorhythmism. The current revival on Mount Athos has been characterized by widespread conversion of long-standing idiorhythmic institutions to cenobitism. Following an age-old pattern of social change on Mount Athos, young brotherhoods, many of them led by charismatic disciples of the modern Athonite hermit and spiritual father, Iosif the Cave-dweller, have moved first into smaller settlements (kellia and skites) and then into depopulated ruling monasteries, which they have converted to cenobitism. As their numbers have grown, fed by the contemporary conservative religious revival, they have colonized and restored run-down and depopulated idiorhythmic monasteries. New wealth that has accompanied the religious revival has enabled these brotherhoods to found new monasteries and missions outside of Athos, as far away as the United States and Canada.

Political Organization. The monastic community is governed, in accord with the constitutional charter of 1924, by a tripartite government. The representative legislative assembly and the representative administrative body (the Holy Community) each consist of twenty members holding one-year terms of office, one from each of the ruling monasteries. The executive is a committee of four monks, the "Holy Epistasia," on which each of the twenty monasteries is represented once every five years in a regular cycle. The chair of the Holy Epistasia rotates among the representatives from the Megisti Lavra, Vatopedi, Iveron, Chilandari, and Dionysiou in the same five-year cycle. In addition, a civil governor appointed by the Greek Ministry of Foreign Affairs is responsible for the general maintenance of law and order, supported by a small office staff, and oversees government functionaries responsible for financial records, forestry, antiquities, etc., plus a small contingent of the Greek National Guard, which maintains several posts on the peninsula.

Social Control and Conflict. The monastic system requires of all monks suppression of the will and all forms of self-assertiveness, to be exercised constantly in relations with other monks, especially elder monks and the abbot or spiritual father. By this system, external conflict among monks is minimized and internal conflict heightened. This internalizing of conflict, linked to the belief that only through the purification of the monk's soul through suppression of his own will is it possible to be receptive to the will of God, contributes to a social order to which all are committed for reasons of personal salvation.

Nevertheless, a number of conflicts characterize Athonite monasticism, both in relation to the secular world and within or among the brotherhoods. As religious professionals who take a strong stand regarding such matters as interdenominational ecumenism and the relations of church and state in "Orthodox" nations, the monks constitute a religious right wing within Eastern Orthodoxy. Their association with conservative grass-roots organizations, which are legitimized by that association, puts them in conflict with ecclesiastical officials whose authority they undermine. Today the Hagiorites are threatened, as well, by a vocal call in Greece for conversion of Mount Athos and the monasteries into a national park with museums. Internally, the Hagiorite community has had difficulties, especially in the past century, with ethnic conflicts. During the last decades before the Russian Revolution, for example, the population of Russian monks swelled so greatly as to create fears among the Greeks of a Russian takeover of the Holy Mountain, a fear that lingers today.

Religion and Expressive Culture

Religious Beliefs and Practices. The preservation of the relics of saints and martyrs, the presence of miracle-working icons in the ruling monasteries, the presence of holy men viewed by pious laypeople as saints, the tradition of the Virgin's protection of the Holy Mountain and all her monks and pilgrims (the monks call it the "Garden of Our Lady"), and recognition and patronage by the Byzantine emperors and the royalty of other Orthodox nations have combined to make this a holy land and place of pilgrimage venerated throughout Eastern Orthodox Christianity. Easter, the commemoration of the resurrection of Christ, is the major pilgrimage event of the year. Each individual monastery also commemorates its dedication day with a festival of all-night psalmody culminating in the liturgy, a litany, and a feast (another major pilgrimage event in the monastery's year). The service expresses through ritual symbols the renewal of blessing on the monastery at the beginning of the monastery's "new year." Pilgrims, at whatever season they come, are brought into the monastery church (catholicon) to venerate the relics and receive blessing from them. Some pilgrims whose spiritual fathers are at an Athonite monastery come for confession, blessing, and spiritual guidance from the spiritual father. Yet another purpose of pilgrimage may be prayer for healing or other aid before a miracle-working icon. These activities, along with participation in the liturgy, represent the spiritual climax of the pilgrimage. For the monks, the pilgrimage festivals are high points in a life whose rhythm is based on the medieval liturgical calendar with its festal and fast periods, its vigils and commemorations of the traditional saints and martyrs. Daily life is structured around observance of the liturgy and services of the canonical hours conducted in the monastic churches, on the medieval almanac of changing hours of light and dark each month, and on the traditional personal regimen of Eastern Orthodox monks, including physical labor ("service") performed for the brotherhood, dietary rules (monks abstain from meat, eating mostly fruits and vegetables, bread, olives, olive oil, and wine), meditation, and continuous prayer. Through meditation, ascetic practices, and suppression of pride and willfulness, monks hope to behold the mystical divine light represented in the biblical account of the transfiguration of Christ, which is understood to be a prefiguration of the apotheosis that is the objective of human life. Since monks must struggle against the sin of pride of accomplishment, they constantly acknowledge personal imperfection and sin, in particular through continuous utterance of the "Jesus Prayer": "Lord Jesus Christ have mercy on me, a sinner." Monks live a life of symbolic death to the world, symbolized in their black robes, which will eventually serve as their burial shrouds. The funeral is a public rite of major importance, for the deceased monk's body, never stiff with rigor mortis, indicates the fulfillment of the monk's hopes. As persons who have died to life and now live "the angelic life," they look forward with hope to immediate resurrection.

Bibliography

Cavarnos, Constantine (1973). _The Holy Mountain_. Belmont, Mass.: Institute for Byzantine and Modern Greek Studies.

Choukas, M. (1935). _Black Angels of Athos_. 2nd ed. London: Constable & Co.; Brattleboro, Vt.: Stephen Daye Press.

Kadas, Sotiris (1979). _Mount Athos: An Illustrated Guide to the Monasteries and Their History_. Athens: Ekdotike Athenon.

Mamalakis, Ioannis (1971). _The Holy Mountain (Athos) through the Ages_ (in Greek). Thessalonica: Society of Macedonian Studies.

Le millénaire du Mont Athos, 963–1963: Études et mélanges (1963). Chevetogne, Belgium: Éditions de Chevetogne.

ROBERT W. ALLISON

Northern Irish

ETHNONYMS: British, Scots Irish, Ulster Irish, Ulster Scots. Historical: Anglo-Irish, Celts, West Britons

Orientation

Identification. Historically, the Northern Irish inhabit the nine-county province of Ulster. In 1920 British sovereignty was retained over six of these counties (Antrim, Armagh, Down, Fermanagh, Londonderry, and Tyrone) by the Government of Ireland Act. The other three counties (Cavan, Donegal, and Monaghan) became part of the Irish Free State. A Protestant minority within Ireland was guaranteed political and economic viability within the six counties.

For most of the population, Irishness and Britishness are not mutually exclusive categories but matters of sentiment and conviction. In 1966, 15 percent of the Roman Catholics and 39 percent of the Protestants claimed "British" national identity while 76 percent and 20 percent, respectively, claimed "Irish." In 1978, after nine years of civil unrest, the number of Catholics asserting British identity remained at 15 percent, but the number of Protestants calling themselves British rose to 67 percent. That same year 69 percent of the Catholics but only 8 percent of the Protestants said they were Irish. Among both denominations, 62 percent considered themselves more like people in the Republic of Ireland than like people in England.

Location. Northern Ireland is located between 54° and 55°20′ N and 5°30′ and 8°15′ W. In area (13,629 square kilometers) it is approximately one-sixth of Ireland. A land boundary of some 450 kilometers separates it from the Irish republic and a sea boundary separates it from Scotland, 20.8 kilometers away. The climate is mild.

Demography. In 1986 the population was 1,578,000. The eastern seaboard, where the provincial capital Belfast is located, had a population density of 111 persons per square kilometer. Total population grew by 1.9 percent between 1981 and 1986. The age structure of Northern Ireland is younger than the rest of the United Kingdom (U.K.), 8.7 percent being under age 5 in 1986. The percentage over 65 is lower at 14.4. The birthrate is high at 18 births per 1,000 population; the national average is 9.9. Just under two-thirds of the population is of Scots and English descent, their forebears having settled in Ulster at the beginning of the seventeenth century. The remaining third is of Irish origin. There has been continuous population movement across the Irish Sea, and many English and Scottish cities have Irish wards. There has also been extensive migration to North America.

Linguistic Affiliation. Two dialect areas—an Ulster Scots zone in the northern and eastern coastal areas and an Ulster Anglo-Irish zone in the inland central, southern, and southwestern parts—follow regional, not religious, patterns. As in the rest of the U.K. and in the Republic of Ireland, class provides the greatest distinction. Irish Gaelic persisted in the westernmost counties until the mid-nineteenth century; Scottish Gaelic dialect traces are found in Antrim. Ulster Irish is considered a cross between Scottish and Irish Gaelic. Gaelic loanwords are common in Northern Irish speech.

History and Cultural Relations

Northern Ireland was fashioned as a distinct political entity within the U.K. with its own devolved government at Stormont Castle in Belfast. In 1972, after four years of civil unrest, the Westminster government resumed direct control. The Northern Irish have strong cultural ties with Australia, Canada, and the United States because of heavy emigration to those countries. Seventeen United States presidents had Ulster forebears.

Northern Irish poets Louis MacNeice, John Hewitt, and

Seamus Heaney have international reputations, as does the flutist James Galway. Many Northern Irish entertainers, broadcasters, novelists, playwrights, and filmmakers are public figures throughout Ireland and the United Kingdom. Seasonal customs in Northern Ireland reflect cultural traditions. The early Celtic Halloween is more important than the Scottish New Year, and mummers who perform folk dramas in a Scots-based dialect do so in distinctively Irish hero-combat plays.

Some sports are played within United Kingdom leagues and associations but most are within Irish leagues, including soccer and cricket. Gaelic sports include Gaelic football, hurling, handball, and camogie. The Gaelic Athletic Association lifted a ban on playing or watching non-Gaelic "foreign" games in 1971. Protestants play soccer, hockey, and cricket at school. International rugby, boxing, athletics, and darts are nondenominational.

Most cultural and social activities take place in neighborhoods and at the county level. Townlands remain important, as do local ceilidhe houses, where folktales and traditional songs are performed. Whether public houses cater only to coreligionists varies with time and place. Cinemas and dance halls are nonsegregated. In some places Catholics and Protestants patronize only shops and services controlled by coreligionists. They support each others' occasional fund-raising activities, fetes, and bazaars, although attendance at such events is almost entirely restricted to coreligionists. Everyday segregation is more acute in working-class urban areas than in small towns and country villages.

Households at the same economic level share a common culture regardless of religious affiliation. This is reflected in standards of living; family relationships; and ideas and attitudes about the role of the sexes, kin, duties of neighbors, good and bad conduct, respect, and officialdom. Nevertheless, the Northern Irish view their society as being fundamentally dichotomized.

Settlements

In 1986 Northern Ireland had the highest rate of new dwellings in the U.K. at 6.5 per 1,000 population. Housing throughout the province was 61 percent owner-occupied, 34 percent rented from local authorities, and 6 percent privately rented. The average cost of a home built in 1986, with mortgage, was 25,700 pounds. Domestic rates at 231 pounds were lower than elsewhere in the U.K.

Economy

Subsistence and Commercial Activities. The gross domestic product (GDP) of Northern Ireland in 1986 was estimated at 6.1 billion pounds, making up 1.9 percent of that of the U.K. as a whole. The provision of public services generated a high proportion (35 percent) of this, as compared with a national average of 23 percent. GDP per head was 3,889 pounds, the lowest in the U.K. The average gross weekly earning for males was 199 pounds, the lowest in the U.K., while that of females was similar to that of most other regions.

Between 1979 and 1987, Northern Ireland had the highest unemployment rate in the U.K., with 35 percent of the Catholic and 17 percent of the Protestant male work force being unemployed. Figures for women were 15 percent and 11 percent, respectively. Social security benefits accounted

for about one-fifth of average household income in 1985–1986, a higher proportion than elsewhere in the U.K. Estimated government expenditure on supplementary benefits was 199 pounds per head, compared with an average of 138 pounds per head elsewhere.

While Northern Ireland clearly is a depressed region within the national economy, the eastern part of the province is more developed than the western, which apart from forestry and tourism is undeveloped. Industrialization around Belfast, migration from the western counties in the nineteenth century due to famine, and the centralization of the economies of London and Dublin in the twentieth century led to markedly uneven regional development. Economic decline has been attributed to structural weaknesses in response to world market changes. An economy narrowly based on marine engineering, shipbuilding, and textiles (linen) employed 55 percent of the manufacturing workforce in 1949 and only 21 percent in 1986. Agriculture suffered a similar contraction from 22 percent of the total labor force in 1949 to less than 4 percent in 1986.

Industrial Arts. Manufacturing industries include engineering and allied trades; tobacco, food, and drink; textiles; and clothing. These employ 21 percent of the population. Agriculture, forestry, and fishing employ 4 percent. Agricultural holdings are small, with only 5.6 percent made up of 50 or more hectares. Dairy products, oats, potatoes, poultry, and eggs were produced on small family farms in 1949. In response to changing demand, the economy has shifted from oats and potatoes to pigs, barley, and cattle. Between 1965 and 1985, mixed farming gave way to the growth, conservation, and utilization of grass. Cattle and milk production account for 34 and 28 percent, respectively, of the total gross output. Cattle number around 1.5 million. Store cattle are imported from the Republic of Ireland for fattening.

Legislation within the European Economic Community (EEC) in 1980 aimed at constructing a common agricultural policy brought changes to the Northern Irish economy. The number of sheep rose to around 1.3 million, but a decline in the number of pigs and poultry followed cereal-price changes. Investment in modernization, including contraction in the number of holdings, led to increased production but a smaller work force. Agricultural gross output rose from 496 million pounds in 1978 to 775.5 million pounds in 1987. State forests occupy 5 percent of the total land area.

The declining economy is attributed to the province's distance from its markets and sources of raw materials. Transportation costs are high. Cross-border schemes between Northern Ireland and the Republic of Ireland and European Community plans hold promise for development in the west. Political unrest deters overseas investment.

Trade. About 74 percent of imports and 82 percent of exports involve trade with the rest of the U.K. Trade with the republic represents about 12 percent of the total.

Division of Labor. Farm labor is divided along age and gender lines, with women and the elderly performing house and farmyard tasks and men and boys working in the fields. Cattle marketing is an exclusively male occupation. Hill farmers cooperate, with neighbors "swapping" labor, but more mechanized lowland farmers do not. In the nonfarming sector of the economy, young women tend to form the lower ranks in offices, businesses, and the professions, and young men tend to be more upwardly mobile.

Land Tenure. Of a total land area of some 1.3 million hectares, about 1.1 million is used for agriculture under an almost universal system of owner occupation. Superimposed on this system is the widespread practice of _conacre_, or seasonal letting of land. This discourages the purchase and amalgamation of land, which modern agriculture requires.

Kinship

Kin Groups and Descent. Descent is bilateral with an emphasis on patrilateral kin. The household is the organizational unit of descent.

Kinship Terminology. English kinship terminology is used. Among Protestants, Christian names often descend within the family; Catholics choose saints' names.

Marriage and Family

Marriage. Marriage is Christian and monogamous. The proportion of marriages solemnized in a religious ceremony (86 percent) far exceeds the national average (59 percent in Scotland; 58 percent in Wales; 52 percent in England). The proportion of the population remarrying (8.7 percent for men and 8.2 percent for women) is the lowest in the U.K. The illegitimacy rate (127 per 1,000) was the lowest in the U.K. in 1986 but is increasing. "Mixed" marriages between Catholics and Protestants are relatively rare, being treated as political actions and viewed with antagonism by both sides. They are more common among the upper and middle classes than among the working class, and in the poorer western rural counties than in urban working-class enclaves. Where kinship networks do cut across the divide, they appear actively to encourage mixed marriages, as on Rathlin Island. A recent increase in integrated schooling may encourage mixed marriages.

Domestic Unit. The nuclear family is the ideal throughout Northern Irish society. Single-parent families are thought to be increasing, particularly in cities, but close kinship ties with siblings and older relatives make them less of a social problem than is the case elsewhere. Most households (61.5 percent) are made up of a husband and wife and their children. Historically, the three-generational stem household was very evident and a modern adaptation existed whereby, in place of the traditional Irish "west room," a bungalow was built nearby for the grandparental generation. Contemporary security measures have increased the familial role of grandparents in house minding, child care, etc. Sibling households are still quite common in the farming community, reflecting the high rate of celibacy and the late age of marriage. Many households contain elderly parents and lodgers (often farm laborers), a reflection of both traditional stem-family residential structure and the modern declining economy and housing shortage. In 1947, the largest households were found among agricultural laborers (4.77), followed by farmers (4.22), factory workers (4.08), shopkeepers (3.35), pensioners (2.68) and artisans (2.60). Overall average household size was 3.96 persons.

Inheritance. Gender is the main determinant of inheritance, but particular modes vary with class. Wealthier farming families practice "tail male" (ultimogeniture). Historically,

neighboring farms were acquired for other sons, but emigration and movement into the professions have lessened the strains of inheritance. Provision of some kind is usually made for daughters.

Socialization. Socialization occurs in the home, at school, in Sunday schools, and in youth organizations, many of which are attached to churches or sociopolitical organizations. Formal education is largely in the hands of religious authorities, although a small number of schools, mainly in rural areas, are nondenominational. The recent establishment of "integrated" schooling is opposed by Catholic church leaders and parents. There are two universities: the Queens University in Belfast and the New University of Ulster in Coleraine. In 1986, 40 percent of the work force had no educational qualifications beyond secondary-school level, a higher proportion than elsewhere in the U.K.

Sociopolitical Organization

Social Organization. The annual parades, open-air festivals, drum and fife bands, and commemorative events of sectarian organizations such as the Protestant Loyal Orange Lodge and the Roman Catholic Ancient Order of Hibernians socialize Protestants and Catholics into separate communities, which crosscut ethnic and age divisions. Each has its own leisure facilities, dances, whist drives, bowling competitions, and the like. In the rural areas, between 30 and 40 percent of the total adult male Protestant population belongs to lodges while spouses and sons belong to ladies' committees and junior lodges or bands. Most members of rural lodges belong to skilled, semiskilled, or unskilled manual occupational categories; few professionals are involved.

Most organizations cutting across the sectarian divide have an occupational or life-experience foundation as in the Ulster Farmers Union, Young Farmer Clubs, the British Legion, and Women's Institutes. Historical or heritage societies based upon village or regional identity and including both Protestants and Catholics in their memberships are new developments.

Political Organization. The Northern Irish deviate from the British political system over one key issue: the question of the province's relation to the rest of the U.K. Voting patterns tend to map the distribution of Catholics and Protestants and there is thus a regional dimension to the vote. Antrim, north and central Down and Armagh, north and central Londonderry, and scattered areas of Fermanagh and Tyrone vote Unionist (i.e., to remain within the United Kingdom). The official Unionist party and Ian Paisley's Democratic party are the largest pro-union parties in Northern Ireland. A large minority (around 34 percent) supports a variety of Irish nationalist and republican candidates seeking reunification with southern Ireland. These include the Social Democratic and Labor party and Sinn Fein (sometimes described as the political wing of the illegal Irish Republican Army). Local election support for Sinn Fein has grown in recent years. The Alliance party bridges the sectarian divide, as do the small Socialist and Workers parties. Voter turnout at national and local elections is heavier than elsewhere in the U.K. After more than twenty years of civil strife, most people support constitutional politics. The Westminster government has pledged that there will be no change in Northern Ireland's constitutional status without majority consent.

Social Control.   The United Kingdom is a signatory to the European Convention on Human Rights and legislation passed in 1973 outlawing discrimination by public bodies, including the government, on the grounds of religious belief or political opinion. While statutory law provides the framework for social control in Northern Ireland, emergency powers were introduced in 1973, including special powers of arrest, nonjury courts, and the proscription of terrorist organizations. Internment without trial was also introduced as a temporary measure and, recently, emergency powers were extended to cover freedom of speech.

Conflict.   As throughout the U.K., most disputes are between people related by marriage. Class conflict has always been muted. Sectarianism has been a source of discrimination and violence since the seventeenth century. The IRA has contested British sovereignty over the six counties since 1920, but the Stormont government contained widespread bloodshed until 1973 when the British army was sent into the province. Loss of life from political violence between 1969 and 1985 amounted to 2,524 persons, of whom 1,507 were civilians. The use of violence as a means of overcoming political differences has declined since the mid-1970s when the police (the Royal Ulster Constabulary) and a local militia (the Ulster Defence Regiment) took over the primary role from the British army. The IRA's campaign was thereafter directed more specifically toward targets in England and Western Europe, and the British and Irish governments began to seek a diplomatic solution to the troubles. By 1990 more people were killed in road accidents in Northern Ireland than in "terrorist" incidents.

Religion

The population of Northern Ireland is 34.9 percent Roman Catholic and 58.2 percent Protestant. Protestants form the majority in all but two (Fermanagh and Tyrone) of the six counties. Presbyterians are most numerous in all but county Fermanagh (where most Protestants belong to the Church of Ireland), a reflection of the Ulster Scots heritage. Evangelical Protestantism came in the early nineteenth century and there are many Methodist, Wesleyan, Pentecostal, and other evangelical congregations in the west of the province. A unique religious sect, the Cooneyites, originated in county Fermanagh.

The diocese and parish boundaries of both the Roman Catholic church and the Church of Ireland straddle the international boundary and many clergy come from the south. Educational and social organizations are closely linked to religious bodies from the cradle to the grave. Medical care is mostly provided by the National Health Service, although some hospitals and hospices are associated with religious foundations.

Catholics and Protestants in Northern Ireland are "endoritualistic." With the rise of the Ecumenical Movement and in response to the cross-community challenge of continuing violence (first met by the Women's Peace Movement), barriers are beginning to fall. Baptisms, weddings, and funerals reflect the religious divide in direct involvement, but indirectly local morality calls for the participation of coresidents and neighbors.

Bibliography

Darby, John, ed. (1985). *Northern Ireland: The Background to the Conflict.* Syracuse: Syracuse University Press.

Harris, Rosemary (1972). *Prejudice and Tolerance in Ulster: A Study of Neighbours and "Strangers" in a Border Community.* Manchester: Manchester University Press.

Heslinga, M. W. (1971). *The Irish Border as a Cultural Divide: A Contribution to the Study of Regionalism in the British Isles.* Assen: Van Gorcum.

Moxon-Browne, Edward (1983). *Nation, Class, and Creed in Northern Ireland.* Aldershot: Gower.

JOAN VINCENT

Norwegians

ETHNONYM: Nordmenn

Orientation

Identification.   The nation of Norway constitutes the western portion of the Scandinavian Peninsula. Its population is substantially of Scandinavian stock, with the exception of Saami and Finns in the north and recent European and other immigrants in the urban south.

Location.   Norway is a narrow, essentially mountainous strip, with an almost 3,200-kilometer coastline to the west and south on the Atlantic Ocean (Norwegian Sea), which is characterized by fjords and numerous islands. Norway shares a long border with Sweden to the east, and shorter boarders with Finland and the Russia to the north and east. Oslo is its capital. It is located at approximately 58° to 73° N and 3° to 31° E. The Gulf Stream assists in producing a continental climate in much of Norway. Despite its northerly location and a short growing season, agriculture and animal husbandry accompany fishing and timbering as primary traditional subsistence occupations. Average yearly rainfall (Oslo) is 68 centimeters.

Demography.   The population of Norway is approximately 4.1 million. The direction of population migration in Norway in recent years has been generally from the country and into the urban centers, the three largest cities currently accounting for approximately one-fourth of the population.

Linguistic Affiliation.   Norwegian is one of the languages of the North Germanic (i.e., Scandinavian) Branch of Germanic languages, which are in turn a branch of the Indo-European Language Family. It is written with the Latin alphabet and is closely related to both Swedish and Danish, the latter having had a strong historical influence on the Norwegian language beginning in the fourteenth century. Today there are two forms of standard written Norwegian. The

Danish-influenced Bokmal is characteristic in urban and up-per-class use. Nynorsk, based on Norway's rural dialects, is associated with independent "Norwegianness" and social egalitarianism. In spoken usage, Norway's mountainous geography has spawned a multitude of local dialects (and local cultural variation in general), although recent urbanization has eroded dialect distinctiveness in some areas.

History and Cultural Relations

Norway was populated by people who are the forerunners of today's Norwegian ethnics as early as 10,000 B.C. Stone Age subsistence in southern Norway was characterized both by foraging and farming. The Bronze Age (1500–500 B.C.) and Iron Ages (500 B.C.–A.D. 400) are clearly demarcated in the archaeological record, the former characterized by rock art, the latter by expanded agriculture and population and by contact with the culture of the Roman Empire. The Germanic migrations of A.D. 500–800 affected primarily the coastal Norwegian population. The Viking Age (A.D. 800–1100), one of exploration, was accompanied by political unification of Norway under a line of kings and the arrival of Catholicism, although growing cultural unification of Norway was interrupted in the fourteenth century by the Black Death. Norway was politically unified with Denmark, as one of its provinces, from 1380 to 1814. Thereafter, it was politically unified with Sweden until 1905, when it gained independence. Norway experienced substantial emigration to North America in the late nineteenth and early twentieth centuries.

Norway is traditionally an ethnically homogeneous society, with the notable exceptions of the Saami and Finnish immigrants in the north and of recent urban immigrants in the south. Cultural and economic conflict characterizes Saami-Norwegian relations, with language use and resource use and allocation being commonly contested issues. Despite substantial cultural similarities with Sweden and Denmark, the colonial history that Norway has experienced with both has strained its relationships with them.

Settlements

Villages are nucleated settlements providing focal points (for marketing, schooling, and religion) for dispersed settlement in the area. Towns are increasing in size, complexity, and degree of interrelatedness to urban centers. The largest cities in Norway are Oslo (approximately 450,000), Bergen (approximately 200,000), and Trondheim (approximately 150,000), with universities in all three (a fourth university is located in Tromsø).

Economy

Subsistence and Commercial Activities. Prior to World War II, the economy was based on timbering, fishing and whaling, metal production (i.e., aluminum, copper), agriculture, and the merchant marine. Since World War II energy production (gas, oil, electricity) has played an increasing role, and the service sector of the economy has grown. A mixed-subsistence base of wage labor and the primary occupations of fishing, farming, or animal husbandry was not uncommon, but it is becoming less prevalent with relative depopulation of rural areas. A typical diet consists of bread, butter, cheese, fish, and meat. Potatoes, cabbage, and carrots are the most

common vegetables, and local berries (lingonberry, cloud berry) are supplemented by imported fruits as sources of vitamin C.

Industrial Arts. Many people, especially in the rural areas, produce crafts, such as knitted or woven goods and various wooden crafts (utensils, bowls, furniture). Regional costumes are a widespread manufacture.

Trade. Open-air produce markets supplement established stores in the summer months.

Division of Labor. The complementarity of female and male roles is a fundamental presumption of Norwegian social structure and is reinforced by a pattern of strong spousal solidarity. "Feminine" and "masculine" behaviors are not strongly distinguished, and decision-making authority is often shared in families. Informal social networks of males and females are, however, substantially segregated. The public/private division of labor is operative in rural areas, with the women performing the majority of domestic duties (i.e., baking, washing, weaving) while the men hold the primary responsibility for such tasks as chopping wood. Farm labor such as making silage, harvesting potatoes, or milking cows often is shared by the entire family.

Land Tenure. Traditionally the small single-family farm was the prevailing type of landholding in rural areas. Gradually the size of these holdings has increased with rural depopulation.

Kinship, Marriage, and Family

Kinship. Kinship is cognatic, with the nuclear family (or less frequently the stem family) as the coresidential group. Residence patterns in rural areas tend to virilocality, whereas in larger towns and urban areas uxorilocality or neolocality are more frequent. Social ties with other cognatic kin living in close physical proximity are significant, but friendship networks and ties of voluntary association also structure everyday interaction in important ways. In modern Norway, no kin-based corporate group exists beyond the nuclear family.

Marriage. After confirmation at about age 14, young Norwegians begin to engage in sexual relations in their mid- to late teens. At formal engagement, sexual relations are openly sanctioned and accompanied by partial or complete cohabitation. Pregnancy is the most common stimulus for marriage. Men are typically 25–30 years of age at marriage and women are typically 20–25 years of age. The divorce rate is relatively low, but it is rising. Personal friction and alcoholism are the most frequently cited reasons for divorce.

Domestic Unit. The nuclear or stem family is the prevalent domestic unit. The stem family consists of a married pair and their unmarried children, plus the parent or parents of one of the spouses. These grandparents often live in a small separate apartment in the same house or in a small separate building near the main house.

Inheritance. Traditional Norwegian inheritance patterns were based on both *odelsrett* (a principle of primogeniture and patriliny) and *asetesrett* (a principle of equal inheritance of all children). In practice in rural areas, eldest sons inherited farms, together with an obligation to pay monetary compensation to other siblings.

Socialization. Norwegian adults consider children as independent individuals who will not be very much influenced by adults, and thus they have a correspondingly democratic approach to child rearing. Harsh discipline, especially corporal punishment, is discouraged, with discussion used as a substitute. Early physical independence is not especially encouraged, but it is welcomed. Avoidance of direct confrontation characterizes relationships. Children construct role models on the behavior of adults rather than on the instructions adults give them for behavior.

Sociopolitical Organization

Social Organization. Norway's system of taxation and social welfare generally precludes extremes of poverty and wealth. Class distinctions between professionals, business people, and working-class people in urban areas are greater than social differentiation in rural areas (the rural merchant-king excepted). Rural elites were and are small in number.

Political Organization. Norway is a constitutional monarchy, divided into nineteen provinces (*fylke*). Of the nine major political parties (including a spectrum from Conservative to Center to Communist), the Labor party has dominated Norwegian politics since the 1930s. The current prime minister, Gro Harlem Brundtland (Labor party), leads a 157-member parliament. Norway's nineteen provinces are in turn divided into counties (*kommune*), each of which has a central administration. Debate of issues is highly valued in county councils. Villages do not have formal councils and local community consciousness may or may not be the norm, as individual independence is also strongly developed.

Social Control. Nonconfrontation and the maintenance of conformity are important Norwegian values. Breaches of law are handled by local sheriffs or by police and are adjudicated in the Norwegian judicial system. Personal relations are characterized by avoidance of expressing strong emotions, rather than open conflict.

Conflict. Norway's early kings (especially Harold Fairhair, c. A.D. 900–940) prevailed in conflicts with local lords to establish centralized leadership; this pattern of internal armed conflict was congruent with simultaneous external Viking conquest. When Norway was ceded by Denmark to Sweden in 1814, the Norwegians attempted unsuccessfully to repel the Swedish army and establish an independent government. Norway's independence from Sweden in 1905 was achieved without military conflict. Norway was occupied by Germany in World War II.

Religion and Expressive Culture

Religious Beliefs and Practices. Lutheranism became the official state religion in Norway in the sixteenth century and remains such, although minority religions (Baptists, Catholics) are also evident. Although membership in the state church is high, many Norwegians are not regular churchgoers, with women generally putting more emphasis on church attendance. High festivals such as Christmas, Easter, and Norwegian Independence Day (Syttende Mai) are ritualized events with national costumes, festive foods, and church attendance integrated into the celebrations.

Arts. Various folk arts, such as rose painting and costume and clothing manufacture, are accompanied by modern forms of visual, literary, and theatrical arts.

Medicine. State-supported socialized medicine fulfills health care needs, with hospital care as a norm for childbirth and serious illnesses. Almost all drugs are dispensed on a prescription basis in pharmacies (*apotek*).

Death and Afterlife. Funerals, like all life-and-death rituals (baptism, confirmation), are generally held in the church. The concept of a continuing spirit after death, which is in accordance with Lutheran theology, is however absent in a significant number of nonchurchgoing Norwegians, approximately 30 percent of the total population.

See also Saami; Finns

Bibliography

Barnes, John A. (1954). "Class and Committee in a Norwegian Island Parish." *Human Relations* 7:39–58.

Barnes, John A. (1957). "Land Rights and Kinship in Two Bremnes Hamlets." *Journal of the Royal Anthropological Institute* 87:31–56.

Barth, Fredrik, ed. (1963). *The Role of the Entrepreneur in Social Change in Northern Norway.* Oslo: Universitetsforlaget.

Eliot, Thomas D., et al. (1960). *Norway's Families.* Philadelphia: University of Pennsylvania Press.

Hollos, Marida (1974). *Growing Up in Flathill.* Oslo: Universitetsforlaget.

KAREN A. LARSON

Occitans

ETHNONYMS: Méridionaux, Midis

Orientation

Identification. Occitans are people who live in the predominantly agricultural French meridional and speak langue d'oc. This language is distinct from langue d'oïl, from which "standard" or official French derived. Both geographic and linguistic factors thus define Occitanie. Today the region is fully integrated into the socioeconomic life of France as a whole but, for historicocultural reasons, the Occitans retain a strong sense of "otherness" from the Paris- or north-dominated larger polity. It is defined, essentially, in terms of its opposition to, or difference from, the France of north of the Paris Basin. This being the case, the present essay will concentrate upon the elements of early Occitanian development that established that difference.

Location. "Occitanie" today consists of thirty departments (French administrative divisions) south of the Loire, bordered on the west by the Atlantic, on the east by the Alps, and on the south by the Pyrenees and the Mediterranean. The northern limits of the region are less clearly defined—with no true natural frontier between the northern and southern territories, this northern border is defined more appropriately in linguistic and cultural terms. Occitan territory largely coincides with six historical provinces: Gascogne, Languedoc, Limousin, Auvergne, Provence, and Dauphiné. One cannot speak of geological or climatic unity for Occitanie. The region's varying sections—the north-central area, dominated by the Central Massif; the western and eastern limits, dominated by mountainous terrain; the very different Atlantic and Mediterranean littorals; and the many fertile river valleys throughout the territory—establish important and distinct ecological zones. Occitanie is located on the border between the temperate and subtropical zones, enjoying on average a higher mean annual temperature than that of the north of France. Summers are, through much of the region, hot and dry. By virtue of its geographic location and environmental conditions, Occitanie comprises the most important agricultural region of France, particularly for cereals, olives, and, of course, some of the world's most famous vineyards.

Demography. Defined by geographical criteria, there are approximately 15 million inhabitants of Occitanie, but not all of these are Occitan according to linguistic and cultural tradition. Of this 15 million, approximately 10 million possess some degree of fluency in one or another of the Occitan dialects, and perhaps 2 million use it in their daily lives. Speakers of Occitan are also found in parts of Catalonia and in villages of the Italian Piedmont, as well as in the Principality of Monaco. In the area today understood as Occitanie, the predominantly rural population is currently suffering a decline in numbers, largely because the region's economy cannot provide employment for much of its youth. Over the past three decades, out-migration by Occitanians for economic reasons and in-migration by well-to-do northerners seeking a romanticized, bucolic life-style have had a profound effect on the local communities and have undermined the geographical-linguistic association of Occitans and Occitanie.

Linguistic Affiliation. Occitan is an Ibero-Romance language, more strongly influenced by Latin than the "standard" French of the Paris Basin and closely related to Catalan. The langue d'oc/langue d'oïl distinction refers to the retention, in Occitan, of the Latinate "oc" as an equivalent for "oui" (the Parisian form is "oïl"). This distinction directly invokes the differences in linguistic development between the two linguistic traditions in France and also implies different degrees of Germanic and Roman sociocultural influences. Within the linguistic tradition called "Occitan" there is, however, a great deal of dialectic diversity. Perhaps because much of the effort, since the late 1800s, to develop a standard Occitan lexicon and orthography has focused upon the Provençal dialect to the neglect of others in the langue d'oc family, Provençal has often been treated as synonymous with Occitan. Within Occitanie, however, there is no consensus accepting such a presumption. Because of the pervasiveness of the French educational system, which employs the langue d'oïl, there are

no longer any purely monolingual speakers of Occitan, and it has come to be considered by many to be a patois used by rustics.

History and Cultural Relations

While there is, in the broadest sense, a geographical and linguistic basis for the designation "Occitan," the developmental trajectory followed by Occitanie that differentiates it from France as a whole is rooted in a series of significant historical and protohistorical events that linked the French meridian more closely with the cultures of the Mediterranean than with that of the Germanic tribes that were much more influential in the north. First to come to the region were the Greeks, who founded Massalia (now Marseille) in 600 B.C. and brought the indigenes of the meridian into the already lively world of Greek-dominated commerce in the Mediterranean. This commercial trade carried with it cultural influences, introducing a Hellenist tradition in architecture and in the layout of urban centers and public monuments that this region shares with the Mediterranean, but not with northern France. The second significant event, or events, was the successive waves of Celts immigrating into the Gallic isthmus, driven there from the north and east by the expansionist movements of Germanic tribes at their backs. Celtic "conquest" of the territory was by settlement rather than by force of arms. By the time the Romans arrived in the mid–second century B.C.—the third profound foreign influence—there already existed a thriving, "modern" Mediterranean culture. The climate favored the adoption of "Mediterranean" crops such as grapes, figs, and grains, while proximity and commercial contact facilitated the adoption of Hellenic modes of social organization and cultural expression.

The Hellenic influence, however strong it may have been on the Mediterranean littoral, was essentially based on commerce and thus was strongly localized to the area of Marseilles. With the coming of Rome's legions, there emerged for the first time a larger meridional unity. Although Roman conquest extended far beyond the southern isthmus that is now, properly speaking, Occitanie, it was primarily in the south that the direct effects of Romanization were felt—for here the Romans established true colonies, rather than simple military outposts. The Romans introduced what are now felt to be distinctive characteristics of the region: cities designed and built according to the Roman model; agricultural enterprise ordered on the principles of the latifundia; military monuments and temples celebrating Roman gods; but, above all, the strong Romanization of the language and the introduction of Roman law to the region.

This ostensible unity did not last. Germanic tribes from the east and north, themselves under constant pressure from the westward expansion of the Huns, were moving westward. By the start of the fifth century, the imperial government of Rome could no longer bar their incursion into the Gaulish territories. Quickly losing its more northern holdings to the invading Vandals and Suevis and, later, the Franks, Rome regrouped and consolidated its presence in the south. Gaul, Brittany, and Spain assumed great importance as a sort of protective buffer zone for Italy. The invaders of the northern part of Gaul took these new territories by force of arms and settled in relatively large numbers. In the south, the newcomers were Visigoths, who constitute the fourth great external influence on the region. The Visigoths approached the annexation of these new lands in a less obtrusive manner than that adopted by the invading tribes in the north. Their settlements were comparatively less numerous—they were not so much interested in land occupation as in administrative and economic control, and so they permitted preexisting cultural practices to coexist with their own.

The first significant historic references to an "Occitan" entity occur in the Middle Ages. This was the time of the region's flowering in the fields of art, science, letters, and philosophy. The various smaller kingdoms of the region at the time were stabilized in the hands of established families—for the most part derived from powerful families of the Gallo-Roman and Gothic periods but also including "made" noble families of Frankish descent, who came to the region during the Carolingian period.

During the 1100s and 1200s, three major houses rose to the status of kingdom (although smaller independent realms had existed in Occitanie prior to this time). These were: Aquitaine, to the west, which later passed through the Plantagenets to English rule for a time; the dynasty of the counts of Saint-Gilles and of Toulouse, in the center and to the east of the region, whose most noted figure was the Count Raimond IV; and finally, in the west, a region in fealty to the Catalans of Spain. The history of the region at this time is essentially the history of the struggles among these three powers.

Losing, in the late 1200s, in the Albigensian Crusades, Occitanie began also to lose its independence, a process completed in 1471, when English Aquitaine was made part of France. Never again an independent political entity (or entities), Occitanie retained its distinctiveness through the retention of its language. The language was banned from official use in 1539, thus beginning its decline in prestige as well as use, although it never disappeared entirely. The poet Mistral, through his work with the Provençal dialect of Occitan in the late 1800s and early 1900s, was one of the first to bring back a certain amount of respect for and appreciation of the language. He and some colleagues established a movement, the Félibrige, dedicated to standardizing Occitan on the basis of the Provençal dialect and developing an orthography with which to write in it. Throughout its history, the Félibrige has suffered from dissension among its members—partly because of its having given pride of place to only one of the many Occitanie dialects, and also because the movement soon took on a political role as well, rather than confining itself to purely linguistic and literary concerns. Its current role has lost much of its former political thrust, giving way in that regard to more militant regionalist movements.

During World War II, the concerns of the Occitan regionalist movements aligned most of their members in support of Petain—exceptions included Simone Weil and René Nelli. During the early postwar years, the Institut d'Estudis Occitans attempted to formulate new approaches to the concept of regionalism, becoming an ideological competitor of the Félibrige. The region's economic problems, arising from the fact that it remains largely agricultural in a national economy that favors industry, has fed the regionalist movement, giving rise to claims of "interior colonization" by the Paris-based government and financial structure. The region today is splintered among rival political factions, which make any concerted efforts for the overall betterment of the region difficult to organize. Perhaps the most influential of these rival movements is the Comitat Occitan d'Estudis e d'Accion, founded in 1961, whose founders first popularized the term "interior colonization" and focused on increasing the autonomy of the local communities within the region. This group, taken over in 1971 by a more militant and revolutionary organization called Lutte Occitane, presses on today in pursuit of the creation of an autonomous Occitanie, and it strongly identifies itself with working-class protest movements throughout France.

Settlements

Occitanie is largely rural in orientation and in organization, although it encompasses important urban centers, the earliest being the Greek-established port city of Marseilles. The historically predominant settlement was the agricultural village, oriented toward meeting the needs of the large estate-farms (latifundia) common to the region. The oldest quarters of today's villages are commonly found on a hillside, at the peak of which may be found the ruins of the "chateau" that once provided the local economic focus for the village. Distinctive of the houses of this old quarter are their red-tiled roofs and their elevated, or "perched," location on the hillside. In much of Occitanie, these old quarters are in ruins, as are the chateaus around which they are clustered. Cities and villages were frequently walled, although the walls are now usually in ruins as well. The larger villages are also oriented around public squares, the site of weekly markets that are still held today and that have been held for perhaps 800 years.

Economy

The economy of Occitanie is largely agricultural, principally concerned with the cultivation of cereals, olives, and other characteristically Mediterranean crops. It is also a notable region for viticulture, the wines of the south of France being among the most well-known and valued in the world—although after viticulture was introduced by the Greeks, they and their Roman successors pronounced the region's product far inferior to the flavored wines of their homelands. Marseilles began as a commercial center for the Greeks and remains an important port on the Mediterranean. Although there has been some industrialization in the region, it remains largely undeveloped in this regard compared to the north. Agriculture has long been practiced according to the extensive-farming concept of the latifundia. Although strongly agricultural, the region has also long possessed a crafts and mercantilist tradition. Tourism, along the Mediterranean littoral in particular, plays an important role in the economy today.

Land Tenure.   The latifundist pattern introduced by the Romans meant that, for most of the region's history, property ownership was concentrated in the hands of a relatively small proportion of the local population. Access to land, for most Occitans, was through leasehold. Most often, this meant farming one or several strips, defined as a single plowed length of field, on one or more estates. This entailed village-wide cooperation, particularly at harvest time, for a great many individual leaseholders might possess harvest rights on a single estate. Ownership of the land itself passed from father to eldest son. Leaseholds were most often handed down generationally as well. Today it is not uncommon for an individual to own a number of noncontiguous plots of land, scattered about the village environs, perhaps as a result of the transfer of leasehold rights to private ownership.

Kinship, Marriage, and Family

Kinship. Descent is bilaterally reckoned, but with a patrilateral emphasis. The patronym is passed on to offspring.

Marriage. Occitanie is a Christian, predominantly Catholic, region, and marriage rules reflect this fact. Monogamy is both the moral and legal norm. Local endogamy is the most common pattern of spousal selection, but it is not specifically prescribed. Divorce, although it does occur, is not approved.

Domestic Unit. Both the nuclear family and the extended family are commonly encountered, with the extended family (broadly speaking, a nuclear family with at least one collateral- or ascendant-generation family member coresident in the household) being more common in rural villages than in urban centers. A newly married son and his spouse may live with the son's parents for a short time immediately after marriage. Postmarital residence with the parents of either spouse, however, is explicitly linked to the particular economic necessities faced by the newly married couple, not to socioculturally defined conditions of propriety.

Socialization. Preschool-age offspring receive their primary care from both parents, although the assumption is that the mother is responsible for most of the day-to-day childcare duties. Children attend local schools, but secondary and postsecondary education may entail leaving the home community, depending on the locally available educational resources. Higher education has tended to emphasize "official" (i.e., northern French) language and culture—a situation that the regionalist movements of Occitanie have attempted to resist, particularly in the last three decades.

Sociopolitical Organization

Occitanie has been part of greater France since the late 1400s and is merged with the larger polity for all administrative and political functions. Regionalist movements have sought to increase local autonomy, but concessions in this area have so far been mostly limited to linguistic and literary spheres. The diversity of interests within Occitanie, both cultural and economic, has hindered the perception and pursuit of regionally defined political, cultural, and economic goals.

Religion and Expressive Culture

Religious Beliefs and Practices. With their arrival in the region, the Greeks introduced the worship of their gods, a religious practice that was supplanted only with great difficulty by Christianity. As late as the late 600s, the Christian church was still encountering opposition, sometimes violent, to its efforts to convert the population. It is perhaps this tenacious retention of pre-Christian practice, as well as the church's willingness to co-opt or incorporate local devotional practice, that explains the novel approaches that characterize early meridional Christianity: a strong interest in cults of the saints and cults of holy relics; a strong monastic tradition; and the numerous holy men, who lived solitary lives of self-abnegation and poverty. This unorthodox approach to Chris-

tianity gave rise to the Occitanian reputation as a "land of heretics," for many practices appeared to the church to be a direct attack upon its doctrine, notably the tendency to decry the accumulation of property by the religious. In the twelfth century, the Albigensian Crusades were fueled by church reaction against the heresy of Catharism, which was strong in the region. This event had more political than religious results—the defeat of the region in this religion-based war marked the end of Occitanian independence and the incorporation of the region into the kingdom of France. This did not, and does not, mean that the region fell placidly into universal acceptance of Rome's dictates. The "tradition" of southern heresy was continued through the 1500s, for the region became a refuge for Calvinists, Huguenots, and other Protestants.

Arts. When one speaks of the art of the Occitans, one speaks first of the troubadours of the Middle Ages, who brought their poetry and celebrations of courtly love to the whole of Europe. But Occitanie is well represented in the spheres of philosophy and literature as well by writers such as Montesquieu, Fenelon, De Sade, Pascal, Zola, Compte, and Valéry. Although these writers wrote in the standard French of their time, rather than in Occitan, they represent what has been called a "meridional humanist" tradition, attesting to the fact that for centuries this region was a center for art, philosophy, and science.

Bibliography

Armengaud, André, and Robert Lafont, eds. (1979). *Histoire d'Occitanie*. Toulouse: Hachette.

Kohler, d'E. (1965). "Observations historiques et sociologiques sur la poésie des troubadours." *Cahiers de Civilisation Médiévale*.

Ladurie, E. Le Roy (1966). *Les Paysans de Languedoc*. Paris.

Ladurie, E. Le Roy (1980). *Carnival in Romans*. Translated by Mary Feeney. New York: George Braziller.

Mussot-Goulard, Renée (1978). *Les Occitans*. Paris: Éditions Albin Michel.

Nelli, René (1978). *Mais enfin qu'est-ce que l'Occitanie*. Toulouse: Edouard Privat.

NANCY E. GRATTON

Orcadians

ETHNONYM: Orkney Islanders

Orientation

Identification.   The Orkney Islands constitute one of the three "Special Island Areas" of Scotland. Prior to the fifteenth century, the Norse were the majority of the population. After 1469, Scottish settlers arrived in increasing numbers and, in time, supplanted the older culture and language. The Romans called the islands "Orcades." Early Irish writers called them "Insi Orc" or "Islands of the Boar."

Location.   The Orkneys are located to the northeast of northern Scotland. They consist of 90 islands, of which only 23 are inhabited. They are separated from Scotland by the 10-kilometer-wide Pentland Firth and are 83 kilometers south of the Shetland Islands. They extend from 58°41′ to 59°24′ N and from 2°22′ to 3°26′ W. The largest island, Mainland, which makes up half the land area, is 39 kilometers long in an east-west direction. The northerly islands are Rousay, Shapinsay, Westray, Papa Westray, Sanday, Stronsay, and the more remote island of North Ronaldsay. The southern islands, separated from Mainland by the inland sea of Scapa Flow, are Hoy and South Ronaldsay. With the exception of high cliffs and hills on the western coasts, the treeless islands consist of broad lowlands and low-lying hills. The spectacular red sandstone sea stack, the Old Man of Hoy, is a famous landmark. The highest point is Ward Hill (549.5 meters) on Hoy.

A subarctic oceanic climate and vegetation pattern prevails. This is conditioned by the Gulf Stream, North Sea, and Atlantic Ocean. Severe winter gales occur at times. The January mean temperature is 4° C and the July mean is 13° C. The annual rainfall averages between 150 and 250 centimeters.

Demography.   In 1981, the population of the Orkney Islands was 19,040, of which 14,900 lived on Mainland. The largest town and the administrative center is Kirkwall (population 4,600 in 1971); Stromness (population 1,477 in 1961) is the only other large town. All other communities are very small. Since 1861, the population has slowly declined.

Linguistic Affiliation.   The local dialect of English is derived from earlier forms of lowland Scottish English. It still retains many words of Norn, the former dialect of Norwegian, which died out in the seventeenth century.

History and Cultural Relations

The islands are famous for their remains of Neolithic, Bronze Age, and Iron Age settlements. Of these, the best-known are Skara Brae, a Neolithic settlement first excavated by V. Gordon Childe in the 1920s; Maeshowe, a Bronze Age chambered cairn; and the Ring of Brogar, a henge-type monument. There are many *brochs* (round stone towers) from the Pictish Iron Age. Viking raiders first appeared in the eighth century; Viking settlers followed during the next few centuries. The emerging Viking-Norse culture, which became Christianized in the early twelfth century, continued until 1468–1469, when the Orkneys and Shetlands were transferred to Scotland as a pledge in lieu of a dowry for the daughter of King Christian I of Denmark and Norway when she married King James III of Scotland. This pledge was never redeemed and, in 1472, Scotland formally annexed the islands. Scottish settlers began arriving after 1230 and their increasing presence influenced the local culture and language. During the late 1500s and early 1600s, the people suffered greatly under the tyrannical rule of the Scottish earls and the feudal system they imposed. During the nineteenth century, these restrictions were eased and agricultural improvements were instituted, resulting in a greatly improved quality of life. In the eighteenth century, 75 percent of the employees of the Hudson's Bay Company in Canada were recruited in the Orkneys. Commercial agriculture in the early twentieth century and the discovery of the North Sea oil in the 1970s brought a new type of economic prosperity to these islands.

Settlements

Since Neolithic times, the Orkneys have been relatively sparsely settled. Even though clustered settlements, such as the village of Skara Brae, were present in the Neolithic period, dispersed farms and houses have been the norm. The few clusters of farmhouses are near crossroads where there is usually a store, a pub, and a garage. During Norse times, the Udal land-tenure system, whereby each child received a share of the farm, led to a highly fragmented system of land tenure and demographic dispersal. Although many of these shares were consolidated into "feudal" estates by the Scottish earls, this system in part persisted. In 1886, the Udal system continued within the framework of the Crofters' Holdings Act and the emergence of commercial beef-cattle production. The largest settlement, Kirkwall, was founded by the Norse in the tenth century. Stromness is the main ferry port linking the islands to northern Scotland.

Economy

Subsistence and Commercial Activities.   The Orkney economy was and still is based on farming; fishing is of minor importance. Fifty-two percent of the land is classified as arable land. In earlier centuries, black oats and bere barley were the staple grains. Kale and (later) potatoes were also important. Every family had a pig, a cow, and a few hens and geese. Because of the cool and rainy growing season, the oats and barley had to be dried in small home kilns. In 1830, and especially after 1850, the estate owners began programs of "agricultural improvements." Fragmented small fields were consolidated, commons were enclosed, soil liming was used to enrich the soil, new grasses for hay were seeded, silage making was encouraged, and beef-cattle raising was encouraged. New, larger breeds of sheep and cattle replaced the smaller, older breeds. Sheep numbers declined, although the ancient sheep still survive on North Ronaldsay. Kelp burning for ash, which was sold to glass makers, ended, and the kelp was used to enrich the soil. Beef, mutton, and other farm products found a ready market in the growing industrial cities of Scotland and England. In the twentieth century, farm mechanization furthered this change to the extent that farming became a business rather than a way of life.

Other sources of livelihood include some fishing and fish processing, a whiskey distillery, cheese making, tourism (in the summer), and the development of the nearby North Sea oil fields (since 1970). Recently, crab and lobster fishing have been developed. Peat, the traditional local fuel, has to a great extent been supplemented by coal, electric power, and now petroleum products.

Industrial Arts. Industrial growth has been inhibited because of the lack of trees, metallic ores, and coal on the islands. Island crafts include some wooden fishing-boat building, a tweed mill, the making of silver jewelry using ancient Celtic and Norse designs, home knitting, and straw-backed chair making.

Trade. Trade in beef cattle, mutton, and frozen and processed fish link Kirkwall and Stromness with the major ports in Scotland. Shops and businesses such as bakeries, printers, food markets, hardware, clothing, and furniture are concentrated in Kirkwall and Stromness, the only towns of any size and importance.

Division of Labor. On the farms and crofts, women did the cooking, baking, dairying, and washing. Between 1900 and 1960, when poultry and egg production was important, women cared for the chickens and controlled the monies from them and the eggs. Men cared for the beef cattle, did the heavy agricultural fieldwork, and fished.

Land Tenure. The land-tenure system is a complex mixture that has evolved from the old Norse Udal system, Scottish feudalism of the fifteenth and sixteenth centuries, the Crofters' Holdings Act, and modern individually owned farms. In the Udal system, each legitimate child inherited part of the land and other property. After the Scottish earls arrived, they gained control of much of the land and became large estate owners. The farmers and others became tenants who paid rents in kind. After the Crofters' Holdings Act of 1886, the rents were fixed and land security was protected. In the twentieth century, the estates were broken up and private use and titles became more important.

Kinship, Marriage, and Family

Kin Groups and Descent. An unfocused variety of cognatic descent is characteristic of the rural areas of Orkney. Within the rural localities, most people are related to each other. Precise kin ties beyond that of first cousin are of little importance. However, people will invoke kinship in order to justify their relations to each other. The older patterns of local endogamy are breaking down as young people who board in Kirkwall to attend secondary school meet individuals from other areas.

Kinship Terminology. Orkney kinship terms follow similar bifurcate-merging patterns in Scotland and the British Isles in general. Relationships to both sides of the family receive equal stress.

Marriage. Weddings have always been an important aspect of social life, especially in the rural farming areas. Local endogamy is common. In the past, young men often delayed marriage for years because of poverty. They would go to Scotland, England, Canada, etc. to earn enough money before returning to marry and settle down. Prior to the formal wedding, announcements and visits took place between the two families. For most people, a marriage was socially valid only if it was performed by a minister in a church. Thursday was considered a lucky day for a wedding. The divorce rate is very low.

Domestic Unit. The basic domestic unit is the nuclear family with neolocal residence. However, on the smaller islands, the housing shortage often forces a young couple to live for varying lengths of time in either his or her parental home. When a house becomes available, they leave.

Inheritance. Today, the farm or the inherited use of farmlands will usually go to one chosen child. Movable property will be passed on to various children. In some cases, land can now be sold to other islanders or even outsiders.

Socialization. The care and training of children was done by the mother, older siblings, and grandmother. In the past, much of this was done in the context of storytelling and rhyme. Homemade wooden toys—especially boats, domestic animals, and windmills—were common. Some villages had schools by the mid-eighteenth century. In 1971, there were twenty-nine local primary schools; only Kirkwall and Stromness had secondary schools. Children from the outer islands who attend secondary schools are boarded in Kirkwall.

Sociopolitical Organization

Social Organization. After 1468, the incoming Scottish earls slowly established a feudal system with large estates and increasing control over the rural population. By the nineteenth century, only a small minority of the farms remained as freehold. Beginning in the early nineteenth century, their control was slowly diminished. The 1886 Crofters' Holdings Act enabled the crofters to regain a high degree of freedom and security on their leaseholds. Today, there are very few distinctions in social rank, especially on the smaller islands.

Political Organization. Between 1973 and 1975, the old county of Orkney was abolished and the Orkneys became one of three Special Island Areas of Scotland. In this new structure, they were allowed to retain a high degree of local authority. The island area operates through the Scottish Office in Edinburgh. Police and fire services are provided through the nearby Highland Region of northern Scotland. The Orkney Island Council has special linkages with London for petroleum and energy development. Other services are provided through various Scottish development agencies.

Social Control. Local "ethnohistorical" pride, island isolation, and a small population are the primary means of social control. No murders have occurred here in over 120 years. On a formal level, the Scottish court system prevails.

Conflict. The major source of local conflict is rooted in the islanders' respect for their original Norse culture and identity. Many islanders resent the recent (post-1970) influx of Scottish and English migrants. Many prefer union with England rather than Scotland. The County Library, which was founded in 1683, the Tankerness House Museum, and the Stromness Museum serve as important centers that enhance island cultural identity.

Religion and Expressive Culture

Religious Beliefs. Since the Reformation, Protestant denominations have replaced the older Celtic-Norse form of Catholicism. The Church of Scotland was established by the Stuarts. Later, the United Presbyterian Church, the Free Church, and the United Secession denominations gained dominance. Saint Magnus Cathedral in Kirkwall, which dates back to 1137, is unique in Britain in that it was deeded over to the Royal Burgh of Kirkwall and does not have a bishop. Most Orcadians are very religious, but the older strict Sabbatarianism has vanished. Today, the churches are important social centers.

Religious Practitioners. Protestant ministers traditionally have been respected as individuals and leaders by most people. However, there has always been some anticlericism over the past two centuries. The people of Harray District on Mainland were regarded as the most devout people.

Ceremonies. The weekly Sunday services are still of importance to many people, especially in the rural and smaller island areas. During the yearly religious cycle, the most important festive days are Yule, New Year's, Candlemas, Easter, Lammas, Harvest Home, and Halloween. On the secular side the annual Ba' (Ball) games on Christmas (Yule) and New Year's are major community events in Kirkwall. The two opposing "teams," the Uppies (uptowners) and the Doonies (downtowners), engage in a "free-for-all football match" on the narrow winding "main" street of Kirkwall.

Arts. The most important local art is the making of sterling silver jewelry; knitting is of less importance. The most important modern Orkney writers have been Edward Muir, Eric Linklater, and, currently, George Mackay Brown of Stromness.

Medicine. The medical services and practices are basically the same as those for the rest of the United Kingdom (i.e., socialized medicine, modern clinics, and hospitalization). Rural doctors are present, but most services are centered in Kirkwall.

Death and Afterlife. Death and funerals were a reminder of the unity of the kin group and all households within the local community. In the past, wakes of eight days were held in the home. The wakes were accompanied by games among the younger people, condolences by others, and an ever-present fear that the ghost of the deceased might return. Drinking of ale and whiskey was an important part of the funeral. The basic Protestant beliefs in heaven and hell prevail.

Bibliography

Bailey, Patrick (1971). *Orkney*. Newton Abbott, U.K.: David & Charles.

Fenton, Alexander (1978). *The Northern Isles: Orkney and Shetland*. Edinburgh: John Donald.

Firth, John (1922). *Reminiscences of an Orkney Parish*. Stromness, Scotland: W. R. Rendall for the Stromness Museum. 2nd ed. 1974.

Marwick, Ernest W. (1975). *The Folklore of Orkney and Shetland*. London: B. T. Batsford.

Theodoratus, Robert J. (1977). "The Orkney Islands: A Bibliographic Survey of Printed Materials on Ethnography, Folklife, Folklore, and Local History." *Behavior Science Research* 12:29–44.

Tulloch, Peter A. (1974). *A Window on North Ronaldsay*. Kirkwall, Scotland: Kirkwall Press.

ROBERT J. THEODORATUS

Pasiegos

ETHNONYMS: none

Orientation

Identification. The Montes de Pas form a high mountain enclave in the Cantabrian range of northern Spain. They straddle the provincial boundaries of Burgos and Cantabria (formerly Santander) at the divide between the Atlantic coast and the *meseta* (plateau). Pasiegos define themselves as those who practice transhumant herding of the Pasiego type or whose forebears did so.

Location. Most Pasiegos live on the northern, or Cantabrian, slope facing the port city of Santander in the three official Pasiego municipalities (townships) of San Pedro del Romeral, San Roque de Riomiera, and Vega de Pas. The population also extends into the montane neighborhoods of adjacent Cantabrian municipalities and, on the Burgos slope, into the montane regions of Espinosa de los Monteros. The Cantabrian side is watered by the high sources of the Rivers Pas and Miera and the Burgos side by the sources of the Trueba. The defining characteristics of areas of Pasiego residence are the pronounced altitudinal variation along the montane rivers and the transhumant herding practiced there. Rivers descend as much as 1,000 meters in a distance of 10 to 15 kilometers. The highest peak in the Montes stands at 1,724 meters and the major passes at about 950 to 1,350 meters. Zones of human use range from the lowest permanent settlements—at 250–350 meters but mostly at 400–750 meters—to the summer meadows around and above the major passes, well over 1,000 meters. The natural grass crop on which the Pasiego economy depends is nourished year-round by rains and mists, with heavy winter snow at the higher altitudes. The low areas of the valleys on the Atlantic slope enjoy temperate winters. Four grass crops are grazed or harvested annually at the bottom of the valleys and two in the high meadows, visited only between May and September. The three official municipalities of the Montes de Pas occupy about 189 square kilometers, or 3.6 percent of Cantabria. Beyond the Montes, on gentler terrain, the conditions that support the rapidly repetitive, sequential exploitation of local meadows and that define the Pasiego way of life are absent.

Demography. The number of non-Pasiegos living in the zone has always been negligible, while about 1,500 Pasiego herders lived adjacent to the official townships in 1970. There were about 4,000 inhabitants in the three municipalities in 1970 and just under 3,000 in 1980. Emigration is, in cattle herding, to towns of the Cantabrian coastal plain and, in commerce and services, to the towns and cities of northern Spain. Emigrants remain emotionally and economically tied to their home zone, especially when lack of schooling hampers their ability to move into the mainstream of Spanish society and beyond herding and the lowest levels of petty commerce. Conditions favoring mobility are improving, and emigrants are increasingly breaking ties of deep dependency on the Montes de Pas. This was not so true earlier; then the community of Pasiego emigrants figured more heavily in the social life of the home zone.

Linguistic Affiliation. The Pasiego dialect of Spanish is one of the so-called Old Leonese Group, which was spoken widely (and written) in northwestern Iberia. It is an evolved archaic Spanish with some Celtic elements of vocabulary. Its affiliations today are principally with rural dialects of Asturias, León, and the rest of Santander. It is no longer spoken throughout entire communities. In the Montes de Pas, the dialect is spoken by the oldest generation and in private life in some but not all homes; its use varies in inverse proportion to the degree of schooling in textbook Spanish. The dialect has long been the object of nostalgic revival by provincial literati and some emigrants with interest in local traditions, but this revival has not enlarged its use within the Pasiego community.

History and Cultural Relations

As far as is known, the Montes de Pas were populated about A.D. 1011 when Sancho, Count of Castile, granted the Monastery of San Salvador at Oña (Burgos) a privilege allowing herders in its extensive dominions to pasture animals there. Herders' entry into the Montes apparently was gradual; permanent settlements are known only later, and for centuries Pasiegos—as the Montes' inhabitants came to be known—depended in civil and religious matters on established centers in the territory of Espinosa de los Monteros. For example, they had to carry their dead over the mountains for burial in Espinosa's territory. Three parishes were established in the Montes in the last half of the sixteenth century, and the three centers were given independent civil and juridical status in 1689. These acts followed a long series of court actions whose records are the principal sources of early Pasiego history. Thus, while Pasiegos are culturally and historically Spanish and do not consider themselves ethnically different from other Spaniards, they have shared a history of marginal statuses and separate legal actions as well as a situation as herders in a remote enclave; these shared experiences have brought them a distinctiveness that is accentuated by the exigencies of transhumant herding. As they emerged into public notice, both as peddlers in the marketplaces of the realm and with the appointment in 1830 of one of their women as wet nurse in the royal household, Pasiegos became the object of writers' curiosity. Considered "too different to be Spanish," a few surmised that Pasiegos must be descended from Moors or Jews. This conjecture spread and Pasiegos came to be viewed, along with such other northern Spanish groups as the Maragatos (León), the Vaqueiros de Alzada (Asturias), or the Agotes (Navarra), as foreigners on Spanish soil. Of these others, the transhumant cattle-herding Vaqueiros de Alzada have the closest cultural, dialectic, and occupational affinities with the Pasiegos.

Settlements

The municipality, or township, is the largest unit of local membership. Each of the three Pasiego municipalities has its town center (*villa*) and rural neighborhoods (*barrios*). Barrios usually correspond to mountain river valleys and thus have a vertical dimension. Within barrios, named meadow clusters are called *praderas*; these are interspersed at different altitudes with municipally held forests and brushlands. Each meadow within a pradera is fully enclosed, bears a housestable structure, and is visited seasonally by its owner or renter. Families move between praderas separately from their neighbors, but most transhumance occurs within single barrios. Much socializing and intermarriage reflect barrio membership or use of high meadows in boundary areas of adjacent barrios. Habitation is dispersed from meadow to meadow, but there is incipient clustering toward the valley bottoms and elsewhere where terrain permits. The town centers are focal points for trade, transport, civil and religious functions, and leisure, though they are distant from the higher meadows. Where Pasiego-type transhumance is practiced in barrios of neighbor municipalities not officially known as Pasiego towns, there is nonetheless a deep sense of community and also intermarriage. The administrative boundaries of the Montes de Pas do not, in the herders' view, separate Pasiegos from non-Pasiegos if they live within the same form of economy.

Economy

Subsistence and Commercial Activities. Cattle herding is the basis of the Pasiego economy. Trade has focused on breeding stock as much as on dairy products. Sheep and goats are less important than in the past, while the herds of Holstein-Friesian cattle have increased since their adoption (at the expense of the native "Pasiego" breed) beginning about 1870. The transhumance system revolves around the cattle meadow. Whole families move between different meadows at single altitudes and between different altitudes. A family might move as many as twenty times a year, between six or seven meadows, ascending the slopes sequentially three times in succession (and once more to harvest grass). Lambs and male calves are sold for meat. Cows are reared for breeding and dairying and sold after their third calving. The hardy, mountain-bred milk cattle are appreciated nationwide. Stock fairs were once local but now are regional. They are the chief public social events of Pasiego secular life. The traditional, labor-intensive manufacture and peddling of butter and cheese have ceded almost entirely to the direct marketing of fresh milk, made possible by improved transport and the industrialization of dairy processing in Cantabria. There is practically no cultivation in the Montes de Pas, as most land is used as meadow or pasture. Hoe culture is confined to occasional cabbage patches. Land once planted in maize (the former bread grain) and beans is now turned to meadow. Wheat bread, potatoes, beans, and other foods are purchased from local storekeepers. The Pasiego economy has had a commercial thrust for a long time. Dairy products and meat (probably lamb and goat) were long marketed in northern regional markets to supplement a subsistence economy. Especially since the adoption of Holstein cattle, Pasiego-bred cattle have supplied the dairy farms of the nation. Pasiegos are also largely responsible for the retail milk supply to the cities and towns of northern Spain. Temporary migrants established urban *vaquerías* (a cow or two stalled in urban neighborhoods providing milk for sale there twice daily). Male calves of urban milk cows were sold for meat and females returned to the Montes de Pas for eventual breeding and sale or service in a vaquería. Urban milk retailing thus existed in symbiotic relation with the stock-breeding economy of the home zone.

Industrial Arts. The chief industrial products of the Montes de Pas are those associated with the transhumant herding life: the combined house/stable called the *cabaña*, made of hewn stone and oak and roofed in slabs of mica schist, and the rudimentary furniture and implements of herding life—the scythes, sleds, pitchforks, rakes, and carrying baskets (*cuévanos*). The carved wooden shoes (*almadreñas*) used in stable and meadow are the principal costume element produced today; the daily and festival dress and handmade leather footgear documented in earlier centuries have long been in disuse.

Trade. Within the community of Pasiegos, trade focuses on the rental or sale of meadows and sometimes of male calves for breeding. These are cash exchanges. There is also some free lending of breeding bulls among friends. Most trade of cattle or other products is with outsiders. However, well-off landlords lend money at favorable rates to poorer members of the community. In the past, community members also entered sharecropping agreements with respect to meadows or herds.

Division of Labor. The division of labor by sex and age is weak among herders. The chief tasks are milking; grazing cattle or other animals (they are never left alone); taking milk to collection points; spreading manure; and cutting, drying, and storing grass at harvest time. All of these are done equally by men, women, and children. Laundering and sewing are the only exclusively female activities. Division of labor by age and sex is more marked among settled, nonherder Pasiegos, and these divisions adhere to general Spanish rural patterns.

Land Tenure. Pasiegos are independent smallholders of their meadowland. Most nonresident owners are emigrants from the zone. The remoteness of the Montes discouraged extensive entry and ownership by feudal powers or the church. Land is a freely circulating commodity; richer families acquire more and poorer ones are forced to rent. Families that are able to live from rental income usually cease active herding. Landownership is the basis of wealth in the community; poorer families measure the number of cattle they can raise against the meadow they own and the rental costs of additional meadow. The poorest herders have raised sheep and goats on common lands without access to cattle meadow.

Kinship, Marriage, and Family

Kin Groups and Descent. Pasiegos share the general Spanish mode of reckoning descent bilaterally. There are no corporate kin groups beyond the nuclear family. No bounded kindred is recognized; beyond the nuclear family, kin are joined only by a diffuse, nonbinding definition of "family" within which particular relationships may be strengthened by friendship or weakened by enmity.

Kinship Terminology. Pasiegos use the bilateral kinship terminology and naming system general to Spain and largely shared in western Europe.

Marriage. Pasiego herders generally marry early, around age 20. Nonherders tend to marry later. Courtship among herders is conducted in the cabaña kitchens; nonherders court in public places. Herder couples may begin to cohabit after posting banns and prior to the wedding ceremony; nonherders do not. Bride and groom, if herders, may live natolocally for up to a year, each doing service to his/her parents, until the first grass harvest after marriage is brought in. They have then earned the marriage portion from both sides. If personal or economic factors favor a less symmetrical arrangement, bride and groom may reside with and help one set of parents and then, probably, expect a better marriage portion from them. When newlyweds separate from senior households, through parental donation, rental, or purchase, they occupy their own cabañas and meadows and start their own herd, usually with cows from their marriage portions. Couples begin families at or even before formal marriage. Families are large and no systematic means of birth control is in use.

Domestic Unit. The nuclear family household is standard but is typically enlarged by the temporary residence of a newlywed child or couple and sometimes by a coresident single or widowed relative. Residents outside the nuclear family, including newlyweds, are lodged by carefully contracted arrangements.

Inheritance. Men and women inherit equally and both carry their property into marriage. The Castilian civil code governing inheritance corresponds with custom and admits some preferential treatment of favored heirs. Property transmission generates anxiety and often open conflict among heirs, since meadow quality varies and parents accept the latitude permitted by the code. Parents sometimes donate their major holdings to their children during their lifetime in exchange for support (these contracts vary and are formally notarized), but many leave transmission until after death. If so, each spouse's property passes separately.

Socialization. Children in the herding community are early socialized into adult roles and independence. Socialization in the nonherding community is into the more complex, role-differentiated social structure familiar in European town life. In both cases, family life is fairly informal and admits open expression of affection and disaffection.

Sociopolitical Organization

Social Organization. The Pasiegos are generally classed low in the Spanish social hierarchy. Herding, petty commerce, and itinerancy are held in lower esteem than agriculture and settled life-styles. Emigrants enter the mainstream of Spanish society as they are educated and forsake the visible trappings of the herding background. Nonherders integrate more rapidly, particularly when they have pursued schooling seriously.

Political Organization. As part of the Spanish state, the Pasiego towns are governed in the same way as other municipalities in the nation, by locally elected councils subject to national administrative and legal codes. Party politics, active since the end of the Franco regime, and formal political activity in general are most concentrated in the settled town centers, of which the barrios are administrative dependents.

Social Control and Conflict. Formal sanctions rest in the legal and policing functions of the Spanish state. Gossip and public censure function to promote conformity to expectations, especially in economic matters, but Pasiego culture tolerates a greater degree of open interpersonal conflict than is found in many Spanish towns. This is supported—perhaps even encouraged—by the dispersed settlement and the number of properties to which most families have access. An angry exchange can lead a person to depart for another cabaña, tied to the rest of the family by their common herding enterprise but not by a lack of facility for independent living. In this setting, marriage and personal relations in general are brittle. Divorce traditionally was impossible and only recently has become a legal possibility, but separation was and is common. Similarly, open conflict between other family members or neighbors is frequent and can lead to long-standing feuds between families and blocs of allies. Homicide is relatively infrequent but not unknown, and physical conflict sometimes follows angry encounters between people of all ages and either sex. Such incidents are brought to local judiciary officials when parties desire, particularly if blood is drawn or property damaged.

Religion and Expressive Culture

Religious Beliefs and Practices. Pasiegos are baptized Roman Catholics whose communities are served by parish priests. The three villas have parish churches but there are fewer chapels in outlying sectors than in denser, more settled populations. Church attendance is highest in the villas; barrio people have less easy access to church and priestly services. Aside from weekly mass, family-observed sacraments, and life-crisis rites, formal religious life is centered on one major fiesta per year and the services of Holy Week. Personal devotions to particular saints are pursued independent of these dates and of the priests, but the occurrence of personal dedications is variable and characterizes only a small part of the community. The Virgin of Valbanuz, celebrated in Selaya on 15 August, is the object of many personal devotions and also of a large regional celebration that attracts many Cantabrians who are not specifically her devotees. Outsiders call the Virgin of Valbanuz "the Virgin of the Pasiegos," but there is no strong basis within the Pasiego community for this claim. There is argument within the community about such things as the efficacy of curses, the truth of superstitions, and the power of witchcraft. Witchcraft is associated exclusively with magical curing practices; there are some known practitioners in the region, including cities, but not in the Montes de Pas.

Arts. The difficult conditions of the herder's life have not inspired many material products beyond the industrial arts. Song or verse and dance (mainly accompanied by tambourine) are as much regional as local but are not highly developed or much performed in public in this part of Spain. Costume and architecture, except for the cabaña, are also as much regional as local in style. In Cantabria, the stone cabaña is considered uniquely Pasiego, but similar structures are in use in other herding zones—in the Pyrenees, in Asturias, and elsewhere.

Medicine. The Pasiego towns are served by resident doctors, local and regional pharmacies, and a major hospital in Santander. The nation's socialized medical system encourages people to seek professional medical care, and most do, though local women sometimes assist each other at childbirth. Veterinary services are crucial to the herding population and have long been available.

Death and Afterlife. Death is dealt with in Roman Catholic tradition. Burial follows within a day, if possible, following a funeral mass. Many emigrants who have lived as adults in the Montes de Pas, left children there, or died unmarried away from the zone are returned there for burial. The cemeteries thus give a sense of the strength of the ties that surmount distance. Funerals were once followed by banquets, one of various traditions once widespread in northern Spain, discouraged by the church, and now mostly in disuse. There are no particularly strong traditions regarding the dead or afterlife that distinguish Pasiegos from other lay Spaniards.

Bibliography

Cátedra Tomás, María (1972). "Notas sobre un pueblo marginado: Los Vaqueros de Alzada (ecología de braña y aldea)." _Revista de Estudios Sociales_ 6:139–164.

Freeman, Susan Tax (1979). _The Pasiegos: Spaniards in No Man's Land._ Chicago: University of Chicago Press.

García-Lomas, G. Adriano (1960). _Los Pasiegos: Estudio crítico, etnográfico y pintoresco (años 1011 a 1960)._ Santander.

Penny, Ralph J. (1969). _El habla pasiega: Ensayo de dialectología montañesa._ London: Tamesis.

Terán, Manuel de (1947). "Vaqueros y _cabañas_ en los Montes de Pas." _Estudios Geográficos_ 8:7–57.

SUSAN TAX FREEMAN

Peloponnesians

ETHNONYMS: none

Orientation

Identification. The Peloponnesos is a large peninsula linked to the Greek mainland by the narrow isthmus of Corinth, cut through by the Corinth Canal in 1892–1893. Its name means "Island of Pelops" (progenitor of the Atreids, of whom Agamemnon and Menelaus of Trojan War fame are the best known). In medieval times it was known as "the Morea" (mulberry tree), either because the peninsula's shape vaguely resembles a mulberry leaf or because it was once the center of a silk industry and abounded with mulberry trees. With an area of 21,379 square kilometers it accounts for just over 16 percent of the total area of modern Greece and comprises 7 nomes: Achaea, Arcadia, Argolis, Corinth, Elis, Laconia, and Messenia. These are further divided into 21 eparchies, 36 municipalities, 1,315 communes or villages, and 2,573 localities or hamlets.

Location.   The Peloponnesos is the southernmost extremity of the Greek mainland. Virtually surrounded by water, no point in the peninsula is more than 50 kilometers from the coast. In the north it is bounded by the Gulf of Corinth, in the east by the Aegean Sea, in the south by the Mediterranean and Sea of Crete, and in the west by the Ionian Sea. Cape Tenaro (also known as Matapan) is the southernmost point of mainland Europe after Tarifa, Spain. Most of the Peloponnesos is mountainous or hilly with small coastal plains around Corinth, Argos, Patras, and Messenia. An upland plain surrounds Tripoli and farther south a smaller flatland lies about Sparta. A chain of mountains, the southern extension of the European Alps, cuts through the peninsula. Prominent peaks include Mount Tayegetos (2,407 meters) above Sparta and Mount Kyllini (2,376 meters) and Mount Aroania (2,341 meters) in the north, all of which are snow-capped half the year. The Alfios, Peneus, and Maritsa are the largest rivers, but none are navigable. There are no lakes of any consequence. The climate of the Peloponnesos is Mediterranean with long hot summers and short wet winters, although there are significant differences between lowland and highland areas and it is difficult to generalize. In the winter temperatures drop well below freezing in the highlands and snowfalls can be heavy, but along the coasts snow rarely falls and temperatures are mild, averaging 10° C in January and 25° C in July compared to 5° C and 24° C for the highlands. Annual precipitation averages 60 centimeters on the coast and 80 centimeters inland.

Demography.   By far the majority of the Peloponnesos's residents are ethnic Greeks, and although there are some minorities, most have assimilated. Most conspicuous are the Tsiganes or Gypsies, who have lived in Greece and other parts of Europe for hundreds of years. In the Peloponnesos, as in other parts of Greece, these people lead a seminomadic existence, traveling about in small pickup trucks trading livestock, selling baskets, caning chairs, sharpening knives, repairing pots, telling fortunes, and begging. There are also Vlach shepherds, whose native language is related to Romanian, and Arvanites (Albanians), who live mainly in the east. Despite Slavic incursions in the early centuries of the Christian era and a relatively large number of Slavic place-names (especially in the south), attempts to identify a Slavic minority in the modern Peloponnesos have failed. The present population of the Peloponnesos is about one million, of which half is rural and the other half urban or semiurban. Overall the population has remained more or less stable for the past thirty years, but there has been a major shift of people from the countryside to the towns and cities of Greece, particularly greater Athens/Piraeus. This movement, along with a limited international migration, continues, but it is much abated from the heyday of the 1960s and 1970s. Major urban centers in the Peloponnesos include Patras, the third-largest city in Greece and an important port with a population of approximately 175,000, Kalamata with about 50,000, Corinth with 25,000, and another half-dozen cities with populations over 10,000.

Linguistic Affiliation.   Virtually all Peloponnesians speak modern Greek, and it is the exclusive language of instruction in all schools. There are distinct regional accents on the peninsula, but no true dialects survive as a principal vehicle of communication. On the other hand, Vlachs and Arvanites frequently use their respective languages among themselves in everyday discourse, although they are fluent in modern Greek as well. A dialect of Greek known as Tsakonian (with ancient roots) was spoken in parts of Laconia, but there are few who remember it today. Likewise, a Maniat dialect disappeared about the same time and, although some older Maniats know a few words of it, the dialect is not spoken by any of them on a regular basis.

History and Cultural Relations

Archaeological excavations have established the presence of Paleolithic occupation in the Peloponnesos, and at least one site, Franchthi Cave in the southeast Argolis, has yielded remains of more or less continuous occupation from the Paleolithic through the Mesolithic and Neolithic periods. During the ensuing Bronze Age the Peloponnesos was the center of the spectacular Mycenaean civilization, which derives its name from the site of Mycenae (near Nauplia), home of Agamemnon, chief of the Greek forces in Homer's account of the Trojan War. The site was excavated about 100 years ago by Heinrich Schliemann, the pioneering German archaeologist who earlier had located and excavated the site of ancient Troy in western Turkey. Sparta, in the southern central Peloponnesos, was the kingdom of Menelaus, brother of Agamemnon and husband of Helen, whose abduction by Paris, son of Troy's King Priam, touched off the Trojan War. Ruins from these and other Mycenaean settlements in the Peloponnesos have been extensively excavated. The Peloponnesians entered a dark age following the collapse of Mycenaean civilization around 1100 B.C. and only became significant again in classical times when Sparta rose as a great power, controlling much of the peninsula and eventually challenging Athens. The resulting Peloponnesian War (431–404 B.C.) ended in victory for the Spartans, but little came of it. Later Corinth gained ascendancy over the region, but soon, like the rest of Greece, the Peloponnesos fell under the sway of the Romans. In A.D. 51–52 Saint Paul lived and preached in Corinth and gradually, in the following decades and centuries, the Peloponnesians were converted to Christianity. During the first millennium of the Christian era the region was out of the limelight. Following the decline of the Roman Empire, it was subjected to barbarian invasions from the north and a general decline of economy and culture. Later it came under the control of the Byzantines and regained its productivity. In the thirteenth century the Franks took over much of the peninsula and for the next six centuries it was controlled alternately by the Franks, Byzantines, Venetians, and Turks. In March 1821 Bishop Germanos of Patras raised the banner of freedom at the Aghia Lavra monastery near Kalavryta, thus beginning the Greek Revolution against the Ottoman Turks. Many of the important battles of the revolution, including the decisive Battle of Navarino in 1827, were fought in the Peloponnesos and the region contributed more than its share of revolutionary leaders, among them Theodore Kolokotronis and Petrobey

Mavromichalis. When independence was achieved in 1830 the Peloponnesians comprised the bulk of the new Greek state, since only a fraction of modern-day Greece was included in the earliest liberated area. The capital was established at Nauplia in 1831 but moved to Athens three years later. It took several decades to integrate all the inhabitants of the Peloponnesos into the new state, and there were pockets of resistance, comprised of citizens who viewed the new state as no better than the Ottomans. Nevertheless, by the turn of the century the region was solidly part of the modern Greek state. The Peloponnesos was once again the scene of fierce fighting in the Greek Civil War of the 1940s, particularly in the period that followed the departure of the German and Italian occupying forces after World War II.

Today cultural relations in the Peloponnesos are stable. There is little animosity between the various segments of the population, nor between the Peloponnesians and other Greeks. Special mention should be made, however, of Mani, a region in the central southernmost part of the peninsula. Its boundaries are a bit vague, but it comprises most of the central peninsula lying south of a line drawn from Kalamata to Gytheion. It is a repository of some traditional culture and is often viewed as a stronghold of individuality and independence. During the last years of Ottoman rule it was never effectively subdued and often defied the Turkish overlords.

Economy

Subsistence and Commercial Activities. As in the past, the economy of the Peloponnesos is largely agricultural and pastoral. There has been some industrialization around the city of Patras, but most Peloponnesian cities have prospered more from agriculture than manufacturing. Until World War II the majority of agriculture was at subsistence level, but in the past three or four decades there has been a shift to more specialized commercial production of grapes, olives, citrus and other fruits, and cereal grains. Pastoralism is still a very significant economic activity in the region, and the Peloponnesos contributes far more than its share of meat and animal products to the national economy. Traditionally much of the herding in the Peloponnesos was transhumant, with shepherds from the highlands descending during the winter months to coastal and other lowland areas. Today transhumance has all but disappeared, and most shepherds remain in one place year-round. Sheep and goats are herded on a fairly large scale and there are also some cattle and pig farms. Other components of the economy include small manufacturing, fishing, the merchant marine, and tourism, this last enterprise being seasonal but a substantial factor in the region's economy nonetheless.

Industrial Arts. Largely in decline, industrial arts are mostly debased mass-production enterprises aimed at the tourist trade.

Trade. The economy is largely a cash economy, fully integrated into the Greek national economy and increasingly internationalized through Greece's membership in the European Community. There are still regional markets and fairs, but they play only a minor role in the overall economy.

Division of Labor. The traditional division of labor whereby women are associated with the house and domestic work while men work outside the home is breaking down in the modern Peloponnesos. Perhaps 30 to 40 percent of all women in the region now have employment outside the home, and rural women have always worked in the fields and orchards alongside the men. Nevertheless, women continue to shoulder the burden of domestic chores, as men rarely contribute in this area.

Land Tenure. Greece has a long tradition of small private land holdings, particularly in the Peloponnesos. There have been few large estates since Greek independence and the expulsion of the Ottoman Turks more than 150 years ago, and even the church has not been a significant landowner in modern times despite the substantial holdings of a few monasteries. A major problem in the past was extensive fragmentation of land because of inheritance laws and dowry practices. With massive out-migration from villages in recent years there has been some consolidation of holdings, and land sales are far more common than in the past. Much poor and marginal land, once cultivated out of necessity, now lies fallow.

Kinship, Marriage, and Family

Kinship. As in the rest of Greece, kinship in the Peloponnesos is bilateral with loosely defined (often patricentric) kindreds being the most significant unit beyond the nuclear family, although there are vestiges of patrilineal clans in Mani and a definite patricentric bias to most kinship reckoning in general. Kinship terminology is symmetrical and virtually identical to the Eskimo system. Fictive kinship, created through marriage and baptismal sponsorship, is a very important means of uniting people and often serves as the basis for economic, political, and social relations outside the true family.

Marriage. Marriage is a prime goal of virtually every Greek, and those who do not marry are looked down upon and pitied. In the Peloponnesos arranged marriage has largely given way to a more open system, although the traditional practice was never very severe and individuals were rarely forced into matches against their will. Nevertheless, arranged marriages sometimes united temperamentally incompatible individuals, and although couples rarely divorced or separated, they often lived virtually separate lives under the same roof. The majority of men and women marry young, averaging 27 for males and 22 for females, slightly older than in the recent past. In the villages postmarital residence is usually virilocal, with couples settling in the husband's village but in a house of their own rather than in his parents' home. Patrilocal residence is still found, but it occurs most often as a temporary arrangement until the couple can establish their own household. Postmarital residence in towns and cities is neolocal, but it often has an uxorilocal slant in that a couple is apt to end up in the neighborhood of the bride's family, especially if she has provided a house or apartment as part of her dowry (a standard practice today).

Domestic Unit. The ideal domestic unit is the nuclear family: husband, wife, and unmarried offspring. However, it is not uncommon, both in rural and in urban areas, to find one or two other individuals in the household, usually a widowed parent of the husband or wife.

Inheritance. By custom and law in Greece, inheritance is partible, bilateral, and equivalent—that is, all children receive equal portions of the estate. The difference is that females traditionally receive their portions in the form of dowries at the time of marriage while males often have to wait for the death of one or both parents to receive their shares, although they may get usufruct rights to land before that time.

Socialization. Socialization takes place mostly within the family, although schools and other formal institutions play an increasingly important role in this regard. For young men, military service, universally compulsory, tends to be an important (and sometimes traumatic) experience that removes them from the indulgent and coddled environment of the family and exposes them to discipline and many new influences.

Sociopolitical Organization

Social Organization. In rural areas social life is remarkably classless and egalitarian. There are often differences in material circumstances among villagers, but they are rarely very great and tend to be less important than reputation and behavior as indicators of social position. One's family situation is also important. A person who makes a good marriage and has well-behaved, successful children (preferably sons) is more respected than a well-to-do individual with no spouse or children. In the towns and cities distinctions are more pronounced and generally depend on one's occupation as well as wealth. Those with some education and nonmanual jobs are usually viewed as superior to workers. Professionals stand at the top of the social order and are usually accorded a great deal of deference. Doctors and lawyers are also usually well compensated for their work.

Political Organization. As citizens of the Greek republic, the inhabitants of the Peloponnesos participate fully in democratic political life, electing representatives to parliament, local mayors, and village council members. Although it once was considered a royalist stronghold, and even today it often is identified with the Right, the Peloponnesos has no real political identity. All political parties are represented and all are active in the region.

Social Control. Members of a national police force maintain control in villages and cities. They are always assigned to regions far away from their homes to minimize possible conflicts of interest. Criminal and civil matters are handled by an extensive system of district, regional, and national courts, which are supplemented by justices of the peace who often travel to villages to mediate disputes. Minor disputes over livestock and crops are usually handled locally by an *agrofylakas* (field warden), although inhabitants have full recourse to formal courts for any matter, serious or trivial.

Conflict. Vendettas and clan feuds, common in Mani during the eighteenth and even nineteenth centuries, have long disappeared and peace reigns in the area. The region suffered terribly during the Axis occupation of World War II—many starved and thousands were killed. In the village of Kalavryta all the males over a certain age, some 1,400 in all, were executed en masse in reprisal for attacks on German soldiers by guerrillas, and many other villages suffered similar punishments. Civil war broke out following the departure of the occupying forces and thousands more were killed, but since then there has been no major conflict in the Peloponnesos.

Religion and Expressive Culture

Religious Beliefs and Practices. Virtually all the inhabitants of the Peloponnesos are Orthodox Christians. Parts of the region were Christianized as early as A.D. 51 when Saint Paul lived and preached in Corinth. Nevertheless, certain "pagan" (pre-Christian) practices are still a part of local worship and festivals. Saints' days are celebrated along with the various Christian holidays, major and minor. Easter is the most important celebration followed by Christmas and the Feast of the Assumption of the Virgin on 15 August. Patras has the largest pre-Lenten carnival in Greece and smaller celebrations take place in every village and town. Village priests preside over local religious affairs, conducting regular services, weddings, baptisms, and funerals. There is a large bishopric at Patras and several others elsewhere as well as numerous monasteries scattered about the peninsula.

Arts. Most traditional arts are rapidly disappearing or are already gone from the Peloponnesos. The region has produced some famous painters of icons and religious frescos in the past, but there is no particular tradition there today. Nor is much left of the traditional music for which the peninsula was once famous, although occasionally one finds an old musician tucked away in a remote village. In Mani and several other places the women still sing the famous *mirologia*, traditional funeral dirges, although even this seems to be a dying art. The Kalamatiano, a dance named after the city of Kalamata, where it presumably originated, is one of the most popular folk dances among Greeks everywhere.

Medicine. Modern scientific and traditional folk medicine are practiced side by side in many parts of the Peloponnesos. A law requiring all Greek doctors to spend up to 18 months in rural areas ensures that every citizen has some access to modern medical care, but folk practices persist and rural people especially often rely on home cures and local bonesetters. In theory, medical care is socialized, but under-the-table payments are common, especially for surgery. Overall the people of the region are healthy and have a high life expectancy and low rates of infant mortality.

Death and Afterlife. The dead are buried within 24 hours of dying and funerals tend to be (next to marriage) the most important rites of passage celebrated in Greece. Memorial services are held at intervals of 6 days, 9 days, 40 days, and one year after death. Relatives can (and frequently do) organize additional services. Three years after interment the bones are exhumed and placed in a box, which is usually stored in a church crypt. Cemeteries are generally well maintained and frequently visited, although in depopulated villages they are likely to be run-down and neglected. Greek Orthodox doctrine stipulates that there is an afterlife; many people appear to believe this, but others clearly do not.

Bibliography

Dimen, Muriel, and Ernestine Friedl, eds. (1976). *Regional Variation in Modern Greece and Cyprus: Toward a Perspective on the Ethnography of Greece.* Annals of the New York Academy of Sciences 268. New York.

Fermor, Patrick Leigh (1958). *Mani: Travels in the Southern Peloponnese.* London: John Murray.

Liddel, Robert (1958). *The Morea.* London: Jonathan Cape.

McDonald, William A., and George R. Rapp, eds. (1972). *The Minnesota Messenia Expedition: Reconstructing a Bronze Age Regional Environment.* Minneapolis: University of Minnesota Press.

National Statistical Service of Greece (1988). *Statistical Yearbook of Greece, 1987.* Athens: National Statistical Service of Greece.

PETER S. ALLEN

Peripatetics

ETHNONYMS: Gypsies, and all corresponding terms in the various European languages (Bohémiens, Cigani, Cingaros, Gitanos, Gitans, Mustalainen, Tataren, Tsiganes, Zigeuner, Zingari, etc.). Travelers or Travellers and all corresponding terms in the various European languages (Gens du Voyage, Rasende, Viajeros, Voyageurs, etc.). Rom or phonetically similar terms (Beaš, Camminanti, Hantrika, Jenischen, Kale, Korrner, Manuš, Minceir, Pavé, Quinquis, Romaničel, Romanies, Rudari, Sinte or Sinti, Woonwagenbewoners, etc.)

Orientation

All complex societies (with a division of labor determined not solely on the basis of sex, with a hierarchical sociopolitical organization, with an economy capable of producing a surplus) leave a potential space for those people referred to, among other terms, as "groups that don't want in." Such a definition is to be understood in both a sociological and an epistemological sense: these groups "don't want in" (1) as far as the hierarchical organization of the society in which they live is concerned, and (2) as far as traditional anthropological categories are concerned. Regarding both these characteristics, one could say that they have been considered by Europeans as "good to think about" symbolically, "good to prohibit" politically, but "indigestible to study" anthropologically. Social anthropology has discovered them only in the last few decades, rejecting the results of the two main theoretical approaches with which they were previously studied: the sociopsychology of disadjustment and positivist, racist criminology. Beyond this rejection, however, no unanimous consensus exists as to how to categorize the "groups that don't want in"; certain scholars consider it erroneous to attempt to create a single defined category. Among the various terms proposed, "peripatetics" has had the greatest theoretical elaboration and today enjoys the greatest consensus. The three main characteristics of the peripatetic groups are: spatial mobility; subsistence based on the sale of goods and/or services outside the group; and endogamy. Since these three features may vary greatly from one group to another, some groups occupy marginal positions that are difficult to define in terms of such a theoretical elaboration. We could thus assert that the main characteristic of the "groups that don't want in" is their extraordinary structural flexibility. The "groups that don't want in" are those who can be categorized as "peripatetics" at certain historical-geographical junctures, but not at others.

Identification. Such groups are currently referred to in Europe as Gypsies and Travellers. The difference between the two categories would appear to reside in their "origin": the former are thought to come from India, the latter to be native Europeans. Since the "origin" is not always verifiable and since several present-day groups may be the result of a fusion between groups of autochthonous origin and groups of an extra-European origin, certain scholars have merged the two terms into "Traveller-Gypsies." In order to maintain the traditional distinction between Gypsies and Travellers, we can subdivide the former into two large sets based on self-denominations: (1) the "Rom" set includes all those groups whose autonym is Rom or one of its phonetic variants (Rom, Róma, Romá, Romje, etc.); (2) the "rom" set includes all those groups that, though having other autonyms, use or formerly used the term "rom," or its variants, with the meaning of "men" or "husband" (Kale, Manuš, Romaničel, Sinti). In some cases, among these last groups, "rom" can also mean "man of our group," thus becoming concurrent with the normally used autonym.

Location. With the possible exception of Iceland and Malta, all European countries are host to a permanent presence of peripatetic groups. Although the three sets we have categorized—"Rom," "rom," and "Travellers"—are represented today in communities throughout the European continent, we can indicate, nevertheless, approximate areas of major concentration, historically speaking. An imaginary line (Rome-Vienna-Prague-Helsinki) divides Gypsy Europe into two parts: the western half is noted for its preponderance of "rom" groups, while in the eastern half there is a large majority of "Rom" groups. This line is only an indication of concentration tendencies—after the great migrations of the nineteenth and twentieth centuries some "rom" communities (especially Sinti) are found in the east and, more importantly, many "Rom" groups have moved to the west. The "Traveller" groups, though in general widely dispersed, also seem to be concentrated in specific regions, which are either marginal or enclaves of the "rom" zone. On the Celtic fringe (Ireland and Scotland), in Scandinavia (but not in Finland) and in the northern Alps (especially the Swiss part, inhabited mainly by Jenischen), these Traveller groups appear to be in the majority. From here, along a corridor running up through Alsace-Lorraine and the Rhine valley (where the Jenischen are outnumbered by "rom" groups, though their number is by no means negligible), we reach the Netherlands, where the local Travellers (Woonwagenbewoners) appear to outnumber the "rom" and "Rom" groups.

Demography. Many estimates have been made as to the numbers of Gypsies and Travellers present in Europe. Here we cite only three: Puxon (1973) counts exactly 4,745,475; Vossen (1983) gives a minimum number of 1,988,000 and a maximum of 5,621,000; Liégeois (1986) calculates a minimum of 3,421,750 and a maximum of 4,935,000. More consistent estimates, however, can be obtained using the same authors' data for areas of larger concentration. Their presence seems concentrated in the Danubian-Carpathian region (the Czech and Slovak Federative Republic; Hungary; the former Yugoslavia; Romania; and Bulgaria) with percentages between 59.1 percent (Puxon) and 64.6 percent (Vossen) of the total European peripatetic population. The southwestern region (Spain and France) is also important with estimates between 15.2 percent (Liégeois) and 18.7 percent (Puxon), whereas percentage estimates for the nations of the former Soviet Union prove to be of little significance, given the lack of more precise data on concentration within this vast territory—between 6 percent (Liégeois) and 10 percent (Puxon). In the rest of Europe there results a more dispersed presence amounting to a percentage somewhere between 12.2 percent (Puxon) and 14.3 percent (Liégeois) of the total Gypsy and Traveller population.

History and Cultural Relations

History. The presence of itinerant groups that lived by trade and handicraft in medieval Europe is fairly well documented. Certain _mangones_ and _occiones,_ horse dealers and metalworkers, were itinerant in Charlemagne's empire (eighth century). In twelfth-century Ireland, certain _tynkers_ were to be found, and at the beginning of the fourteenth century nomads by the name of _sculuara_ were the subject of one of the king of Sweden's decrees. In addition to the continual presence of these groups of presumably autochthonous origin, medieval Europe would seem to be scoured now and then by foreign groups: "Egyptian" acrobats visit Greece, Macedonia, and Spain, while an "Ethiopian" group given to magic artistry visits Italy, Spain, France, and England during the thirteenth century. However, undoubtedly at the start of the fifteenth century Western exotic nomads began to invade western Europe. Their presence in the Balkans had already been noted during the previous two centuries. Although Europeans used many names to describe these foreigners, two are by far the most common: "Egyptians" in the Atlantic regions, which was to become "Gitanos" in Spanish, "Gitans" in French, "Gypsies" in English, etc.; and "Cigani" (a term whose etymon is dubious—perhaps from the Greek word "Atsinganoi") used in central-eastern Europe with several variants: "Zigeuner" in German, "Zingari" in Italian, "Cingani" in modern Latin, etc. The two terms overlap in many regions. The relationships established between the newcomers and the local peripatetic groups do not appear to have been always univocal. Although it may be true that modern literature notes several cases of "counterfeit Egyptians," that is, people of the so-called "dangerous classes" joining bands of Gypsies or passing themselves off as Gypsies, it is equally true that foreign peripatetics often kept their identity distinct from that of the local ones. As far back as the sixteenth century, one anonymous author compared the two groups and demonstrated their diversity through ethnographic and linguistic data. Language research, in fact, dates back to the end of the eighteenth century and plays an important role in the study of the history of the exotic peripatetics' migrations, by making the connection between Romani (the language of the Gypsies) and the neo-Sanskrit languages of India. The race to discover the Gypsies' Indian origins (the region of India they came from) and the era of their departure was, thus, initiated. Different interpretations of certain

phonological and lexicological features have resulted in moving the "country" of origin, from central India either to northwest India or to the region of present-day Afghanistan. The date of departure is still uncertain; the date currently proposed is A.D. 1000, though some scholars date this as far back as the seventh or eighth century A.D. Linguists maintain that the numerous terms in the Romani language of non-Indian origin (above all Persian, Armenian, and Greek) are proof of the journey undertaken from India to Europe. According to a recent hypothesis, however, during the Middle Ages, the Romani language could have been a sort of lingua franca, used along the trade routes connecting Europe to the East. This hypothesis implies that the present-day European Gypsies, albeit speakers of neo-Indian dialects, may not be the direct descendants of peoples living in India today. According to linguists, however, the Gypsies who came to Europe spoke an essentially unitary language, which then became more and more diversified as a result of the borrowings from the languages of the European people among whom they settled or among whom they practiced their nomadism. On the basis of these borrowings, the linguists identify six or seven major Romani dialectal groups, still in use today or spoken up to the last century.

Cultural Relations. The patterns of Gypsy dispersion and settlement within modern Europe are practically unknown and consequently so are the modalities of the ethnogenesis of the Gypsy groups as they appear today. Nevertheless, two factors would appear to be at the basis of such modalities: the external relationships with non-Gypsies and the inter-Gypsy relationships. As far as the former are concerned, we can distinguish, very schematically, two political approaches adopted by European governments towards Gypsy populations: the "western" approach, aimed at the annihilation of the Gypsies, and the "Danubian" approach, aimed at the exploitation of Gypsy labor. The western approach consisted of thousands of banishments, mass imprisonment, deportation to American and African colonies, Gypsy hunting for rewards, with the resulting genocide, and, at the best, attempts at forced assimilation. The culmination of this tradition is the genocide of the Nazi period when more than half a million Gypsies were exterminated. This figure does not bear true witness, however, to the real proportions of the Holocaust, since the Gypsy presence in some areas occupied by the German forces and their allies was diminished by 80 percent. The "Danubian" approach, in contrast, saw the insertion of Gypsies in the servitude and slavery systems of southeastern Europe. Here the Gypsies were never submitted to the "western" type of mass extermination. Therefore, they have become an important part of the overall population in many eastern European countries—and not only in those countries where mixed marriages between Gypsies and non-Gypsies were formally forbidden by law—and have for the most part become sedentary. The Gypsy disequilibrium in demographic terms between the Danubian-Carpathian region and the rest of Europe is a result of these two different political approaches. This disequilibrium has had at least two consequences. In the west the Gypsy groups have subdivided themselves mainly on a regional basis, practicing a sort of commercial eclecticism consistent with their resistance to annihilation. The dozens of subdivisions derive from this situation: the Sinti, for example, call themselves "Prussian" Sinti,

"German" Sinti, "Austrian" Sinti, "Marchigiani" Sinti (from the region in central Italy called the Marches), etc. In southeast Europe, on the other hand, the subdivisions, in addition to being regional, have also been of a professional nature. Compelled by public authorities or by economic expediency in the wake of growing demographic pressure to differentiate their professions, the Gypsy groups have often adopted ergonyms with the function of ethnonyms: Kalderaš and its variants (coppersmiths), Čurara (sieve makers), etc. This phenomenon has been seen by certain authors as a survival of the Indian caste system among the Gypsies, whereas we are, in all probability, dealing with a situation that has its origins in the Balkans. Another consequence of the demographic disequilibrium has been the Gypsies' periodic movements from the Danubian-Carpathian region to other parts of Europe, which tend to take place during periods of economic or political hardship suffered by the non-Gypsy population in the region. Thus large groups of Rom arrived in western Europe during the second half of the nineteenth century (after the abolition of slavery in Moldavia and Walachia, in 1865, but above all at the time of the Balkan states' struggle for independence against the Turks) and at the start of the twentieth century. Other groups, after a stay in Russia, took refuge in the West following the events of 1917; others from the south of Yugoslavia began to migrate to Western Europe from the beginning of the 1960s in order to escape from the local economic crisis; others continue to flee en masse from disaster-struck post-Ceausescu Romania.

These great migratory movements have always been accompanied by smaller, virtually imperceptible group movements from one region to another. In all probability, these smaller movements have contributed more than anything else to the present Gypsy disposition in Europe. One example will suffice: the Romaničel are today present only in Great Britain (apart from North America and Australia), yet the same ethnonym has been noted in Spain and France for the nineteenth century. This would lead us to believe that the Romaničel once frequented much vaster zones than they do today. Toward the end of the eighteenth century and the beginning of the nineteenth, for reasons still unknown, there was a sort of "explosion" of the Sinti present in the Germanic countries, who gradually penetrated into the neighboring states. In some cases, they remained in the minority in relation to the Gypsy groups already present, but sometimes they perhaps "Sinticized" the local Romaničel (this is probably the case for France). In both the greater and the smaller migratory movements, there also appears to be a sort of autoregulation, because of "internal" pressures of a politicoeconomic nature. The settlement in new territories is always, in fact, made simpler when the presence of other groups is scarce or when the newcomers start to occupy "economic niches" that have yet to be exploited. The Gypsy populations, though nowadays largely sedentary, without doubt have constituted and continue to constitute the main "producers" of peripatetic groups; however, the non-Gypsy populations have always been a potential reservoir. The Jenischen in the Germanic countries and certain Swedish Rasenede appear to have formed a distinct identity only as late as the seventeenth and eighteenth centuries, while Dutch Woonwagenbewoners seem to have an even shorter history, dating from the nineteenth and twentieth centuries.

Peripatetic groups therefore are useful as special observatories for the study of ethnogenesis in highly stratified societies. Furthermore, given their great capacity to adapt—which requires a structural flexibility that is hard to find in other populations and which enables them to escape any sort of systematic classification—they should be considered worthy of careful and urgent research.

See also Bulgarian Gypsies; Gitanos; Gypsies and Caravan Dwellers in the Netherlands; Irish Travellers; Piemontese Sinti; Rom of Czechoslovakia; Scandinavian Peripatetics; Slovensko Roma; Spanish Rom; Vlach Gypsies of Hungary; Xoraxané Romá

Bibliography

Fraser, Angus (1990). "Counterfeit Egyptians." Paper read at the Annual Meeting of the Gypsy Lore Society, Staten Island, N.Y.

Gmelch, Sharon B. (1986). "Groups That Don't Want In: Gypsies and Other Artisan, Trader, and Entertainer Minorities." *Annual Review of Anthropology* 15:307–330.

Hancock, Ian (1987). *The Pariah Syndrome.* Ann Arbor, Mich.: Karoma.

Hancock, Ian (1988). "The Development of Romani Linguistics." In *Languages and Cultures*, edited by M. A. Jazayery and W. Winter, 182–223. New York: Mouton de Gruyter.

Liégeois, Jean-Pierre (1986). *Gypsies and Travellers.* Strasbourg: Council of Europe, Council for Cultural Co-Operation.

"De Nubianis erronibus, quos Itali Cingaros appellant, eorumque lingua" and "De idiotismo quorundam Erronum a Nubianis non admodum absimilium" (1597). In *De literis et lingua Getarum siue Gothorum*, edited by C. Vulanius, 100–109. Lugduni Batavorun [Leiden]: Apud Raphelengium.

Okely, Judith (1983). *The Traveller-Gypsies.* Cambridge: Cambridge University Press.

Puxon, Grattan (1973). *Rom: Europe's Gypsies.* London: Minority Rights Group.

Rao, Aparna (1987). "The Concept of Peripatetics: An Introduction." In *The Other Nomads*, edited by A. Rao. Cologne: Böhlau.

Vossen, Rüdiger (1983). *Zigeuner.* Frankfurt: M. Ullstein.

LEONARDO PIASERE

Piemontese

ETHNONYM: Piedmontese

Orientation

The term "Piemonte" refers to both a geographical entity—as an administrative district of the Italian state—and to a linguistic entity, distinct enough from Standard Italian to be treated as a language in its own right. Piemonte is comprised of the districts of Alessandria, Asti, Cuneo, Navarra, Turin, and Vercelli. It is bordered on the west by France, on the north by Val d'Aosta District and by Switzerland, on the east by Lombardy, and, between its southern border and the Ligurian Sea, by Liguria. Its principal city is Turin (Torino). The northern portion of the region is subalpine, with the remainder formed by the northern Italian plain. Piemonte is a part of "continental Italy," as distinct from "peninsular Italy" to the south. It is exposed to polar air in winter and warm winds off the Atlantic in summer. Winters are characterized by fog and frost, with snow at elevations above 1,500 meters. The portion of Piemonte that verges on the Alps differs climatically from the plains region, in part because the latter enjoys the shelter from winds provided by mountains on three of its sides. In the plains region, while temperatures may drop to below freezing in winter, snow is rare.

Piemonte is one of the more densely populated of Italy's regions, with more than 4.5 million inhabitants. Much of its population growth in recent decades has been fueled by immigrants from the economically depressed regions of southern Italy, who are drawn northward by the possibility of employment in Piemontese (and Lombardian and Ligurian) industries.

Piemontese is a Gallo-Italian dialect, along with Lombard, Ligurian, and Emilian. Illiteracy, historically a problem in Italy because of its wide range of linguistic diversity, occurs at a substantially lower rate for Piemonte than for any other administrative region of the country. This may in part be the result of the long-standing tradition of lay education that distinguishes Piemonte (and its neighbor, Lombardy) from the rest of the country.

Settlements

In Piemonte, one finds both major urban centers and nucleated rural villages. In agricultural regions, the towns and villages provide services, shops, and administrative institutions for the smallhold farms that surround them.

Economy

Piemontese agriculture is characterized by smallhold peasant farms. Traditional crops centered on wheat production, and in the early twentieth century, farm mechanization and successful land-reclamation practices gave rise to markedly increased yields, compared to other agricultural regions in the nation. With the introduction of new techniques, old systems of land tenure (sharecropping and small-plot rentals) gave way to a method of agriculture involving limited-company ownership.

Manufacture was strongly established in the region by the final quarter of the 1800s, and it emphasized the production of silk, cotton, and wool. Other industry included mining, engineering and metals, ceramics, and glassmaking. In the early twentieth century, Italy's "breakthrough" into the then-revolutionary industry of auto manufacture was led by Fiat, founded in 1912 in Turin. This breakthrough led to the development of several subsidiary industries, including coach works, tire factories, and the manufacture of automotive parts. This development resulted in Piemonte becoming a major car-manufacturing center for Europe, and it established the region as a key element of the "industrial triangle" (demarked by Turin, Milan, and Genoa) wherein most industrial development in twentieth-century Italy has taken place.

Unlike the women in the south, Piemontese women fully participate in economic life—there is no preferential social status accorded to women who do not work outside the home. In the agricultural areas of the region, women and men work side by side in the shared enterprise of farm production. In manufacturing, there is a certain association of women with particular industries—they are more strongly represented than men in textile production, for example.

Kinship

Piemontese recognize descent through both the maternal and paternal lines. The single most important kinship unit is the nuclear family, which operates in relative autonomy. Multigenerational extended families are not uncommon, however, particularly in agricultural regions. The normative expectation is that people ought to give assistance to maternal and paternal kin whenever needed, but in practice such aid tends to depend on the economic resources available in a given family.

Marriage and Family

Late marriage is most common, with average ages at time of marriage being about 28 for men and 24 for women, and with many individuals remaining unmarried well into their 30s. Until fairly recently, Italian civil codes held that adultery could only be committed by women and that divorce was not possible—although a man could have his marriage annulled on the grounds of adultery or on discovering that his bride was not a virgin. Legal policy encouraged large families, with the sale or purchase of contraceptive devices being illegal until 1971. Still, Piemonte's average family size has through most of this century been less than two children per married couple. Although abortions became legal in Italy only in 1978, the practice was not unknown prior to that time. Civil marriages have become common since the 1970s, with the legalization of divorce.

Family structure is, as noted previously, strongly influenced by socioeconomic factors. Whether nuclear or extended, the family is normatively thought to form a tight, unified group when confronting the outside world. Within the family itself, however, dissension is not uncommon, as individual interests (such as competing claims to heritable property) and personality clashes often cause problems among siblings. Within the household, the wife plays a strong decision-making role, often extending to control of the family budget.

Responsibility for the care and socialization of children during the early years of life falls to the mother. As the child grows older, the church and schools take on much of the socialization process.

Sociopolitical Organization

There is a strong army tradition in Piemonte; since the 1800s its soldiers have dominated the officer corps of the national army. This dominance was also apparent in the upper ranks of the civil service throughout the nineteenth century. Although regarded as "honest" in its aims and efforts, this Piemontese dominance in the early state was not suited to the task of developing a modern state structure. The system's reliance on personal contacts and the "politics of influence" made the transition to a twentieth-century bureaucratic model of government difficult.

Modern Italy has been described as possessing a "party-dominated" political system, driven more by the influential leaders of the political parties than by formal governmental institutions. Characteristic of such a system is a strong reliance on patronage. Until the mid-twentieth century, government was based on a nineteenth-century document (the Albertine Statute) that originally provided the constitutional basis for the then Kingdom of Piedmont and Sardinia and later for the united Italian state. In 1948, a new constitution established a parliamentary republic for all of Italy. Under this constitution the head of state (president) occupied a primarily ceremonial office. Decision making was the province of a Council of Ministers, and legislation was to be the responsibility of two houses of parliament.

Strong local government has a long history in Italy. The local unit of governing is the commune, which consists of an urban center plus its surrounding area. The commune is governed by an elected municipal council. Within the commune, many governmental services and decision-making powers are vested in neighborhood councils. Thus, much of day-to-day government is quite decentralized.

Regional government—based on regional councils—takes two forms in Italy. Five regions (Friuli-Venezia Giulia, Sardinia, Sicily, Trentino-Alto Adige, and Val d'Aosta) have extensive autonomy granted them by the Italian constitution. All the others, including Piemonte, are "ordinary" regions and are more directly subject to national authority.

Religion and Expressive Culture

Catholicism is the majority religion throughout Italy, but one Protestant group in particular, the Waldensians, is important in Piemonte. The original members of this group, begun as a movement within the Roman Catholic church but considered heretical, were excommunicated in 1177. The Waldensians did not formally join the Protestants until 1532. Although freedom of religion is constitutionally guaranteed, provisions of the constitution effectively make Roman Catholicism a state religion. Since the late 1960s, many of the privileges constitutionally accorded the Roman Catholic church have gradually been eliminated or reduced.

Piemonte participates in the National Health System, the purpose of which is to extend free health-care services to all Italian citizens and resident foreigners.

See also Piemontese Sinti

Bibliography

Clark, Martin (1984). *Modern Italy: 1871–1982*. Longman: London.

Le regioni italiane e l'Europa: Atti del Convegno internazionale promosso e organizzato dalla Regione Piemonte (1976). Milan: A. Giuffore.

NANCY E. GRATTON

Piemontese Sinti

ETHNONYMS: Sinti Piemontesi, Sinti Pimuntezi

Orientation

Identification. The Piemontese Sinti of northern Italy are one of a number of related peripatetic or formerly peripatetic groups including the Hungarian Sinti, Sinti Lombardi, the Gaškane Manuš ("German" Manuš), the Valče Manuš ("French" Manuš), and the Prajštike Manuš ("Prussian" or "Alsacian" Manuš).

Location. While the Piemontese Sinti were for some time centered in Piedmont valleys of northern Italy, they are now found scattered over a broader area, including Piedmont, Lombardy, Tuscany, and Latium provinces in Italy, Switzerland, and France.

Demography. The population of the entire group is difficult to estimate, although it is likely that they number somewhere between 10,000 and 15,000.

Linguistic Affiliation. The Piemontese Sinti speak a regional dialect of the "Sinti-Manuš" language, which evidently originated in ancient northeastern India. The dialect includes a high proportion of loanwords from French, Provençal, and Piedmontese, although unlike other Sinti dialects there are relatively few loanwords from German. The dialect is still spoken in the more traditional Sinti communities but is declining in use in communities where children attend the local schools.

History and Cultural Relations

The Piemontese Sinti are one of a number of groups called Gypsies who are descended from peoples who migrated west from India about 1,000 years ago. Why these people left India is unknown, although in 1011 a Persian poet, Firdousi, in his *Book of the Kings* mentions a group of 10,000 musicians called Luri sent from India to entertain his people. Whether the Luri are the ancestors of the current-day Gypsy groups is unknown, although linguistic evidence indicates that Gypsy ancestors did live in Persia and the Byzantine Empire. The arrival of Sinti ancestors in Europe may go back to the arrival of the Turks in the fifteenth century, and evidently involved two waves of emigration. The first wave involved a people commonly called the Vlachs who settled in central Europe where they were enslaved in Romanian principalities. The second wave, which included the Sinti's ancestors, settled in western Europe. The first Gypsy settlements in the Piedmont date to somewhere between 1410 and 1430, a period when they were already present in what are now south Germany, Switzerland, and France. By the close of the fifteenth century the Piemontese constituted a sizable population in Piedmont as they were paid large sums of money by the government not to settle in the cities. The contemporary Piemontese Sinti are probably descendants of these fifteenth-century immigrants; their surnames are the same as those registered in the civil status books of the 1450s.

The Piemontese reject the labels "Gypsy" and "Bohemian," viewing themselves instead as a distinct group. They also see themselves as standing in opposition to the Gadže (sedentary, peasants), a belief which tends to align them with other peripatetic groups on the basis of a traditional or current nomadic way of life. The Gypsy/Gadže opposition thus represents the dichotomy between sedentarism and nomadism. This opposition is reflected in long-term mistrust between the two groups, reflected in attempts at various times to assimilate the Sinti, remove them from the Piedmont, or exclude them from the government. Hostilities have also occurred between different Piemontese groups, largely caused by the practice of similar economic activities and competition over economic niches. Despite conflicts with the Gadže, the Sinti have been much influenced by the Gadže, and, in fact, the unique features of each Sinti group tend to reflect local customs and beliefs borrowed from non-Sinti neighbors. In the past, when the Sinti were largely nomadic, these borrowings had little chance of turning the Sinti into Gadže. Contemporary settled groups, however, are facing strong assimilation pressures from compulsory public education for their children, television, and contact with the urban, industrialized world.

Settlements

Until the close of World War II the Piemontese lived in horse-drawn wagons and traveled about in small groups of five or six families each, setting up camp on the outskirts of villages. By the 1950s, most had replaced their wagons and horses with automobiles and trailers. Today, many continue to reside in trailers, whether they are nomadic or not. Many wealthy Piemontese also live in permanent houses or villas while poorer ones live in slum housing. The vast majority now lives in urban areas, on the edges of cities such as Turin, Cuneo, Marseille, Nice, Lyon, and Paris. As a general rule, Sinti households in a village all tend to be located in the same neighborhood.

Economy

Subsistence and Commercial Activities.   With their tradition of nomadism, it is not surprising that the Sinti shun agricultural work. Generally, they practice crafts and trades such as horse dealing and knife sharpening; such economic activities are compatible with a nomadic life-style because they can be quickly discontinued, and they require small inventories and little productive equipment. Economic activities generally are based on the exploitation of the non-Gypsy world; in-group trading activities are considerably less exploitative. Despite the variety of activities, all Piemontese

work has three major characteristics: mobility, autonomy, and when trading, haggling to obtain the highest price. The expression used by the Sinti to define their work brings this last characteristic home: *džava te mangav*, meaning "I am going to ask for." As a result of this work ethic, they have difficulty adapting to sedentary work and even young people who accept wage labor usually quit after a short time.

Industrial Arts.   Traditional activities included basket making, rebottoming, knife grinding, horse dealing, reprocessing discarded metal, and seasonal farming. Some people were musicians and circus managers. Women peddled haberdashery and items made by the men, and engaged in palm reading and begging. Although most of these activities still exist, second-hand car dealing has replaced horse dealing, and trade activities have become more important than craft production. Thus, many Piemontese now sell goods at markets, with the wealthiest selling Oriental carpets, precious stones, and gold jewelry. Reprocessing of discarded materials from the industrialized society has also become an important economic activity in recent times.

Division of Labor.   As noted above, the division of labor is largely on the basis of gender. In general, a woman's work produces a small yet steady income that covers day-to-day family expenses while a man's work produces income used for the purchase of expensive items or adds to the family's prestige. In difficult times, however, this division is set aside so that everyone helps provide for the family.

Kinship

Kin Groups and Descent.   The word *sinti* following a possessive adjective means "parents" in a general sense. Used in a more limited sense, it refers to a whole group of related households that travel and camp together. This traveling group is usually composed of consanguineal kin. While each household is an independent economic unit, in difficult times they are expected to help each other. The Piemontese kinship system is bilateral, with an emphasis on the patriline as reflected in a preference for patrilocal residence and the use of patricentered surnames.

Kinship Terminology.   Piemontese kin terms conform to the Eskimo pattern.

Marriage and Family

Marriage.   The age of marriage has increased as the Piemontese have shifted from a nomadic to a settled lifestyle. Because of public education and the decline of training in Piemontese crafts, the young often delay marriage, thus also denying themselves the status of adults in the community. Premarital sexual relations are also more common now than in the past and virginity at marriage for females is now more an ideal than a reality. Marriages are common between both first and second cousins. Marriage is by elopement, with a respected man acting as a go-between for the couple and their parents. The marriage is then officially recognized through a religious service and a feast attended by both families. The parents help the couple set up a household, with patrilocal residence more common than matrilocal. Divorce is rare, but when it does occur the woman and her children are cared for by her family.

Domestic Unit. The nuclear family is the basic residential and economic unit, although it is often closely linked to four or five other families.

Inheritance. Except for a few personal items, such as jewelry or pictures kept in a secret place, property of the deceased is either burned or sold to non-Sinti without haggling. The proceeds from the sale are spent on the deceased.

Socialization. Sinti infants are cared for closely by their mothers, who look after them day and night, react immediately to their cries, and sometimes nurse them until they are four years of age. This indulgent nurturing fits well with Sinti values, which stress the avoidance of frustrating situations and catering to individual needs. Consequently, parents prefer to talk to their children and convince them to obey rather than to punish them. As they get older, children are expected to help in return for what they receive and eventually are deemed able to make their own judgments about how they use their time. This indulgent-permissive socialization process produces adult Sinti who are able to work autonomously, live a nomadic life-style, and bargain effectively with customers.

Sociopolitical Organization

Social Organization. The Piemontese do not have formal social classes, although wealth differences between families are noted.

Political Organization. The Piemontese are a culture without a clearly defined territory and without a leader, despite legends of Gypsy kings. The authority of an elder extends beyond the family only when it is accompanied by respect. Those elders play a crucial role in making important decisions and in settling conflicts.

Social Control and Conflict. In general, community pressure tends to control the behavior of individuals. Community control is effective because of the communal nature of Piemontese life and because of the absence of private places in the camp. When conflicts cannot be resolved peacefully, families may leave or be ostracized from the group.

Religion and Expressive Culture

Religious Beliefs and Practices. Most Piemontese are Roman Catholics. Piemontese Catholicism, however, stresses relatively minor cults (e.g., the cult of Saint Sarah) and pilgrimages, and gives less attention to the major beliefs and practices of Catholicism. For at least the last ten years, the Piemontese, like other European Gypsies, have been drawn to evangelical Pentecostalism. Pentecostalism is particularly appealing to Gypsies for a variety of reasons. First, it stresses miracle cures and divine revelation, practices that have always attracted Gypsies, as indicated by their regular participation in pilgrimages. Second, it easily integrates with Gypsy practices; for example, the Pentecostal ministry does not require celibacy, as does Catholicism, and hundreds of Gypsies have become ministers and preach in their native langauge. And, third, the movement involves events that regularly bring diverse elements of the European Gypsy community together.

Arts. Singing and music composition are the major artistic activities, with music composed for performance on guitars.

Medicine. Some Sinti women have a great knowledge of medicinal plants, while others seem to have a gift for fortune-telling, as indicated by their regular non-Sinti clientele.

Death and Afterlife. The Piemontese believe in an afterlife, and they fear malevolent deeds (*mule*) perpetrated by the dead. Consequently, they try to respectfully ignore the deceased, try not to speak about them, and destroy their material possessions. *Xa tre mule!* ("Eat your dead!") is the most spiteful insult one Sinti can say to another.

Bibliography

Formoso, Bernard (1986). *Tsiganes et sédentaires: La reproduction culturelle d'une société*. Paris: l'Harmattan.

Formoso, Bernard, and Georges Calvet (1987). *Lexique tsigane: Dialecte sinto piémontais*. Paris: Publications Orientalistes de France.

Franceze, Sergio (1989). "La situation culturelle des Sinti Piémontais au Piémont." In *Tsiganes: Identité, évolution*, edited by Patrick Williams. Paris: Syros Editions.

Partisani, Sergio (1972). "Glossario del dialetto zingaro piemontese." *Lacio Drom* 6:11–32.

Winstedt, Eric O. (1910). "La Bella Chiavina: A French or Piedmont Gypsy Tale." *Journal of the Gypsy Lore Society*, n.s. 3:242–253.

BERNARD FORMOSO

Poles

ETHNONYMS: Polacy, Polak/Polka, Polen, Poliak, Poliane, Polyak

Orientation

Identification. Poles speak Polish and the overwhelming majority are Roman Catholics. Although Poles reside worldwide, most live in Poland and their name for their country is Polska.

Location. Poland is located in the center of Europe between 49° and 54°50′ N and 14°7′ and 24°8′ E. In the United States and western Europe, Poland is thought to be in eastern Europe; in Poland the country is considered to be in central Europe. Poland is bounded by Lithuania and the Baltic Sea on the north, the independent republics of Russia, Belarus, and Ukraine on the north and east, the Czech and Slovak Federative Republic on the south, and Germany on the west. Poland is mainly an open lowland plain, as 75 percent of the land is less than 200 meters above sea level, with drainage to the Baltic in the north. The north consists of the swamps and dunes of the Baltic coastal plain. Southward is a belt of glacial-origin lakes. Farther south are the central low-lands with agricultural (Lower Silesia and Great Poland) and industrial areas. South of these lowlands are the Little Poland Uplands and the Little Poland Lowlands with deposits of coal, iron, lead, and zinc. This is Poland's most important in-dustrial area. At the country's southern border are the Carpathians and their foothills, with a large rural population and medium-sized towns. Deposits of salt, sulfur, natural gas, and oil are found here. Poland lies in the temperate zone, and its climate is transitory from oceanic to continental. In gen-eral, the warmest area is in the southwest and the coldest in the northeast. The country can be divided into twenty-one agricultural and climatic divisions with six seasons. The high-est recorded temperature is 40.2° C and the lowest −42° C. The mean annual temperatures range from 8° C to 6° C, ex-cept in the mountains where the temperatures decrease with altitude.

Demography.   There are 51 million Poles worldwide; 38 million live in Poland, while 13 million live outside the coun-try. Of those residing abroad, the vast majority live in the United States, Belarus, and Ukraine. Significant Polish pop-ulations also are found in Australia, Brazil, Canada, France, and the United Kingdom. Ethnically, Poland is one of the most homogeneous (over 98 percent Polish) countries in the world. Ukrainians constitute the largest minority followed by Belarusians, Slovaks, Russians, Gypsies, Lithuanians, and Greeks and Macedonians. Because of the genocide perpe-trated by Germans during World War II and subsequent emi-gration, the formerly sizable Jewish minority has all but disappeared.

Linguistic Affiliation.   The Polish language belongs to the West Slavic Group of languages of the Indo-European Fam-ily, which is a part of the Nostratic Macrofamily. The Poles use the Latin alphabet. The spelling of foreign words diffused into Polish usually is changed to reflect Polish alphabetical values. Literary Polish has been developing since the six-teenth century. It is based mainly on the speech of the Polish upper class and the Great Polish and Little Polish dialects. As a result of universal education and mass migration, literary Polish is becoming more homogeneous and more widely used. However, most Poles can still identify an individual's place of origin by his/her speech. The main dialects are Great Polish, Kashubian (which has its own orthography and literature), Kuyavian, Little Polish, Mazowian, Pomeranian, and Silesian.

Settlements

Sixty-one percent of Poland's population is urban. Warsaw (Warszawa), the capital of the country and its largest city, has a population of 1.7 million. Four other cities (Lodz, Krakow, Wroclaw, and Poznan) have over 500,000 inhabitants each. In rural areas, people live predominantly in villages. In the eastern portion of the country, the street village type predom-inates; in the western areas, other types are more common. Farmsteads are surrounded by a fence and have several build-ings located around an open center with the family dwelling facing the road. Traditionally, buildings were wooden with thatched roofs; now they are built of masonry with fireproof roofs.

History and Cultural Relations

We do not know when and where the ancestors of the Poles originated. Some hypothesize that the original home of the Indo-European speakers was in the territory covered by mod-ern Poland or its vicinity. It is generally agreed, though, that by 4,000 years ago the Poles' Slavic ancestors inhabited much of what was to become modern Poland. By the ninth century, some of the Slavic tribes were beginning to form states. Mieszko I of the Piast dynasty founded a state in the western part of modern Poland. In A.D. 966, he married a Bohemian princess and accepted Christianity. This date is considered to be the beginning of the Polish state. For the next thousand years, Polish history has been influenced by the fact that the country has no natural boundaries to the east and west. This has meant that there has been constant strife with the Ger-mans, the Poles' western neighbors, with the Russian states to the east, and, for a while, with the Balts to the north. At times, two of these groups would combine to attack a third. Thus, in 1226, Prince Conrad of Mazovia invited the Teu-tonic Knights, a German crusading order, to help fight the Prussians, a group of Baltic tribes living in what later became known as East Prussia. The consequences of this invitation were removed only after World War II when Poland expelled the Germans remaining in the Polish part of East Prussia and in today's western Poland. In 1382, the Lithuanian Grand Duke Jagiello married Jadwiga, a Polish princess, and formed a Polish-Lithuanian state. Poland-Lithuania was quite suc-cessful and became one of the largest states in Europe. Its ter-ritory covered much of present-day Poland as well as considerable portions of what is now Belarus and Ukraine. For the commonwealth, the "golden age" was in the sixteenth century, which was marked by peace and prosperity in the Polish lands and by considerable achievements in the arts and sciences. By the middle of the seventeenth century, polit-ical decline had set in. Among the reasons for this decline was that the nobility had enormous power and independence vis à vis the state and often used it to further their private interests at the expense of the commonweal. The gentry elected the country's kings, and the kings acted more like managers than rulers. In 1652, the Sejm, the Polish diet, introduced the *liberum veto*. This meant that all legislation had to pass unan-imously. By the late eighteenth century, Poland-Lithuania had become so weak that the Russians and Germans, specifi-cally the Austrians and the Germanic Prussians, divided Po-land between themselves, even making an agreement that the very name "Poland" would not be used officially. It was not until the end of World War I when the Austrian empire col-lapsed and the Russian and German empires had been weak-ened that Poland regained its unity and independence only to be divided again between the Soviet Union and Nazi Ger-many in 1939. At the end of World War II, however, Poland regained political unity, albeit under the Soviet Union's suze-rainty. In 1989, the Soviets no longer supported the Polish Communist government, and the Poles were able to begin de-mocracy and a market economy.

Poles consider themselves to be affiliated with Western European culture. They see their allegiance to the Roman Catholic church and their use of the Latin alphabet as indica-tors of this orientation. In recent times, their main economic, technological, and fine-arts affiliations and influences have been with the West.

Economy

Subsistence and Commercial Activities. Farming produces 13 percent of the GNP and employs 28.5 percent of the labor force. The major field crops are potatoes, sugar beets, wheat, rye, barley, and oats. Poultry, cattle (mostly dairy), pigs, sheep, and horses are the main domestic animals. Tractors and other farm machinery are becoming increasingly more common. Industry accounts for 41 percent of the GNP and employs 28.5 percent of the labor force. The main industrial products are chemicals, ferrous metals, machinery, and consumer goods (e.g., household appliances, shoes, and textiles). Coal, the main industrial and household fuel, is also a chief export.

Industrial Arts. Rural areas support local artisans such as blacksmiths, cobblers, tailors, and seamstresses. Some people, primarily in the south, make handicrafts patterned after the traditional folk culture. In most parts of the country, rural people specialize in farming. Crafts and home industries are gradually disappearing in favor of industrialized goods purchased in stores.

Trade. Trade is a mixture of government-owned and -operated outlets, private retail and service shops, and fairs and markets where farmers sell their products to each other and to city dwellers. As of 1991 the government was attempting to convert the nation's planned economy to a market one. To this end, joint ventures with Westerners and other forms of free enterprise have been promoted. It is impossible to predict the final form that these economic institutions will take.

Division of Labor. By law, men and women have equal rights and pay. In practice, the average woman earns less than the average man and, even if employed outside of the home, has to do almost all the housework.

Land Tenure. The majority (77 percent) of farmland is privately held. Most private farms are not single, compact fields but are scattered, multiple strips. State farms occupy 19 percent of the farm land; 4 percent is held by collective farms and 0.4 percent by agricultural associations. It is anticipated that most of the land in the "communal" sector will be "privatized."

Kinship, Marriage, and Family

Kinship. The Poles use Eskimo-type kin terms. The ideal is the extended family. Kindreds may assemble for funerals and weddings. Kinship and extended kin ties are important when one attempts to manipulate the formal kin system in order to obtain scarce goods and resources.

Marriage. The expectation is that marriage will be monogamous, but increasing numbers of people are practicing serial monogamy. In rural areas, dowries are given. Marriages tend to be class-endogamous and in rural areas village-exogamous. Ideally, residence should be neolocal or virilocal, especially with farming groups and the upper classes. Because of the urban housing shortage many individuals are forced even after marriage to continue living separately with their own parents. Immediately after World War II, divorce was easy to obtain. More recently it has become more difficult, but divorce still is obtainable. Socially, a certain stigma is attached to a divorced woman.

Domestic Unit. Ideally, the household consists of the nuclear family or a stem extended family, with the aged parents of one of the spouses and adult unmarried children. In fact, a large number of households are single-parent families. A significant portion of households consist of married or divorced daughters with their children, a type of household called a _susu_.

Inheritance. A father used to be able to divide the inheritance in any way he chose. Currently, he faces certain legal restraints (frequently evaded in practice) on the minimum size of landholdings and inheritance payments by farming people to city residents. The inheritance system does not work well. It generates strong antagonisms and frequent lawsuits among heirs.

Socialization. Great emphasis is placed on good manners and etiquette—children who misbehave are considered "impolite." Boys, in particular, are raised to be brave, independent, self-reliant, and tough. Patriotism is also inculcated. Among farming people and workers, physical punishment is common; upper-class people tend to use psychological punishment. The father should be respected and obeyed. Ideally, the mother is kind and often mediates between the father, who is the stern disciplinarian, and the children. Since frequently both parents work outside the home, the grandparents play an important role in raising the children, especially in the cities.

Sociopolitical Organization

Social Organization. In rural areas, there are the peasants and the gentry. In urban areas, there are the workers, the "intelligentsia" (artists, writers, university-educated professionals, and the upper-echelon white-collar workers), and the old "new class." The "new class," the _nomenclatura_, consists of the upper echelons of the Communist party and the state apparatus (the two categories overlap). They have lost the political power that enabled them to assume important posts in Soviet-dominated Poland and are now attempting by both legal and illegal means to retain economic power. Since World War II, the gentry and intelligentsia have been losing their social distinctions, and the peasants have been migrating to the cities and joining the workers.

Political Organization. The political structure is changing rapidly and dramatically, and it is impossible to predict its final form. Poles are struggling with the aftereffects of Soviet domination, but as yet Polish society has not reached a consensus regarding the form the new political structure should take. There is ongoing strife regarding the proper functions and powers of the president, the government (i.e., the prime minister and the various ministries and administrative bodies), and the parliament. The parliament consists of a 100-member Senate and the Sejm with 460 seats. In addition to government at the national level, there are regional and local self-governments. Since 1975, the country has been divided into 49 _voivodships_ (regional territorial units) and 2,404 local administrative bodies. At both levels there are self-governing legislative bodies and executives. Another area of disagreement concerns the function and structure of the political parties. A basic issue is whether the political structure should encourage ideologically committed parties or ones whose aim is to gain power, with ideological purity being a secondary concern. Another subject of debate is the future role of Solidarity and of labor unions in general—should Solidarity become a political party or should it remain a labor union whose primary concern is the welfare of workers and peasants? These conflicts stem from the fact that from 1940 to 1989 the government forbade any organizations except government-sponsored ones. The society was deliberately atomized. Today, organizations must be created by people with no experience in organizing and self-government.

Social Control.   Families, kin, and neighbors exert strong informal social control, especially in rural areas. The mechanisms range from ridicule and gossip to ostracism, physical punishment, and surreptitious attacks on property. The formal system consists of courts with appointed judges and prosecuting attorneys. There also are provisions for policing and incarceration. The most commonly seen police are the uniformed militia (MO). Currently, the legal system and the police are being changed to transform them from instruments of oppression into agencies for the protection of Polish citizens. The judges and prosecuting attorneys are being retrained to prepare them for their new roles and some of the more notorious police units have been or are being disbanded.

Conflict.   For the past 1,000 years, the Poles' main conflicts have been with their western neighbors, the Germans, and with the Russians, their eastern neighbors. When the Polish state was weak or nonexistent, wars between their neighbors were fought on Polish territory. This was especially the case during World War II when the Soviet Union and Germany initially divided Poland between themselves and pursued the same policy of killing Poles who might assume leadership roles. In 1941, Germany attacked the Soviet Union and drove its armies from Poland. About three years later, the Soviets reconquered Poland. During the war years, the Poles had several undergrounds fighting whatever foreign army was occupying Poland at the time. The best-known partisan units were the Home Army (AK), which owed allegiance to the Polish government in exile in London. The last vestiges of the partisans were not liquidated until the early 1950s.

Religion and Expressive Culture

Religious Beliefs and Practices.   Over 90 percent of the population has been baptized into the Catholic church, and 78 percent attend religious services regularly. The Roman Catholic church has great moral authority, in part because historically it has been the one organization the Polish people felt was opposed to foreign political and ideological domination. An additional twenty-five religious groups are officially recognized. In 1975, the Polish Autocephalous Orthodox, Lutheran, and Uniate denominations had over 100,000 adherents each. In some rural areas, folk beliefs and practices are found in addition to the religious dogma and services of the formal religions.

Arts.   The Poles, especially in the upper classes, have been deeply immersed in all the great movements of Western culture. The fine arts and architecture have been and are a part of the general European culture. Folk crafts were much more regionalized and are falling into desuetude, despite government attempts to revive them.

Medicine.   Social insurance for health service covers free treatment for workers employed 2,000 hours per year, their families, students, invalids, pensioners, and, since 1972, private farmers. The state-operated system employs pharmacists, physicians, dentists, and nurses in hospitals, sanatoriums, clinics, pharmacies, and ambulance services. The system emphasizes preventive medical care, with special emphasis on immunization and intervention in trauma and contagious diseases. Patients, at their own expense, also may visit medical professionals in private practice. The medical system is currently in a crisis situation because of a shortage of resources.

Bibliography

Barnett, Clifford R. (1958). *Poland: Its People, Its Society, Its Culture.* New Haven: HRAF Press.

Graham, Lawrence S., and Maria K. Ciechocinska, eds. (1987). *The Polish Dilemma: Views from Within.* Boulder, Colo.: Westview Press.

Hann, C. M. (1985). *A Village without Solidarity: Polish Peasants in Years of Crisis.* New Haven: Yale University Press.

Kolankiewicz, George, and Paul G. Lewis (1988). *Poland: Politics, Economics, and Society.* New York: Pinter.

Wedel, Janina (1986). *The Private Poland.* New York: Facts on File.

ANDRIS SKREIJA

Pomaks

ETHNONYMS: Bulgarian Muslims, Bulgaro-Mohamedanin

Orientation

The term "Pomak" refers to Bulgarians who converted to Islam during the Ottoman occupation, beginning in the latter portion of the 1300s. During the Communist period of forced assimilation in Bulgaria (1970s and 1980s), the term disappeared from official use. Since the 1989 democratic reforms, however, Pomaks are quite active in public political life. The region of Pomak origin is principally the Rhodope Mountains and the southeast slopes of the Pirin, but because of a series of population exchanges there are a large number of Pomaks in both Greece and Turkey.

The total Pomak population, worldwide, is estimated to be at least 300,000 to 400,000, of which perhaps 75,000 are currently living in Bulgaria. However, this last figure is difficult to verify, as Bulgaria has not provided census data broken down into ethnic minorities. The Muslim settlements of the Rhodope Mountains are currently enjoying a certain demographic growth relative to Christian villages of the region, partly because of a higher birthrate and the fact that Pomak villages appear to be less affected by processes of urbanization.

The language spoken is a dialect of Bulgarian, with some introduced elements from Turkish.

History and Cultural Relations

The conversion to Islam that gave rise to the Pomaks may have begun as long ago as the early 1370s, and Pomak tradition holds that this conversion was accomplished forcibly, though there is little historical evidence that this was the case—it may be that here, as elsewhere, conversion was effected through economic, legal, and religious pressure. Still, the local perception of forced conversion is reinforced in indigenous song and legend. Adoption of Islam was not complete initially, and at first it may have consisted of minor changes in local practice and the adoption of a Muslim name, but as time went on the Pomaks took on other Muslim practices (e.g., the veiling of women). While Pomaks and Christians generally have interacted with little or no conflict, in those areas where Pomaks constituted a majority there was likely to be little or no reason for contact with Christian outsiders. In 1944, Bulgaria came under the control of a Communist regime, which instituted a policy of ethnic assimilation, profoundly suppressing the indigenous culture. (Since 1989, however, Pomaks have regained many cultural freedoms.) In addition, a trend toward cash cropping and the mechanization of farm work have reduced the self-sufficiency and isolation of Pomak villages. In 1950, many Pomaks took advantage of a legal option to claim Turkish as their national identity and thus to emigrate to Turkey. Over the past several decades, the modernization of transportation and communications have drawn the Pomaks more and more into mainstream Bulgarian life, but they have maintained some degree of distinctiveness nonetheless.

Settlements

Pomak villages are nucleated, surrounded by the fields and pastures that form the venue for their peasant farming economy. The traditional two-storied house serves as both a dwelling, on the upper floor, and a byre or animal stable, on the lower. These buildings are constructed of stone, wood, and clay, and traditionally they were topped by a sloping slate roof. Recently brick and cinderblock, as well as ceramic tiles for the roofs, have been introduced as building materials.

Economy

The Pomak economy centers upon agriculture, with animal husbandry (some cows, plus sheep and goats) constituting a second important element of it. Major crops are rye, barley, corn, flax, hemp, potatoes, and tobacco. Bread, potatoes, and beans, as well as yogurt and cheeses, lamb and goat meat, constitute the diet. The farm household traditionally functioned as a largely autonomous, self-sufficient production and consumption unit, with most necessary tasks carried out by its members. However, communal work parties are regularly organized for larger projects, such as construction, or the production of handiwork (spinning, tobacco stringing). Tasks are allocated according to age and sex, and in the work parties, men and women tend to work separately. Pomak women are renowned weavers. Land and property are inherited patrilineally, by and large.

Kinship, Marriage, and Family

Pomaks trace descent patrilineally. Marriages were and continue to be arranged between the families of the prospective spouses, and they occur when both the bride and groom are still in their mid- to late teens, with the groom generally being only slightly older than the bride. Before marriage, the bride handcrafts a dowry of household items and clothing (carpets, blankets, clothing, and gifts for wedding guests). Polygyny, though countenanced by Islam, was never a frequent occurrence, and currently it is barred by law.

The Pomak household is made up of a patrilineally ordered extended family (_zadruga_), which traditionally constituted the unit of both subsistence production and consumption.

Religion and Expressive Culture

Pomak religion, notwithstanding the Islamic influence, retains Christian and pre-Christian elements as well, and is grounded in the agricultural cycle. Rituals commemorating the feast days of certain Christian saints continue to be observed, while other ceremonial occasions, such as weddings, combine elements of both Christian and Muslim practice. While the Ramadan fast and other Muslim ritual occasions were once observed, these customs have fallen into disuse. The relative isolation of the Pomaks from mainstream Islam has allowed a certain syncretist tendency to continue unhindered.

Bibliography

Silverman, Carol (1984). "Pomaks." In _Muslim Peoples: A World Ethnographic Survey_, edited by Richard V. Weekes, 612–616. Westport, Conn.: Greenwood Press.

CAROL SILVERMAN

Pontic

ETHNONYMS: none

Pontic refers to speakers of the Pontic language who currently reside in Greece, in the suburbs of Athens and Piraeus. Pontic speakers also live in the United States, Canada, and perhaps on the Black Sea coast of Turkey. Pontic is a non-Indo-European language of ancient Asia Minor with no known affiliations to other languages. Pontic speakers immigrated to Greece in the 1920s and 1930s from Black Sea communities where Greeks had lived for centuries. The use of Pontic is declining in Greece where younger people more often speak modern Greek.

Bibliography

Danoff, Charles M. (1962). "Pontos Euxeinos." *Pauly-Wissowa Realencyclopädie*, supp. 9:865–1175.

Portuguese

ETHNONYMS: none

Orientation

Location. Continental Portugal occupies approximately one-sixth of the Iberian Peninsula in western Europe. It is bordered on the south and west by the Atlantic Ocean and on the east and north by Spain. Portuguese also inhabit the islands of the Azores and Madeira in the Atlantic. As a result of colonial expansion and of massive emigration in the nineteenth and twentieth centuries, Portuguese-speaking peoples live in Asia, Africa, South America, the United States, Canada, Australia, and northwestern Europe.

Demography. In 1984 the population of continental and island Portugal was estimated at 10,128,000. The population increased during the twentieth century until the 1960s, when it declined by more than 200,000 because of the extensive emigration to northern Europe after 1961. In the 1970s, the population of continental Portugal increased by more than a quarter of a million, largely as a result of the *retornados*, the settlers who returned to Portugal from Africa after decolonization. By comparison with other nations of Europe, Portugal has a high birthrate, though this rate is regionally differentiated and has declined in recent years. In 1985 the birthrate was 12.5 and the death rate 9.6.

Linguistic Affiliation. The Portuguese language has largely Latin roots, though some words are Arabic in origin. Portuguese was made the official language under the reign of King Dinis (1279–1325). Unlike Spain, continental Portugal demonstrates a high degree of linguistic homogeneity.

History and Cultural Relations

Humans have inhabited Portugal since Paleolithic times. Over the course of prehistory and history, various peoples have settled in the region, though the modern Portuguese trace their descent to the Lusitanians, a branch of the Iberian populations that spread over the peninsula in the third millennium B.C. Lusitanians made contact with Celtic peoples who moved into the region after 900 B.C. Roman armies invaded the Iberian Peninsula in 212 B.C. The Romans established important towns at the present-day sites of Braga, Porto, Beja, and Lisbon. An invasion of Swabians in the fifth century A.D. and of Moors in the eighth century A.D. added new elements to the Portuguese population, though Moorish influence was much stronger in the south than in the north. Portugal emerged as an independent kingdom in 1140 with its capital in the northern city of Guimarães. As part of the reconquest, whereby the Moors were pushed out of the penin-

sula, Lisbon was made the capital in 1298 and the boundaries of Portugal as they exist today were definitively determined. Early statehood and a national identity with deep historical roots are the basis of the relative homogeneity of Portuguese society. In the fifteenth century the Portuguese inaugurated their age of discovery and for three centuries built and expanded their empire. The loss of Brazil in 1822 and a series of economic and political crises led to a decline in the world position of the Portuguese during the nineteenth century. The monarchy was eliminated in 1910 with the establishment of the First Portuguese Republic, and this in turn was replaced by the authoritarian dictatorship of António Salazar in 1926. Salazar formed his New State in 1932 on corporatist political principles. The Salazarist regime survived until 1974, when it was overthrown by a group of military men frustrated by the hopelessness of the colonial wars in Africa, wars that had escalated after 1961. The entire African colonial system was dismantled after 1974. In the late 1980s the Portuguese turned their attention toward Europe to become part of the European Community. However, linguistic and other cultural ties with former colonies, including Brazil, are maintained.

Economy

Subsistence and Commercial Activities. The subsistence and commercial activities of the Portuguese vary regionally. The Azores are largely agricultural, with some islands depending primarily on dairying and meat production and others on a combination of cattle raising, whaling, fishing, and small-scale agriculture (sugar beets, tea, tobacco, and vegetables). These activities have been supplemented by more than a century of emigration to the United States. Madeira also relies on agriculture (wine, bananas, sugarcane), fishing, and whaling, in addition to small-scale cottage industry and tourism. The embroidery industry, introduced by an Englishwoman in the middle of the nineteenth century, employs approximately 70,000 female workers. Large numbers of Madeirans have emigrated to South Africa and, to a lesser extent, to Canada. The people of the Algarve are engaged in agriculture, fishing, and tourism. Cash-crop agriculture (wheat, olives, cork) predominates in the Alentejo. In central continental Portugal, a variety of irrigated grains (wheat, corn, rice) are cultivated on medium-sized family farms. The peasants of northern continental Portugal cultivate maize (rye in the northeast), potatoes, wine grapes, and vegetables. Many also raise dairy cattle. Along the coastline are populations engaged in fishing. Fish canning is an important export-oriented industry. Like the Azores, the local economies of northern Portugal have been supplemented by centuries of emigration, and as a result men have developed artisan skills as masons, carpenters, etc. Around the cities of Braga, Porto, and Guimarães there is a population of worker-peasants who are employed in the old and important textile industry. Furniture making, food processing, winemaking, and pulp and paper production are among the other industrial activities in this region. Heavier industry (steelworking, shipbuilding, iron production) and the bulk of the industrial working class are concentrated in the Lisbon-Setubal region in the south. In recent years, the construction industry has become important in several parts of the country.

In 1984 there were 4,695,700 Portuguese counted in the labor force. Of these, 22 percent were engaged in agriculture, forestry, and fishing; 22 percent in manufacturing; 13 percent in distribution and hotels; 8 percent in construction; 27 percent in other sectors; and 8 percent unemployed. The estimated national income per person was $1,820. Labor force figures frequently underestimate the participation of women who, since Roman times, have been making important contributions to the rural economy of northern Portugal. Some anthropologists view these activities as the basis of significant economic and political power accorded to peasant women. Bourgeois and upper-class women, on the other hand, were at one time restricted to the domestic sphere. This situation has changed significantly in the last twenty years as women have received advanced education, professional training, and full legal equality.

Land Tenure. Portugal is characterized by significant regional variations in patterns of land tenure. In the southernmost district of continental Portugal, the Algarve, landholdings are small and cultivated by owners, tenants, or sharecroppers. The region between the Algarve and the Tagus River, the Alentejo, has traditionally been a region of low population density, latifundia that originated in the Roman estate system, and landless day laborers. Prior to 1974, approximately 500 absentee landlords owned the bulk of the land and were disinterested in capital investment and agricultural development. The agrarian reform movement of the post-1974 period altered the system of land tenure in the south, though some of the early "revolutionary" expropriations have been restored to their original owners. By contrast, the north of the country is characterized by much greater population density (higher in the northeast), land fragmentation, "minifundia" that originated with the system brought by the Germanic invaders of the fifth and sixth centuries, and subsistence peasants. These peasants (_lavradores_) own, rent, and/or sharecrop several fields scattered throughout a village and in neighboring villages. Most of the farms are of less than 3 hectares. Although they are not as numerous here as in southern Portugal, there is also a population of landless day laborers (_jornaleiros_) in northern Portugal, many of whom are women. Jornaleiros provide supplemental labor to the peasant household. In the much less densely populated region of northeastern Portugal, ethnographers have described a form of communal property ownership and communal farming that survived well into the twentieth century.

Kinship, Marriage, and Family

Kinship and Domestic Groups. Although all Portuguese reckon kinship bilaterally, the structure of domestic groups and the kinship links that are emphasized vary by both region and social class. Portuguese kinship terms have Latin roots, with the exception of the Greek roots of _tio_ (uncle) and _tia_ (aunt). In northern Portugal, nicknames (_apelidos_) are extremely important as terms of reference. Some anthropologists have suggested that they connote moral equivalence in otherwise socially stratified rural communities. In the northwest, nicknames serve to identify localized kin groups linked through females. In this region there is a preference for uxorilocality and uxorivicinality, both of which can be linked to male emigration. At some point in the domestic cycle, households in northern Portugal tend to be complex, many of them composed of a three-generation stem family. Some villages of the northeast follow a custom of natalocal residence for many

years after marriage. In southern Portugal, however, a household usually is a nuclear family. The obligations between friends sometimes are felt to be more important than those between kin. Among the rural peasantry, particularly in the northwest, household headship is held jointly by a married couple, who are referred to as _o patrão_ and _a patroa_. By contrast, among urban bourgeois groups and in the south the concept of a dominant male head of household is more prevalent. Spiritual kinship ties are established at baptism and marriage. Kin are frequently chosen to serve as godparents (_padrinhos_), and when this arrangement occurs the godparent-godchild relationship takes precedence over the kinship relationship.

Marriage. The marriage rate has demonstrated a progressive rise during the twentieth century. Age at marriage has been characterized by both spatial and temporal variation—that is, marriage generally occurs later in the north than in the south, though differences are slowly disappearing. In southern Portugal there are significant numbers of consensual unions, and northern Portugal has had high rates of permanent spinsterhood. Although it has declined since 1930, the illegitimacy rate formerly was high in rural northern Portugal. It remains high in Porto and Lisbon. Marriage has generally been class-endogamous and there is a tendency, though by no means a rule, for villages to be endogamous. Although the Catholic church traditionally prohibited cousin marriage within the fourth degree (inclusive of third cousins), dispensations as well as unions between first cousins were by no means unusual among all classes of Portuguese society. This kind of marriage was traditionally associated with a desire to rejoin divided properties.

Inheritance. In accordance with the Civil Code of 1867, the Portuguese practice partible inheritance. Parents, however, have the right to dispose freely of a third share (_terço_) of their property, and women share the right to both receive and bestow property. (The Civil Code of 1978 did not significantly change the articles pertaining to these practices.) Among the peasants of northern Portugal, where inheritance is generally postmortem, parents use the promise of the terço as a form of old-age security by marrying a child, often a daughter, into the household. At their death, this child becomes the owner of the house (_casa_). The rest of the property is divided equally among all heirs. _Partilhas_, whether in the north or the south, can be an occasion for friction between siblings since land is variable in quality. Some peasants hold land under long-term lease agreements; traditionally these agreements also were passed on "for three lives" in one piece to one heir, their value being calculated against the total assets. The Civil Code of 1867 eliminated the system of entailed estates (_vínculos_) that made it possible for wealthier classes to pass on property to a single heir, usually by a rule of male primogeniture. Wealthier landowners have been able to keep property intact by having one heir buy out the interests of his siblings.

Sociopolitical Organization

Social Organization. Salazarist Portugal was a hierarchical society with a small upper class composed of latifundists, industrialists, financiers, top military personnel, the Catholic episcopate, university professors, and other professionals; a small middle class composed of people in the service sector;

and a mass of urban and rural poor. Since 1960, as urbanization has progressed, a lower-middle class of skilled workers and technicians has emerged.

Political Organization.   Before 1974, the Portuguese state was based on corporative bodies that in theory channeled class interests but in practice were often circumvented by means of personal contacts. Electoral politics were absent. Between 1974—when the Salazar regime was bloodlessly overthrown—and 1976, the Portuguese established a constitutional democratic representative system. Recently, some of the more socialist clauses of the 1976 constitution have been revised. At the local level, villages are still run by a parish council (*junta da frequesia*), the members of which are elected by village households. Throughout the Salazar period, the juntas had little real power and few economic resources of their own, though the members had local prominence. They depended on the *câmara*, the administrative body in the county seat, and today the câmara is still the important unit of political organization and administration. Since 1974 political parties and agricultural cooperatives have assumed importance, though participation varies by region. The other important local social institutions are the religious brotherhoods (*confrarias*). Traditionally they served as lending institutions; today they are largely ceremonial and cover funeral expenses.

Religion and Expressive Culture

Religious Beliefs.   The bulk of the Portuguese population is nominally Catholic. During its history, Portugal has experienced waves of political anticlericalism—in the latter half of the eighteenth century; during the 1830s, when religious orders were banned and church properties were confiscated; and under the First Portuguese Republic, when education was secularized, properties again confiscated, folk celebrations restricted, and religious orders abolished. Under Salazar, Portugal experienced a religious revival, and the position of the local priest in the villages throughout the country was greatly enhanced. Since 1974, however, this position has been challenged, and in recent years there has been a decline in the number of clergy. A form of "pious" anticlericalism exists among the people who view the priest as a spiritual leader on the one hand and a man like every other man on the other. Religiosity is generally weaker in Lisbon and in the south of continental Portugal and stronger in the center, in the north, and on the islands. Portuguese Catholicism has produced fewer mystics than that of Spain, and people develop personal relationships with particular saints who are never represented with the suffering and anguish that characterizes some Spanish representations. Much of Portuguese religious life exists beyond the official structures of the Catholic church.

Ceremonies.   The rhythms of local village life are marked by various celebrations honoring the saints. *Romarias* (pilgrimages) to regional shrines are a central feature of religious practice, especially in northern Portugal. Portuguese villagers also celebrate an annual *festa* (generally but not always to honor the patron saint) that includes a procession and combines elements of both the sacred and the secular. In the Azores, the festas of the Holy Ghost (Espírito Santo) predominate. In conjunction with these festas people fulfill religious vows (*promessas*). Cults of death, magical practices, sorcery (*feitiço*), witchcraft (*bruxeria*), which is largely associated with notions of illness and healing, and beliefs in envy (*inveja*) that invokes the evil eye are still part of the belief system of many Portuguese.

Arts.   Craftspeople can be found throughout Portugal. The rugs made in Arraiolas (in southern Portugal) are well known internationally. Women of the north and the island of Madeira produce embroidered goods, many of which are sold to tourists. This is also true of pottery, which varies in style according to geographic region. Artistic expression is also evident in the items that are produced for decorating the floats carried in religious processions.

Medicine.   Modern medical practice now reaches all sectors of Portuguese society. Few women, for example, give birth at home, a practice that was common into the 1960s. Good health is often associated with what is natural, and changes in the diet (the consumption of unnatural and synthetic foodstuffs) are frequently cited as the cause of diseases such as stomach cancer. Folk medical practices are still prevalent in some parts of the country. Curers use a combination of prayer, religious paraphernalia, and traditional and modern medicines in their healing. Among some Azorean Portuguese at home and abroad there is a high incidence of Machado-Joseph disease. It is an inherited disorder of the central nervous system, colloquially known as the "stumbling disease" because the carriers demonstrate a staggering and lurching gait, spasticity, and uncoordinated body movements.

Death and Afterlife.   Death is a fundamental part of Portuguese village life. Church bells toll to send the message that a neighbor (*vizinho*) has passed away. In some parts of Portugal the gates and doors of the dead person's house are opened to allow anyone to enter, and relatives begin to wail around a body prepared for viewing. Burial is in local cemeteries, and family graves are well tended by living kin. Each village has several burial societies (confrarias) to which individuals belong in order to help defray the costs of a funeral and help pay for commemorative masses that continue for several years after death. All Saints' Day is an occasion for special reverence for those who have departed. Mourning is signified by the wearing of black; a widow will generally wear black for the rest of her life, while other kin remain in mourning for varying lengths of time depending on their age and relationship to the deceased. Portugal is also characterized by various cults of death—for example, beliefs about souls in purgatory or incorrupt bodies. Such beliefs are by no means confined to rural areas; in Portuguese cities a network of spirit mediums who can contact the dead for the living has arisen.

Bibliography

Brettell, Caroline (1986). *Men Who Migrate, Women Who Wait: Population and History in a Portuguese Parish*. Princeton: Princeton University Press.

Cutileiro, José (1971). *A Portuguese Rural Society*. Oxford: Clarendon Press.

Keefe, Eugene K., et al. (1977). *Area Handbook for Portugal*. Washington, D.C.: Foreign Area Studies of American University.

O'Neill, Brian (1987). _Social Inequality in a Portuguese Hamlet_. London: Cambridge University Press.

Pina-Cabral, João de (1986). _Sons of Adam, Daughters of Eve: The Peasant Worldview of the Alto Minho_. Oxford: Clarendon Press.

Robinson, Richard (1979). _Contemporary Portugal_. London: George Allen & Unwin.

CAROLINE B. BRETTELL

Provencal

ETHNONYM: Provençal

Orientation

Identification. Provence is one of the twenty regions that constitute the Republic of France. These regions correspond to the pre-1789 division of the country into provinces. Provence refers to a region in the southeasternmost part of France and it includes the departments of the Alpes-de-Haute-Provence, the Hautes-Alpes (also known as the Basses-Alpes), the Alpes-Maritimes, the Bouches-du-Rhône, the Var, and the Vaucluse.

Location. The region is delimited on the north by the departments of the Rhône-Alpes region and on the west by the departments of the region of Languedoc. The southernmost departments of Provence touch the Mediterranean Sea, and the principality of Monaco in the southeastern corner of Provence is generally considered part of the region. The Italian border represents the eastern boundary of the region. Provence is located approximately at 44° N and 6 to 8° E. Topographically, Provence can be divided into three zones—an alpine zone in the northeast, an intermediate zone of hills between the mountains, and a third zone of river valley plains in the west and the coast in the south. The hills and highlands are cut by gorges, rocky plateaus, and valleys of the Rhône, the Durance, and the Verdun rivers. Extending from the delta of the Rhône through Monaco to Italy is the famous narrow strip of coastline called the Côte d'Azur. The port cities of Marseille and Toulon and the well-known cities of the French Riviera, Cannes, Saint Tropez, and Nice, are all situated on this coast. The climate of the coast is Mediterranean in character consisting of long hot and dry summers, warm autumns, and relatively mild winters, though the mistral, a chilly wind from the inland mountains, prevails in the winter months. The interior of Provence has a climate that is more continental in character. Average annual precipitation ranges from 50 to 150 centimeters. The annual temperatures vary from highs averaging in the upper 20s to lower 30s Celsius. The average low temperatures for the region range from 15° C on the coast to 5° C in the interior.

Linguistic Affiliation. Within Provence, French represents the official language; however, Provençal is often spoken for everyday purposes, especially among the rural elderly of the region. Provençal is a dialect of Languedoc or the Occitan language, a Romance language once spoken throughout southern France. "Languedoc" comes from the langue d'oc, a language using _oc_ for "yes" (from the Latin _hoc ille_). The langue d'oïl was once spoken only in northern France. The Occitan dialects are more closely related to Spanish than to French. Provençal refers both to the dialect of Languedoc spoken in the region of Provence and to the literary language, the language of the troubadours of medieval twelfth- to fourteenth-century France and northern Spain. There is some degree of controversy over the extent to which Provençal is used in contemporary France. Recently, however, intellectuals and some politicians have launched campaigns to preserve local culture and language. So Provençal has come to be taught in schools, and Provençal history, literature, poetry, and festivals are all undergoing revival.

Demography. The population of Provence in 1990 exceeded 4 million, with about 75 percent concentrated along the coast. The rapid growth in population after World War II (from 2 million in 1950 to the current total) is attributed to the large numbers of immigrants who have settled in the Provence area. In the immediate post–World War II period, immigration from Italy and Spain rose to meet the demand for labor in reconstructing France. More recently, with the collapse of the French colonial empires in Indochina and North Africa, colonial subjects came to France in search of work. Many residents of Provence issue from the former French colonies in North Africa. In Marseille, for example, roughly one-sixth of the population is Muslim Arab, and a large number among them are recent immigrants to France. Refugees from Vietnam, Cambodia, and Palestine have come also to settle throughout France and in Provence.

History and Cultural Relations

At the end of the second century B.C., when what is now France was partly under Roman rule, Provence was the first Roman _provincia_ (hence the name Provence) beyond the Alps. With the breakdown of the Roman Empire, about 536, Provence fell under Carolingian rule (in the second Frankish dynasty founded by Charlemagne), after suffering successive invasions by the Franks from the north. Following the collapse of the Carolingian Empire in the ninth century and until the beginning of the eleventh century, Provence formed part of a series of kingdoms set up between France and Germany. By the end of the tenth century, a local dynasty (which had led the defense against the invasion by Muslims) dominated the area and acquired for its leader the title of count of Provence. In 1113, this dynasty ended, the House of Barcelona gained the title, and Provence fell to Spanish rule from Catalonia for over a century. Under Catalonian-Spanish rule, Provençal cities grew, becoming important centers for trade with Spain. Troubadour poetry, Romanesque architecture, and the use of a language very similar to Latin were characteristic of this period. In the thirteenth century, the Albigensian crusade was launched by the Catholic church to suppress the Cathari sect of southern France, which was considered heretic. The crusade consolidated the influence of the papacy and northern France. The popes acquired certain territories in northern Provence and took up residence in Avignon from 1309 to 1377. The domination of Provence by the north dates from around 1246, with the extension of the rule of the Angevin dynasty, started by Charles of Anjou, brother of Louis IX. During this period, the administrative autonomy of Provence prevailed with the development of the estates that had the power to approve taxes and to help rule the province in times of disorder. In 1481, Provence was willed to the king of France, and from the sixteenth to the eighteenth century, control by the king grew and the power of the estates decreased. After the revolution of 1789, Provence lost all its political institutions, and in 1790 the first division of the province into departments occurred.

Contemporary France is inhabited by a culturally diverse population, though white native French represent the numerical majority. While Spanish and Italian immigrants have been more easily absorbed into the dominant culture, visible minority groups are less easily absorbed and tolerated. As the economic recession has reduced the demand for labor, resulting in job scarcity, ethnic tensions have grown. In the 1970s, racial intolerance became the political platform of the Right and ultra-Right parties of France. Interracial conflict is especially evident in areas with a large population of visible minority groups, such as Marseille, which represents one of the main ports of entry for the migrants from North Africa. In the rural areas, social interaction between French families and families of North African origin is highly attenuated and limited usually to the workplace.

Settlements

Roughly 65 percent of the population of Provence is concentrated in the urban areas surrounding Avignon in the Vaucluse, in Marseille, and on the Côte d'Azur. The remaining 35 percent of the population lives in villages scattered throughout the region. In the middle of the nineteenth century, the population of the hinterland of Provence began to decline as people migrated to the coastal areas in search of employment in a developing industrial and commercial economy. The inhabitants of rural Provence live together in nucleated villages that are surrounded by fields worked by local farmers and agricultural laborers. Older houses in Provence are constructed of stone and covered by red roof tiles, while more recent dwellings are made of brick and stucco and are also covered by red roof tiles.

Economy

Subsistence and Commercial Activities.   The economy of Provence is based on a combination of agriculture, industry, and tourism. The agricultural economy is highly diversified, mixing the cultivation of cash and subsistence crops with animal rearing. Sheep, goats, and cattle are raised in the highlands and foothills of Provence. On the plateau of Valensole, which is cut by the Durance River, mixed grains are grown, including corn, wheat, sorghum, barley, and oats. Viticulture takes up the greatest proportion of the arable land, and vineyards cover almost all of the southern half of Provence, leaving a small area in the Rhône Valley and the river valley of the Durance for the cultivation of fruits and vegetables. Groves of fruit and olive trees as well as flowers are often interspersed with vineyards. Half the agricultural output is ex-

ported outside the region to large urban centers within France and also abroad to Germany, the Netherlands, and Great Britain. The other half of the agricultural output is primarily sold in local markets and a small proportion is retained by the producers for home consumption. The number of people employed in agriculture has been declining since 1954.

Some small, older industries that were developed in the eighteenth and the nineteenth centuries, such as building-materials fabrication, food processing, and textile manufacture, are scattered throughout the region. However, more recently developed industries tend to be concentrated around Avignon, Marseille, Aix-en-Provence, and Toulon. These industries include the agro-alimentary, steel, armaments, electronics, energy, and chemical industries. Much of the immigrant population constitutes the labor force in the industrial sector of the Provence economy. The economic recession of the 1980s, economic restructuring, and the transformation of technology have resulted in a reduction of employment in industry. Tourism is also a significant sector of the economy of Provence. In contrast to both agriculture and industry, the tourist economy and the service sector of the economy have grown, absorbing much of the labor force rendered redundant in industry and agriculture.

Trade.   Periodic markets, supermarkets, and "hypermarkets" service the population of Provence. The small open-air markets in the villages of the hinterland and the tourist centers along the coast are outlets for the sale of local handicrafts, such as lace, perfume, sweets, pottery, and for local farm products.

Division of Labor.   In the division of labor in rural Provence, men are primarily responsible for executing the tasks of farm production, while women are responsible for the domestic tasks. This division represents the conceptual ideal and is seldom met in practice. Women often perform farm work in the fields on the family holding. Available children and the elderly are also enlisted to aid in the fields. Most rural households survive on the basis of mixing farm work with wage work, and husbands, wives, sons, and daughters may be involved in nonfarm wage work. While women are often involved in farm work, performing a range of light and heavy tasks, married men seldom perform domestic tasks such as cooking and cleaning.

Land Tenure.   Land is privately owned, rented, or sharecropped. A farmer may operate a holding that is partly sharecropped and partly owned. Sharecropping arrangements are often made with absentee owners who wish to maintain some agricultural land while not working it. The conditions of each sharecropping contract differ, but generally the owner receives one-third of the revenues generated on the sharecropped land. The sharecropper receives two-thirds of the revenues and provides the equipment and inputs, as well as labor. In rental arrangements, the tenant farmer pays a fixed rent to the owner of the land. The average size of the farms in this region is 11.5 hectares, which is half the national average. Sixty percent of the farming population operate holdings of less than 5 hectares. Because of the relatively small size of the holdings, most rural households combine some form of wage work with agricultural work.

Kinship, Marriage, and Family

Kin Groups and Descent. The "conjugal unit" is commonly referred to as the *famille*. It consists of a husband and wife and their unmarried offspring. The term *ménage* refers to "household," which consists of a coresidential kin core and its dependents. It is usually used interchangeably with famille. Kinship or *parenté* is reckoned bilaterally, and it is applied to both affinal and consanguineal kin.

Marriage. In rural Provence, women and men tend to marry in their early twenties. There is no strict postmarital residence rule, but the newly married couple tends to reside in a separate residence, close to the location of their principal source of income. In farm households this of course means close to the holdings operated by the farmer. In rural Provence, the preferred marriage partner is a person who owns land.

Domestic Unit. The ménage in rural Provence may consist of many arrangements. In some households, several generations may live together and grandparents, parents, and children may take meals together and participate in the running of the household and the farm. Other households may consist only of a couple and their unmarried children. Other domestic arrangements may involve kin living under the same roof, but in different quarters, forming separate households.

Inheritance. In the late eighteenth century, the Napoleonic Code abolished primogeniture, and all legitimate offspring, female and male, came to be legally entitled to an equal share of their parents' estate. The division of property in practice in rural Provence may take a variety of forms. For example, land may be distributed among sons and cash and movable property distributed among daughters. The different forms of property division respond to the pressure preventing, if possible, the further fragmentation of already small holdings.

Sociopolitical Organization

Social Organization. The villages of Provence tend to be stratified on the basis of landownership. Families who own and operate large agricultural holdings tend to enjoy both wealth and prestige compared with the landless segment of the village population. However, wealth does not necessarily confer political rank and influence. Since the economies of rural villages are complex, with villagers earning incomes from diverse sources, some villagers may become relatively wealthy earning incomes as owners of local businesses, such as hotels, cafés, butcher shops, and hardware stores. The wealthiest members of the village do not necessarily monopolize local power, as efforts often are made to elect officials who reflect the diversity in wealth and occupation at the local level. Hence, landless agricultural laborers, housewives, and schoolteachers have been elected to serve on municipal councils, as well as large and small farmers.

Political Organization. France is a constitutional republic, headed by an elected president, who forms the government. The president is responsible for the appointment of government ministers and the prime minister. France also has a parliamentary system, which is composed of two houses of elected representatives, the National Assembly and the Senate. The main units of local government are the departments, the communes, and the overseas territories. The department is composed of from 11 to 70 cantons. Cantons are in turn composed of communes, which are the smallest administrative units in France. Each commune has a municipal council headed by a mayor, which is composed of elected representatives who sit for six-year terms. The main political parties in France include the Gaullist party, the Rassemblement du Peuple Français (RPR). The Socialist party of France (PSF) forms the current government of France headed by François Mitterrand. Other important parties are the Communist party (PCF) and the ultra-Right National Front party (PFN).

Social Conflict. One of the main sources of social conflict is political allegiances. These differences become most apparent around election time, when animosities between supporters of the various political parties at the local level can develop into brawls in public places as well as attacks on private property. Political allegiances often reflect class differences in the local population, as agricultural laborers as well as small farmers historically have tended to support the parties of the Left while large landowners have tended to support the parties of the Right. Conflicts between agricultural laborers and their employers revolve around wage rates, conditions of work, and terms of employment, and differences over these issues have often resulted in strikes and work stoppages.

Religion and Expressive Culture

Religious Beliefs. The dominant religion in rural Provence is Catholicism; however, because of the significant numbers of Muslim Arabic residents, Islam represents an important religious force. The majority of people in Provence observe the holy days and participate in the cycle of festivities of the Catholic church. Thus, Epiphany, All Souls' Day, Assumption, Candlemas, and Lent are celebrated. One of the most prominent festivals is Carnaval, which is held during Holy Week at Easter. Carnaval has enjoyed a revival in rural villages in Provence and Languedoc. While the specific rites and ceremonies may vary from one region to another and from one village to another, the reemergence of Carnaval is linked to a revival of Occitan customs, language, and culture. This revival has also occurred in the arts.

Arts. The music and poetry of the troubadours is being revived in Provence as part of a movement to preserve regional identity against the dominant French identity. Written in the Occitan language, troubadour art forms flourished in medieval Provence. Occitan literature and the Occitan language itself also have become part of school curriculums at the local level.

Medicine. Villages are served by licensed medical practitioners (i.e., doctors and nurses), who make their rounds visiting patients in their homes as well as tending to them in their offices. One doctor or nurse may serve several villages in close proximity to one another. Most large villages contain a pharmacy that stocks standard pharmaceutical products as well as homeopathic medicines. Homeopathic remedies as well as naturopathy are used in conjunction with "scientific" medicine. Medical knowledge itself is not the strict domain of medical practitioners, as many villagers, especially the elderly, are familiar with the medicinal properties of a wide variety of herbal plants that grow wild in the countryside. These plants are collected, dried, and brewed into teas that are used as medical remedies for many ailments.

Bibliography

Atlas economie régional (1987). Marseille: Chambre Régionale de Commerce et d'Industrie, Provence Alpes Côte d'Azur Corse.

Busquet, Raoul, V.-L. Bourilly, and Maurice Agulhon (1986). *Histoire de la Provence*. Paris: Presses Universitaires de France.

Forster, R., and O. Ranum, eds. (1977). *Rural Society in France*. Baltimore: Johns Hopkins University Press.

Wylie, Lawrence (1956). *Village in the Vaucluse*. Cambridge, Mass.: Harvard University Press.

WINNIE V. LEM

Romanians

ETHNONYMS: Aromans, Karavlachs, Kutzovlachs, Macedoromans, Megloromans, Moldavians, Roumanians, Rumanians, Vlachs, Vlatzii, Wallachs

Orientation

Identification. There is disagreement about the origin of the name "Romanian." It is generally thought to derive from the region's Roman conquerers. In 1965 the state's name was changed to Romania from Rumania to emphasize its Western origins.

Location. Romania is located between 44° and 48° N and 21° and 48° E. Romania is bordered by Bulgaria to the south, Yugoslavia to the southwest, Hungary to the west and northwest, Moldova and Ukraine to the north and northeast, and the Black Sea to the east. The climate is central European with hot summers and cold winters. Romania is comprised of four geographic regions. South of the Carpathian massif is the fertile Wallachian Plain, which extends to the Danube River, the border between Romania and Yugoslavia and Bulgaria. East of the Carpathians is the Moldavian Steppe, a region of rolling hills and fertile soil, which is duplicated by the Dobrogean Steppe that extends between the Danube and the Black Sea. The Transylvanian Plateau is an upland of small, low-lying, forested mountain ranges interspersed with river-cut valleys.

Demography. In 1989 the Romanian population was about 24,000,000, of which 75 percent was classified as Romanian ethnics. Other large Romanian populations live in the former republics of Yugoslavia, Moldova (formerly the Moldavian SSR and, prior to World War II, a Romanian province), Ukraine, the United States, Canada, and Australia.

Linguistic Affiliation. Romanian has a Latin grammar with a few Slavic elements. The vocabulary mixes Latin, Slav, and Turkic elements.

History and Cultural Relations

Romanian history has been shaped by the Romanian people's perceived struggle for territorial integrity and an independent state, concerns intensified by the ethnic heterogeneity of the Romanian lands. The most numerically important ethnic minorities are Hungarian speakers (Magyar and, formerly, Szekler), German speakers (Saxons and Swabians), Gypsies (Romani), Jews, and diverse Slavic populations. Relations have been most difficult with Hungarian speakers because of the proximity of the Hungarian state and questions about Transylvanian sovereignty, which itself involves two distinct theories of Romanian ethnogenesis. According to Romanian historians, Romanians originated from the interbreeding of the Roman legions with autochthonous Geto-Dacians after Rome's occupation of Dacia in the first century A.D. Romanians assert that after Rome withdrew south of the Danube, this hybrid population remained in the Carpathian area in loose confederations of transhumant pastoralists. Hungarian historians disagree and maintain that Romanians withdrew totally, leaving Transylvania open for in-migrating Magyars. Romanian-Hungarian relations have remained tense as control of Transylvania, now part of Romania, has shifted repeatedly. Furthermore, Romanians recall the extreme restriction of their legal rights when the province was Magyardominated. Relations with German speakers and others have been somewhat less charged. Saxons and Swabians generally are considered to have had a modernizing influence; Jews, however, historically suffered from restrictive property laws that tracked them into commercial and renter roles, prompting occasional anti-Semitic excess during times of peasant unrest such as the rebellion of 1907. Gypsies especially serve as a negative reference group for Romanians. Gypsies in Romania date to the fourteenth and fifteenth centuries, when many of their groups were enslaved; they were not emancipated fully until 1848. Although Gypsies have served crucial economic functions for Romanian society (e.g., stock keeping, metalsmithing, brick and tile making), they are still marginalized. Official policy now considers all minorities except Gypsies as "coinhabiting nationalities," with proportional representation in official bodies, though without a separate territorial base.

Settlements

The Carpathian Hills are considered the zone of original Romanian settlement. In fourteenth- and fifteenth-century Moldavia and Wallachia the market-oriented grain trade transformed kin relations, fostered ownership of some villages and regions, and spawned population shifts to lowland plains. Romanians remaining in uplands established villages extending along river bottoms in a dispersed pattern. Urban centers were populated extensively by non-Romanians; Greeks and Turks in the south, Magyar and German speakers in Transylvania and Banat (the southwest), Jews and German speakers in Bucovina (the northeast). A western European commercial class was found throughout the country as well. Socialist development has encouraged more balanced rural-urban population distribution. Regional settlement patterns are now undergoing great change, with attempts at social engineering occurring via the policy of systemization. Under this policy, less populous villages are razed, larger villages developed into towns servicing a network of villages, and major cities closed to most new immigration. Restrictions are also placed on rural construction. New peasant homes must be two stories for multifamily occupancy, and apartment construction has been greatly expanded. Systemization has recently been intensified. Out of 13,000 villages, 7,000 are to be razed, with the affected population to be moved elsewhere.

Economy

Subsistence and Commercial Activities. Before feudalism, Romanian villagers were subsistence-based agropastoralists. The feudal grain trade shifted many of these populations to lowland maize production. Villages exhibited a diversity of activities geared to local environmental potentials and the provisioning of a peasant economy. Often villages specialized in one activity to the extent that their inhabitants were identified by others accordingly. Mountain communities used forests and meadows extensively, often collectively pasturing sheep and cattle and giving access to forest by lottery or membership in religious associations. Production of wine and fruit brandies also figured prominently in some local economies. Reciprocal labor was common as neighbors and kin worked together during times of concerted need. Feudal villages also were characterized by work gangs (*claca*) called together by local nobles. Joint labor was also performed on church lands. Collective and state farms dominate rural areas today, and much of the rural population also commutes to jobs in industry. Use of personal connections in economic exchange and informal "second-economy" production is also common.

Industrial Arts. A wide range of trades was practiced including sawmilling, wool and other fiber processing, tanning, metalsmithing, and woodworking. The clothing industry was especially well developed. Women produced for this and also specialized in weaving and embroidery for the domestic economy. Subregions were identified by a unique blouse and apron style.

Trade. Overland trade routes between Asia and Europe traversed the Romanian lands but were monopolized mainly by non-Romanians. Extensive cross-Carpathian trade in hides, local crafts, and agricultural products linked Romanian communities on both sides of the mountains until terminated by the nineteenth-century customs wars between Austro-Hungary and the Romanian Kingdom. In order to protect Romanian economic independence, trade policy, currently and in the past, has often been protectionist. Today Romania exports finished goods (wood products, clothing, shoes) to the West while machine tools, tractors, and capital goods go to

the third world. Romania continued as a member of the Soviet–East European Council of Mutual Economic Assistance. Seriously in debt in the early 1980s, Romania greatly expanded exports of food, effecting rationing and local shortage within the country.

Division of Labor. Although Romanians are said to be patriarchal, the sexual division of labor is not rigorous. Men and women were both involved in nearly all agricultural tasks, with women only enjoined from operating plows. Traditionally, cooking and weaving were exclusively female occupations, though men were and are quite active in child rearing and other domestic activities. Previously, multiethnic regions had ethnic divisions of labor. In pre–World War I Transylvania (and to a lesser extent Banat) Romanians were mainly small-scale peasant producers (serfs before 1848), while Hungarians dominated government and were owners of large estates, and German speakers were bankers, shopkeepers, commercial farmers, and professionals. Socialism spurred equality in the division of labor. Women entered the nondomestic work force in large numbers and ethnic divisions were discouraged. However, development has since spawned rapid change. Rural men have left agriculture for industry, leaving women and the elderly as the main source of collective farm labor. Women are again impelled to domestic labor by rigorous state pronatalist policies.

Land Tenure. Traditional Romanian villages were corporate groups led by an assembly of agnatically related household heads who decided periodic land redistribution to community members. Feudalism brought great concentrations of land ownership, especially in plains regions, and its end in 1848 did little to limit this. The land reform of 1920–1921 was successful in developing an extensive class of small landholders. With socialism, land was nationalized in state farms or collectivized. Collective farmers receive access to an annual use plot from the farm if they satisfy farm-labor requirements. A small number of private peasants are still found in mountainous zones, though estate size is circumscribed by law.

Kinship

Kin Groups and Descent. Romanian kinship is bilateral (with patrilateral preference), generating an expanding network of increasingly distant kin and quasi-kin family, kindred, region, and nation. Kin relations also extend to one's children's affines and to one's children's baptismal and marriage sponsors.

Kinship Terminology. Kin terms follow the Eskimo system with considerable local and regional variation in terminology.

Marriage and Family

Marriage. Village and regional endogamy was widespread in pre-Socialist Romania. The incest taboo was extended to first cousins and second-cousin marriage was frequent. Marriage partners were sought from households of roughly similar social status. Postmarital residence was either viri- or uxorilocal, with the former being preferred. The marriage feast was generally held in the household where the newly married couple was to reside. The godparent role is emphasized in some regions. Godparents sit at the center of the head table, invite their own friends and family to the wedding, and are treated with great respect by the bride, the groom, and their families. Despite the Socialist government's requirement of a civil wedding, religious ceremonies are still common.

Domestic Unit.   In rural areas three-generation stem families predominated and are still common. Although an artifact of peasant economics, they are still functional for socialist conditions as the labor they generate enables access to the diverse but limited socialist resource base available.

Inheritance.   Partible inheritance was both customary and legally mandated. A slightly larger share of the rural patrimony was retained by the household heir for care of elderly parents. In this, male primogeniture was the ideal, though ultimogeniture of either sex was more likely.

Socialization.   Romanians dote on their children, though gentle expressions of love can quickly turn to intense tongue lashings and beating. Children are admonished with the phrase, "You haven't the right," suggesting an emphasis on knowing one's place. In the past children were raised to be "good householders," though today formal education is encouraged.

Sociopolitical Organization

Social Organization.   Romanian village social organization differed widely across regions and between villages, as the oft-cited proverb "There are as many customs as peasant huts" suggests. Households and their webs of bilateral kin were the base of local social organization. One important nonkin tie was godparenthood (*nasie*), which linked families across generations in a formalized set of rights and obligations. Because of the costs of godparenthood, multifamily sponsors were generally wealthier villagers, while sponsored households served as political clients and occasional labor for the wealthy. Neighborhood relations were also important as they determined women's participation in nightly winter working bees (*sezitoare*) and in some regions defined mutual assistance, burial, and cooperative labor associations. Communities also sponsored one or more young men's age associations (*ceata feciorilor*), mainly active during Christmas season when the ceata organized Christmas dances. In return for pastries, money, and drink they caroled each household while courting eligible young women. It was mandatory that ceata leaders marry the following year.

Political Organization.   Communal villages were led by councils of elders. Feudalism destroyed this system and replaced it with patrimonialism. With its end, and especially after the land reform of 1920–1921, villages gained greater degrees of autonomy and again were regulated by councils generally comprised of ten to fifteen male landowning heads of households. These councils tended to be dominated by the wealthy. Local politics are now organized by state and party. The post of mayor and first party secretary are unified, and commune deputies are elected from a range of party-supported candidates.

Social Control.   The face-to-face relations and demands of village life were the basis for traditional social control. Propriety was necessary to marry well and receive the support of co-villagers. Kin relations and respect for elders also checked inappropriate behavior, as did ostracism and the belief that thieves, drunks, or the shiftless suffered after death. Village councils adjudicated most disputes, with great effort being made to keep these cases from proceeding to provincial- or state-level bodies. Local judicial commissions are now state-appointed, and state trials are often held locally with the population invited to attend.

Conflict.   Traditionally intravillage conflict was over land and inheritance issues. Conflicts between young men of neighboring villages over boundary issues, personal affronts, or questions of faith were also not uncommon.

Religion and Expressive Culture

Religious Beliefs.   Romanians adopted Eastern Orthodoxy in the late ninth to early tenth centuries. In Transylvania Eastern Catholicism/Uniatism was established in the eighteenth century in a Habsburg attempt to encourage Romanian loyalty. Uniatism and Orthodoxy were unified by state decree after World War II. Rural religion was eclectic: nature worship, pilgrimages to sites of miracles, and belief in a pantheon of both good and evil spirits mixed with Christian belief. Quasipolitical religious cults like Hosts of the Lord (Oastea Domnului) developed between the world wars, and currently a variety of Protestant sects are attracting increased numbers of adherents. Traditional beliefs recognized the Trinity and a number of other spirits and forces, both benevolent and malign. The latter include *vircolaci*, *strigoi*, and *moroi* (witches, undead human and animal spirits) that brought illness and death to their former communities. Beneficial forces included white magic practiced by sorceresses and the curative powers of Whitsuntide dancers.

Religious practice and education is now legally limited and controlled by the state Ministry of Cults.

Religious Practitioners.   Orthodox and Uniate priests served pre-Socialist era communities as advisers, social arbiters, and leading economic figures. The churches owned extensive lands and priests received labor and other needs gratis from citizens. Even today priests receive the best of the annual vintage and other gifts. However, as state employees, Orthodox priests now find their community activism restricted by the government.

Arts.   Traditional arts focused on the production of utilitarian household objects or religious items. Woven and embroidered clothing, rugs, and wall hangings were especially well developed, as was the carving of decorative wood gates, grave markers, and utensils. Transylvania's icons, painted on glass, and the painted monasteries of Moldavia are world-reknowned. The interwar period also saw a flowering of Romanian art, best exemplified by the work of the sculptor Constantin Brancusi. Currently, plastic arts are widely emphasized.

Medicine.   Traditional folk medicine made extensive use of locally grown plants prepared as teas or poultices. Some plants such as garlic and wormwood were thought to be especially efficacious. As illness was often attributed to spirit possession, various kinds of healing rituals were also used. Although less respected in the past, physicians today are afforded high social status in Romanian communities.

Death and Afterlife.   Although Christian belief in heaven and hell is common, a practical streak frequently denies the reality of the afterlife. In either case, death is not feared and is fairly well integrated into daily life. The dead are generally thought to need similar things as the living (e.g., food, light, money), and these elements figure prominently in funerary ritual. The cemetery is a great focus of meaning in Romanian village culture and creation of elaborate funerary art, crypts, and epitaphs characterizes many villages. Death is publicly commemorated by close family at six-week, six-month, and one-year intervals—and more often than that if dreams of the deceased interfere with the living.

Bibliography

Kligman, Gail (1988). _Wedding of the Dead: Ritual, Poetics, and Popular Culture in Transylvania._ Berkeley: University of California Press.

Shafir, Michael (1985). _Romania: Politics, Economics, and Society._ Boulder, Colo.: Lynne Rienner.

Stahl, Henri (1972). _Traditional Romanian Village Communities: Subjection and Capitalist Penetration._ London: Cambridge University Press.

DAVID A. KIDECKEL

Romansch

ETHNONYM: Rhaetians

The Romansch, or Rhaetians, are speakers of the Romansch language who live in the canton of Graubunden (Grisons), in Switzerland. They number approximately 65,000 today, a figure that reflects a reversal of a demographic trend toward depopulation that reached its nadir in the early 1940s. Romansch is a member of the Rhaeto-Romansch Language Family, derived from the vernacular Latin. It is related to Ladin and Friuli, but all three are separate languages. The Romansch, as fully integrated members of the larger Swiss polity, are perhaps more accurately thought of as a linguistically and historically defined group, rather than as a unique ethnic or cultural unit.

The territory of the Romansch was known prior to 1814 as Upper Rhaetia and Churraetien, among other names, and as the Grisons or Graubunden in the fifteenth century. The origins of the Romansch people are unclear. Archaeological evidence shows the influence of Illyrian, Celtic, and Etruscan cultures. Although Roman occupation, begun in 15 B.C., brought vernacular Latin to a wide territory, the geographical isolation of the Romansch territory permitted it to develop into a separate dialect—and later a distinct language in its own right—rather rapidly.

The ancient territory of the Romansch was called Raetia, which consisted of the modern canton of Graubunden, as well as eastern Switzerland south of Lake Constance, a large portion of the Tirol, and part of northern Lombardy. Its capital was at Chur. The Raetians were cattle breeders and timber cutters for the most part, though they practiced agriculture as well. In the fifth and sixth centuries A.D., Roman authority declined and the government of the region passed to the duchy of Alemannia. The Frankish kings spent the period of the sixth to ninth centuries attempting to secure control over this territory, as well as the lands of Swabia. Raetia's importance to the Franks lay in the fact that its capital commanded the eastern access routes to Italy, and thus it was of strategic as well as economic concern. In the tenth century, German kings began to try to take control of the region. By the 1300s, Raetia belonged entirely to German rule and was split up into territories. Some came under the rule of feudal lords, others under the authority of ecclesiastics (e.g., the bishopric of Chur). During this time, a number of autonomous peasant communities in the region grouped together to form the Gray League (Grau Bund or Grisons), the League of God's House (Gotteshausbund), and the League of the Ten Jurisdictions, all three of which formed a confederated republic that allied itself with the Swiss Confederacy. These three groups became known as the "Gray Leagues" (French "Grisons" or German "Graubunden"), from which the name of the modern Romansch territory is derived.

The period of German control over the region caused a serious setback for the Romansch language, for the language of the rulers supplanted the local tongue in literature and official business. However, the provincial autonomy maintained in the area of the "Gray Leagues" served to preserve large pockets of Romansch speakers and militated against successful government suppression of the language. Romansch is now listed as one of the four national languages of Switzerland (along with German, French, and Italian), although it does not have official language status. Its written form dates from the sixteenth century. The first printed books in the language appeared during the Reformation and display the religious concerns of that era. Thus the earliest printed works in Romansch were Bible translations, hymnals, religious tracts, and prayer books. However, it was not until the later nineteenth century that the Romansch language established a strong secular literary tradition, a movement largely inspired by concerns that German and Italian were beginning to supplant Romansch through the incursion of their idioms. It became an important enterprise among historians and linguists to develop dictionaries and grammars for Romansch in order to preserve its linguistic integrity. By the early 1900s, a great effort was made to preserve the oral traditions, folk customs, music, and other cultural elements of the Romansch past, which has since been followed by a revival of the use of Romansch in the development of contemporary literature, particularly in the realm of poetry.

Because the Romansch do not live in a linguistically and culturally homogeneous territory, there is little today to distinguish them economically, socially, and culturally from their German- and Italian-speaking fellow canton inhabitants. Even the remote agricultural villages, long a stronghold for isolated, homogeneous Romansch communities, are in decline as they lose their young people to the attractions of employment in the cities and in the tourist industry. Romansch is taught in primary schools, but the only language of instruction at the secondary level is German. Biweekly newspapers are published in Romansch and its linguistic relative, Ladin, and there is a church-produced weekly (_La Casa Paterna_), but there are no daily newspapers published in the language. The efforts of scholars to preserve the folk culture and oral traditions of the Romansch have been largely replaced by efforts to establish and develop a lively contemporary literature. It has become more important to the Romansch to preserve their autonomy and to develop in today's world than to preserve some idealized version of past cultural practice, and the Swiss federal government has shown a willingness to respect these goals.

See also German Swiss; Swiss, Italian

Bibliography

Bezzola, Reto R., ed. (1971). *The Curly Horned Cow.* London.

Lansel, Peider (1937). *The Raeto-Romans.* Chur, Switzerland: Uniun dals Grischs.

Luck, James Murray (1985). *A History of Switzerland. The First 100,000 Years: Before the Beginnings to the Days of the Present.* Palo Alto, Calif.: Society for the Promotion of Science and Scholarship.

NANCY E. GRATTON

Rominche

ETHNONYMS: Romanies, Travelers, Traveller Gypsies

Orientation

The Rominche, Romanies, or Travelers are the Gypsies of Great Britain. It is estimated that there are well in excess of 20,000 individuals, possibly 8,000 to 9,000 families, of Rominche stock in England and in Wales. The languages spoken by the Rominche include Anglo-Romany, Romani, Shelta (Gammon), and "Cant."

History and Cultural Relations

The Rominche appear to have arrived in Britain in the early sixteenth century, and from the start they were associated with exotic occupations such as fortune-telling. As was the case elsewhere in Europe, deportations began soon after their arrival, at least by mid-century, where it was decreed lawful that those who would not leave the British Isles could be imprisoned or executed. They were prosecuted as vagrants, with punishments ranging from forced labor (to cure them of their supposed "idleness") to the death penalty until as late as 1783. Even those who associated with Gypsies were subject to punishment, up to and including imprisonment. Banishment policies on the part of the British government resurfaced in strength in the twentieth century.

Settlements

Rominche settlements of preference are temporary encampments of caravans (trailers), pulled up into a circle to form a single entrance to the space thereby enclosed. The main windows face inward into the circle. Waste is disposed of outside of the circle and well away from the settlement. Government policy, embodied in the 1968 Caravan Sites Act, has tried to make the Rominche sedentary. The approach has been to set up caravan parks, screened from public view by bushes, trees, or other such barriers, but this runs contrary to Rominche preference.

Economy

The Rominche economy is largely independent of wage labor, relying instead on the sale of goods and services. Traditional occupations include the following: (1) sales of goods that may be either bulk-purchased manufactured items or second-hand merchandise, fruits and vegetables from barrows, horses and dogs, or items of their own manufacture such as baskets, wood carvings, and charms; (2) sales of services such as trash and scrap clearing, gardening, wagon construction, knife grinding, or fortune-telling. The preference for self-employment is strong, because it permits greater flexibility and mobility. However, some wage labor is taken, particularly for seasonal work on farms. Work that takes one away from the encampment usually is considered to be the province of adult males, with the exception of "calling" at houses in search of cast-off items that may be repaired and resold. Most stringent of all is the restriction of horse trading to men. Women may also earn for the household by fortune-telling and by sharp trading at fairs.

Kinship

A Rominche is considered as such by reference to parentage—that is, at least one parent must be Rominche. "Didikois" is the usual term applied to "half-breeds," while non-Rominche are called "Gorgios." Kinship is recognized bilaterally, but it is usually reckoned rather shallowly: for most purposes, only the grandparental through grandchild generations are counted. First, and possibly second, cousins are considered too closely related for marriage. One's recognized circle of kin have moral obligations to provide assistance and loyalty in times of trouble. Naming practices are used to emphasize personal associations—for example, a woman can elect upon marriage to retain her father's name, to take on her husband's name, or to reject both in favor of her mother's surname.

Marriage and Family

Average age at marriage is 16–17 for women, 18–19 for men. Elopements are common. The permanent, monogamous union is the ideal, but separation and remarriage are easily achieved and do not involve legal action. In such cases, the children usually stay in the care of the mother. There are prohibitions against marriage to a Gorgio, to a first or second cousin, and to a much older or much younger mate. Violations of these prohibitions do occur, however. In the case of marriage to a Gorgio, the status of the "outsider" spouse will always be ambiguous—acceptance is never complete. Weddings are celebrated with a party to which the close cognates of the bride and groom, plus additional kin and affines, are invited. Many fights occur during weddings. Upon marriage, the new couple sets up a separate trailer unit from that of their parents, but they may choose to live near either set of in-laws. A good wife is expected to be submissive and helpful and to follow her husband. Children are highly prized, but they are not romanticized. At a very early age they are presumed to be capable of helping out, particularly by caring for their younger siblings and by accompanying their mother when she goes "calling." Rominche rarely willingly send their children for formal schooling, which has frequently caused conflicts between the Rominche way of life and the expectations of the state. Children are fully involved in adult society, except with regards to sex—there is a strong cultural denial of children's sexuality.

Sociopolitical Organization

Groups of Rominche are formed according to principles of territorial proximity, shared experiences, and economic cooperation. Such groups are extremely flexible, and there is little or no formal system of leadership beyond the level of the household. Deference is accorded to elders, but advanced age does not guarantee authority. Among adults, the practice is to offer advice, rather than to issue commands. If a leader of sorts arises, his authority is based on charisma. There are larger organizations that have formed in recent decades to look after the interests of Rominche in Great Britain: the Gypsy Council; the Association of Gypsy and Romany Organizations; the Association of Traveling People; the Romany Guild; and the Southern Gypsy Council. These groups exist largely to minimize confrontations with Gorgios.

Religion and Expressive Culture

Rominche culture is in many ways influenced by their opposition to Gorgios. Pollution beliefs are a strong example of this: food is "dirty" or "polluted" if even the shadow of a Gorgio falls upon it. The Rominche believe in and fear *mulo*, or ghosts, and much funerary practice is dedicated to confound the mulo of the deceased and speed him away from the living. Death should ideally occur away from the encampment—Rominche are most willing to send the terminally ill to hospitals to ensure that this is the case. There is also a very strong aversion to handling the corpse, which is a job they consider more suited to a Gorgio. Any Rominche in the vicinity of a death may attend the funeral, but there is a prohibition on all discord, so either rivalries must be set aside or the parties to such rivalries must stay away from a funeral. The day before the ceremony, the body is brought in an open coffin to a trailer in the camp. Traditionally its clothes are put on inside out, in an attempt to confuse the mulo. Two fires are lit to frighten off other mulo—one for men, one for women—around which groups of people keep vigil. Only postmenopausal women may sit up with the corpse in the trailer itself. Periodically someone will enter the trailer to look at the body and touch its face "so that it can be forgotten." When the corpse is brought out of the house, the attendees, all dressed in black, form a circle around the door, to witness the start of its final journey. The widow(er) and close cognates are expected to display dramatic expressions of grief, but affines are expected to maintain decorum and remain in the background. When the Rominche still traveled in wagons, the tradition was to burn it upon the death of its owner and to give the eldest son the iron frame left behind by the fire. Today it is the practice to purchase a cheap trailer into which the body is brought, and that trailer, rather than the one that had served as the deceased's residence, is what is burned. The procession to the grave site is solemn, conceived of by the mourners as the deceased's "last time to travel." Favorite possessions are traditionally buried with the corpse, so that the ghost won't be tempted to return for them.

Bibliography

Adams, Barbara, Judith Okely, David Morgan, and David Smith (1975). *Gypsies and Government Policy in England*. London: Heineman.

Okely, Judith (1983). *The Traveller Gypsies*. Cambridge: Cambridge University Press.

NANCY E. GRATTON

Rom of Czechoslovakia

ETHNONYMS: Cikán, Gypsies, Tsiganes, Zigeuner

Orientation

Identification. Rom is the name applied to people of Indian origin who migrated out of India about 1,000 years ago and today are commonly referred to as Gypsies. Although outsiders view all Gypsies as being the same, there were and remain castelike distinctions between different Rom groups based on occupational specialization and language. Although the Rom are now found throughout the world, caste-based restrictions are still followed by some, including the prohibition of marriage between members of different groups. The name "Rom" is derived from the name of an ancient Indian caste, "Dom," whose subcastes practiced occupations such as blacksmithing, basket weaving, and music making. "Dom" is derived from the Sanskrit word *damaru*, meaning "drum." The label "Gypsy" is derived from "Egyptianos," incorrectly suggesting an Egyptian origin for the European Rom. The labels "Cikán," "Zigeuner," and "Tsiganes" all suggest ancestry among the *athinganoi*, a group of musicians in Asia Minor. In Czechoslovakia, "Cikán" was a derogatory term that was officially replaced by "Rom" in 1989.

Location. Three Rom groups are found in the Czech and Slovak Federative Republic: Slovak Roms (about 80 percent of the Rom population), Hungarian Roms (about 10 percent), and Vlaxi (about 10 percent). About one-third live in the Czech part of the republic and about two-thirds in the Slovak section. There are also a few German Rom (Sinti) and Hungarian Rom families.

Demography. According to information from the National Committees (local, district and regional administrative centers), in 1987 there were 383,000 Rom in Czechoslovakia. This is probably an underestimation, as only those Rom who came to the attention of government social workers are counted. Thus, the actual number of Rom is probably close to a half-million. The Rom birthrate is about twice that of non-Roms, and projections point to a Rom population of one million in 2020.

Linguistic Affiliation.   Roms speak dialects of Romani, which is classified in the Indian Group of Indo-European languages and which is related to Hindi, Punjabi, Rajasthani, and other Indian languages. Each Rom group speaks a distinct dialect. Dialect differences evidently existed at the time of migration out of India and have been further broadened through contact with different non-Rom groups in the regions where Rom settled. In general, Czechoslovakian Roms are bilingual or even trilingual, speaking some combination of Romani/Slovak/Czech/Hungarian. While Romani has disappeared among the Czech Rom, a majority of Slovak Rom still use Romani, although its use is decreasing in the youngest generation.

History and Cultural Relations

As mentioned above, the Rom are descendants of groups who left India about 1,000 years ago. The first document written about "Gypsies" in Europe was by a Mount Athos (Greece) monk in the twelfth century and describes them as blacksmiths. A medieval legend about a "gypsy" blacksmith who made nails for crucifixions spread throughout Europe. Other ancient accounts note that "gypsies" were musicians, for example in the Turkish army. The first reference to Roms in the region that is now Czechoslovakia dates to the fifteenth century. Because non-Gypsies (*gadžos*) never distinguished the different Rom groups from one another, we do not have a record of which groups "came and went." The history of the Rom in what are now Czech versus Slovak regions differs greatly. In Czech areas, the number of Rom was always small and they remained largely itinerant, until they were exterminated at Osweinenczim during World War II, when the area was a "German protectorate." Of 8,000 Rom, only about 200 escaped death. The German extermination policy was the culmination of a long history of persecution of the Czech Rom. Various laws and directives dating back to 1539 decreed that "gypsies should be evicted/banished out of the country" or even killed. In 1697 King Leopold issued an edict declaring that Gypsies should be considered outlaws. And, as late as 1710, in the Czech town of Beroun, the law stipulated that one who "murders a gypsy, should not be accused of any crime."

In Slovakia conditions were better. The Hungarian noblemen who ruled the region allowed Rom to settle on the outskirts of villages and work for the peasants as blacksmiths, basket weavers, and musicians. They were also drafted as soldiers in the various regional armies. Thus, the Slovak and Hungarian Rom were sedentary as early as the 1700s. Only the Vlaxi remained peripatetic, until 1959 when a sedentarianization law was passed. In 1761 the Empress Maria Theresa enacted an "assimilation decree" that Gypsies in both the Czech and Slovak regions be assimilated into the general population. Toward this end, "Úji-Magyar" replaced Gypsy as the official group label, Rom were forced to settle on farms, Rom surnames were replaced by Christian ones, the

speaking of Romani was outlawed, and Rom children were placed with non-Rom farm families for reeducation. Although this effort failed, the Slovak and Hungarian Rom slowly have been assimilated, largely through economic relations with their gadžo neighbors. During World War II, while the Slovak Rom did escape mass extermination, they too were persecuted: men were sent to labor camps, they were banned from cities, Rom settlements were moved to isolated locations, and some settlements were burned and Rom killed as punishment for participating in the partisan movement. After the war, many Slovak Rom emigrated to Czech regions where they settled near towns, often in areas previously inhabited by the Germans who were exiled.

In recent times, Rom officially were labeled "citizens of gypsy origin" by the Socialist government and were viewed as the "relics of a decaying ethnic" and underdeveloped culture that blocked the national goals of social integration and assimilation. This official position led to attempts to disperse the Rom among the general population and to ban the use of Romani. In 1969 a group of educated Rom formed the Union of Roms (Svaz Cikánu-Romu) and demanded official recognition of the Rom language and culture. The union disbanded in 1973, but informal Rom ethnic identity efforts persisted, such as amateur theater groups, a Romani language school in Prague, and petitions to the government. In 1989, the assimilation policy was reversed when the Presidium of the Communist party supported a new policy encouraging ethnic freedom for the Rom.

Settlements

As noted above, the Rom are now largely sedentary. In the Czech region of the republic they live mostly in towns, scattered among the gadžo. In the Slovak area about 70 percent live in villages, although some isolated settlements still exist.

Economy

In the past, the Rom provided specialized services such as blacksmithing and basket weaving for the nearby rural peasant and villager populations. They were usually paid with food; only the *lavutara* (musicians) were paid with money. However, because of assimilation and a high Rom birthrate, this economic relationship gradually declined in importance and was replaced by unskilled or semiskilled wage labor such as seasonal farm work, brick making, and well digging, as well as recycling scrap materials and peddling small wares. Thus, many Rom have been absorbed into the national economy, with the notable exceptions of the *úri* lavutara (gentleman musicians who play in wine bars and cafés) and the *handlara* (pig dealers). Pig dealers were often men who had emigrated to the United States to earn money and then returned home and used their wealth to establish a pig-dealing business. Some became very wealthy, even to the point of lending money to gadžo villagers. While high rates of illiteracy (70 percent for Roms over 60 years of age) have kept the Rom at the low end of the occupational scale, the number of middle school and university graduates is increasing rapidly.

Kinship, Marriage, and Family

Marriage.   Traditionally, marriages were arranged by the parents of the man and the woman. Cousin marriage was forbidden and was considered the worst of all crimes. Upon marriage, the wife went to live with the husband's family and became a _bori_ (daughter-in-law and sister-in-law) in that family. Women were subordinate to men, although women procured everyday food for the family. On the other hand, _daj_ (mother) was a sacred position and the high-status _baro phral_ (eldest son) protected her from inevitable violence by her husband. As she got older, a woman's status increased and she was often respected for her knowledge of healing and dreams.

Family.   The _familija_ and the _fajta_ were and still are the basic organizational units. The fajta is a patri/matrilineal lineage group. The familija is an extended family of from three to five generations, the members of which used to all reside in the same _kher_ (house) or in the same neighborhood. Familija and fajta are also economic units; music bands consist of fathers, sons/brothers, and cousins, and in blacksmith families, the fathers did the smithing, mothers peddled the products, and children helped to blow the bellows. Families commonly _sikhavel zor_ (showed their strength) by having the sons stand in front of the dwelling and lift heavy objects.

Sociopolitical Organization

Social Organization.   Caste relations regulated contact between different Rom settlements. A basic division was that between the _žuže_ Roma ("clean" Roms who did not eat "polluted" meat) who would never visit a settlement of _degeša_ (those who eat horse and dog meat). Žuže Roma were usually _lavutara_ (musicians), _charti_ (blacksmiths), or _handlara_ (pig dealers) and they were generally wealthier than the degeša who were _butakere_ (day laborers), brick makers, or scrap-material recyclers. Despite the high level of economic assimilation, social distance between Roms and gadžos is maintained and intermarriage is rare.

Political Organization.   The nature of Rom-Czechoslovakian relations is discussed earlier in the section on History and Cultural Relations. Within the Rom settlements, the leader is the _chibalo/vajda_ who serves as an intermediary with the local government officials. Despite wealth distinctions between communities, strong pressures toward equality minimize status distinctions within communities.

Conflict and Social Control.   Although serious disputes might lead to fights, people try to avoid open conflict. A peacemaking formula is to say "Roma sam" ("We are Roms"), meaning, "Let us be united," "Let us not fight." Ethical principles, unwritten laws, various sanctions, and the concepts of "_paťiv_" (honor, respect, proper behavior) and _ladž_ (shame, dishonesty) are central forces in maintaining ethnic identity and social order in Rom communities. Rom conceptions of the ideal male and female are especially well defined. A "Paťivalo Rom" is a man who shares food with others, offers shelter to a stranger (Rom), doesn't offend anyone, may be unfaithful to his wife but doesn't leave her, cares for his children, drinks but doesn't get drunk, doesn't get polluted by eating taboo foods, etc. A "Paťivali Romni" is a woman who is never unfaithful to her husband,

never leaves her children, is an obedient bori, can _anel maro_ ("bring bread," i.e., procure food), is _žuži_ (is clean, i.e., follows all the complicated rules of ritual cleanliness), etc. Traditional sanctions included _ladž_ (public shame—jeering at, spitting at, or mocking a wrongdoer); _mariben_ (beatings) for women; and cutting the hair of an adulterous woman. The most severe punishment was excommunication (Vlaxi call it _marime_, Czech Roms call it _prastapen_, while Slovak Roms have no word for it).

Religion and Expressive Culture

Religion.   Rom religion is best described as a set of beliefs rather than as a system of organized belief. Many features of Hinduism are still apparent. For example, the belief that whatever you do will sooner or later "come back to you" reflects karma law. Older Roms believe in rebirth, with the soul of a deceased Rom born in the body of a child. Most common is the belief that _mule phiren_ (spirits of the dead) can influence the affairs of the living by taking revenge, fulfilling a wish, bringing a warning, etc. Roms use the services of local clergymen for life-cycle events such as _bolipen_ (baptism) and burial, to witness an oath, and to exorcise a _mulo_.

Arts.   Rom art forms are rich and varied and are manifested in _čardašis_ (dance), _gila_ (songs), _paramisa_ (tales), and narrations, riddles, proverbs, etc. Songs are sung by women and especially by young girls. _Čorikane gila_ are traditional, slow songs full of emotion, speaking about hunger, poverty, sorrow, loneliness, etc. _Čardaša_ are amusing couplets that accompany dancing. Through these songs, feeling are expressed, messages conveyed, improper behavior criticized, and important events described. Each singer usually adds some improvised lines to the standard lyrics. Today, elements of popular music are transformed by Rom musicians into creative new forms for performance by Rom folk groups. Traditionally, paramisa were told by men at gatherings that lasted for hours. Today, with families more widely dispersed and televisions in every home, paramisa gatherings are no longer regular events and take place mainly at wakes. Rom literature and Rom graphic and plastic arts are recent phenomena, with Ruda Dzurko's glass pictures being the best-known example.

Bibliography

Horváthová, Emilia (1964). _Cigáni na Slovensku_. Bratislava.

Hübschmannová, Milena (1972). "What Can Sociology Suggest about Origins of the Rom." _Archiv Orientální_. Prague.

Nečas, Ctibor (1939–1945). _Osudy Českych a Slovenský ch Cikánů_. Brno: UJEP.

Romské Obyvatelstvo Podle Sčítání Lidu, Domů a Bytů (1970). Prague: Federal Statisticky Urad.

MILENA HÜBSCHMANNOVÁ

Saami

ETHNONYMS: Saami, Sámi, Sapmi; formerly Fenni, "Finn," Lapp

Orientation

Identification. Saami speak various dialects of the Saami language, and/or the national languages, within northern Norway, Sweden, Finland, and Russia's Kola Peninsula, and nominally follow the religions of the dominant society. "Sapmi," or "Same-eatnam," refers to traditional Saami regions others have called "Lapland." The terms "Lapp" and "Lapland" were used mainly by non-Saami, and the derivations of both "Lapp" and "Saami" are contested. Contemporary areas designated "Finnmark" and "Lappmark" constitute but a small portion of Sapmi.

Location. Saami inhabit much of the tundra, taiga, and coastal zones north of 62° N in Norway and Sweden, 66° N in Finland, and 67° N on the Kola peninsula. These arctic and subarctic regions enjoy a climate moderated by the gulf stream, with winters seldom dipping below −40° C (in the far north, without sun for up to two months), and summers occasionally reaching 25° C (sometimes with midnight sun for up to two months).

Demography. There have been no adequate censuses of Saami. Any estimate of their population depends on the operational definition of Saamihood as much as on quality of sampling, but they number very roughly 1 percent of the populations in their overarching countries. Representative figures around 1982 suggest a total of 40,000 to 60,000 in Norway, 15,000 in Sweden, 4,000 in Finland, and less than 2,000 in Russia—of which about 70 percent speaks Saami and 10 percent breeds reindeer. All in all, the roughly 7,000 Saami dependent on reindeer management as a livelihood herd and husband around 450,000 head. While the majority of Saami resides in the traditional northern regions, the largest concentrations of Saami are today in their national capital cities, to which migration has been most intense in the period since World War II.

Linguistic Affiliation. The Saami language is in the Western Division of the Finno-Ugric Branch of the Uralic Family. Its closest linguistic relatives include Finnish, Estonian, Livonian, Votic, Veps, Mordvin, Mari, and Permian. Northern, southern, and eastern dialects of Saami mirror traditional habits of resource utilization, cutting across contemporary national boundaries. Saami inflection (of nouns, verbs, pronouns, and adjectives) involves infixes, from alteration of intersyllabic consonant values as well as suffixes. Morphology is highly productive through noun-noun apposition, nuanced verbal and adverbial forms, prepositions, postpositions, and other deictic constructions. Stress is on the first and alternating syllables. Orthographies inspired by Scandinavian, Finnish, and Russian conventions were first devised and disseminated by missionaries in the sixteenth century. Mid-twentieth century efforts for Nordic Saami solidarity have resulted in refinement and consolidation of these orthographies by linguists and native speakers. This writing system follows the Roman alphabet with supplemental symbols and diacritics.

History and Cultural Relations

Hunting and gathering ancestors of present-day herding, farming, fishing, mixed-economy, and entrepreneurial Saami entered northern Fennoscandia from the east by several routes and separate migrations and over several millennia. During these waves, Saami traversed some areas already sparsely settled by other peoples and languages before establishing themselves in present-day Sapmi. Here, cultural and linguistic contact arose with the later northern movements of Scandinavian, Finnish, and Russian peoples in the current era. Earliest contacts in the historic period came through traders, tax collectors, and missionaries. Periods of intense proselytization and forced assimilation led some individual Saami as well as whole regional groups into the dominant national culture and language, facilitated by the phenotypic indistinguishability of the Saami. More pluralistic national policies in the late twentieth century have stemmed the trend of assimilation. Saami today have full rights as citizens and participate in the same educational, religious, and political institutions as other members of their dominant cultures, at the same time as they actively champion their ethnic status.

Settlements

Saami settlements range in size and permanence, since part of the population is seasonally nomadic. More permanent villages and towns range from a few families to a few thousand individuals. In the latter case, Saami inhabitants may be in the minority, being interspersed with members of the dominant culture, some of very recent entry. Both encampments and settlements are predicated on local resource utilization, and are often along waterways affording access by boat in summer and by sled and snowmobile on winter ice. Contemporary transportation relaxes these constraints on settlement, at the same time as social conventions such as schooling and consumer habits impose other demands and opportunities leading to centralization. In the literature, occasionally "village" refers to a reindeer-herding, an administrative, or a territorial unit, rather than to a settlement per se.

Various forms of permanent and portable housing exist, often juxtaposed in the same settlement or even on the same household plot. Earlier types of construction include tents, sod huts, and frame dwellings, and these persist as homes (or are diverted to other purposes such as storage of food and equipment, smoking of meat and fish, or work stations). Contemporary homes are built to national standards, with central heating and running water; social life centers on the kitchen. Particularly in the more mobile reindeer-breeding segment of the population, some families manage more than one permanent dwelling and numerous portable ones. The tents and huts are round, organized around a central, usually open, fire. Any bare ground will be covered first with birch twigs and then by reindeer hides. Small items such as cooking utensils are stored in one or more chests opposite the entry.

Economy

Subsistence and Commercial Activities. The reindeer is best described as semidomesticated and half wild. Dogs assist in reindeer herding and are sometimes kept as pets. Less frequently, goats may provide milk for household consumption. Commercial farmers may raise sheep and cattle. Pets other than dogs are seldom encountered. Originally hunters, especially of wild reindeer, some Saami converted to domestic reindeer breeding in the most recent half-millennium. Today, several forms of reindeer management, all essentially oriented to a cash market, support as much as 35 percent of the population in some regions, while other regions have only some combination of farming, fishing, hunting, and commercial activity. Even though reindeer management is a minority occupation of this ethnic minority group, it has largely shaped the stereotype of Saamihood and has been recognized in law as the only justification for special Saami rights. Through both indigenous identification with the reindeer and extrinsic policies controlling but also privileging reindeer management, this occupation continues to be an emblem of the Saami despite some ambivalence and even resentment by the sedentary majority of Saami and other northern dwellers. Farming centers on sheep- and bovine-meat production and some dairy cattle; these animals require shelter and provisioning up to eight months a year. No grains other than barley thrive at these latitudes, but potatoes have been grown since their arrival in the early 1800s. Freshwater fishing focuses on salmon, char, trout, and whitefish, the smaller species available year-round and not just in the open water of summer. Ocean fishing brings in greater quantities of cod, halibut, haddock, coalfish, and sole. Some Saami hunt ptarmigan, small mammals, European elk, and reindeer predators. Wild berries, abundant in season, are collected by all.

Industrial Arts and Trade. Reindeer hide, antler, and bone provide raw materials for footwear, clothing, and utensils. Saami men etch distinctive decorations on the antler sheaths of their knives. Wood is also an important material, especially burls from birch for the carving of shallow cups and containers. Basketry and root-weaving artisans execute utilitarian and decorative wares, and other specialists spin pewter thread to be sewn onto leather and fabric. All these naturally harvested products and manufactures are used in the household; they are also sold commercially and used in barter between sedentary and nomadic Saami and among Saami generally, with local and distant non-Saami, and with tourists. The post-World-War II road system has promoted the increase of communications, services, circulation of goods, tourism, and nonindigenous resource extraction. Larger towns have local shops and national chains as well as municipal offices, slaughterhouses, handicraft centers, and museums.

Division of Labor. Today, the sexual division of labor is both more and less pronounced than in earlier times. Reindeer herding and husbandry now falls more into the hands of men, while women are tied down by the need to maintain and utilize the conveniences of modern housing, compulsory schooling for their children, and transportation. In the farming sector, women do most chores with seasonal assistance by men, who may spend other seasons in hunting, fishing, and/or wage labor. Overall, women do the majority of crafts with soft materials, men with hard materials; men slaughter; both genders cook and tend children; men control snowmobiles and women cars. It is common for at least one member of each family to contribute a wage income to the household

economy. Higher education and nontraditional professions especially attract sedentary men and nomadic women.

Land Tenure. The Saami reindeer-grazing regions of Fennoscandia are divided into administrative units, only sometimes commensurate with traditional utilization practices. The nation-states grant the Saami special resource privileges (including reindeer grazing, hunting, fishing, and use of timber) on these crown and public lands. However, state ownership of these lands is still contested by Saami organizations. Saami immemorial rights of usufruct have been confirmed in a number of important court cases. The issue of Saami land rights has continually been investigated by government commissions and brought before international courts of law. With but few exceptions, reindeer management is a right reserved for Saami in Norway and Sweden. Any Finnish citizen living in the Finnish reindeer herding region has the right to manage reindeer. On the Kola Peninsula, Saami herders mix with those of other native herding peoples.

Kinship

Kin Groups and Descent. Traditionally, the basic kin group in the reindeer-management sector has been based on a flexible and seasonally fluctuating affiliation, usually consisting of consanguineal kin of the same generation living in a loosely defined territory. This kin group is called a _siida_. Variations of the siida organization persist today, though often subsumed by larger extrinsic units. Individuals resort to a kindred-type structure in locating friends, mates, assistance, and godparents. Descent is bilateral.

Kinship Terminology. Kinship terminology is bifurcate in first ascending generation, with special terms for mother's older and younger sisters and for father's older and younger brothers. Cousins are classified as semisiblings, both differentiated by gender. Classificatory grandmother and grandfather terms generalize when addressing and referring to older persons. Affines have marked terms. Most individuals will be related to each other by more than one consanguineal, affinal, or fictive kinship link.

Marriage and Family

Marriage. Marriage is monogamous. Sometimes cross cousins or double cross cousins marry, which is advantageous for nucleation of herding groups. Constraints on marriage include compatibility of the partners' subsistence bases. The merging of two large reindeer livestock holdings or two very small holdings would each be marginally viable arrangements (given some combination of labor requirements, pasturage availability, and herd controllability), as would be the marriage of two persons having the responsibilities associated with ultimogeniture, or two persons committed to incommensurable livelihoods. Within these limits, individuals usually choose their own mates, marrying sometimes after a family has been started. Postmarital residence is neolocal, although flexible, as in the case of an ultimogeniture heir apparent, who remains at home. When a newly formed family continues in the subsistence livelihood of one or another of the spouses, they reside so as to take advantage of their familiarity with the area. Divorce seldom occurs, either formally or informally.

Domestic Unit. The domestic unit is the nuclear family, from which individuals disperse and regroup (also across household lines) owing to activities requiring constant mobility.

Inheritance. In reindeer-breeding families, each individual, regardless of age or gender, owns livestock. Saami inheritance is constrained by the various practices of the dominant society. Following Saami tradition, however, inheritance of parental dwellings, plots, livestock, resource-utilization locations, and other wealth—as well as the responsibility of caring for elderly parents—will commonly fall to the youngest child.

Socialization. Children learn at their own pace through opportunistic imitation. They are seldom explicitly instructed or disciplined. Versatility and individuality are rewarded.

Sociopolitical Organization

Social Organization. Saami society is open, fluid, acephalous, and relatively egalitarian. Members of the reindeer-breeding sector enjoy higher prestige within the society and more attention from without. In some regions dominated by non-Saami, the ranking has placed the reindeer breeders last. In their core areas, the nomadic and sedentary sectors integrate symbiotically. Saami reside in parliamentary democracies with and without constitutional monarchies, as well as in the former USSR. When expeditious, Saami can appear to defer to the national majority culture.

Political Organization. In earlier times, the largest though noncorporate group, the siida, was based on resource utilization, and its consensual leader was, and still can be, active, but only in unusual circumstances. Although poorly represented in the governing structures of contemporary society, Saami have initiated a number of their own general- and special-interest organizations, the latter responsive to subsistence interests. Saami have also been active participants in the fourth-world movement since its inception in the early 1970s.

Social Control. Until the eighteenth century, social control was informal and relatively nonproblematic. In the absence of any hierarchical regulating mechanisms, some disturbances such as reindeer theft could escalate. With the court and religious systems of the encroaching dominant societies, Saami found alternatives in formal administration and litigation while maintaining informal controls through persuasion, gossip, sorcery, and relocation (forced or voluntary).

Conflict. Saami history reveals little endemic conflict other than competition, often between reindeer-breeding units. The exception was a massacre in 1852 in which the two victims were non-Saami. In recent times, however, conflict is more prominent, centering on protests of encroachments on Saami areas through resource extraction (hydroelectric power, mining, logging), by communication networks (roads, snowmobile routes, boat and air lines, and power lines), through usurpation of land (by recreational, tourist, and military activities), and by pollution (most recently nuclear contamination from Chernobyl).

Religion and Expressive Culture

Religious Beliefs. The ecstatic shamanic tradition has been subsumed but not utterly eradicated by state churches, whose missionizing nominally converted most Saami by the end of the eighteenth century. Most Saami belong to the evangelical Lutheran faith of the dominant culture, while some retain a nineteenth-century syncretic institution named Laestadianism after its charismatic founder.

According to Saami traditions, various spirits reside in and around prominent geographical locales, such as natural outcroppings and encampment sites. The shamanic drum of old commemorated a host of cosmological forces associated with space, time, weather, animals, and social categories. Saami folklore contains abundant references to people of the underworld and a giant troll-like figure. Other spirits correspond to once-living beings, as do ghosts of infanticide casualties.

Religious Practitioners. Male pastors from the dominant society service most Lutheran churches in Saami areas; Laestadian practitioners are usually recruited from the Saami and Finnish populations. Laestadian practitioners also perform in the folk-medicine arena, and are male. Self-styled shamans of both genders serve the medical and sorcery needs of their kin, friends, neighbors, and trading partners. Not all healers are shamans, however, and not all shamans are healers.

Ceremonies. The most elaborate ceremony in former times, congruent with that of other circumpolar peoples, was associated with the bear hunt. The Saami observe the regular Christian life-cycle rituals. Laestadian meetings are held in some of the same places as church services and also in secular buildings and homes. Healing rituals, whether Laestadian or shamanic, usually take place in the home of a patient or during a meeting.

Arts. Most utilitarian arts and crafts are done by all, while specialists such as knife makers, basket makers, and silversmiths render decorative wares. Summer tourism and year-round exports have become important in the local economy. To protect themselves against imitation, Saami handicraft professionals mark their produce with a special seal. A number of Saami have attained international recognition in nontraditional graphic art forms and literature. The vocal arts are represented by the chantlike *yoik*, which has become a recognized musical form.

Medicine. Indigenous beliefs and practices (such as the stopping of blood) are grounded in the knowledge and skills of the patient, a family member, or a shaman. Remedies are readily available in nature for human, reindeer, and dog maladies. In addition and within limits, these sparsely settled outlying regions receive medical and veterinary services in line with those of the rest of the country.

Death and Afterlife. Saami have a higher-than-average incidence of cardiovascular disease; males in their early years are at risk for accidental death, and in earlier times, a certain toll was taken by childbirth. Barring such mortality, Saami are often active in their 80s. In the past, if burdensome to the family, the elderly boarded with sedentary people, wandered off, or were left behind to die. The funeral and burial follow national custom, usually Lutheran. Saami do not speculate much about afterlife. In pre-Christian and earlier Christian times, when frozen or rocky terrain precluded burial, interment or temporary interment utilized trees and cairns.

Bibliography

Anderson, Myrdene (1978). *Saami Ethnoecology: Resource Management in Norwegian Lapland*. Ann Arbor, Mich.: University Microfilms.

Beach, Hugh (1981). *Case of Tuorpon Saameby in Northern Sweden*. Uppsala Studies in Cultural Anthropology, 3. Uppsala: Almqvist & Wiksell.

Ingold, Tim (1976). *Skolt Lapps Today*. Cambridge: Cambridge University Press.

Paine, Robert (1965). *Coast Lapp Society*. Vol. 2, *Study of Economic Development and Social Values*. Oslo: Universitetsforlaget.

Pelto, Pertti J. (1962). *Individualism in Skolt Lapp Society*. Kansatieteellinen Arkisto, 16. Helsinki: Suomen Muinaismuistoyhdistys.

Vorren, Ornulv, and Ernest Manker (1962). *Lapp Life and Customs*. Oxford: Oxford University Press.

MYRDENE ANDERSON AND HUGH BEACH

Sarakatsani

ETHNONYM: Vlachs

Orientation

Identification. The Sarakatsani are transhumant sheep- and goatherders of continental Greece. Their non-Sarakatsani neighbors refer to them as "Vlachs," a reference to their seasonal migrations in search of pasturage for their flocks. This term is, however, misleading, for it suggests a cultural or linguistic relationship with the Kousovlachs and Albanian Vlachs, ethnic minorities who speak an entirely different language than the Greek dialect used by the Sarakatsani.

Location. Sarakatsani live in the Pindus massif and the southern fringes of the Rhodope mountain range of northwestern continental Greece. They are found in greatest numbers in the provinces of Epirus, Thessaly, Macedonia, and Thrace. The demands of their sheepherding life-style require them to spend half the year (May to November) high in the mountains, until the winter snows set in and they have to seek the more benign climate of the coastal plains on which to graze their flocks.

Demography. Census data do not specify figures for the Sarakatsani as a discrete group; firm population figures are not available. In the late 1950s their number was estimated to be somewhere in the vicinity of 80,000 throughout Greece.

Linguistic Affiliation. The Sarakatsani speak a local dialect of Greek.

History and Cultural Relations

Linguistic, cultural, and historical evidence indicates that the Sarakatsani descend from pre-Classical pastoralists indigenous to the region in which they are found today. However, this evidence is by no means conclusive. There is a dearth of references to any peoples called Sarakatsani in any chronicles, even up to the eighteenth century. Scholarly interest in the Sarakatsani only arose around the time of the Balkan Wars (1912–1913). Competition for the territory on which they grazed their sheep was played out by larger political interests: the Turks and Greeks have long vied for control over the region, and the Ottomans only ceded the last portion of the territory to Greece in 1913. Throughout these struggles between the larger political units, the Sarakatsani maintained their identity as Christians and preserved their pastoral lifestyle, although not without a few concessions to the administrative demands of the national units under which they lived. Since the early part of this century, the Sarakatsani have been subject to Greek administration, which has had both positive and negative effects upon their way of life.

Settlements

Traditional Sarakatsani settlements were located on or near their leased grazing lands both during summers and winters. Dwellings were of two types, with the most characteristic being a domed hut, framed of branches and covered with thatch. The second type was a wood-beamed, thatched, rectangular structure. In both types, the centerpiece of the dwelling was a stone hearth. The floors and walls were plastered with mud and mule dung. Since the late 1930s, national requirements for the registration of citizens has led many if not most Sarakatsani to adopt as legal residence the villages associated with summer grazing lands, and many Sarakatsani have since bought houses in such villages. During the winter, however, their settlement patterns still follow the more traditional configuration: a group of cooperating households, generally linked by ties of kinship or marriage, build their houses in a cluster on flat land close to the leased pasturage, with supporting structures (for the cheese merchant and cheese maker) nearby. Pens for goats and folds for newborn lambs and nursing ewes are built close to the settlement. This complex is called the *stani*, a term also used to refer to the cooperative group sharing the leased land.

Economy

Sarakatsani life centers year-round on the needs of their flocks. The demands of this pastoralist economy vary with the seasons, with winter being by far the most arduous and time-consuming because lambing occurs then. The protection and general care of the flocks, shearing, and milking are done by the men and boys. The women are responsible for building the dwellings, sheepfolds, and goat pens for the care of newborn lambs and kids, for child care and the domestic tasks of cooking and sewing, as well as for preparing, spinning, and dying the shorn wool. In addition, women try to keep chickens, the eggs of which provide them with their only personal source of income. That income is used to purchase dyes in the village. In summer villages, women keep household vegetable gardens, and in winter women and girls gather wild vegetables and herbs to supplement the family diet. The pasturage used by a stani is leased, with the head of each participating family paying a share at the end of each season to the stani leader (*tselingas*), in whose name the lease was originally taken.

Kinship

The Sarakatsani kindred is a bilaterally reckoned extension of the conjugal family: the descendants of a man's maternal and paternal grandparents provide the field from which his recognized kin are drawn. There is, however, a strong patrilineal bias, and when reckoning descent—as opposed to determining contemporary family relationships—lineage membership is calculated along the paternal line alone. Contemporary kin relationships are not counted beyond the degree of the second cousin. Within the kindred, the family constitutes the significant unit and is, unlike the larger network of personal relations of the kindred, a corporate group.

Marriage and Family

Marriage.   Sarakatsani marriages are arranged, with the initiative in such arrangements taken by the family of the prospective husband in consultation with members of the kindred. There can be no marriage between two members of the same kindred. The bride must bring with her into the marriage a dowry of household furnishings, clothing, and, more recently, sheep or their cash equivalent. The husband's contribution to the wealth of the new household is his share in the flocks held by his father, but these remain held in common by his paternal joint household until some years after his marriage. The newly established couple initially takes up residence near the husband's family of origin. Divorce is unknown and remarriage after widowhood is unthinkable.

Domestic Unit.   The extended family has at its core a conjugal pair, and includes their unmarried offspring, and, often, their young married sons and their wives.

Inheritance.   Inheritance, considered as the disposition of an individual's property and wealth at the time of his or her death, is largely through males: sons inherit a share of the flocks and property owned by their fathers and mothers. However, household goods may pass to daughters, and prestige—or lack thereof—of the family is visited on all surviving offspring, regardless of gender.

Socialization.   When children are very young, child care is the province of the mother. When boys are old enough to help with the flocks, they accompany their fathers and are taught the skills they will someday need. Similarly, girls learn through observing and assisting their mothers.

Sociopolitical Organization

Social Organization.   The Sarakatsani kindred constitutes a network of shared obligations and, to a degree, cooperation in situations concerning the honor of its members. Within the summer villages they are conscious, as well, of their opposition to non-Sarakatsani neighbors. However, the organizational unit of most profound importance is that smaller collection of kin and affines that constitutes the stani, for survival depends upon the members of this group. Care of the flocks requires, minimally, the cooperative efforts of five or so active, adult men.

Political Organization.   The Sarakatsani do not constitute an independent political unit within the larger Greek polity, nor even within the local village. Dealings with authorities, whether local or national, tend to be conducted in terms of patronage, which is sought, and extended, to individual families.

Social Control and Conflict.   The concept of "honor" is of great importance to the Sarakatsani. The behavior of any member of a family reflects back upon all its members. Therefore, the avoidance of negative public opinion, particularly as expressed in gossip, provides a strong incentive to live up to the values and standards of propriety held by the community as a whole. Men have as their duty the protection of the family's honor, and are therefore watchful of the behavior of the rest of the household. In the wider field of village and national interests, the Sarakatsani are subject to local statutes and Greek law.

Religion and Expressive Culture

Religious Beliefs.   The Sarakatsani are Christian and associated with the Greek Orthodox Church. However, their participation in the institutional forms of the church is not particularly marked. Although not particularly concerned with formal participation, Sarakatsani believe strongly in the concepts of God the Father, Christ, and the Virgin Mary. God is seen in strongly paternalistic terms, as protector and provider, as judge and as punisher of evil deeds. Folk beliefs in such things as the "evil eye," and in a complex of Panhellenic spirits, are interwoven with Christian beliefs. On the whole, religious life centers upon the family rather than the church, except for the observance of specific feast days in the liturgical calendar. Each hut shelters an icon or icons upon which family devotions focus.

Religious Practitioners.   The family is thought to be a reflection of the relationship expressed among God, the Virgin, and Christ. The father, as family head, is thus responsible for the spiritual life of the family. The Sarakatsani do not have formally recognized religious practitioners, and each household constitutes an autonomous religious community. There is a belief in the efficacy of magic (e.g., in the casting or warding off of the evil eye). Again, however, there are no formally recognized magical specialists among the Sarakatsani.

Ceremonies.   The Sarakatsani honor the feast days of Saint George and Saint Demetrius, which fall just before the seasonal migrations in spring and early winter, respectively. For Saint George's feast day, a family kills a lamb in the saint's honor, a ritual that also marks Christmas and the Feast of the Assumption. Easter week is the most important ritual period in Sarakatsani religious life. Other ceremonial events, outside the formal Christian calendar, are weddings and funerals.

Arts.   Sarakatsani folk art consists of song, dance, poetry, and some decorative sculpture in wood, as well as elaborate embroidery such as that which adorns their traditional costume. Principal motives used in sculpture and embroidery are geometrical shapes and human and plant representations.

Medicine. The Sarakatsani employ a number of folk remedies that make use of herbs, honey, lamb's blood, or a combination thereof.

Death and Afterlife. Funerals are ritual occasions that involve not only the immediate family of the deceased but also the members of the larger kindred. Funerary practice is consistent with that of the church. Mourning is most marked among the women, and most of all by the widow. Beliefs in the afterlife are conditioned by the teachings of the church, though flavored to some degree by traditions deriving from pre-Christian folk religion.

Bibliography

Campbell, J. K. (1964). _Honour, Family, and Patronage: A Study of Institutions and Moral Values in a Greek Mountain Community._ Oxford: Clarendon Press.

Kabbadias, Georgios B. (1965). _Nomadic Shepherds of the Mediterranean: The Sarakatsani of Greece._ Translated by Frieda Shütze. Paris: Gauthier-Villars.

NANCY E. GRATTON

Sardinians

ETHNONYMS: i Sardi (Italian), su Populu Sardu (Sardinian)

Orientation

Identification. Sardinians are the inhabitants of the island of Sardinia, today an autonomous region of Italy. Sardinians see themselves as a distinct ethnic group while being Italian by nationality.

Location. The island of Sardinia lies in the central Mediterranean Sea, 184 kilometers north of the African coast, 208 kilometers west of the Italian port city of Civitavecchia, and separated from Corsica to the north by the 11-kilometer-wide Straits of Bonifacio. With an area of 24,090 square kilometers, Sardinia is the second-largest Mediterranean island, after Sicily. The island consists primarily of mountainous plateaus, rising gradually from the west and forming the Gennargentu Range in east-central Sardinia, with its highest peak, Punta La Marmora, at 1,834 meters; the eastern plateaus plunge dramatically into the sea. Most of the land area of Sardinia is unsuitable for agriculture; the most important exception is the Campidano Plain, a corridor of fertile lowlands in the southwest stretching from the Gulf of Cagliari to the Gulf of Oristano. Forests, too, cover a relatively small area; most of these are of cork oaks, an important natural resource of the island. Two-thirds of the island is covered by the degraded vegetation characteristic of the Mediterranean, called maquis (Italian, _macchia_), much of which is suitable for pastoralism.

Sardinia has a typical Mediterranean climate of mild, wet winters and hot, dry summers. At lower elevations, from sea level to 450 meters, the summer drought can last five months, although above 900 meters the dry period is reduced to three months. The mean annual rainfall (at Cagliari, sea-level) is 48 centimeters; however, the amount of rainfall is highly variable from year to year.

Demography. Sardinia has roughly 1.6 million inhabitants and is the least densely populated region of Italy. The two main urban centers are Cagliari, the regional and provincial capital in the south, and Sassari, a provincial capital in the north; the two other provincial capitals, Oristano and Nuoro, are rapidly growing towns that serve as local urban centers.

Linguistic Affiliation. Most Sardinians speak standard Italian as well as their local Sardinian language, although Sardinian is now declining in urban areas. Sardinian is a family of related dialects that derive from the ancient Latin of the Romans. There is no standard form of Sardinian. There are small pockets of populations that speak other colonial languages, such as Catalonian Spanish, which is still spoken in Alghero.

History and Cultural Relations

Sardinia has been inhabited since prehistoric times. The primary evidence of the proto-Sardic people and culture are the _nuraghi_, ancient, conical-shaped stone dwellings, of which about 6,500 have been identified; little else is known about these original Sardinians. The Phoenicians, mainly interested in trade, established peaceful contacts with the Sardinians around 1000 B.C. They were followed by the Carthaginians during the sixth century B.C., who warred with the Sardinians and conquered much of the island, as did the Romans from 238 B.C.; these two periods of domination were militarily, economically, and politically quite similar. The changes imposed by these powers have influenced the development of the island ever since. Interested only in exploiting the fertile plains and mineral-rich hills, the invaders conquered and occupied only the lowland areas, where latifundist estates and mines were established. The indigenous peoples either were subjugated or sought refuge in the highlands, which the Romans called "the land of the barbarians," the region known as Barbagia today. Thus Sardinia was divided into two socioeconomic subregions: the foreign-dominated agricultural lowlands and the independent but impoverished agropastoral highlands; this separation has characterized Sardinia until present times. The Vandals conquered Sardinia in A.D. 455, but throughout their eighty-year domination they, too, failed to penetrate the mountain refuge areas. Sardinia became a province of Byzantium in A.D. 534; by the eighth century, however, the authorities began gradually to withdraw, ushering in a period of autonomous government, an indigenous renaissance based on communal landholdings and administration by local assemblies of freemen. The absence of a strong military power on the island was a temptation to both the pirates and the pope: Pisa and Genoa allied with the Sardinians to oust the Arabs, staying on to compete among themselves for dominance. From 1323 to 1478, Aragon fought for control of the island, initiating four centuries of Spanish domination. Spanish feudalism was essentially parasitic, feeding an absentee aristocracy, which led to economic isolation and stagnation in Sardinia; Spanish exploitation primarily took the form of taxation, which left communities relatively free to organize production according to traditional forms. Thus, the subsistence-oriented economies based on agriculture in the lowlands and pastoralism in the highlands persisted in Sardinia much longer than in the rest of Europe, and the island became more and more of an underdeveloped backwater. In the nineteenth century, Sardinia passed to Savoy under treaty, and was incorporated into the Italian state with unification in 1860. The greatest changes in Sardinian society have been since World War II, as the Italian state has instituted policies to stimulate development and modernization throughout the *mezzogiorno* (southern Italy).

Settlements

The majority of the population lives in nucleated settlements situated away from the coasts, with a typical village having between 1,500 and 4,000 inhabitants. The coasts were largely abandoned until modern times, both because malaria (endemic until 1952) was more prevalent in the low-lying coastal areas and because inland villages were safer from pirate attacks, which were common until the early 1800s. Cagliari, with its excellent natural harbor and centuries-old urban tradition, is a notable exception to this rule. Sardinian houses, which may reach several stories high, were constructed of unmortared stone; cement blocks are more common today, however.

Economy

Subsistence and Commercial Activities. In the highlands, subsistence was based on pastoralism and small-scale agriculture. In the lowlands, agriculture was more intensive and livestock of less importance. Sheep and goats provided milk, which was processed into cheese; chickens laid eggs; household gardens provided vegetables and fruits; vineyards yielded grapes, which were made into wine; olive trees were harvested to produce oil; and grain was sown for bread. Pigs were raised, wild game hunted, and, occasionally, lambs slaughtered for meat. The local economy provided all the elements of a well-balanced diet; unfortunately, until recently, most villagers were too poor to enjoy such a variety. Fishing has never been a major part of the Sardinian subsistence or economy. Donkeys provided transportation and animal power for the lower classes, horses for the well-to-do. Cows were sometimes raised for milk and dogs were kept for hunting. Today, the traditional subsistence economy has been replaced by a market economy. Agriculture has diminished because only a few crops are profitable in competition with imports from the European Community (EC) and elsewhere. Pastoralism remains an important sector in the modern economy, although much of the milk is now sold to cooperatives that produce the distinctive *pecorino* sheep's cheese in modern dairies for sale and export.

Until recently, the Sardinian economy had been oriented primarily to subsistence, commerce was restricted to the dominating elites, and industry was limited to household handicrafts. Today, the service sector, including government employment and small business, employs more Sardinians than any other. Household handicrafts have all but disappeared, although a small-crafts industry produces items for the tourist and export markets. Industrialization has not been very successful in Sardinia, despite massive inputs from the central government. Mining (which is in decline) and petrochemical processing are the two major industries. Tourism is an important and expanding part of the economy in coastal areas.

Trade. Sardinia imports most manufactured goods and exports primary products (wine, cheese, vegetables) from the agro-pastoral sector. Sardinia also exports labor in the form of unemployed workers migrating to the industrial centers in northern Italy or west-central Europe and imports money in the form of subsidies, aid, pensions and remittances from migrant workers.

Division of Labor. The traditional division of labor was structured along gender lines. Men's roles were centered away from the home, while women's were centered in the home. Peasant men worked in the fields to grow the wheat while the women worked at home to transform it into bread. The shepherds who were away with the flocks most of the time were always male; the women worked closer to home, producing cheese, raising other domestic animals, and gardening. In pastoral communities, agricultural work was shared by both men and women, although some tasks were designated as male or female. Today, women are responsible for domestic tasks and child care. This division of labor is reflected symbolically in the community, where certain areas are designated as male territory (the bars, piazza, and pasture) and others as the female domain (the house and the neighborhood). The household is seen as having both a male and a female head, both recognized decision makers, the men directing activities outside of the household and the women inside, with the women storing, processing, and marketing much of the total product of men's and women's work, and, as well, mediating between the adult men of the household. Major economic expenditures are decided jointly.

Land Tenure. Land may be held privately or communally. In the agricultural lowlands most land is privately owned, but most of the pastoral communities have maintained some of their property as communal grazing land to which all village members have rights. Privately owned land is often rented out to the landless or those with inadequate land of their own.

Kinship, Marriage, and Family

Kin Groups and Descent. Kinship is an important factor in an individual's social network, but corporate kin groups do not exist. Descent is bilateral.

Marriage. Marriage is monogamous and indissoluble; divorce, although legal today, is rare. Marriage has been village-endogamous, but this custom is now in decline. In pastoral communities young people typically married late, the female average age being 25 and the male 35. A shepherd proved his ability to support a family by supplying the house, and (ideally) assuming independent control of a flock. Postmarital residence is neolocal with a preference for living near kin.

Domestic Unit. The household is the most fundamental unit in Sardinian society. The household is minimally composed of a husband and wife; no unmarried person leaves the natal household to live alone. Unmarried adults may form households with siblings or other close relatives; widows often live with their married daughters (but never with their married sons), while widowers with no unmarried close kin constitute the only category of individuals who typically live alone (but they will be cared for by a close female relative). All adult household members are expected to contribute to the household economy.

Inheritance. Property is divided equally between the surviving members of the nuclear family, including the spouse and all children. Inheritance may be divided before death, retaining only a portion for subsistence, which will be divided after death.

Socialization. The primary responsibility for socialization rests with the mother, although the father may be responsible for teaching his livelihood (e.g., shepherding) to his sons. The moral conduct of the children is considered to reflect on the mother most strongly. Socialization emphasizes one's community reputation and the fulfillment of one's social roles. For example, young boys are encouraged to spend their free time away from home with other young boys, and young girls are expected to spend their free time with other girls and women within the domestic/neighborhood sphere as much as possible. Both boys and girls risk ridicule if they fail to fulfill these gender-specific expectations.

Sociopolitical Organization

Social Organization. The most important social institutions in an individual's life are the household and the village/ _commune_, each with specific rights and obligations of membership. Social relations beyond the household consist primarily of ego-centered networks of individuals: much time and effort is expended to develop and maintain these kin and friendship networks as these provide the people to whom one turns in times of need. Shepherds and others whose occupations take them beyond village boundaries extend their networks to selected individuals in other villages and/or in regional centers. Collectively the shepherds of a region form a moral community called _noi pastori_, "we shepherds," which sets the norms within which cooperation and competition in the pastures take place. Relations between poorer and richer and less and more powerful take the form of patron-client ties.

Political Organization. Sardinia is an autonomous region of Italy, the regional government having limited authority over internal affairs. The region is divided into four provinces. The lowest level in the hierarchy of authority is the commune, one or two settlements and an associated territory, which democratically elects a council to govern local affairs. Affiliation to regional and national political parties— Christian Democrats, Socialists, Communists, Sardinian Nationalists—often corresponds to alliances and factions in villages and vertical patronage ties to government authorities.

Social Control. At the community level, social control is primarily informal, directed toward the high cultural value accorded to one's honor, or social reputation, which is based upon fulfilling social obligations toward others and effectively protecting the resources of one's family (but not focused upon the "purity" of women). Gossip is therefore an important element of social control. This is effective because one's social networks rest on one's honor: a man without honor is a man without friends and without support in difficult times. In fact, in the highland areas, the code of honor continues a complex legal tradition, including the ethics of sheep rustling

and the _vendetta_, retaliation against another family for offences against the property and well-being of one's own family. Today, these local traditions of social control are often in conflict with the state-level controls, national law and police enforcement; the traditional forms of social control persist, however, because the people continue to find them more effective than state intervention.

Religion and Expressive Culture

Religious Beliefs and Practices. Sardinia was converted to Christianity in the Middle Ages and continues to be predominantly Roman Catholic. Every village has one or several churches. Religious ceremonies include both official church rituals and popular local feasts (_feste_), such as saint's day celebrations. Life-cycle rituals continue to be church-sponsored, even among Sardinians who are otherwise not active in religious affairs.

Arts. Local handicrafts such as weaving, basketry, woodwork, and leatherwork are still appreciated by most Sardinians, but are today the work of specialists. Sardinian music and poetry also continue to be popular. New art forms are also being incorporated, often in such distinctive ways as the politically inspired murals painted on houses in many villages and towns.

Bibliography

Angioni, Giulio (1982). _Rapporti di produzione e cultura subalterna: Contadini in Sardegna_. Cagliari: Editrice Democratica Sarda.

Berger, Allen (1986). "Cooperation, Conflict, and Production Environment in Highland Sardinia: A Study of the Associational Life of Transhumant Shepherds." Ph.D. dissertation, Columbia University.

Brigaglia, Manlio, ed. (1982). _La Sardegna enciclopedia_. 3 vols. Cagliari: Edizioni della Torre. Reprint. 1988.

Meloni, Benedetto (1984). _Famiglie di pastori_. Turin: Rosenberg & Sellier.

Moss, David (1979). "Bandits and Boundaries in Sardinia." _Man_, n.s. 14:477–496.

Schweizer, Peter (1988). _Shepherds, Workers, Intellectuals: Culture and Centre-Periphery Relationships in a Sardinian Village_. Stockholm Studies in Social Anthropology, no. 18. University of Stockholm.

Weingrod, Alex, and Emma Morin (1971). "'Post-Peasants': The Character of Contemporary Sardinian Society." _Comparative Studies in Society and History_ 13:301–324.

LISA-MARLENE EDELSWARD AND PHILIP CARL SALZMAN

Scandinavian Peripatetics

ETHNONYMS: Finnish Kaale, Natmandsfolk (Denmark), Tatere (Norway), Tattare (Sweden)

People identified as Gypsies began arriving in the Scandinavian countries as early as 1500. Today, peoples traditionally identified as either Gypsies or Travellers are found in Denmark, Finland, Norway, and Sweden. Population estimates covering both groups for the early 1980s are: 1,000–1,500 (Denmark); 5,000–7,000 (Finland); 250–500 (Norway); and 6,000–10,000 (Sweden).

Soon after their arrival in Scandinavia, these peoples experienced the same discrimination as in other nations. Sweden first enacted discriminatory laws in 1560, and banished all peripatetics in 1637. They were afforded full legal rights only in 1954. The same pattern holds for Denmark, which began persecutions in 1536, Norway, whose persecutions began in 1687, and Finland, which moved Gypsies to the Russian border in 1660. Peripatetic peoples in these countries are now largely settled, and discrimination has eased. In the mid-1960s, the Gypsy population of Denmark was increased by people migrating from Yugoslavia. In 1973 the Nordic Council of Romanies was founded, which served as an umbrella organization for other smaller associations representing Gypsy and Traveller groups in the Scandinavian countries.

Bibliography

Alanen, I. (1970). *The Gypsies of Finland*. Helsinki: Helsinki University.

Barth, F. (1955). "The Social Organization of a Pariah Group in Norway." *Norveg* 5:125-143.

Gronfors, M. (1977). *Blood Feuding among Finnish Gypsies*. Research Report no. 21, Department of Sociology, University of Helsinki.

Gronfors, M. (1979). *Ethnic Minorities and Deviance: The Relationship between Finnish Gypsies and the Police*. Helsinki: Helsingin Yliopisto.

Mohammed-Salih, M. (1985). "The Position of Gypsies in Finnish Society." Ph.D. Thesis, University of Manchester, England.

Takman, J. (1976). *The Gypsies in Sweden: A Soci-Medical Study*. Stockholm: LiberForlag.

Trankell, I., and A. Trankell (1968). "Problems of the Swedish Gypsies." *Scandinavian Journal of Education Research* 12:141-214.

Sephardic Jews

ETHNONYM: Oriental Jews

Orientation

Strictly speaking, Sephardic Jews (singular, Sephardi; plural, Sephardim) are descendants of Jews who lived in Spain or Portugal before they were expelled from the former in 1492. The name "Sephardim" is derived from "Sephard," the term used by Jews in medieval times to refer to the Iberian Peninsula. Also included in the Sephardic category are Conversos (Marranos, New Christians, Judeos, Chuetas), Jews who were forced to convert to Catholicism in Spain and Portugal but continued to practice Judaism and maintain their Jewish identity in secret. Today, the label "Sephardic Jew" is often used in a broader sense to include all Jews who follow Sephardic religious practice, as contrasted with those who follow Ashkenazic traditions. Because of the dissemination of Sephardic publications and, after 1492, the resettlement of Sephardic Jews throughout the Middle East and North Africa, many Jews from these regions are today classified as Sephardim, whether or not they are descended from Jews from the Iberian Peninsula.

Language

One major distinction between Sephardic and Ashkenazic Jews was language. The language of Sephardic Judaism was Ladino (Judeo-Spanish, Judezmo, Hakatia), which originated in Spain and was later spoken in Sephardic communities in Turkey, North Africa, and the Balkans. Ladino is best described as a dialect of Castilian Spanish, with loanwords from Hebrew, Turkish, and other languages. Originally, Ladino was written with Hebrew characters and later with the Latin alphabet. It is unlikely that Ladino is now the day-to-day language in any Sephardic community, as most Sephardic Jews now speak the language of the nations where they live. However, there are individuals who still speak Ladino, and systematic efforts are under way to record the language. Sephardic Jews in Portugal and in diaspora communities mainly spoke Portuguese, although many also spoke Spanish.

Sephardic Judaism has an especially rich literature including religious works written in Hebrew, literature written in Spanish and Ladino, translations into Spanish and Ladino, political tracts written and translated into various languages, biblical commentaries, inspirational works, and a rich folk literature in Ladino, featuring ballads (*romancero*), a number of which have now been recorded and are still performed.

Location

Although the first date of Jewish settlement in Spain is unknown, it is believed that Jews lived on the Iberian Peninsula as early as Roman times. Between 100 and 300 C.E. large Jewish populations had settled in towns in southeastern Spain, and the region south of Cordoba became a region of major Jewish settlement. Jews lived as farmers and landowners under the Visigoths, but they also suffered various persecutions; in 689 all were reduced to the status of slaves. In 711

Arab Muslims conquered the region and granted Jews religious, though not complete economic or political, freedom, and the period described as the "golden age" of Spanish Jewry began. This golden age lasted roughly to near the end of the fourteenth century and saw the advancement of many Jews in instrumental roles as political advisers and physicians and the development of Sephardic Jewish traditions in poetry, literature, philosophy, and biblical interpretation. Jews were active participants in Spanish society, and many felt that they were Spanish as well as Jewish. In 1136 the practice of Judaism was prohibited and Jews began to suffer from increased persecution, although restrictions were less in the Christian north, where the community continued to thrive. But beginning in 1391, the Jewish community came under increasing pressure, entire communities disappeared, and the golden age ended. From that point on, the Spanish Jewish community was regularly persecuted: restrictions were placed on participation in public life, many were forced to convert to Christianity, Jews and their property were attacked, and they were finally expulsed from Spain in 1492. Estimates place the number of Jews who left Spain at anywhere from 50,000 to 250,000. Most went to lands in what was then the Ottoman Empire (modern-day Turkey, Greece, and the Balkans), Portugal, and Italy (especially northern Italy). In 1496 Portugal moved to expulse all Jews, but in 1497 substituted a policy of forced conversion. Near the close of the next century a second diaspora of Sephardic Jews took place, this time involving Conversos from Portugal who moved to the Netherlands, and later to England, northern Europe, and the New World. Some of these Conversos reestablished their Jewish identity, while others assimilated into the Christian population. The third major movement of the Sephardim has taken place since World War II, with the settlement of many Middle Eastern and North African Sephardim in Israel, immigration to the United States, and migration from North Africa to France and Spain.

If we use the broad definition of Sephardic Jew, the countries with the largest Sephardic populations in the 1980s (all figures are estimates) were Israel (1.7 million), the United States (350,000), and France (260,000). Other countries with large Sephardic populations include Argentina (34,000), Brazil (30,000), Italy (30,000), Turkey (22,000), Mexico (15,000), Morocco (13,000), and Spain (12,000). For the most part, in most countries of the New World (i.e., Argentina, Brazil, the United States) where Sephardic Jews (sometimes Conversos) formed the earliest Jewish communities, they are now far outnumbered by the descendants of Ashkenazic Jews whose ancestors arrived later. Similarly, diaspora communities founded by Conversos in Europe eventually disappeared as the Conversos either assimilated or reasserted their Jewish identity. However, Converso communities are reported as still existing in Mexico and on Majorca.

Religion

As with Ashkenazic Jews, Sephardim follow the Babylonian tradition, and they view the Babylonian Talmud as the ultimate guide to belief and practice. In matters involving religious law, Sephardim follow Joseph Caro's codification, the Shulhan Arukh, which is more permissive in many ways than Ashkenazic religious law. Sephardim and Ashkenazim differ not only in degree of permissiveness on some matters (espe-

cially dietary rules) but also in religious practice. Differences involve variations in religious garb for rabbis, the use of ritual decorations, the internal organization of the synagogue, texts recited at specific times, terms used for ritual objects and practices, melodies in chants, and the pronunciation of Hebrew. While many of these distinctions are minor, adherence to them by Sephardic Jews is today an important marker of Sephardic identity in a Jewish world largely dominated by the Ashkenazim. In Israel today, there are both Sephardic and Ashkenazic chief rabbis.

See also Andalusians

Bibliography

Bunis, David M. (1981). _Sephardic Studies: A Research Bibliography Incorporating Judezmo Language, Literature and Folklore, and Historical Background._ New York: Garland.

Elazar, Daniel J. (1989). _The Other Jews: The Sephardim Today._ New York: Basic Books.

Encyclopaedia Judaica (1971). New York: Macmillan.

Lerman, Antony (1989). _The Jewish Communities of the World._ London: Macmillan.

Moore, Kenneth (1977). _Those of the Street—The Catholic Jews of Mallorca._ South Bend, Ind.: University of Notre Dame Press.

Raphael, Chaim (1985). _The Road from Babylon: The Story of Sephardi and Oriental Jews._ New York: Harper & Row.

Speake, Graham (1984). _Atlas of the Jewish World._ New York: Facts on File.

Tapia, Claude (1986). _Les juifs sepharades en France, 1965–1985: Études psychosociologiques et historiques._ Paris: L'Harmattan.

DAVID LEVINSON

Serbs

ETHNONYM: Srbi

Orientation

Identification. Serbia is the larger of the two remaining republics that constitute the Federated Republic of Yugoslavia as of 1992. Ethnically homogeneous within Serbia proper, the republic also contains two autonomous provinces. The autonomous province of Vojvodina in the north is mainly Serbian but also contains large minorities of Romanians and Hungarians. The province of Kosmet (Kosovo-Metohija) is located in southern Serbia and has a majority Albanian Muslim population in which Serbs are a minority. Substantial Serbian populations live in the neighboring republic of Montenegro and in the independent states of Croatia and Bosnia and Herzegovina.

Location.   Serbia is bounded on the north by Hungary, on the east by Romania and Bulgaria, on the south by Albania and Macedonia, and on the west by the Yugoslav republic of Montenegro, Bosnia and Herzegovina, and Croatia. Its location is approximately 42–45° N and 19°30′–23° E. Geographically, Serbia is two-thirds highlands and one-third rolling plains. Šumadija, the agricultural heartland of Serbia, lies west of the Morava River valley, just south of Belgrade. The climate of the plains is markedly continental consisting of dry, warm summers, long, humid autumns, and cold, dry winters. The growing season begins in mid-March and runs through November. Average annual precipitation is 76 centimeters. Temperatures vary from an average high of 23° C in July to 1.6° C in January, the coldest month. Within these patterns, however, considerable variations exist, with recorded highs well over 38° C and lows down to below −10° C.

Demography.   The population of Yugoslavia in 1990 was estimated at 23,864,000. At this time some 8,591,000 individuals (36 percent) were identified as ethnically Serbian, making them the largest ethnic group in the country.

Linguistic Affiliation.   Serbs speak mainly the Ekavian Subdialect of the Štokavian Dialect of Serbo-Croatian, a South Slavic language from the Slavic Branch of Indo-European. Slovene, Macedonian (both spoken in other former Yugoslav republics), and Bulgarian are the closest related languages. The Serbs still prefer the use of the Serbian Cyrillic alphabet, which differentiates them from the Croats who use the Latin alphabet. In recent years this situation has changed somewhat with street signs, bus routes, etc. being written in both scripts, but Cyrillic remains the alphabet of choice for official documents and newspapers.

History and Cultural Relations

Early Serbian migration into the then largely unpopulated Balkan Peninsula dates to about A.D. 500–600. Moving south from the area adjacent to the Carpathian Mountains, these early settlers arrived with their flocks and herds. The first Serbian state dates to the middle of the ninth century. By the fourteenth and fifteenth centuries, however, internal warfare had facilitated Ottoman conquest of the region. For the Serbs, this conquest is still symbolically remembered today by the defeat at Kosovo Polje (Kosovo Plain) in 1389. Modern settlement of the region dates to the 1700s and the wane of Ottoman power in the area. Prior to this time, much of the population had fled Ottoman conquest and remained in the Dinaric Alps to the west. By 1830, after years of continuous rebellion including the First Revolt of 1804 and the Second Revolt in 1815, Turkey was forced to recognize Serbia as an autonomous principality. Serbia was later proclaimed an independent state in 1882, but it was not until 1918 that the first Kingdom of Serbs, Croats, and Slovenes was established. The modern socialist state of Yugoslavia emerged out of World War II and the concomitant civil struggle between Mihailovic's Chetniks and Tito's Partisans.

Modern former Yugoslavia was an ethnically diverse and complicated state. Recent economic hardships coupled with political tensions have resulted in the flaring up of historical ethnic tensions between Croats and Serbs and between Muslims and Serbs. With the Croatian moves toward independence in 1990–1991, full-scale civil war between Croatia and the Serbian-dominated federal army erupted in the summer of 1991, after Croatia and Slovenia declared their independence. Also threatening at the present time are the tensions in the Kosovo between Serbs and Albanians fueled by growing Serbian nationalism. Yugoslavia is formally nonaligned.

Settlements

Traditionally, neighborhoods or hamlets within villages were composed of closely related kin belonging to the same *vamilija* (lineage). Today, however, the population of Serbia is predominantly urban: over the past decades a tremendous shift of population to urban centers has occurred. Only about one in every four Serbs now lives in the countryside. Peasant villages in the Šumadija tend to be dispersed in small clusters, with each house surrounded by its own orchards, fields, and outbuildings. Three other types of settlements are found also. Agglomerated villages, in which houses are crowded together along narrow, crooked streets, are found mainly in eastern and southern Serbia. The cross-road village, with its evenly spaced houses and well-planned appearance, can be seen near Belgrade and in the lower Morava Valley. Finally, the *ciflik*, walled and densely packed villages created by Turkish landlords during the period of Ottoman domination of the area, are found in southern Serbia near the Macedonian border.

Houses ideally are made of brick and stucco with tile roofs. Wood dwellings, which were common historically, are considered inferior. A pattern of paying as you go in building, rather than financing through mortgage, means that a new house sometimes takes years to build.

Economy

Subsistence and Commercial Activities.   The pre–World War II economy was based primarily on subsistence agriculture with a concentration on wheat and maize. Oats and barley are grown as market crops. Raising of pigs, cattle, and sheep was also important. Postwar modernization and urbanization have resulted in decreased dependence on agriculture. Most rural households have a diversified economic base that includes at least some wage earning. Some Serbian males (between 4 and 5 percent) work outside the country, predominantly in western European industry. The former Yugoslavia as a whole was noted for its labor policy of worker self-management.

A typical diet historically consisted primarily of bread and a variety of stews in a lard base. Fruits and vegetables were normally available on a seasonal basis. Lamb was reserved for holidays and other festivities. Cheese is made and eaten, but milk is rarely drunk. (Kefir is more common.) An important change over the last few decades has been the switch to the use of sunflower oil in cooking.

Industrial Arts.   Many people engage in part-time craftwork, particularly in the manufacture of wood and metal utensils, tools, and furniture.

Trade.   In addition to Western-style stores and shopping centers, open-air markets (*pijaca*) with an array of fresh meats and produce, as well as handicrafts, are common.

Division of Labor. An emerging social pattern is the so-called "feminization" of agriculture as households with male factory workers maintain a diversified resource base. Previously, labor tended to be divided into inside (female) and outside (male) activities. For example, baking, cheese making, weaving, cleaning, and washing were almost exclusively female jobs while chopping wood and most agricultural tasks were men's work. In urban areas, a similar pattern of women working outside the household also has emerged.

Land Tenure. Despite a Socialist government, the vast majority of land is held privately. Attempts in the late 1940s and early 1950s to socialize landholdings met with staunch peasant resistance and were eventually abandoned. Although a few large collectives remain, most peasants continue to work their own land. Current law limits private holdings to 10 hectares, but contiguous holdings by different family members often allow joint working of larger parcels. Recently, the government has made some attempts to develop plans for reorganizing private holdings, which have become increasingly fragmented, into more productive integrated holdings. This attempt has been poorly received.

Kinship

Kin Groups. The most important kinship group after the *zadruga*, or extended family household, is the vamilija (lineage). Tracing descent patrilineally from a common known ancestor, sharing a common last name, and having the same patron saint, a vamilija nonetheless lacks the corporate functions normally associated with true lineage structure. Lineages are exogamous, and the bonds created by marriages between them are socially important. In addition, the fictive kin relationships created by godfatherhood (*kumstvo*) and blood brotherhood (*pobratimstvo*) are important social ties.

Descent. Descent is strictly agnatic, and to die without male heirs is one of the worst personal tragedies that can befall a traditional Serbian peasant. Village society is built on the matrix of male kin relationships as expressed in lineage structures and the relationships between them. Knowledge of this matrix, and one's place in it, are important in knowing who you are and where you came from. It is common for rural men to be able to recall accurately several hundred living and deceased male relatives spanning eight, or even ten, generations.

Kinship Terminology. Serbian kinship terminology is complicated and does not fit readily into conventional categories. On the first ascending generation, however, terminology is bifurcate-collateral for males and lineal for females. In general, terms for consanguineal kin are more specific than for affines. For example, a cover term, *sna* or *snaja*, can be applied to all in-marrying females.

Marriage and Family

Marriage. In rural Serbia where marriage and childbearing have remained important symbols of adult status, the age at marriage has remained low. Both men and women typically marry in their early twenties and immediately start a family. Postmarital residence is almost exclusively patrilocal. Matrilocal residence is a possibility only in cases where no sons are present. Such in-marrying males are commonly referred to as a *domazet*. Traditionally, marriages were often arranged. In urban areas, where living space is less available, marriage may be delayed until later. Legal abortion is a principal means of birth control. Divorce has become increasingly common in the postwar era.

Domestic Unit. The zadruga, or South Slavic extended-family household, is the most prevalent rural domestic unit even to this day. Even in cities, domestic units often contain extended-family members. Historically, zadrugas consisted of married brothers, their wives, and children. Households of ten or more members were common. These extended-family households functioned as single units of production and provided a common defense. Normally, married brothers would remain together until after the death of their father, but as their own families matured, the household would be divided. Often this went so far as actually disassembling the dwelling and evenly dividing the building materials. Today these households are typically smaller and lineally, rather than laterally, extended. Nonetheless, most rural Serbs continue to live in extended-family households. There has not been the pattern of family nuclearization so often associated with modernization.

Inheritance. Historically, land inheritance was strictly through male lines of descent. Land was divided equally between a man's sons when the household was divided. Men without male heirs would frequently seek to find an in-marrying son-in-law (a practice counter to the norm of patrilocal residence). Post–World War II legal codes specify bilateral inheritance, although the laws are still frequently circumvented.

Socialization. Corporal punishment is a common means of discipline. Emphasis has traditionally been placed on respect for adults and the aged and on conformity to household goals. It is not uncommon today, however, to hear people complaining that children no longer respect their parents and often ignore their wishes.

Sociopolitical Organization

Yugoslavia is a Socialist federated republic with separate heads of state and government. The Communist party as embodied in the National Front remained the principal political force in the country until the late 1980s. After Tito's death in 1980 and the establishment of a collective presidency to replace him, the head of the collective presidency had been rotated between members representing each republic and the two Serbian autonomous regions. By 1991, however, the central government was in danger of disintegrating and the national Communist party, under its old framework, had been dissolved. Late in 1991, Croatia and Slovenia withdrew from the republic and declared their independence. War between the Serb-dominated national army and Croatians has left Serbia in control of some territory within Croatia. The Serbian republic's government remains headed by ex-Communists, as of early summer 1992.

Social Organization. The class structure of modern Serbia is occupational and simple. Some pure agriculturalists remain in rural areas, but most households combine agriculture with some wage earning. Landless working people also exist. Successful peasant agriculturalists may still be esteemed, but the urban upper commercial class now wields real political power.

Political Organization. Administrative divisions below the republic level have been reorganized several times since 1945. Village and other local councils are important to local affairs. Village council members are locally elected and responsible for the exercise of federal and republic government policies at the local level, as well as deciding policy on local affairs. Membership in the Communist party is not a prerequisite to being elected.

Social Control. Public opinion and tradition, coupled with a well-developed federal court system, are important to conflict resolution and the maintenance of conformity.

Conflict. Serbian history is fraught with warfare, both internal and external. Centuries of war with the Turks is a common theme in traditional oral epic poetry and is an important symbol of solidarity against the outside world. Serbia, and the former Yugoslavia as a whole, were decimated in both the First and Second World Wars.

Religion and Expressive Culture

Religious Beliefs. Serbian Orthodoxy is the principal religion of Serbia. However, holiday (rather than weekly) church attendance is the norm. Easter is the most important general religious holiday.

Religious Practitioners. In addition to the village priest and Western medical facilities, help may also be solicited from a *vračara*, typically an older woman.

Supernaturals. The saints are highly revered in Serbian Orthodoxy, and in Serbia each clan or lineage has its own patron saint from whom help may be solicited.

Ceremonies. The most important holiday in addition to the church calendar is the *slava*, or feast of the patron saint, held on the saint's day. Every family has a patron saint who is inherited through the male line. Formerly, these were lavish affairs often lasting three days.

Arts. Serbian culture is noted both for its traditional oral epic poetry, recited with an accompanying *gusle* (a single-horsehair string instrument stroked with a bow), and its naive art painting movement.

Medicine. Modernization has meant increased access to Western medical facilities. Women now give birth in hospitals rather than at home. However, for some types of illnesses, help is still solicited from a vračar or vračara. Illness may be attributed to many causes, and self-diagnosis has been important to the decision to seek help from a folk practitioner or Western-style physician.

Death and Afterlife. Peasant society readily accepts death as part of life, but in contrast to church theology its concept of the afterlife is more one of a continued life in heaven. Funerals are held the day after death. The dead continue to serve an important integrative function both in terms of lineage recall and lineage solidarity. Large graveyard feasts traditionally are held one week, forty days, six months, and one year after the death.

Bibliography

Federal Statistical Office (1983). *Statistički kalendar Jugoslavije* (Statistical pocket book of Yugoslavia). Belgrade.

Halpern, Joel M. (1967). *A Serbian Village*. Rev. ed., illustrated. New York: Harper & Row.

Halpern, Joel M., and Barbara Kerewsky-Halpern (1972). *A Serbian Village in Historical Perspective*. New York: Holt, Rinehart & Winston. Rev. ed. 1986. Prospect Heights, Ill.: Waveland Press.

Hammel, Eugene A. (1968). *Alternative Social Structures and Ritual Relations in the Balkans*. Englewood Cliffs, N.J.: Prentice-Hall.

Lodge, Olive (1941). *Peasant Life in Jugoslavia*. London: Seeley, Service & Co.

Simic, Andrei (1973). *The Peasant Urbanites*. New York: Seminar Press.

RICHARD A. WAGNER

Shetlanders

ETHNONYMS: Shetland, Zetland; older forms were Hetland, Hjaltland, Yealtland, Yetland

Orientation

Identification. The Shetland Islands constitute a "Special Island Area" of modern Scotland. Prior to the fifteenth century the islands had a Norse population and culture. After 1469, large numbers of Scottish settlers began to arrive. Although English is spoken today, the inhabitants tend to identify with their Norwegian ancestors.

Location. The Shetlands are the northernmost area of Scotland. They consist of about 100 islands of which only 19 to 20 are inhabited. The main cluster of islands is 83 kilometers northeast of the Orkney Islands, 160 kilometers northeast of Scotland and approximately 356.4 kilometers from Bergen, Norway. The core island group extends from 59°48′ N to 60°52′ N and from 0°45′ to 1°45′ W. The main islands are Mainland (the largest island), Unst, Yell, Fetlar, Whalsay, Bersay, Papa Stour, Foula, and Fair Island. The total land mass is 1,407 square kilometers. Most of the islands are low, treeless, and have extensive boggy peat areas. The highest point, Ronas Hill, is 453 meters high. The coastline has many small indented bays (*wicks*) and low indented fjords (*voes*).

A subarctic oceanic climate and vegetation pattern exists. Because of the Gulf Stream and Atlantic waters, the climate is relatively humid and mild though severe winter gales occur. The summers are cool with long hours of daylight. About 52 to 116 centimeters of rainfall occur annually. At Lerwick, the average annual temperature is 7.1° C and the January mean is 3.4° C.

Demography. In 1988, the estimated population of the Shetlands was 22,364. The one large town is Lerwick. All other communities are very small. A significant percentage of the population lives on scattered farms or crofts. Since 1860, the population has continually declined.

Linguistic Affiliation. The local dialect of English is derived from earlier forms of Scottish English. It contains many words of Norn, the dialect of Norwegian once spoken there.

History and Cultural Relations

The remains of Neolithic and Bronze- and Iron-Age settlements are present. These were followed by early Celtic and/or Pictish settlements. The Celtic/Pictish Christian period came to an abrupt end around A.D. 800 with the arrival of the Viking raiders and settlers. The new Viking-Norse culture continued until 1468-1469 when the Orkney and Shetland Islands were transferred to Scotland. This was done as a pledge in lieu of a dowry for the daughter of King Christian I of Denmark and Norway when she married King James III of Scotland. The pledge was never redeemed, and in 1472 Scotland formally annexed the islands. Before 1469, many Scots had moved to the islands; after 1469, their numbers continually increased. With this came a decline of the older Norse culture and language. During the late 1500s and early 1600s, the people became indentured laborers under the local Scottish lairds (lords). The inhabitants also became more isolated from Norway. They were increasingly influenced by Dutch and German fishermen and the Scottish clergy. By the nineteenth century, the people had been reduced to a serflike status. In the mid-nineteenth century, they were freed from this and large numbers began to leave. The discovery of North Sea oil in the early 1970s has helped to stabilize life, reverse the population decline, and bring economic and social change to the islands.

Settlements

From the Neolithic period to the present day, the Shetlands have always been sparsely settled. Although clustered settlements were present from the early times, dispersed homesteads were and remain the norm. Most farmsteads and settlements were and are on small bays or sheltered coastal sites. This has given the inhabitants easy access to both arable land and rich coastal fishing sites. The town of Lerwick was founded by the Norsemen. Its excellent sheltered harbor is still a major fishing and fish-processing port. Scalloway, the provincial capital in the early 1600s, is now a village. Shetland is famous for its prehistoric sites (e.g., Mousa Brock, Clickimin Brock [near Lerwick], and Jarlshoff, with its Neolithic, Bronze-Age, Iron-Age, and Viking settlement continuum).

Economy

Subsistence and Commercial Activities. The traditional economy was based on fishing as a commercial activity and subsistence agriculture for household needs. The rich local fishing banks were first exploited in the fourteenth century, and the dried cod and herring were marketed through the Hanseatic League. In later times, Lerwick became an increasingly important gathering place for North Sea fishermen. In the twentieth century, refrigeration, fish filleting, and large trawlers have contributed to the present serious depletion of many fishing grounds. The main fishing season for herring,

cod, pollock, and halibut is from May through August; the season for haddock is October to March. Recently, lobster fishing has also become important.

The small family farm or croft is the basic rural unit. These average between two and four hectares in size and usually include pasturage and peat-cutting (for fuel) rights on the common lands. The traditional crops were barley, cabbage or kale, black oats, turnips, rutabagas or swedes, and potatoes. A five-year cycle of crop rotation and fallowing was practiced. Spade cultivation was practiced until the late eighteenth century when simple scratch plows (ards) became more common. In the past, small breeds of sheep and cattle, the Shetland pony, pigs, and geese were the main livestock. Sheep and wool production have increased in importance since 1870, whereas cattle have declined. Today, larger breeds of cattle and sheep have replaced the older breeds.

Industrial Arts. Because the islands are treeless and lack metallic ores, industrial growth is inhibited. Those crafts present include fishing-boat construction with timber from Norway, cooperage (fish barrels), and blacksmithing. Many fishing boats were built in Norway.

Trade. Trade in frozen and processed fish links Lerwick with the major Scottish, English, Dutch, German, and Scandinavian ports. Traditional shops (bakeries, printers, clothing stores, food markets, hardware shops, etc.) are concentrated in Lerwick, the only town of any importance.

Division of Labor. On the crofts, women tended the milk cows, pigs, and poultry; baited the lines of fishing hooks; cured the hay; helped cultivate the vegetable gardens; dried and transported peat; and knitted sweaters and stockings. Men fished, built boats, spaded the gardens, and plowed the fields. Neighborhood cooperative labor exchanges were important for house building, haying, peat cutting, harvesting, and fishing crews.

Land Tenure. A croft by both law and tradition cannot be subdivided. One child will be chosen to inherit it. However, the other siblings usually have access to the croft's produce, can work on the croft, and even build their houses on it.

Kinship

Kin Groups and Descent. An unfocused variety of cognatic descent is characteristic in the crofting townships. Within the local group, most people are related to each other. In a functional sense, precise kin ties are of little importance beyond that of first cousin. However, people will invoke the concepts of "lineage" or "kindred" to justify their associations with others in the community. Kinship is usually the basis for membership in fishing-boat crews. Strong patterns of local endogamy tend to reinforce feelings of local kin solidarity.

Kinship Terminology. Shetland kinship terms follow similar bifurcate-merging patterns in Scotland and the British Isles. Relationships to both sides of the family receive equal stress.

Marriage and Family

Marriage. Weddings are an important aspect of social life, especially in the rural areas. Local endogamy is common. Courtship usually occurs in the late fall and winter. Prior to the wedding, formal announcements and visits occur between the families of the bride and groom. In the past, processions of relatives walked from the home to the church and finally to the bride's parental home for the reception. Today, automobiles are used. Until this century, first-cousin marriages were not allowed. In the past, divorces were very rare.

Domestic Unit. The basic domestic unit is the nuclear family with neolocal residence. Today, many young couples reside with his or her parents for up to two years until they can find or build a house. Traditionally, individuals and their families pooled their resources to furnish the house and provide agricultural tools. Large families were once common; today, they are not.

Inheritance. By law, only one chosen child inherits the farm. The others receive goods, tools, furniture, etc., at the time of their marriages. Traditionally, names were also inherited: the oldest son was named after the father's father, the oldest daughter for the mother's mother, the second son after the mother's father, and the second daughter after the father's mother.

Socialization. The care and training of children was done by the mother, older siblings, and grandmothers. Local schools are important. Those seeking upper-level schooling were sent to board at Lerwick.

Sociopolitical Organization

Social Organization. Until 1872, a rigid, serflike class system prevailed. The local laird-merchants totally controlled the lives of the crofter-fishermen. All fish had to be marketed through specific merchants, emigration was forbidden, and goods at high prices (truck system) could only be purchased from shops controlled by the lairds who also controlled the lands. After 1872, this system was abolished, and the crofters and others gained their personal freedom. Today, Shetland society is characterized by having a high degree of egalitarianism.

Political Organization. Between 1973 and 1975, the old county was abolished and Shetland became one of three "Special Island Areas" of Scotland. In this way, they were allowed to retain a high degree of local authority. The Island Area operates through the Scottish Office in Edinburgh. Police and fire services are provided through the Highland Region of northern Scotland. The Shetland Island Council has special linkages with London for petroleum and energy development. Other services are provided through various Scottish development agencies.

Social Control. On the local level, Norse ethnic pride and insular isolation are the primary means of social control. On a formal level, the Scottish court system prevails. Drunkenness and drunken brawling account for 80 percent of the court cases. The major source of local conflict is rooted in the islanders' strong sense of Norse cultural identity. On several occasions, local officials have stated that they prefer union with England to union with Scotland. The county library and its adjacent museum serve as important centers for both education and local identity.

Religion and Expressive Culture

Religious Beliefs. Since the Reformation, Protestant denominations have been dominant. The Stuarts established episcopacy. Since the early eighteenth century, Presbyterianism has increasingly gained strength. Most Shetlanders are very open and tolerant toward all Christian denominations. Traditionally, religion has played an important role as a moral power. Today, religious indifference is common. Until recently, many older folk beliefs in *trows* (fairies), *selkies* (seal people), ghosts, and witchcraft were present.

Religious Practitioners. Protestant ministers have been and still are respected leaders among Shetlanders. Today, this is even true for those who are indifferent to religion.

Ceremonies. The weekly Sunday services are still of importance to many people. In the yearly cycle, the following are most important: Christmas, New Year's Day, Candlemas (2 February), Good Friday, and Easter. The most important secular ritual (at Lerwick) is Up-Helly-Aa in late January. This involves the yearlong building of a large "model" Viking ship and its procession to and burning in the harbor. The key male participants are dressed as Vikings.

Arts. The important local arts are knitting fine woolen sweaters and shawls, making sterling silver jewelry, and folk fiddling. The most popular tunes are reels.

Medicine. Medical beliefs and practices are basically the same as in the United Kingdom (i.e., socialized medicine, surgeons, modern clinics, and hospitals. These are centered in Lerwick).

Death and Afterlife. Death and funerals were a reminder of the unity of the kin group and all households in the local community. Wakes were once held in the home of the deceased. Neighbors visited and offered condolences. Then the coffin bearers and others formed a procession to the church for the service. Burial was in the churchyard. Unbaptized children were buried in a separate place. In the past, it was forbidden to utter the name of the deceased as that might bring the ghost back. The basic Protestant beliefs in heaven and hell prevail.

Bibliography

Button, John (1978). *The Shetland Way of Oil: Reactions of a Small Community to Big Business.* Sandwick, Shetland: Thuleprint.

Cohen, Anthony P. (1987). *Whalsey: Symbol, Segement, and Boundary in a Shetland Island Community.* Manchester: Manchester University Press.

Fenton, Alexander. (1978). *The Northern Isles: Orkney and Shetland.* Edinburgh: John Donald.

Marwick, Ernest W. (1975). *The Folklore of Orkney and Shetland.* London: B. T. Batsford.

Nicolson, James R. (1978). *Traditional Life in Shetland.* London: Robert Hale.

Theodoratus, Robert J. (1979). "The Shetland Islands: A Bibliographic Survey of Printed Materials on Ethnography, Folk Life, Folklore, and Local History." *Behavior Science Research* 14:159–187.

ROBERT J. THEODORATUS

Sicilians

ETHNONYM: Siciliani

Orientation

Identification. Sicily is the largest island in the Mediterranean Sea. The name derives from the Sicels, a people who settled Sicily in prehistoric times. Currently a semiautonomous region of the Republic of Italy, Sicily, for administrative functions, also includes adjacent minor islands.

Location. Sicily is located at the center of the Mediterranean, between 36° and 38° N and 12° and 15° E. Triangular-shaped, the island has an area of 25,500 square kilometers. Only 144 kilometers from Tunisia in North Africa, Sicily has historically been a bridge between Africa and Europe, and between the eastern and western Mediterranean. The island is separated from the Italian mainland to the northeast by the Strait of Messina. Sicily is mainly mountainous and hilly. On the east coast, Mount Etna, an active volcano, is Sicily's highest peak. The largest lowland, the Plain of Catania, is located nearby. Other lowlands are also located along the coasts. Much of the topography in the interior consists of rugged, deforested hills. Sicily has a typical Mediterranean climate of moderate, wet winters and hot, dry summers; the lack of summer rain, together with insufficient irrigation, has profoundly affected agriculture.

Demography. With an estimated population of slightly more than 5 million in 1987, Sicily contained somewhat less than one-tenth of the population of Italy. Emigration because of lack of work has depopulated the interior, whose towns and villages are composed mainly of the very young and the very old. The movement of people has proceeded from the interior to the coastal cities and from the island overseas. Waves of emigration from the island have been occurring for at least a century, initially to destinations such as the United States, and more recently to industrialized areas of northern Italy and Europe.

Linguistic Affiliation. The native language of most Sicilians is a Romance language, derived mainly from Latin. The vocabulary includes many words borrowed from Arabic and from other cultures that influenced Sicily. Although often classified as a southern Italian dialect, the local language is usually mutually unintelligible with the national language. As a result of the past isolation of towns, noticeable differences in local vocabulary and pronunciation still persist and are important social markers to Sicilians. Owing to the influence of television, the school system, and other unifying phenomena, most Sicilians, particularly the younger people, are bilingual in their native language and in the national language of Italy.

History and Cultural Relations

Sicily's geographic position and formerly rich agricultural resources have made it a crossroads of cultures. For most of its long history, Sicily has been subject to foreign rule. The island was first populated perhaps before 20,000 B.C. Notable among the various groups of early colonizers and settlers were the Greeks, who arrived in the eighth century B.C. Sicily subsequently became the first province of Rome, which it served as a producer of wheat. The Romans introduced latifundia, large estates owned by absentee landlords and farmed by a subject population. This method of organizing agriculture, in which those who actually work the land are separated from the owners through chains of middlemen or brokers, has been a feature of Sicily for much of its history and indeed persisted until fairly recently. Colonizers and settlers subsequent to the Romans include Byzantine Greeks in the sixth century A.D. and Muslims from North Africa, who ruled Sicily for approximately 200 years beginning in the ninth century. The conquest of the island by the Norman French in the eleventh century inaugurated a new pattern of rulers from northern and western Europe. Under the Normans and in the ensuing period, Sicily had a culture unique in Europe, based on a mixture of northwestern European, Arabic, and Byzantine elements. The island experienced a period of strong local rule under Emperor Frederick II in the thirteenth century. At the end of the thirteenth century, while Sicily was controlled by the Angevins of France, Sicilians rebelled in the Sicilian Vespers. However, this uprising resulted in a centuries-long period of rule by dynasties of Spain. Throughout the following centuries, while a representative of the foreign ruler nominally held authority, power was in fact exercised for the most part by the local nobility, the large landowners of the island. In the nineteenth century, Sicily was ruled from the Italian mainland by the Bourbon dynasty based in Naples, in a state called the Kingdom of the Two Sicilies. During the movement for national Italian unification, the Italian military hero Garibaldi joined Sicily to the mainland; in 1861, Sicily became part of the newly constituted kingdom of Italy whose ruling dynasty was the House of Savoy, based in Turin. In 1946 special autonomous status was granted by the government of Italy to the region of Sicily to appease a separatist movement that had been active at the end of World War II. Italy became a republic after World War II and is a member of the European Community.

Settlements

The capital of Sicily, Palermo, and other major cities such as Catania, Messina, Syracuse, and Agrigento are located along the coasts, which are the most densely populated areas of Sicily. In the interior, nucleated settlement patterns leave the countryside largely uninhabited. A typical Sicilian interior town is situated on a hilltop. The urban orientation is also reflected in the importance in every town of a large square or piazza, the center of the community's formal representation. Typically located in the piazza are the main church, the town hall, commercial institutions, and coffee bars. Often emerging from the piazza is the street on which Sicilians take their ritual stroll on Sundays, feast days, or in the evenings. This promenade (_passeggiata_) is an expression of the gregariousness of the people, their enjoyment in creating theater and in observing each other. Outside the main square, houses directly adjoin one another in dense settlements. Traditional peasant homes, usually one or two rooms, contained people and animals. Wages from migration are used to modernize and enlarge homes by adding floors. A typical home today might consist of several stories, with one or two rooms to a floor. While the piazza and other formal spaces are in normal hours reserved for the activities of women, who, especially in small towns, live in semiseclusion and venture into public spaces only for specific purposes. A recent settlement pattern made possible by emigrant remittances tends toward suburbanization on formerly cultivated land.

Economy

Subsistence and Commercial Activities. The interior economy is based on extensive dry agriculture, whereas more profitable irrigated agriculture and industries are located along the coast. Wheat has long been the major crop of interior Sicily. Herding of sheep and goats, important in the past, has declined. Other significant agricultural products are vines, olives, almonds, hazelnuts, walnuts, and garden crops. Sicily is Italy's largest producer of citrus fruits. Fishing, especially for tuna and sardines, is important to the regional economy. Industries based on petroleum are located in the southeast of the island. Other industries, such as those based on the transformation of agricultural and fishing products, are also located along the coasts. Services, retailing, and the public sector are major sources of employment. While Italy is one of the world's largest economic powers, Sicily and southern Italy in general experience underdevelopment and unemployment. Migrant workers are now the most important export of Sicily, and their savings are crucial to the economy. Staples of the Sicilian diet are bread and pasta, olive oil, tomato sauce, vegetables and fruit, cheeses such as *pecorino* and ricotta, nuts, and wine. Meat has recently become a significant addition to the diet.

Industrial Arts. Trades connected with construction prosper. While several towns are still noted for the production of colorful ceramics, other artisanal activity has almost entirely disappeared because of the availability of inexpensive imported consumer goods.

Trade. Stores and open-air markets are supplemented by itinerant tradesmen who ply their wares with characteristic cries through local streets on foot or by truck.

Division of Labor. Sicily has long had a rather rigid division of labor. Men have performed most agricultural work, with the exception of harvests, such as those of grapes and olives, in which the whole family participated. While women no longer spin, weave, or raise chickens, in the interior they still transform agricultural products for food, cook, maintain the home, and raise children. In the larger towns and cities, and as migrants, increasing numbers of women work outside the home.

Land Tenure. In the past, most land was held by an absentee-landlord class of the nobility and their successors in large estates, called latifundia or *feudi*. The majority of the population had access to land either as sharecroppers on short-term contracts or as wage laborers hired for the day (*braccianti*). Following land redistributions, particularly in the post-World War II period, land is now more widely distributed among the population. However, most families own only several hectares of land, often plots of poor quality, lacking irrigation, and dispersed in the countryside. As a result of emigration, much of the land is once again owned by absentee landlords.

Kinship

Kin Groups and Descent. The most important social unit is the nuclear family, the basis of self-identity and location in the community. The cultural concept of honor identifies loyalty to the family as the major social allegiance. Bilateral kin outside the nuclear family may share in a corporate reputation. Relations of spiritual kinship established during baptism, marriage, or confirmation extend alliances beyond the nuclear family.

Kinship Terminology. Kin classification follows the Eskimo system.

Marriage and Family

Marriage. Sicilians consider marriage socially necessary to attain full status as an adult. The most important achievement in the lives of parents is to establish their children in good marriages. Traditionally, people tended to marry within the town, although current patterns of mobility have been altering this situation. People still marry within their social class. Although legal, divorce is infrequent.

Domestic Unit. The ideal domestic unit is the married couple and children living independently as a viable economic and social unit. It is also common for parents, in remodeling their home, to build separate floors for their married children. In a recent domestic pattern, parents working abroad send their children back to Sicily to live with grandparents so as to maintain the children's cultural identity.

Inheritance. Partible inheritance is traditional. Women have been more likely to receive a larger share of their inheritance at the time of marriage, as a dowry in the form of a trousseau of embroidered and lace white wear and household goods, or money, and possibly a house. Men usually received land and agricultural implements, and possibly a house, either at marriage or at the death of their parents. As part of their rapidly increasing integration into a market economy, many families now favor education for their children as a form of inheritance.

Socialization. As children mature, they are taught to subject their wishes to the interests of the family. The Catholic church is an important agent of socialization, as is education. Most Sicilians now complete high school. Older generations have lost some of their authority to adolescent peer groups.

Sociopolitical Organization

Social Organization. Sicily has long had a stratified social system. A small minority of the population controls material resources and the allocation of employment. The most salient factor in the lives of the majority of the population is lack of work. Most families pool earnings from agriculture, salaries, and wage labor, or emigrate in an attempt to better their condition. Recently, even some working-class families are turning to university education as a means of economic advancement.

Political Organization. Sicily is an autonomous region of Italy with an elected parliament, which elects a cabinet and president. The island is divided into provinces and communes, which are the local administrative units. Communes hold elections for mayor and other administrative officials. The political parties control access to a large percentage of employment possibilities and to other necessities of life. Formal political authority lies almost exclusively in the hands of men.

Social Control. Police forces and the judiciary, as well as public opinion with its mechanisms of gossip and ridicule, help maintain order. In addition, the dependence of the majority of the population on assistance from those in control of resources in order to survive creates vertical patron-client ties, which exert pressure against challenging the status quo.

Conflict. Western Sicily in particular is known for the existence of associations engaging in violent activities, often called "mafia." The origins of this phenomenon are often attributed to the important role played by intermediaries between the absentee large landowners and the dispossessed population, in the absence of other effective government. Organized crime has moved from its traditional rural base into urban, national, and international activities.

Religion and Expressive Culture

Religious Beliefs. Christianity was introduced to the island soon after the origin of the religion. Almost all Sicilians are Roman Catholic. Devotion to Mary in her maternal role is particularly strong, and she, as well as saints such as Joseph, Agatha, Anthony, Lucy, and Rosalia, are revered as intercessors. Many people engage in reciprocal exchange relations with these supernatural patrons, through vows that promise lighting of candles, participation in processions, or pilgrimages. Recently, Protestant denominations have been attracting converts.

Religious Practitioners. Roman Catholic priests are the major religious practitioners.

Ceremonies. Each town has a patron saint, whose feast day (*festa*) is considered the most important local holiday, the symbol of town identity. As migrants return from the north, markets or fairs are held and public entertainment is offered. On this date and for major church feast days, images of the sacred figures are taken out of the church and carried through the streets to the people in lengthy processions. On 19 March in many communities, women make elaborate altars of food in their homes to honor Saint Joseph.

Arts. Traditional Sicilian arts included puppetry and peasant carts brightly painted with historic scenes. Itinerant storytellers also kept themes of chivalry and honor alive. Sicily is known for its elaborate pastries and sweets, formerly made in some places by convent nuns. Women still embroider and make fine lace linens not only to dower their daughters, but also for sale. Noted Sicilian writers include Giovanni Verga, Luigi Pirandello, Giuseppe Tomasi di Lampedusa, and Leonardo Sciascia.

Medicine. Most Sicilians now have access to modern medical facilities. Folk healers may still be consulted by some people, often to supplement modern medicine.

Death and Afterlife. After death, the soul journeys to purgatory, and then to heaven or hell. In the funeral, the casket is carried through the town to the cemetery on a bed of rose petals. Periods of wearing black in mourning are rigidly prescribed by degree of relation to the deceased, and widows may wear mourning clothes for the rest of their lives as a symbol of family identity.

Bibliography

Chapman, Charlotte Gower (1971). *Milocca: A Sicilian Village*. Cambridge, Mass.: Schenkman.

Di Lampedusa, Giuseppe Tomasi (1960). *The Leopard*. New York: Pantheon.

Finley, M. I., Denis Mack Smith, and Christopher Duggan (1987). *A History of Sicily*. New York: Viking Press.

King, Russell (1973). *Sicily*. Harrisburg, Pa.: Stackpole.

Schneider, Jane, and Peter Schneider (1976). *Culture and Political Economy in Western Sicily*. New York: Academic Press.

PAMELA QUAGGIOTTO

Silesians

ETHNONYMS: Schlesien (German), Silésie, Slask (Polish), Slezko (Czech)

The name "Silesia" refers to a large, lozenge-shaped region in central Europe, mainly in the upper basin of the Oder River, which lies to the northeast of the Sudetic Mountains. The Oder River forms the northeastern border of the territory. Germany lies along its western border, and Czechoslovakia bounds it to the south. Today, this region is treated as two separate entities: Upper Silesia, which is a part of Germany; and Lower Silesia, which is part of Poland. The total number of German-speaking Poles is 1,400,000, but this figure is not broken down regionally. In the city of Opole, around which German-speaking Polish Silesia is centered, 300,000 residents registered themselves as being of German descent in 1990. In Germany's Upper Silesia, Polish speakers number approximately 100,000.

The earliest known inhabitants of Silesia were Celts who came from Bohemia and Moravia around 400 B.C. Later, Germanic and Teutonic tribes (Cimbri, Lugi, and Vandals) entered the territory from the north. One branch of these incoming groups, the Silingi, arrived in the first century A.D. and remained in the region for the next 500 years. These Silingi established permanent settlements and participated in trade relations with the Roman Empire that were maintained until well into the fourth century. The arrival of the Burgundians in A.D. 300 disrupted the trade of the region, but did not succeed in routing the Silingi people. In the sixth and seventh centuries A.D., Slavonic tribes pushed into the region from the east to settle in the fertile lowlands, and by the ninth century the region was exclusively populated by Slavs. The history of the region from this time onward was for centuries the history of wars for territory—fought between Slavs and Teutons, and between Poles and Prussians—so that the region's population came to include Germans, Poles, Czechs, Slovaks, Moravians, and Wends. In the tenth century it became a wholly Polish possession, but was separated from Poland in 1163 and divided into a number of autonomous duchies ruled by branches of the Polish Piast dynastic family. Because of the custom of partitioning heritable lands practiced by Silesia's ruling families, the region became divided over time into a great many small principalities that were too small to retain their independence. Over two centuries Silesia underwent a gradual process of Germanization and was incorporated into Bohemia in 1355. Religious wars of the early 1400s also left their mark on the region. These wars most often took on the additional character of interethnic hostilities, and they resulted in the plundering and burning of many Silesian cities and towns. In 1526, Silesia became a possession of the Austrian house of the Hapsburgs, who brought a period of relative peace and stability to the area, but the Thirty Years' War again brought destruction to Silesia and forced another period of rebuilding. The First and Second Silesian Wars (1740–1745) resulted in the return of the region to German possession for a time. In 1741–1742, Silesia was conquered by Frederick the Great, and the bulk of historical Silesia was formally ceded to Prussia in 1763. From this date the history of Silesia is split between that of Upper Silesia, by far the larger portion of the territory, which was under Prussian rule, and Lower (Austrian) Silesia, now a part of Poland.

"Silesian," in today's literature, has come to refer to two distinct groups: "Polish-speaking Prussians" and "German-speaking Poles." Both these groups exist as cultural and ethnic minority enclaves within the larger political entity that serves as their host. The Polish-speaking Silesian population in Germany sought throughout the 1800s to maintain a Polish linguistic and religious identity, particularly in the face of the *Kulturkampf,* launched by Germany in 1872 as an effort to insulate the Reich against regionalism, ethnic nationalism, and Catholicism. In Poland, this development resulted in a closing of Polish ranks against all things German, which had the effect of sensitizing the German-speaking communities of Lower Silesia to their own ethnic and linguistic roots. In both portions of Silesia, the minority populations have, over time, become fully integrated into their respective host economies, but in both cases there remained, and remains, a high level of national consciousness and a will to resist political assimilation.

The two world wars of this century once again visited Silesia with devastation, but of the two conflicts, it was World War II that had the greater impact on Polish Silesia. When the territory was occupied by the Germans during the Nazi conquest of Poland, the German-speaking population found itself briefly raised from the national minority status it had so long known. After World War II, the region was occupied first by Soviet soldiers, later to be returned to Polish control. This postwar period is remembered among Silesians as a time of terror and looting, and the Polish policy of "verification" required that Silesian residents show proof of Polish descent to avoid deportation to Germany. Later there was a great influx of immigrants, numbering in the hundreds of thousands, brought from eastern Polish territories when their lands were ceded to the Soviet Union by the agreements at Yalta. Today, German-speaking Silesians are concentrated in the southeastern part of the region, centering on the city of Opole.

The region is rich in coal reserves, and its economy has long been based upon mining and heavy industry, with some agriculture in the fertile lands of the Oder basin. In Polish Silesia, where the German population's assimilation has been less thorough than that of German Silesia's Poles, the houses and villages retain a distinctly German flavor. The language still spoken in this small territory is derived from a German lexical base modified with Polish endings and incorporating some Czech as well. German ethnic identification here was suppressed under Communist rule, but was never crushed. With the installation of the Solidarity-led Government, there has been a resurgence in expressions of German ethnic identification among Polish Silesians.

Ties with Germany, which were never wholly severed, have been strengthened with the recent relaxation of travel restrictions between Eastern and Western Europe, enabling many young German-speaking Silesians to travel to Germany in search of work. For most German ethnics in Polish Silesia, the recent overthrow of 45 years of Communist rule has brought a sense of renewal and the hope that their German ethnic and linguistic identification may be translated into political gains.

Bibliography

Rose, William (1935). *The Drama of Upper Silesia: A Regional Study.* Brattleboro, Vt.: Stephen Day.

Wynot, Edward D., Jr. (1974). "The Case of German Schools in Polish Upper Silesia, 1922-1939." *Polish Review* 19(2): 47–69.

NANCY E. GRATTON

Slav Macedonians

ETHNONYMS: Macedonians, Skopje Slavs, Vardar Slavs

Orientation

Identification.   The name "Macedonia" has been used since 1944 to indicate the Yugoslav republic that has its capital at Skopje. The name itself is a controversial misapplication of the name used for the ancient Hellenic kingdom of Philip of Macedonia and Alexander the Great, which included much of the area today occupied by that Yugoslav republic as well as the Greek province of that name. The Slavic inhabitants of the republic are called Macedonians, although names such as Slav Macedonians are used to distinguish them from the Greek Macedonians who live in the northern Greek province of Macedonia.

Location.   Macedonia, the geographical region, stretches from 42°20′ to 40°00′ N and from 20°30′ to 24°50′ E. In the north it is bounded by the Šar and Črna mountains, on the east by the Rhodope Massif and the Nestos (Mesta) River, on the south by the Vistritsa River and the Aegean Sea, and in the west by the Pindus Range, Lake Dhrid, and Albania. Within these boundaries the area of Macedonia is approximately 64,500 square kilometers (25,000 square miles), roughly the size of West Virginia. Of this area about 34,965 square kilometers lie within the borders of Greece, 6,575 square kilometers within Bulgaria, 1,036 square kilometers within Albania, and about 22,015 square kilometers within what used to be Yugoslavia. The Slav Macedonians are primarily limited to the latter region, or Vardar Macedonia, a mountainous forested land of breathtaking beauty. The landscape is characterized by precipitous cliffs and narrow valleys, and it is dissected by the Vardar River and its tributaries.

Demography.   Census figures originating from the Socialist Republic of Macedonia over the past few decades have met with heavy criticism, especially from the Albanian minority of the former republic. Of the roughly 1.9 million people (1981) living in the republic, it is estimated that no more than 1.2 million are Slav Macedonians, with the balance of the population consisting of Albanians, Vlachs, Gypsies, and a number of other, smaller minorities. The government at Skopje repeatedly has been accused of inflating the numbers of Slav Macedonians at the expense of Albanians, who claim to represent more than 30 percent of the population rather than the officially recognized 17 percent. This, if true, would bring the population of Slav Macedonians to about one million. Although there are no hard numbers on the Slav Macedonians living abroad, it is possible that there might be as many as a quarter of a million, most of whom live in Australia, Germany, Canada, and the United States.

Linguistic Affiliation.   The official language in use at Skopje is called "Macedonian," and it was created soon after World War II under the supervision of the Communist government of Marshal Tito. This new language is based on a Slavic dialect spoken in the areas of Prilep and Titov Veleš. Because the dialect was inadequate as an official language, it was enriched with vocabulary borrowed from several other languages, mainly Serbian and Bulgarian. By the end of the 1940s, this "Macedonian" language had become the language used in all levels of education, the mass media, and literature. The various dialects traditionally spoken by the Slavs of Macedonia are closely related to Bulgarian, belonging to the Macedono-Bulgarian Subgroup of the Southern Branch of Slavic languages. Despite the existence of an official language, the Slav dialects are still in use today, especially in the rural areas. Old Church Slavonic, the liturgical language of Slav Orthodoxy during the Middle Ages, was based on a Slav dialect of Macedonia, although its grammar and vocabulary seem to have included a number of Old Bulgarian features.

History and Cultural Relations

The people who are today called "Macedonians" are descendants of Slavic tribes who settled in Macedonia during the sixth and seventh centuries A.D. They were called "Sclavini" by the Byzantines, and they were looked upon as uncouth barbarians. Late in the seventh century, the Proto-Bulgarians crossed the Danube and came into contact with the "Sclavini." Out of the mixture of the two peoples emerged the Bulgarians, who eventually established a state that included a large part of Macedonia. During the ninth century, two Greek brothers from Thessaloniki (Salonika), Cyril and Methodius, were instrumental in the conversion of the Slavs to Christianity. They were also responsible for the creation of an alphabet, the Glagolitic, out of which evolved the Cyrillic. By the end of the tenth century, there existed two Bulgarian king-

doms. The kingdom in the west had its capital in Ohrid and covered much of Macedonia. The claims of certain Yugoslav historians that the Western Bulgarian Kingdom was the first Macedonian state have been proven erroneous. On the contrary, evidence suggests that at that time there did not yet exist a "Macedonian" consciousness and that the Slavs of Macedonia regarded themselves as Bulgarians. In any case, the Western Bulgarian Kingdom lasted only a few years until its conquest by the Byzantines. It was not until a couple of centuries later that the second Bulgarian state was able to emerge, only to be swallowed up by an expanding Serbian kingdom, which soon fell under Ottoman control, lasting until 1912. In 1870 the Ottomans aided in the creation of a Bulgarian Orthodox church, which established its independence from the patriarchate of Constantinople. It was at about this time that a movement was begun in Macedonia by the Slavs to join Macedonia to an independent Bulgarian state, which finally happened in 1878. The union lasted only a few months and Macedonia fell once again under Turkish control. Terrorist organizations, armed and guided by Bulgarians, agitated for liberation from the Turks. With the defeat of the Turks in the Balkan Wars (1912, 1913), Macedonia was divided between Greece, Serbia, and Bulgaria. By the 1920s, with the exchange of populations between the Balkan states, almost all the Slavs had crossed into either Bulgaria or Serbia. It was at about that time that the Comintern (the Communist International) called for the creation of an independent Macedonia and the recognition of a "Macedonian" nationality. A sentiment of separateness had developed among the Slavs of Macedonia during the previous decades. Although they still viewed themselves as Bulgarians, they now emphasized their regional identity as "Macedonians." In this struggle for a new identity they were aided by the Communist parties in Bulgaria, Greece, and Yugoslavia. When Communists came into power in Yugoslavia, Macedonia became a province, or socialist republic, of the Yugoslav federation. The Slavs of Macedonia were then used by Tito as tools in his expansionist policy, which envisioned the creation of a "Greater Macedonia" to include Greek Macedonia and thus to gain access to the Aegean Sea. It should be noted that there is no connection between the Macedonians of the time of Alexander the Great, who were related to other Hellenic tribes, and the Macedonians of today, who are of Slavic origin and related to the Bulgarians. As a result of the region's turbulent history, the "Macedonian question" is the source of great tension in the central Balkan region.

Settlements

The Slavs of Macedonia traditionally were peasants living in small villages scattered about the countryside. The village house was typically a one-story building of two or three rooms. These houses were invariably connected to a small barn or stable, which doubled as a storeroom. Most of the villages were to be found on the foothills of mountains or near streams and rivers. Since the end of the Second World War there has been a steadily climbing rate of urbanization, which has resulted in the abandonment of hundreds of rural settlements. Most peasants migrated to large towns such as Prilep, Vitola, Titov Veleš, and Skopje. Many migrated to Belgrade, the federal capital, and still others went abroad.

Economy

Subsistence and Commercial Activities.   As a result of Yugoslav industrial policy, enterprises employing more than five people could not be privately owned. This resulted in the proliferation of either very small businesses or large state-regulated enterprises. Subsistence agriculture has declined in importance. Commercial activity has become concentrated in the towns.

Industrial Arts.   Macedonia has many mines for the extraction of iron, zinc, and chromium. Large textile factories have replaced the small, family-based looms that existed until World War II. The region is famous for its tobacco, the cultivation and processing of which provides jobs for thousands of people. Hydroelectric plants dot the landscape, taking advantage of the abundant water supply of the region.

Trade.   Macedonia is a net exporter of electric power, mostly to parts of Yugoslavia. It also exports mining products. Aside from tobacco, which is the single largest export, it also exports textiles, leather, porcelain, glass, and cement. In return it imports industrial and agricultural machinery as well as a wide array of food and consumer products. Formerly, most of the import-export business with foreign countries was handled through the federal capital at Belgrade.

Division of Labor.   With the advent of industrialization under communism, Macedonia's traditional division of labor broke down to yield to the demands of industry. In the traditional peasant society women were responsible for the household upkeep and child rearing, as well as assisting men in the fields. During periods when intense labor was required, the children and elderly of both sexes became involved in the fields as well.

Land Tenure.   Small peasant landholdings for the most part were replaced by large cooperatives as a result of the Yugoslav policies. These cooperatives fell into two distinct categories: 1) the "general agricultural cooperatives," which were more like purchase and sale organizations where members were allowed to keep their own small plots; and 2) the "peasant work cooperatives," where labor, equipment, and land were pooled and members were bound by three-year contracts.

Kinship

Kin Groups and Descent.   With the advent of communism, the older social organization into *zadrugas* (clans) weakened. Nevertheless, the patrilocal extended family still plays an important role among the Slav Macedonians. The society has strong unilineal characteristics of descent, including the institution of unilateral sponsorship called *kumstvo* (godparenthood). The existence of the extended family was necessary for farming and herding, clearing of land, defense, and military servitude. When the group became too large, it fissioned into smaller groups. However, the patron saints of each group were retained even after a group's division. Over time, very distant agnates (up to the fourteenth generation), who possess the same patron saint, celebrate an annual feast (*slava*) in its honor. Men celebrate their fathers' slava, women that of their husbands. Each patriline is related to another patriline through kumstvo, which constitutes a much stronger and more permanent relationship than affinal ties.

Often the alliance of kumstvo is formed with another group in order to prevent an affinal tie. The marriage is permitted only if kumstvo is dissolved. However, in 90 percent of cases the godfather of a male child is also related to the marriage or baptismal sponsor of the godchild's father, and kumstvo is further inherited by the male members of the group, so dissolution of such alliances is unlikely. Kumstvo is given in exchange for important favors, friendship, and avoidance of enmity. The relationship is not reciprocal. Rather, the group tries to obtain prestige through such alliance.

Kinship Terminology.   The genealogical reckoning is primarily agnatic. Kinship terminology distinguishes father's brother (*stric*) from the mother's brother (*ujak*), as well as using a special word to indicate sister's or daughter's husband (*zet*) and a woman married to a set of brothers (*jetrva*). On the agnatic side, marriage is forbidden up to the ninth generation, while the matrilineal first cousins could be regarded as possible mates if it was not for the canonical prohibition. Residence is virilocal. The wife's family lives in another place, and there is a special term used to refer to that group. Both husband and wife use special terms for the kin group with which they do not live (wife's), and neither has a term for the group of residence (husband's), which is considered home. Other than gender distinction, there is no differentiation in cousin terminology.

Marriage and Family

Marriage.   It used to be the case that marriages were arranged, usually by older women related to the prospective bride and groom. Often these marriages took the form of alliances between clans. Dowry was commonly paid by the family of the bride to the groom in the form of animals, land, or household necessities. The bride would then move to the groom's family house or nearby. The exception occurred when the bride's family had no male heirs, in which case the groom might move in with the bride's family. Divorce was extremely rare, virtually nonexistent, although remarriage of widowed men was common practice.

Domestic Unit.   The basic household unit was that of the extended family, which often included three or more generations related patrilineally.

Inheritance.   Land and flocks were traditionally divided equally among the sons, the eldest son remaining in the family residence and his brothers building their homes in the vicinity. The family treasures such as linens and gold jewelry were given to the daughters on their weddings as a dowry. In absence of sons, the oldest daughter would receive *miraz*, the property that otherwise would have belonged to the male heirs.

Sociopolitical Organization

During the Middle Ages the sociopolitical organization of Slav Macedonians centered on the zadruga, in which the elders acted as heads. Each zadruga had its roots in a single nuclear family (ranging in size from a group of father, mother, and one or more married sons to a group of eighty members). The segments of zadruga were always closer to each other than to any other agnatic group, owning contiguous plots of land and houses. It was the responsibility of the zadruga to provide the dowry and divide property among the male members. The need for self-reliance reinforced the power of the zadruga, which often was the epicenter around which villages grew. There existed a loose federation of clans whose chiefs were autocratic and elected by open ballot. Successive occupations by other people weakened this system of self-governance, although even today the extended patrilocal family is of great importance to the Slav Macedonians. With the advent of communism after World War II the Slav Macedonians were formed into a socialist republic, thus participating in the former Yugoslav federation of six republics and two autonomous regions.

Conflict.   Under Ottoman oppression the institution of brigandage grew in importance among Slav Macedonians. Guerrilla bands known as _hayduks_ were formed to settle scores with Ottomans by attacking caravans and plundering feudal estates. The hayduks consisted mostly of displaced peasants whose fame grew among the oppressed populace, reaching mythic proportions and instituting them as national heroes. At the turn of the century, guerrilla bands from Serbia, Bulgaria, and Greece fought not only against the Turks but also against each other over the future of Macedonia. The most recent conflict consists of the Macedonian claims on the Greek city of Thessaloniki and their newly proclaimed independence, which, as of mid-1992, has been recognized only by Bulgaria and Turkey.

Religious and Expressive Culture

Religious Beliefs.   The majority of Slav Macedonians are Orthodox Christians. Most belong to the Macedonian Orthodox church (MOC), which was established in 1958 with the help of Marshal Tito. This is a rare example of a Communist leader actually supporting the establishment and welfare of a religious body. To this day the MOC is not recognized by any of the Orthodox patriarchates and churches. The reason behind this lack of recognition is the realization that the creation of the MOC was politically motivated on the part of the Yugoslav Communists, engineered to weaken the power and influence of the Serbian church, and intended to lend more legitimacy to the newly established "Macedonian" nation. Despite the political problems surrounding the MOC, the Slav Macedonians uphold similar dogmas and liturgical practices as their Orthodox neighbors in Yugoslavia, Bulgaria, and Greece. Central elements of their belief are the primacy of the Holy Trinity and the importance of saints as examples of Christian living. During the Middle Ages a heresy known as Bogumilism spread throughout the central Balkan Peninsula. It was a mixture of Christianity and Manichaean teachings, which held that there is a constant eternal struggle between good and evil, light and darkness. God is the creator of the soul, which is perfect and good, whereas Satan is the creator of the body, which is imperfect and impure. The Bogumils believed only in the New Testament and rejected church sacraments. (A related heresy in western Europe is known as Catharism.) Slav Macedonians joined the heresy in large numbers and suffered persecution by the civil and ecclesiastical authorities. Eventually, Bogumilism weakened and disappeared, thus closing the chapter of a very interesting part of the history of Slavs in Macedonia.

Religious Practitioners.   The importance of the Orthodox clergy in Slav Macedonian history and culture cannot be underestimated. During the centuries under Ottoman domina-tion it was the clergy who maintained a sense of continuity of culture. Often enough the priest was the only literate person in the village, sometimes functioning as a teacher as well.

Ceremonies.   As is the case among other Balkan peoples, the saints of the Orthodox church appear to have replaced ancient pagan deities and many of the ceremonies of the church can be viewed as a continuation of pagan rites and festivals. For example, beliefs in thunder being caused by the chariot of Saint Elijah as it is driven over the sky, or in fertility rites involving slaughter of a rooster or a lamb to assist conception in a sterile woman, are remnants of ancient pre-Christian beliefs and practices. The celebration of Christmas is of great importance and the customs surrounding the occasion can be traced back to pagan winter celebrations akin to the Roman Saturnalia. Easter has been delegated a second place, but it still may be considered as a continuation of ancient festivities of Dionysus. Women then color eggs red, which is considered the color of life. The Easter festivities are connected with the pagan spring rites, celebrated to ensure fertility of humans, beasts, and fields.

Arts.   A long tradition of Christian iconography among the Slav Macedonians has left many splendid examples in the hundreds of churches and monasteries. Although Slav Macedonian iconography was heavily influenced by Byzantine art, there was a definite move away from the stylized Byzantine rigidity, with a strong emphasis on nature and the addition of a three-dimensional perspective. Another aspect of artistic expression can be found in the colorful female peasant costumes that are still worn by the older women. The variations from region to region are bewildering and stand in sharp contrast to the all-black clothing sometimes seen worn by women in Serbia, Greece, and Italy. Embroidery motifs borrow heavily from ancient themes such as depictions of mythological animals, bears' paws, and geometric figures. The traditional Slav Macedonian round dance (_oro_) is a highly intricate, fast-stepping dance whose origin can be traced back for centuries. Similar dances are called _horos_ in Greece, _horo_ in Bulgaria, and _hora_ in Romania. The music is rich but has highly irregular rhythms. Polyrhythmic combinations are common. _Lazarice_ are folk songs sung by girls on Saint Lazarus's Day, related to pagan spring songs. _Kraljice_ are sung on Saint George's Day.

Medicine.   Modern medical science has replaced healing practices that traditionally fell within the domain of older women. Dancing around sick people, as a form of exorcism, was part of the ancient healing practices to ward off evil spirits causing the illness. The "evil eye" was also believed responsible for causing illness in babies and animals and even inanimate objects such as houses.

Death and Afterlife.   Among the Slav Macedonians the twelve days from Christmas to Epiphany are dedicated to the reverence of the dead, during which period their souls wander about the living and participate in everyday life. Evil souls are believed to be found among the rest of the souls, so a dance known as _dzamala_ is performed to chase them away. In the dance, dancers representing the world of the living fight with and defeat dancers representing the underworld. As Christians, they believe in an afterlife along the lines held by the Orthodox church, but, as can be seen, ancient Slavic beliefs do find a place in modern practi

Bibliography

Andriote, N. P. (1960). "History of the Name 'Macedonia.'" *Balkan Studies 1.*

Apostolski, M., and Polenakovich, H., eds. (1974). *The Socialist Republic of Macedonia.* Skopje.

Barker, E. (1950). *Macedonia.* London: Royal Institute of International Affairs.

Hammel, E. A. (1968). *Alternative Social Structures and Ritual Relations in the Balkans.* Englewood Cliffs, N.J.: Prentice-Hall.

Pribichevich, S. (1982). *Macedonia: Its People and History.* University Park: Pennsylvania State University Press.

Semiz, D. (1928). "Rusija i Borba Srbije za Vardarsku Dolinu." *Nova Europa.* Zagreb.

Tašković, D. (1951). *Bogomilstvoto i Njegovoto Istorisko Značenje.* Skopje.

West, R. (1941). *Black Lamb and Grey Falcon.* New York: Viking Press.

VESNA GARBER

Slovaks

ETHNONYMS: Slováci, Slovák

Orientation

Identification.   The Slovaks are Western Slavs who speak Slovak and live in Slovakia, the easternmost third of Czechoslovakia, in 1992 renamed the Czech and Slovak Federative Republic. Slovaks are most closely related to two other Slavic peoples located to their west: Moravians and Czechs.

Location.   Slovakia is located between 47° and 50° N and 17° and 23° E. Slovakia occupies an area of approximately 49,995 square kilometers and is bounded on the north by Poland, on the east by Ukraine, on the south by Hungary, on the southwest by Austria, and on the west by the Czech republic of the Czech and Slovak Federative Republic. The topography of Slovakia is extremely varied, ranging from the Carpathian Mountains in the north to the Danube Basin and fertile plains in the south and west. The climate is typical of continental Europe with hot summers and cold, snowy winters.

Demography.   The 1986 estimated population of Slovakia was 5,200,000 with Slovaks constituting 88 percent of that number. About 1,000,000 live outside Slovakia, with approximately 750,000 residing in the United States and others scattered throughout Europe, Canada, and South America. The population density in Slovakia averages 106 persons per square kilometer, and the population is growing at an estimated rate of 0.3 percent per year. Hungarians, Ukrainians (Rusins), Poles, Romany peoples, and Germans account for the remaining 12 percent of Slovakia's population.

Linguistic Affiliation.   Slovak is a Western Slavic language (along with Czech and Polish) of the Indo-European Language Family. It is most closely related to, but distinct from, Czech. Slovak is an inflected language, and stress is fixed on the first syllable of a word; words of more than three syllables also have a secondary accent. Generally, Slovak words have as many syllables as they have vowels. Some words appear composed entirely or mostly of consonants: *smrt'* (death); *slnko* (sun); *srdce* (heart); and *yrt* (bore, drill boring). There are three genders (masculine, feminine, neuter) and forty-three letters. The three main dialects represent western, central, and eastern subareas of Slovakia. The dialect spoken in central Slovakia was the one adopted by Slovak scholars as the norm.

History and Cultural Relations

Slavs who became known as the Slovaks settled between the Danube River and the Carpathian Mountains of east-central Europe by the fifth or sixth centuries A.D. and have occupied that territory continuously. Evidence of growing cultural complexity, from tribe to prefeudal alliances to feudal state, is found in their permanent settlements in the Váh, Nitra, Torysa, Ipel', and Morava river valleys. The settlement of Nitra became the home of the Slovak princes and the location of the first Christian church in east-central Europe. During the reign of King Svatopluk (A.D. 870–894), the Great Moravian Empire of the Slovaks reached its greatest development and size, consisting of some one million inhabitants and 350,000 square kilometers, including Polish and Czech subjects. After Svatopluk's death and the defections of Czech and Polish peoples, the Magyars (Hungarians) began to invade Slovak lands. The Magyars controlled Slovakia from the time of the battle of Bratislava in A.D. 907 to the end of World War I. About midway into the millennium of Hungarian rule, the Turkish invasion of 1526–1683 reduced the Magyar kingdom to the size of modern-day Slovakia.

The first half of the nineteenth century marked the beginning of a Slovak national renaissance and desire for ethnic independence as a minority in the Austro-Hungarian Empire, but in 1868 the Hungarians initiated a formal program of assimilation or "Magyarization." Hungarian was declared the official language in Slovakia, the last three Slovak secondary schools were closed, and in 1869, the Matica Slovenská (the Slovak Institute of Sciences and Arts founded in 1863) was suppressed. As World War I got under way, Slovaks in the United States urged Czech-Americans to join in efforts to promote a joint nation and by 1919, the federated state of Czecho-Slovakia was established and recognized to be a union of two ethnic groups.

The Czechs, who were more numerous and powerful, soon insisted on Czechoslovak unitarism in an effort to eliminate the national individuality of Slovakia. Slovak relations with the Czechs worsened until Czecho-Slovakia disintegrated in 1938–1939. The Slovak Republic (1939–1945) was established as the result of growing international pressures and became dependent on Hitler's Germany. In 1944, anti-Nazi Slovak partisans mounted an armed rebellion, but they were quickly crushed by German forces who reportedly killed 30,000 Slovaks while Soviet troops waited in the nearby Carpathian Mountains. The nation of Czechoslovakia was reconstituted at the end of World War II; by 1949 Communists had gained total control of the country and Slovaks were once again placed in a subordinate position by the Prague government.

When the "Czech Spring" movement emerged in 1968 under the leadership of a Slovak, Alexander Dubcek, it was crushed by a Soviet-led invasion of Warsaw Pact troops who occupied the entire Czechoslovak Socialist Republic, including Slovakia. In November 1989, the Czech dissident playwright, Vaclav Havel, led the Civic Forum party in the "Velvet Revolution," a peaceful overthrow of the republic's Communist government. Public against Violence was the Slovak counterpart of Civic Forum. National elections were held in 1990, and the name of the country was changed to the Czech and Slovak Federative Republic. In 1991, a vocal Slovak nationalistic party called Movement for a Democratic Slovakia began to demand independence for Slovakia. Its showing in the June 1992 elections further widened the rift between the Czech and Slovak republics.

Settlements

Slovaks live in small hamlets or colonies, villages, towns, and cities. The hamlet or colony (*osada*) typically contains less than ten households of closely related people, usually with a common surname, which may also be the name of the community. The village (*dedina*) can have upwards of 3,000 to 4,000 people, frequently including the inhabitants of the surrounding hamlets. A town (*mesto*) commonly has a population in excess of 5,000 and a city (*velkomesto*) many thousands more. The largest cities of Slovakia are Bratislava, the capital (417,100), and Košice (222,200). Traditional Slovak homes in hamlets and villages were constructed of plastered-over mud bricks in western Slovakia or wood in the heavily forested regions of central and eastern Slovakia. Roofs were thatched or shingled. Typical peasant homes built in the eighteenth and nineteenth centuries contain one room, or at most, two rooms: a kitchen that would also double as a bedroom, and a separate room that would serve as a bedroom by night and a room to entertain guests by day. A large oven would be accessed from the kitchen, while the body of the oven would extend into the second room where it would provide a warm surface for children to sleep on. Sometimes additional rooms were added linearly to this basic design to accommodate families of married sons or daughters and/or provide for the sheltering of livestock. Many hamlets still exhibit this traditional Slovak house, though most now have tile roofs. Villages in present-day Slovakia usually contain a jumble of varied house types, from the basic two-room plan of a detached home to the newer four- or six-unit two-story apartment houses. Cinder blocks and fired bricks have replaced mud bricks and wood as building materials, and indoor plumbing has been the norm for three decades even in rural areas. Stepwise migration, with people leaving hamlets and villages for larger communities (cities), is ongoing throughout Slovakia. In some regions, nearly 10 percent of the hamlets have been abandoned over the past fifteen years.

Economy

Subsistence and Commercial Activities. During the many centuries of Magyar rule when nearly all the land of Slovakia was owned by Hungarian nobility, most Slovaks were peasants (actually landless serfs). They cultivated the land, growing and harvesting crops for the manor. Initially, the fertile plains in the west and south were heavily populated, but by the twelfth century A.D., Slovaks began moving into the central region, which was more suited to animal husbandry. Other Slovaks were court servants and their villages were named for their trades or occupations. They worked at making metal pots, being forest wardens, fishing, goldsmithing, etc. The years of Magyar rule resulted in a mostly peasant Slovak population. Agriculture is still extremely important in late-twentieth-century Slovakia, with key crops such as rye, wheat, corn, clover, potatoes, and sugar beets being grown since the 1950s on large collective farms. Vineyards and wine making are important in the region surrounding Bratislava, while the spas of Piešt'any, Trenčianski, Teplice, and Bardejov still attract foreign visitors. Many rural families keep gardens, fruit trees, and livestock and thus do not experience the frequent shortages in urban stores. Barter is still active in Slovak villages, with families that keep chickens trading eggs for milk with neighbors who have cows. For several decades there also has been an active black market for all sorts of commodities, such as building materials, parts for motor scooters, and currency. In recent decades Slovakia received an economic boost during the tenure of Gustav Husak, a Slovak who took national office in 1968 and served as president of the Czechoslovak Socialist Republic from 1975 until 1989. However, the steelworks, chemicals industry, and aluminum works established in Slovakia during the Husak years are experiencing difficulties as the economy languishes in the post–cold war era.

Industrial Arts. Slovakia has a long tradition of ceramic manufacturing, lace making and embroidery, linen and wool garment making, wood carving, metalworking, and the sewing of traditional costumes.

Trade. Prior to the twentieth century, Slovak trade was controlled by the Magyars. Routes leading into Slovakia from the west were popular entryways for enemies of the Hungarians, so these roads were frequently gated and guarded. On numerous occasions, the Slovak lands were devastated by invading armies. Therefore, growth of trade with neighboring groups was difficult. During the era of the Council of Mutual Economic Assistance, Slovakia was an active trade participant, but remained primarily agricultural. Light industry (underwear manufacturing) and the growing importance of the amount of electricity being generated by Slovakia's nuclear power facility in the village of Jaslovské-Bohunice have been emerging as significant economic factors in recent years, along with the development of some heavy industry. Now with the demise of COMECON, new trade problems have appeared and old ones have grown worse. Some Slovak collective farms are moving toward a farm-co-op type of arrangement, which will entail local control of production and the ability to enter directly into an assortment of economic relationships.

Division of Labor. The traditional division of labor was by age and sex. In peasant agricultural life, adult males tended to the draft animals and performed the heavier tasks in the fields, such as plowing. Adult females would plant, weed, and help with the harvest. Children of both sexes could be placed in charge of the family's geese, cows, or other livestock to take to pasture. In addition, girls would be expected to help their mothers and boys would be sent to work alongside their fathers. In the home, the bulk of child-rearing responsibility fell to the females of the household. Women cooked, tended the household gardens, stripped the geese of feathers to make the featherbeds, cleaned the house and immediate yard areas, washed the clothes, wove, and performed all the other sorts of handiwork, such as lace making and embroidery.

Formal schooling for peasant children even in the first quarter of the twentieth century rarely went beyond the third grade. Learning a trade, such as tailoring, enabled boys to live in a village or town and not be locked into agricultural activities. Some men worked at trades in addition to cultivating crops and keeping livestock. Some girls might learn to be midwives or traditional curers from their mothers or grandmothers.

Land Tenure.   Prior to the onset of Magyar rule, property was probably held and used in common by related individuals, as is reported for many Slavic groups. Feudalism resulted in vast numbers of landless peasants, so that by the twentieth century, Slovaks were emigrating at a rate second only to the Irish. With the establishment of Czechoslovakia after World War II, land reform brought some degree of prosperity to those who held plots. In the 1950s, land was once again confiscated as large collective farms were established. There are now measures to repatriate land taken by the Communists, but few individuals expect to return to the agricultural pursuits of their fathers or grandfathers and will probably sell the land for cash.

Kinship

Kin Groups and Descent.   Modern Slovak kinship is bilateral, resulting in large numbers of relatives. In many regions, Slovaks can travel to village after village and continue to find individuals with whom they share some kin relationship. In the past, Slovaks were patrilineal, organized in male-headed units termed *rod* (sing.), and were virilocal. The term for a small village, dedina, is derived from a kin term for elderly male relative or grandfather, *dedo*. Several families, closely related through males, formed residence colonies. This pattern survives today in the tiny hamlets that surround Slovak villages. The modern term for family in Slovak is *rodina*.

Kinship Terminology.   Although Slovaks now exhibit bilateral kinship and are moving toward an essentially Eskimo terminology, they retain a Hawaiian-type terminology for Ego's generation: terms for brother and sister are, respectively, *brat* and *sestra*, while male cousins are called *bratanec* and female cousins *sesternica*. In many parts of Slovakia and especially in rural areas, portions of what was once a descriptive kinship system is still in use. For example, there are different terms for father, mother, father's brother, mother's brother, father's brother's wife, mother's brother's wife, brother's son, sister's son, brother's daughter, and sister's daughter.

Marriage and Family

Marriage.   Slovaks practice monogamy, with divorce and remarriage becoming a frequent occurrence in the last quarter of the twentieth century. In the past, there was a high degree of village endogamy or, at least, local endogamy (marriage within a group of villages representing a particular regional enclave). Religious endogamy is still prevalent, but is growing less important. In the past, everyone married and staying single was not possible, save for those unable to secure a spouse because of disability. Dowry was important, with cash being the preferred item. A daughter ordinarily could not marry until her female relatives had completed a set of featherbeds for her, her prospective husband, and their first offspring. There was a strong emphasis on virilocal residence. On the day of the wedding, the groom and his entourage would arrive at the bride's home and, after her attendants had sent several imposters outside to "trick" him, they would finally send the bride out. She would then bid a ritual farewell to her parents and be carried off with her possessions in a wagon to the groom's home. At some point following the ceremony, her wedding headdress would be removed and the distinctive, folded cap of a married woman would be placed on her head, accompanied by the singing of another ritual song. Once she was in her husband's home, her mother-in-law would call her *nevesta* (bride) for several months, and she would be assigned many of the heavy household chores. Today postmarital residence is ambilocal and even neolocal when financial circumstances permit or when employment cannot be secured near relatives.

Domestic Unit.   Increasingly, the domestic unit is the nuclear family. However, the extended family, three generations deep, was once the norm and can still be found in villages and hamlets. Some homes have an additional room or two at the end of a house to provide a separate kitchen or bedroom for a son's wife and children.

Inheritance.   Inheritance is partible. In the past, if a peasant family had some land, the brother or brothers might attempt to buy out the sister's share and thereby provide her with some dowry while keeping enough land to farm. Partible inheritance reduced landholdings in some areas to small ribbons of land that were ultimately too small to support a family. Today, grown children of deceased parents feud over shares in houses. The married offspring who occupies the parents' home is forced either to sell it and divide the proceeds or to come up with the cash to pay off the claims of siblings.

Socialization.   Babies remained under the care of their mothers, who would take them into the fields. Young children were placed in the care of their grandmothers, most commonly their father's mother. When they reached about the age of 7, children would be assigned chores usually specific to their gender; both boys and girls would be sent off with geese, cows, or sheep to tend. The Communist government established preschools throughout Slovakia by the 1970s, thus changing the old pattern of socialization. Liberal maternal leaves permitted new mothers to stay home with pay. These factors have combined to lessen the degree of cultural continuity across the generations. Today formal education is compulsory, but in the past it was common for Slovak peasant children to leave school in the early grades with many dropping out after the third grade to go to work.

Sociopolitical Organization

Social Organization. In hamlets the basis of social organization is a loose grouping of related families and in villages, one or more groups of households. This local organization takes responsibility for villagewide events such as facilitating weddings and funerals. The leadership of the collective farms in the rural sector took over some of these activities and certainly was responsible for directing the work force in the villages. Informal, voluntary associations of amateur musicians exist on the village level and play for various events, including the end-of-the-school-year procession and the end-of-the-harvest celebration. Males, related and unrelated, congregate nightly in the village bar to play cards, drink, and visit. Females, related and unrelated, visit in the evenings and do a considerable amount of the planning for communal events.

Political Organization. Prior to 1990, the Slovak Socialist Republic of the Czechoslovak Socialist Republic was divided into eighteen administrative districts (*okres*), each with a large town or city serving as a district seat. The boundaries of the districts were drawn in 1949 and correspond somewhat to yet older political divisions, *župa,* that were in place from 1886. The Slovak Republic of the Czech and Slovak Federative Republic instituted a local government system of elected mayors and councils in 1990 several months after holding elections for national representatives, republic representatives, and national and republic leaders. Therefore, at least on the community level, the prospect is for more flexibility in local decision making.

Social Control. Widely accepted expectations and obligations among the peasants who lived in virtual daily contact with one another resulted in broad compliance within the parameters of acceptable behavior. Antisocial behavior would ordinarily be dealt with directly by the offender's and victim's relatives in order to maintain harmony in the community. As communities grow larger and more diverse, disputes more frequently are settled in the courts.

Conflict. Today there is still conflict over inheritance and, with the changes since 1990, renewed conflict over land occurs as the government attempts to repatriate plots confiscated by the Communist government since the 1950s. Theft from the collective farms and from village construction may be overlooked if the offender is a local person, but intruders from other villages (operating at night) are confronted outright by local men, who may beat the thief, relieve him of his loot, and then telephone the police the next morning when the post office opens. Villages do not have police in residence.

Religion and Expressive Culture

Religious Beliefs. Cyril and Methodius brought Christianity to the Slovaks in the ninth century, but there are numerous examples of an earlier, widespread, traditional religion characterized by a pantheon of supernatural beings. Among them is Morena, the goddess of death who, represented by a straw doll, is still ritually "drowned" in the first meltwater of the spring by a group of young girls in some mountain villages. Some Christian Slovaks, even those educated beyond high school and holding professional positions in villages, still believe in the existence of witches, ghosts, and the evil eye. The vast majority of Slovaks are Roman Catholic, but there is a strong minority presence of Protestants (Evangelical Lutherans), especially in western Slovakia, where many villages have churches of both faiths and some have only a Lutheran one. Jewish Slovaks, once numerous in some villages, towns, and cities, lost their lives in the Holocaust; businesses and farm plots were confiscated and sold off to Christian Slovaks by banks and other agencies during the years of the independent Slovak Republic. Few synagogues remain and Jewish Slovak cemeteries in the villages are abandoned and in ruin.

Religious Practitioners. Full-time religious practitioners, Roman Catholic priests and Evangelical (Lutheran) pastors, experienced diminished influence and authority between 1949 and 1989. Sermons or any departure from the prescribed liturgy were required to be tape-recorded for review by a government official. Secular authorities held full control over their activities and priests or pastors could be jailed if they held religious services during government-mandated harvest periods. In 1990, some Roman Catholic priests began taking an active role in local and national politics by promoting one candidate or one party over another to their parishioners. Slovaks also recognize part-time religious practitioners who are traditional curers and mostly female.

Ceremonies. Historically, Slovaks observed an annual round of rituals common to European agricultural peoples that were ultimately linked with and incorporated into events in the Christian calendar. On the village level, these rituals involved virtually everyone and provided settings for village cohesion and solidarity.

Arts. Wood carving, embroidery, lace making, burn etching in wood, egg painting, ceramics, and weaving were and still are the traditional arts. There are also very rich folk dance, folk music, and folk song traditions that distinguish one Slovak region from another, along with the sewing of distinctive regional costumes. The *fujara,* a shepherd's giant flute held vertically in front of the body when played, is a particularly Slovak instrument. Hviezdoslav (1849–1921), the pseudonym of Pavol Országh, is probably the best-known Slovak poet.

Medicine. Until fairly recent times, Slovak peasants relied on the knowledge of traditional curers to diagnose their illnesses and provide them with appropriate remedies. Rural populations also shared popular cures among themselves and had extensive information about how to make teas and poultices to relieve certain symptoms and about which plants to use to stem bleeding. Curers were still diagnosing evil eye in the 1970s through a particular divination ritual. Modern Slovak medical care on the village level revolves around the clinic, a community building where patients come to be treated by the regional dentist, pediatrician, obstetrician/gynecologist, and general practitioner who stop by at regular intervals. Usually the resident health-care delivery system consists of a midwife/paramedic and a nurse. Pharmacies in towns display colored charts bearing drawings of medicinal plants and urge people not to destroy them. Although modern medicine is mostly relied upon and doctors with formal educations are trusted, Slovaks in some areas still believe that certain illnesses and symptoms are the work of witches or the evil eye and will seek out traditional curers.

Death and Afterlife.   Christian Slovaks believe in an afterlife, and burials are primarily inhumations in conventional cemeteries. Pre-Christian Slovaks apparently cremated the dead, placed the ashes in ceramic urns, interred them with grave goods of various types, and then covered these features with clay and stone mounds. Death is not borne lightly by the surviving relatives and friends. In the recent past, the deceased was washed and prepared for burial at home, with a wooden coffin being made as soon as possible and brought to the house. The family then kept vigil with the corpse through the night and visitors paid respects the next day, at which time a religious service would be held in the church and then the coffin would be carried off for burial. Normally, a funeral procession would form and walk through the village, accompanied by the village band. Widows would adopt black skirts, aprons, vests, and sweaters as permanent attire following the death of a spouse.

Bibliography

Kirschbaum, Joseph M., ed. (1978). *Slovak Culture through the Centuries*. Toronto: Slovak World Congress.

Mikus, Joseph A. (1977). *Slovakia and the Slovaks*. Washington, D.C.: Three Continents Press.

Oddo, Gilbert L. (1960). *Slovakia and Its People*. New York: Robert Speller & Sons.

Pleuvza, Viliam, and Jozef Vladár, general eds. (1984). *Slovenská Socialistická Republika: Encyklopedický prehl'ad. Priroda, dejiny, hospodárstvo, kultúra*. Bratislava: Slovensky Akademie Vied.

Seton-Watson, R. W. (1943). *A History of the Czechs and Slovaks*. Hutchinson & Co. Reprint. 1965. Hamden, Conn.: Archon.

JANET POLLAK

Slovenes

ETHNONYMS: Krainisch, Slovenec (plural, Slovenci), Slovenian, Slovenski, Wendisch, Windisch

Orientation

Identification.   Slovenia was the northwesternmost republic of Yugoslavia; it is now an independent state. The name "Slovenec" is derived from the common name for the Slavs, which is the equivalent of the Greek "Sklavenos" (Romanian "Slavjanin"; Czech, Slovak "Slovan"). There is disagreement about the origin of the word for the Slavs. It is thought to derive either from the word *slava* (glory) or from the word *slovo* (word), referring to those who speak clearly, as opposed to the neighboring Germans who do not. (The Slavic root *nem*, which forms the word for German, *nemec*, also forms words meaning mute.)

Location.   Slovenia is situated in the Karst Plateau and the Julian Alps. It is drained by the Sava and Drava rivers. It is bordered on the north by Austria, on the southwest by Italy, and by the former Yugoslav republic of Croatia, another now independent state, on the south and east. It also shares a small border to the east with Hungary. Slovenia is located between 49° and 50° N and 12° and 19° E. Its area is 20,251 square kilometers. The largest part of Slovenia is mountainous. Much of the land is karstic, rugged and stony. Only a small eastern section lies within the Pannonian Plain. Summers are short, often cool, and sometimes rainy. Winters are cold but not severe.

Demography.   Compared to Serbia's, Slovenia's population increase has been gradual, growing in urban sections and generally declining in rural ones since 1891 because of exhaustion of free land. According to census figures, in 1921 the Slovene population was 1.05 million; in 1931, 1,266,604; in 1948, 1,439,800; and in 1961, 1,584,368. The latest population figure (1990) is 1,891,864. Population density in 1990 was 93 persons per square kilometer. Large Slovene populations also live in southern Austria and in the United States (especially in Cleveland, Ohio; Pennsylvania; and Minnesota).

Linguistic Affiliation.   The Slovene language, one of the South Slavic Group of the Slavic Family, is one of the most archaic of the Slavic languages. It includes thirty-six dialects, and twenty-nine subdialects, many of which are distinct enough to be unintelligible to Slovene speakers of different areas.

History and Cultural Relations

In the area that is today Slovenia, early Iron Age settlements attributed to Illyrians came under Roman control by 14 B.C. By A.D. 650 Slavic tribes, including the Slovenes, were in full possession of Illyria. In the middle of the seventh century Slovenes were included in the Slavic union led by King Samo (617–658). Later the Slovenes came under the domination of the Franks and became the object of intensive Christian proselytizing, particularly under Charlemagne (768–814). During the Middle Ages Slovene lands became part of the Holy Roman Empire and by the middle of the fourteenth century, Hapsburg domination over the duchies of Carinthia and Carniola was established and continued until 1918, with the brief interruption of the Napoleonic conquest of Carniola (1809–1813).

By the tenth century German lords and the Catholic church represented the feudal order. The peasants were burdened with various feudal obligations. By the sixteenth century the Reformation encouraged the rise of Slovene national consciousness and the Slovene language was adopted in church services. In 1584 the first Slovene grammar appeared. But the Counter Reformation was successful in opposing Protestantism. From the fifteenth to the seventeenth centuries there were peasant revolts. Problems were mitigated by the enlightened policy of agrarian reform under Maria Theresa (1740–1780) and her son Joseph II (1780–1790). In 1848 when all serf obligations were abolished, Slovene national consciousness culminated in the call for the creation of a Slovenian kingdom under Austria. The years from 1848 to 1918 saw mixed developments since, in spite of improvements in agricultural practices, taxes increased, as did land subdivisions and mortgaging of farms. The agrarian crisis of the 1890s that followed forced large numbers of peasants to emigrate to the United States.

In 1918, with the end of Austrian rule, the new South Slav state was formed, initially called the Kingdom of the Serbs, Croats, and Slovenes and later named Yugoslavia. World War II saw the fall of the Yugoslav government, and on 2 April 1941 the Germans invaded Yugoslavia, giving rise to the Partisan movement. Slovenia was occupied by the Germans except in the southwest section, which was controlled by the Italians, and a small area of Prekomurje, which fell to the Hungarians. On 29 November 1945 the Federal People's Republic of Yugoslavia was formed, and Slovenia gained a part of the Istrian Peninsula and the territory surrounding Trieste as well as certain regions west of the Italian city of Goricia. More stringent land reforms followed that did not greatly help the situation in Slovenia, where there were not many rich peasants with enough land to be distributed. The program of collectivization of the land was introduced in 1948 and, while the bulk of the peasant holdings remained private, the peasant economy became strictly regulated by the Communist program. In 1948 Yugoslavia broke with the Cominform and introduced regional autonomy, which culminated in the Constitutional Law of 1953 giving considerable authority to local government bodies, the people's committees (_narodni odbor_). In 1955 the Law on Organization of Communes and Districts instituted the communal system. In April 1963 the constitution of the Socialist Federal Republic of Yugoslavia became law. In 1971 the decision was made to establish a collective presidency, which President Tito encouraged. In 1974 a new Yugoslav constitution was introduced. Since Tito's death, on 4 May 1980, economic and national problems have increased. On 22 January 1990 the Communist party of Yugoslavia renounced its constitutionally guaranteed leading role in society and called on parliament to enact political pluralism leading to a multiparty system. In the spring of 1990 the Slovene Communists lost in the elections and Slovenia then advocated turning Yugoslavia into a loose federation of allied states. A Slovene secessionist movement gained strength and succeeded in establishing independence in 1991. Slovenia has its own militia, which the national government had declared illegal prior to independence, and has established its own currency.

Settlements

In the most typical settlements, called planned or long villages, houses were lined up close together on either side of the road with the narrow end of the house facing the road, or houses were built only on one side of the road, or houses faced a central square with a church. In areas where the topography permitted, land surrounding the village was divided into open fields or sections, which in turn were subdivided into long parallel fields or strips. Traditionally each peasant possessed one or more strips in each section of the village land, and all villagers cooperated in a villagewide system of crop rotation (_kolobarjenje_). After the harvest the fields were opened for pasturing the cattle of the entire village. Houses were made of stone with attached sheds for animals, which

contained a stove to cook food for pigs (_kuhinja_). Detached wooden barns were for storage of hay and cattle fodder. Houses were one-and-one-half stories with two rooms and no cellar. In the kitchen was a raised hearth on which an open fire burned vented by a hole in the ceiling. Meat was stored in the attic. Roofs were thatched. The second room was the main room, heated by a large tiled stove. Tile roofs date from after World War II. Today modernization has proceeded with revenues from factory work and with remittances from family members who have migrated to cities and to foreign countries. Electrification, piped water, electric stoves and refrigerators, and house enlargements are among the improvements. Apartment buildings have grown up around factories and in urban centers. Tourism and urban development have given cities a very modern appearance.

Economy

Subsistence and Commercial Activities. Farming, livestock raising, and forestry have been the traditional rural occupations of peasants. Agricultural land is limited by rugged mountains, stony valleys, and karstic soil. Only at high altitudes are alpine black soils found. Slovenia does not produce enough grain for its own needs and must rely on imports. The main crops are wheat on the flat areas; rye, barley, and oats at higher elevations; and maize, clover, and potatoes. Turnips, carrots, beets, and cabbages are cultivated for animal as well as for human consumption. The animal economy includes milk cows, beef cattle, pigs, sheep in the mountains, and poultry. Horse and oxen for draft, the traditional sources of power, have been replaced by tractors, but only in the post–World War II period. Forest exploitation has been important for Slovene peasants, who owned 90 percent of the woodland by the period between the two wars. Furniture factories and sawmills are often close to peasant villages. Traditional methods of distribution included exchanges in regional markets. Industrialization began in the nineteenth century aided by the construction of a railroad line connecting Trieste and Ljubljana. Slovenia's resources include natural gas, oil, mercury, coal, lead, silver, and zinc. Iron, steel, and aluminum are produced. Slovenia produces considerable electrical energy. There are also paper, textile, wood, and chemical industries. While in 1900 75 percent of the population was engaged in agriculture, by 1960 this figure was reduced to 32.3 percent and a large portion of these worked part-time in factories. Of all the former Yugoslav republics, Slovenia was the most industrialized and urbanized and had the highest per capita income.

Industrial Arts. The traditional village included artisans such as tailors, weavers, cobblers, smiths, carpenters, and millers, and their products provided for most of the villagers' needs.

Trade. Villagewide and regional markets once dominated local trade, where cattle were traded and textiles, tools, rope, sweets, etc. were sold. Now there are inns and stores in the countryside providing for the village needs. Horse smuggling was common in the interwar period, when horses were bought in Croatia and sold in Italy. In the modern period much of the rural trade has been controlled by cooperative farms, to which cattle, hogs, potatoes, lumber, hay, etc. are sold at prices the peasants consider unfavorable. Consequently rural areas have attempted to develop their own specialties not demanded by the cooperatives, such as breeding hogs and selling young pigs, thereby circumventing official channels. Today Slovenia imports wheat and industrial products from the West and exports wood and textile products, nonferrous metal products, livestock, and numerous other commodities. Slovenia is attempting to increase capital-intensive and specialized industries and reduce exporting of lumber and meat in order to compete on the world market.

Division of Labor.   The traditional Slovene family was patriarchal and extended. Division of labor by sex was clear but not rigid. Women carried the main burden of the fieldwork, cutting and raking hay, digging potatoes, planting, weeding, hoeing, and caring for the crops throughout the year. Women also milked the cows, cared for the pigs, made everyday clothes and linen, prepared the food and cared for the children. Men scythed or mowed, fed the cattle, plowed, repaired buildings and tools, lumbered, and carted wood, etc. But today both men and women may work in the factory and divide up the fieldwork more informally. Other activities also divided the sexes. Thus only men and boys played ball in the *balina* fields. Young boys, but not girls, could sleep in barns at night. Men peopled the local inns. Typically boys helped the father and girls, the mother. Village specialists had far less land and engaged in weaving, forging, carpentry, etc.; some villagers owned sawmills and were millers.

Land Tenure.   Various traces of evidence suggest ancient landholdings may have been held jointly by brothers. The joint family, or South Slavic *zadruga*, it is suggested, was then modified and equal division was practiced. When land became increasingly scarce by the fourteenth century, partible inheritance was replaced by impartible inheritance with a preference for primogeniture. Disinherited brothers, unless they married women who inherited land, were forced to emigrate, to turn to specialized village crafts, or become day laborers. In the modern period, primogeniture has broken down since many sons prefer to leave rural life for factories or specialized training, leaving only a younger son or a daughter to maintain the land and homestead. However, the rule of impartibility is generally maintained since landholdings are too small to be further subdivided.

Kinship

Kin Groups and Descent.   Kinship is bilateral with a patrilineal emphasis. The typical kin group was the stem family composed of the patriarch head (*gospodar*), his wife, their children, various unmarried collateral relatives of the gospodar, and the wife and offspring of the eldest son. The presence of common surnames, archival records, and legends suggest that lineage relations existed between dominant joint families.

Marriage and the Family

Marriage.   Traditionally, village or regional endogamy was preferred. Marriages were arranged by parents and involved bargaining over dowry and inheritance. Preferred residence was virilocal, but it was sometimes uxorilocal if the inheritor of the land was a daughter. The aim was to gain land in a marriage, and thus a peasant with little land might try to marry his son to an inheriting woman. Weddings were the occasion of a *veselica*, a celebration with feasting, music, games, etc.,

and might extend over three days. Civil marriages in the postwar period have not replaced religious marriages, which, however, are much briefer than formerly. Divorce, while permitted by civil law, is still relatively rare in rural areas.

Domestic Unit.   The large stem family with many children has become smaller, increasingly being replaced by a small extended family or a nuclear family composed of parents, one to three children, and one or more members of the older generation.

Inheritance.   Land is inherited by the rules of impartibility and primogeniture when possible. Women are granted dowries and may inherit land if there is no son. The son also inherits money and animals. While status is not inherited, traditionally the son of a craftsman tended to follow his father's occupation; however, in the modern period education and factory work have opened opportunities to all strata and both sexes.

Socialization.   Children are welcomed, with sons preferred. Swaddling is no longer practiced, but a restraining nightgown may be used for the first year. Schooling is universal and education beyond high school is desired by the younger generation.

Sociopolitical Organization

Social Organization.   The family is tied to other families by relations among kin and relations to godparents and neighbors. Traditionally, villagewide activities were organized by the church, by singing societies, by firemens' organizations, which included other activities such as dramatic productions, and by veselicas at many occasions such as weddings, threshing, and the *kolina* festivities when a pig was slaughtered. Additionally, regional markets were centers for social interaction of all kinds. All these activities have declined in the modern period. Traditionally there were clear differences in social status in the peasant village. The highest status was occupied by the largest landowners and in some areas by the millers who owned larger forest reserves. Middle peasants were next, and the landless or semilandless craftsmen had the lowest status. In the postwar period peasants who became political functionaries occupied an ambiguous status, having a measure of power but often coming from the landless class. Status also became far more fluid as factory work and educational activities expanded.

Political Organization.   The post-1848 village was ruled by an elected village council under the village head (*podžupan*), who was subordinate to the *občina*, a council representing a number of villages, which in turn was subordinated to the district. This structure was successively altered under the Communist regime and the communal system. Local village government lost much of its autonomy, being replaced by people's committees (narodni odbor) at the občina and district level. After 1955 the communal system was instituted. The commune replaced the občina as the basic political unit and local units were further consolidated. Full-time peasants had less rights and were less fully represented than others.

Social Control.   In the traditional village social control was informally exercised through face-to-face relations, gossip, social ostracism, the power of the local Catholic church and the village council, and only secondarily by the legal mechanisms of the state. In the postwar period local methods largely have been replaced by official ones.

Conflict.   Traditionally conflicts between villages over such issues as boundary disputes, inheritance, rights to forest land, and road construction were settled by the village council or local courts. Postwar conflicts such as those between the village and the cooperative farms no longer are settled locally. Ethnic antagonisms between Slovenes and the representatives of the southern nationalities have been sources of tensions.

Religion and Expressive Culture

Religious Beliefs.   The main religious beliefs of the Slovenes are those of the Roman Catholic church. While legends relate activities of witches and magical forces, such themes are intermixed with Christian dogma.

Religious Practitioners and Ceremonies.   In the prewar period the parish was supported by a church tax administered by the village council and the priest was paid by the state and received remuneration from parishioners for his services, which included: hearing confessions; religious education for children; and officiation at masses, baptisms, confirmations, marriages, and funerals. The religious calendar was full and well observed, including pilgrimages to large churches with stops at wayside shrines and general celebrations on religious holidays. In the postwar period the activities and power of the Catholic church were seriously curtailed, although the priests attempted to continue to offer their services and the Catholic religion remained a strong moral force. In the post-Communist period, of course, the church has considerably greater latitude.

Arts.   Traditional arts included decorative motifs on buildings such as barns, gravestone decorations, and religious carvings and paintings in churches following central European styles. In peasant houses one saw colorful tile stoves, wall stippling giving the impression of wallpaper, woven cloths, wooden carvings on boxes and other items, and hand-carved simple furniture. Local folk art declined during the Communist period, becoming commercialized and standardized and being sold primarily in tourist-orientated state-controlled stores, but there has been a rich growth of modern architecture and painting in urban centers.

Medicine.   Modern medicine has penetrated the rural area. Children receive inoculations, chest X rays are available to everyone, and most children are born in hospitals. Peasants receive health insurance, although coverage has been limited as compared to that available to workers. While local cures and traditional herbs are still used, the primary curer is the medical doctor.

Death and Afterlife.   Funerals follow traditional Catholic customs. The body is placed in an open coffin in the house for forty-eight hours while friends and relatives pay a last call and sprinkle the body with holy water or salt. After the coffin is closed, it is placed in the open door, and the priest invokes a benediction and leads prayer. There follows the funeral mass at the church, a graveside benediction, the burial, and then the funeral feast. For eight days thereafter friends visit the family of the deceased and pray, eat, and drink together. Finally, there are additional requiem masses thirteen and eighteen days later.

Bibliography

Grafenauer, Bogo (1954–1962). *Zgodovina slovenskega naroda* (History of the Slovene people). 5 vols. Ljubljana: Kmečka Knjiga.

Hočevar, Toussaint (1965). *The Structure of the Slovenian Economy, 1848–1963*. New York: Studia Slovenica.

Mal, Josip (1928). *Zgodovina slovenskega naroda: Najnovejša doba* (History of the Slovene nation: The modern period). Celje: Druzba sv. Mohorja.

Melik, Anton (1963). *Slovenija: Geografski opis* (Slovenia: A geographic description). Ljubljana: Slovenska Matica.

Slovene Studies (1979–   ). Journal of the Society for Slovene Studies. University of Alberta. Edmonton, Canada.

Winner, Irene (1971). *A Slovenian Village: Zerovnica*. Providence: Brown University Press.

IRENE PORTIS-WINNER

Slovensko Roma

ETHNONYMS: Māre Roma, Māre Romora, Roma, Roma Sloveni, Romora

Orientation

Identification.   The Slovenian Roma are a small Gypsy group, the main nucleus of which came to Italy during the 1940s from northern Yugoslavia. Together with the Croatian Roma (Roma Hervati) and the Istrian Roma (Roma Istriani) they form a fairly homogeneous group, both culturally and linguistically, which is clearly distinguished from other Gypsy groups in Italy. From a socioeconomic point of view, the Roma can be said to be a peripatetic group (an endogamous group that bases its subsistence on the sale of goods and services to the surrounding non-Gypsy population and that adopts strategies of spatial mobility).

Location and Demography.   The Roma in Italy are concentrated in the northeast of the country; small groups are also found in central Italy. There are no general census reports directly concerning them. On the basis of fragmentary and approximate reports carried out on a local level, one may hazard a guess that the number of Roma in Italy at present is about 1,000.

Linguistic Affiliation.   The Slovenian Roma speak a dialect of the Romani (Gypsy) language, classified by some linguists as a West Balkan Gypsy dialect. Compared to most of the Gypsy dialects of Indian origin spoken in Europe, it possesses certain unique features (the absence of the article, the presence of the infinitive, special adjectival inflections, etc.).

The Roma also speak standard Italian as well as the Italian dialects spoken by the surrounding non-Gypsy populations. Only the elderly are still able to speak Slovenian.

History and Cultural Relations

The history of the Roma is closely connected, on the one hand, to the history of the surrounding European populations and, on the other, to the attempts made by the latter to assimilate the Gypsies. Linguistically related to some groups living today in Macedonia and Bulgaria, the Roma appear to be the descendants of a Gypsy group that reached the Croatian and Slovenian regions via the Adriatic coast. The first documents to cite them with certainty date from the first half of the nineteenth century, by which time they were already established in Croatia and Istria and had started to move into the Dolenjska region (southern Slovenia). They were divided into bands comprised of only a few families and exercised a circumscript nomadism, setting up camp on the outskirts of villages and in woods. They took to horse trading and working as blacksmiths with an essentially rural non-Gypsy clientele. Another important activity (exclusively female and juvenile) was begging. The Hapsburgs and the various regional governments tried to assimilate the Roma by outlawing nomadism and even, in certain cases, forbidding their commercial activities. Such a policy resulted, toward the end of the last century, in the virtual sedentarization of many families who came to live on the outskirts of villages and small towns, forming in certain cases real Gypsy "colonies." Sedentarization, proletarization, and schooling were the means adopted by the government of the new Yugoslav state in their attempts to assimilate the Roma. During World II War they suffered from the genocide of the Nazi army and of the Croatian Fascists. Many of them were slaughtered in their encampments or taken to concentration camps in Croatia and central Europe. The Italian Fascist army, which had occupied a part of Slovenia, also deported hundreds of Roma to Italy. After the arrival of the allied forces in Italy, the Roma fled from the concentration camps but remained in the country, restricting their presence to the northeast. The policies of assimilation developed in Italy (from the 1960s onward), though attempts at sedentarization, schooling, and evangelization have been absorbed by the Roma, who continue to manifest and reproduce a peculiar identity. The attempts at compulsory schooling, in particular, are negated by the Roma by means of a refined system of school absenteeism, based on an ideological consideration: in their opinion literacy is something for the non-Gypsies and is of no value to the Roma themselves.

Settlements

One of the most peculiar aspects of the Roma's settlements is their immersion and dispersion in the midst of the Gadje (non-Gypsies). In order to maintain dispersion, based on economic and sociopolitical considerations, they are both nomadic and sedentary. Most of the Roma live in caravans and camp in locales that are either less than ideal or specially prepared by the local authorities, on the outskirts of town. However, a number of families live in permanent dwellings, ranging from simple huts to luxurious villas. A fair degree of mobility is, nevertheless, found even among those living in fixed abodes; removals are frequent and they often alternate between house and caravan. Dispersion is achieved by maintaining a minimal density of Roma in any given locality. A local group rarely consists of more than fifteen nuclear families.

Economy

Subsistence and Commercial Activities. Adaptability and flexibility are characteristic of the Roma's economic practice; they tend to avoid salaried jobs as much as possible in order to retain a total control over what they do with their time. They tend to occupy a commercial niche, in part left free by the non-Gypsies, and, if necessary, they engage in more than one activity at a time. Over the last hundred years the Roma have engaged in activities typical of peripatetic groups: the sale of goods, the sale of services, and the occasional and temporary sale of labor to the non-Gypsies. In Slovenia they worked, above all, as smiths, making or repairing the small tools used by the non-Gypsies for agricultural purposes; they also acted as horse dealers and every so often worked for wages as gravel makers on the roads. The women and children were mainly beggars; begging often involved an exchange of goods for services: the Gypsy women would enter peasant farmers' houses, reciting spells that would bring prosperity to the household and receiving food and clothing in exchange. By the beginning of the twentieth century, the Roma had already begun to abandon working as smiths. In Italy, until the sixties, they were mainly involved in horse dealing and begging, while in more recent times they have developed activities connected with the sale of used metals, used cars, fruit, precious objects, and even real estate. Only a few families have continued to practice horse dealing, while begging has been replaced in part by requests for church and public assistance. Some families, albeit discontinuously, will accept salaried labor connected with seasonal fruit harvesting.

Kinship

Kin Groups and Descent. Kinship provides the base for the socioterritorial organization, even though the Roma themselves do not propagate any marked kinship ideology. They recognize a bilateral kindred (*slahta*), a pragmatic rather than cognitive category, which includes first cousins, beyond which the confines become somewhat imprecise. Affines are not considered kin. Even if kinship is bilateral, certain practices demonstrate a patrilineal ideology—for instance, their preference for forming local groups based on a nucleus of married brothers. There are no corporate groups; their genealogical memory is impaired by the censorship resulting from the fact that it is prohibited to mention the name of a dead relative and usually goes back no farther than the second ascending generation.

Kinship Terminology. The Roma have a Sudanese system with descriptive terms based on the six elementary kin terms denoting father, mother, son, daughter, brother, and sister. For the vocative, first names are always used, except when speaking to small children; in this case the terms for "mother" and "father" are used reciprocally and also as terms of affection toward the children in general.

Marriage and Family

Marriage. The Roma practice marriage by elopement, following which consent must be given by both families. It is on such occasions that the more violent feuds may break out. There are no formalized exchange units, but ethnographic data demonstrate that despite the apparent "freedom" of choice, the patrilines tend to practice a sort of delayed exchange, following an irregular triad model A>B>C>A by means of marriages with consanguines or affines' consanguines. Apart from the nuclear family, where incest is frowned on, the only exogamous group would appear to be the set of the patrilateral parallel cousins, whereas endogamy is practiced toward non-Gypsies and toward a few different Gypsy groups. Postmarital residence follows three fairly distinct phases: uxorilocality immediately after the marriage, followed by a period of bilocality, which leads to virilocal residence. Divorce does exist, but it always involves a high level of conflict and requires the divorced man and woman to live in separate local groups.

Domestic Unit. Roma ideology stresses the autonomy of the nuclear family. Each family always must have its own home (mobile or fixed) distinct from other families, be economically self-sufficient, and be free to move. Commercial associations between two or three families are always temporary and short-lived.

Inheritance. The Roma have developed a system of "respect for the dead," which involves, among other things, the destruction of the goods belonging to a deceased person. The destruction involves either burning the possessions (even a caravan, a car, or money) or selling them to a non-Gypsy. In the latter case, the money received from the sale is used to decorate the tomb. Very few objects escape destruction (a knife, a watch, and so on): they are chosen and kept individually by the members of the family in memory of the deceased. Apart from this modest passage of goods of a symbolic nature, there is no other economic inheritance. There is, therefore, no accumulation of wealth that passes from one generation to another. However, the system of respect encourages the family not to abandon the locale in which the deceased is buried; therefore one can say that the deceased "leaves" the survivors an exploitable commercial territory.

Sociopolitical Organization

Social Organization and Political Organization. The only recognized authority is the father/husband within the domestic unit. Otherwise the Roma have an acephalous organization based on local groups of about ten families. A local group is formed by a nucleus of married brothers, to which can be added bilateral kin, whose presence is more or less fluid. Every local group expects a commercial monopoly over the territory where it is camped and will be prepared to make sure it is observed. It is possible for a leader to emerge in a local group (usually one of the brothers), even though he is not officially recognized by all the members. For many families nomadism is limited to movement from one local group to another.

Social Control and Conflict. The more serious conflicts arise from disagreements over marriages or commercial activities. The Roma do not have any formal council. The resolution of a conflict always results from a settlement obtained by mediators assigned by one of the two parties. For other matters, social control is spread widely: every head of family has a gun, which serves more as a deterrent against possible violence aimed at his own family than as an offensive instrument. A violent conflict is made official by pronouncing "Eat your dead!" against the other party. Thus the conflict is extended to the group that has the same dead "to respect," the core of which is a group of brothers. Often, the fear of having the formula pronounced against one is a good enough reason for settling a dispute immediately. Social control may also involve requesting non-Gypsy police intervention.

Religion and Expressive Culture

Religious Beliefs and Practices. The Roma consider themselves to be Christians and turn to divinities of the Catholic church. Each local group is tied to a particular saint (called *devloro*, "little God") and to his sanctuary. The saints have a non-Gypsy nature, as indeed do the ministers of the cult, who are all non-Gypsies: the Catholic priest and the faith healer. The former is considered above all the intermediary between the living and the dead; the latter (devloro or *hailigo gadjo*, i.e., "little God" or "non-Gypsy saint") is called upon in cases of illness.

Death and Afterlife. As mentioned above, the Roma follow a complex system of respect for the dead, a system that involves all social spheres. The various ways of showing respect are pursued by the family of the deceased and by anyone else who wishes to show respect. The respect involves a taboo on mentioning the deceased's name, the destruction of his or her possessions, the abandonment of the place where he or she died, and the decision to avoid doing something the deceased loved to do (for example, listening to a certain song, using a certain tool, eating a special dish). The respect also involves frequent visits to the cemetery (where the dead Roma are buried in the midst of the dead non-Gypsies, just as living Roma live in the midst of living non-Gypsies), no exhibition of photos of the deceased, and the substitution of red objects for black ones. As already noted, the group practicing respect acts as a group of defense/offense in cases of conflict.

Bibliography

Dick Zatta, Jane (1988). *Gli Zingari, i Roma: Una cultura ai confini*. Padua: C.I.D.I.

Piasere, Leonardo (1985). *Māre Roma: Catégories humaines et structure sociale*. Paris: Études et Documents Balkaniques et Méditerranéens.

Štrukelj, Pavla (1980). *Romi na Slovenskem*. Ljubljana: Cankarjeva Založba.

LEONARDO PIASERE

Sorbs

ETHNONYMS: Lusatian Serbs, Lusatians, Wends

Orientation

Identification.   The Sorbs are an officially recognized national minority of Germany. While they do not constitute a separate political unit, they maintain a distinctive linguistic and cultural identity. The name "Sorb" derives from "Srbi" in their own language, and it rightly suggests a relationship to peoples elsewhere called "Serbs," but "Sorb" is preferable in that it is more specific. Similarly, the terms "Lusatian" and "Lusatian Serbs" are imprecise. "Wend" was long the designation of this group, but because it has negative connotations it is no longer in official usage. Nearly all information regarding the Sorbs is available only in Slavonic languages. The material for this article was taken from the one English-language study of the Sorbs, written by Dr. Gerald Stone of Hertford College, Oxford.

Location.   The Sorbs inhabit the Lusatian region of Germany, which extends from approximately 80 kilometers southeast of Berlin to the Polish border on the east and the border of the Czech and Slovak Federative Republic in the south. The Niesse River separates the easternmost Sorbs from their Polish neighbors, and the Spree River runs from north to south through the length of the territory. The region itself is divided into two separate territories, each distinct from the other both topographically and linguistically. Upper Lusatia, in the southern part of the region, is predominantly flatland and is the more fertile territory; Lower Lusatia is dominated by wetlands and forest. These two environmental zones are separated by the "Serbska hola" (Sorbian heath), with its sandy soils, stands of conifers, and the brown coal deposits that contribute importantly to the region's economy. The two principal Sorbian towns are Bautzen and Cottbus.

Linguistic Affiliation.   A debate continues as to whether Lower and Upper Sorbian (also called Lower and Upper Wend) constitute two dialects of a single language or are two distinct languages. Together they make up the Sorbian Subgroup of the West Slavonic Group of the Indo-European Language Family. Sorbian is closely related to Serbian, though as distinct languages, not as related dialects of one language. Whether we treat them as two separate languages or as two major dialects of a single language, each consists of several lesser dialects, six such dialects having been identified for Upper Sorbian, three for Lower Sorbian. Whether or not spoken Sorbian should be considered as consisting of two separate languages, there are clearly two distinct written forms.

Demography.   The Sorbian-speaking population in Germany was estimated in 1976 to be between 60,000 and 70,000. Today nearly all Sorbs are bilingual in Sorbian and German.

History and Cultural Relations

Since the year 806, the history of the Sorbian people has been one of conquest and reconquest by others. Their earliest forebears were the Luzici (in Lower Lusatia) and the Milceni (in Upper Lusatia), two Slavonic tribes who migrated westward into the current Sorbian territory from the lands just to the east of the Oder River sometime in the fifth or sixth centuries A.D. The political autonomy they enjoyed during those early centuries was brought to an end in 806 by Karl, son of Charlemagne. Although the region changed political hands several times, the Sorbs never again attained anything approximating an independent political existence. Although their conquerors were, at various times, Polish, Czech, and Bohemian, they were most often and most thoroughly under Germanic rule. The Christianization of the Sorbs began early, with the Moravian missions possibly arriving as early as the ninth century. But it was the Reformation, with Lutheranism's preference for the use of the vernacular, that provided the impetus to develop a written language. The development and maintenance of a specifically Sorbian literature, and thus the possibility of maintaining a separate Sorbian cultural identity in the face of German policies of colonization and assimilation, were linked to the religion of the region in another way as well—a sizable minority of Sorbs never converted from Catholicism. The Catholic church, recognizing the importance of these communicants in an otherwise Protestant region, established the Wendish Seminary in Prague in 1706, providing a place where Sorbian students could become literate not just in German but in their own language as well. The 1700s and 1800s brought other changes to the Sorbian people. Once a rural population barred by law from participating in the life of the towns and banned from membership in the trade guilds, they were suddenly free to leave the land and enter wage labor. The linkage of the region to the rest of Germany by railroad in the mid-1800s brought Sorbian villages into more direct contact with the larger society, and by the 1880s the major industries of modern-day Lusatia—brown coal, iron, and glass making—were firmly established. All these changes contributed to the development of a literate Sorbian bourgeoisie, which responded readily to the Panslavic movement that arose in Prague in the mid-1800s, slowing the rush to "germanicization" and permitting the florescence of a specifically Sorbian literary culture. Although both the Weimar Republic and the Nazi regime sought to restrain Sorbian efforts toward independence, the sense of a particularly Sorbian national identity never faltered. At the end of World War II, Soviet policies broke up the large landholdings of Lusatia, converted them back into agriculture, and introduced statutes that made Sorbian an official language. The special position of the Sorbs as an official national minority continued to be recognized after the Soviet Occupation Zone became the German Democratic Republic.

Settlements

In the past, Sorbs lived in rural villages, and as recently as 1945 many of these villages had exclusively Sorbian populations. Since 1945 the populations of all Lusatian communities have become a mixture of German and Sorbian peoples. While most Sorbs today live in houses of modern design and construction, the traditional house was built of wood, was gabled, and had a thatched roof. The woodwork was highly carved and colorfully painted.

Economy

The Sorbs were once restricted to a rural life-style, barred by law from participating in the trade guilds of the towns. But when serfdom was abolished in the early to mid-1800s, such restrictions were eased. There is now no single economic activity in which the Sorbs specialize. The region is largely agricultural, but the coal and iron industries, as well as glass manufacturing, are well developed and quite important. Sorbs participate fully in the life of the towns of the region, at all socioeconomic levels and in all fields of endeavor. Land and other property is privately owned.

Kinship, Marriage, and Family

Kinship. Sorbian kinship reckoning does not differ from the pattern followed by their German neighbors; it is bilateral, but with a strong patrilineal bias. Whether this was the case earlier in their history, prior to their "germanization," is unclear.

Marriage. There appears to be some preference for Sorbian endogamy. Marriage is monogamous. Weddings are religious as well as secular events.

Domestic Unit. The Sorbian household centers on the nuclear family (husband, wife, and their offspring) and tends today to be neolocal, at least in the towns. In the organization of the household, as in many other elements of day-to-day life, Sorbs differ little from the practices of their German neighbors.

Inheritance. Although property can be inherited by either sons or daughters, there is a bias toward sons over daughters.

Socialization. The distinctive elements of Sorbian culture, which are found in language and literature, music, women's costumes, and certain religious and secular traditions, are passed along through all three of the principal institutions of socialization: parents, the church, and the schools. Specific institutions dedicated to the maintenance of a specifically Sorbian cultural identity include the Domowina groups (first established in 1912, banned by the Nazi regime in 1937, and reestablished in 1945). Domowina groups are dedicated to "the advancement of creative cultural activity," and through their sponsorship of a variety of cultural performances (concerts, films, folk music, and the like), as well as through their direct involvement in local Sorbian schools, they seek to keep Sorbian traditions, particularly in the arts, alive and accessible to the population.

Sociopolitical Organization

The Sorbs are integrated into the social and political life of their communities, and they have no specific organizational units of their own other than the Domowina groups (discussed earlier). Membership in the Domowina and its local units (Serbski Domy, "Sorbian Houses") is voluntary, and, though popular, Domowina membership does not extend throughout the Sorbian-speaking population.

Religion and Expressive Culture

Religious Beliefs. The Christianization of the Sorbian people began as early as the ninth century, with the influence of the Moravian mission. Since the Reformation, Sorbs have been predominantly Protestant, specifically Lutheran, but one area to the northwest of Bautzen remained, and remains today, Catholic. Local legends refer to a number of mythical creatures, the best known of which is the Waterman, a trickster figure who inhabits local bodies of water and who can disguise himself as a human, animal, or fish. Traditional folktales of the region feature a lively cast of ghosts, witches, and magical serpents.

Religious Practitioners. Formal religious practice based in the churches is led by either German or Sorbian priests and ministers. There has long been an emphasis on training priests and ministers in the Sorbian tongue; the Lutheran emphasis on the use of the vernacular was one factor in this development, and the need of the Catholic church to maintain a stronghold in a predominantly Protestant region was another.

Ceremonies. There are a number of specifically Sorbian traditions that may be grouped loosely under the category of "ceremonies," some of which are linked to the religious calendar. These include the use of decorated Easter eggs in a children's game similar to playing "marbles"; a ritual "walking of the borders," wherein the populace of a village makes a procession around the newly planted fields while singing hymns; and the Easter Ride, wherein formally dressed villagers ride off on decorated horses to visit a neighboring community bearing the altar cross and banners of their own village church. Many of these traditions are thought to have their roots in pre-Christian fertility rites. Another important event, recently fallen into disuse, was called the Spinning Evening, which took place on winter nights. Groups of up to twelve unmarried girls would meet regularly in one house over the period from 11 October to Ash Wednesday and share in the work of spinning. During these meetings there was much gossip, storytelling, and song. These Spinning Evenings were important because they provided a venue for passing along much of Sorbian oral history, folklore, and traditional music through the generations. In the past there were a number of ceremonies tied specifically to the celebration of the harvest. Today, life-cycle celebrations such as weddings and funerals are occasions for the adoption of special forms of the national costume.

Arts. Sorbian folk art is preserved in national costume and in the elaborate dying and decorating of Easter eggs. The distinctive Sorbian national dress is today worn only by women, and it includes extremely large hoods. While there has been some modification of the costume, reflecting the influence of fashion, traditionally it was made of brightly colored, heavy material and was highly embroidered. The specifics of the costume, the materials used, and the colors of the fabric vary somewhat across the villages of the region. The decoration of Easter eggs is not a specifically Sorbian art, as it is found throughout the Slavonic peoples, but it has achieved a special importance among the Sorbs and currently is undergoing an increased popularity. The visual arts are encouraged by the Circle of Sorbian Artists, founded in 1924. Sorbian literature is also highly developed and is encouraged by the Domowina People's Press. This literature includes nonfiction treatments of both traditional and scholarly themes, as well as poetry and fiction. The Sorbian People's Theatre was founded in 1948, but there are few Sorbian playwrights, so most performances are of the translated works of others. Music was always an important aspect of Sorbian life, particularly choral music performed by groups of young women in such venues as the Spinning Evenings. Of traditional Sorbian instruments only two are still played: the three-fingered fiddle and the bagpipes. There are a number of published collections of traditional folk songs. The earliest compositions were hymns for the most part, but secular composition began at least by the mid- to late 1700s. There is a lively Sorbian interest in choral movement; its most prolific and best-known practitioner is Jurij Winar, who has also published poetry and fiction.

Medicine. There is no information regarding indigenous Sorbian medical practices. As members of the larger German community Sorbs participate in the same health-care system as their non-Sorbian neighbors.

Death and Afterlife. Sorbian beliefs and practices regarding death and the afterlife are consistent with Christian teachings. Funerals are one of the ritual occasions for which Sorbian women will don national dress. The color of mourning, for the Sorbs, is white.

Bibliography

Stone, Gerald (1972). *The Smallest Slavonic Nation: The Sorbs of Lusatia*. London: Athlone Press.

NANCY E. GRATTON

Spaniards

ETHNONYMS: none

Spaniards are citizens of Spain (España), which occupies an area of 504,750 square kilometers and in 1990 had an estimated population of 39,623,000. The Castilian form of Spanish is the national language. Ninety percent of Spaniards are Roman Catholic. Although the regional cultures were unified in the fifteenth century, regional distinctions based on history, territorial ties, and language remain strong. The major regional cultures are the Andalusians, Basques, Castilians, Catalans, Galicians, and the Leonese. Smaller distinctive cultural groups include Gitanos, Rom, Sephardic Jews, and various cultural isolates who live by farming and herding. These include the Agotes, Maragotes, Pasiegos, and Vaqueros de Alzada.

See Andalusians; Balearics; Basques; Castilians; Catalans (Països Catalans); Galicians; Gitanos; Leonese; Pasiegos; Sephardic Jews; Spanish Rom

Bibliography

Kurian, George T. (1990). *Encyclopedia of the First World*. 2 vols. New York: Facts on File.

Worldmark Encyclopedia of the Nations (1988). 7th ed. New York: Worldmark Press.

Spanish Rom

ETHNONYMS: Hungaros, Zingaros

Orientation

Identification and Location. The Rom are a Gypsy group of wide distribution in Europe and the Americas. The Rom are scattered throughout Spain in small communities. By and large they make their living through metalworking, and small, relatively sedentary communities tend to be located in industrial, urban, and resort centers. Some Rom who do metalworking or operate small circuses continue to engage in a more nomadic life-style. These mobile groups tend also to travel through Portugal, France, and Italy.

Demography. There are comparatively few Rom on the Iberian Peninsula. At any one time there are at most several hundred of them in Spain and Portugal.

Linguistic Affiliation. Gypsies generally speak Romany, which is classified by linguists as belonging to the Indo-Iranian division of the Indo-European Language Family. The varieties of Romany that the Rom speak are called the Vlach dialects. Vlach Romany has a conservative Indic basic vocabulary and grammar. It has eight or nine noun cases and a complex system of functional verbal suffixes. Although Vlach "common" or basic vocabulary items are of Indian origin, Vlach also contains numerous (1,000+) Romanian loanwords. The Spanish Rom also speak Spanish, and the nomadic groups speak the languages of nearby European countries in addition to their own dialects.

History and Cultural Relations

Linguistic and genetical evidence indicates that the "original" Gypsies were an Indian ethnic group that migrated out of the subcontinent around A.D. 1000. Passing through Byzantium, they spread through the Balkans during the fourteenth century and reached Russia, Scandinavia, the British Isles, France, and Spain in the fifteenth century. The Spanish descendants of these early migrants are called "Gitanos" and today, as in past centuries, they constitute the majority of Spanish Gypsies. The Gitanos retained much of their Romany lexicon, which was called "Caló" until well into the nineteenth century; but they quickly forgot its Indic grammar. The Rom, on the other hand, did not arrive in western Europe, including Spain and Portugal, much before 1850. Until about that date they had been attached, in a kind of serfdom, to the still-feudal Romanian economy; hence a considerable admixture of Romanian words is evident in their Romany. Reportedly, a nomadic band of metalworking Gypsies camped on the outskirts of the Portuguese city of Fonte Nova in 1869, and their kitchenware was of such fine quality that it left the city's resident Neopolitan craftsmen speechless. Another report from Portugal in 1883 describes a nomadic band of metalworkers, at least two of whom spoke "perfect Spanish," and relates that they were returning to Spain. They spoke a "special language" that was not Caló, and they did not like to be compared with the Gitanos. Both descriptions refer to the people involved as "Hungarian Gypsies" (Ciganos Hungaros) and leave little doubt that these folk were Rom, and that, as such, the Rom had entered Iberia soon after the Romanian diaspora.

Settlements

The size and distribution of settlements are structured by the availability of metalwork. The latter consists of industrial cutting tools to be sharpened, repaired, and tempered and industrial kitchenware to be cleaned, tinned, and repaired. Hence, small nuclei of several extended families cluster in urban, industrial, and resort areas. Other groups of thirty to forty people are nomadic and travel from work site to work site. Mixed types also occur.

Economy

Metalwork is always done on a contractual basis for non-Gypsy or Gazé businessmen. Each Gypsy male head of an extended family has his clientele of repeat customers, some of which have "been in the family" over several generations. All family heads constantly search for new clients. Often several family heads enter into joint ventures and share proceeds. Interfamily solidarity is a paramount economic focus for the Rom in that significant capital is invested back into the multifamily local group in the form of elaborate ritual drinking and feasting. Women are charged with domestic responsibilities, but they help with metalwork and sometimes are called on to deal with difficult Gazé customers. The Spanish Rom and other European Rom see a sort of economic "golden age" of their people as ending in the post–World War II era, when great urban and resort hotels began to replace their large collections of valuable copper pots and pans, which required constant tinning and repair, with stainless steel. Spain, in particular, is seen by Rom to have suffered from the effects of this technological innovation. Many Rom see Spain as _xalardó_ or "finished" in an economic sense. Many European and American Rom also view their Spanish cousins as being somewhat old-fashioned and traditional. In a related sense, European Rom perceive Spain as a particularly good place to be "Gypsy" (i.e., as a sort of "vacation" spot in which to spend the money they have made elsewhere in Europe). Some of the few small circuses that find their way in and out of Spain are run by Moldováya or Bayása Gypsies, who lost much of their Romany during the "Romanian captivity" but who have relearned it from the Rom they associate with in various parts of Europe. Finally, Rom from South America have found their way recently into Spanish tourist centers, where they make their living by telling fortunes. They tend to keep their distance from the Spanish Rom proper, who frown on the practice because they believe it exposes their women to danger.

Kinship, Marriage, and Family

Kin Groups and Descent. In the Rom kinship system, kin terms are, with the exception of affinal labels, similar to those in English. The European Rom, including the Spanish Rom, divide themselves into three "tribes" or _vítsi_: the Kalderása, the Lovára, and the Tšurára. Although Rom concede that small linguistic and social differences distinguish one _vitsa_ from another, all Rom consider themselves related to all other Rom by ties of consanguinity and affinity, as well as by a common culture and language. Marriages can occur both within and across vitsa lines, and one can claim membership to either father's or mother's tribe. The vitsi are not corporate groups.

Marriage. Ideally, the kin of a marriageable young man (a _romoṛo_) seek out a Rom girl (a _šei_) for him to marry. The boy's kin arrange a series of feasts "to honor" the girl's kin. Then at a formal ritual (_mangimós_), a bride-price in gold coins is negotiated. A wedding usually follows. Many Spanish Rom dislike the idea of a bride-price and take pains to keep their married daughters close by. They also require that the young people involved consent to the union. Occasionally Rom men will marry Gazé women or Gitano women. There is a strong taboo on Rom women marrying Gazé men. Patrilocality is the ideal, but matrilocality also occurs.

Sociopolitical Organization

The Spanish Rom have no formal leaders, and coercion of any sort is frowned on. Occasionally, rich Gypsy men might influence others by example and persuasion, but never by threat.

Religion and Expressive Culture

Religious Beliefs and Practices. The Spanish Rom are nominally Catholics. Some are devoted to the cults of Iberian folk saints and healers. They are very devoted to the memory of their dead, especially their recent dead. They believe these recent dead can intervene for ill or for good in the affairs of the living. The Spanish Rom have no folk healers and strongly believe in Western medicine.

Arts. The Rom are aware that they have a certain style that permeates and unifies many aspects of their everyday life including speech, food preparation, manners, dress, the arrangement of space, and the ritual preparation of tea. They value this style, which they denote by the adverb _romanés_ (in the Gypsy way) and are aware that it is admired by many of their Gazé and Gitano neighbors.

Bibliography

Cohn, Werner (1969). "Some Comparisons between Gypsy (North American _rom_) and American Kinship Terms." _American Anthropologist_ 71:476–482.

Gjerdman, O., and E. Ljungberg (1963). _The Language of the Swedish Coppersmith Gipsy Johan Dimitri Taikon._ Uppsala: A.-B Lundequistska Bokhandeln.

Mulcahy, F. D. (1988). "Material and Non-Material Resources, or Why the Gypsies Have No Vises." _Technology in Society_ 10:457–467.

Yoors, Jan (1987). _The Gypsies._ Prospect Heights, Ill.: Waveland Press.

Yoors, Jan (1988). _Crossing._ Prospect Heights, Ill.: Waveland Press.

F. D. MULCAHY

Swedes

ETHNONYMS: none

Orientation

Identification. The origin of the name "Swedes" (*svenskar*) is *swaensker*, which means "from Svealand."

Location. Sweden is located between 55° and 69° N and 24° E. Sweden lies in northwestern Europe in the Scandinavian Peninsula bounded by Norway in the west, Finland in the northeast, Denmark in the southwest, the Gulf of Bothnia in the east, the Baltic Sea in the southeast, and the North Sea in the southwest. Sweden's main regions are, from the north, the northern mountain and lake region named Norrland; the lowlands of central Sweden known as Svealand; the low Småland highlands and the plains of Skåne, both areas in Götaland. Sweden has a coastline that is sometimes rocky and consists of large archipelagoes, *skärgård*. About 15 percent of the country lies within the Arctic Circle, and the climatic differences in the country are substantial. Snow is found in the mountainous regions in the north for approximately eight months out of the year, but in the south only about one month. The waters of the west coast are almost always ice-free, but the northern Baltic is usually ice-covered from November to May. The growing period is about three months in the north and eight in the south.

Demography. In 1990 the Swedish population was about 8,590,630, including a Saami population in Lappland and a Finnish-speaking group, Tornedalians, along the border of Finland, both consisting of approximately 15,000–17,000 persons.

Linguistic Affiliation. The Swedish language belongs to the North Germanic (Scandinavian) Subgroup of the Germanic languages. It is related to Norwegian, Danish, Icelandic, and Faroese. It has been influenced by German, French, English, and Finnish. The Saami and the Tornedalians understand and speak Swedish, but they form special linguistic groups. Immigration to Sweden after World War II has created many new language groups.

History and Cultural Relations

It is most likely that the first migrations to Sweden occurred about 12,000 B.C. when tribes of reindeer hunters followed the herds from the Continent to Sweden. The Sviones (Swedes) are mentioned by Tacitus (A.D. 98); this indicates that trade links between the Roman Empire and Scandinavia existed. During the Iron Age (500 B.C.–A.D. 1050) the Lake Mälaren valley, in central Sweden, became an influential area, with the Svea tribe in the leading position. The Vikings (c. A.D. 800–1050) were traders who made voyages to many of the Christian countries of Europe. Many of them stayed in countries such as France, England, and Scotland. Many geographical names in these countries are of Scandinavian origin. The Vikings controlled several trade routes in contemporary eastern Russia, but from the tenth century they began to lose their foothold in this market. During the period of 800–1050 Sweden was frequently visited by Christian missionaries from France, Norway, Denmark, Russia, and Germany. Toward the end of the tenth century, Sweden had been transformed into a Christian kingdom and a united state. In the thirteenth-century Swedish "crusades," Sweden—with the double goal of Christianization and conquest—moved against Finland and the eastern Baltic coast. By the mid-thirteenth century, several Hansa merchants were established in Sweden, and an increase in trade with the Hansa cities followed. German involvement in Scandinavia led to the unification of Scandinavian countries in 1397 under the Kalmar Union; this lasted until 1448. In the following period Sweden was involved in wars with Finland and crushed a Danish attempt to recreate a union. During the seventeenth century Sweden constituted a major power consisting of present-day Sweden, Finland, Ingermanland, Estonia, Latvia, and smaller areas in northern Germany. The country was involved in war for over a hundred years, and Swedish soldiers were in Germany, Czechoslovakia, Russia, and the Baltic States. After 1721 all overseas Swedish provinces were lost with the exception of Finland and Pomerania. In the beginning of the nineteenth century, Sweden became involved in new wars with Denmark and Russia, and Finland was lost to Russia in 1809. This political border was drawn right through a former culturally homogeneous area—Tornedalen—and thus Sweden obtained a Finnish-speaking minority at the border with Finland. From 1814 to 1905 Sweden was unified with Norway. During World War II, from which Sweden was spared, thousands of refugees came to Sweden, mainly from Denmark, Norway, and Finland but also from Estonia, Latvia, and Lithuania. Before this time Sweden was unusually homogeneous in language and ethnic stock, although it had had an immigration of Germans, Walloons, Dutch, and Scots from the Middle Ages on. But since World War II Sweden has had a net immigration of about 600,000 people, primarily from the European continent but also from Latin America, Asia, and the Middle Eastern countries.

Today there are representatives of 166 different nations living in Sweden. The number of ethnic groups is even higher. There is also a Swedish minority in North America. During the nineteenth century, over a million Swedes emigrated because of difficult living conditions.

Settlements

As a result of variations in ecological conditions and inheritance practices, there have been large variations between villages in different parts of the country. Traditionally, the largest villages were in Dalecarlia, in the valley of Norrland, and on the rich plains of Skåne. There are also variations in the form of the villages. In Dalecarlia the houses have often been built in irregular and open clusters (*klungbyar*, cluster villages). In other parts, the villages have had a more closed and regular structure, as for example in Svealand and Götaland where the villages were often built as a row of houses (*radbyar*, row villages). In Skåne the villages have often been constructed around an open place (*rundby*, circle villages). There have been five main forms of traditional housing design in the Swedish villages. The northern Swedish farmyard consisted of several buildings around a grassy yard. In the central Swedish yards the main house and the farmhouse were separated by a building, often a stable with a gate. The third type (Gothic) had a long, rectangular form, with the farmhouse separated from the main house by a fence. The western Swedish type was an irregular and loose construction of houses. The southern Swedish farmyard consisted of four long row houses built together. These square houses in Skåne were built with brick, and clay was applied over a stick frame. In the rest of the country, wood has been the most common construction material. Houses built in contemporary Sweden are basically the same throughout the country. Because of urbanization many empty houses are now used as summer houses. The relatively few castles and manors are found only in southern and central Sweden.

Economy

Subsistence and Commercial Activities.   Preindustrial Sweden was an agrarian country. Farming was the most common subsistence activity, always combined with stock raising and often with forestry, handicraft, trade, and transportation. Farming was combined with fishing along the coasts and around the many big lakes. Today agriculture has diminished. In 1990 it employed only 3.3 percent of the working population. The main agricultural products are dairy produce, meat, cereals, and potatoes.

Industrial Arts.   Iron ore and lumber are the basic raw materials. Besides lumber, the modern forest industry produces paper, board, pulp, rayon, plastics, and turpentine. Sweden also is able to exploit hydroelectric power thanks to its many rivers with waterfalls. The country has two big car manufacturing companies (Volvo and Saab), a telecommunications industry (Ericsson), a manufacturer of roller and ball bearings (SKF), a producer of household appliances (Electrolux), and a company producing electric motors, steam turbines, and equipment for hydroelectric power plants (ASEA-Brown Bovery).

Trade.   About one-half of the industrial production is exported. Iron, steel, and forest products—such as paper and paper board—are important as well as different kinds of manufactured commodities, especially machinery and transportation equipment. Sweden's largest export markets are Germany, the United States, the United Kingdom, and Norway, in that order. Engineering products, cars and other motor vehicles, machinery, computers, chemical products, fuel, and crude oil dominate the imports to Sweden. The supplying countries are Germany, the United Kingdom, the United States, and Denmark.

Division of Labor.   In the old peasant society, cattle raising was female work, while horses were part of the male world. Threshing was regarded mainly as men's work, but in eastern Dalecarlia it belonged to the women's sphere. Women from this area even worked as professional threshers during seasonal work periods. Textile production has been a female job, except in Halland, where men, boys, and women traditionally produced knitwear for sale. The general tendency is that in areas where agriculture has been a sideline, women have carried out several tasks that traditionally belonged to the male sphere in typical agricultural areas. Child labor was usual in preindustrial Sweden as well as during the first period of industrialization (1850–1900). Children worked in the sawmills, factories, glassworks, and ironworks. In contemporary Sweden, ethnic niches have started to emerge. There are restaurants owned by Chinese, pizza shops, sweet stalls, and small grill-restaurants owned by immigrants from the Middle Eastern countries. Assyrians and Syrians are involved in traditional trades such as tailoring and shoemaking. Together with Kurds and Turks, they also trade in fruit and vegetables.

Land Tenure.   Before 1827, when a statute on enclosures (_laga skifte_) was passed, the fields of each farm were split up in several small lots in various places. The agricultural modernization of 1827 meant that the fields of each farm could be assembled together in a compact area. These enclosures of land took place during the entire nineteenth century and changed the countryside radically. At the end of 1940, a new wave of structural rationalization began with the goal of creating larger and more productive units. In 1988 only 8.7 percent of Sweden's land area was utilized for agriculture. The majority farms are privately owned. An estimated 69.6 percent of the country's area is covered by forest and woodland. Corporations and other private owners control at least three-quarters of the nation's forest land and timbering.

Kinship

Kinship and Descent.   Swedish kinship is bilateral and cognatic. Generally the kinship system follows the same rules of other European peoples. Except for the family, kin groups have been of little importance as a focus of social organization during the most recent centuries.

Kinship Terminology.   Kin terms follow the Eskimo system with local and regional variations in terminology. In some regions in northern Sweden, cousins are numbered from first to fourth. They can be called, as for example in northern Värmland, _tvämänningar, tremänningar, fyrmänningar, femmänningar_. In central and southern Sweden the words _syssling, brylling, pyssling_ are used instead of the number of the cousins.

Marriage and Family

Marriage.   In preindustrial Sweden, marriage was an economic agreement between two families and not, as today, a private affair. The marriage ritual included exchanges of gifts and economic transactions between the two families. The dowry that the bride should bring into the marriage was carefully stipulated. This dowry, as well as a gift she got from her husband, belonged to her. In cases of childlessness, the dowry went back to the wife's family. Because of economic and social differences in Sweden, there have been variations in the degree of parental control over marriage partners. Strategic marriages, even sibling exchange, have been much more common among the wealthy farmers in the south than among the poor forest dwellers in the north. During the last twenty years, cohabitation without marriage (to _sambo, sam_ meaning "together with" and _bo_ meaning "live") has increased. This form usually precedes a marriage, and it is not unusual to have children before marrying. In 1988 a law was passed making the partners in sambo relationships almost spouses. The divorce rate has risen during the last two decades: twice as many marriages end in divorce now as compared to 1960.

Domestic Unit.   The dominant domestic units in the peasant society were the small, extended, and nuclear families. Today the most common type is the nuclear family.

Inheritance.   Until 1845 peasant daughters inherited half as much as their brothers. In 1845 equal rights of inheritance were legally stipulated. In reality, however, there were variations in inheritance practice. Many farmers, for example, on the isle of Gotland, on the plains of Skåne, and in the valley of Mälaren, had male primogeniture. Male ultimogeniture also existed. Other families practiced partible inheritance, for example in Dalecarlia and certain parts of Norrland.

Socialization.   Characteristically, young children in Swedish peasant society participated in adult tasks. The children learned about working life through observation, imitation, and practice rather than by education. In three-generational domestic units, grandparents played an important role in raising children. In contemporary Swedish families it is common for both parents to work, and all children over 18 months are entitled to a place in a daily-care center up to the age of 6 years. There are also open preschools where preschoolers can meet a few times weekly in the company of a guardian. "Leisure time centers" are available for children ages 7–12 whose parents are working or studying. These centers are open before and after school and during vacations.

Sociopolitical Organization

Social Organization.   Strong patriarchalism was characteristic of the preindustrial family unit. In northern Sweden the master often kept his role until his death, but in the rest of the country it was normal for him to hand over the leadership to the younger generation during his later years. The older couple was then "retired" (på undantag, sytning), and were supported for the rest of their lives. Even though the family was the basic production unit, there was also a great need for cooperation in larger units. In preindustrial Sweden there existed a large number of corporations, which were constructed through cooperation and/or joint ownership. The structure of these corporations was often nonhierarchical. If there was a leader, he was primus inter pares (first among equals).

Political Organization.   In preindustrial Sweden owning land was a condition for taking part in local policy. The communal villages were led by a council of the landed gentry. An alderman could be chosen, but it was more common that the job was shared by rotation. Contemporary Sweden has been famous for its "middle way"—a Socialist but non-Communist policy. Sweden is a constitutional monarchy. The hereditary monarch is head of state but has very limited formal prerogatives. Executive power rests with the cabinet (regeringen), which is responsible to the parliament (Riksdag). In 1971 the unicameral Riksdag was introduced. Its 349 members are elected for three years by universal suffrage. The country is divided into 24 counties and 279 municipalities; local governments are responsible for important parts of public administration.

Social Control.   Since the 1930s, the relationship between Swedish employees and employers has been characterized by the "Swedish model." This model implies negotiations between the government, employers, and the trade unions, and as a result cooperation is typical in Swedish working life. Since the general strike in 1909, strikes have been rare.

Conflict.   Sweden is not a member of any political or military alliance and pursues a policy of neutrality. The Swedes have lived in peace for over 170 years.

Religion and Expressive Culture

Religious Beliefs.   At birth all Swedes automatically become members of the Lutheran Protestant State Church, but they have the right to leave the church. Ninety-two percent of the Swedish population belongs to it. The majority of people do not go to church regularly, but most children are baptized and confirmed, and most Swedes are married and buried by the church. During the nineteenth century there were many pietistic movements characterized by a puritan life-style. In the north of Sweden the Laestadian movement is still vital. Swedish peasant society believed that the landscape was crowded with various supernatural beings.

Religious Practitioners.   Shamans were part of the Saami religion and are considered prophets of the Laestadian movement. Today the ministers of the Lutheran Protestant State Church are both male and female.

Ceremonies.   There are not many religious ceremonies in contemporary Sweden. Certainly some celebrations have a religious origin—Advent, Lucia, Christmas, Easter, and Whitsuntide—but only a minority of the Swedes think of these celebrations as religious.

Arts.   Swedish folk art and handicrafts present many regional variations because of differences in the availability of raw materials. Straw products were usual in Skåne, whereas birch-bark products were common in Norrland. The Saami made, and still make, richly ornamented knives and spoons from reindeer horn. In Dalecarlia human hair was used to produce rings, necklaces, and brooches, which were sold all over Sweden until 1925, when they went out of fashion. The traditional Swedish textiles are wool and flax. A weaving technique used mainly in south and western Sweden is röllakan. Dalecarlia is famous for its wall painting. Blacksmithing is another handicraft with a long tradition. Folk art is noticeable in the modern design of glassware, ceramics, woodwork, textiles, furniture, silver, and stainless steel.

Medicine.   Traditional folk medicine made use of magical objects as well as locally grown plants. As illness was often attributed to spirit possession, various kinds of healing rituals were also used. These were mainly readings, for example of charms, and various types of curing by local healers' or priests' touch. Medical knowledge was passed from one generation to the next. During the nineteenth century, several literate healers read official medical books. They picked up fragments of information from these books, which they combined with their traditional knowledge. Sometimes this led to conflicts between local healers and district medical officers and sometimes to a division of labor, with local healers often being respected for their ability to cure allergies and various skin diseases.

Death and Afterlife.   Beliefs in a life after death certainly influenced the daily life in preindustrial Sweden. Currently, such beliefs are not integrated into everyday life but are privately held. The Tornedalians in the north still practice a funeral ritual, which in earlier days was common in several areas. Immediately after the death the family, neighbors, and close friends gather around the deceased, in his or her home, and "sing him/her out." Two weeks after this ritual, the formal funeral takes place in the church.

Bibliography

Bringéus, Nils-Arvid, ed. (1973). _Arbete och redskap: Materiell folkkultur på svensk landsbygd före industrialismen._ Lund: CWK Gleerup Bokförlag.

Daun, Åke (1989). _Svensk mentalitet: Ett jämförande perspektiv._ Stockholm: Raben & Sjögren.

Frykman, Jonas, and Orvar Löfgren (1987). _Culture Builders: A Historical Anthropology of Middle-Class Life._ New Brunswick and London: Rutgers University Press.

Hellspong, Mats, and Orvar Löfgren (1974). _Land och stad: Svenska samhällstyper och livsformer från medeltid till nutid._ Lund: CWK Gleerup Bokförlag.

Himmelstrand, Ulf, and Göran Svensson, eds. (1988). _Sverige-vardag och struktur: Sociologer beskriver det svenska samhället._ Stockholm: Norstedts.

Stromberg, Peter G. (1986). _Symbols of a Community: The Cultural System of a Swedish Church._ Tucson: University of Arizona Press.

Svanberg, Ingvar, and Harald Runblom, eds. (1990). _Det mångkulturella Sverige: En handbok om etniska grupper och minoriteter._ Stockholm: Gidlunds Bokförlag.

LENA GERHOLM

Swiss

ETHNONYMS: none

The Swiss are citizens of the nation of Switzerland (Swiss Confederation). Switzerland is located in central Europe and covers 41,295 square kilometers of territory. The estimated population for 1990 is 6,628,000. Switzerland is a pluralistic society with about 65 percent of the population German-speaking, 18 percent French-speaking, 12 percent Italian-speaking, and about 1 percent Romansch-speaking. The population is split about equally between Catholics and Protestants. Politically, Switzerland is divided into twenty cantons and six half-cantons. The Swiss Confederation was founded in 1291 when three cantons joined together for defensive purposes and gradually expanded over the centuries. Switzerland is known today for its military neutrality, banking industry, and as the headquarters for many international organizations.

See German Swiss; Jurassians; Romansch; Swiss, Italian

Bibliography

Kurian, George T. (1990). _Encyclopedia of the First World._ 2 Vols. New York: Facts on File.

Worldmark Encyclopedia of the Nations (1988). 7th ed. New York: Worldmark Press.

Swiss, Italian

ETHNONYMS: Graubunden, Grigioni Italiano, Italiani in Svizzera, Svizzera Meridionale, Svizzeri Italiani, Ticino

Orientation

Identification. The canton of Ticino was named by Napoleon in 1803 after the main river of the region. The name "Grigioni" is derived from the "grey league" founded in the fourteenth century.

Location. Italian-speaking people in Switzerland reside in two cantons: Ticino and Grigioni (Graubunden in German) (Mesolcina, Calanca, Bregaglia, and Poschiavo valleys). Except for one village (Bivio, in Grigioni), they are all situated south of the Alps (Svizzera Meridionale). All the rivers lead to the Italian Lombardic plain of the Po River. The region is located at 46° N and between 8° and 11° E. To the north are the cantons of Valais, Uri, and Grigioni. Ceneri Mountain divides Ticino in two parts. To describe the climate, we have to distinguish among the plains, the hills/mountains, and the Alps: the differences in temperature, hours of sunshine, and altitude are considerable. The landscape is characterized by many steep and wooded valleys (such as the Centovalli). On the plains the lakes influence the climate so that even exotic plants grow in the open air. In general, the climate south of the Alps is characterized by dry, sunny winters, with little fog and sometimes heavy snowfall; rainy springs; sunny summers with frequent thundershowers; and autumns with dry periods, alternating with strong rainfalls. In recent years, air pollution has adversely affected the climate and its reputation.

Demography. Before the nineteenth century, emigration from the valleys was seasonal or yearly and then mainly to cities in Switzerland and Italy, but there was also emigration to France, England, Germany, Austria, Hungary, Poland, and Russia. In the nineteenth century, permanent emigration took place to North and South America and to Australia. (In 1830, 12,000 passports were issued.)

Italian workers began coming to Switzerland to construct the San Gottardo railway at the end of the nineteenth and beginning of the twentieth century. During the twentieth century, the population of the Ticino (but not Grigioni Italiano and the Centovalli, Maggia, Verzasca, Leventina, Blenio areas) has doubled. There has been constant population growth in the cities so that today over 70 percent of the population lives there. In 1990 the population in the Svizzera Meridionale was about 6 percent of the Swiss population (i.e., 300,000 people). About 20 percent of the population in the Ticino is Italian by nationality.

If we define Swiss Italians on the basis of language, we must also count the 400,000 or so Italian migrants (beyond those who are naturalized citizens and their children) living in all parts of Switzerland. In most of the Swiss cantons, one will find Italian immigration centers, Italian consulates, private Italian schools, or other services to support Italian culture.

Linguistic Affiliation.   The identity of the Swiss Italians reflects the history of minorities within minorities. In Europe, Switzerland consists of German, French, Italian, and Romansch minority groups. Within Switzerland, French, Italian, and Romansch people are minority groups. The Grigioni Italiano live in a canton that has the smallest linguistic minority in Switzerland—the Romansch—besides the German-speaking majority.

Written Italian in Switzerland is the same as in Italy, with some dialectal differences. It has a Latin grammar, with Celtic, Gallic, and Lombardic elements. The dialects spoken by native Swiss Italians are an important element of their ethnic identity. To speak the Swiss Italian dialect affords a social distinction in most Swiss Italian regions, though the elite of Lugano emphasize standard Italian and the Locarnese prefer to use their own dialect. The Italian language is disappearing in two of the four valleys of the Grigioni Italiano (Bregaglia, Poschiavo), which are economically and politically dependent on the German-speaking capital of their canton. The valleys of Calanca and Mesolcina are geographically attached to Ticino, where their language is used in the press and in education.

History and Cultural Relations

The desire to control the alpine transit roads was the reason for wars that greatly affected the Swiss Italian population. The first alpine passages were the Passo di Spluga and the Bernina (Bregaglia) in the second century A.D. After the fall of the Roman Empire, Ticino was dominated in turn by the Lombardic lords, monasteries or the church, and German rulers or lords; and from the fifteenth century to the French Revolution, it fell under the domination of the other Swiss cantons. Leventina and Blenio were independent and had a democratic political system for a short time in the twelfth century. With the creation of the different leagues of the Grigioni in the fourteenth and fifteenth centuries, the Bregaglia and the Mesolcina/Calanda were organized as independent regions.

Because of fear of foreign domination by France or Austria if the regions were integrated into the Napoleonic Republica Cisalpina, Ticino became a free republic and a canton of Switzerland in 1803. The end of tax-free trade with Italy in 1848 and the incorporation of Ticino into the bishopric of Basle and Lugano in 1888 bound Ticino to Switzerland.

The railway through the San Gottardo, which opened in 1882, brought little economic or industrial development. Only the German Swiss profited, as the taxes to use the trains were too high for the people of Ticino to pay. The attitude of the people of Ticino toward Italian unification and fascism displays another facet of Swiss Italian identity. During the Italian Fascist movement, sympathy for fascism grew and the desire for incorporation into Italy (*irredentismo*) grew in Ticino. But, as tradition changed into folklore, the Swiss Italian regional culture became a harmless "Ticinesità." Reasons for this shift may be related to post–World War II relations of Ticino with the German Swiss, Germany, and Italy and concern such issues as economic development, tourism, and migration.

Settlements

The first known settlers in Ticino were the Leponzi (Leventina), Brenni (Blenio), and Insubrii (Isole di Brissago). In the alpine valleys, the villages were situated on the steep slopes. The transhumance of the pastoralists in the alpine valleys involved residing in summer homes in the Alps (Monti, Rustici); during the winter months, people from Maggia and Verzasca descended to the lakesides of the Lago Maggiore. Today, houses are built closely together. In the Leventina and the Blenio, they are made of wood, while elsewhere they are constructed from stone. The roofs are of granite in the Sopraceneri and of bricks in the Sottoceneri. On the lakesides and in the Sottoceneri, the architecture of the houses is similar to the Lombardic style. Castles, marketplaces, and churches were built and maintained by the ruling families, the lords, and the church. They show the influence of Roman architecture. During the German Swiss occupation few public buildings were constructed, as the German Swiss lords did not want to invest in an occupied territory.

Economy

Subsistence and Commercial Activities.   In 1900 about 60 percent of the population still lived by family-based agriculture. In the Sottoceneri, long-term land leasing to tenants was the primary economic arrangement and mode of production. Hunting at one time also played a role. Fishing was an economic activity on the lakesides, but as pollution has increased, fishing in the Lago Ceresio has been prohibited. Entire families are sometimes involved with a single trade such as bricklaying, plastering, carpentry, chestnut selling, chimney sweeping, or baking. Cottage industries also exist: for example, straw is woven in Valle Onsernone; cotton and silk, woven mainly in Sottoceneri and mainly by women, was another source of income until the 1930s. Mountain farming has now ended as it is not profitable. Today 80 percent of the farms are for second incomes, are smaller than 5 hectares, and produce less than 5 percent of the economic product. Some of the abandoned farms have been taken over by the *neorurali,* young urban German Swiss.

Industrialization in Ticino began in the second half of the nineteenth century. Capitalistic industrialization was, until the 1950s, local and traditional (half of the enterprises are still family-owned). Modernization of the economy in the 1950s and 1960s took place rapidly. Today, service (tourism, banking) is the most important sector. The banking sector grew explosively in the 1970s as foreign capital was transferred to Switzerland (Ticino is the Hong Kong of Switzerland). In general, industry in Ticino is oriented toward labor-intensive production, as the required pool of low-paid workers (Italian) is assured. Raw materials are imported from abroad, and half-finished industrial products arrive either from German Switzerland or from abroad. Export is to German Switzerland, Italy, or other countries. The banks have become internationalized (44 percent of the banks in the

Ticino are foreign-owned). The industrial survival of the Ticino depends on reacting to the European marketplace.

Industrial Arts. Cattle, cheese (_formaggio di paglia_), wine, and other goods—game (in the nineteenth century), skins, fish, charcoal, larch, chestnut, crystal, marble, granite—are sold at Lombardic marketplaces. The main industries at the turn of the century were food, wood, clothing, railway production, hydroelectric power, granite, tobacco, and metallurgic products. The last three are threatened today by structural changes and low-cost production elsewhere. Microelectronic and precision instruments are manufactured today as well. Construction is one of the most stable activities.

Trade. San Gottardo is the most important of the Swiss alpine passages. Today road transport (a street tunnel opened in 1980) of goods and tourist traffic during holidays is responsible for notorious traffic jams in Ticino. From Roman times the alpine passages have been used for warfare expeditions. Men were recruited as soldiers and as transporters of goods. Most of the time, taxes and tributes were paid to the respective regional lords and/or the church for protection from enemies.

Division of Labor. Public prestige is afforded primarily to men (the vote was given to women in Switzerland only in 1971). The head of the traditional agricultural families were men but as they migrated, the main work in agriculture was done by women, elderly people, and children. Women performed all the farm work (household, cattle, hay making), while the same cannot be said of men. The traditional pattern of sharing work (general reciprocity, open networks) is taken over by families of the _neorurali_. Even though equality in employment is the law, the idea is still widespread that a man must earn more than a woman, and when spouses are taxed together, the official form is only addressed to the man. Average salaries in Ticino are 20 percent lower than in Switzerland in general, and some women earn half of what other women earn in German Swiss towns.

Land Tenure. Land or forests in the communities can be owned privately, by several kin of the same family, or by the _patriziato_ (the old community of the bourgeoisie). Land is attributed or loaned and work or profit is distributed by vote of the assisting persons. Land sharing (based on traditional Roman laws) is a barrier to land reform as agricultural plots become too small to be cultivated effectively.

With the development of tourism, the "sale of the Ticino" began. Since 1970 several laws have limited land sales—a limitation on selling to outsiders, a stipulation that agricultural land has to be used as such, and a limit on second residences.

Kinship

Kin Groups and Descent. Children take their father's name if their parents are married. The kinship system is cognatic, with a patrilineal preference. In general, the more people in a family rooted in the village context and the larger the family, the more important the kin group becomes. Traditionally, one's godfather and godmother were of social importance. Modernity, economic mobility, and urbanization have eroded the role of the localized kin group.

Kinship Terminology. Cousin terms follow the Eskimo system.

Marriage and Family

Marriage. Regional and village endogamy was the rule in the past. Young people met on church visits and at church festivals and feasts. Informal, secret meetings of the future spouses (_kiltgang_) existed in the alpine valleys. For the engagement, a man offered a gift (_dotta_) to the woman, which was taken as a promise of marriage. Today young people meet within peer groups, at discos and sporting events, at school, or at work. In urban centers young people often live together before marriage and get married when the woman is pregnant. Normally the wedding is of three parts: legal, religious, and celebratory. The bride and the groom are led to church by their witness. Rice as a sign of fertility is thrown on the spouses after the religious ceremony. The celebration takes place in a restaurant or in a community room and consists of a banquet, wedding cake, fireworks, and music. Depending on the importance of kin and on one's financial status, only the next of kin or also aunts and uncles and friends are invited to the party. Cousins are invited to the religious ceremony, for a drink afterward, and for lunch. Postmarital residence depends on the working place of the husband and economic opportunities and is usually neolocal.

Domestic Unit. Extended nuclear families with grandparents or other kin in the same household are rather rare. Economic mobility encourages nuclear families or one-person households and second residences (_pendolarismo_).

Inheritance. Roman law as a historical base of inheritance rules demands a division of property. Sometimes this leads to a situation where houses cannot be renovated or sold because the heirs cannot be located or do not agree.

Socialization. The growing role of public social institutions has reduced the socialization role of the family and has intensified generational conflicts. For young people, owning a car signifies freedom and also produces a high traffic-death rate among young men. In the valleys, family gatherings for Sunday lunches at the house of the grandmother (_mamma/nonna_) are common and highly valued.

Sociopolitical Organization

Social Organization. Besides the local open-air restaurants (_grotto_), which serve as informal, public meeting places, in the villages there are a variety of associations, although they have lost their initial political or religious significance. On the level of regional ethnic identity, the ideals of conserving nature and preserving tradition are emphasized. The activities and ceremonies of the _confraternità_ association are centered on a church patron. A Catholic movement with slightly fundamentalist or traditionalist tendencies, called "Communione e liberazione," supports them and the religious processions they organize. Traditional music bands (_fanfare_) with political significance (radical-liberal vs. Christian-Democrat bands of the villages in the nineteenth century) are today mostly apolitical. Shooting associations from the same epoch and sporting clubs, founded from the 1920s on, today organize carnivals, summer parties, and walking tours.

Quite a few cultural events and festivities (_festa dei fiori_ as an imitation of the _fêtes des vendanges_ of Vevey, the May dance, and polenta and risotto banquets) were introduced in

Ticino. They are attempts to add a folkloric element to the culture and are also tourist attractions.

Political Organization. The political organization of Switzerland is federalistic and democratic. It is structured on the levels of the confederation, the cantons, the districts (only juridical), and the community. There is a parliament (*gran consiglio del Ticino*, general assembly of the community) and an executive branch (*consiglieri dello stato, consiglieri della commune*), with members elected to four-year terms in a proportional election.

In the middle of the nineteenth century, Ticino was known as liberal and there was a broad support for the Lombardic liberation movement. The political pattern of the nineteenth century (liberals vs. conservatives) is still alive, despite the introduction of the Social Democratic party in the 1920s and its splinter groups. But neither the liberals (Partito Liberale Radicale) nor the Christian Democrats (PCD) can command an absolute majority today. In the last fifteen years four new parties joined in elections: Diritti Democratici Ticinesi; Partito Socialista dei Lavoratori; Partito Sozioliberale Federalisti Europei; and the Lega Lombarda. Those political groups show where the political future of Ticino lies. The elections are no longer major political battles, as the number of people who vote has shrunk (as everywhere else in Switzerland) to an average of a third or a half of the population.

Social Control. In urban centers where anonymity is growing, publicity in the press has assumed a role in social control. Until recently, social control in the villages was exercised by the church, the political party, and the family. Today these institutions have weakened considerably.

Conflict. Coexistence with the German Swiss neorurali is an example of conflict in the village context today. They are also called *capelloni*, because of the long hair some of them once wore; today this term is used for any man wearing long hair and dressing alternatively. As the neorurali differ from the natives in ideology and values, their alternative life-style is subject to gossip, rumors, and even legal sanctions (prohibition of settlement). Thus, the presence of the neorurali triggers feelings of anger among the Italian Swiss about their own "miserable" past and the colonizing German Swiss of the past and the present.

Religion and Expressive Culture

Religious Beliefs. In the Swiss Italian region there was space for an autonomous, anarchistic, esoteric *monte verità*. Newspapers give a good view of popular beliefs, as they are full of advertisements by fortune-tellers, therapists, and problem solvers. Officially, most Swiss Italians are Catholic. Archaeological remains from graves provide evidence of Etruscan, Celtic, Gallic, and Roman customs and goddesses. The Swiss Italians were Christianized already in the fourth century and some villages still celebrate Ambrosian rites. In the alpine valleys (Leventina, Blenio) people were Christianized from the north. During the Reformation, Italian refugees were accepted in Mesolcina, Bregaglia, Poschiavo, and Locarno. As the Grigioni Italiano were under foreign domination, the Reformation could develop freely but it did not have a lasting influence. Catholic Ticino was influenced considerably by the Catholic Swiss cantons, which by law prohibited the Reformed church from remaining in dominated

areas. Until the formal separation of church and state, the population was under the control of the churches and monasteries. Recently, many monasteries and community churches have been abandoned because of a shortage of priests. Italian priests are often found in the valleys.

Arts. The cultural (linguistic, intellectual, architectural, art-historical, and artistic) center of Swiss Italy lies in Italy (Milan). The sculptor Giacometti from Bregaglia (Stampa), who was known locally, had to exhibit first in Paris and Milan before he was recognized in Ticino. The same can be said of Brignoni, the artist and ethnographic collector. Swiss Italian literature emphasizes regional culture and identity. There are regional programs for theater, music, and arts education. There is no Swiss Italian university (four American universities around Lugano and business centers in nearby Lombardia were recently opened).

In the last thirty years nearly every valley has opened a local ethnographic museum. Many of the objects are also sold as souvenirs: wooden backpacks (*gerla*); copper pots; bast-covered chairs; *pergolas, peperonis,* and *maïs* of plastic; open wooden shoes (*zoccoli*); and special mugs (*boccalino*).

Medicine. Because of the climate, a growing segment of the economy focuses on the construction of private hospitals and old-age homes. At the beginning of the century hospitals for the treatment of tuberculosis were famous. Because of a lack of confidence in modern medicine, there is a movement among the middle class toward traditional methods of healing. Traditional knowledge about medical plants and healers is being studied. Modern medicine is still regularly used for major health problems.

Death and Afterlife. Beliefs about the afterlife are shaped by the Christian tradition. In villages today the deceased are no longer kept at home until the funeral, and wakes are less common. A community room is now used for this purpose. At funerals the church is more or less filled, depending on the public status of the dead. At times there is a "fanfare" played. After the service the procession goes to the churchyard, where the last prayers and rites take place. The churchyard is built at the edge of the village and protected by walls. The burial places show differences depending on traditional, economic, political, and social status.

Bibliography

Franscini, Stefano (1987). *La Svizzera italiana.* Edited by Virgilio Gilardoni. 4 vols. Bellinzona: Casagrande.

Frisch, Max (1981). *Der Mensch erscheint im Holozän.* Frankfurt: Suhrkamp.

Martini, Plinio (1970). *Il fondo del sacco.* Bellinzona: Casagrande.

Nessi, Alberto (1986). *Rabbia di vento.* Bellinzona: Casagrande.

Ratti, Remigio, et al. (1990). *Il Ticino—Regione aperta.* Locarno: Armando Dado Editore.

BARBARA WALDIS

Tiroleans

ETHNONYM: Tyroleans

Orientation

The Tirol is an alpine province of western Austria, bounded by Germany to the north and Italy to the south. "Tirol" was originally a family name, derived from a castle near Merano in what is now Italy. In 1248, the counts of Tirol received lands from the bishop of Brixen, and by 1271 they had nearly replaced the power of the church throughout the region. In 1363, control of the area passed to the Habsburgs, with whom it remained until 1918. The region was effectively Catholicized during the Counter-Reformation. After World War I, Italy received South Tirol, with its large German-speaking population, and has retained it to this day. The principal towns of Tirol are Innsbruck, Kufstein, Lienz, and Solbad Hall. The population of the region is just under 600,000.

The majority of Tiroleans live in nucleated communities, generally located in river valleys, surrounded by the lands on which they earn their livelihoods. In each village one finds shops, administrative institutions, a school, and a church.

Economy

Tiroleans are predominantly pasture farmers—largely of wheat and rye—and livestock breeders, with some dairying and silviculture as well. While agriculture and stock raising have long been dominant, the location of the Tirol—controlling passes between the Mediterranean and transalpine Europe—made commerce an important factor in the economy as well. One of the most important commercial centers of the area historically has been located at Bozen, in South Tirol, since the Middle Ages. There is some mining in the region: coal, iron, lead, zinc, copper, and magnesite. Also important to the modern Tirolean economy are textile mills and some other small, specialized industries, particularly those to do with the tourist trade.

Agriculture is based on the privately owned family farm, ownership of which passed from one generation to the next impartibly, generally along the male line and according to the principle of primogeniture. Noninheriting siblings had three basic alternatives: to stay on as dependents of the heir, if the land was able to support them; to hire themselves out to other farms in the region; or to migrate in search of employment in the lowland towns or beyond. Until recently, agriculture retained its traditional subsistence orientation, but production for market has in the last several decades gained in importance, and nearly all households are now to some degree dependent on cash income.

Kinship, Marriage, and Family

Kinship terminology specifies lineal relations, while merging into collective terms all those individuals who stand in collateral relationship to the household head. There are special terms for first and second cousins.

Only through marriage does an individual acquire full recognition as an adult in the community. Marriages in the Tirol tend to be village-endogamous—indeed, most marriages occur between individuals of the same neighborhood within the village. It is within the neighborhood—a group of four to six of the local farm properties—that the closest relations of interhousehold cooperation and friendship arise, and intermarriage between such households serves to strengthen these bonds. Individuals who did not inherit land have great difficulty in marrying, for they are wholly dependent on their inheriting sibling for their support. A man generally did not marry until he was financially able to support a wife. Long courtships were the rule, and they depended on the approval of the bride by the siblings of the marrying male. A dowry is required and generally consists of furnishings for the marital household. It is often the bride-to-be herself, rather than her family, who earns the money to be invested in the dowry. The wedding is an event of villagewide import, celebrated in the church. Upon marriage, the wife usually comes to live in the farm household of her husband; it is far less common for a man to go to live on the bride's family estate. Information on divorce is unavailable.

With marriage, a new domestic unit is established, with the husband serving also as head of household—except on the rare occasion when a noninheriting sibling marries. Generally speaking, however, dependent male siblings who remain on the family farm remain unmarried, so this circumstance does not arise with any great frequency. The household consists of the heir to the farm, his wife, their unmarried children, and any siblings of the heir that the farmstead can employ and who choose to stay on. The Tirolean tradition of impartibility according to the principle of primogeniture serves to keep the major portion of an estate's land undivided, but it is not absolutely applied. Smaller parcels of land can be, and are, divided among a number of heirs. At times, a firstborn son is unwilling to wait until his father relinquishes control of the family estate and so leaves the farmstead. In addition, even those who are excluded from inheriting ownership of the property may be bequeathed rights to a living from the land (i.e., rights to ownership of a room within the house and usufruct rights of a portion of the land itself).

The early socialization of the Tirolean child is the responsibility of the mother. The family is adult-centered rather than child-centered, and children are taught early on to conduct themselves politely, even formally, in the presence of adults. Discipline is not harsh, but it relies principally on sending the misbehaving child from the room. Play is unstructured, and in early childhood, boys and girls may play together. By the age of 7 or 8, however, children are expected to begin to assume some of the responsibilities of adults, taking on chores appropriate to their sex. Herding is a boy's pursuit, housework is a girl's, and both are expected to help in the fields, especially during harvest times. Children begin school at about the age of 6, and are required to attend until they reach the age of 14. Most children do not go on beyond this point, but opportunities do exist for high-school education and beyond.

Sociopolitical Organization

The basic social unit of the Tirol is the neighborhood, consisting of four to six neighboring farm households. Cooperative tasks are organized within this group under the leadership of the several household heads, who share ties of friendship and trust through long association with one another. The hierarchical relations that characterize the farm household, with the owner-heir at the head, have implications beyond simple household and interhousehold activities as well. Those who serve as head of household also tend to monopolize political activity in the village, hold village-council office, and dominate the decision-making processes regarding village concerns. Tirol communities enjoy self-government; each one has its own mayor, elected community council, and regulatory committees.

Religion

Tirol is a Catholic region, and it has been so since the Counter-Reformation. Local communities provide a residence and farm lands for the local priest. Attendance at mass and membership in ecclesiastical organizations are expected of all members of the community. Baptism, confession, and communion are important rituals, and marriage is consecrated by the local priest. Each of the religious organizations (there are separate ones for married and unmarried men, and married and unmarried women) sponsor special masses over the course of the year. At the approach of death, the priest provides the sacrament of extreme unction.

Bibliography

Cole, John W., and Phillip S. Katz (1973). "Knecht to Arbeiter: The Proletarianization Process in South Tyrol." In *Studies in European Society: The Worker-Peasants in Europe*, 39–66. The Hague: Mouton.

Cole, John W., and Eric R. Wolf (1974). *The Hidden Frontier: Ecology and Ethnicity in an Alpine Valley*. New York: Academic Press.

Crowe, Patricia W. (1981). "Community Size and Social Relationships: A Comparison of Urban and Rural Social Patterns in Tirol." *Anthropological Quarterly* 54:210–229.

NANCY E. GRATTON

Tory Islanders

ETHNONYMS: Oilean Thoraighe, Torach, Tor Inis (archaic)

Orientation

Identification. Tory Island is a small island off the coast of County Donegal in the extreme northwest of Ireland. Politically it is part of the Republic of Ireland (Eire).

Location. The island, roughly 5 kilometers long and 1.6 kilometers at its widest, is oriented in a west-east direction and is 14 kilometers from the nearest landfall on the mainland. The cliffs on the north side rise to as much as 120 me-

ters and protect the southern slopes from the sea, making a little agriculture possible. The climate is mild and temperate, with temperatures never reaching much more than 21° C in summer, or much less than 2° C in winter. Annual precipitation (average 102 centimeters) is somewhat lower than on the mainland, but storms of up to gale force 9 are common and the channel is known for its rough crosstides. The official growing season starts on 17 March (Saint Patrick's day) and continues to early October.

Demography. The population of Tory (with a fairly even sex ratio) is approximately 300. An accurate estimate is hard to establish because migrant laboring leads to a high population in the summer and low in the winter. The first census (1841) showed 399 (191 males, 208 females), and that of 1961, 264 (146 males, 118 females). The population of Ireland declined by one-half over the same period. In both cases emigration is the major factor, but high fertility (Tory net reproduction rate = 1.6) prevents further decline.

Linguistic Affiliation. The islanders speak as a first language the northern dialect of Irish Gaelic, which has strong affinities with its daughter dialect, Scots Gaelic, as spoken in the highlands and islands of Scotland. Both are related to Welsh, Breton, and Cornish (extinct) as members of the once-widespread Celtic Branch of the Indo-European Language Family. Many islanders also speak English with varying degrees of fluency depending on degree of contact. English is taught as a second language in school, and some people are literate in both languages. Spoken Gaelic is now heavily loaded with English loanwords, but these are easily Gaelicized and assimilated.

History and Cultural Relations

The earliest remains on Tory are those of an Iron Age hill fort. The next earliest are a round tower and associated buildings thought to be part of the monastery founded there by Saint Columba (Columkille) in about A.D. 550. Later it was seized by the Norsemen around A.D. 700 to 800. Various annals show it was a key strategic location in the control of the northern coast and was often in contention. In 733 Dougall the Second, king of Scotland, seized it; because it had harbored refugees from the Armada, the English "devastated" it in 1595. In 1609 it was still in Irish hands, but by 1653 it had passed to an English Protestant. In 1832 a lighthouse and Lloyd's signal station were built. In 1903 the Congested Districts Board for Ireland purchased the island from Benjamin Joule, who had owned it since 1861. A gunboat sent to collect the local taxes in 1884 sank with all hands. In 1922 Tory became part of the Republic of Ireland along with County Donegal. The islanders are fiercely independent and wish to run their own affairs, but they are increasingly dependent on government subsidies. They have a favored status as native Gaelic speakers, and government policy subsidizes such enclaves.

Settlements

Three settlements are named for their respective locations: West Town, Middle Town, and East Town. West/Middle Town, with 42 households, has the harbor, the church and church hall, the graveyard, the school, and the two shops. East Town, a little more than a kilometer away, has none of these. Each township's fields surround it in long strips. Beyond these are the peat bogs (largely exhausted) and the grazing land.

Economy

Subsistence and Commercial Activities. The subsistence economy of Tory is of the "crofter" type: basic agriculture on small plots averaging 2–3 acres planted with potatoes, barley, oats, and hay, supplemented by garden produce, poultry, some sheep, a few cattle, donkeys (for plowing), and inshore fishing from small coracles. Larger boats were built in the late nineteenth century, and a herring-curing station was opened by the Congested Districts Board. This fishing industry employed 100 men and boys and most of the women and girls. Kelp (an algae from which iodine is extracted) was gathered and dried. These industries declined and lobster is now the main cash crop, with winter migrant labor providing capital for the summer lobster season.

Industrial Arts. The islanders build their own boats from imported materials. Houses formerly were built from local stone and thatched, but more recently commercial concrete blocks are imported and roofs are slated. Farm implements were ingeniously constructed from driftwood and iron scavenged from wrecks. When sheep were plentiful, wool was carded and spun, and then knitted—there were no looms. Illicit whiskey (poteen) was distilled from barley. Today clothing, implements, etc. are bought from the mainland. Even so, the shore is still meticulously divided by lot each year so that the flotsam and jetsam can be harvested.

Trade. The major cash crop is fish, but it was hard to get fresh fish to market in time. The curing station solved this problem, but when the herring moved and the station was abandoned the islanders turned to inshore lobster fishing, with contracts from continental lobster trawlers, which also provide the pots.

Division of Labor. Traditionally the division of labor was strictly by gender: the men and boys fished and did the heavy agricultural and building work; the women and girls attended to the domestic chores, the children, the poultry, and the gardens. The curing station provided the first female wage work. When migrant laboring began after World War II, it was the men who left the island. Recently the unmarried women have started leaving. The traditional division of labor still exists. A few specialists now exist in the shops and government positions.

Land Tenure. Traditional land tenure was on the "rundale" system, usually described as a group of blood kin holding land "in common." The mechanics of this are obscure, but the Tory system suggests the following: it is a system of usufruct in which all the heirs of the "owner" have a claim on the use of his or her land, but all do not pursue the claim. They leave one of their number to farm it. On the owner's death, the land would go to the immediate heirs, but in default of heirs it would revert to the next closest descendants of the original owner. The fragmentation associated with systems of partible inheritance is avoided by the concept of the "land of the marriage." When a couple marries, it is provided with a basic amount of land from the patrimony of one or the other set of parents. A brother, for example, who marries a woman with land, is not supposed to claim land from his siblings. The idea is that each household, not each person, should end up with much the same amount of land, and this ideal is surprisingly well realized. Official records show a dominance of male "owners," but questioning about claims showed that 33 percent of land was in female hands. Women are less likely than men to press claims, but have equal rights to the use of the land.

Kinship, Marriage, and Family

Kin Groups and Descent. Kinship is reckoned bilaterally and the main category of kin is the _clann_ (pl. _clanna_). These are all the descendants, over five to seven generations, of a known ancestor, and are known after him (for example, clann Eoghain, the descendants of Owen [Eugene]). Obviously, as with all cognatic descent groups, these clanna overlap. Four major groups dominate the genealogical scene and account for 80 percent of all living members. In the recitation of genealogy, these are given first in full, even where they overlap, and then the other 18 or so are "referred" to them. The ultimate ancestors date from the 1780s and seem to have been holders of land. The system of personal naming (kinship terms are very little used) parallels this descent system. Thus individuals are known by a first (baptismal) name and then the names of lineal ancestors, male and female. In genealogical theory, all names should converge on the clann ancestor, and this means that a person will have as many sets of names as recognized ancestors. This is not realized, however, and people take the names of the clann to which they have the strongest allegiance, while recognizing that other "strings" are possible. For practical purposes an individual will use only a few of the names. The other major kinship category is _muintir_, an Ego-centered bilateral kindred including affines. This would be "kinship" as the majority of the islanders know it, precise genealogical knowledge belonging to specialists.

Marriage. Marriage is governed by the Catholic church and is therefore monogamous and without divorce. Because of the parental resistance to marriage—they regret the loss of a family member—and unless there is an illegitimate child (a not unusual occurrence) it is often late (average 29) and surreptitious. Marriage is rarely celebrated. A couple will drop their work, go to the church with the witnesses, and then come back and resume where they left off. Until recently marriage was largely endogamous to the island, but now there are more out-marriages. Men, but rarely women, marry into the island from time to time.

Domestic Unit. The ideal household on Tory is nuclear, and some 50 percent of marriages achieve this ideal. But it often conflicts with another ideal of sibling solidarity. Because marriage is late, many siblings already have established households by the time at least one parent dies, and they do not want to leave these on marriage. Thus, it was (and is) the custom, for the couple to remain in their respective natal homes. This form of natalocal residence is not fixed, since couples move in and out of this state, but older marriage partners tend to stay thus separated, with the husband becoming a privileged "visitor." Children stay with the mother. Up to 40 percent of marriages involved natalocal residence in the past, and some 20 percent were still so as late as 1970. The husbands in these marriages farm their wives' land, and contribute to their upkeep.

Inheritance.   After the land, the house is the most important item of inheritance. Ideally the house should go with the land, but a compromise often occurs. Thus a son who marries a woman with a house will surrender the parental house to his sister(s); or a brother will take the house and his sister's husband will build on the land she inherited. A compromise is not always reached, however, and bitter disputes very often occur. Written wills are virtually unknown on Tory and old parents will usually make a disposition of property before death.

Socialization.   Child rearing is very relaxed. Until nurses interfered, weaning was as late as three years, and children still suckle casually until that age. The relationship with the mother is very close and dependent. Nowadays children go to school at age five; in the past they would have gradually assumed adult responsibilities at a very early age. Young children are mostly unsupervised and corporal punishment is used rarely.

Sociopolitical Organization

Social Organization.   No social classes or other differentiations of status exist on the island. The professionals are respected but they have no special privileges. The acknowledged "ancient" families—Duggans, Doohans, and Rogers—have some status, but no special benefits. The islanders are individualists but will work together for common aims. Hauling in boats is a community activity.

Political Organization.   Official authority emanates from the parish, the county, and ultimately the Dublin government. This sits lightly on the islanders. The islanders vote in local and national elections, and since they hold a block of votes in a marginal constituency, they are able to command some patronage. Otherwise the island is self-governing. In the past there was a "king" (*an Riogh*), a descendant of the old Brehon lawgivers, who arbitrated disputes and supervised the drawing of lots for the shore division.

Social Control.   This is purely informal, with most discipline occuring within families. The curate will attempt to exert influence and will be listened to up to a point. The power of custom (*beas*) is strong, and often quoted. The wise counsel of the old is the strongest force for social control.

Conflict.   Conflict over inheritance is by far the most serious form. Most conflict is individual or between families, and long-standing quarrels occasionally break out into open fighting. This is inevitably between unmarried male protagonists and is mitigated by the intervention of relatives who restrain the fighters, and mediators who attempt reconciliation.

Religion and Expressive Culture

Religious Beliefs and Practices.   The islanders are all practicing Roman Catholics, but church authority is weak. They are certainly devout and attend to all the religious observances. There is a pilgrimage (*turus*) with stations of the cross completing a circuit of the island. The island is sacred to St. Columba and very proud of its association with the saint. There is a whole literature of prayers and cures and several shrines. Only since about 1880 has there been a permanent priest on the island, and the moral authority of the church has yet to take hold. The curates all deplore the casual attitude to illegitimacy and marriage, to little avail. The is-

landers supplement their orthodox beliefs with rich lore concerning legendary gods, ghosts, and fairies. In the absence of a priest, the oldest member of the Duggan family, which in legend welcomed Columba to the island, leads the flock in prayers at an ancient stone altar.

Arts.   There are few plastic arts on the island. The main arts are singing, storytelling, and traditional Irish dancing. Much pride is taken in performance. The telling of stories varies from the classical myth cycles, told by the older men, to fairy and ghost stories, told by the old women, and anecdotes about island life and history, told by anyone. Many islanders are excellent musicians, playing the fiddle, accordion, banjo, and tin whistle.

Medicine.   This is now officially administered by a resident nurse, but is supplemented by herbal cures, spells, midwifery, and prayers known to the old women. In the past this was the only medicine available.

Death and Afterlife.   The islanders subscribe to the official Catholic beliefs, but they supplement them with an active belief in ghosts, who are supposed to be souls in purgatory working out their time of penance. They are rarely harmful, but are an omen of death. A major festival is that of All Souls' Eve when a meal is left out overnight so that dead souls may feast on its essence. When an old person dies, the attitude is that a soul that has lived its allotted span is being taken to eternal life, and this is celebrated by a wake to console the relatives and to keep the newly dead spirit away from the house.

See also Gaels (Irish)

Bibliography

Fox, Robin (1978). *The Tory Islanders: A People of the Celtic Fringe*. Cambridge: Cambridge University Press.

Hamilton, J. N. (1974). *The Irish of Tory Island*. Studies in Irish Language and Literature, vol. 3. Belfast: Queen's University of Belfast.

ROBIN FOX

Transylvanian Ethnic Groups

ETHNONYMS: Magyarok (Hungarians), Romāni (Romanians), Sachsen (Saxons), Schwaben (Swabians), Srbi (Serbians)

Orientation

Identification.   Transylvania is a multiethnic region located in the present-day state of Romania. Its principal ethnic groups, or nationalities, are Romanians, Hungarians, and Germans; there are also Serbs, Gypsies, and Jews in the region, as well as small numbers of others (such as Armenians). It is difficult to give basic facts about Transylvania, since members of the different groups—particularly the Romanians and Hungarians—disagree on fundamental points of information.

Location.   Disagreement begins with the territory to which the label "Transylvania" applies (since the region does not now have any administrative status, there are no political boundaries to simplify the problem of its designation). Some people use the term to include all the territory of Romania west and north of the watershed of the southern and eastern Carpathian Mountains, to the Hungarian and Ukrainian borders. Others use it in a narrower sense, to refer to the central plateau (400–600 meters in elevation) encircled by the eastern, southern, and western Carpathians; the remaining areas between this plateau and the Hungarian and Ukrainian borders are then called Banat, Crişana, and Maramureş. The former, more inclusive definition (somewhat more common) will be used here. Transylvania thus defined lies between approximately 45.5° and 48° N and 20.5° and 26° E. It occupies 41.9 percent of the total surface area of Romania. The climate is continental, with relatively dry, warm summers and cold winters.

Demography.   Population figures for the different groups are another area of disagreement. Romanian statistics gave the country's population, as of 31 December 1988, as 23,112,000; of this, the counties of Transylvania comprised 35 percent, distributed in 16 of Romania's 39 counties. Official statistics showing Romania's ethnic groups by county or region have not been published for many years. Even the national percentages for each group (not published since 1977) are disputed, Hungarians claiming that the official statistics understate the numbers of Hungarians in Romania. Since it is therefore impossible to say exactly what proportions each nationality represents of the Transylvanian population, only estimates are available. In 1977, official figures gave the national population as 89.1 percent Romanian, 7.7 percent Hungarian, 1.5 percent German, and .2 percent Serbian (down from 1966 percentages of 85.7 percent, 9.1 percent, 2.2 percent, and .3 percent). Given that most Hungarians, Germans, and Serbs in Romania lived in Transylvania, the approximate proportions for Transylvania's nationalities as of 1977 were: slightly more than 70 percent for Romanians, about 22 percent for Hungarians, about 4.3 percent for Germans, and about .6 percent for Serbs. Extensive emigration of Germans during the late 1970s and 1980s reduced their numbers from the roughly 325,000 of the 1977 census; informal estimates as of 1990 put them at 200,000 to 250,000. The figure often used for Hungarians as of 1990 was about 2,000,000 (some Hungarian sources put the number as high as 2,500,000). Until accurate statistics are collected and published, it is probably safest to speak of Hungarians as constituting about 8 percent of the population of Romania and about one-fourth of Transylvania. Gypsies were generally underenumerated and often did not declare Gypsy identity, making it impossible to state the size of this minority. While these population figures may seem vague, figures offering greater precision are probably motivated by one or another group's bias and cannot be accepted with confidence.

The Hungarian and German minorities are concentrated in different parts of Transylvania. Hungarians are most numerous in the eastern counties of Harghita and Covasna, the north-central city of Cluj (Hungarian: Kolozsvar), the surrounding Cluj and Mureş counties, and the western portions of the counties of Satu Mareş Arad, Bihor, and Timiş (all bordering on Hungary). Germans are concentrated in southern Transylvania, particularly the cities of Brassov (German: Kronstadt) and Sibiu (German: Hermannstadt) and their environs. Serbs are found largely in the city of Timişoara and the counties of Timiş and Caraş-Severin, which border on Serbia. Romanians and Gypsies are found in all parts of the region, somewhat less numerous in the two eastern counties (Harghita and Covasna) where Hungarians have their highest densities.

Linguistic Affiliation.   Each of Transylvania's major ethnic groups is distinguished from the others by both language and religious affiliation. The language of Transylvanian Romanians is Romanian, a Romance language of the Indo-European Family having some elements of Slavic vocabulary and grammar. Although some differences in pronunciation and lexicon exist among them, the speech of Transylvanian Romanians is fully intelligible both among themselves and with Romanians from elsewhere in the country. Hungarian, of the Finno-Ugrian Language Family, is the first language of Transylvanian Hungarians. While it is marked by regionalisms and other features that distinguish it from the language spoken in Hungary, Hungarian-speakers from Transylvania and Hungary have no difficulty in understanding one another. Particularly during the sixteenth and seventeenth centuries, when the heartland of Hungary was occupied by the Ottomans and Transylvania was a quasi-independent principality, many Hungarians came to regard Transylvanian Hungarian as the proper literary form; from this has come their present notion that Transylvanian Hungarian is the "purest" form of this language. Transylvania's Germans are all schooled in High German (Hochdeutsch) and, through it, they communicate freely both with one another and with Germans from Austria, Germany, and Switzerland. Domestically, however, many of them use one of two dialects that are not mutually comprehensible, known as Saxon and Swabian. These were brought into the region in two different waves of migration, one in the twelfth and thirteenth centuries, the other in the eighteenth (see History below). The differences between Saxon and Swabian, together with the tendency for Swabian-speakers to be concentrated in southwestern Transylvania and Saxon-speakers in the southcentral and southeastern zones, meant that up to 1940, speakers of Saxon and Swabian did not often intermarry. Following World War II, the numbers of Germans declined markedly, not just from the emigration of the 1970s and 1980s but also from deportation and exile between 1945 and 1951, which halved Romania's prewar German minority of nearly 700,000. This, together with the increased social and geographical mobility of Germans under Communist-party rule, led to increased intermarriage between Swabians and Saxons (such couples usually spoke Hochdeutsch in the home, rather than either dialect).

Of Romania's other groups, Serbs speak the South Slavic language known as Serbo-Croatian, comprehensible to Serbs from Yugoslavia. Gypsies employ both Romani (of the Indo-Iranian Subfamily of Indo-European) and Romanian; many of them also speak Hungarian and/or Serbian, from their circuits across the borders of the three countries. Jews may have as their domestic language Yiddish, Romanian, or Hungarian, the latter two depending in part on which nationality they or their families had oriented to historically; many Transylvanian Jews do not know Yiddish.

Religion

Each of Transylvania's three principal nationalities is divided across two or more religions. Most Transylvanian Romanians belong to either the Romanian (Eastern) Orthodox church or the Uniate church (a hybrid of Eastern Orthodoxy and Roman Catholicism that the Habsburgs created in the late 1600s, with the aim of Catholicizing Transylvania's Romanians). Some Transylvanian Romanians stayed with the Uniate church even after the Communists forcibly rejoined it with the Orthodox Church in 1948. In addition, as of about 1960 small but growing numbers of Romanians converted to one or another Protestant sect, of which the most significant are the Pentecostals, Seventh-Day Adventists, Jehovah's Witnesses, and Baptists. Among the other ethnic groups, only Serbs share the Orthodox religion with Romanians; the faiths practiced by Romanians are otherwise unique to them. Hungarians in Transylvania have historically belonged to three faiths: Roman Catholicism, Calvinism, and Unitarianism. Swabian Germans were generally (although not universally) Roman Catholic, and Saxons were Lutheran. These historical religious attachments diminished to some extent during the Communist period as secularization and official atheism eroded religious practice. The different faiths continue, however, to be more or less exclusive to the different ethnic groups, only Roman Catholicism being shared (by some Hungarians and some Swabians). (While both Serbs and Romanians are Orthodox, each group orients to its own patriarch—of, respectively, the Serbian and Romanian Orthodox Churches.)

History

The history of the different groups in Transylvania is the area of greatest disagreement between Romanians and Hungarians. Few facts are beyond dispute. It seems certain that the ancestral population of modern Romanians derives from the mixture of two groups on the territory of Transylvania: Dacians, an important group at the margins of the Roman empire, and Romans, who conquered the territory of the Dacians in A.D. 105–106 and brought in substantial numbers of colonists to fortify this easternmost border of the empire. Admixtures of Slavs during their migrations of the seventh to eighth centuries further augmented Romania's heritage. Hungarians arrived in the Danube basin at the end of the ninth century A.D. (the date usually accepted is 896) and, having established their control over the plains in what is now central and eastern Hungary, gradually moved into the Transylvanian region during the tenth and eleventh centuries, consolidating their hold over it by the twelfth century. Disagreement begins here, centering on whether or not a population ancestral to today's Romanians was already inhabiting the area when the Hungarians moved in. Hungarian histories claim that the territory Hungarians settled was empty, the local population having moved out with the Roman retreat from Dacia in 271; Romanians claim that their forebears had stayed in Transylvania, perhaps not in the open spaces but in the foothills, where they had retreated to escape the nomads (Goths, Avars, Khazars, etc.) whose invasion had prompted

the Roman retreat. It is difficult to adjudicate between these positions. The way of life of ancestral Romanians did not readily lend itself to producing concrete remains for archaeologists to find. Although both sides invoke archaeology to support their positions, the degree of political investment and patriotic sentiment even among outstanding scholars on both sides obviates neutral scientific interpretation. The matter is further complicated by the fact that the ethnic labels "Hungarian" and "Romanian" as now understood are inapplicable to the tenth and eleventh centuries; current theories of ethnic processes do not unequivocally support the notion that these ethnic groups formed in antiquity and evolved with no changes in their identity into the present, as both Hungarian and Romanian sides presume.

The argument between Hungarians and Romanians concerning first settlement of Transylvania is linked to their claims to the territory. Following the Hungarian conquest, Transylvania became the eastern rampart of the Hungarian kingdom; it was ruled by a *voivod*, or military leader, charged with defending Christian Hungary from the Mongols, Petchenegs, Cumans, and other groups raiding from the Asian steppes. The cultured and largely Hungarian nobility of the region participated in the glories of the Renaissance courts of the Hungarian kings; speakers of Romanian, by contrast, were illiterate and uncultured serfs. The region gained importance for Hungarians following the defeat of their army by the Ottomans in 1526, after which the kingdom's center of gravity moved into the Transylvanian hills that the Turks did not manage to subdue fully. For Hungarians, Transylvania was an integral part of their historical kingdom and ought to have remained part of it into the present. By the time population statistics began to be collected in the 1700s, however, Romanians outnumbered Hungarians and Germans; to the argument based on numbers the Romanians added their own historical arguments, marshaling scraps of documentary evidence from medieval Hungarian and Byzantine sources to buttress their claim that Romanians had been constantly present since the Roman conquest. At first, the goal of this argument was to obtain civic rights for Romanians in Hungary, not to bring the territory under Romanian control. Only late in the nineteenth century did Romanians begin to demand that Transylvania be severed from Hungary and joined with the kingdom of Romania. This was finally accomplished in the wake of World War I, as the victorious powers awarded Transylvania to their Romanian allies (Hungary had been on the losing side). This award was seen by Romanians as the just recognition of their historic rights and by Hungarians as the unjust usurpation of theirs. Between these two exclusive claims, each with its accompanying arsenal of scientific and historical arguments, there is no easy reconciliation.

The history of the German presence in Transylvania is less contested. During the twelfth and thirteenth centuries, Hungary's kings invited colonists from the Rhineland and Flanders to settle in Transylvania, granting them privileges and self-governance; their role was to secure the eastern borderland of the Hungarian kingdom, increase agricultural output, and serve as a counterweight to the power of certain Hungarian nobles. These settlers formed the ancestral population of the Saxons. Several centuries later, following Austrian expulsion of the Ottomans from Hungary, Habsburg emperors brought a second series of colonists from the area around the Black Forest, settling them in the eastern plain of the Danube basin (the Banat). Once again, the aim was to secure otherwise vulnerable spaces, increase agricultural productivity, and provide a counterweight to the powerful nobles of Hungary. The descendants of these settlers were the modern-day Swabians (found not only in Transylvania but also in eastern Hungary and northern Yugoslavia). On the question of Romanian-Hungarian priority in Transylvania, German-language scholarship tended to take the Hungarian side when Transylvania was part of Hungary, later becoming somewhat more equivocal.

Contemporary Relations

Under the last decade of the rule of Communist dictator Nicolae Ceausescu (1965–1989), relations between Hungarians and Romanians worsened but rarely broke out into open conflict owing to the high level of police repression. Following Ceausescu's overthrow in December 1989, a brief period of interethnic harmony gave way to overt tensions as Hungarians promptly demanded the educational, political, and linguistic freedoms suppressed under Ceauşescu and Romanians reacted with anger, at least partly fomented by the remnants of Ceauşescu's security apparatus. The voices of those who continued to call for mutual cooperation tended to be lost in the outbreak of nationalism on both sides. As for Transylvania's Germans, the proportions of their emigration from Romania suggest that they will cease to be a significant minority presence in Transylvania within a generation. Relations between them and other ethnic groups had in any case been more peaceable than those between Romanians and Hungarians.

See also Germans; Hungarians; Romanians

Bibliography

Daicoviciu, Constantin, et al. (1961). *Din Istoria Transilvaniei* (From the history of Transylvania). Bucharest: Ed. Academiei.

Köpeczi, Béla, et al. (1986). *Erdély Története* (History of Transylvania). 3 vols. Budapest: Akadémiai Kiadó.

McArthur, Marilyn S. (1981). "The Politics of Identity: Transylvanian Saxons in Socialist Romania." Ph.D. dissertation, University of Massachusetts, Amherst.

Paikert, G. C. (1967). *The Danube Swabians: German Populations in Hungary, Rumania, and Yugoslavia and Hitler's Impact on Their Patterns*. The Hague: Martinus Nijhoff.

Pamlényi, Ervin, ed. (1975). *A History of Hungary*. London: Collet's.

Prodan, David (1971). *Supplex Libellus Valachorum*. Bucharest: Ed. Academiei.

Seton-Watson, R. W. (1934). *A History of the Roumanians*. Cambridge: Cambridge University Press.

Verdery, Katherine (1983). *Transylvanian Villagers: Three Centuries of Political, Economic, and Ethnic Change*. Berkeley and Los Angeles: University of California Press.

KATHERINE VERDERY

Tsakonians

ETHNONYM: Tzakonians

Tsakonians are a pastoral people of Greece. Their numbers have been estimated at anywhere from 300 to 10,000 and they reside on the eastern coast of the Peloponnesos. In the summer they tend their flocks in the mountains west of Leonidi, and their winters are spent in Leonidi and other nearby towns. Tsakonian is a dialect of Greek and is related to, though not mutually intelligible with, modern Greek. It is derived from the dialect of ancient Greek spoken by Spartans in Laconia.

Bibliography

Thumb, Albert (1894). "Die ethnographische Stellung der Zokonen." *Indogermanische Forschung* 4:195–213.

Tuscans

ETHNONYMS: none

Tuscans are the people of the central Italian region of Tuscany, located on the Tyrrhenian Sea. Tuscany, covering some 22,991 square kilometers, contains the provinces of Massa-Carrara, Lucca, Pistoia, Firenze, Livorno, Pisa, Arezzo, Sienna, and Grosseto. The population was estimated at about 3,600,000 in 1983. The name derives from the Etruscans, a tribal people who settled the region in about 1000 B.C. As in all of Italy, the population is predominantly Roman Catholic. Tuscany has long been and remains a major cultural and artistic center in Italy. The capital is Florence, with other major cities including Siena, Pisa, Livorno, Lucca, and Piombino. The Tuscan dialect of Tuscany is the basis for Standard Italian. In addition to its art and culture, Tuscany is also a major agricultural region. The primary crops are wheat, olives (and olive oil), grapes, and other fruits and vegetables. Chianti is the best-known of the wines produced in the region. Cattle, pigs, poultry, and horses are also raised. Major industries include metallurgy, chemicals, and textiles, with tourism important along the coast and in major cultural centers such as Florence and Pisa.

From an economic and cultural perspective, Tuscany is part of what is called central Italy, a designation encompassing parts of Tuscany, Emilia, Marches, Umbria, Lazio, and Abruzzi-Molise. Within central Italy there are significant differences between life in the urban and rural locales and between life in the agricultural interior and on the seacoasts.

Anthropological interest has mainly focused on the "traditional" peasant communities of the interior plains. Central Italy is often contrasted with southern Italy, with the latter considered by some to be economically and socially backward.

The interior plains of Tuscany and neighboring Umbria until recently displayed many typical features of traditional rural central Italian economic and social organization. While some of these typical features remain, the region has been experiencing continual change since the end of World War II, as discussed at the end of this essay. The following is a summary of traditional rural economic and social organization. Communities consisted of a central town surrounded by individual farms. The landowners (*padrone*) lived in town; the tenant farming families lived on the farms. Each farm was a largely self-sufficient unit, farmed by the same family for a number of generations. If a landowner owned eight to ten contiguous farms, they were operated as a *frattoria* for joint production and distribution.

The ideal peasant family was a three- to four-generation patrilocal extended family. Thus, these families were often large (twenty or more persons) and were headed by the senior male, the *mezzadro*. The relationship between the tenant and the landowner was defined by the *mezzadria* contract, usually renewed on a year-to-year basis. In general, the owner provided the land, working capital, and equipment while the peasant and his family provided the labor. In return for their labor, the family got about 50 percent of the crop and 50 percent of the proceeds from sales. There was a clear class distinction between owner and peasants, with the former also playing a patron role for the latter. As the region has been integrated into the national and international economic system, this patron role has disappeared.

In addition to the owner-tenant relationship, other important features of the traditional social organization included a strong sense of being neighbors (*vicini*) among neighboring farmers and work exchange (*aiutarella*) between farms.

Major changes in this traditional pattern of organization include smaller farms, more owners of land with each owning less land, more absentee owners, a movement of farmers off the land, commercialization of agriculture and wider involvement in distribution networks, increased mechanization, smaller families, and collective ownership of farms.

Bibliography

Silverman, Sydel F. (1965). "Patronage and Community-Nation Relationships in Central Italy." *Ethnology* 4:172–189.

Vlach Gypsies of Hungary

ETHNONYMS: Rom or (occasional plural) Roma; also known in Hungarian by Magyar (Hungarian) compatriots as Olah Cigany

Orientation

Identification. Vlach Gypsies are one branch of the Romany-speaking Gypsies who lived for several hundred years in Romania until they began migrating to other parts of the world in the middle of the nineteenth century. The majority of Vlach Gypsies now live in Hungary, Czechoslovakia, and Romania. In Hungary they are mostly found in the eastern and northern regions of the country. The origin of the ethnonym "Rom" is obscure, though one Hungarian scholar has speculatively suggested it might derive from the north Indian Dom caste. The term "vlach" (Hungarian *olah*) derives from the association of these Gypsies with the old Romanian principality of Wallachia. The Hungarian word *cigany* (Gypsy) is found in the Hungarian language from the Middle Ages and is cognate with terms for Gypsies in other European languages such as German *zigeuner*. "Cigany" has negative connotations of deceit and laziness. The term "Rom" distinguishes Vlach Gypsies from other Gypsy groups in Hungary such as Romanian-speaking "Boyash" Gypsies and Hungarian speaking "Romungro" Gypsies.

Location. Gypsies tend not to rely directly on the natural environment for their livelihood; instead, they are dependent on human environments, so they live wherever the non-Gypsy environment provides them with the human resources they need to carry out their economic activities. Since at least the early 1960s, when nomadism was suppressed in Hungary, the Rom (like most Gypsies in eastern Europe) have been more sedentary. Today, Rom are as likely to be found in towns as in villages, but almost always in the poorer areas. Large concentrations of Rom reside in the inner cities of Budapest, Pecs, and Miskolc.

Demography. Approximately 100,000 Rom live in Hungary today; this figure accounts for 20 percent of all the Gypsies in the country. When the Rom migrated into Hungary after their liberation from slavery in the Romanian principalities of Wallachia and Moldavia, some moved on to western Europe and even to the New World. The majority remained in the countries that came under Russian control after World War II. We do not know what percentage of the world's Rom live in modern Hungary.

Linguistic Affiliation. Rom speak Romany (also spelled "Romani") or Romanes as they say. The vocabulary items of the Romany spoken by any one group of Rom are deeply influenced by the country where they happen to reside. The syntactical structure remains more constant. Romany spoken in Hungary belongs to the Balkanic Language Group. Some 800 words or so of its basic vocabulary (words that are shared throughout all variants of Romany spoken around the world today) are of north Indian, Persian, and Armenian origin. Romany spoken in Hungary seems to have become recently homogenized, with the merging of alternate dialects, possibly as an expression of growing ethnic self-awareness. Scholars disagree about the extent to which Romany across the world may be treated as one language—certainly Rom manage to communicate in it wherever they find one another.

History and Cultural Affiliations

Intense scholarly dispute persists regarding the "origins" of the Gypsies. On the basis of one interpretation of the linguistic evidence, Gypsies clearly came from north India sometime after the Mogul invasions, perhaps in the tenth century. Another theory propounded by Dr. J. Okely in the United Kingdom suggests that Gypsies are the result of indigenous people marrying into a trading diaspora population speaking a trading pidgin of north Indian derivation. On the basis of their Romanian-influenced dialect, scholars presume that modern Hungarian Rom were slaves to feudal lords and monasteries in Moldavia and Wallachia from their appearance in the Middle Ages until the mid-nineteenth century. Rom have cordial relations with other Romany-speaking Gypsies in Hungary and elsewhere but for the most part scorn those Gypsies who have attempted assimilation into Hungarian society (such as the Romungro Gypsies). Non-Gypsies are known as _gazo_ (plural _gaze_), which Rom translate as "peasant" whether the non-Gypsy concerned is a peasant, a teacher, or otherwise employed. Non-Gypsies are known as "peasants" because of their involvement in productive labor. Gypsies, by contrast, are involved in trade and exchanging the products of non-Gypsy laborers. Relations between the two groups are for the most part hostile.

Settlements

Gypsy settlements tend to be formed from clusters of related Rom. In rural areas settlements are most commonly located on the edge of villages. Traditionally Gypsies used to make their own sunken mud houses and cave houses. Today, prosperous Gypsies may buy old peasant cottages. Poorer Gypsies will still live in hovels. In towns Gypsies are normally placed in municipal housing. Whenever Gypsies move into an area the Magyar residents tend to move out, thus creating de facto if not de jure ghettos.

Economy

Subsistence and Commercial Activities. The most important fact about the Rom economy is that they have never used land productively; this they leave to the non-Gypsies. In feudal Europe, Rom had a reputation as blacksmiths and musicians; both professions were considered tainted or "infamous," construed as either polluting or socially dangerous. Now Rom engage, if possible, in various forms of trade, especially with horses, antiques, and (most recently) secondhand cars. Other goods (e.g., nylon sheeting) may be scavenged from municipal rubbish heaps and then sold back to the gaze (non-Gypsies). For most Rom, trade provides an insufficient income to support a family, and, therefore, they take wage-labor jobs in factories and collective farms. When Hungary had a Socialist government, all citizens were obliged to have a registered workplace. This law had been introduced, it was said, to prevent middlemen from "sponging off society," and Gypsies were at times persecuted for trying to avoid "honorable work." A Rom family will often keep a few (two to six) piglets for fattening and later sale to the slaughterhouse. These piglets, fed on bread and other garbage scavenged from

urban housing estates, provide a crucial extra source of cash income. Food is always purchased in shops, though a particular type of unleavened bread (_bokholi_) is made by Rom women and thought to be truly Gypsy food.

Industrial Arts. Gypsies produce little apart from metalwork either for their own use or for sale. Rather than make, for example, brush brooms himself, a Rom will buy the material and employ a gazo to make them for him before selling them back to gaze in the markets of rural Hungary.

Trade. Rom trade is primarily in horses. Cart horses are needed by Hungarian peasants to work their "household plots," and Rom are the middlemen who organize the circulation of these animals. Horses play an important symbolic role in the self-definition of the Hungarian "proper peasant," and so, by controlling the trade in these animals, Gypsies have acquired a position of control in the Hungarian marketplace. Rom more recently have begun to take over the secondhand car market in Budapest, the capital of Hungary. Rom say that they can dominate in the market because they have the ability to "talk people into parting with their money." The wit and personal skills of the Rom trader are celebrated in contrast to the plodding ardor of the peasantlike non-Gypsy. Trade is an activity that Rom engage in together, and the spoils of trade tend to be split equally between those who cooperate on a deal.

Division of Labor. Both men and women from the age of 14–16 engage in wage labor. Horse trading and other symbolically elaborated marketing activities are the preserve of male Rom, as it is considered unlucky for a (fertile) woman to interfere in such. Rom women tend to be more involved in scavenging industrial refuse, which they sell alongside their husbands at the horse fairs. They also raise the piglets that provide income for subsidizing the horse trade, which is itself by no means always profitable. There are no formal occupational specializations according to age or sex.

Land Tenure. Rom own no productive land. Houses, however, may be owned and sold to other Rom or non-Gypsies.

Kinship

Kin Groups and Descent. There are no formalized kin groups among the Vlach Rom, nor is an ideology of shared descent important in conceiving social relations. Rather, shared identity is talked of primarily in terms of shared activity at the present time. If one lives like a Rom, sharing one's life with other Rom, one is a Rom. In line with this ideology of identity through shared activity, Gypsies think of themselves as a "brotherhood" open to anyone who fully participates in the communal rituals.

Kinship Terminology. In traditional terms Rom terminology is of the Eskimo type. However, men of any age or relation to the speaker are most commonly referred to and addressed as "boys" and women likewise as "girls." This use of kin terms seems to accord with the antidescent ideology of "brotherhood."

Marriage and Family

Marriage. There are no explicit marriage rules; rather, a Rom expresses a series of preferences: spouses should be

Rom, known to the family, not first cousins, and from good families, etc. Most marriages are within a small circle of kin, and, despite articulated preferences, many marriages are now among first cousins. Postmarital residence tends to alternate for several years but becomes virilocal after several children are born. Divorce and remarriage in the early years of marriage is frequent, although previous marriages are a taboo subject to discuss in public.

Domestic Unit.   Two-generation households are the norm. Once all the children have left the parental home, they are often replaced by grandchildren, so old people rarely live alone. Families of eight or more children were traditionally common, with three to five offspring now being the norm.

Socialization.   Children are *the* focus of Rom communities and are treated with great tolerance and generosity. Male children are treated preferentially, and values of autonomy, independence, and agonistic display are cultivated, especially in them. Girls are taught to acquire a sense of "shame." Children are taught a brazen, even aggressive stance with non-Gypsy children; girls, for instance, may appear to drop their "shame" with the "shameless" non-Gypsy to "fool" them. After the purificatory rite of baptism there are no initiation rites. All Rom children receive some formal education in state schools, where they have often suffered from discriminatory practices.

Sociopolitical Organization

Social Organization.   Rom communities are extremely egalitarian in values, despite marked economic inequalities among households. To be "proud" and appear to stand above one's fellow Rom is unacceptable and is interpreted by fellow Gypsies as a desire to leave the community and assimilate into the non-Gypsy population. Economic inequalities have developed primarily from success in manipulating the second or "black" economy, but they have not given rise to social stratification of Rom into different classes. Rom tend to look down on other groups of Gypsies.

Political Organization.   In accordance with their egalitarian social philosophy and fierce individualism, Rom strongly resist any official leadership. Occasionally *vajda* (bosses) arise when non-Gypsy authorities conspire with a prominent Gypsy to control access to some limitable resource, but the authority of such men is always contingent on their ability to "serve up" the non-Gypsies. There are no councils among Rom, nor are there institutions for communal decision making.

Social Control.   Lack of "respect" is the most common cause of informal dispute. Trickery in horse deals or other business also features prominently in conflicts. The collapse of a marriage likewise raises such disputes. In these last instances Rom may resort to the Kris, a council of Rom arbitrators who may suggest various forms of recompense. The judgment of such arbitrators is not binding and so disputes that reach a Kris can last many months until both parties accept a compromise.

Conflict.   Rom are often in conflict with non-Gypsy authorities and others over rights of residence, matters of school attendance, accusations of theft, etc. In such disputes Rom are at a distinct disadvantage, given their lack of ease with formal non-Gypsy procedures. During the last years of the So-

cialist period, Rom formed their own national associations, which are expected to play an increasingly prominent part in future political life in Hungary.

Religion and Expressive Culture

Religious Beliefs.   Rom religion, like Rom culture in general, is an elaborate conversation with or commentary on the religion of surrounding non-Gypsies. O Del (God) and Sunto Maria (Holy Mary) are the two main benevolent forces in the universe. Jesus appears occasionally in Rom belief but mostly as a young boy. Pilgrimages provide the most common occasions for public supplication, devotion, and prayer, some of which attract large Rom gatherings. Although formally adherents of the Catholic faith, Rom have a cosmology that is only tangentially related to Catholic doctrine (see later discussion of death).

Religious Practitioners.   *Drabarni* (old female curers) are still found among Rom but otherwise Rom have no mystical/religious specialists. Each Rom relates to God, Mary, and the saints directly. Priests of the official church are unequivocally feared and held in contempt because Gypsies presume their public virtue conceals private vices of lechery, gluttony, and alcoholism. But they are also essential to maintain Gypsy purity since they provide a sort of moral cleansing for polluted Gypsies. To see a priest is unlucky and dealings with them tend to be mediated by Gypsy women.

Ceremonies.   Baptism, request for a bride/marriage, and burial are the three major life-cycle rituals, but only the first and last are celebrated in a church. At these rites the impurities associated with natural bodily processes of birth and death are unceremoniously disposed of onto the priest in order for the Gypsies to purify themselves. The priest's and the Gypsies' interpretation of the same ritual event are thus decidedly at odds. The main ceremonial form of Gypsy life is the *mulatsago*, in which men gather together, eat, drink, and then sing about the trials, tribulations, and joys of being one of the Gypsy brothers. These celebrations help create an integrated image of Gypsy society.

Arts.   Individual Rom have established themselves as poets, painters, and dancers of international note. Most Rom pride themselves on their singing and dancing skills. Rom tend to sing in groups, each group singing a song chosen and particularly associated with one of their members. The songs normally are mournful laments. Traditionally, certain ballads were also sung by Rom but these are now hard to record in Hungary. Several records have spread the fame of Hungarian Rom singers. Gypsy dance is known among the wider family of eastern European dance types.

Medicine.   Rom have their own cures for a number of minor ailments, especially ones that afflict children. Rom greatly fear treatment in non-Gypsy hospitals, which, because of their association with childbirth and death, are thought to be polluting and therefore unhealthy places. Rom tend to have more health problems than non-Gypsies, partly because Rom often do wage labor under difficult conditions.

Death and Afterlife.   At death, a gradual process of separation of the living from the deceased begins. Until burial the soul or "dream" of the deceased remains nearby, attached to the body. A continual wake is held around the body, and at times when the soul is likely to be present (between midnight and dawn), favorite songs and tales of the deceased are performed. At burial the body is, in effect, handed over to the priest and the church for safekeeping, with the soul remaining in the Gypsies' care: a nice inversion of church ideology. For at least one year the soul may return to visit the living as a _mulo_ (dead person/ghost). Gypsies pay for masses to be sung to complete the process of separation. Feasts for the deceased (_pomana_) are held at anniversaries.

Bibliography

Kaminski, I. M. (1980). _The State of Ambiguity: Studies of Gypsy Refugees_. Anthropological Research, University of Gothenburg.

Kenedi, J. (1986). "Why Is the Gypsy the Scapegoat and Not the Jew?" _East European Reporter_ 2:1.

Stewart, M. (1989). "True Speech: Song and the Moral Order of a Vlach Gypsy Community." _Man_, n.s. 24:79–102.

Stewart, M. (1990). "Gypsies, Work, and Civil Society." In _Market Economy and Civil Society in Hungary_, edited by J. Hann.

Tomka, M. (1984). "The Gypsy Craftsmen of Europe." _Unesco Courier_, October 1984 (special issue on the Gypsies).

MICHAEL STEWART

Vlachs

ETHNONYMS: Aromuni, Cincari, Vlasi

Orientation

Identification. The name "Vlachs" refers to the old Balkan ethnic group whose members are descendants of romanized and grecized Paleo-Balkan and Indo-European populations: Illyrians and Thracians. Also, the Vlachs are a recent ethnic substratum in northeast Serbia formed by Romanians and Romanized Slav immigrants from Romania.

Location. Small groups of Vlachs have survived a diaspora, mostly in the central Balkan mountain regions, in northern Greece (Thessaly, Epirus), Bulgaria, Romania, and Yugoslavia. In the former Yugoslavia Vlachs are found in eastern Istria (Croatia) between the towns of Trieste and Rijeka, in Macedonia near Kruševo and Bitola, and in Serbia near Pirot and on the mountain of Kopaonik. Vlachs in northeast Serbia live in the region delimited by the rivers of Velika Morava to the west, Timok to the east, and Danube to the north, and by the mountain of Rtanj to the south.

Demography. As there is no generally accepted criteria for determining who should be considered a Vlach, and because their assimilation with Slavs and other populations is rather intense, it is difficult to determine their exact number. Historical data show that at the beginning of the nineteenth century about 400,000 to 500,000 Vlachs lived on the Balkan Peninsula. However, it is assumed that today there are about 50,000 to 60,000 Vlachs, of which 20 percent live in the former Yugoslavia. The population of Yugoslavia in 1981 was 22,425,000, while 32,071 individuals or 0.1 percent listed themselves as Vlachs. They are most numerous in Serbia (25,596) and Macedonia (6,392).

Linguistic Affiliation. The Vlach language developed from vernacular Latin. It is similar to Romanian, with which it shares many common forms both in grammar and phonetics. However, the differences between the two languages are so great, particularly in Vlach vocabulary, which abounds with Slavic, Albanian, and Greek elements, that the average Romanian cannot understand the Vlach language. Because of frequent migrations, isolated mountain life, and the separate development of individual Vlach groups, several dialects have been formed. Generally, Vlachs are bilingual, speaking both the language of the population living in their immediate proximity and the Vlach language, which they use for internal local communication. In the southeast regions of the Balkan Peninsula they also accepted Greek as a more prestigious language, whereas in the western parts of the Balkans the Vlach language completely disappeared (except in Istria), although it left clear traces in both toponymy and anthroponymy.

History and Cultural Relations

During the sixth and seventh centuries A.D., under the pressure of the Slavs and other peoples advancing from the north to the Balkan Peninsula, the autochthonous Balkan populations retreated to the southern and western regions. Those who took refuge in inaccessible high mountains of the central and southern Balkans and adopted a nomadic way of life managed to survive and eventually developed into a distinct group. This process probably took place in the region of Pind in Greece, where their core remains today and from which they have dispersed for centuries. In the tenth century a large Vlach group still lived on the mountain of Pind, in Thessaly, Epirus, and Macedonia. Another group spread through the mountains of the Balkan Peninsula, between the Black Sea and the Adriatic, in the Adriatic hinterland and towns of the Adriatic coast. From the twelfth to the fourteenth centuries, because of their nomadic way of life, they spread considerably through what was then Serbia, Bosnia, Herzegovina, and Croatia, moving as far north as the Polish Carpathians. From the fifteenth century, during the time of the Turkish invasion of the Balkans, the Vlachs as nomadic cattle breeders became included in the economic life of the Turkish Empire and were granted certain privileges. During this time they even formed some permanent villages. However, the crises and conflicts that affected the Turkish Empire from the seventeenth to the nineteenth centuries resulted in the persecution of nomadic Vlachs. Ali Pasha Janjinski (1744–1822) was the most cruel of the Turkish overlords, destroying the Vlachs' native country in Pind and scattering Vlach families to different parts of the Balkan Peninsula. Some Vlachs remained faithful to a nomadic way of life and sheep breeding, while others traveled to find work in towns and abandoned the traditional occupations. Further development of socioeconomic, historical, and political relationships was not favorable to nomadic cattle raising nor to the Vlachs, so they began to assimilate with the surrounding ethnic groups. Vlachs in northeast Serbia immigrated mostly at the end of the eighteenth and the start of the nineteenth centuries from the territory of present-day Romania.

In their dispersion, individual Vlach groups maintain cultural relations with different Slavic, Albanian, Greek, and Romanian ethnic groups, living with them in peaceful coexistence with frequent contacts and intermixing. Vlachs in northeast Serbia have equal rights and obligations with the predominant Serbian population, although they do not have their own schools or other cultural and social institutions, newspapers, etc.

Settlements

Traditional settlements of nomadic Vlachs are summer dwellings (*katuni*), situated on high mountains near springs and good pastures. Tents made of black felt (rolled wool) or log cabins built of reed, brushwood, and branches, covered with a thatch of straw of circular or rectangular shape, are crowded together. Temporary winter settlements are somewhat larger than summer ones, as more family groups gather together. Permanent Vlach villages are usually situated along steep mountain slopes with spacious houses closely set together. Since World War II the Vlachs in northeast Serbia have built large brick houses, comfortably furnished and including small gardens, as a considerable number of their population work abroad in western Europe. However, they still generally prefer their old houses situated nearby.

Economy

Subsistence and Commercial Activities. The basic occupation of Vlachs is sheep breeding, including the production of milk and dairy products. The main food on all occasions is "white meat" (cheese, milk, cream, and sour cream) and bread, and only occasionally potatoes and meat. Winter food provisions are meager, except for dairy products and bacon. Their most popular drink is whey, the liquid that remains after cheese is curdled. They exchange sheep products for some agricultural products with farmers. They process wood, leather, and wool and make clothes from home-produced and -worked wool. Clothes are made from felt produced by rolling or beating woolen cloth left in the color of the natural wool or dyed with dark stains. The costume consists of a long tunic-shirt, worn next to the skin, a sleeveless coat, a red yarn belt, several layers of woolen stockings and over them sandals (*opanci*) of rawhide formed on a last and with woven thongs of sheep guts. Women wear a woolen apron decorated with braids and loops. A large cloak with a hood (*kabanica*) and a small brimless cap are typically worn. Vlachs in northeast Serbia, in addition to sheep and cattle breeding, are also engaged in mining, gold panning, and the production of charcoal. In lowlands near the Danube, they are engaged in farming, fruit growing, and viticulture.

Industrial Arts. The Vlach herders are good tailors and wood-carvers. Those who settled in towns are professional artisans, particularly shoemakers, tinsmiths, coppersmiths, goldsmiths, and construction workers. They are also successful bankers and innkeepers.

Trade. Vlachs in towns are known as good tradespeople who own small oriental shops with handicraft products. For herders, exchange of goods is common.

Division of Labor. Labor is traditionally divided into male and female activities. Milking, cheese making, weaving, cleaning, washing, cooking, and care of children are exclusively female responsibilities, whereas tending pasture, chopping wood, handicrafts, and trade are men's work.

Land Tenure. Pastures, water, and forests are collective property, and every family of the group has equal rights to them. In addition, each lineage has its own pastures that are inviolable. Frequently, a number of families of the same or different lineages are joined into a larger group (*tajfe*), and together they rent pastures, process milk, and sell dairy products, so that a community spirit permeates all group activities.

Kinship, Marriage, and Family

Kinship. The most important kinship group is the patriarchal extended family formed by married brothers and their offspring. Herders usually have many children, from eight to twelve. Several families of a common descent form a lineage (*soj* or *fara*). The surnames of lineages are permanent and the members of seven to fifteen generations are known genealogically. Descent is agnatic and kinship terminology is highly elaborated. Blood brotherhood (*pobratimstvo*) and godfatherhood (*kumstvo*) are highly respected and socially important.

Marriage. Exogamous marriage and patrilocal residence are preferred. However, matrilocal residence is possible when there is no male heir in a family, and such an in-marrying male is called a *domazet*. Marriages are traditionally arranged by parents. Age at marriage is exceptionally low, and early marriages are a common and socially imposed phenomenon. It is generally believed that a girl will grow old if she does not marry immediately after puberty.

Domestic Unit. The extended family is the most frequent domestic unit, which is a unit of production, consumption, and common defense.

Inheritance. Land inheritance, both traditionally and today, is primarily through male lines of descent.

Socialization. Children are taught always to respect their elders and never to oppose them. They are more afraid of their fathers than of their mothers; corporal punishment is common. Small children are carried everywhere in a small cradle slung on their mother's back. In addition to the parents, father's and mother's brothers and cousins also show considerable care for the children. Male children are generally more protected than female ones, while the borderline between childhood and adolescence for both sexes is the age of 15, which coincides with sexual and biological maturity.

Sociopolitical Organization

Throughout history, the Vlachs never succeeded in forming their own state. By the end of the eighteenth century in the Albanian town of Moskopolje, a national movement was organized but it never involved all Vlachs. Although they are not numerous, they do live on a comparatively great territory because they are dispersed as ethnic islands among other peoples. Individual Vlach groups—especially herders in winter settlements—maintain frequent mutual contacts. Movements from one regional group to another are rather common. This behavior contributes to intermixing and to the maintenance of ethnic identity. Although the Vlachs had been relatively homogeneous, following the Balkan Wars (1876–1878 and 1912–1918) the territory in which they live was politically divided so that communication between Vlachs in Albania, Yugoslavia, Greece, Bulgaria, and Romania became very difficult. They were not allowed to cross state borders with their flocks and herds.

Social Organization. The social position of the Vlachs was determined by the opposition between the sedentary populations and the mobile nomads, clearly distinguished in Old Serbian and Croatian laws. Serbian laws of the Middle Ages, for example, prohibited marriages between sedentary Serbs and Vlach nomads in order to preserve a sedentary economic national character. Mountains and forests in the Middle Ages were treated legally almost as a dead zone, and their inhabitant herders were free from laws that applied to sedentary populations. Consequently, Vlachs have always had their own autonomous internal organization. Patriarchal families were grouped in lineages or groups of lineages (_tajfas_) headed by _čelnik_ or _ćehaja_. This head shepherd was supreme chief with great authority. His word was always obeyed and he governed a group of 20 to 200 families with 10,000 sheep, paying taxes and tributes and taking care of trade and other group activities.

Social Control. Traditional norms regulate the relationship between the individual and the group. The place and the role of the house and family is strictly determined within this structure.

Conflict. Self-managed communities (katuni) were closed in their autonomous world and their members organized their own defense. Conflicts between two neighboring communities were usually over pasture rights, and every offense gave rise to fierce animosity, plundering, and killings, which sometimes turned into a series of bloody revenges. Isolated in high mountains, the Vlachs represented the main outposts of resistance in fights with the Turks.

Religion and Expressive Culture

Religious Beliefs and Practices. Generally, Vlachs accepted the same religion as the other populations in the region in which they lived. Today, the majority of Vlachs belong to the Orthodox church, characteristic for the eastern Balkans; Vlachs in the western Balkans are Catholics; and only a small number are Muslims. Nonetheless, they also persistently preserve their ancient practices and beliefs, which are respected and maintained as ethnic, cultural, and moral traits. This belief system clearly defines the relationship of the individual self with the material and spiritual world. Every-thing related to human beings and existence usually is attributed to fate. Although they celebrate all the main holidays of the formal church calendar, they rarely attend church for these occasions, celebrating instead among themselves; they do not call the priest for requiem masses and they do not marry in church. Even if they come to church, they disturb prayers by dancing and singing. The Orthodox Vlachs celebrate the important Orthodox holiday _slava_, feast of the patron saint, but for them it is primarily a cult dedicated to land fertility. Fortune-telling and sorcery are a common part of all aspects of social and religious life.

Arts. Vlachs developed all types of oral folk literature, epic and lyric songs, ballads, proverbs, and riddles. However, their creative work lacks fantastic beings and events. Tattooing as body decoration has been preserved up to the present in some Vlach groups.

Medicine. Traditional ways of healing still play an important role, particularly with mountain herders who live far from medical institutions. Vlachs cure the majority of illnesses with simple devices, mostly plants and their infusions, by themselves or with the help of a folk practitioner.

Death and Afterlife. Vlachs have a deeply rooted belief in life after death and very elaborate funeral rites. The dead are highly respected and imaginary contact with them is held on many occasions and in different ways, are to ensure the afterlife of the soul. In northeast Serbia, requiem masses are held for both the living and the dead in the same way, in the form of feasts that often develop into real orgies. Twice a day, three times a week for forty days, prayers are held to forty-four dead and forty-four live kin, and everything is accompanied by abundant food, music, and dances for the souls. The custom of disinterment forty days after death is still present there, although prohibited by law.

Bibliography

Cvijić, Jovan (1966). _Balkansko poluostrvo i južnoslovenske zemlje_ (The Balkan Peninsula and the South Slavic lands). 2nd ed. Belgrade: Lavod za Izdavanje Udžbenika.

Drobnjaković, Borivoje (1960). _Etnologija naroda Jugoslavije_ [Ethnology of peoples in Yugoslavia]. Belgrade: Lavod za Izdavanje Udžbenika.

Federal Statistical Office (1982). _Statisticki bilten Jugoslavije_ [Statistical bulletin of Yugoslavia]. Belgrade: Lavod za Izdavanje Udžbenika.

Skok, Petar (1926). _Rumunska literatura o balkanskim Vlasima_ [Romanian literature on Balkanic Vlachs]. Skopje: Glasnik Skopskog Naučnog Društva.

ANITA SUJOLDŽIĆ

Walloons

Orientation

Identification. In the broad sense of the word "Walloon" is the name given to the autochthons of Wallonia inhabiting the Belgian provinces of Hainaut, Namur, Luxembourg, Liège (except for the German cantons in the east), and the district of Nivelles in Brabant. A small percent of the population (centered on people over age 65) still speak Walloon regularly. French is the native language of the vast majority, though there is a particular accent that distinguishes it from the standard French of France. The term "Walha" was used by the ancient Germans to designate romanized Celtic tribes. From this word, "Walloon" was derived (*walon* in Walloon and *waal* in Flemish). "Belgian" refers to a citizen of Belgium, which includes both the Walloons and the Flemish.

Location. Belgium lies to the north of France, the west of Germany and the south of Holland. The provinces that comprise Wallonia (approximately 17,000 square kilometers) are roughly located in the southern half of Belgium. The Walloon landscape ranges from low plateaus to wooded hills in the southeast. To the north live the Flemish, who are separated by a linguistic, rather than a geographic border. Two major rivers cross Wallonia, the Escaut and the Meuse. The weather is cool and rainy year round. The higher elevations of the Ardennes (694 meters is the highest point) receive up to 50 days of snow in a year, as opposed to around five days of snow for the rest of the country.

Demography. The total population of Wallonia is 3,200,000, with 191 persons per square kilometer. Four hundred sixteen thousand, or 13 percent of this population, are foreigners. Most of these foreigners come from southern Europe, with increasing numbers from North Africa. The number of births per thousand stood at 15.5 in 1963, dropping to less than 11.7 by 1983. The death rate is 12.9 per thousand (1983). Age stratification in 1981 is: 0-14, 20 percent; 15-24, 16 percent; 24-64, 50 percent; 65+, 14 percent.

Linguistic Affiliation. Walloon is a Gallo-Romance dialect of the Indo-European Language Family. Being so close to the dialect border, Walloon shares certain sounds and structures with Germanic dialects, but the base of the language is Romance. Walloon can be divided into Eastern Walloon (with Liège as its capital), Central Walloon (Namur), and Western Walloon (Charleroi, La Louvière, Nivelles). Other dialect areas in southern Wallonia, which still form part of the same general dialect region though they are not called "Walloon," are: Picard or Rouchi (Mons, Ath, Tournai, Mouscron), Gaumais (or Lorraine of Belgium), and Champenois.

History and Cultural Relations

Belgium has been aptly called "the crossroads of Europe." Its tribes, which were probably Celtic, were colonized by the Romans for the first three centuries of the first millennium. In the fourth and fifth centuries the Franks invaded from the north. Their settlement was sparse in Wallonia, which en- sured the continuation of Romance dialects. The city of Liège, the largest city and cultural capital of Wallonia, was designated as a Catholic see in the seventh century. Under Carolingian suzerainty (A.D. 752–918), it became an international center of learning. It then became the seat of a large independent principality and evolved into an important city during the late Middle Ages and early modern period. Burgundian dukes annexed Wallonia and Flanders at the end of the fourteenth century, except for the principality of Liège. The Burgundian territories were passed on to Spain and then Austria. In 1789 the people of Liège drove out their leader, the Prince Bishop, and together with the rest of Belgium joined the Republic of France in 1795. In 1815 Belgium fell under the leadership of William I of Holland. This only lasted until 1830, when Belgium revolted and won her independence. Since this time there has been conflict over linguistic rights within the state.

Settlements

There are two major types of traditional farms in the countryside. In the central region structures are built in a quadrilateral. In the Ardennes and Gaumais, they are built along a single axis. Chateau-farms are scattered throughout the region. The majority of the population is urbanized, and the predominant type of house is a brick row house of several stories. Whether in the village or the city, a Catholic church is never far away.

Economy

Subsistence and Commercial Activities. Sugar beets are a common cash crop in the countryside. What is not turned into sugar is used as animal fodder. Wheat and potatoes are other common crops. Belgium's holdings in central Africa led to the importation of cocoa, which was developed into the world-renowned Belgian chocolate. In 1982, Belgians consumed over 7 kilos of chocolate per capita. Many artisanal chocolate operations exist throughout Wallonia. Local breweries also used to be a common sight. Nowadays there is still an extremely wide choice of beers, but production is not so localized. Walloons drink a lot of Flemish beer, too, but they always know which ones are made in Wallonia. Straight gin, called *pèkèt*, is also a popular alcoholic drink. The milk has an especially high fat content, which translates into extremely rich butter, cream, and cheese. A simple local cheese, *makèye*, is eaten most often on slices of bread as *tartines*, a common breakfast and supper. The heavy meal of the day is eaten at noon, often including a pork dish, potatoes, and salad with mayonnaise. Soups are a common first course at the midday meal and supper. A four o'clock *goûter* often consists of a piece of pie and coffee.

Belgium has one of the highest daily per capita caloric consumption rates in the world. Coffee is widely drunk. Some families keep a thermos filled all day long. Pork is the cheapest and most widely consumed meat, and hams from the Ardennes are a delicacy known throughout Europe. Mussels imported from Flanders and Holland are a favorite dish along with french-fried potatoes. Fried potatoes can be bought at almost any time of the day on most every street corner, with a variety of sauces available. Several types of waffles can also be readily purchased, often hot out of the oven.

Industrial Arts. Owing to the presence of coal and good river transportation, Wallonia has been an important center of iron and steel production since the Middle Ages. By the beginning of the eighteenth century, coal-burning machines used for the pumping and draining of mines were installed in Liège, greatly increasing production. Wallonia was the first region on the European continent to undergo the Industrial Revolution. Many of the early industrialists came from England. Verviers became an important textile center while the coal mines around Liège, Charleroi, and the Borinage gave birth to the steel industry. As early as the fifteenth century, Wallonia was supplying firearms to the king of Spain. Nowadays the arms industry is centered in the National Arms Factory in Herstal. The crystal factory, Val St. Lambert, had a world reputation at one time, but it is now closed. In the past, women made lace in the home, but very few continue to do so.

Trade. Wallonia has long carried on trade with neighboring European countries. The excellent canal, river, and railway systems of Belgium facilitated the transport of both imports and exports. However, the Walloon coal mines are now shut down and the steel industry is in a critical decline. The food industry has begun exporting more, but on the whole, trade has decreased dramatically in the last twenty years. In 1980 the unemployment rate in Wallonia was 14.5 percent.

Division of Labor. Walloon women have been working outside the home since the Industrial Revolution, though they still earn less than men since they are concentrated in low-paying industries such as textiles and clothing and are not proportionately represented in upper management. Factories began running day-care centers for the children of their female employees in the nineteenth century. Today the state operates numerous day-care centers around the country. Women are still primarily responsible for keeping the home.

Land Tenure. As in England, the introduction of the capitalist order during the eighteenth century, in combination with several disastrous agricultural years, led to the impoverishment of the countryside and the beginning of the exodus into the cities to compete for factory jobs. Today only about 4 percent of the population makes its living from agriculture.

Kinship, Marriage, and Family

Kinship. Walloon kinship is bilateral. The nuclear family predominates as a household group.

Marriage. Wallonia has a rising divorce rate and a falling marriage rate. Monogamy or consecutive monogamy are the two acceptable marriage types. People are free to choose their own marriage partners. Average age of marriage is mid- to late twenties. (It has decreased over the last century.) Usually people marry within their own socioeconomic class. Upon marriage, most young people set up their own household. They may take children to their parents' house so that grandmothers can babysit.

Domestic Unit. The nuclear family is the norm. An elderly parent often moves in with the family of one of her (sometimes his) children, but it is very common for old people to live alone.

Socialization. Children undergo a different socialization process depending on whether their families are working-class, middle-class, or upper-class. For instance, working-class families value getting a job early more than they do the pursuit of higher education. The opposite is the case among the middle and upper classes. There are 54 nationally certified day-care centers throughout Wallonia, which charge a minimal amount along a sliding scale. A great emphasis is placed on equality in these centers. They even supply clothes so that children are not differentiated on this basis. Upper-class families make more use of hired private nannies. Ninety percent of the Belgians aged 2½ to 5 are in preschool. Education is compulsory for children between ages 6 and 14.

Sociopolitical Organization

Belgium is a parliamentary democracy under a constitutional monarchy. The king is the titular head of the state and the prime minister, who is chosen from among leaders of major political parties represented in parliament, is the head of government. Elections are held at four-year intervals.

Social Organization. Belgium is a Western, industrial, class-based society. Clubs and associations, based on shared personal interests or backgrounds, proliferate. What political party one belongs to is almost always an important criterion when choosing an organization.

Political Organization. The Socialist party claims the most adherents in Wallonia (36.3 percent of the vote in 1981). Other political parties are the Christian Socialists, the Liberals, the Walloon Assembly, the Communists, and the Ecologists. Trade unions are very important. The first three parties named run their own trade unions.

Social Control. The Belgian armed forces and police force (including national gendarmerie and municipal, rural, and criminal police) exercise control over the region.

Conflict. Belgium, throughout its history, has been used as a frequent battlefield in wars that originated outside its borders. Even though Belgium claimed neutrality in both world wars, its countryside was decimated. The two major conflicts in Wallonia today are between the leftist and conservative political parties and between the Flemish and the Walloons.

Religion and Expressive Culture

Religious Beliefs. Wallonia is an area of dying Catholicism. Many parish churches have had to close owing to a lack of attendance. Communion, confession, baptism, and religious marriages are all on the decline. Many older people may attend church only occasionally, but keep statues of the Virgin Mary in their windows. Lourdes in southwestern France is a popular place of pilgrimage. Beauraing and Banneaux are the two most popular places of pilgrimage in Wallonia. Several saints' processions have been revived in recent times, though often because of an interest in folkloric practices rather than renewed religious faith. Some of these even include religious reversals, such as a fake priest handing out slices of cucumber instead of hosts. The immigrants from southern Europe are usually more observant of Catholic rituals than the Walloons. The immigrants from North Africa and Turkey are beginning to call for more support of the Islamic religion. Wallonia is also the home of small numbers of Protestants, Jews, Russian Orthodox, and Greek Orthodox.

Religious Practitioners. Wallonia used to have several monasteries that produced an important number of clergymen. Today, very few boys choose a religious career.

Ceremonies. Baptisms, first communions, and marriages are rites of passage marked by celebrations. Many nonreligious Walloons have begun celebrating laic communions for their children. Carnival has numerous faces around Wallonia. Generally, an entire village dons identical costumes. Most famous among these is the Carnival of Binche.

Arts. Belgium has been known for her painters since the late Middle Ages. While many of the most famous painters were Flemish, Walloons were represented as well. Wallonia is perhaps better known for its contributions to modern art by the surrealists René Magritte and Alfred Delvaux. There have been several internationally known Walloon writers. Probably the best-known in the United States is Georges Simenon, the mystery writer and creator of Maigret. Folk arts are alive and well in Wallonia, with numerous processions of giants, mock military marches, and a thriving rod-puppet theater.

Medicine. There are 2.1 doctors per thousand Wallonians, and 4.77 hospital beds. Medical care is subsidized by the state.

Death and Afterlife. The devil is a popular figure in Walloon folklore, and belief in an afterlife is probably still fairly strong. Funerals vary from open casket to cremation. Friends of the deceased usually give speeches honoring him or her at the funeral. All Saints' Day, at which time spirits are thought to return to the earth, occurs on 4 November. On this day, many families go to the cemetery and clean the tombs of their ancestors.

Bibliography

CRISP (1982). *Dossier pour Wallonie 2000.* Brussels: CRISP dossier no. 15.

Hasquin, Hervé (1982). *Historiographie et politique: Essai sur l'histoire de Belgique et la Wallonie.* Mont-sur-Marchienne: Édition Institut Jules Destrée.

Lejeune, Rita, and Jacques Stinnon (1978). *Wallonie: Le pays et les hommes.* Liège: Marche Romane.

Turney-High, Harry Holbert (1953). *Château Gérard: The Life and Times of a Walloon Village.* Columbia: University of South Carolina Press.

Wickman, Stephen B., ed. (1985). *Belgium: A Country Study.* Washington, D.C.: U.S. Government Printing Office; Brussels: La Renaissance du Livre.

JOAN GROSS

Welsh

ETHNONYM: Cymry (pronounced kamrī)

Orientation

Identification. The principality of Wales is one of the four "countries" constituting the United Kingdom of Great Britain and Northern Ireland. Though once ethnically homogeneous, Wales has had a steady influx of English-speaking settlers since the twelfth century. Prior to 1974 there were thirteen internal divisions or counties; in 1974 these were redrawn into eight counties.

Location. Wales is a wide peninsula that extends into the Irish Sea on the west coast of the island of Great Britain. The northern shore begins at the Dee Estuary and Liverpool Bay, the western shore borders on Saint George's Channel and the Irish Sea, and the south shore consists of the Severn Estuary and the Bristol Channel. The peninsula consists of four major regions. The interior plateaus and uplands are characterized by a shorter growing season, relatively infertile acid soils, and high rainfall. The northwestern and west coastal lowlands or "Welsh Heartland" has a milder climate, longer growing season, and better soils. The "Anglicized Lowlands" along the south coast and the English border have relatively good soils and a more productive agricultural economy. Finally, "Industrialized Wales" is centered in the hills, valleys, and coastal cities of the south.

The Welsh climate is part of the North Atlantic maritime pattern with relatively heavy rainfall and high humidity throughout the year. Along the coast the amount of rainfall varies between 76 and 80.9 centimeters per year. The annual mean temperature is around 10.4° C with the January mean around 5° C and the July and August mean around 16° C. At times the higher uplands are subject to heavy winter snowstorms.

Demography. As of 1988 the population of Wales was estimated at 2,805,000, of which 76 percent was urban and 24 percent rural. Given the official status of both the English and Welsh languages and the differing degrees of bilingualism, it is impossible to determine the exact numbers of individuals who ethnically identify as Welsh. The uplands, north, and west are relatively thinly populated. All the large cities (Cardiff, Swansea, and Newport) are in the relatively densely populated southern industrial belt.

Linguistic Affiliation. Both Welsh and English are official languages. During the past two centuries the percentage of Welsh speakers has continued to decline. In 1901 about half the people spoke Welsh; today this is about 20 percent. Welsh is one of the Celtic languages. It is closest to Breton in France. Other related languages are Irish and Scottish Gaelic. In recent years there has been an increasing recognition and use of Welsh in Wales.

History and Cultural Relations

The Celtic conquest of Wales occurred only a few centuries before the Roman conquest of Britain in A.D. 70. The Romans withdrew in A.D. 383. This was followed by the arrival of Christian missionaries from Ireland and the Anglo-Saxon invasions from the east. After the seventh century the Welsh were increasingly isolated from the rest of Europe by the expanding Saxon kingdoms. From this time until the arrival of the Normans, Welsh history can be characterized as a complex pattern of internal disputes between its small kingdoms, shifting alliances between different factions, and a constant series of petty wars between these groups and the Saxon kingdoms. During the ninth and tenth centuries, there was some success at unification, the establishment of a code of laws along with increasing Saxon legal and cultural influences. Between 1066 and the early twelfth century, Norman colonies, towns, and forts along the east and south further isolated the Welsh. In 1282 the Anglo-Norman conquest of Wales was completed, and between 1400 and 1410 the last Welsh revolt was suppressed. Finally in 1536 the Act of Union occurred whereby Wales was made a principality of England, English became the official language, and English law became dominant.

From about 1750 to 1900 much of Welsh life was greatly changed by the industrial revolution and the Methodist-Calvinist religious revivals. The development of coal and iron mining and smelting in the south resulted in massive movements of Welsh workers to the south. Large numbers of English workers also arrived. This division between the urban-industrial south and the rural-agrarian center and north still remains. The Wesleyan and nonconformist religious movements stimulated a shift away from the established church and provided a new core of Welsh ethnic consciousness.

Settlements

Traditionally, Wales was a land of dispersed homesteads and small hamlets. The medieval Code of Hywell Dda specified that a hamlet could consist of no more than nine houses or hearths. This pattern was a reflection of the old economy based upon subsistence farming and transhumance dairying with the winter base camp (_hendre_) at a lower elevation and the summer camp (_havod_) in the uplands. The earliest towns were those founded by the Normans in the south and the coastal strips. After the English conquest in 1292, county administrative and market towns were established, but these usually remained centers of English social life. During the industrialization of the south, larger towns and cities arose but the older rural pattern remained in the uplands and the north.

In the mining communities of the southern vales, slate-roofed and stone-walled row houses often stretch for miles along the valley slopes. Most of these were built in the late nineteenth century.

Economy

Subsistence and Commercial Activities. Since the 1830s, the Welsh economy developed into a bifurcated pattern between the rural uplands and the southern industrial regions. In the uplands, the Welsh Heartland, and the north, the older self-sufficient agricultural, dairying, and sheepherding way of life was increasingly drawn into the larger regional and national economic networks. The most important agricultural products included wheat, barley, oats, dairy products, beef, mutton, and lamb. Potatoes, poultry, vegetables, and fruits were important for household use and local mar-

kets. In today's urban markets most of these are now supplied by English producers. Most dairy products are produced and marketed locally.

Beginning in the 1840s the Welsh economy increasingly shifted to coal mining, iron and steel production, and tin plating in the industrial south. Since 1950 these have drastically declined and are being replaced by light industry, plastics, and chemical- and electronic-equipment manufacturing. The recent development of the deep-water oil port, refinery, and petrochemical complex at Milford Haven has been the one major change. Slate mining remains important in the north.

Industrial Arts. Up to 1930 every locality had a wide range of local craftsmen such as blacksmiths, tanners, clog makers, coopers, etc. By the 1940s these were declining and by the 1950s they had virtually ceased to exist.

Trade. Today one finds a mixture of traditional shops, open-air markets, supermarkets, shopping centers, large department stores, and weekly farmers' open-air markets.

Division of Labor. In the rural areas women traditionally were in charge of food production, dairying activities, and care of the cattle and poultry, whereas men did the heavier work in the fields, pastures, and hedges. Cooperative exchanges of labor, farm machinery, and farm laborers were essential. With the commercialization of dairying and poultry raising, women's labor load has increased. Modern machines have almost ended the labor exchanges. Costly machines are cooperatively purchased.

Land Tenure. Western and southern Wales was once a land of minor gentry; elsewhere there were small owner-occupied farms. Today the gentry is gone and the small farms predominate. A heavy turnover of ownership for small holdings is normal.

Kinship

Kin Groups and Descent. The core kin group is the bilateral kindred. Within this group the household and relationships of the first degree (parents, siblings, and children) are the most important. Second-degree relationships (grandparents, uncles, aunts, first cousins, nieces, nephews, and grandchildren) are also important as are those of the third degree (siblings of grandparents and children of first cousins and of nieces and nephews). Both consanguineal and affinal links are important in tracing one's relationships to others in the locality and expressing "community solidarity," reciprocal obligations, and needs. Ideally, people should remain loyal; otherwise, they risk social isolation. Interconnections between kindreds tend to bind everyone together into larger groups of "kin," which form the bases for local identity. Older individuals can often trace interrelationships between everyone in a locality back 130–150 years. The kindred also influences membership in religious groups, political affiliation, marriage alliances, and general social interaction. Marriage between kin closer than second cousins is rare. The oldest son in a family is commonly named after the paternal grandfather, the second son after the father, and the first and second daughters after the grandmothers.

Kinship Terminology. Welsh kinship terminology follows a bifurcate-merging pattern as among the English. In some areas there are differing terms for consanguineal as opposed to affinal relatives. Personal or individual preferences often lead to stressing one side of the family as opposed to the other. Lifelong nicknames based upon negative or humorous traits are common.

Marriage and Family

Marriage. Traditionally, a son's marriage was his important transition to independence and adulthood. This concluded his major economic obligations to his parents. At this time they provided him with a farm, the implements, and livestock. There was a tendency to marry within the local community if possible. Sons usually married in their late twenties or early thirties and daughters in their mid- or late twenties. The percentage of bachelors was relatively high. Courtship tended to be very lengthy. Today the number of children per family generally ranges between one and three.

Domestic Unit. The basic domestic unit is the nuclear family, which consists of either the husband and wife or the parents and their children. In the latter case this often includes unmarried adult sons acting as unpaid farm workers. A widow or widower who gave up farming traditionally preferred to live with a married daughter. A chosen son, in most cases a younger son, commonly inherited the parental farm.

Inheritance. From medieval times to the present each child has been entitled to his/her share of inheritance. Older siblings usually receive their shares in the form of purchased land, furnishings, and other goods at the time of their marriage; the chosen heir, often the youngest son, succeeds to the parental land. The sex of the children, movement to the city, and other circumstances can influence these inheritance patterns.

Socialization. Traditionally discipline was maintained through a combination of corporal punishment, moral example, and religious teachings and exhortations, especially in the context of the nonconformist chapels. These were reinforced by an emphasis on the importance of schooling and knowledge in general.

Sociopolitical Organization

Wales is a principality that is governed from Whitehall in London. Since 1964, when the position of Secretary of State for Wales was established, an increasing degree of administrative autonomy for Wales has evolved. All British political parties are represented, although the Labor Party is strongest in the industrial south. The Welsh Nationalist Party (Plaid Cymru) and other separatist groups are small but vocal.

Social Organization. Wales was and remains far less class-conscious than England. After the Union of 1536, whereby authority was centralized in London, the aristocrats drifted away and Wales increasingly became a land of smallholders. The Acts of Enclosure were never applied in Wales. A large liberal-oriented working class and an egalitarian middle class have emerged in the industrial south.

Political Organization. In 1974 the internal political organization of Wales was simplified and Monmouthshire, now Gwent, was transferred to Wales. Sparsely populated counties in the north and central uplands were amalgamated and Glamorgan was divided into three new counties. The eight counties were subdivided into thirty-seven districts, and

Cardiff retained its status as a city and capital of Wales. Each county and administrative district has its own elected council.

Social Control. On the local level gossip, religious values, and ethnic pride are the primary means of social control. Above this, the British court system prevails. Both English and Welsh are used in the courts.

Conflict. Welsh history was dominated by centuries of military and social conflict with the English and internal dissention. The nineteenth and twentieth centuries have seen the rise of a Welsh cultural revival and ethnic consciousness in the face of a decline in the use of the Welsh language. Much of this revival has centered around the musical and literary competitions of the Welsh *eisteddfod*, Welsh religiosity, literary societies, and the efforts to have Welsh recognized as one of the official languages in Wales.

Religion and Expressive Culture

Religious Beliefs. Various Protestant churches are dominant in Wales. In 1536 the Church of England became the official faith of the Welsh; by the early nineteenth century, the majority of the Welsh were nonconformists: Calvinist-Methodists, Congregationalists, Baptists, Presbyterians, Unitarians, etc. In 1914 the Church of England was declared no longer the official church of Wales, but the four ancient cathedrals retain their importance for all denominations.

Religious Practitioners. Ministers are respected leaders and moral exhorters in their individual parishes.

Ceremonies. The most important services are the weekly Sunday services and special evening prayer services. Others are Christmas eve and morning services, New Year's Eve, Palm Sunday, Easter, and Harvest Home. Saint David's Day (1 March) for the Patron Saint of Wales has increasingly become a secular holiday related to ethnic consciousness. Bible study, or Sunday schools with age-graded groups for young people and adults, have traditionally been important.

Arts. The local and national literary, musical, and cultural eisteddfods are the core of the Welsh arts. The Welsh poetic tradition remains uniquely strong even today.

Medicine. Medical beliefs and practices are basically the same as those in modern England (i.e., socialized medicine with physicians, surgeons, modern clinics, and hospitals).

Death and Afterlife. Death and the ensuing funeral, with the gathering of the kindred, were traditionally the great reminder of family unity. Every local household was expected to have at least one representative at the funeral and the feast provided for by the family of the deceased afterwards. In the past, careful note was made as to who was and was not there. In some areas the list from the funeral guest book was published in the local newspaper. The basic Protestant belief in the soul going either to heaven or hell was common among the Welsh.

Bibliography

Jenkins, David, Emrys Jones, T. Jones Hughes, and Trefor M. Owen (1962). *Welsh Rural Communities.* Cardiff: University of Wales Press.

Jenkins, J. Geraint (1976). _Life and Tradition in Rural Wales._ London: J. M. Dent & Sons.

Jones, R. Brinley, ed. (1972). _Anatomy of Wales._ Peterston-Super-Ely, Wales: Gwerin.

Owen, Trefor M. (1974). _Welsh Folk Customs._ 3rd ed. Cardiff: National Museum of Wales, Welsh Folk Museum.

Rees, Alwyn D. (1950). _Life in a Welsh Countryside._ Cardiff: University of Wales Press.

ROBERT J. THEODORATUS

Xoraxané Romá

ETHNONYMS: Arlija, Arnuta (i.e., "Albanians"), Čergaša, Gurbéti, Romá, Xoraxané Romá (i.e., "Turkish" Romá)

Orientation

Identification.   The Xoraxané Romá are a heterogeneous Gypsy group, found in the south of former and current Yugoslavia, particularly in those regions that once belonged to the Ottoman Empire. In order to escape the economic crisis in southern Yugoslavia, they began, like many Yugoslavs, to emigrate to Western Europe in the 1960s (and have continued to do so up to the present day). The Xoraxané described here migrated from the Yugoslavian region of Kosovo and arrived in Italy at the end of the 1960s.

Location and Demography.   The Xoraxané Romá in Italy today are nomads and tend to set up camp on the outskirts of large and medium towns. They travel widely throughout Italy and are today found in virtually all regions, including Sicily and Sardinia. Because many families traveled back and forth between Yugoslavia and Italy prior to the Yugoslav civil war, their numerical presence in Italy is extremely variable and very difficult to calculate. One can estimate a population numbering between 5,000 and 10,000, though no census has ever been made.

Linguistic Affiliation.   The Xoraxané Romá speak a Gypsy dialect, which has been considerably influenced lexically by the languages of the region of origin (i.e., Serbian and Albanian). The Gurbeti, who arrived in Yugoslavia from Romania at the beginning of the nineteenth century, speak a Gypsy dialect, called "Vlax" by gypsiologists, with strong Serbian and Albanian influences. The Xoraxané also speak Serbian and Albanian fluently, and also a mangled Italian.

History and Cultural Relations

Having lived for centuries in regions under the domination of the Ottoman Empire, the Xoraxané are noted even today for the cultural influences they have received from the surrounding non-Gypsy Muslim populations. In fact the term "Xoraxané" is used as a distinguishing mark in relation to the "Christian Romá," called "Dassikané Romá" or "Gadjikané Romá" (i.e., "Serbian Romá" or "non-Gypsy Romá"). They are very numerous in the regions that were the south of Yugoslavia (numbering a few hundred thousand) and it would seem they developed relatively early permanent settlements, both rural and urban. Today one can find Xoraxané Romá in France, Belgium, the Netherlands, Germany, Austria, and Denmark, as well as in Italy. Even though they consider the West to be a "halter's" (beggar's) paradise, their living conditions are far from easy. Most arrive in Italy illegally and remain without the residence permit required of them as foreign citizens. This unlawful status leads them to continual struggles with officials, as do their economic activities, which are considered illegal under Italian law. During the 1970s the Italian police used mass roundups and escorted them over the Italian/Yugoslavian border, but the Romá always managed to return. During the 1980s several Italian city councils, especially those in large municipalities, adopted a policy of integration by means of the usual system of schooling, job-training schemes, and the setting up of special campsites; nevertheless, the Xoraxané's position in Italy today remains difficult. Among the Gypsy groups in Italy, the Xoraxané is the group that appears to best accept schooling and literacy. Even most of the adults can read and write, evidently as a result of the partial success of the Yugoslavian policies regarding mandatory school attendance; in fact, it is not an accident that in Kosovo and Macedonia there are cultural circles organized by Romá that have produced notable literary works.

Settlements

Although they are sedentary in their country of origin, once in Italy the Xoraxané become nomadic. They live in tents (the ordinary tents one uses for camping) or in caravans they buy from the Italian Gypsies. They go in for large encampments (comprising as many as a hundred people); for traveling they use cars or trains; and, in most cases, they move on only when forced to do so by police intervention. Such intervention renders highly fluid the composition of the local groups, which are prevalently, though not exclusively, formed on a basis of bilateral kinship ties.

Economy

Although they pursue various activities and are partially involved in salaried jobs in what was Yugoslavia, few of the Xoraxané arriving in Italy today intend to sell their labor. Although some try to make a living through small commercial activities, like the sale of used paper for recycling, most of them live by begging and petty theft. Only the Xoraxané originating from Bosnia are involved in the coppersmith trade. Begging is considered a real trade and, among the Xoraxané from the Kosovo region, it can be followed by all the members of a household—men, women, the elderly, and children—

although only the women tend to do it on a day-to-day basis. The women prefer begging in town centers, halting along the busiest streets or outside churches, and they do not try to hide the fact that they are Gypsies. The men, however, prefer begging door-to-door and pretend to be non-Gypsy cripples, political refugees, or Yugoslavian, Romanian, or Lebanese earthquake victims. They all see the town in which they are encamped as their principal, though not their only, begging area. The town of temporary residence is in fact the center of an economic area that extends as far as other nearby towns, reached daily by the Romá by means of public transport. On account of the woman's domestic duties, the extension of her economic area is somewhat limited in relation to the man's: a woman may travel as far as 50–60 kilometers from her encampment in order to beg, while a man may go as far as 100–150 kilometers. Petty theft is practiced above all by children, since the latter cannot be punished under Italian law. This has led, in recent years, to some families "renting" children for a sum of money from relatives or friends in Yugoslavia. For this reason, certain Romá have been condemned by the Italian law courts as "slave traders." The Romá themselves declare that a month's begging in Italy can earn you as much money as 3–4 months' salaried work in Yugoslavia. Some families, therefore, organize their migration in great detail; some members of the household remain in Yugoslavia, while others go to Italy to beg for a few months. In this way life in Italy is seen only as a "period of production," while the earnings are spent in Yugoslavia.

Kinship

Kin Groups and Descent.   The Xoraxané Romá recognize a bilateral kindred (*familja*) which, in theory, includes third cousins. In practice there is no rigid dividing line, and the composition will often depend on genealogical memory. This memory certainly reaches as far back as the third ascending generation, but for the most part only as far as the lineals are concerned; the collaterals are more easily forgotten. Within the kindred great stress is placed on the patriline, though this in no way constitutes a formalized corporate group. Eponymous ancestors do not exist. The patrilineal ideology, symbolized in the transmission of blood, is in evidence above all where blood feuds are concerned. The maternal uncle has a rather peculiar position: if his sister's son is killed, he can seek revenge (within certain time limits); sexual intercourse between himself and the wife of his sister's son is considered incestuous (whereas it is not considered so between a paternal uncle and his nephew's wife).

Kinship Terminology.   The terminology makes a clear distinction between consanguineal and affinal terms. The consanguine terminology is of the Sudanese type with elements of the Eskimo type, while the affinal terminology is of a type that can be defined as "Greek." The terminological system is not, however, uniform throughout all Xoraxané groups.

Marriage and Family

Marriage.   The norm requires a preliminary agreement between the families of both parties plus the payment of bridewealth (either in cash or in gold). A promise of marriage can be made while the future bride and bridegroom are still children. Elopement is an accepted possibility for a couple who wish to go against their parents' wishes. The incest taboo stretches as far as first cousins and includes the following affinal relationships: daughter-in-law/father-in-law, son-in-law/mother-in-law, bride's father/bridegroom's mother, bride's mother/bridegroom's father, maternal uncle/nephew's wife. The bilateral kindred as previously described is, in theory, an exogamous group, though one can note several exceptions to the rule. The exogamy, again in theory, concerns all the members of Ego's kindred in relation to all the members of the kindred of Ego's godfather. The postmarital residence is generally virilocal, with some cases of neolocality. Divorce is possible and is ideologically accepted. Polygyny is practiced (in this case the first wife has a predominant role), though monogamy is much more common.

Domestic Unit.   As well as bilateral kindred, the term *familja* also denotes the extended family and the nuclear family. The expression *barí familja* (i.e., "big familja") can refer to a group containing all the descendants of a living person, or to a group of coresidents made up of one or more nuclear families. One must distinguish, therefore, between a barí familja of descendance, following cognatic lines, and a barí familja of residence, made up from rules following virilocality. In the development of the domestic cycle, the virilocality is not permanent: a married son will usually leave his father's family when another brother gets married and replaces him in the paternal home (house or caravan). The father's family, however, remains a point of reference and of solidarity. Another type of "great" family is made up from the polygynous family; here the dyads of mother/children assume great importance, seeing that the cowives have separate homes and can even live in different towns. Each cowife with her children forms an autonomous residential unit, and the husband divides his time between one unit and another.

Inheritance.   The norm, which is not always followed, is that the youngest married son should inherit everything. This rule of ultimogeniture is in keeping with the chain development of the virilocality: the last son to marry and who lives with his father becomes, at the death of the latter, head of the household and must look after his widowed mother and any young unmarried siblings.

Sociopolitical Organization

Social and Political Organization.   Outside the domestic unit there are no recognized "chiefs" or units that act as centers of power. Among the Xoraxané the only inequalities are those depending on age and sex. The acephalous character, however, does not prevent the recognition of *baró* Rom (great Rom), a prestigious title given to the head of family who is also head of a large barí familja of descendance and whose reputation is impeccable. The domestic units, independent from each other both politically and economically, form the basis for the local groups. The latter are, in Italy, ever-changing and very unstable and do not expect a monopoly over a given territory: every domestic unit can move freely and camp with any family with whom they are on good terms. This movement is hindered only by the surrounding non-Gypsies and sometimes by non-Xoraxané Gypsies, who wish to have nothing to do with the Xoraxané Romá, whom they see as trespassers.

Social Control and Conflict. For the Romá the institution of the blood-feud, or merely the threat of such a feud, is a fundamental guarantee of order. The feud, which in theory foresees the intervention only of patrilineal relatives and, within certain time limits, the intervention of the murdered person's maternal uncle, can in practice be put into effect by the nonpatrilineal relatives as well. The cognatic structure constitutes a notable restraint on prolonging a feud: the relatives common to both parties in a dispute can become peacemakers. In order officially to "repacify the blood," as the Xoraxané put it—that is, to end a feud—there exists an ad hoc institution. This is a formal trial by a council composed of an unfixed number of "great Romá" and called a *plešnóra*, which must be requested by both contenders. The plešnóra decides who is right and who is wrong and establishes the sum of "blood wealth" to be paid. A contender who refuses to accept the plešnóra's verdict risks a blood feud with the plešnóra itself.

Religion and Expressive Culture

Religion. The Xoraxané call themselves Muslims, though religious practice is held to be a private affair. The nonpracticing Xoraxané are in no way censured. In Italy, where there are no mosques, the practicing Muslim Xoraxané content themselves with observing Ramadan, not eating pork, and invoking Allah in moments of need. Many have begun to have their children baptized according to the Christian rites, but they continue to call themselves Muslims. Messianic movements that have met with success among other Gypsy groups in Italy (e.g., the Rom Kalderash and some Sinti groups) do not seem to interest the Xoraxané.

Death and Afterlife. When possible, the Xoraxané will take their dead to Yugoslavia in order to bury them according to Muslim ritual. They believe in the return of the dead (especially for those who meet a violent death) in the form of vampires (*coxané*). These are believed to possess superhuman aspects and to become incarnate in children. Some say the vampires exist only in Yugoslavia, while others swear they have seen them in Italy.

Bibliography

Lockwood, William G. (1986). "East European Gypsies in Western Europe: The Social and Cultural Adaptation of the Xoraxané." *Nomadic Peoples* 21–22:63–70.

Piasere, Leonardo (1987). "In Search of New Niches: The Productive Organization of the Peripatetic Xoraxané in Italy." In *The Other Nomads*, edited by A. Rao, 111–32. Cologne: Böhlau.

Piasere, Leonardo (1990). *Popoli delle discariche*. Rome: CISU.

LEONARDO PIASERE

Glossary

affine   A relative by marriage.

agglutinative language   A language in which morphemes are combined into words without substantially modifying their form or losing their meaning.

agnatic descent. *See* patrilineal descent

Alps   A mountain system of south-central Europe that extends for about 1,200 kilometers. The system has three ranges—northern in southeastern France and northwestern Italy, central in north-central Italy and southern Switzerland, and eastern in parts of Germany, Yugoslavia, and Austria.

ancestor spirits   Ghosts of deceased relatives who are believed to have supernatural powers that can influence the lives of the living.

animal husbandry. *See* pastoralism

archipelago   A sea or broad expanse of water interspersed with islands or groups of islands; the term often is used for island groups themselves.

Asia Minor   Also known as Anatolia, the peninsula of land that forms the Asian portion of Turkey.

autarkic   Economically self-sufficient.

Balkans   The easternmost of the three major peninsulas of southern Europe and the collective name for the nations located there—Bosnia and Herzegovina, Slovenia, Croatia, Yugoslavia, Romania, Albania, Bulgaria, Greece, and the European section of Turkey.

bilateral descent   The practice of tracing kinship affiliation more or less equally through both the female and male line.

blood feud (vendetta)   A conflict between two groups (usually families or other kin groups) in a society. The feud usually involves violence or the threat of violence as a means of avenging some wrongdoing against a member of one of the groups. Feuds often are motivated by a desire to protect or restore a member's honor.

Bronze Age   The third stage in the development of Western civilization, characterized by the production and use of bronze tools and objects. The Bronze Age, which began in Europe in Greece about 3000 B.C. and ended about 1000 B.C., followed the Neolithic period and preceded the Iron Age.

Byzantine Empire   The eastern half of the Roman Empire that survived the fall of the western half and lasted until 1453, when it fell to the Turks. The capital at Constantinople was established in A.D. 330.

Carpathian Mountains   A mountain range in east-central Europe in the Czech and Slovak Federative Republic, Poland, Hungary, Romania, and nations that were formerly part of the Soviet Union.

Celts   An Indo-European people of Iron Age and pre-Roman Europe who ranged from the British Isles to Asia Minor. Modern-day descendants of the Celts include the Irish, Highland Scots, Welsh, Cornish, and Bretons.

clan, sib   A group of unilineally affiliated kin who usually reside in the same community and share common property.

classificatory kin terms   Kinship terms, such as aunt, that designate several categories of distinct relatives, such as mother's sister and father's sister.

cognates   Words that belong to different languages but have similar sounds and meanings.

cognatic kin   Kin related to one another through the female line.

collaterals   A person's relatives not related to him or her as ascendants or descendants; one's uncle, aunt, cousin, brother, sister, niece, nephew.

constitutional democracy   A form of government in which the actual affairs of government are carried out by elected officials who act in accord with a national constitution.

constitutional monarchy   A form of government in which a monarch (king or queen) is the legal head of state but the actual affairs of government are carried out by elected officials who act in accord with a national constitution.

continental climate   In the Köppen system, a climate characterized by large seasonal temperature variations, with hot summers, cold winters, and year-round precipitation.

cousin, cross   Children of one's parents' siblings of the opposite sex—one's father's sisters' and mother's brothers' children.

cousin, parallel   Children of one's parents' siblings of the same sex—one's father's brothers' and mother's sisters' children.

cross cousin. *See* cousin, cross

Cyrillic alphabet   A writing system developed in the ninth century for Slavic languages. Russian, Serbian, Bulgarian, and other Slavic languages today are written with somewhat different versions of the basic Cyrillic alphabet.

descriptive kin terms   Kinship terms that are used to distinguish different categories of relatives such as mother or father.

diglossia   The coexistence of two forms of the same language in a culture or community. Often one is the literary form and the other is the domestic form. The term is also sometimes used in reference to groups who regularly use two different languages.

displaced person   An individual forced to leave his or her homeland as a result of World War II.

dowry   The practice of a bride's kin giving substantial property or wealth to the groom or his kin before or at the time of marriage.

Ego   In kinship studies "Ego" is a male or female whom the anthropologist arbitrarily designates as the reference point for a particular kinship diagram or discussion of kinship terminology.

endogamy   Marriage within a specific group or social category of which the person is a member, such as one's caste or community.

English common law   A legal system in which laws are based on the decisions rendered in prior judicial cases. Common law developed in England, beginning in the eleventh century.

Enlightenment   A social and philosophical movement of the eighteenth century that emphasized the use of reason and scientific explanation, rational thinking, and the questioning of traditional authority.

European Community (EC)   A political and economic association of twelve Western European nations, formally founded in 1992 and to be established in 1993 following ratification by the parliaments of the member nations.

European Economic Community (EEC)   Also known as the Common Market, an economic association of Western European nations founded in 1957. It has been replaced by the European Community.

evil eye   An idea that a person can cause harm to another by simply wishing him or her harm (casting the evil eye).

exogamy   Marriage outside a specific group or social category of which the person is a member, such as one's clan or community.

fictive kin   Individuals referred to or addressed with kin terms and treated as kin, although they are neither affines nor consanguines.

foreign workers. *See* guest workers

Franks   A Germanic people who occupied Gaul and formed a kingdom that replaced the fallen Roman government in the fifth and sixth centuries A.D. The Frankish kingdom is considered to be the beginning of modern France.

freehold land   Ownership of land for an indefinite period of time, such as for life.

Gauls   People located in what is now France, Belgium, western Germany, and northern Italy from about the fifth century B.C. until about the sixth century A.D. The Gauls were considerably influenced by Rome and were an important repository of Roman culture following the decline of the Roman Empire.

glasnost ("openness")   Part of Mikhail Gorbachev's new policy set in motion in 1987. *See also* perestroika

godparenthood   A category of fictive kin with important obligations between the members. The social relations of godparent-godchild are especially important in many southern European cultures.

Great Tradition, Little Tradition   Terms first used by the anthropologist Robert Redfield to contrast the formal, literate tradition of a civilization with its variant manifestations at a local and rural level. Elements of the Little Tradition are thought to be continually absorbed into the Great Tradition through a process called *universalization*.

Gregorian calendar   A slight revision of the Julian calendar that was adopted in Great Britain and the American colonies in 1752. Most Roman Catholic countries adopted it immediately, with Protestant countries adopting it later, and Eastern Orthodox countries in the twentieth century.

guest workers   People from one nation (usually men) who live and work temporarily in another nation; for example, Italians in Switzerland.

Gypsy   A generic term for a diverse group of people who live or formerly lived a nomadic life-style. *See article* Peripatetics

homeopathic medicine A system of medical treatment developed in the nineteenth century based on the belief that "like cures like." Thus, treatments such as drugs or the application of heat are used to cure ailments that would be caused by their application to people free of the ailment. For example, quinine is given to persons with malaria because quinine causes symptoms of malaria when given to healthy persons.

Huns A nomadic people who invaded and ruled areas of southeastern Europe from about A.D. 370 until they were defeated by a coalition of other groups in A.D. 455.

Indo-European languages A family of languages spoken in Europe, Southwest Asia, and South Asia. Modern Indo-European languages are believed to be descended from a single language thought to have been spoken about 5,000 years ago in the region north of the Black Sea.

Industrial Revolution An economic transformation marked by the decline of small-scale, domestic production of goods and the rise of large-scale, centralized mass production and distribution based on power-driven machines.

Iron Age The fourth stage in the development of Western civilization, characterized by the production and use of iron tools and objects. Beginning in southeastern Europe in about 1200 B.C., the Iron Age followed the Bronze Age.

Jansenism A religious movement of the seventeenth and eighteenth centuries in central Europe and especially France that maintained that freedom of will did not exist and that only a portion of humankind would be redeemed through Jesus Christ, with the rest being damned to hell.

Julian calendar A calendar introduced in Rome in 46 B.C. that established the 365-day year with twelve months and the 366-day year every fourth year. This calendar was retained by Eastern Orthodox countries into the twentieth century and is still used in church calendars.

kindred The bilateral kin group of close kin who may be expected to be present and to participate on important ceremonial occasions, usually in the absence of unilineal descent.

kinship Family relationship, whether traced through marital ties or through blood and descent.

kin terms, Eskimo A system of kinship terminology in which cousins are distinguished from brothers and sisters, but no distinction is made between cross and parallel cousins. Sometimes also called European kin terms.

kin terms, Iroquois A system of kinship terminology in which parallel cousins are referred to by the same terms used for brothers and sisters but cross cousins are identified by different terms.

Köppen system A system of climatic classification developed in 1900 based on mathematical values assigned to temperature and rainfall. The system is named for its developer, the German climatologist Wladimir Köppen (b. 1846, d. 1940).

latifundia Large estates of the Roman Empire that were often the local or regional centers of political and economic power. Large estates based on the latifundia model existed in many regions of Europe up to the present time, for example in Italy and Spain. Typically the land was owned by a single family and passed on through inheritance, with the land actually being worked by serfs.

levirate The practice of requiring a man to marry his brother's widow.

lineage A unilineal (whether patrilineal or matrilineal) kin group that traces kinship affiliation from a common, known ancestor and extends through a number of generations.

linguistic minority A national minority population that is comprised of speakers of a language that is different from the national language; for example, the Ladin in Italy.

Little Tradition. *See* Great Tradition, Little Tradition

matrilineal descent The practice of tracing kinship affiliation only through the female line.

Mediterranean climate In the Köppen system, a climate characterized by hot, dry summers and cool, wet winters.

middleman minority A term used to describe an ethnic or racial group that occupies a middle economic position between the supplier and the consumer in a national, regional, or local economy. Usually the group is segregated from the rest of society because of racial or ethnic differences.

monogamy Marriage between one man and one woman at a time.

Moors The Muslim population of Spain.

Napoleonic (Continental) legal system A system of law and justice derived from the Napoleonic Code. It was an important early influence on the legal systems developed in many nations in the nineteenth century but has been much revised in the twentieth century.

national minority A minority population in one nation that is comprised of people from another nation; for example, Albanians in Italy.

NATO (North Atlantic Treaty Organization) A military alliance of North American and European nations formed in 1949 as a response to Soviet domination of eastern and central Europe. With the fall of communism in Europe and the disintegration of the Soviet Union, the future role of NATO is unclear.

Neolithic period A stage in the development of human culture characterized by the use of polished or ground stone tools. It follows the Paleolithic period and precedes the Bronze Age.

neolocal residence The practice of a newly married couple living apart from the immediate kin of either party.

Ottoman Empire Empire created by Turkish peoples in what is now Asian Turkey from 1300 to 1922.

parallel cousin. *See* cousin, parallel

parliamentary democracy A form of democratic government in which the elected legislature has control over the making and administration of the law.

partible inheritance An estate of inheritance that may be divided.

pastoralism A type of subsistence economy based on the herding of domesticated grazing animals such as sheep or cattle.

patois A dialect of a language spoken by a specific social or occupational group in a multicultural environment.

patrilineal descent The practice of tracing kinship affiliation only through the male line.

peasant, peasantry Small-scale agriculturalists producing only subsistence crops, perhaps in combination with some fishing, animal husbandry, or hunting. They live in villages in a larger state, but participate little in the state's commerce or cultural activities. Today, many peasants rely on mechanized farming and are involved in the national economy, so they are called "post-peasants" by anthropologists.

perestroika ("reconstruction") Part of Mikhail Gorbachev's new policy set in motion in 1987. *See also* glasnost

Perigord A specific phase of the Paleolithic period in western Europe characterized by the use of narrow pointed-flint knife blades.

peripatetic A generic term used by social scientists and others to refer to peoples previously called "Gypsies" or "Travellers." *See article* Peripatetics

primogeniture A rule of inheritance that gives the exclusive right of inheritance to the first-born son.

Pyrenees A mountain range in southwestern Europe that forms a boundary between France and Spain.

Reformation A revolution in the Catholic church in the sixteenth century that led to the development of Protestantism.

refugee An individual who has left his or her homeland as a result of political events in that nation or for other political reasons.

Roman Empire The state centered in Rome, founded as a republic in 509 B.C., established as an empire in 27 B.C., the western half of which collapsed in the fifth century A.D. The Roman Empire was the dominant force in the Mediterranean region, North Africa, and much of Europe.

Roman law The legal system of the Roman Empire, including both unwritten and written law, the latter including legislation, edicts, judicial interpretations, and codes of emperors.

Scandinavians A generic term of reference for Swedes, Finns, Norwegians, and Danes.

seer One who foresees the future.

serf In medieval Europe, a tenant farmer who subsisted by farming land owned by a lord or landowner. Serfs were generally bound to the land they farmed and their rights to move from the land were greatly restricted.

Slavs (Slavic peoples) A generic term for peoples who speak Slavic languages: in Europe, it encompasses Serbs, Croats, Slovenes, Bulgarians, Macedonians, Czechs, Slovaks, Sorbs, Poles, Russians, Ukrainians, and Belorussians.

social class stratification A form of social organization in a society in which individuals or groups are ranked in a hierarchical system based both on ascribed and achieved status.

sorcery The use of supernatural forces to further the interests of the sorcerer, primarily through formulas and the ritual manipulation of material objects.

stem family A residential group composed of a nuclear family and one or more additional members who do not comprise a second nuclear family.

subarctic climate In the Köppen system, a climate characterized by a long, cold winter with low humidity and relatively little precipitation, mainly in the form of snow.

teknonymy The practice of addressing a person after the name of his wife or his or her child rather than by the individual name. For example, "Bill" is called "Father of John."

transhumance Seasonal movements of a society or community. It may involve seasonal shifts in food production between hunting and gathering, horticulture, and the movement of herds to more favorable locations.

Turks (Turkic peoples) A generic term that refers to modern-day descendants of the people who formed an empire that extended from the Black Sea east to Mongolia in the sixth century A.D.

unilineal descent The practice of tracing kinship affiliation through only one line, either the matriline or the patriline.

United Kingdom Also known as Britain or Great Britain, the term refers to England, Scotland, Wales, and Northern Ireland.

urbanization A sociodemographic process through which an increasingly large percentage of a nation's population resides in cities or urban areas.

uterine descent. *See* matrilineal descent

Vandals　A Germanic people who raided southern Europe from their kingdom in North Africa, which existed from 429 to 534 A.D.

witchcraft　The use of supernatural forces to control or harm another person. Unlike sorcery, witchcraft does not require the use of special rituals, formulas, or ritual objects.

zadruga　A form of extended family organization found primarily in cultures in the Balkan region. The family is generally extended either generationally through grown children and their families living with parents or laterally through brothers and their families living together. Zadrugas are no longer the norm and have been generally replaced by nuclear families.

Filmography

The following is a list of films and videos on Europe and European cultures. The list is not meant to be complete; rather, it is a sampling of documentary films available from distributors in North America. Listing a film or video does not constitute an endorsement by the volume editor or any of the summary authors, nor does the absence of a film represent any sort of nonendorsement. Abbreviations for names of distributors are provided at the end of each citation. The full name and address may be found in the directory of distributors that follows the index to the filmography. Many of these films are also available through the Extension Media Center of the University of California at Berkeley and/or the Audio-Visual Services of the Pennsylvania State University, indicated by (EMC) or (PS) at the end of the citation.

1. *Across the Tracks—Vlach Gypsies in Hungary.* (Vlach Gypsies) 1988. Color, 52 minutes, VHS. FI.
2. *Aegean Sponge Divers.* (Greece) 1974. Color, 27 minutes, VHS, U-mat. EMC.
3. *An Invisible Enemy.* (Saami) 1987. Color, 52 minutes, VHS. FI.
3a. *Anastenaria.* (Greece) 1969. B&W, 17 minutes, 16mm. HARP (EMC).
4. *Ancient Moderns: Greek Island Art and Culture 2000–3000 B.C.* (Cyclades) 1979. Color, 19 minutes, 16mm. EBEC (PS).
5. *Anglo-Saxon England.* (England) 1971. Color, 22 minutes, 16mm. IFB (PS).
6. *Are You a Racist?* (English) 1986. BBC for the Horizon Series. Color, 49 minutes, VHS, U-mat. PSUPCR (PS).
7. *The Basques of Santazi.* (Basques) 1987. Color, 51 minutes, VHS. FI.
8. *Biquefarre.* (French farming) 1983. Georges Rouquier. Color, 90 minutes, 16mm. NYF.
9. *Brendan Behan's Dublin.* (Ireland) 1968. Color, 29 minutes, 16mm. IFB (EMC).
10. *Cave Dwellers of the Old Stone Age.* (Europe, prehistory) 1960. Color, 18 minutes, 16mm. EBEC (EMC).
11. *The Country between the Sands.* (Iceland) 1974. Color, 29 minutes, 16mm. PS.
12. *Crystal Year.* (England) 1966. Legacy Series. B&W, 30 minutes, 16mm. IU (EMC).
13. *Drifters.* (North Sea Trawling) 1929. John Grierson. B&W, 40 minutes, silent, 16mm. WaU.

14. *East and West.* (Sicily, Spain, southern France, Islam) 1983. World of Islam Series. Color, 30 minutes, VHS. PS.
15. *The Family of Man.* (Poles) 1966. B&W, 23 minutes, 16mm. PS.
16. *The Farming of Fish.* (Norwegians) 1977. Paul Tasker and Rex Tasker for the National Film Board of Canada. Color, 58 minutes, 16mm. NFBC (PS).
17. *Farrébique.* (French farming) 1947. Georges Rouquier. B&W, 100 minutes, 16mm. NYF.
18. *Federico Garcia Lorca y Su Granada.* (Andalusia) 1974. Color, 24 minutes, 16mm. BFS (EMC).
19. *Une Ferme Belge.* (Belgian farming) 1972. Color, 11 minutes, 16mm. WLacU.
20. *Fire on Heimaey.* (Iceland) 1975. Color, 31 minutes, 16mm. PS.
21. *Flamenco.* (Spain) 1986. Color, 70 minutes, VHS. FFHS (PS).
22. *Four Families.* (French) 1959. B&W, 60 minutes, 16mm. McGH (EMC).
23. *Geel: A Changing Tradition.* (Belgium) 1967. Stephen White for Swedish Television. Color, 40 minutes, 16mm. (EMC) (PS).
24. *Heritage: Civilization and the Jews, 2—The Power of the Word.* (Jews) 1984. Produced by WNET. Color, 59 minutes, 16mm. FI (PS).
25. *Heritage: Civilization and the Jews, 3—The Shaping of Traditions.* (Jews) 1984. Produced by WNET. Color, 59 minutes, 16mm. FI (PS).
26. *Heritage: Civilization and the Jews, 4—The Crucible of Europe.* (Jews) 1984. Produced by WNET. Color, 61 minutes, 16mm. FI (PS).
27. *Heritage: Civilization and the Jews, 5—The Search for Deliverance.* (Jews) 1984. Produced by WNET. Color, 59 minutes, 16mm. FI (PS).
28. *Heritage: Civilization and the Jews, 6—Roads from the Ghetto.* (Jews) 1984. Produced by WNET. Color, 59 minutes, 16mm. FI (PS).
29. *Heritage: Civilization and the Jews, 8—Out of the Ashes.* (Jews) 1984. Produced by WNET. Color, 59 minutes, 16mm. FI (PS).
30. *Kypseli: Women and Men Apart—A Divided Reality.* (Greeks) 1976. Color, 40 minutes, VHS, U-mat. EMC.
31. *Land without Bread.* (Hurdanos) 1932. Directed by Luis Buñuel. B&W, 31 minutes, 16mm. DER (EMC).
32. *The Last Whalers.* (Portuguese, Azores) 1973. Color, 20 minutes, 16mm. IFF (EMC).
33. *Life Chances.* (Cypriots) 1970. B&W, 43 minutes, 16mm. LONSE (EMC).

34. *The Long Search: 4—Catholicism: Rome, Leeds, and the Desert.* (England, Spain, Italy, Catholicism) 1977. Produced by the BBC. Color, 53 minutes, 16mm. AMBVP (PS).

35. *The Long Search: 6—Orthodox Christianity: The Rumanian Solution.* (Romanians, Orthodox Christianity) 1977. Produced by the BBC. Color, 53 minutes, 16mm. AMBVP (EMC) (PS).

36. *Man of Aran.* (Irish Gaels) 1934. Directed by Robert Flaherty. B&W, 77 minutes, 16mm. FI (PS).

37. *Matador.* (Spain) 1983. Color, 50 minutes, VHS. FFHS (PS).

38. *Misery in the Borinage.* (Belgian miners) 1933. Henri Storck. B&W, 28 minutes, 16mm. IaU, CtU.

39. *Music.* (England) 1970. Color, 51 minutes, 16mm. FI (EMC).

40. *Out of the Fiery Furnace: 2—Swords and Ploughshares.* (Europe, history) 1983. Produced by Robert Raymond. Color, 58 minutes, VHS. PUBTEL (PS).

41. *Out of the Fiery Furnace: 4—The Revolution of Necessity.* (Europe, history) 1983. Produced by Robert Raymond. Color, 58 minutes, VHS. PUBTEL (PS).

42. *Paris: The Belly and the Heart.* (France) 1973. Towards the Year 2000 Series. Color, 22 minutes, 16mm. DA (EMC).

43. *People of the River Neretva.* (Yugoslavia) 1966. Produced by Zagreb Films. B&W, 18 minutes, 16mm. PS.

44. *Pepe's Family.* (Andalusians) 1978. Produced by Jerome Mintz. B&W, 38 minutes, 16mm. IU (PS).

45. *Poland: The Will to Be.* (Poland) 1979. Color, 58 minutes, 16mm. PYRAMID (EMC).

46. *Prehistoric Man in Europe.* (Europe, prehistory) 1965. Color, 23 minutes, 16mm. IFB (PS).

47. *Romanian Village Life.* (Romanians) 1972. Produced by Julien Bryan. Color, 15 minutes, 16mm. IFF (PS).

48. *The Shoemaker (El Zapatero).* (Andalusians) 1976. Produced by Jerome Mintz. B&W, 33 minutes, 16mm. IU (PS).

49. *The Story of English: 4—The Guid Scots Tongue.* (Scots) 1986. Color, 60 minutes, VHS. FI (PS).

50. *The Story of English: 8—The Loaded Weapon.* (Irish) 1986. Color, 60 minutes, VHS. FI (PS).

51. *Suffer the Little Children.* (Northern Irish) 1972. Produced by NBC. Color, 52 minutes, 16mm. FI (PS).

52. *Tale of Two Irelands.* (Northern Ireland) 1975. Produced by CBS News. B&W, 50 minutes, 16mm. CBSNEWS (EMC).

53. *Tale of Two Rivers.* (France) 1974. Color, 40 minutes, VHS, U-mat. EMC.

54. *34 Years after Hitler.* (Germany) 1979. Produced by CBS. Color, 19 minutes, 16mm. CAROUSEL (EMC).

55. *The Village.* (Irish Gaels) 1968. Directed by Mark McCarty and Paul Hockings. B&W, 70 minutes, 16mm. EMC (PS).

56. *Village Dances of Yugoslavia.* (Macedonia, Serbia, Slovenia, Croatia) 1982. Color, 60 minutes, 16mm. IFA (EMC).

57. *The Visit.* (Calabrians) 1967. B&W, 28 minutes, 16mm. (EMC).

58. *Viva San Fermin.* (Spain) 1983. Produced by John McDonald. Color, 48 minutes, VHS. PS.

59. *Vlach Gypsies.* (Vlach Gypsies) 1988. Produced and directed by John Blake. Color, 58 minutes. Grenada Television.

60. *Western Europe: A New Look.* (Europe, western) 1986. Produced by Sam Bryan. Color, 24 minutes, 16mm. IFF (PS).

61. *Yeats Country.* (Ireland) 1965. Color, 18 minutes, 16mm. IFB (EMC).

62. *Yugoslavia.* (Yugoslavia) 1987. Nations of the World Series. Color, 27 minutes, VHS. NGS (EMC).

Index to Filmography

Directory of Distributors

Ethnonym Index

This index provides some of the alternative names and the names of major subgroups for cultures covered in this volume. The culture names that are entry titles are in boldface.

Albanians
Albanois—**Albanians**
Alemanes—**Germans**
Allemands—**Germans**
Alsatians
Andalucians—**Andalusians**
Andalusians
Anglo-Irish—**Northern Irish**
Aquitaine
Arbëresh—**Albanians**
Arlija—**Xoraxané Romá**
Arnauts—**Albanians**
Arnuta—**Xoraxané Romá**
Aromans—**Romanians**
Aromuni—**Vlachs**
Arvanits—**Albanians**
Arvernes—**Auvergnats**
Ashkenazic Jews
Athonite Monks—**Mouth Athos**
Austrians
Auvergnats
Aveyronnais
Azoreans

Balearics
Basques
Bavarians
Beaš—**Peripatetics**
Belgians
Belgians—**Flemish; Walloons**
Bergamasco
Black Portuguese—**Cape Verdeans**
Bohémiens—**Peripatetics**
Bosnian Muslims
Bourguignons—**Burgundians**
Brava—**Cape Verdeans**
Breizhiz—**Bretons**
Bretoned—**Bretons**
Bretons
British—**Northern Irish**
Buitenlandse Zigeuners—**Gypsies and Caravan Dwellers in the Netherlands**
Bulgarian Gypsies
Bulgarian Muslims—**Pomaks**
Bulgarians
Bulgarini—**Bulgarians**

Bulgaro-Mohamedanin—**Pomaks**
Bulgars—**Bulgarians**
Burgenländer—**Austrians**
Burgundians

Calabrese
Calabrians—**Calabrese**
Camminanti—**Peripatetics**
Canarians
Canary Islanders—**Canarians**
Cape Verdeans
Cassubians—**Kashubians**
Castilians
Catalans (Països Catalans)
Catalonians—**Catalans (Països Catalans)**
Cěch—**Czechs**
Celtic—**Highland Scots**
Celts—**Gaels (Irish); Highland Scots; Northern Irish**
Čergaša—**Xoraxané Romá**
Češi—**Czechs**
Cigani—**Peripatetics**
Cikán—**Rom of Czechoslovakia**
Cincari—**Vlachs**
Cingaros—**Peripatetics**
Cornish
Corses—**Corsicans**
Corsi—**Corsicans**
Corsicans
Cretans
Crioul—**Cape Verdeans**
Crnogorci—**Montenegrins**
Croatians—**Croats**
Croats
Cyclades
Cymry—**Welsh**
Cypriots
Czechs

Dalmatians
Danes
Deutschen—**Germans**
Deutschen Shweiz—**German Swiss**
Dolomites—**Ladin**
Dutch
Dutchmen and Dutchwomen—**Dutch**

Eftanissiotes—**Ionians**
Eireanneach—**Irish**
Ellines—**Greeks**
Engl—**English**
English
Eskualdunak—**Basques**
Euskaldunak—**Basques**

Faroe Islanders
Fenni—**Saami**
Finn—**Saami**
Finnish Kaale—**Scandinavian Peripatetics**
Finns
Flamencos—**Flemish**
Flanders—**Flemish**
Flemings—**Flemish**
Flemish
Føroyingar—**Faroe Islanders**
French
French-Flemish—**Flemish**
Frisians
Friulano—**Friuli**
Friulans—**Friuli**
Friuli
Friulians—**Friuli**
Frysk—**Frisians**

Gaedhils—**Gaels (Irish)**
Gaels (Irish)
Gagauz
Galego—**Galicians**
Galicians
Gallego—**Galicians**
Gens du Voyage—**Peripatetics**
Germans
German Swiss
Gitanos
Gitanos—**Peripatetics**
Gitans—**Peripatetics**
Graubunden—**Swiss, Italian**
Greeks
Greek-Speaking Jews of Greece
Griegos—**Greek-Speaking Jews of Greece**
Grigioni Italiano—**Swiss, Italian**

295

The Editors

Editor in Chief
David Levinson (Ph.D., State University of New York at Buffalo) is vice-president of the Human Relations Area Files in New Haven, Connecticut. He is a cultural anthropologist whose primary research interests are in social issues, worldwide comparative research, and social theory. He has conducted research on homelessness, alcohol abuse, aggression, family relations, and ethnicity. Among his dozens of publications are the award-winning text *Toward Explaining Human Culture* (with Martin J. Malone), *The Tribal Living Book* (with David Sherwood), and *Family Violence in Cross-Cultural Perspective*. Dr. Levinson also teaches anthropology at Albertus Magnus College in New Haven, Connecticut.

Volume Editor
Linda A. Bennett (M.A., Indiana University; Ph.D., American University), professor of anthropology at Memphis State University, is editor of the Professional Series of the American Anthropological Association. She is a sociocultural anthropologist with a strong focus on applied clinical research and has a particular interest in the study of alcohol and other drugs. In American society, she has studied family rituals and their impact on intergenerational patterns of alcoholism, and she is coauthor of *The Alcoholic Family* and coeditor of *The American Experience with Alcohol: Contrasting Cultural Perspectives*. In the former Yugoslavia, especially Croatia, she has studied alcoholism treatment and the social history of the temperance movement, and she is co-principal investigator of a study of biological and cultural microdifferentiation of rural populations in Middle Dalmatia. Active in the National Association of the Practice of Anthropology and the Society for Applied Anthropology, she is the author of *Bridges for Changing Times: Local Practitioner Organizations in American Anthropology*. Dr. Bennett is also clinical professor in the Department of Psychiatry at the University of Tennessee Health Science Center and adjunct professor of anthropology at the University of Pittsburgh.